International Corporate Finance

J. Ashok Robin

The McGraw-Hill/Irwin Series in Finance, Insurance and Real Estate

The McGraw·Hill Companies

INTERNATIONAL CORPORATE FINANCE
International Edition 2011

Exclusive rights by McGraw-Hill Education (Asia), for manufacture and export. This book cannot be re-exported from the country to which it is sold by McGraw-Hill. This International Edition is not to be sold or purchased in North America and contains content that is different from its North American version.

10 09 08 07 06 05 04 03 02 01
20 15 14 13 12 11
CTP SLP

When ordering this title, use ISBN 978-007-132586-8 or MHID 007-132586-7

Printed in Singapore

www.mhhe.com

My family and friends—especially ones afar—
whom I do not get to see as much as I should.

About the Author

J. Ashok Robin, a native of India, was brought up in Coimbatore, a mid-size industrial city in the southern state of Tamilnadu. He did his undergraduate work at the Government Arts College in that city. Later, he moved to the United States, completing his MBA and PhD at SUNY-Buffalo. Currently, he is Professor of Finance at the Rochester Institute of Technology, and he was recently named as the Madelon & Richard Rosett Chair for Research. He lives in Rochester, New York. When he is not writing or teaching, he enjoys traveling—visits to Italy and India are especially cherished. He has published articles on a variety of topics in accounting and finance in journals such as the *Journal of Accounting and Economics, Financial Management, Review of Accounting Studies,* and *Journal of Financial Research.* Having taught international finance courses to graduate as well as undergraduate students for more than 15 years, he decided to use his experience to write this book, which is his first.

Brief Contents

Contents

The economic affairs of all nations are connected one to another. This connection was amply demonstrated during the recent economic crisis. The discipline of international finance explores the workings of the financial world in this interconnected global setting. As such, International Corporate Finance covers a wide range of topics. This text focuses on a key player in this financial world: multinational corporations (MNCs). By applying general financial concepts and procedures, the text explains the conduct of financial management in MNCs. Because most corporations are either directly or indirectly affected by multinational entities and have a global exposure, a study of MNC financial management has broad applicability.

Intended Audience

International Corporate Finance is a compact, corporate-focused text designed for use in an international corporate course at both the undergraduate and graduate levels.

International Corporate Finance offers in-depth coverage of critical international corporate finance topics including risk management, capital budgeting, financing, working capital management, and acquisitions and alliances. Strong coverage of these and other key topics provides direct value to students embarking on corporate careers.

This text has 15 chapters, and most courses will be able to cover the majority of them if desired. The text offers flexibility to those instructors who may wish to supplement the text with additional readings and cases.

Key Features

- Focus on Problem-Solving. Most chapters have numerical examples and a rich multitude of end-of-chapter problems that help reinforce instances to convey key points.

- Minicases. Each chapter has a minicase (using the same firm) that offers an opportunity for students to apply concepts covered throughout the chapter. Many of these cases contain information about real-world firms to illustrate to students how the concepts to the text relate to the everyday world. Each minicase is designed to be completed with 1–3 hours of work and can be used for a 20–30 minute class discussion.

Preface

The economic affairs of all nations are connected one to another. This connection was amply demonstrated during the recent economic crisis. The discipline of international finance explores the workings of the financial world in this interconnected global setting. As such, *International Corporate Finance* covers a wide range of topics. This text focuses on a key player in this financial world: multinational corporations (MNCs). By applying general financial concepts and procedures, the text explains the conduct of financial management in MNCs. Because most corporations are either directly or indirectly affected by multinational entities and have a global exposure, a study of MNC financial management has broad applicability.

Intended Audience

International Corporate Finance is a compact, corporate-focused text designed for use in an international corporate course at both the undergraduate and graduate levels.

International Corporate Finance offers in-depth coverage of critical international corporate finance topics including risk management, capital budgeting, financing, working capital management, and acquisitions and alliances. Strong coverage of these and other key topics provides direct value to students embarking on corporate careers.

This text has 15 chapters, and most courses will be able to cover the majority of them if desired. The text offers flexibility to those instructors who may wish to supplement the text with additional readings and cases.

Key Features

- **Focus on Problem-Solving.** Most chapters have numerical examples and a rich and varied selection of end-of-chapter problems. This helps instructors to convey key points in a logical manner.

- **Excel Spreadsheets.** Most quantitative examples are formulated using spreadsheet logic. The solutions to end-of-chapter problems are also formulated in Excel, offering students numerous templates for exploration and learning. Students who use this text and who use the solutions files will enhance their spreadsheet skills. Because many careers in finance require a high level of spreadsheet proficiency, students obtain tangible benefits.

- **Current Examples.** The text is interspersed with numerous real-world examples. This is particularly useful for bringing the topics to life for students without field experience. These examples concern firms in diverse industries and diverse countries and serve to increase students' awareness of global issues. This book has many examples from emerging markets: U.S. as well as non-U.S. students can relate to these examples.

- **Credit Crisis of 2007–2008.** The credit crisis of 2007–2008 is one of the most significant events in recent times, and many examples allude to this event. Without a doubt, this crisis has affected financial practice (e.g., a heightened sensitivity to counterparty risk), so it is important to convey this cutting-edge material. More generally, students learn to appreciate the dynamic nature of the financial world.

- **Minicases.** Each chapter has a minicase (using the same firm) that offers an opportunity for students to apply concepts covered throughout the chapter. Many of these cases contain information about real-world firms to illustrate to students how the concepts in the text relate to the everyday world. Each minicase is designed to be completed with 1–3 hours of work and can be used for a 20–30 minute class discussion.

Content and Organization

Chapters 1–5 describe the international environment and discuss currency-related issues (markets, valuation, derivatives, forecasting). A noteworthy feature is strong coverage of currency derivatives, including Eurocurrency derivatives in Chapter 3. This set of chapters provides a compact foundation so that core corporate material can quickly follow.

Chapters 6–9 form the core corporate risk management and capital budgeting material, which builds on the foundation of Chapters 1–5. Noteworthy is a two-chapter sequence on capital budgeting. These chapters cover a wide range of material, including the use of the real options methods to value projects. Because the financial analysis of projects is a key function in MNCs, this depth in capital budgeting adds significant value for the student.

Chapters 10–11 discuss financing strategies (long-term and short-term) as well as their connection to overall firm strategy. Long-term financing is linked to strategic considerations, and short-term financing is linked to operational working capital considerations. An efficient treatment of relevant theories (e.g., international CAPM) allows space for a robust discussion of practical financing issues (e.g., how currency risk and agency costs affect financing choices).

Chapter 12 is unique, focusing on methods by which firms penetrate markets and demonstrating M&A and joint venture valuation. Because these two methods in particular form the bulk of foreign direct investment by MNCs, this material is of great use to students in their careers.

Chapters 13–15 cover several important topics. They discuss trade methods, trade finance, taxation, currency/hedge accounting, and international diversification/investing.

Wherever possible, chapters have been constructed as independent units. This allows instructors to change the order of the chapters and thus construct a "custom" textbook for their course. For example, one can switch the order of Chapters 3 (Currency and Eurocurrency Derivatives) and 4 (Currency Systems and Valuation); instructors may also cover capital budgeting (Chapters 8 and 9) before currency exposure (Chapters 6 and 7).

Supplements

To assist with course preparation, the following ancillaries are available on the Online Learning Center at www.mhhe.com/robin:

- **Sample Syllabi.** Although most instructors will construct their own, sample syllabi are available to reduce start-up time for some instructors.

- **PowerPoint Presentation.** Prepared by the author, PowerPoint slides are provided for each chapter. These files include images and tables from the text and are easily customizable to suit various teaching styles.

- **Solutions Manual.** Prepared by the author, the manual includes solutions to end-of-chapter problems provided in Excel format. These files are painstakingly constructed to not only use Excel formulas for calculations but also display the algebraic formulas behind the calculations. These files are user friendly and customizable. Importantly, students can use many of the solutions as templates for exploration of concepts. The solutions to the mini-cases are also provided in the Excel format.

- **Excel Chapter Examples.** Significant numerical examples are provided in Excel spreadsheets. This will aid students' comprehension of key topics as they work through the chapters.

- **Test Bank.** Prepared by Robert Allen, Columbia Southern University, multiple-choice questions and a problems section offer a variety of questions to meet any instructor's quizzing and testing needs.

Acknowledgments

I wish to thank students at the Rochester Institute of Technology who used prior versions of this book. I am grateful for their honest feedback, which helped me improve the text. Special thanks to my students Min Zhu and Mouna Pyneni for an insightful review of key chapters.

I am grateful to the following individuals for their insights and suggestions for this text:

Robert Allen
Columbia Southern University

CW Anderson
University of Kansas

Bulent Aybar
Southern New Hampshire University

John Barkoulas
Georgia Southern University

Shumel Baruch
University of Utah

Deanne Butchey
Florida International University

Reid W. Click
George Washington University

Marie E. deBoyrie
New Mexico State University

Andres DeMaskey
Villanova University

Laura Field
Penn State University

Ali N. Garba
University of Wisconsin-Milwaukee

Delio E. Gianturco
George Mason University

Mark D. Griffiths
Miami University

Joel Harper
Oklahoma State University

John Hatem
Georgia State University

Pankaj K. Jain
University of Memphis

Joan C. Junkus
DePaul University

April Knill
Florida State University

Junsoon Lee
University of Alabama

Darius Miller
Southern Methodist University

Simona Mola
Arizona State University

Atsuyuki Naka
University of New Orleans

RS Nappinnai
Iowa State University

Mattias Nilsson
University of Colorado at Boulder

Karim Pakravan
DePaul University

Rolando Pelaez
University of Houston-Downtown

R. Scott Perlin
Baruch College/CUNY

John E. Petersen
George Mason University

Ramkishen S. Rajan
George Mason University

Mitchell Ratner
Rider University

Ebru Reis
Miami University

Benedicte Reyes
Monmouth University

Stephen Siegel
University of Washington

Tie Su
University of Miami

Antoinette Tessmer
Michigan State University

Cathyann D. Tully
Monmouth University

Nilufer Usmen
Montclair State University

Anand Venkateswaran
Northeastern University

Rahul Verma
University of Houston-Downtown

Nafeesa Yunus
University of Baltimore

Emilio Zarruk
Florida Atlantic University

I would like to express special thanks to the McGraw Hill editorial and production professionals who showed patience and skill in working with this rookie author. Special thanks are due to Michele Janicek, Executive Editor, who provided the dose of encouragement that made the difference, Katherine Mau, Editorial Coordinator, who kept me focused and on task, JaNoel Lowe, Copy Editor, who had the unenviable task of processing my writing, and Lindsay Burt, Production Manager, who got it all done at the end.

J. Ashok Robin

CHAPTER ONE

Introduction

International or global business activity by corporations presents unique financial management challenges. Consider the much admired firm Toyota Motors, which seeks to consolidate its leading position in the global auto industry. Toyota has faced issues concerning how to do the following:

Structure financing for its annual capital expenditure and investments, which are currently estimated at $30 billion.

Enter new markets such as India.

Optimize its global production strategy as it expands to new markets.

Estimate risks from currency changes.

Respond to shifts in currency markets such as the devaluation of the U.S. dollar.

Evaluate risks of operating in countries with political or economic turmoil.

Evaluate investments in new technologies.

Financial models and methods can help Toyota and other global firms address these and similar issues. This book discusses the global business environment and the use of financial models and methods in the global setting. Although the approach used in this book has many similarities with those in standard financial texts, the global context requires a different mindset and awareness as well an understanding of the customization or modification of standard financial models. For instance, certain risks such as currency risk and country risk are unique to the global setting. Furthermore, a global setting is much more dynamic than a purely domestic setting. This means that, among other things, managers seek flexibility in operations, but how can one evaluate flexibility? These are some interesting international corporate finance issues covered in this book.

Global issues affect the financial management practices of many entities including corporations, governments, and financial institutions. The focus of this book is on corporations. This is reflected in its title, *International Corporate Finance*. Most of the discussions in the text are in the framework of problems that global corporations known as **multinational corporations (MNCs)** face. Global factors such as currency values affect many purely domestic firms as well as MNCs. Foreign participation in an industry can occur by competing with foreign companies, having foreign customers, or using foreign suppliers. As long as they engage in some foreign activity, firms are subject to the influence of global factors. Hence, many issues discussed in this book apply equally to domestic firms.

This introductory chapter has two main objectives. First, it describes the global business environment in which MNCs operate. In particular, it discusses ways in which the world is becoming increasingly integrated and therefore affects MNCs. Second, it discusses the organization and management of MNCs. In short, this chapter is an introduction to globalization and MNC activity, specifically the following:

- Description of various ways in which globalization occurs and why this is important for corporations.
- Study of neoclassical and contemporary theories explaining international trade.

- Scope of cor~~ ~~ity.
- Overview of special risks faced by MNCs.
- Financial management issues that MNCs encounter.

1.1 Globalization

This section discusses the concept of globalization and its various forms. Next, it discusses factors contributing to globalization. It also analyzes the ways firms contribute to globalization and are in turn affected by it.

Globalization refers to international integration[1] and represents the cross-border movement of goods, services, money, and people. From a business standpoint, it refers to the economic integration of nations that is reflected in various types of cross-border activity such as the movement of:

- **Goods.** The movement of goods across borders, also known as *international trade,* is perhaps the foremost element of globalization. It integrates consumers and producers globally. Daimler AG, for instance, sells automobiles built in Germany around the world.
- **Services.** Increasingly, services such as tourism and consulting are being conducted across borders. The Walt Disney Company, for instance, attracts many Asians to its theme parks in the United States.
- **People.** Countries are increasingly allowing foreign citizens to reside and work within their borders. Because of the European Union agreement, Romanians seeking better labor market opportunities, for example, can emigrate to more affluent European nations.
- **Money.** Investors are increasingly able to purchase foreign assets. Such purchases involve either financial assets such as stocks and bonds or real assets such as farms and factories.

Although the word *globalization* was coined recently, the idea as well as the activity is not new. International trade, for instance, has existed for millennia. Two thousand years ago, the famous Silk Route connected East and West Asia and covered 8,000 arduous kilometers. Ancient civilizations along the Mediterranean traded with one another: Amphorae in ancient sunken vessels bear silent testimony. People in the Roman Empire moved across borders. Late 20th century developments have, however, elevated globalization to new levels. For example, only in recent decades have services and money flowed easily across borders and international trade has been pervasive enough for ordinary citizens to experience its effects. Globalization is expected by many to accelerate in the 21st century.

EXAMPLE 1.1	Is globalization good? It depends on whom you ask. In the United States, the auto factory workers in Detroit who lost their jobs because of Japanese competition or the textile workers in Charlotte who lost their jobs because of imports from low-cost nations such as Bangladesh would certainly say no. The U.S. customer who buys low-cost goods from Walmart—an importer of goods from foreign countries—may actually welcome globalization. Economists usually agree that globalization is good because they believe it raises the standard of living for global citizens, but recent events have amply demonstrated the dark side of globalization. Because of interconnectedness, events in a major country such as the United States tend to unduly influence other countries. The crisis that originated in the housing market in the United States in 2007 eventually became a full-blown global crisis in 2008. Virtually all financial markets worldwide were affected; the most severely affected arguably were emerging economies, whose stock and currency markets took massive hits.

Political and Socioeconomic Factors Influencing Globalization

Political and socioeconomic factors influence globalization. This section focuses on the economic situation at the end of World War II, trade agreements, the political movements toward freedom, and the rise of Asia.

[1] In a contemporary classic, *The World Is Flat: A Brief History of the Twenty-First Century*, Thomas Friedman (New York: Farrar, Straus and Giroux, 2005) discusses why technology and brilliant individuals are connecting the globe so that it feels as though it were flat.

The End of World War II

The end of the war in 1945 influenced many political and economic events. One was the increased involvement of the United States in European and world affairs. Another was the interest of nations in multilateral cooperation, especially in economic issues. This interest and the decades of peace following the war encouraged international trade as well as other manifestations of globalization. In fact, many experts consider globalization to be a post-World War II, 20th century phenomenon. Others consider the 19th century to be the first era of globalization and the post-World War II era to be the second and more significant era. The postwar era also coincides with the rise of MNCs.

Trade Agreements

Countries have increasingly come to believe that engaging in international trade could improve the welfare of their citizens. In recent decades, the World Trade Organization (WTO) agreements and the North American Free Trade Agreement (NAFTA), for example, have brought substantial blocks of countries into trade zones with fewer tariffs and other restrictions. The objective of these agreements is to foster and enable the movement of goods and services across borders by eliminating quotas, taxes, and other impediments. These agreements depend on multilateral negotiations and enforcement rather than having governments take unilateral actions resulting in a cycle of governments retaliating against one another by increasing restrictions. The resulting trade wars often hurt all parties. Multilateralism—joint coordinated action by all countries—has the potential to overcome these unilateral actions.

More than 100 nations are signatories to the WTO and similar agreements. These agreements have helped the world to generate a 15 percent annual growth in trade over the last 50 years. However, much needs to be done to ensure a higher level of trade and reduce frictions. Key unresolved issues include agricultural subsidies in industrialized nations, market access in developing nations, and intellectual property protection internationally. Trade agreements also have inherent limitations because of their focus on tariffs and quotas: They often overlook the informal and subtle barriers that many nations erect.

Political Change away from Socialist Systems

The dismantling of the Soviet Union, the gradual movement away from other socialist regimes, and the liberation of eastern European nations such as Poland and Hungary have advanced globalization. A widespread belief is that political freedom often precedes and presages economic freedom. Citizens in socialist systems are not allowed to consume as they please, nor are they allowed to conduct economic activity freely; even when certain economic freedoms are granted to citizens, those freedoms do not extend to cross-border activity, which increases when political freedoms are obtained.

EXAMPLE 1.2	The Czech Republic was once totally isolated from the global economic system, but following its "Velvet Revolution" of 1989, the country has made significant economic progress. Its national income has increased significantly, it has attracted foreign capital, and its business sector has been restructured. Firms such as Skoda Motors have become global players. The path to progress has not been easy: Czechs had to solve legal and political issues before advancing the country's economic reform including taxation, labor relations, regulation of information, and corporate governance.

Rise of Asia

For much of the 20th century, the United States and European nations dominated the global economic system because of the size of their economies (see Exhibit 1.1), but this is unlikely to continue in the 21st century. During the 1970s, Japan was the first outside nation to break into this elite club by exploiting its expertise in electronics and automobiles and creating global markets for its products. Other Asian countries such as Singapore, Hong Kong (now a part of China), and Korea next made important breakthroughs. Although these Asian "Tigers" initially specialized in low-cost manufactured products, they now form the critical supply chain for high-technology products.

EXHIBIT 1.1
Population and Gross Domestic Product (2007)

Sources: *http://siteresources. worldbank.org/DATASTATISTICS/ Resources/POP.pdf* and *http://siteresources.worldbank.org/ DATASTATISTICS/Resources/GDP. pdf* (accessed January 15, 2009).

Country	Population in Millions	Gross Domestic Products in Trillions (USD)
United States	302	13.8
Japan	128	4.4
China	1,320	3.3
Germany	82	3.3
United Kingdom	61	2.7
France	62	2.6
Canada	33	1.3
Russia	142	1.3
India	1,123	1.2

Two populous Asian nations, India and China, currently are experiencing high rates of economic growth and dramatic transformation and have gained both economic and political power.[2] Consequently, they have more input in decisions concerning the global economic system and have the potential to change the global business landscape.

Technology, Innovation, and Globalization

The post–World War era of globalization coincides with an era of technology and innovation including telecommunications connectivity, Internet connectivity, and shipping innovation.

The Telecommunication Revolution

Cross-border flow of information is itself a manifestation of globalization but more importantly enables cross-border economic activity. Telecommunication is the key technology that contributes to this flow. Readily available telephony services and rapidly decreasing costs enable a higher volume of international transactions. Consider a German importer of garments who is able to communicate easily with a supplier in Sri Lanka, a U.S. importer of shoes that is able to communicate inexpensively with its suppliers in Brazil, and a U.K. bank that is able to outsource its customer support function to India and decrease costs.

EXAMPLE 1.3

Mobile telephony has changed the business landscape in emerging economies. Economically disadvantaged nations have historically had poor infrastructure in telecommunications, which inhibited business activities. Large areas in India, Brazil, and China have been inaccessible by telephone. Many factors contributed to this including difficult geography, insufficient resources, and the presence of inept government monopolies in the telecommunications industry. In the last decade with the introduction of mobile phones, however, the situation has changed dramatically. Not only has connectivity greatly improved but also emerging economies have actually innovated in the deployment of mobile telephony. In India, for instance, service providers such as Bharti Airtel use a lean business model (operating with fewer resources) whose networks are outsourced to third parties such as Nokia. This allows pricing at significantly lower rates than those in developed countries. This innovation has spurred national growth and international trade.[3]

Internet Age

The Internet is a global electronic communications network with more than a billion users (see Exhibit 1.2) that leverages the use of the telecommunications infrastructure. The pace of

---

[2] The recently coined acronym BRIC refers to the emerging economies of Brazil, Russia, India, and China as a collective force.

[3] The benefits of technologies such as mobile telephony also extend to average citizens. In a famous study, Robert Jensen found that both consumers and fishermen benefit when wholesalers contact the fishermen using cell phones before the catch is brought ashore. The resulting exchange of information via a phone call enables the fishermen to unload their catch at the best possible beach or market. See Robert Jensen, "The Digital Provide: Information (Technology), Market Performance, and Welfare in the South Indian Fisheries Sector," *Quarterly Journal of Economics* 122, no. 3 (2007), 879–924.

EXHIBIT 1.2
Internet Usage (2008)

Source: *http://internetworldstats.com/stats.htm* (accessed January 16, 2009).

Country/Region	Internet Users (millions)	Penetration (% of population)
Africa	51	5.3%
Asia	579	15.3
Europe	385	48.1
Middle East	42	21.3
North America	248	73.6
Latin America/Caribbean	139	24.1
Oceania/Australia	20	59.5

technological innovation is so breathtaking that we forget that e-mail has existed only since the 1980s. This ubiquitous method of communicating has revolutionized the conduct of business. Succeeding innovations such as electronic commerce have brought together suppliers and consumers from diverse nations. Technology has the capability to span national borders and overcome difficulties that firms face in selling or sourcing products overseas. Easier and cheaper access to the Internet is to some extent a consequence of large investments in fiber optics during the dot com boom of the 1990s.

Recent breakthroughs in the deployment of broadband Internet are promising by enabling, for example, research and development (R&D) teams in different countries to collaborate with one another, banks to process trade documents efficiently in centralized and low-cost locations such as Dubai, and medical data to be transferred for transcription and storage in low-cost locations such as India. New and innovative business models emerge every day. No industry is immune to radical changes, it appears.

Sea and Air Shipping

Only about one-quarter of all international trade involves trade between countries that share a land border. In most other cases, goods need to be shipped by air or by sea, the vast majority by sea because of its significantly lower costs. A major innovation in sea shipping in the latter half of the 20th century is *containerization*. This is the use of standard sized cargo boxes called *containers* that typically measure 20′ by 8.5′ by 8.5′. This innovation has reduced shipping costs and, more importantly, improved shipping quality.[4] Container shipping makes loading and unloading ships easier and also facilitates transfers between trucks, ships, and railroad cars. Containerization has also led to innovative ship design for carrying only containers and using space efficiently. Innovation in propulsion technology (e.g., wind power) is likely in the near future because of the recent rise in oil prices.

Although more than 95 percent of shipping is by sea, an increasing percentage of high-value goods are shipped by air. Firms are motivated to use air shipping when time is important. Goods shipped from Asia to North America may take three weeks by sea but only one to two days by air. Although fuel price becomes a significant factor, innovation in air shipping has led to significant cost reductions in the last few decades. The trend is toward increased use of air shipping.

1.2 Theories of International Trade and Industry Location

International trade (broadly described as the movement of goods and services) is the most important component of globalization. This section uses the classical theory of comparative advantage and contemporary theories such as the product cycle and new theories to explain why international trade is increasing. It also discusses theories of agglomeration or industry location.[5]

---

[4] David Hummels, "Transportation Costs and International Trade in the Second Era of Globalization," *Journal of Economic Perspectives* 21, no. 3 (2007), 131–154.

[5] There are a variety of sources for theories of trade. One comprehensive text is *International Trade* by Luis A. Rivera-Batiz and Maria-Angels Oliva (New York: Oxford University Press, 2003).

Classical and Neoclassical Theories of Trade

Classical Version

theory of comparative advantage

The *theory of comparative advantage* explains why Canada exports wheat and why France exports wine.

According to the **theory of comparative advantage** proposed by the 19th century economist David Ricardo, nations exhibit different levels of productivity. The key input is assumed to be labor but because of various levels of technology, countries have relative advantages in producing only certain products. For instance, countries such as Japan have high labor productivity in manufacturing vehicles (because of advanced manufacturing technology) and hence export vehicles. Others countries such as Canada exhibit high labor productivity in growing wheat and therefore export it. Trade resulting from comparative advantage benefits all nations because it allows countries to change their productive capacity to only those products for which they have a comparative advantage. The theory of comparative advantage should not be confused with the theory of absolute advantage. Comparative advantage does not mean that goods are produced only by the lowest costs producer.

EXAMPLE 1.4

The original example offered by Ricardo best explains comparative advantage without invoking absolute advantage. England and Portugal produce wine and cloth. Portugal produces the least expensive wine and cloth. However, comparing the two goods, Portugal finds it relatively cheaper to produce wine and England finds it relatively cheaper to produce cloth. If Portugal shifts some of its production from cloth to wine, it can then ship the excess wine to England and receive cloth in return. Conversely, England shifts production from wine to cloth and benefits from trading with Portugal, which also benefits from this trade.

Neoclassical Version of the Comparative Advantage Theory

The neoclassical Heckscher and Ohlin (HO) model offers a deeper understanding of comparative advantage. The HO model explains the situation in terms of factor abundance instead of technology. In this model, productivity differences are explained by the relative abundance of factors of production. A country that has relatively more capital (per worker) may focus on capital-intensive industries. Likewise, a country that has abundant labor may produce labor-intensive products such as textiles. The United States, which has capital abundance, produces and exports planes and jet engines to India because of the capital-intensive nature of these industries. In return, India, which has labor abundance, produces and exports T-shirts to the United States because of labor intensity in the textile industry. See Exhibit 1.3 for imports and exports of a sample of countries.

The theory of comparative advantage is an important one in economics. In addition to explaining patterns of trade, it finds application in the design of complex financial contracts such as swaps (discussed in Chapter 10). As a trade theory, however, this concept has become increasingly less relevant because of increasing levels of cross-border mobility of factors of production (e.g., raw materials, capital) contrary to model assumptions. For instance, capital and knowledge increasingly flow across borders. Furthermore, forces such as knowledge, technology, and innovation are shaping the business world to a greater extent than labor productivity.

EXHIBIT 1.3
Imports and Exports of Selected Countries

Country	Exports	Imports
China	Electronics, consumer goods, computers, apparel, machinery	Capital goods, chemicals, oil, steel, airplanes
Germany	Automobiles, machines, electronics, chemicals	Automobiles, computers, petroleum, textiles, food
India	Food, jewelry, textiles, leather, minerals, machinery	Petroleum, chemicals, plastics, pharmaceuticals, electronics, airplanes
Russia	Petroleum, natural gas, wood products, minerals	Food, consumer goods, capital goods, textiles
United States	Capital goods, airplanes, grains, computers, software	Textiles, electronics, automobiles, petroleum

Other Theories of International Trade

This section summarizes several recent models and ideas that explain bilateral and multilateral trade.

Imperfect Markets Theory

Because imperfect markets block the cross-border movement of inputs to a product, countries specialize only in certain products and trade with one another to obtain others. According to the **imperfect markets theory**, international trade is a consequence of market impediments that restrict the free flow of resources across borders. In actuality, resources such as raw materials, energy, labor, and management are not easily transferable across borders. Even when transfers are possible, they have significant transaction costs. This inhibits the movement of the factors of production and forces countries to specialize in certain industries.

Consider this application of the imperfect markets theory. India is perhaps the largest global source of software engineers. Information technology (IT) in India serves U.S. corporate customers. Because imperfect markets for labor caused by regulatory impediments and transaction costs inhibit the ability of U.S. corporations to hire these engineers, they outsource their work to engineers working in Indian firms.

Gravity Theory

Gravity theory explains trade between two nations (bilateral trade). The quantity of bilateral trade is hypothesized to be positively related to the countries' size (measured by gross national product) and negatively related to distance. For instance, the United States tends to trade more with Germany because both nations are large and affluent. At the same time, the United States trades a lot with Mexico because of proximity.

Product Life Cycle Theory

The **product life cycle theory** is attributable to Vernon and others; it relates to competitive advantages arising from innovation. When a nation's products are first introduced in global markets, they have a clear competitive advantage because of R&D, innovation, or other advantages, for example, that are not easily overcome. As the technology becomes standardized, less expensive, and more readily available, competitors in foreign countries take market share in their countries first and later in international markets. Finally, foreign competitors become strong enough to pose a challenge in the originating country's markets. The U.S. consumer electronics industry went through such a cycle.

Firm-Level Product Cycle Theory

The firm-level product cycle theory states that a firm initially produces and sells in its domestic market. Over time, the firm exports in order to enjoy economies of scale and perhaps to overcome stagnation in its domestic markets. Next, the firm considers producing its products in foreign locations because it needs, for example, to have flexibility, to save transportation costs, to be close to the customer, and so on. The Chinese appliance manufacturer Haier is an example of this theory. After establishing its business in China during the past two decades, Haier is now trying to compete in global markets.

New Trade Theory

Krugman and other writers proposed the **new trade theory** that focuses on other factors affecting international trade such as consumer preferences and economies of scale. Consumers seek variety and producers seek economies of scale. Consumers demand differentiated products with similar qualities. For instance, consumers prefer variety in wine and clothes. If each variety requires fixed production costs, firms (and countries) will specialize in certain varieties. In the wine industry, for instance, Chilean producers specialize in wines made from the cabernet sauvignon grape, and Australian producers specialize in wines made from the Syrah grape. By engaging in trade, producers' volumes rise, and they benefit from decreasing average production costs. An interesting feature of this theory is that it explains why countries simultaneously import and export the same product. This follows from the fact that in a given country, the variety demanded by consumers will exceed the variety supplied by its producers, leading consumers to import from other nations. The United Kingdom, for instance, is both an exporter and importer of automobiles. The United States also is both an exporter and an importer of commercial airplanes. In fact, intraindustry trade is a significant component of total trade especially for developed nations where consumers demand great variety in products. This theory is quite useful in explaining trade data.

Theories of Industry Location

As globalization intensified competition among nations, scholars sought to understand why certain industries were situated in specific geographic locations, why certain countries export certain products, and why MNCs set up certain business divisions in particular locations. The following sections summarize these trade theories of location.

Industry Agglomeration Theory

industry agglomeration theory
Location theories such as the *industry agglomeration theory* explain why the computer software industry thrives in the Silicon Valley.

Why did the computer software industry come together, or agglomerate, in the Silicon Valley area of California? Why is the financial industry located in centers such as New York and London? Why are computer notebook components manufactured in Taiwan? The **industry agglomeration theory** explains that industries agglomerate because of positive *externalities* such as exchange of ideas (knowledge spillover), labor market pooling, and development of ancillary industries. In the Silicon Valley, for instance, an R&D network spanning corporations and universities results in knowledge spillover, benefitting software firms located in the area. In New York, for example, investment banks and other financial institutions share a pool of highly skilled labor. In Taiwan, personal computer manufacturers obtain inputs from a large network of component manufacturers.

Porter's Diamond Theory

One version of the industry agglomeration theory, **Porter's Diamond theory**, identifies four factors that explain why certain nations have advantages in producing certain products:

- **Factor conditions.** Inputs such as skilled labor as well as transportation and other infrastructure are available.
- **Demand conditions.** The domestic market for the products and services in question is vibrant.
- **Related and supporting industries.** Suppliers and other ancillaries are available.
- **Firm strategy, structure, and rivalry.** Rivalry between producers in the home market creates an efficient setting for the industry.

EXAMPLE 1.5

Tirupur, located in the southern Indian state of Tamilnadu, was a boom town in the 1990s for only one reason: It annually exported more than $1 billion of knitted garments to European and North American markets. Tirupur's success can be explained using agglomeration theories. Garment manufacturing, despite advances in past decades, requires much skilled labor. Thousands of factories in Tirupur employ nearly a quarter of a million skilled employees and have created a vibrant pool of skilled labor. This industry originally located in Tirupur because of its proximity to Coimbatore and its cotton-spinning industry. Spinners provide the thread that is then knitted into jersey fabric. Tirupur was initially viewed as a low-cost area compared to Coimbatore. Over time, crucial ancillaries such as knitting, dyeing, mercerizing, embroidery, and printing were developed in and around Tirupur, which has a vibrant entrepreneurial culture with great rivalry between various producers. Observers have noted that when wealthy residents meet, even in formal social functions such as weddings, they engage in industry-related gossip such as speculation about which firm recently landed a large order or whether a new labeling machine is performing well at a friend's factory. Tirupur is no longer a low-cost producer because of rising labor costs. It is facing intense competition from other Asian countries such as Bangladesh. Tirupur is now attempting to move up the value chain and produce more value-added products such as custom-made garments.

1.3 MNCs, Foreign Direct Investment Strategy, and Globalization

MNCs engage in **foreign direct investment (FDI)** by which they acquire ownership in foreign branches, subsidiaries, and affiliates. Although thousands of firms may fit the definition of an MNC, people generally consider only large firms that conduct business in many foreign countries to be true MNCs. These firms (e.g., Applied Materials and General Electric) typically have billions of U.S. dollars (USD) in foreign sales and thousands of employees in overseas locations. And, unlike the situation of the 1960s and 1970s when most MNCs were U.S.-based corporations, today's roster of MNCs includes firms from many different countries including non-U.S. firms such as Nokia (Finland), Hyundai (Korea), Acer (Taiwan), Tata Motors (India), Norilsk Nickel (Russia), and Embraer (Brazil). Increasingly, MNCs are now coming from emerging economies.

MNCs face significant costs in setting up foreign operations. Because of geographical distance and resulting transaction costs, a purely local firm should in principle be able to operate a business more efficiently than an MNC. This means that MNCs conduct FDI activity only if other benefits offset these transaction costs. The following theories that suggest value-producing strategies for MNCs explain these advantages.[6]

Dunning's OLI Model

Dunning's **OLI model** explains that firms become MNCs because of ownership, location, and internalization advantages.

Ownership Advantages

An MNC owns specialized firm-level assets such as intellectual property, production technologies, brands, and reputation and can leverage these assets in global activity and enjoy an advantage over local firms. Coca-Cola, for instance, has a brand image and formulas for soft drinks that it uses globally. One caveat is that licensing (allowing a foreign firm to produce and sell for a fee) may offer a simpler alternative to an FDI for exploiting ownership advantages.

Location Advantages

Factors such as taxes, availability of inputs, transportation costs, and other transaction costs may be so advantageous to cause an MNC to favor producing goods in the country where it will sell them. For instance, Hyundai finds producing cars in Chennai for the Indian market an advantage because of the tax incentives and low-cost labor there.

Internalization Advantages

A firm may be considered a nexus of contracts in the sense that there are contracts between the firm and various parties such as suppliers and customers. Sometimes contracting with external parties may pose difficulties, so firms choose to keep activities within the firm's current boundaries. This is the case, for instance, for firms that do not trust entities in foreign countries with their know-how. This may explain why Boeing prefers to have its own maintenance operations in China and India rather than transferring knowledge to entities in other countries to perform the same function.

Knowledge Capital

knowledge capital
One important reason why firms expand overseas and become MNCs is that they have specific and unique advantages such as proprietary product and process knowledge (known as *knowledge capital*).

The OLI model and others by various authors are sometimes referred as the knowledge capital approach to FDI. It is based on the understanding that MNCs differ from other firms because they have considerable knowledge capital that they use extensively. For example, they hold

---

[6] A number of authors are credited with theories related to MNCs. Many ideas in the following section are explained in James Markusen, *Multinational Firms and the Theory of International Trade* (Cambridge, MA: MIT Press, 2002). He is one of the leading authors on MNCs.

patents and have developed specific technologies and are innovative. Markusen, who coined the term *knowledge capital,* explains the central role it plays:

- Knowledge capital, relative to physical capital, can be easily transmitted to a foreign location. For example, technologies and processes can be easily communicated and used to create a foreign plant.
- Knowledge capital requires skilled labor. MNCs are often headquartered in countries with abundant skilled labor. Thus, MNCs can generate knowledge capital in their home country and export this capital to foreign locations.

MNCs as Facilitators of Globalization

Foreign direct investment is a key MNC activity, but it is only one aspect of globalization. Consider the following examples that illustrate the variety of MNC activities (including FDI) that facilitate globalization:

- MNCs are skilled in moving goods and selling them across borders. For instance, Hewlett Packard is successful in selling computer hardware and services in Europe. Thus, MNCs are facilitators of international trade.
- MNCs are skilled in making investments in foreign assets. In fact, this is a core competency that explains FDI activity. Volkswagen, for example, has a record of successfully setting up plants in developing countries. It has multiple plants in China and now has its first one in India to manufacture its Polo model.
- MNCs are skilled in various forms of business contracting. In addition to FDI in its strict sense (establishing subsidiaries), MNCs engage in cross-border joint ventures, licensing agreements, and other forms of business activities. Such activities involve cross-border movement of goods, services, and capital and thus increase globalization.
- MNCs are skilled in moving people across borders. In a controversial practice, U.S. insurance firms such as Aetna outsource information technology (IT) work to Indian firms such as Infosys. Some of the work is accomplished by "importing" Indian software engineers to work in the firm's home country. In some respects, however, this is not very different from the practice of U.S.-based MNCs sending executives to work abroad in subsidiaries.
- Perhaps not directly relevant to the business world, one should not forget the role of MNCs in global cultural integration. Firms such as Nike, Coca-Cola, and Apple are cultural as well as business icons.

Other entities (e.g., governments, nongovernmental agencies) also engage in cross-border activities, but MNCs are particularly suited to them. MNCs have specialized skills as well as the financial resources to engage in global activities. Some well-known U.S.-based MNCs are identified in Exhibit 1.4. These firms, many of which are household names, derive billions of U.S. dollars in sales overseas by conducting complex international operations (e.g., IBM derives USD 62 billion of revenues from foreign countries). The extent of international operations is also indicated by their foreign assets (e.g., Johnson & Johnson has USD 21 billion in foreign assets).

EXHIBIT 1.4
Foreign Revenues and Assets of Selected MNCs (2007)

Source: Marketwatch.com (accessed June 15, 2008).

Company	Foreign Revenue (USD billions)	Foreign Revenue (%)	Foreign Assets (USD billions)	Foreign Assets (%)
Exxon	269	69%	87	72%
Ford Motor	79	46	21	30
IBM	62	63	6	49
Hewlett-Packard	69	67	3	45
Microsoft	20	39	0	9
Nike	10	63	0.7	46
Coca-Cola	21	74	6	68
Johnson & Johnson	29	47	21	49
Eastman Kodak	6	59	0.5	30

EXHIBIT 1.5
Intel's Revenue by Geographic Regions, 2007

Source: Intel Annual Report 2007.

Country/Region	Revenues (%)
Americas	20%
Europe	19
Asia-Pacific	51
Japan	10

MNC Activity: The Intel Example

The U.S.-based semiconductor firm Intel performs an incredible range of cross-border activity. It sells products in more than 100 countries and derives more than 50 percent of its revenues and income from foreign sources. See Exhibit 1.5 for the geographic sources for its year 2007 revenues. Note the extent of diversification across various regions.

However, foreign sales represent only one aspect of Intel's worldwide operations. Consider the following additional aspects:

- Investments in foreign firms.
- Acquisition of many foreign firms.
- Operation of software development centers in many countries.
- Production of semiconductor chips in many countries.
- Sourcing of materials and supplies from many countries.

These activities can be explained by the theories of international trade. For example, consider Intel's locating a software center in India to take advantage of the supply of Indian software engineers. It would take this action because of market inefficiencies that make the movement of labor across borders difficult. The comparative advantage theory would explain why Intel obtains supplies from countries such as Indonesia and Taiwan that have particular types of manufacturing expertise.

The wide variety of MNC activities as evident in the Intel example suggests an alternative definition of MNC: a firm that operates seamlessly across national borders. In the extreme, an MNC operates as though there are no national borders. Today, hundreds of firms fit this alternative definition. Previously, firms in only a few industries such as petroleum, automobiles, and pharmaceuticals had global operations. Today, many firms in industries including telecommunications, semiconductors, personal computer hardware and software, and financial services operate globally. More and more non-U.S. firms fit this definition of MNC.

1.4 Special Risks Faced by MNCs

Operating in the global landscape is challenging. Firms face various risks that increase the volatility of their cash flows. By appropriately managing these risks, however, MNCs can produce value for their investors. The following sections discuss several specific risks. This discussion provides an introduction to this key aspect of this topic. Detailed discussions are found in later chapters.

Currency Risk

A firm faces currency risk when its financial performance (cash flows) responds to changes in currency values. Consequently, its cash flows reflect a certain level of increased variation or risk. This heightened variation has the potential to disrupt the firm and decrease its value. Consider the simplest global activity: selling products in overseas markets. This activity results in earning revenues denominated in foreign currencies that are then converted to the domestic currency. A decrease in the value of the foreign currency relative to the domestic currency would lower revenues.

EXAMPLE 1.6

Consider the French luxury goods firm Moet Hennessy Louis Vuitton (LVMH). When it sells fashion products in the United Kingdom, it converts its British pound revenues into Euros. If the pound weakens, the amount of Euro-equivalent revenues is lower. Because currency values influence the firm's cash flows, LMVH faces currency risk. Chapters 4 and 5 discuss why currency values change over time; this currency volatility induces uncertain cash flows for MNCs and other firms.

Currency risk can be a complex issue because MNCs face exposure to multiple currencies. Consider firms such as General Electric that operate in many countries and are therefore exposed to a *portfolio* of currencies. Financial models for risk and diversification provide appropriate tools to understand currency risk in such a setting. However, some aspects of currency risk require much more sophisticated analyses than the mere estimation of diversification effects. For example, firms may have competitors from other countries whose cost basis is in other currencies. In this case, changes in currency values could have multifaceted effects on the corporations; among effects are the prices and quantities of goods sold. Chapters 6 and 7 explore these ideas and ways to manage currency risk.

Economic Risk

Economic risk refers to the variation in cash flows caused by changes in macroeconomic conditions. In the context of international finance, it refers to the risks inherent in foreign economies. Influential economic factors are economic growth, inflation, interest rates, and employment. Because of increasing levels of integration, certain economic factors assume common values worldwide. For instance, inflation in energy prices is highly correlated across nations. Nevertheless, most economic factors have an imperfect correlation. An MNC wishing to operate in a particular country should carefully evaluate its economic risk factors.

Consider the example of a U.S.-based MNC operating a subsidiary in Italy as a brief illustration of how economic risk factors such as growth and inflation in Italy can influence the performance of this firm.

- The first factor to consider is economic growth, which would lead to increased product demand in Italy. On the other hand, a recession in Italy would adversely affect product demand. The impact of economic growth is especially evident if the firm is producing and selling durable goods. Basic economic theory states that people tend to decrease consumption of durable goods during recessions.

- The second economic risk factor is inflation. High inflation would increase the cost of goods sold and adversely affect profitability. Inflation in output prices could result from inflation either in the cost of inputs such as oil and steel or in labor costs.

- Other factors also can affect the firm's performance. Labor relations is one such factor. In Italy, a large proportion of the labor force is unionized. Unions there and in other European nations are able to conduct strikes and curtail operations more than unions in the United States.

Political and Regulatory Risk

Political (and regulatory) risks in foreign countries result from potential action by governmental and regulatory authorities. It has been said that only MNCs operating in emerging markets face this type of risk, but this is not quite true. MNCs face political risks even in developed nations. Generally speaking, firms are subject to all types of regulation pertaining to operational issues such as pollution, labor relations, and customer relations; governance issues such as shareholder rights and board of director's composition/responsibilities; and financial issues such as taxation, remittance of funds, and financing. MNCs need to have a core competency in dealing with regulations in multiple countries.

EXAMPLE 1.7

Consider a European pharmaceutical firm such as AstraZeneca or GlaxoSmithKline that operates subsidiaries in the United States. These firms are subject to political risks arising from actions taken by U.S. legislators. Examples of legislation that could adversely affect these firms are laws setting price limits or restricting drug marketing. An analysis of a country's political environment may reveal the extent of these risk factors. For example, one recent development is prescription drug price increases and their adverse consequences on private as well as government insurance programs. Because of public outcry over this problem, the pharmaceutical industry in the United States could anticipate a heightened level of risk in the near future, which would likely pose adverse consequences for pharmaceutical firms. For instance, the U.S. government could attempt to control drug costs in the Medicare program, which aids senior citizens, by restricting drug access or by cutting drug reimbursement prices.

Variation in Business Practices

Global differences in culture, tradition, conventions, and regulations invariably affect business methods. An MNC should be adept at assessing a nation's cultural and business climates and altering its business methods appropriately. Business practices that could be affected include labor, customer, and supplier relations as well as corporate governance. Consider the example of customer relations in Japan. Typical Japanese customers demand a higher level of personalized service than typical U.S. customers. Thus, U.S. firms conducting business in Japan need to structure their distribution systems and marketing strategies differently to meet the needs of the Japanese customer. From an economic perspective, one may consider such variations as a corporate risk factor.

Countries differ in their levels of transparency with respect to rules and regulations. Often, nations with low levels of transparency have powerful bureaucracies, making an effective relationship with key bureaucrats important. A learning curve appears to exist in this aspect, especially when dealing with emerging economies such as those of India and China. For this reason, MNCs often set up limited operations in a foreign country to learn about its regulatory climate first. After gaining confidence and knowledge, they can extend their involvement. Such sequential MNC activity is explained by the *real options* model discussed in Chapter 9.

1.5 Corporate Governance of MNCs

MNCs are complex organizations especially regarding their overall organization and the relationship between various entities such as managers, investors, and external markets. The term *corporate governance* refers to the rules, processes, and laws regulating and controlling firms. This section discusses MNCs' goals and explains how MNCs differ from domestic firms and the various internal and external corporate governance mechanisms they can employ. It also describes global differences in corporate governance.

MNC Goals and the Agency Problem

As with other corporations, an MNC's key goal is to *maximize shareholder wealth*. Various analytical frameworks and rationales can justify this goal; the two most compelling reasons are presented here. First, from a narrow legal perspective, shareholders are owners of the firm and therefore have *property rights* that transcend the rights of other parties such as employees, managers, and the community. These property rights are reflected, for instance, in shareholders' rights to govern the firm by electing directors and taking other actions. Second, from a broad economic perspective, maximization of shareholder wealth benefits society at large. Firms allocate resources to their most productive uses, in turn helping to generate economic growth.

Like domestic firms, MNCs face challenges in achieving their goal to maximize shareholder wealth. The *principal-agent* model explains the fact that shareholders are viewed as principals who assign tasks to managers who act as their agents. A well-known fact is that agents prefer

agency costs
MNCs face high agency costs because they are large, geographically dispersed, and decentralized.

decisions that increase their own welfare rather than the welfare of their principals, creating agency costs (loss of value because of the presence of agents). For example, many corporate takeovers are motivated by managerial motives to increase their own wealth or power, but these motives do not benefit shareholders. An important goal of corporate governance, therefore, is to reduce the incidence and impact of such antishareholder behavior. Additional goals may relate to the protection of other stakeholders such as creditors, employees, and society at large.

While the underlying principal-agent issues are similar for MNCs, MNCs face higher agency costs for the following reasons:

- MNCs are typically very large firms with geographically dispersed operations.
- MNCs usually produce and sell a large number of products and services.
- MNCs tend to have greater decentralization, especially with respect to foreign subsidiaries.

These differences exacerbate the agency problem. Thus, an MNC needs to pay close attention to various mechanisms to alleviate the agency problem. The following sections briefly discuss these mechanisms.

Internal Governance and Monitoring Mechanisms

Various mechanisms within the corporation are available to reduce agency costs. Two of them are the corporation's organization structure and board of directors.

Organizational Structure

An important mechanism for controlling agency costs is the firm's organization. One organizational variable is the degree of *centralization* or the extent to which decisions are concentrated at the top of the organization. From an economic perspective, the optimal degree of centralization depends on the trade-off between two types of costs. The first is the *cost of information transmission,* or the cost of transferring information from lower-level units to upper-level decision-making units. An MNC with a production operation in Taiwan may face this cost in regard to various decisions about production such as the type of raw materials to use, the sources to obtain them, and the contractual relationship with labor. MNCs with high information transmission costs should decentralize. The second is the agency cost between top and lower-level management. If agency costs are high, MNCs should centralize. In a comparison of an MNC to a normal firm, geographical distances are likely to create difficulties in information transmission for MNCs and, hence, the need for more decentralization.

Board of Directors

Firms also depend on nonmanagerial monitoring, especially of top management. They use the *board of directors* as this mechanism. Shareholders elect the directors, usually during the annual shareholders meeting. Shareholders who are unable to attend the meeting are allowed to submit their proxies (votes) by mail. In theory, shareholders control the board, but their ability to do so is actually weak for two reasons. First, the insiders such as the CEO often chair the board and have control over the process of nominating directors. Second, because of apathy and/or lack of economic incentives, many shareholders do not participate in the firm's governance.

By optimally structuring the board of directors, firms can increase the quality of management decisions. Boards that are reasonably small (10 or fewer members) and include a large number of independent directors best serve the interests of shareholders. Furthermore, it is important to minimize the influence of the CEO and other top managers on the board.

External Monitoring Mechanisms

External monitoring mechanisms, which are outside the firm's domain, relate to the corporate governance climate in a country. Markets play a vital role as do shareholder monitoring, analyst coverage, and the market for corporate control.

Shareholder Monitoring

Shareholders are keenly interested in the financial results of the corporations they own. They demand information about the firm's performance and act on this information. Regulation mandates some of the information, but firms themselves initiate others to help reach certain objectives such as lowering the cost of capital. Firms typically publish accounting information such as income statements, balance sheets, and the statement of cash flows. In addition, firms use signals such as dividends, share repurchases, and earnings projections. In the United States, firms also cultivate relationships with analysts, who collect information regarding the firm and produce reports about it for their clients.

The cumulative effect of such information dissemination is that investors obtain both good and bad news about firms and use this information to properly value their securities and make buy/sell decisions. These buy/sell decisions and their effect on share prices help discipline managerial behavior. For example, consider a firm divulging bad news. The resulting fall in stock prices reduces its ability to obtain financing at favorable terms, thus limiting its growth opportunities. The firm also may become an attractive takeover target. MNCs, principally because they are larger firms and face greater regulatory requirements for information dissemination concerning its operations, offer increased opportunity for shareholder monitoring.

Analyst Coverage

MNCs differ from other firms in that they tend to be larger and attract a great deal of scrutiny from shareholders and financial institutions. One way to measure investor scrutiny is to count the number of financial analysts following a firm. These analysts belong to (Wall Street) investment banking firms such as Morgan Stanley and Merrill Lynch. At least 10 analysts follow a typical MNC; they maintain various levels of contacts with the firm, and these contacts and the reports they generate help shareholders to monitor the MNC and its management.

Market for Corporate Control

The market for corporate control conducts transactions such as mergers that result in changes in the control of firms.[7] A firm that is controlled suboptimally (that is, managed inefficiently) becomes the takeover target of another firm or group of investors. The goal of these transactions is to strengthen the management of corporate assets and to control them better, resulting in increased value. *Mergers and acquisitions* are key transactions in the market for corporate control. Other methods to change control include large investors' submission of their nominees for the board and/or seeking a change in top management. Such changes are achieved through negotiations between large investors and the management team or through a *proxy contest* in which one person or, more likely, a group solicits other shareholders' votes to approve new directors who are expected to bring about corporate change.

A common belief is that MNCs are too large to be taken over and therefore are immune to the corporate control market's discipline. This is no longer true, however; large acquisitions are made possible by a relatively new method known as a *stock transaction* through which the acquirer uses its own shares instead of paying cash for an acquisition. This method allows transactions involving tens of billions of dollars. See Chapter 12 for more information concerning mergers and related transactions.

U.S. or Anglo-Saxon Governance Model

governance model
The U.S. or Anglo-Saxon *governance model* is characterized by independent boards, incentive contracts for managers and transparency in financial reporting.

U.S. financial markets are often considered the healthiest in the world.[8] The U.S. governance model—geared toward public markets and arms-length contracting—is a consequence of traditions adopted from the United Kingdom. For this reason, it is sometimes referred to as the U.S. or Anglo-Saxon governance model. The United Kingdom, Canada, and Australia have similar governance.

[7] Henry Manne, "Mergers and the Market for Corporate Control," *Journal of Political Economy* 73, no. 2 (1965), pp. 110–120.

[8] No market appears safe from spectacular failure. The global credit crisis of 2007–2008 originated with U.S. markets and appears to have put the global economy in a tailspin.

Despite high-profile scandals such as those involving Enron and WorldCom, the U.S. governance model is considered to be a good one. Its salient features include the following:

- U.S. corporations tend to have so-called independent boards of directors dominated by directors who are not subject to the influence of the firm's insiders. Government and stock exchange regulations mandate independent boards.

- U.S. managers typically have compensation contracts based on performance and resulting in the award of stock options in an attempt to align their objectives with those of shareholders.

- U.S. laws protect minority stockholders from acts of expropriation. In particular, because of the well-defined and well-enforced legal system, managers and other insiders are held legally accountable to all shareholders including minority shareholders.

- U.S. accounting practices are geared toward rapid transmission of relevant financial information to investors. This produces a certain level of transparency by which external parties are able to see a firm's true status.

Governance Practices in European and Asian Countries

Although the use of the U.S. model of governance is increasing and other nations are imitating aspects of it, governance features of firms in Europe and Asia differ significantly from those in the United States.

Board Structure

Board structure and composition vary across countries. Firms in the United States and other countries following the Anglo-Saxon governance model have single-tier boards containing insiders (managers) as well as outsiders. Most continental European nations, however, have two-tier boards: the management board composed of executives and the supervisory board of outsiders and labor representatives. In Germany, for example, regulations stipulate that half the supervisory board be made up of labor representatives. Another difference relates to the presence of large shareholders. In the United States, outside blockholders (large unaffiliated shareholders) often serve as directors as members of the board. This is less common in other countries. Finally, the pool of professional directors is larger in the United States than in European and Asian nations.

Family Control

In many countries, closely knit families commonly own a majority of the voting shares, hold critical managerial positions, dominate the board of directors, and operate large corporations. This is especially true in Asian countries such as Taiwan, China, and Malaysia and in European countries such as France and Italy. Family control, however, can inhibit internal and external monitoring. For instance, the threat of a takeover of a family-controlled firm is not credible and cannot cause a change in management practices. Consequently, high holdings by insiders may lead to suboptimal corporate performance and correspondingly low firm value.

Market for Corporate Control

The effectiveness of the market for corporate control in United States and other countries also differs. The U.S. market is particularly active and effective. In the United States, investments banks such as Goldman Sachs serve as intermediaries and facilitate this market. In recent years, increasing merger activity has occurred in many European countries such as the United Kingdom, France, and Germany. Much of this European activity is pan-national and triggered by the European Economic and Monetary Union (EMU). However, various regulations impede takeovers in non-U.S. nations. Organized labor is one particularly effective deterrent to takeovers in Europe. Because of the strong labor interests represented in boards and the explicit regulatory powers given to labor unions, they have the power to veto transactions. The recent veto of the proposed takeover of the troubled Italian airline Alitalia by unions illustrates their power. In Asia, because of family control of firms and other impediments, the market for corporate control is in a far worse condition with a lower probability of a merger transaction and reduced threat to insiders. This leads to the conclusion that the market for corporate control is rather ineffective in non-U.S. settings.

Accounting Transparency

In the United States, public corporations are required to follow generally accepted accounting principles (GAAP), which emphasize the need for transparency and for serving the interests of external parties such as stockholders and bondholders. GAAP does provide flexibility, and U.S. firms often choose conservative options in accounting in response to pressure brought to bear by investors. But transparency and conservatism are not always found in non-U.S. settings because of different legal systems and different forms of corporate governance in other countries. In particular, European countries such as Germany and France and Asian countries such as Japan and Malaysia do not follow U.S. practices. In Japan, banks are major capital providers, and because bank financing is private in nature, monitoring takes a different and more direct form. Banks often place their representatives on the board of corporations they finance. Financial reporting, therefore, is not critical for monitoring Japanese firms.

Minority Shareholder Rights

In countries with weak legal systems, interests of minority stockholders are often violated. Majority stockholders can potentially transfer assets of a firm at below market prices to an external entity under their control. Unlike the minority shareholders who lose because of the lower value of the firm that has sold assets at below market prices, the majority shareholders stand to gain because of the higher value of the external entity that has purchased assets at below market prices. Weak legal systems do not allow minority shareholders to challenge such transactions effectively. This diabolical problem is a fact of life in many eastern European and Asian countries. Czechs have coined a term indicating expropriation from minority shareholders: **tunneling**. Expropriation and other governance problems tend to dampen investor interest in the securities of emerging markets. In turn, this reduces the stock of financial capital available for economic activity in these countries.

In summary, a wide variety of corporate governance strategies are used around the world. The U.S. model stressing public contracting is considered the best model currently, but alternative models stressing private contracting are also prevalent.

1.6 International Financial Management Issues

So far, this chapter has discussed the global setting and the role of MNCs. From these discussions, we can make the following inferences about financial management issues pertaining to MNCs.

- **Understanding the Environment.** MNCs conduct FDI to generate value for their shareholders. To operate effectively, MNCs must understand the global environment. Among the many financial factors affecting an MNC, a critical one relates to international financial markets. In particular, MNCs must thoroughly understand foreign exchange markets, which are discussed in Chapters 2–5.

- **Managing Currency Risk.** Currency risk is perhaps the most important special risk that an MNC faces and is therefore covered in detail in this text. At a fundamental level, currency risk arises from the fact that MNC revenues and expenses are themselves related to currency values. Once currency risk is quantified, firms decide on whether and how to mitigate such risk, perhaps by using operational and financial methods. Chapters 6 and 7 address this topic.

- **International Project Analysis.** In conducing FDI, MNCs evaluate foreign projects. Large MNCs must make hundreds of these decisions annually. The lack of precision in cash flow estimates, the impact of regulations and taxes, country and currency risk factors, and agency problems are some of the issues confronting the decision maker. These issues are discussed in Chapters 8 and 9.

- **Global Financing.** MNCs are capital-intensive enterprises. How do MNCs finance their projects? What is the cost of capital? How can an MNC exploit global markets to lower financing costs and gain a competitive advantage over its peers? This is the subject of Chapters 10 and 11.

- **Global Operations.** The remaining chapters cover miscellaneous topics of interest to MNCs as well as other market participants. Chapter 12 discusses alternate forms of FDI such as joint ventures and mergers. Chapter 13 discusses how MNCs and other entities can process imports and exports. Chapter 14 discusses issues of international accounting. Chapter 15 discusses international investments from the perspective of investors.

Summary

- The extent of global business activity has increased dramatically. Factors influencing globalization include trade agreements such as the WTO and NAFTA, the rise of the Internet, and innovation in communication technologies.
- International trade is a win–win proposition that occurs because nations have comparative advantages in producing certain products.
- Today's MNCs not only sell their products in multiple countries but also undertake a wide range of activities in multiple locations. These activities include research and development, production, and sourcing components.
- MNCs leverage their knowledge capital to maximize shareholder wealth. Using this capital as well as their expertise in structuring complex overseas businesses, they overcome the transaction costs of operating overseas.
- MNCs are constrained by risk factors such as currency risk, economic risk, political risk, and regulatory risk. Evaluating and managing them are vital to an MNC's success.
- MNCs face considerable agency costs, so they need to design effective organizational and governance structures. In particular, MNCs need to determine the optimal level of decentralization to facilitate operations and the optimal board structure to facilitate monitoring.
- Globally, internal and external corporate governance practices vary widely with perhaps the best practices evident in the United States.

Questions

1. **MNC Definition.** What is an MNC? Provide three examples of MNCs from (a) the United States, (b) a non-U.S. but developed nation, and (c) an emerging market. In your estimate, which category of countries has long-standing (i.e., listed for a long period of time) firms and which has young firms?
2. **Globalization.** Define *globalization*. What forms of globalization are of more interest to the businessperson? What forms are of more interest to the general person? Explain differences in the perspectives of the two people.
3. **Movement of Goods.** Is the movement of goods—one form of globalization also known as *international trade*—a recent phenomenon? Use your knowledge of business history as well as current affairs in answering this question.
4. **Global Agreements and Globalization.** What kind of agreements lead to globalization? Are these multilateral or bilateral agreements? What are their typical features?
5. **Freedom and Growth.** Is there a connection between freedom and economic growth? Use historical as well as contemporary examples to support your answer.
6. **Impact of Technology.** "Technology and innovation inevitably lead to globalization." Support this statement by providing at least two recent examples.
7. **Transportation.** What transportation innovations have occurred in recent decades? What are recent trends? In your answer, address all forms of transportations.
8. **Comparative Advantage Theory.** Explain the comparative advantage theory of trade with an example. Distinguish between the classical and neoclassical versions of this theory.
9. **Trade Theory.** Few theories of trade explain why a country might simultaneously export and import the same product. For instance, the United States is simultaneously an exporter and importer of airplanes. What theory explains this phenomenon?

10. **Trade Theory.** In the past few decades, the United States has shown strength in various industries—steel, automobiles, and consumer electronics to name a few—only to see other countries ultimately prevail in these industries. What theory explains this empirical fact? Are current areas of U.S. industrial strength destined to follow the same pattern in the next 10 to 20 years?

11. **Location Theory.** Using theories of industry agglomeration, explain the location of (a) business process (human resources, accounting, etc) outsourcing firms in Bangalore, India, and (b) financial services firms in New York City.

12. **MNC Theory.** What is the OLI model? How does it differ from the knowledge capital model? Based on your judgment of global business conditions as well as your understanding of these models, do you expect more or fewer MNCs in the future?

13. **MNC Risks.** "MNCs face greater risks than purely domestic firms." What are some of the arguments supporting and disproving this statement?

14. **MNC Agency Costs.** Explain why MNCs face higher levels of agency costs than purely domestic firms.

15. **Centralization versus Decentralization.** Are most MNCs centralized or decentralized? What are some advantages and disadvantages of choosing one organizational form over another?

16. **Comparative Corporate Governance.** Define *corporate governance*. What are some differences between corporate governance in the United States and in Asia?

17. **Corporate Governance Issues.** What is *tunneling?* In what scenarios does tunneling occur? What are the consequences for a firm exhibiting this problem? What are the consequences for the growth rate of an economy where tunneling is rampant?

18. **Monitoring Systems.** Consider a firm based in Korea (you may want to think of Samsung Electronics). Based on your understanding of global corporate governance norms, assess the efficacy of internal and external controls for this firm in comparison to a U.S. firm.

Extensions

1. **Bilateral Trade between Developed Nations.** (See http://www.state.gov/r/pa/ei/bgn/3180 .htm.) The U.S. Department of State Web site with information on Ireland (accessed July 28, 2008) states the following regarding its imports/exports from/to the United States:

   In 2005, U.S. exports to Ireland were valued at $9 billion while Irish exports to the United States totaled $28 billion, according to the U.S. Department of Commerce. The range of U.S. exports includes electrical components and equipment, computers and peripherals, drugs and pharmaceuticals, and livestock feed. Irish exports to the United States represent approximately 20 percent of all Irish exports and have roughly the same value as Irish exports to the United Kingdom (inclusive of Northern Ireland). Exports to the United States include alcoholic beverages, chemicals and related products, electronic data processing equipment, electrical machinery, textiles and clothing, and glassware. According to Ireland's Central Statistical Office, Irish exports to the United States from January to September 2006 rose by 7 percent compared to the same period in 2005 while Irish imports from the United States from January to September 2006 fell by 14 percent compared to the same period in 2005.

   Use theories of international trade to explain this bilateral trade relationship. In your opinion is this a large volume of trade?

2. **Bilateral Trade and Entities.** The U.S. Department of State Web information on Mexico (http://www.state.gov/r/pa/ei/bgn/35749.htm, accessed July 28, 2007) states the following:

   Mexico is among the world's most open economies, but it is dependent on trade with the U.S., which bought about 82 percent of its exports in 2007. Top U.S. exports to Mexico include electronic equipment, motor vehicle parts, and chemicals. Top Mexican exports to the U.S. include petroleum, cars, and electronic equipment.

Does this list provide clues about the types of entities conducting cross-border trade between the United States and Mexico? Explain.

3. **Bilateral Trade between Developed and Developing Nation.** The U.S. Department of State Web information on Peru (http://www.state.gov/r/pa/ei/bgn/35762.htm, accessed July 28, 2007) states the following:

Peru registered a trade surplus of $8.8 billion in 2006. Exports reached $23.7 billion, partially as a result of high mineral prices. Peru's major trading partners are the U.S., China, EU, Chile and Japan. In 2006, 23.0 percent of exports went to the U.S. ($5.9 billion) and 16.0 percent of imports came from the U.S. ($2.9 billion). Exports include gold, copper, fishmeal, petroleum, zinc, textiles, apparel, asparagus and coffee. Imports include machinery, vehicles, processed food, petroleum and steel. Peru belongs to the Andean Community, the Asia-Pacific Economic Cooperation (APEC) forum, and the World Trade Organization (WTO).

Use theories of trade to explain these data.

4. **Corporate Governance in Emerging Markets.** Pyramidal ownership structures are common in many Asian, European, and South American countries. Usually, a founding family has control over a firm that in turn has control over other firms. The founding family is thus at the top of the pyramid and can control all firms lower on the pyramid. Consider this simple example. A family owns 50 percent of firm A that in turn owns 50 percent of firm B that in turn owns 50 percent of firm C. The family's direct ownership of firm C is 50 percent × 50 percent × 50 percent and equals 12.5 percent, by no means a majority, yet it is able to control C fully. What are the costs and benefits of such an ownership structure?

Case

Clover Machines: *Determining a Global Strategy*

Clover Machines is a U.S.-based manufacturer of a wide range of commercial, construction, and agricultural machines. Initially, most of its sales were domestic with a small presence in western European markets, especially France and Italy. Clover is organized in three divisions. Its commercial division makes machines for contractors and businesses; its main products are utility tractors and mowing machines. Its construction division makes machines for mostly large-scale construction firms; its main products are dump trucks, loaders, and dozers. Its agricultural division makes farm equipment; its main products are tractors and combines with various attachments such as balers.

Clover faces a mature home market. Sales during the past five years have been growing at a modest rate of 2 percent, but input prices have been rising faster. Steel is an important input raw material and because of rising global demand—primarily from Asian economies such as China and India—steel prices have risen at more than three times the rate of inflation. Labor prices have also risen, primarily due to rising health care and regulatory costs. Clover has been searching for ways to increase cash flows. As in the auto industry, the farm and construction machinery industry has evolved over time to include a vast supplier network. Clover's suppliers are mostly national and located near its Chicago, Illinois, headquarters.

Clover is blessed with many positives, the most important of which is the domestic and global boom in agricultural products. U.S. agriculture is on the upswing for many reasons. Considerable farm lands, rising productivity, and burgeoning global markets contribute to a good if not spectacular forecast for agriculture as well as agricultural machinery. The United States has been the world's leading agricultural exporter, currently exporting more than USD

50 billion worth of corn, wheat, soybeans, and other grains. Globally, agricultural production is growing at a fast rate, especially in South America and Asia; even moribund markets such as Europe are emerging. Except for its presence in southern Europe, Clover has not penetrated the global agricultural machine markets. Thus, potential for future expansion is great.

As far as construction is concerned, recent events such as the credit crisis of 2007–2008 severely affected U.S. construction, but global construction is booming in far-flung places such as Dubai, Mumbai, and Shanghai. Clover has little or no market share in these foreign markets. The same is true for its commercial machines. Key markets are in North America where Clover has a presence, but it is not yet addressing the growing markets in Europe and Asia.

Laura Brooks, Clover's CEO, is concerned about the firm's strategy. Since its inception 30 years ago, the firm has survived and prospered and now employs 10,000 people and has a market capitalization of USD 10 billion. However, a recent 15 percent dip in Clover's stock price coincides with the market's general unease about the future direction of the firm. Ms. Brooks believes that both revenues and expenses need to be managed better but that revenue enhancement may be the more important of the two. With increased revenues, Clover can achieve greater economies of scale, which alone can mitigate some of the firm's cost pressures. Ms. Brooks notes that gross margins are running at 30 percent but had earlier been as high as 40 percent. She wonders whether the firm can simply fine-tune its business model (keeping it primarily domestic) or needs to use innovative ways to remake itself.

1. Why was Clover able to flourish in the U.S. setting? Are there theories of location that justify its continued existence in the United States in addition to globalizing to a larger extent?

2. According to data on the Internet and other sources, is an increased penetration abroad, especially in agricultural machines, justified? What theories of globalization would support such a move by Clover?

3. What are ways in which Clover can contain costs? Explain the advantages and disadvantages of alternative methods of production and distribution.

4. For this particular industry (earth moving and other machines), explain the best method of penetrating foreign markets in Asia, Europe, and South America. What organization design would facilitate this method? What are alternatives?

5. Global warming is predicted to impact agriculture because of shifting optimal locations for various crops and increased variability in weather conditions. What are the advantages and disadvantages of this for Clover? Can you think of other risk factors for the firm?

Appendix 1

Example of Comparative Advantage

Consider the following example involving two countries: the United States and Germany. Assume that the United States has a comparative advantage in manufacturing computers and that Germany has a comparative advantage in manufacturing cars. We can show that both countries will be better off with international trade if the United States buys cars from Germany and Germany buys computers from the United States.

Identification of Comparative Advantage

Let's start by considering the inputs needed to manufacture the two products. In the United States, 50 units of inputs are needed to produce one car and 20 units are needed to produce one computer. You may consider inputs as resources used (e.g., labor hours or national currency units). In Germany, 60 units are needed to produce one car and 40 units are needed to produce one computer. Thus, on a comparative basis, the United States has an advantage in producing computers and Germany has an advantage in producing cars. One way to understand the idea of comparative advantage is to calculate the ratio of inputs needed for cars to computers for the two countries. This ratio is 2.5 (=50/20) for the United States because a car requires 50 units of inputs and a computer needs 20 units. The ratio of inputs for Germany is 1.5 (=60/40).

Current Production and Consumption

Consider the current situation. The United States produces (and consumes) 20 cars and 10 computers; Germany produces (and consumes) 10 cars and 20 computers. Thus, the total (global) production of cars is 30 and the total production of computers is 30. The inputs used by the United States and Germany in their production of cars and computers are calculated as follows:

$$\text{Total inputs (United States)} = 20 \times 50 + 10 \times 20 = 1,200$$
$$\text{Total inputs (Germany)} = 10 \times 60 + 20 \times 40 = 1,400$$

Exchange of Cars for Computers

To understand how international trade benefits both countries, assume that the existing consumption pattern is unchanged. Given these constraints, consider a scenario in which the United States switches some of its production from cars to computers and Germany switches from computers to cars. We can show that by trading cars for computers, both countries will be better off.

Benefits of International Trade

Assume that the United States exports 10 computers to Germany and in return imports 5 cars. Thus, the United States would produce 15 cars and 20 computers while Germany would produce 15 cars and 10 computers. The inputs needed are as follows:

$$\text{Total inputs (United States)} = 15 \times 50 + 20 \times 20 = 1,150$$
$$\text{Total inputs (Germany)} = 15 \times 60 + 10 \times 40 = 1,300$$

We see that the same overall production (i.e., 30 cars and 30 computers) is achieved using fewer resources, a savings for both countries. Therefore, international trade maintains the same level of consumption for both countries while requiring fewer resources.

International Trade and Economic Growth

International trade is a source of both efficiency and economic growth (see Exhibit 1A.1). If the two countries decide to use their productive capacities fully, the 50 units of inputs saved by the United States and the 100 units of inputs saved by Germany can be used to produce the following additional products:

- **United States.** The 50 units of savings can be used to produce 1 additional car or 2.5 additional computers.
- **Germany.** The 100 units of savings can be used to produce 1.67 additional cars or 2.5 additional computers.

Other Inferences

Exhibit 1.6 includes additional issues of interest. One is the equilibrium exchange rate between the two countries. The United States imports 5 cars requiring 300 units of input in Germany and exports 10 computers requiring 200 units of input in the United States. Thus,

EXHIBIT 1.6
Illustration of
Comparative Advantage

	United States	Germany	Total
Production Inputs			
Cars	50	60	
Computers	20	40	
Comparative advantage ratio of cars to computers	2.5	1.5	
Current Production			
Cars	20	10	30
Computers	10	20	30
Inputs needed	1,200	1,400	2,600
Production with International Trade			
Cars	15	15	30
Computers	20	10	30
Inputs needed	1,150	1,300	2,450
Savings in resources	50	100	
U.S. imports of cars	5		
U.S. export of computers	10		

300 units of German input are equivalent to 200 units of U.S. input. Assuming that each unit of input equals one unit of the currency, the equilibrium exchange rate would reflect 3 units of the Germany currency for 2 units of the U.S. currency. In other words, 1 U.S. dollar would equal 1.5 Euro. However, this is only one of many possible solutions. In practice, the result would depend on other factors such as the relative bargaining ability of the two nations, consumer preferences, and labor rates.

CHAPTER TWO

International Financial Markets: Structure and Innovation

Financial globalization occurs when money moves across borders. This cross-border flow of money is sometimes motivated by foreign direct investment (FDI, the acquisition of real assets) and at other times by investments in financial assets. What financial markets enable this movement of money and what are their features? What types of instruments are traded in these markets? We answer these questions in this chapter by studying foreign exchange markets as well as international money and capital markets.

MNCs participate in foreign exchange markets for obvious reasons: They conduct numerous transactions with foreign entities. MNCs participate in international money markets on both sides: They obtain funding and use these markets for investing excess cash. Finally, MNCs participate in international debt and equity markets to obtain low-cost funding. To understand MNCs' financial management practices, it is important to learn about these markets.

A key theme in this chapter is globalization and innovation in financial markets. The **Euro markets** that developed in the 1950s are famous examples of financial innovation. With original roots in London, today they are global rather than European markets. The Eurodollar and the Eurobond markets—vital components of the Euro markets—are multi-trillion-dollar markets and provide financing as well as investing opportunities to MNCs. MNCs are not the only beneficiaries of these markets. Investors also use them to arbitrage or diversify their portfolios. The importance of the Euro markets is perhaps underscored by the fact that key indicators from those such as London Interbank Offered Rate (LIBOR) interest rates are more widely followed than indicators such as the Treasury bill rate from U.S. markets.

In particular, in this chapter, we discuss:

- The structure of global currency markets, focusing on how currencies are quoted and traded as well as the motives for currency transactions.
- The structure of the international money markets and features of key instruments such as the Eurodollar.
- The structure of the intermediate maturity notes market and a description of the floating rate note.
- The market for Eurobonds.
- A brief description of global stock markets.

2.1 Foreign Exchange Markets

Currencies are exchanged or traded in foreign exchange (FX) markets. In this chapter, we focus on transactions in currency *spot markets* through which counterparties enter into agreements and immediately exchange currencies. In later chapters, we discuss other important components of currency markets that have more complex transactions involving future exchanges.[1]

Foreign exchange markets are large global markets with average daily transactions exceeding a trillion dollars. Trading in foreign exchange takes place in electronic over-the-counter (OTC) markets dominated by large multinational banks such as Citicorp and BNP Paribas. Other important participants include MNCs, nonbank financial institutions (pension funds, insurance companies, investment funds) and governments.

In general, an entity participates in this market for three reasons:

- MNCs and others have business-related needs to buy or sell foreign exchange.
- Banks and other intermediaries profit from facilitating foreign exchange transactions.
- Investment funds have portfolio-related needs to buy and sell foreign exchange.

The following section provides a description of foreign exchange markets. We discuss MNC participation in foreign exchange markets, the structure of foreign exchange markets, foreign exchange quotation systems, key currencies, and recent market trends.

MNC Participation in Foreign Exchange Markets

MNCs are important participants in the foreign exchange markets. Their transactions with foreign subsidiaries, affiliates, customers, and suppliers require foreign currencies. However, MNCs are not the sole beneficiaries of foreign exchange markets. Banks and other financial institutions such as pension funds, insurance firms, and mutual funds are also important participants.

In general, MNC demand for foreign exchange transactions arises from three sources, two of which are related to global trade and the third related to global investments:

- The production of goods and services involves transactions between firms and their suppliers. When suppliers are located in foreign countries, payments are needed in the currencies of these countries. If Dell Computer sources liquid crystal display (LCD) screens from a Japanese firm, Dell either requires the conversion of U.S. dollars (USD) to Japanese yen (JPY), or if it pays with USD, the Japanese firm requires the conversion from USD to JPY.
- The sale of goods and services may generate the need for a currency conversion. Thus, when Dell sells computers in Europe, it ultimately must convert European currencies received in payment such as the euro (EUR) and pound (GBP) to USD.
- The third source of demand for foreign exchange transactions relates to cross-border investments. Firms invest money to set up production and research and development (R&D) facilities in other countries or to buy assets and/or firms in other countries. An example is Cisco's investment of USD 150 million to create a software and research center in Bangalore, India. If the parent finances the plant, this amount would have to be converted from USD into rupees (INR).

Other Participants in Foreign Exchange Markets

While our focus in on MNCs, it is important to recognize the role of other participants in foreign exchange markets. We next discuss the role of banks, nonbank financial institutions, governments, and individuals.

Banks

interbank market
Large banks such as Deutsche Bank, MNCs and governments are participants in the *interbank foreign exchange market*.

The most important players in foreign exchange markets are banks. They not only conduct considerable transactions to meet their needs as well as those of their customers but also play the role of intermediary. In fact, the main foreign exchange market is known as the **interbank market**, indicating the vital role of banks that serve as dealers: banks buy as well as sell various currencies and therefore provide liquidity.

---

[1] Chapter 3 discusses currency derivatives such as currency forwards, currency futures, and currency options. Chapter 10 discusses currency swaps.

Other Financial Institutions

Compared to banks, other entities play a different and less important role. While the main "commodity" transacted by banks is money (cash or near cash), nonbank financial institutions transact in different instruments. For instance, mutual funds transact in stocks and other financial instruments. So, a mutual fund may desire to convert funds into another currency to purchase foreign stocks. One particular institution that has gained notoriety lately is hedge funds (unregulated funds catering to wealthy investors) that have become increasingly large players in foreign exchange markets. Hedge funds often take large speculative positions in currencies. They also try to profit from a discrepancy in currency values in various markets.[2]

Governments

Governments hold currencies for various purposes. Sometimes these holdings serve as a store of value: The central banks of many countries hold USD or EUR for this purpose. At other times, governments buy and sell currencies to manipulate the value of their own currency: The U.S. **Federal Reserve Bank**, for instance, may sell its holdings of EUR for USD to increase the USD's value.[3]

Individuals

Individuals typically purchase rather than sell foreign currencies. A common motive is travel. When individuals travel to foreign destinations, they need foreign currency for meals, lodging, and other purchases. Individuals may also demand currencies to invest directly in foreign assets such as stocks, bonds, and real estate. Naturally, direct sales of foreign assets may put individuals in the position of selling foreign currencies.

Market Characteristics: Size and Currencies

Market Size

The demand for foreign exchange transactions is increasing for the following reasons. The rise in global trade spurred by global trading agreements such as the **World Trade Organization (WTO)** and **North American Free Trade Agreement (NAFTA)** clearly indicates the increasing need for currency transactions. This rise in global trade is coinciding with a wave of consumerism around the world. But this is only part of the story. The dismantling of national restrictions on foreign investments has also gained impetus, leading to more capital flows across borders. Increased global trade and increased global investments together indicate a rising demand for foreign exchange transactions. As a result, the daily volume of transactions in the broadly defined foreign exchange markets is about USD 3 trillion. Of this amount, USD 1 trillion represents spot transactions and the rest contains two special kinds of foreign exchange transactions, called *forwards* and *foreign exchange swap agreements,* respectively. As mentioned previously, we discuss forwards and foreign exchange swaps in a later chapter.

The size of the foreign exchange market dwarfs all other financial markets and offers extreme liquidity. Transactions are easy and inexpensive to execute, and more important, large transactions are possible without moving market prices. The average foreign exchange transaction of about USD 4 million underscores the size of the market.

Currencies Traded

Most transactions in the foreign exchange market involve USD. There are two reasons for this dominance. First, the U.S. economy constitutes one-quarter of the global economy. In addition, many countries such as Japan, Korea, Taiwan, and China depend on their trade with the United States. This dependence contributes to transactions involving USD. Also, because of the USD's importance, even transactions not involving U.S. entities are often conducted

---

[2] The strategies involved in exploiting currency value discrepancies are known as *currency arbitrage.* This is discussed in Chapter 5.

[3] The role of governments in currency markets is discussed in Chapter 4.

EXHIBIT 2.1

Major Currencies' Share of Daily Turnover

Source: Bank for International Settlements, 2007 Triennial Central Bank Survey.

Currency	April 1998	April 2007
USD	87%	86%
DEM*	30	N/A
EUR	N/A	37
JPY	21	17
GBP	11	15
CHF†	7	7

*The German mark (DEM) was the dominant European currency in the pre-EUR era.
†Swiss francs.

in the dollar. Second, the USD is often used as an intermediary or **vehicle currency** in foreign exchange transactions. For example, an Indian importer of machinery from Japan might convert INR to USD (the vehicle currency in this transaction) and then convert USD to JPY to pay the Japanese exporter. Other important currencies are the EUR, GBP, and JPY. Not surprisingly, the most important currency pairs traded are USD/EUR, USD/JPY, and USD/GBP, constituting more than 50 percent of currency trading. The relative importance of currencies is practically unchanged in the last decade (see Exhibit 2.1).

Market Structure

Most transactions in the foreign exchange markets are conducted over electronic networks in a manner similar to stock trading on the National Association of Security Dealers Automated Quotations (NASDAQ). Firms such as Reuters and Bloomberg operate the electronic networks, which are used to transmit quotes to participants. Banks are important dealers in such networks, and some have deployed their own proprietary interfaces. In this section, we consider the structure of the foreign exchange market by examining key players and their roles. Because markets inevitably involve information transmission, technology plays a key and ever-increasing role.

Market Makers

A well-functioning market requires the presence of market makers who serve as actual or de facto "designated" dealers. For example, on the New York Stock Exchange (NYSE), exchange-designated firms such as Spear, Leeds and Kellogg serve as market makers. Market makers are ready to buy as well as sell at any given moment, ensuring liquidity. Although not explicitly designated, large money center banks such as Citicorp and JP Morgan Chase de facto perform this function in the foreign exchange market. As market makers, these banks communicate the prices at which they are willing to buy or sell a particular currency to other market participants.

bid and ask
The market maker will buy at the lower *bid* price and sell at the higher *ask* price. The difference is the profit.

Bid and ask represent the prices at which market makers are willing to buy and sell, respectively, a certain currency. While the market makers profit from the **bid-ask spread**, they bear the risk of carrying a currency inventory. For example, a bank making the market in JPY would at any point in time carry either a positive (i.e., long) or negative (i.e., short) JPY inventory. A bank long on JPY would generate losses when the JPY falls and a bank short on JPY would generate losses when the JPY rises. To give a numerical example, if the current value of JPY is USD 0.01, a bank short on JPY 10 million will lose USD 4,000 if the spot value increases to USD 0.0104. This happens because the liability associated with the short position rises from USD 100,000 (JPY 10 million × USD 0.01) to USD 104,000 (JPY 10 million × USD 0.0104).

Dealers and Brokers

Dealers and/or brokers may also facilitate transactions. As with stock trading, dealers take net positions in the traded item. Unlike market makers, dealers do not assume the responsibility of making a market and hence do not feel compelled to provide liquidity to markets. They buy and sell only when it is profitable. Brokers also provide a valuable function: In contrast to dealers and market makers, brokers do not assume the risk of currency inventory. They

EXHIBIT 2.2

Top Five Foreign
Exchange Dealers, 2008

Source: Euromoney, foreign
exchange survey 2008, http://www.
euromoney.com/Poll/3301/
PollsAndAwards/Foreign-Exchange.
html (accessed November 20, 2008).

Dealer	Market Share (percent)
Deutsche Bank	21.70
UBS	15.80
Barclay's Capital	9.12
Citi	7.49
Royal Bank of Scotland (RBS)	7.30

match buyers with sellers and earn commissions on transactions. See Exhibit 2.2 for the top five foreign exchange dealers.

Settlement

When a transaction is completed in the foreign exchange markets, complex electronic accounting systems handle the clearing functions. At the heart of these systems is the method by which funds are transferred between entities. A *clearing system* is essentially a secured network that processes financial messages or instructions. Key features are efficiency, speed, and security. It is no coincidence, then, that the most commonly used system has the acronym **SWIFT**, which stands for **Society for Worldwide Interbank Financial Telecommunications**. It originated in Belgium as a cooperative endeavor of major financial institutions and markets itself as a provider of "secure financial messaging services." SWIFT processes about 15 million financial messages a day. In the United States, however, competing systems are used for financial settlements. Commonly used U.S. systems are the **Fedwire** and **Clearing House Interbank Payments System (CHIPS)**. A U.K. system similar to CHIPS is **Clearing House Automated Payment System (CHAPS)**. All of these systems achieve funds transfer electronically (by "wire").

To understand how these settlement systems work, consider the Fedwire system. As the name implies, the 12 Federal Reserve Banks of the United States operate it. Because member banks keep mandatory reserve balances with the Federal Reserve, funds transfer is achieved by making accounting debit and credit entries to reflect a transaction between two banks. Thus, if an MNC wanted to transfer funds to another MNC, the transfer would be effected by changing the Federal Reserve balances of the banks of these two firms; simultaneously, the banks can adjust the account balances of the two MNCs. Major banks centered in New York operate the second U.S. system, CHIPS. These banks have created a reporting system that at the end of each day flags whether a certain bank has a net debit or credit situation with respect to all other banks in the CHIPS system. Use of the Fedwire system to change the balances of banks with the Federal Reserve corrects net debit and credit situations daily. Thus, the CHIPS system is a netting system that efficiently processes a large number of transactions by aggregating them and processing only the net amounts.

Foreign Exchange Quotations

Currency quotations can be direct or indirect. Direct quotes express the value of a foreign currency in terms of the domestic currency. Thus, from the U.S. perspective, a quotation of "USD 1.25 per EUR" is a direct quote. This means that 1 EUR is worth USD 1.25. (Yes, the cappuccino for a euro in Venice costs you a buck and a quarter!) This is the most direct way of conveying the price of any item, whether it is a bar of chocolate or a foreign currency. For example, a person who says that a gallon of gas is USD 2.00 is expressing the value of gas in terms of the currency USD. Similarly, the direct quote for the EUR expresses the value of the EUR in terms of the currency USD. Using a more technical term, we can say that in both instances, the domestic currency serves as the *numeraire*.

Indirect quotes express the value of the domestic currency in terms of the foreign currency. As an example of an indirect quote, the EUR may be quoted as "EUR 0.80 per USD." The numeraire is no longer the domestic currency USD but is the foreign currency EUR. With normal commodities or assets, we rarely use this system of quotation. One exception with normal commodities perhaps arises in grocery shops where the price of candy bars might be listed as "2 candy bars per dollar." Converting an indirect quote to a direct quote simply requires taking the inverse (1/x) of the quote. In the indirect quote for candy bars, it is easy to understand that the direct quote is USD 0.50 per bar. Similarly, the indirect quote of "EUR 0.80 per USD" can be converted to a direct quote of "USD 1.25 per EUR" by noting that 1/0.80 equals 1.25 (see Exhibit 2.3). Note that the ratio of EUR to USD is maintained regardless of whether the quote is direct (1:1.25) or indirect (0.80:1).

Most currencies are quoted directly. However, certain currencies, especially those with low value, are quoted indirectly. To avoid confusion about whether a quote is direct or indirect, market participants used a standardized system (see Exhibit 2.4). Each currency quote contains

EXHIBIT 2.3
Direct versus Indirect Quotes (from U.S. perspective)

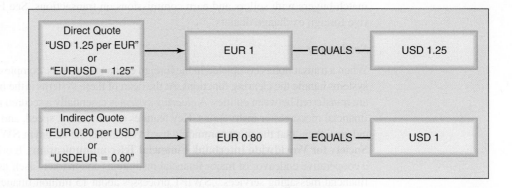

EXHIBIT 2.4
Currency Quotations

http://www.bloomberg.com/markets/currencies/asiapac_currencies.html.

World Currencies

	AMERICAS	**ASIA/PACIFIC**	EUROPE/AFRICA/MIDDLE EAST		
CURRENCY	**VALUE**	**CHANGE**	**% CHANGE**	**TIME**	
USD-JPY	94.1940	0.0095	0.0101%	23:54	
USD-HKD	7.7504	0.0000	0.0000%	23:53	
AUD-USD	0.8374	0.0017	0.2028%	23:53	
NZD-USD	0.6873	0.0030	0.4384%	23:53	
USD-SGD	1.4420	-0.0002	-0.0138%	23:53	
USD-TWD	32.9160	-0.0015	-0.0046%	23:53	
USD-KRW	1246.3750	-1.7750	-0.1422%	23:53	
USD-PHP	48.7250	0.2150	0.4432%	23:51	
USD-IDR	10055.0000	25.0000	0.2492%	23:36	
USD-INR	48.8170	0.0550	0.1128%	23:53	
USD-CNY	6.8316	-0.0004	-0.0051%	23:53	
USD-MYR	3.5272	0.0078	0.2202%	23:40	
USD-THB	34.0150	-0.0050	-0.0147%	23:54	

Currency Calculator ▸

When the U.S. dollar is listed first, the valuation is expressed as the number of the units of the other currency per U.S. dollar. When another currency is listed first, the valuation is expressed as the number of U.S. dollars per currency unit.

Currency key

USD:	U.S. Dollar	**JPY:**	Japanese Yen
HKD:	Hong Kong Dollar	**AUD:**	Australian Dollar
NZD:	New Zealand Dollar	**SGD:**	Singapore Dollar
TWD:	New Taiwanese Dollar	**KRW:**	South Korean Won
PHP:	Philippine Peso	**IDR:**	Indonesian Rupiah
INR:	Indian Rupee	**CNY:**	Chinese Yuan (Renminbi)
MYR:	Malaysian Ringgit	**THB:**	Thai Baht

Unless indicated otherwise: intraday data is at least 15 minutes delayed; mutual fund NAVs are updated at the close of every market day; all prices are in the local currency; Time is ET.

two components: the currency pair and the numerical quote. A set of six characters identifies the currency pair. The first three letters identifies the **base currency**—one that is being bought or sold—and the last three letters identifies the **terms currency**—the one used to buy or sell the base currency. International Organization for Standardization (ISO) codes are used to identify each currency. Hyphens or slashes are sometimes used to separate the two currencies. At other times, no separator is used. For simplicity, we use no separator in this text. The numerical quote represents the number of units of the terms currency equivalent to one unit of the base currency. For example, a quote of EURUSD = 1.25 means that 1.0 unit of the base currency (EUR) equals 1.25 units of the terms currency (USD). From the U.S. perspective, direct quotes require the dollar as the terms currency as in JPYUSD, EURUSD, GBPUSD, and so on.

The uncertainty of whether a quote is direct or indirect causes endless grief for students of international finance. Consider three pieces of advice in this regard. First, determine the base currency: It is either mentioned first in the currency pair or it is prominently mentioned in narrative form as in "the euro was quoted at...." Second, obtain knowledge of the relative values of currencies. For instance, it is important to know that today, the USD is more valuable than the JPY but less valuable than the GBP. Use this knowledge to decipher quotes. Finally, in your own calculations, consistently use direct quotes when possible.

International Organization for Standardization (ISO) codes
Currency quotes displayed in trading terminals use the three-letter *ISO code* to denote each currency. Because each quote involves two currencies, a total of six letters are used.

Bid-Ask Spread and Transaction Costs

Earlier we introduced the concept of bid and ask quotes. Recall that the spread represents profits for currency dealers. Equivalently, the spread represents an important component of transaction costs for MNCs and other users of currency markets. Liquid currencies have low spreads, and illiquid currencies have high spreads. Because currencies have different value thresholds or levels—the JPY is worth a few cents while the GBP is worth more than a dollar—the bid-ask spread is sometimes converted into a percentage form using the following equation:

$$Bid\text{-}Ask\ spread\ percent = (Ask\text{-}Bid)/Ask$$

EXAMPLE 2.1

A bank is quoting EURUSD at 1.5511 – 1.5514. The bank transacts with two different MNCs. MNC A purchases EUR 10 million and MNC B sells EUR 10 million. Estimate cash flow for the three parties. What is the bid-ask spread percent?

Solution:

Cash flow for MNC A = −USD 10,000,000 × 1.5514

$$= -USD\ 15,514,000$$

Cash flow for MNC B = +USD 10,000,000 × 1.5511

$$= +USD\ 15,511,000$$

Cash flow for bank = +USD 15,514.000 − USD 15,511,000

$$= +USD\ 3,000$$

Percent bid-ask for EURUSD $= \dfrac{1.5514 - 1.5511}{1.5514} = 0.01934\%$

Discussion: The bid-ask percent also represents the profit percent (profit relative to transaction size) for the bank. In this example,

0.01934% × 15,514,000 = 3,000

The bid-ask spread can also be calculated using indirect quotes as follows:

Percent bid-ask for USDEUR $= \dfrac{\dfrac{1}{1.5511} - \dfrac{1}{1.5514}}{\dfrac{1}{1.5511}} = 0.01934\%.$

Note that the bid and ask quotes are reversed in this case: The inverse of the ask quote for EURUSD is the bid quote for USDEUR.

Transaction costs for MNCs typically contain two components: bid-ask spread and commissions or fees. One useful method of estimating total transaction costs is to determine the difference between total cash flows with and without transaction costs. Cash flows with transactions costs are the actual cash flows pertaining to an MNC transaction. Cash flows without transaction costs are the hypothetical cash flows with no commissions assumed to be paid and with the conversion rate at the midpoint between bid and ask.

EXAMPLE 2.2

A Brazilian mining firm wishes to purchase USD 400,000 to make payment toward equipment purchased from a U.S. firm. It approaches Unibanco for a quote. Assume that Unibanco quotes USDBRL at 1.4015 − 1.4037 (BRL indicates Brazilian real). Also Unibanco imposes a commission of BRL 200 on each transaction. Calculate the amount paid by the Brazilian firm to purchase the USD. Assuming that the "true" market price for USD is the midpoint between bid and ask, estimate the percent of transaction costs the firm paid.

Solution:

Actual amount paid toward USD purchase $= 400,000 \times 1.4037 + 200 = BRL\ 561,680$

Hypothetical amount paid (w/o transaction costs) $= 400,000 \times \dfrac{1.4015 + 1.4037}{2} = BRL\ 561,040$

Transaction costs $= BRL\ 561,680 - BRL\ 561,040 = BRL\ 640$

Transaction costs percent $= \dfrac{640}{561,040} = 0.114\%$

Discussion: The total transaction costs for the MNC may be broken into commissions of BRL 200 and the spread of BRL 440. Note that this is a single-trip, not a round-trip transaction. Therefore, the MNC is bearing costs related to only one-half of the bid-ask spread. (Round-trip spread is BRL 880, calculated as the per unit spread of 0.0022 multiplied by 400,000.

Currency quotes typically use four or more decimal points. For major currencies, bid and ask quotes typically differ only in the fourth decimal. Nevertheless, because of large transaction sizes, these differences matter. In currency transactions and indeed in any financial transaction, it is important to calculate total transaction costs, not just focus on commissions.

Currency Cross Rates

In a given country, a foreign currency may be quoted directly or indirectly relative to its own currency. Quotes may also be found, however, by relating one foreign currency to another foreign currency. Such quotes are known as **cross rates**. These rates may be inferred from either direct or indirect quotes on the two currencies as follows:

EXAMPLE 2.3

The EUR is quoted directly and indirectly relative to USD at 1.5514 and 0.64458, respectively. The JPY is quoted directly and indirectly relative to the USD at 0.0100 and 100.00, respectively. Calculate the cross rate between EUR and JPY using the direct and indirect quote approaches.

Solution:

Method I: Direct Quote Method

Value of EUR expressed in JPY $=$ EURJPY

$=$ Direct quote of EUR/Direct quote of JPY

$= 1.5514/0.0100$

$= 155.14$

> ***Method II: Indirect Quote Method***
>
> Value of EUR expressed in JPY = EURJPY
>
> = Indirect quote of JPY/Indirect quote of EUR
>
> = 100.00/0.64458
>
> = 155.14
>
> ***Note:*** A third method, using a mixture of direct and indirect quotes, is also available. To solve this problem, use the following equation:
>
> EURJPY = EURUSD × USDJPY

Foreign Exchange Markets: 24-Hour Trading

The five important centers for foreign exchange trading are New York, London, Singapore, Zurich, and Tokyo. This is reflected in country-level statistics in Exhibit 2.5. Of these markets, London is the most important, despite the relative unimportance of the British pound. This is because of the historical importance paid to currency trading by London based banks. London also is aided by the fact that its time zone is ideally positioned to help its trading day overlap with Asia as well as the United States. Morning trading in London overlaps with afternoon trading in Singapore. Afternoon trading in London overlaps with morning trading in New York. Thus, during regular hours of trading in London, overseas orders from Asian as well as U.S. customers can be accommodated.

Given the geographic dispersal of foreign exchange centers, the market is truly open for 24 hours. Thus, it is possible for major players to continuously transact in foreign currencies, yet the frequency of trading is more concentrated during morning hours in New York when London is also active.

Foreign Exchange Market Trends

The **Bank of International Settlements (BIS)** produces a triennial central bank survey providing information on currency markets. The most recent survey (2007) identified the following trends:

- The volume of transactions is increasing rapidly. Average daily spot transactions reported in 2001, 2004, and 2007 are USD 387 billion, USD 631 billion, and USD 1,005 billion, respectively.
- Since the mid-1990s, trading in foreign exchange swaps exceeded trading in spot currencies. This is an important phenomenon explained later in the text in the discussion of currency risk and its mitigation. This trend strengthened in 2007.
- Nonbank institutions such as hedge funds, mutual funds, pension funds, and insurance companies increased in importance. While banks are still the biggest players in currency markets, their market share is decreasing.
- The market share of the four largest currencies fell, indicating the rising importance of other currencies. Although the USDEUR pair continued to dominate trading, the share of emerging market currencies increased to about 20 percent.

Another important trend relates to the impact of technology and innovation. In the recent decade, many online trading platforms such as FXall and FXConnect have been introduced,

EXHIBIT 2.5
Geographical Distribution of Foreign Exchange Trading

Source: Bank for International Settlements, 2007 Triennial Central Bank Survey.

Location	April 1998	April 2007
United Kingdom	33%	34%
United States	18	17
Japan	7	6
Singapore	7	6
Switzerland	4	6

providing less expensive alternatives for currency transactions. These developments are especially beneficial to MNCs that typically relied on banks to execute currency transactions. MNCs not only save costs by accessing online trading but also increase transaction execution speed. The rising trading volume continues to attract new entrants. FXMarketSpace is the most recent and is a joint venture between the Chicago Mercantile Exchange and Reuters and bills itself as the first centrally cleared OTC foreign exchange trading platform.

2.2 International Money Markets

In the latter half of the 20th century, international money markets developed to benefit MNCs and other parties. In purely domestic money markets, residents of a country borrow and lend in their own currency. In contrast, in international money markets, transactions are entered into by nonresidents in various currencies or by residents in foreign currencies. Traditionally, the term **Eurocurrency market** has been applied to an important subset of the international money market in which lending and borrowing of currencies occur outside their respective countries. The prefix *euro* is slightly misleading because these markets are truly global today.

International Banking: Classifying Transactions

An important component of international money markets is international banking. Bankers participate in money markets by borrowing and lending. When such activity occurs across currency or residency borders, they are said to participate in international money markets. The following identifies some conventions recently used by BIS, the main reporting entity for banking data.

The term *international* is used to denote a *foreign aspect* in one of two dimensions: entity and currency. Thus, international transactions are transactions with nonresidents or transactions in a foreign currency. Cross-border and foreign currency transactions are subsets as depicted in Exhibit 2.6. International transactions are shown to occur in three possible ways: transactions with nonresidents in a domestic currency (B), transactions with residents in a foreign currency (D), and transactions with nonresidents in a foreign currency (C). Cross-border transactions comprise B and C, and foreign currency transactions comprise C and D. BIS appears to have relabeled positions previously known as *Eurocurrency positions* as *foreign currency positions* presumably to avoid confusion with the currency EUR. The *euro* prefix and its connotation of "foreign currency" continue in practical usage, however.

EXHIBIT 2.6
Classification of Banking Positions

Source: BIS, Guide to the International Banking Statistics, 2003.

	Residents	Nonresidents
Domestic currency	A	B
Foreign currency	D	C

B + C = External or cross-border positions
C + D = Foreign currency positions (also known as *Eurocurrency*)
B + C + D = International positions
A + B + C + D = Global positions

EXAMPLE 2.4

Consider the following transactions of a French bank. It accepts two deposits from a French citizen: EUR 5,000 and USD 10,000. It also accepts two deposits from a Japanese citizen: JPY 2,500,000 and EUR 8,000. Classify these deposits.

Solution:

External positions = JYP 2,500,000 + EUR 8,000

Foreign currency positions = USD 10,000 + JPY 2,500,000

International positions = USD 10,000 + JPY 2,500,000 + EUR 8,000

Global positions = USD 10,000 + JYP 2,500,000 + EUR 13,000

EXHIBIT 2.7
Cross-Border Banking,
September 2007
(USD billion)

Source: Bank for International
Settlements.

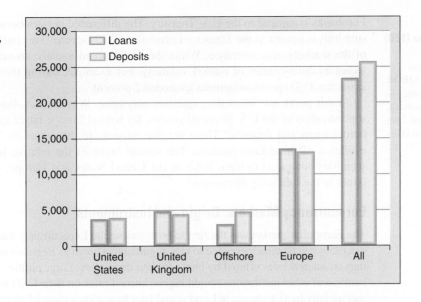

What are the frequency and importance of international banking transactions? See Exhibit 2.7 for information on cross-border loans and deposits reported by banks to BIS. Cross-border loans and deposits exceed USD 20 trillion; most of this activity occurs in European and foreign banks. We also note the importance of banks in the United Kingdom, and we explain this phenomenon in the next section.

Eurodollars and LIBOR

Banks report that most of their foreign currency deposits (and loans) are denominated in the USD. This is in line with the statistics on currency trading reported earlier. In fact, the USD is used in about 50 percent of these deposits. The EUR follows with a 20 percent share. Other important currencies are GBP, JPY, and CHF. Eurocurrency or foreign currency transactions in the USD are called **Eurodollar** transactions. Similarly, foreign currency transactions involving the euro, yen, and pound are called *Euroeuro, Euroyen,* and *Europound,* respectively. Banks active in the Eurocurrency markets are known as *Eurobanks.*

Market participants closely follow the Eurodollar market. The key indicator for this market is the **London Inter Bank Offered Rate (LIBOR)**, the rate Eurobanks offer for loans to other institutions. The LIBOR indicator is widely used in financial contracting around the world. In the United States, the LIBOR is commonly used to benchmark floating interest rates in mortgage contracts. A mortgage quoted at LIBOR plus 175 basis points would mean that the homeowner (the borrower) pays the prevailing LIBOR rate plus 1.75 percent as interest.

Because LIBOR is pervasive in financial contracting, we need a deeper understanding of what exactly it means. LIBOR is not a single rate but comprises a set of rates based on various currencies and maturities. These rates, compiled by the British Banker's Association and disseminated at 11 a.m. Greenwich Mean Time, reflect rates at which banks are willing to lend to each other. The actual methodology for LIBOR fixing is explained in detail on the Web site www.bba.org.uk. Another indicator, not as commonly followed, is the London Interbank Bid Rate (LIBID), which represents the rate "bid" by Eurobanks for accepting deposits. The spread between LIBOR and LIBID represents the ask-bid differential for the Eurodollar market.

Why has the LIBOR emerged as the key indicator of Eurocurrency markets? The answer lies in the roots of this market in London as well as the fact that London is still the most important center for the Euro markets. While LIBOR rates prevail for most currencies, Euro Interbank Offered Rate (EURIBOR) rates compiled by the European Banking Federation are more commonly used for the EUR.

A rate often compared with the LIBOR is the yield on U.S. Treasury bills. LIBOR rates are higher than that of the Treasury bill because markets perceive a higher default risk with

Treasury-Eurodollar (TED) spread

The *TED* spread—the difference between LIBOR and the U.S. T-Bill rate—is normally around 1 percent but at times exceeded 2 percent during the credit crisis of 2007–2008.

Eurobanks compared to the U.S. Treasury. The difference in rates between LIBOR and Treasury bills is known as the Treasury-Eurodollar (TED) spread. This indicator reflects the level of the market's risk tolerance. While the TED spread usually hovers around 1 percent, it increases during times of market volatility. For example, during the credit crisis of 2007–2008, the TED spread sometimes exceeded 2 percent.

At this point, one interesting question may arise. Why do U.S.-based banks, with all the sophistication of the U.S. financial system, lag behind Europe-based banks in terms of cross-border loans and deposits? There are two answers to this question. The first involves the evolution of these Euro markets. The second involves the relative importance of tradable securities compared to bank IOUs in the United States and Europe. We address these two issues in the following discussion.

Eurocurrency Markets: Origin and Instruments

The Eurodollar market was the first to arise among the Eurocurrency markets. Its emergence in the 1950s can be directly related to U.S. regulations known as *Regulation Q* that prescribed ceilings on interest rates offered by banks to their depositors. Large entities such as MNCs, central banks, and other institutions sought higher interest rates on their USD holdings. This need was met initially by U.K. banks in London and later by a wide variety of global banks in London and elsewhere. The rise of the Eurodollar market can also be linked to persistent U.S. current account deficits (disparity between exports and imports) that led to external holdings of the USD. Many believe that these two factors—deposit ceiling regulations and U.S. current account deficits—are the most relevant factors explaining the development of the Eurodollar.[4] Recent research[5] shows the Eurodollar market started when the English Midland Bank aggressively sought USD deposits in 1955. At that time, U.S. regulations placed a ceiling of 1 percent on 30-day deposits. The Midland Bank was able to offer a small premium to rates offered by U.S. banks and obtain funds at a cheap rate. The heavy demand for loans in the United Kingdom at that time meant that Midland was able to profit from these deposits. Initially, the Bank of England was concerned about such nonconventional banking strategies but later realized that allowing innovation was in the best interests of preserving London's status as a financial center.

Over time, other currencies such as the German mark (precursor to the EUR), JPY, and GBP were deposited. Also, transactions were no longer confined to London. Other financial centers such as New York, Singapore, and Tokyo as well as offshore centers such as the Bahamas entered the fray. Soon, the Eurocurrency markets became a large global market, and today it is a multi-trillion-dollar market.

A principal feature of Euro markets is their lack of regulation. For instance, if a U.S. bank accepts local deposits, it is required to hold a certain fraction as a reserve. These and other normal requirements in banking were not applied to Eurocurrency transactions. There is an interesting parallel between the Euro markets and the Internet. Both are global phenomena that are unregulated principally because of the difficulties of enforcing regulations. Both have experienced growth because of this very feature—lack of regulation—and because of the anonymity offered to users.

The vast majority of the transactions in the Eurocurrency markets are private unsecured transactions. However, the issue of financial instruments that can then be traded in secondary markets is a growing trend. The two key financial instruments in the Eurocurrency markets are the Euro commercial paper and the Euro certificate of deposit. The **Euro commercial paper (ECP)** is an IOU with an average maturity of about six months. The issuers are primarily MNCs that view this market as a viable alternative to the domestic (i.e., U.S.) commercial paper market. The *Euro certificate of deposit (ECD)* is the international counterpart to bank CDs. These are deposits in banks outside the United States. ECPs and ECDs are traded in

---

[4] Some point to Soviet-bloc nations' reluctance to make USD deposits in U.S. banks as a reason for the emergence of the Eurodollar market. Details that are now apparent about the origins of the Eurodollar market do not bear out this interesting view.

[5] See Catherine Schenk, "The Origins of the Eurodollar Market in London: 1955–1963," *Explorations in Economic History* 35 (1998), pp. 221–238.

secondary markets that benefit the entity making the loan in many ways. First, this trading provides a way of cashing out. Second, it allows certain entities to specialize in originating the loan and others to invest in it. More generally, liquidity brings additional participants and helps make the market more efficient.

Calculating Returns on a Eurodollar Deposit

Consider an MNC making a deposit of $3 million for 60 days at a stated (or quoted) rate of 5 percent. Using the convention that interest on Eurodollar deposits is calculated on a simple interest "actual/360" basis,[6] we calculate the future value of the deposit as:

$$FV = 3{,}000{,}000 \times \left(1 + 5\% \times \frac{60}{360}\right) = 3{,}025{,}000$$

The annualized return earned by the MNC can be calculated as:

$$\text{Effective annual return} = \left(\frac{3{,}025{,}000}{3{,}000{,}000}\right)^{365/60} - 1 = 5.178\%$$

The term within parentheses equals 1-plus return for 60 days. This is compounded (that is, raised to power 365/60) to equal 1-plus return for the year. Subtract 1 from the resulting 1-plus return to find the effective annual return.

An effective annual return of 5.178 percent simply means that a present value (PV) of USD 1,000 would produce a future value (FV) of USD 1,051.78 in one year. In the preceding example, a simple interest LIBOR rate of 5 percent in a 60-day contract produced this "annualized" result. In financial markets, one encounters other interest rate conventions such as annual compounding and continuous compounding. An annual compounding rate of 5.178 percent would be consistent with an effective annual return of 5.178 percent. However, with continuous compounding, a smaller rate would produce the same end result.

EXAMPLE 2.5

Suppose a Eurobank offers a deposit with an effective annual return of 5.178 percent. A local bank offers a deposit but uses the continuous compounding method to calculate interest. What is the continuous compounded rate that produces an effective annual return of 5.178 percent?

Solution:
The equivalent continuous compounded rate is the value X that satisfies:

$$e^X = 1 + 5.178\%$$

To solve for X, take the natural log of both sides of the equation. This cancels out the exponent function and produces:

Continuous compounded rate $= X = ln\,(1 + 5.178 \text{ percent}) = 5.048$ percent.

If the local bank offers a rate higher than 5.048 percent, its deposit would be preferred.

2.3 International Debt Markets

International debt markets are markets where medium-term (1–5 years) and long-term (>5 years) debt instruments are issued and traded. BIS reports their total size at USD 21 trillion in 2007 (see Exhibit 2.8). They are a much larger market than the international money markets

---

[6] There are literally hundreds of interest rate conventions. Conventions in money markets fall into one of these two general approaches: actual/360 (also called n/360) and 30/360. U.S. money markets follow versions of the 30/360 convention, and Eurocurrency money markets follow versions of the actual/360 convention. Both calculate simple interest but differ in subtle ways. As an example of the difference between the two conventions, consider a six-month period. The 30/360 convention assumes 30 days to a month, so six months is translated to 180/360; instead, actual/360 produces either 182/360 or 183/360. To keep things simple in this text—while being faithful to conventions in money markets—we use the actual/360 convention flexibly: When possible, we state clearly the value (in days) for actual, and when dealing with months, we simply convert using 30 days per month.

EXHIBIT 2.8
International Debt Securities: Amounts Outstanding on December 2007 (Billions USD)

Source: Bank for International Settlements.

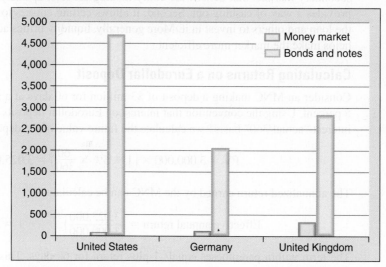

A. Residence of Issuer

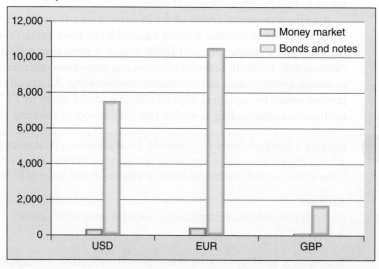

B. Currency of Issue

(ratio of almost 20:1) because large entities including governments, financial institutions, and MNCs use these markets for large-scale financing. U.S., German, and British issuers (by residence) dominate. Key currencies are therefore the USD, EUR, and GBP.

As with money markets, international debt markets contain cross-border and Euro components. In the following sections, we focus on the Euro (that is, foreign currency) components of these markets: the medium-term Eurocredit and the long-term Eurobond markets. MNCs are active participants in both of these markets.

Eurocredits

The Eurocredit market is characterized by medium-term maturities, typically ranging from one to five years. In contrast to the Eurocurrency market that mostly comprises non-negotiable instruments, this market consists of financial instruments. The main instrument is the **floating rate note (FRN)**. These are floating rate financial instruments with coupon interest linked to the LIBOR or other indicative rates such as the EURIBOR.

Coupon Interest Calculation

The coupon payment in an FRN is usually specified as "LIBOR + X." For example, consider a five-year USD-denominated FRN with a face value of USD 1 million. Suppose the annual coupon is specified as "LIBOR plus 125 basis points"; interest payments reset every 12 months. This means that the annual coupon payments—although paid at the end of each year—are determined at the beginning of the year, at which time the reference LIBOR rate is noted. The coupon payment is calculated as the product of the face value and the sum of LIBOR and 1.25 percent (because 1 basis point equals 0.01 percent).

EXAMPLE 2.6

Consider the five-year FRN just described with a coupon rate of "LIBOR plus 125 basis points." If today's value of LIBOR is 6.25 percent, what is the coupon payment at the end of the first year? What is the coupon payment at the end of the second year?

Solution:

Par value = USD 1 million

Coupon rate (1st year) = 6.25 percent + 1.25 percent = 7.5 percent

Coupon payment (1st year) = USD 1 million $\times$ 7.5% = USD 75,000

Coupon rate (2nd year) = Unknown (depends on prevailing market rates)

Coupon payment (2nd year) = Unknown (depends on prevailing market rates)

Discussion: In a floating rate instrument such as the FRN, coupon payments depend on future movement in interest rates. Thus, decision makers need to forecast interest rates in order to forecast cash flows. While the general topic of forecasting interest rates is beyond the scope of this text, it is useful to make the following observations about available methods:

- If one assumes that interest rate changes are random, the best estimate of a future interest rate is its current value. By using the method in this example, the expected interest rate in the second year is 6.25 percent and the expected coupon rate is 7.5 percent; this implies a coupon payment of USD 75,000 in the second year also.
- Future interest rates may also be inferred by comparing short-term and long-term rates. Theories that support this method are known as *term structure theories*.
- A final method is to use certain "futures" markets to infer future interest rates: this idea is developed in Chapter 3 in the discussion on Eurocurrency derivatives.

Fixed rate instruments in the Eurocredit markets are called *Euronotes*. In practice, however, they tend to be called **Eurobonds** because, with the exception of maturity, they share all other features of Eurobonds. The following discussion of Eurobonds is therefore relevant also to Euronotes.

Eurobonds: Origins

The precursor to the Eurobond is the foreign bond. A *foreign bond* is a bond issued in a particular country by a foreign issuer and denominated in the country's own currency. The issuance of foreign bonds dates back to the 19th century when various governments issued GBP-denominated bonds in England. Today, foreign bond markets are active in many countries. Some prominent examples follow. *Yankee bonds* are USD-denominated bonds issued in the United States by foreign entities such as foreign-based MNCs and foreign governments. *Samurai bonds* are JPY-denominated bonds issued in Japan by non-Japanese entities. Other examples are *kangaroo bonds* (Australia) and *kauri bonds* (New Zealand).

Eurobonds differ from foreign bonds in one important dimension. Like Eurodollar and Eurocurrency instruments, a mismatch for Eurobonds exists between the country (and region) of issue and the currency denomination of the bond. Thus, when a U.S.-based MNC issues a

EXHIBIT 2.9

**Anatomy of the
Eurobond Market
1980–2000**

Source: Anouk Claes, Marc J. K.
De Ceuster and Ruud Polfliet,
"Anatomy of the Eurobond
Market 1980–2000," European
Financial Management 8,
no. 3 (2002), pp. 373–386.

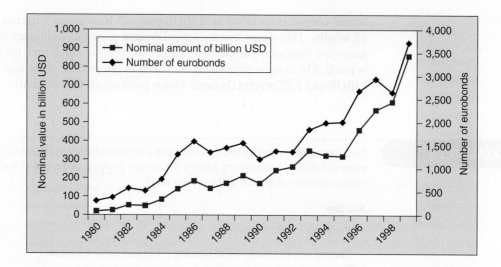

USD-denominated bond in Japan, the bond is categorized as a Eurobond. In this example, there is a mismatch between the location of issue (Japan) and the currency denomination (USD).[7]

The Eurobond market essentially started in the 1960s in response to a tax change in the United States.[8] At that time, the United States was running current account deficits and was searching for ways to decrease the supply of USD abroad. The *Interest Equalization Act* attempted to stem the outflow of funds from the United States to foreign countries by penalizing the issuance of Yankee bonds in the United States. The penalty arose in the form of payments from the issuers to the U.S. Treasury reflecting the interest rate benefits of issuing the bond in the United States. This penalty is estimated to have increased the cost of borrowing by about 1 percent. Consequently, foreign issuers took their business away to European centers and hence started the Eurobond market. At the same time, the U.S. government also created the Office of Foreign Direct Investment Control that prevented U.S. firms from borrowing in the United States for foreign investments. This added further impetus to the Eurobond market.

In 1963, investment bankers at S. G. Warburg of London devised the first Eurobond. On behalf of their client, the Italian highway authority, the Autostrade, they designed a bond that would be privately placed in Europe. This bond was a humble one by today's standards; it was a USD 15 million, 15-year bond. The key innovation was in designing an instrument that avoided national regulatory scrutiny. Two elements contributed to this effect. First, the bond was viewed as a global instrument and, hence, not under the jurisdiction of any one nation's regulatory bodies. Second, the private placement of the bond indicated that it was not being sold at the retail level; normally, regulators scrutinize public retail activity and not private wholesale activity.

Over time, MNCs, institutions, and governmental agencies obtained funds in the Eurobond market to make it the multi-trillion-dollar market it is today. See Exhibit 2.9 for the size of the market and Exhibit 2.10 for the variety of its issuers, currencies, and maturities. Issuers include industrial firms (Wolters Kluwer), financial institutions (Credit Suisse), and public utilities (Tokyo Electric). Currencies include the USD and EUR. Maturities range from 2 to 10 years.

Who are investors in Eurobonds? At least initially, the majority of the investors were European banks and financial institutions. Individual investors in Europe also participated indirectly through their accounts at these institutions. In the 1980s and 1990s when the Eurobond market developed

---

[7] This traditional definition appears to be unraveling after the introduction of the EUR. According to Peristiani and Santos, "Prior to the introduction of the euro in 2002, a Eurobond represented a bearer security offered by issuers domiciled in any country but issued in other than the country's currency. After the introduction of the euro, this distinction became redundant because the euro began to function as a common denominator for many European issuers. Eurobonds are underwritten by international syndicate of banks and are not subject to national regulation." (Peristiani and Santos, 2008, "Has the U.S. Bond Market Lost Its Edge to the Eurobond Market." It is available at SSRN: http://ssrn.com/abstract=1100018.)

[8] Merton Miller, "Financial Innovation: The Last Twenty Years and the Next," *Journal of Financial and Quantitative Analysis* 21 (1986), pp. 459–471.

EXHIBIT 2.10

A Day in the Life of the Eurobond Market

Excerpted from the *Wall Street Journal*, "New Securities Issues," April 4, 2008.

Credit Suisse—1.25 billion euro self-led bond issue was priced, according to a person familiar with the deal. Terms: maturity: April 8, 2010; coupon: 60 basis points more than three-month euro interbank offered rate; reoffer: 99.809; payment: April 8, 2008; spread: 70 basis points more than three-month Euribor; ratings: Aa1 (Moody's), double-A minus (S&P), AA- (Fitch Inc.); denominations: 50,000 euros; 1,000 euros; listing: Luxembourg.

Societe Generale—1.25 billion euros self-led bond issue was priced, according to a person familiar with the deal. Terms: maturity: April 15, 2010; coupon: 60 basis points more than three-month Euribor; reoffer: 99.866; payment: April 15, 2008; spread: 67 basis points more than three-month Euribor; ratings: Aa2 (Moody's), double-A minus (S&P), AA- (Fitch).

Tokyo Electric Power Co.—50 billion yen of five-year bonds was priced through Daiwa Securities SMBC, Nomura Securities, Mitsubishi UFJ Securities, underwriters said. Terms: maturity: April 25, 2013; coupon: 1.094%; price: 100; yield: 1.094% (No. 247 JGB plus 26 basis points); payment: April 25, 2008; ratings: Aa2 (Moody's), double-A (S&P), AA+ (R&I), AAA (JCR).

Tokyo Electric Power Co.—50 billion yen of 10-year bonds in Japan were priced through Nikko Citigroup Securities, Mizuho Securities, Goldman Sachs Securities, underwriters said. Terms: maturity: April 25, 2018; coupon: 1.64%; price: 100; yield: 1.64% (No. 291 JGB plus 27 basis points); payment: April 25; ratings: Aa2 (Moody's), double-A (S&P), AA+ (R&I), AAA (JCR).

UBS AG—1 billion euro self-led bond issue was priced, according to a person familiar with the deal. Terms: maturity: perpetual; coupon: 8.836%; reoffer: par; payment: April 3, 2008; spread: 465 basis points more than midswaps; ratings: Aa3 (Moody's), A (S&P), A+ (Fitch); denominations: 50,000 euros; listing: Luxembourg; interest: annual.

Wolters Kluwer—750 million euro bond was priced through Deutsche Bank, ING and Rabobank, lead managers of the transaction said. Terms: maturity, April 10, 2018; coupon 6.375%; reoffer: 99.654; payment: April 10, 2008; spread: 198 basis points more than midswaps; ratings: Baa1 (Moody's), triple-B plus (S & P); denominations: 50,000 euros, 1,000 euros; listing: Luxembourg.

dramatically, experts referred to the typical individual investor as the "Belgian dentist." This was a reference to wealthy investors primarily in countries such as Belgium, Germany, and Switzerland who preferred investments in Eurobonds not only to generate low-risk income but also to save on taxes. Eurobonds have traditionally been unregistered instruments and facilitated tax avoidance; however, there are indications that this feature of Eurobonds is changing.

Features of Eurobonds and Their Markets

Because initial investors in Eurobonds have been European individuals and institutions, European traditions have dictated the features of Eurobonds. Unlike U.S. bonds paying coupon interest semiannually, Eurobonds pay coupon interest annually. More important, Eurobonds are bearer instruments, affording anonymity to their holders. Bearer instruments provide to holders bearer coupons that can be exchanged for cash. These bearer coupons do not identify the holders unlike U.S. bonds that register the identity of holders. But demand for anonymity also arises from institutions. Banks, hedge funds, and other institutions may also value anonymity not from a tax perspective but from a trading and asset strategy perspective.

In addition to annual coupons and bearer form, Eurobonds exhibit the following features[9]:

Eurobonds

Eurobond issues are usually large issues denominated in key currencies such as the USD, EUR, and JPY.

- The three main currencies are the USD, EUR, and JPY. The JPY is losing market share, probably because of the long-running economic crisis in Japan. The EUR is gaining market share to emerge as the leading currency.

- The median issue size is around USD 100 million.

- Maturities are equally dispersed in the three categories: 1–5, 5–10, and 10–15 years.

- Roughly 75 percent are fixed-rate, 20 percent floating-rate, and 5 percent convertible bonds.

- About 10 percent are callable. This means that the issuer can repurchase the bonds at predetermined terms.

[9] Anouk Claes, Marc J. K. De Ceuster and Ruud Polfliet, "Anatomy of the Eurobond Market 1980–2000," *European Financial Management* 8, no. 3 (2002), pp. 373–386.

Most investors in Eurobonds hold the instruments for the duration of the bond. However, some investors demand liquidity. Hence, over time, secondary markets have developed in places such as London and Luxembourg. Despite the development of exchange trading, most transactions are conducted in OTC markets.

Recent Developments in Debt Markets

Financial markets tend to evolve faster than other markets because of the ease with which money moves from one entity to another and the ease with which financial contracts can be written and enforced. So, it is no surprise that during the recent decade, many interesting developments occurred in debt markets. In the following sections, we discuss three such developments.

Deregulation

A major player in listing and trading Eurobonds—Luxembourg Stock Exchange—recently launched the *Euro Multilateral Trading Facility (MTF)* market for trading securities in a less regulated environment. Issuers are relieved of the burden of preparing detailed prospectuses. Furthermore, it has less onerous requirements for financial reporting. These relaxed rules are offset by the requirement that denominations be at least EUR 50,000, ensuring that market participants are larger players and therefore able to gather information through other means for conducting due diligence.

MNCs' Preference for Eurobonds

The U.S. bond markets have traditionally been the largest source of debt capital for corporations. Its strength relative to the Eurobond market has been on the wane, and in 2005, the situation reversed with more issuances in the Eurobond market compared to the U.S. bond market.[10] This trend is expected to continue. Additionally, some Eurobond issues are mega-issues (more than one billion USD) simultaneously offered in multiple markets.

A *global bond* is essentially a Eurobond that is simultaneously issued in multiple regions around the world. Typically, global bonds are issued in North America, Europe, and Asia simultaneously. A wide variety of market participants invest in these bonds. Global bonds tend to be much larger—often exceeding USD 1 billion—and more liquid than Eurobonds. See Exhibit 2.11 for details of an actual issue:

EXHIBIT 2.11
Global Bonds

Source: *treasury.worldbank.org*

Worldbanks' Global Bond Issue

Amount: EUR 1.5 billion
Settlement date: May 30, 2007
Maturity Date: June 1, 2010
Issue/Re-offer price: 99.767%
Coupon: 4.25% annually
Spread: 5 basis points over the underlying government benchmark
Denomination: EUR 1,000 and multiples thereof
Format: Registered Notes
Listing: Luxembourg
Clearing Systems: Euroclear and Clearstream Luxembourg
Investor Region: Middle East and Africa 26%, Asia 17%, N. America 4%, Germany 7%, France 3%, Italy 3%, Other Europe 40%
Investor type: Central Banks and Official Institutions 70%, Banks 14%, Fund Managers 10%, Pension and Insurance funds 6%

---

[10] Stavros Peristiani, "Evaluating the Relative Strength of the U.S. Capital Markets," *Current Issues in Economics and Finance* (Federal Reserve Bank of New York) 13 (July 2007).

Complexity

One exotic component of debt markets contains what are known as *structured products*. These are typically asset-backed instruments with complex features. For instance, *collateralized debt obligations (CDO)* are backed by risky assets such as mortgages and issued in tranches (classes) with varying levels of risk. Markets for structured assets developed in a period of decreasing risk tolerance particularly during 2003–2005. Global issues of CDOs and other structured products, mostly denominated in USD and EUR, exceeded half a trillion USD in 2006. The credit crisis of 2007–2008 has increased risk aversion and has adversely affected this market.

2.4 Global Equity Markets

Equity markets are those in which corporate shares are issued and traded. In this section, we primarily discuss the secondary markets in which shares, once issued, are subsequently traded. We discuss the share issuance process and the primary markets in detail in Chapter 10. Because the U.S. equity markets are the largest and most important component of global equity markets, we start with their descriptions.

U.S. Equity Markets

Today, even after declines related to the credit crisis of 2007–2008, U.S. equity markets remain a prominent component of global equity markets. This prominence is reflected in the following factors:

- Market capitalization, measured by the market value of shares outstanding, of U.S. firms is a significant fraction of the market capitalization of the entire world. This is testament to the strength of U.S. capital markets as well as the economy.
- The U.S. equity markets provide more liquidity, measured in terms of trading volume, than any other equity market in the world.
- U.S. equity markets are sophisticated enough to allow the trading of shares of emerging firms, especially in the high technology arena.
- Finally, the U.S. equity markets have shown a great ability to innovate trading practices.

The two important stock markets in the United States are the **New York Stock Exchange (NYSE)** and the *National Association of Security Dealers Automated Quotations (NASDAQ)*. Market statistics from 2007 in Exhibit 2.12 indicate that the NYSE and the NASDAQ have market capitalization of roughly USD 16 trillion and USD 4 trillion, respectively. The total for these two U.S. markets, USD 20 trillion, is roughly one-third of the global market capitalization of USD 60 trillion. However, this share has been trending down.

Other Exchanges

Other large markets are Tokyo, Euronext, and London, each with a market capitalization of about USD 4 trillion. However, the equity market landscape is changing dramatically. In the

EXHIBIT 2.12
Leading Stock Markets (2007)

Source: *http://www. world-exchanges.org/statistics/ annual/equity-markets* (accessed January 16, 2009).

	Market Cap (USD Billion)	Average Daily Turnover (USD Billion)
NYSE Group	15,651	119
Tokyo SE Group	4,331	26
Euronext	4,223	22
NASDAQ	4,014	61
London SE	3,852	41
Shanghai SE	3,694	17
Hong Kong Exchanges	2,654	9
TSX Group	2,187	6
Deutsche Börse	2,105	17
Bombay SE	1,819	1

recent decade, equity markets have boomed in many emerging economies. Stock exchanges (SE) such as Shanghai SE and Bombay SE are increasing in market capitalization.

Trading and Liquidity

The 10 largest exchanges form a combined daily turnover exceeding USD 300 billion. Although smaller than the trading volume of about USD 1 trillion in the spot foreign exchange markets, this is still a considerable figure, implying high levels of liquidity in stock markets.

Unlike currency markets, stock markets are not 24-hour markets today. For example, the NYSE conducts trading between the hours of 9:30 a.m. and 4:00 p.m. Trading takes place in a physical location using a process known as the *open outcry process*. Although the NYSE is transitioning to increased levels of electronic trading, extending trading into evening and night hours will be difficult. To do so will require additional staffing by securities firms. Such expansion is expensive and may not justify the benefits of 24-hour trading. These issues recently came to the fore when the NYSE considered extending trading hours and solicited feedback: Retail customers applauded the proposed move while financial institutions balked.

While the NYSE represents traditional markets, the NASDAQ uses a different trading system similar to the one used in the Interbank currency market. Using computers and telecommunications, a virtual market is created for buyers and sellers to transact by exchanging bid and ask quotations. Such a trading paradigm perhaps lends itself more easily to the needs of round-the-clock trading. Electronic stock exchanges such as Instinet known as *electronic communications networks (ECN)* cater to the demands of evening and early morning trading for large institutional clients. Retail clients, however, are by and large precluded from after-hours markets. But there is no denying the movement toward continuous trading.

Cross-Border Listing

Deregulation and financial globalization have resulted in the following forces. First, investors are demanding access to equity instruments issued by foreign entities. U.S. investors, for instance, demand stocks issued by firms located in Japan, Germany, and other foreign countries. (This issue was discussed in Chapter 1.) Second, corporations are demanding access to cross-border sources of equity capital. Indian firms, for instance, are interested in listing their shares in U.S. exchanges.

These forces have led to certain interesting developments, especially in the United States. Various exchanges, such as the NYSE, have devised mechanisms to permit U.S. investors to trade in foreign equities. Furthermore, non-U.S. firms have been able to conduct financing transactions in the United States by issuing equities. These issues are discussed in depth in Chapter 10.

Recent Developments in Global Equity Markets

During the recent decade, many developments have occurred in global equity markets. In the following sections, we summarize certain key developments.

Incorporation of Exchanges

As a consequence of rising demand for financial transactions, exchanges have themselves become more businesslike. Many have incorporated as public firms, issued shares, and become more attuned to cash flows and shareholder wealth maximization. The NYSE was structured as a for-profit corporation with publicly held shares in 2006. Other exchanges such as NYMEX and CME are also publicly traded corporations.

Consolidation

As exchanges sought opportunities especially in nontraditional products such as derivatives or beyond their national boundaries, they engaged in collaborative efforts. In extreme cases, exchanges merged their operations. In 2007, the NYSE merged with Euronext to create the most comprehensive and largest financial exchange in the world.

Rise of Emerging Markets

The recent decade was the decade of emerging market equities. Bourses (exchanges) in Brazil, Russia, India, and China (so-called **BRIC** nations) boomed. Listings in these exchanges also expanded dramatically. Predictably, leading exchanges in developed nations are exploring joint venture opportunities in emerging markets. The NYSE has one such venture with the Bombay SE.

Private Equity Markets

In contrast to pubic equity markets—shares are issued and traded in exchanges and public markets—private equity (PE) results in private shareholding. PE financing mostly takes two forms: venture capital (VC) funding and buyout funding. VC funding arises during a firm's early stages The United States has been a pioneer in VC funding, but two recent crises—the NASDAQ collapse of 2000 and the credit crisis of 2007–2008—have severely affected VC activity in the United States. Buyout activities—private investors buy a stake in a public firm, often taking it private—have also been adversely affected. An interesting development in private equity is the rise of the so-called sovereign funds: giant funds (usually with capitalization approaching USD 1 trillion) launched by cash-rich governments of countries such as the United Arab Emirates (UAE) and Singapore.

Summary

- Currencies are traded in foreign exchange markets. These markets, dominated by large global banks, are the largest financial markets.
- Eurocurrency markets are short-term money markets dominated by Eurobanks' lending and borrowing. Like foreign exchange markets, this is a multi-trillion market. The main component of this market is the Eurodollar market involving transactions in the USD. LIBOR is a key interest rate in the Eurodollar market.
- Eurocredit markets are medium-term debt markets. The main instrument is the FRN with coupons linked to LIBOR. This market is not as large as the Eurocurrency market.
- The Eurobond market is even larger than the Eurocurrency market and involves bonds denominated in a currency different from the currency of the country that issued the bonds. Bonds denominated in the EUR predominate.
- The Eurobond market has recently experienced rather large issues, often exceeding USD 1 billion and issued simultaneously in North America, Europe, and Asia. These issues are classified as global bonds.
- The most important global stock market is the U.S. market, accounting for about one-third of global capitalization. Current trends indicate that stock exchanges around the world are consolidating.

Questions

1. **Foreign Exchange Market.** How large is the foreign exchange market? What drives demand for transactions in it?
2. **Foreign Exchange Market.** Why is the foreign exchange market a 24-hour market?
3. **Bid-Ask Quotes.** What are bid and ask quotations? What are some factors determining the spread between bid and ask values?
4. **Direct versus Indirect Quotes.** What are direct and indirect currency quotes? How can direct quotes be converted into indirect quotes? Give examples of currencies that are quoted indirectly in the United States.
5. **Banks in FX Trading.** Give examples of large U.S. banks involved in foreign exchange trading. Globally, which nation's banks are the leading foreign exchange dealers?
6. **Other Entities in FX Trading.** Try using key words such as "foreign exchange" or "buy foreign currency" on a search site such as Google. What types of businesses appear on

the first page? In particular, who are the advertisers of the sponsored links? Enter some of these Web sites and determine the business models of these advertisers, and then relate them to material learned in this chapter.

7. **FX Market Location.** Which location is the most important for foreign exchange trading and why?

8. **Oil Prices and FX Trading.** Assume that the price of oil increases by 40 percent in a particular year because of political instability in a major oil-producing country. Consequently, transportation costs rise. Explain how this rise affects the number of transactions in the foreign exchange market.

9. **Eurobonds Market.** What are Eurobonds? How do they differ from domestic bonds? What factors led to the birth and growth of Eurobonds? Where are they traded?

10. **Eurobonds Issue Considerations.** Formans is a grocery store chain operating in the Midwest (United States). The firm is interested in expanding the number of stores from 200 to 250 in the next three years. Forman's CFO, Ron Mittal, is considering various options for issuing debt. Forman's investment banker raises the possibility of a USD 50 million issue in the Eurobond market. Comment on the viability and desirability of this alternative.

11. **Foreign versus Eurobonds.** An Australian firm wishes to make a debt issue. Explain to its CFO the difference between foreign bonds and Eurobonds. Which of these two bonds is issued and traded in a more global market? Which alternative is probably better for this firm and why?

12. **Eurocurrency Market.** What are Eurocurrency markets? What is the approximate size of this market?

13. **FRN Description.** What are FRNs? What types of issuers might be interested in this instrument?

14. **Eurodollar Market.** How did the Eurodollar markets develop? Evaluate their current importance.

15. **Global Equity Markets.** What are the major stock exchanges in the world? Which one is the largest and why? What are current developments in equity markets?

16. **Global Equity Markets.** Why are stock exchanges consolidating? Give an example of a recent attempt at consolidation.

17. **Global Integration of Markets.** We are living in an era of globalization. In terms of global integration of markets, which has occurred first, (a) market for goods or (b) market for capital? Explain.

18. **Euro Debt and Firms.** Why are euro debt markets attractive to corporate issuers?

19. **U.S. Equity Markets.** Why are non-U.S. entities interested in tapping U.S. equity markets?

Problems

1. **Currency Conversion.** An MNC converts USD 215,000 into BRL 395,000. Assume zero commissions and fees.
   a. What is the BRLUSD exchange rate?
   b. What is the USDBRL exchange rate?

2. **Currency Conversion.** The Oriental Mercantile Bank, headquartered in Singapore, services many U.S.-based MNC clients. Assume that it quotes SGDUSD at 0.7352–0.7358 (SGD refers to Singapore dollars). Assume zero commissions and fees. A U.S. customer wishes to obtain SGD 2 million for payment to a Singapore supplier. How many USD are necessary to make the conversion?

3. **Currency Conversion.** Use data from problem 2. Assume instead that a U.S. customer is receiving SGD 40,000 from a customer in Singapore and wishes to convert this amount into USD. What is the amount received in USD?

4. **Bid-Ask Spread.** A U.S. bank is quoting 1.22 and 1.24 for EURUSD. What is the bid-ask spread in absolute terms? What is the spread in percentage terms?

5. **Bid-Ask Spread.** A U.S. bank is quoting 103 and 104 for USDJPY. What is the bid-ask spread in absolute terms? What is the spread in percentage terms?

6. **Comparing Bid-Ask Spreads.** Consider the quotations in the following table offered by the Chong Hing Bank of Hong Kong for currency transactions. Calculate the bid-ask spread (absolute and percent) and identify the least and most costly spread. In words, explain the significance of your findings.

Currency Pair	Bid	Ask
USDHKD	7.6211	7.6219
SGDHKD	5.9998	6.0012
EURHKD	11.1882	11.1895
JPYHKD	0.0748	0.0751

7. **Comparing Bid-Ask Spreads.** Use data from problem 6 concerning Chong Hing Bank. The table has direct quotes from the Hong Kong bank's perspective. Convert the table into indirect quotes and recalculate bid-ask spreads (absolute and percent). Which currency appears to be the most expensive to trade?

8. **Evaluation of Transaction Costs.** An MNC wishes to sell EUR 2 million that it received from a French customer and obtain its domestic currency (USD). The following alternatives are available. Determine which bank provides the highest amount of USD.

Bank	Currency Pair	Bid	Ask	Commission
A	EURUSD	1.4512	1.4519	USD 250
B	EURUSD	1.4511	1.4520	USD 100
C	USDEUR	0.6890	0.6891	USD 150

9. **Evaluation of Transaction Costs.** Use data from problem 8. Assume that an MNC transacts with bank A to convert EUR 500,000 into USD. Estimate total transaction costs in absolute and percentage terms.

10. **Transaction Costs and Bank Profits.** Consider again the data presented in problem 8. Assume that bank B transacts with two customers. The first customer purchases EUR 5 million and the second customer sells EUR 5 million. What is the profit made by bank B? Break down profits into spread and commissions.

11. **Cross-Currency Quotes.** Consider the following currency quotes. Fill in the missing values:

Currency Pair	Quote
USDJPY	108
EURJPY	156
HKDJPY	17
USDEUR	?
USDHKD	?

12. **LIBOR Deposit FV and Effective Rate.** Microsoft has excess cash of USD 2 billion that it uses to make a 90-day Eurodollar deposit. Assume that 90-day LIBOR equals 4.2 percent (actual/360 convention). How much interest does Microsoft earn? What is FV? What is the effective annual return?

13. **LIBOR Deposit Effective Rate.** Assume that 180-day LIBOR equals 5.4 percent (actual/360 convention). Calculate the effective annual return. Also calculate the continuously compounded interest rate that will provide an equivalent annual return.

14. **Inferring LIBOR Rate.** Dell makes a Eurodollar deposit for 180 days and earns an effective annual return of 3.8 percent. What is 180-day LIBOR (actual/360 convention)?

15. **Inferring LIBOR Rate.** An MNC makes a Eurodollar deposit for 270 days and earns an effective annual return of 4.1 percent. What is the 270-day LIBOR (actual/360 convention)?

16. **LIBOR versus Other Rates.** Waste Management, a U.S. firm, has a surplus amount of USD 20 million available for 180 days. Its U.S. banker offers a fixed-rate deposit with interest calculated using a continuously compounded rate of 5 percent.

    a. Calculate the FV of the deposit.

    b. Assume that Eurobanks compete for this deposit and offer an interest rate using the actual/360 convention. At what rate will these Eurobanks be attractive to Waste Management?

17. **FRN and Expected Cash Flows.** A U.S. firm issues a three-year FRN with a face value of $175,000. The coupon is set at LIBOR plus 40 basis points and is paid annually. The coupon rate is set at the beginning of the year. The firm's CEO notes that the one-year LIBOR rate is 4.2 percent. Calculate the year 1 expected cash flow related to this debt issue.

Extension

Term Structure and FRN Cash Flows. A firm issues a two-year USD-denominated FRN at LIBOR plus 60 basis points. Face value is USD 1 million. Payments are made annually and fixed using LIBOR rates at the beginning of the year. The one-year LIBOR rate is 4 percent. The two-year LIBOR is not widely available: The British Bankers' Association, which disseminates LIBOR rates, provides rates for maturities of only one year or less. However, a financial analyst working for the firm gathers information on an alternate reference interest rate and notes that the two-year rate exceeds the one-year rate by 1 percent. This suggests that the two-year LIBOR rate, were it to exist, would be 5 percent (that is, 4 percent plus 1 percent). Calculate the coupon payments. [*Hint:* Suppose the rate for the second year is X percent. One version of the term structure theory implies that the FV of USD 1 will be identical whether we earn (a) interest at 5 percent for two years or (b) 4 percent in the first year and X percent in the second year.]

Case

Clover Machines: *Dabbling in International Markets?*

Financial policies at Clover had remained traditional and oriented toward domestic markets. The firm has built a good reputation in U.S. equity and debt markets with conservative financial practices. The firm is followed by 16 Wall Street analysts; this is at the upper end of the distribution of number of analysts per firm. Brian Bent, CFO of Clover Machines, takes pride in noting that these analysts' tight dispersion of earnings forecasts is a sign of transparency and efficient management of information flow to key market participants.

Meanwhile, Clover Machines continues its operational push abroad. Following revisions to its strategic plan, it has set up subsidiaries in South America and Asia to add to its subsidiaries in Europe. Consequently, Clover expects its foreign revenues to rise from a current level of 12 percent of total revenues to 15 percent in the coming year. A long-term goal is to increase this ratio to 40 percent. Clover also expects higher margins in foreign sales compared to domestic sales. But current margins in foreign sales are lower because of operating leverage and other factors. One-time set up costs can be quite large and require significant financing. Additional financing is probably required in the foreseeable future to improve infrastructure for foreign operations.

Mr. Bent wishes to be proactive in structuring Clover's financing strategy. Although the firm has good relations with Wall Street firms and is confident of refreshing its liquidity through commercial paper issues in the United States, Clover needs to assess whether global financial markets offer better opportunities. Furthermore, internal financing is constrained by Clover's long-standing dividend policy: Its dividend payout ratio has fluctuated around 25 percent. A radical departure from this ratio would send worrisome signals to analysts. He tasks a junior financial analyst, Cheng Peng, to prepare a report on financing opportunities in international financial markets.

In his report to the CFO, Mr. Peng identifies the following opportunities:

- Medium-term notes denominated in EUR paying EURIBOR + 30 basis points, interest payable annually and maturing in four years. Currently EURIBOR is 4.3 percent. Mr. Peng expects a slowdown in the Eurozone and a resulting decrease in rates, making this floating rate instrument attractive. EURUSD is currently 1.60, and volatility estimates indicate a range of 1.50–1.70 in the future. Issue price is 99 percent.

- A Eurobond issue denominated in USD with a fixed rate of 5.2 percent. The bond matures in 10 years. Standard & Poor's will probably rate the bond AA. Issue price is 101 percent.

- A Samurai bond with a fixed rate of 1.9 percent. The bond matures in 10 years. This bond will likely not have an active secondary market. Issue price is 97 percent. Samurai bonds are denominated in JPY. The Japanese economy is weak right now, and prospects for a speedy turnaround appear bleak.

Mr. Bent carefully reads Mr. Peng's report. He jots down the following questions to be resolved in a follow-up conversation:

1. What are overall benefits of tapping international markets? Does it make sense for Clover given its success in using domestic capital markets?

2. Why did the report contain no mention of foreign equity markets?

3. What are general pros and cons of medium-term versus long-term debt financing? Floating versus fixed rate? Given Clover's current situation, is one approach generically better than another without giving consideration of financing specifics?

4. What are the pros and cons of tapping the Eurobond market? Does Clover fit the profile of firms using this market? What are preconditions for successful participation?

5. Clover does not have any business in Japan. Given this, does it make any sense to obtain JPY financing? What might be the downside of the attractive rate that is offered?

6. The report shows no indication or model of how to translate the effects of obtaining floating rate financing. Mr. Bent resolves to ask Mr. Peng to construct a spreadsheet—using plausible scenarios—to demonstrate cash flow consequences of the floating rate note.

Appendix 2

Autodealing: Technology and Innovation in Currency Markets[11]

Autodealing refers to algorithmic trading models that employ electronic price feeds to generate dealable prices and transact based on dealable prices. Autodealing has come about as the result of a variety of developments in the foreign exchange marketplace and has itself further transformed the functioning of that market.

Foreign exchange electronic dealing began in the bank-to-bank market in the early 1990s when dealing systems developed by EBS and Reuters enabled the automatic matching of trading interests of large market-making banks. Today, these systems provide electronic brokering for foreign exchange transactions, allowing member banks to trade various currency crosses with one another by way of electronically posting bids and offers and striking at various price levels. These trades are electronically matched between banks that have established bilateral credit lines within the systems. The counterparties to a transaction are not identified until after the deal is struck. The trading platforms feed the transaction information into banks' downstream settlement systems, enabling deal settlement through the regular settlement practices of the member banks.

---

[11] Excerpted from "Autodealing: Market Impact and Best Practices Recommendations," Foreign Exchange Committee, New York Federal Reserve Bank, 2006.

Financial institutions worldwide now use electronic brokering. More recently, electronic brokers have spun off products to allow nonbank institutions to access interbank liquidity. These dealing systems also provide credit management and deal control. The features provided by electronic brokering platforms have dramatically increased deal flow frequency, contributed to deeper liquidity, and increased controls on the extension of counterparty credit in the foreign exchange market.

Indeed, electronic brokering services have given rise to autodealing strategies in the foreign exchange market. In the late 1990s, banks with substantial capital and well-developed proprietary trading technologies began to deliver electronic pricing and trading capabilities to their clients directly. This changing market landscape was characterized by a consolidation of secondary market share and a concentration of liquidity when banks merged, the cost of developing competitive proprietary customer platforms increased, and margins shrank.

These developments in technology and market concentration led to the growth of so-called white labeling—the sale of a comprehensive trading system by a large global bank or technology vendor to a smaller bank. Large banks marketed white-labeling services to access additional client transaction volume and earn the fees associated with providing these comprehensive trading systems. Clients benefited by gaining access to liquidity and more efficient trading platforms without incurring the associated capital expenditure. By using white-labeling services, client banks were able to outsource their market risk to the larger bank.

White-labeling solutions were followed swiftly by the introduction of bank- and vendor-owned multidealer electronic marketplaces in which secondary market participants could access liquidity from multiple bank sources in competition. The offerings in this category currently include FXall, FXConnect, Hotspot, Lava, and Currenex. Multibank platforms began with a request-for-quote protocol; next, some of these platforms moved to a streaming, executable price model; and currently, a few even offer market-making capabilities not unlike the interbank platforms.

To trade in multibank streaming executable price and market-making environments, secondary market participants need readily available access to credit from multiple counterparties. This need has been met by the introduction of prime-brokerage services, which have enabled substantial growth in the trading volume on these multidealer portals. A prime-broker bank allows the client to deal in the bank's name subject to a "give up" after the trade is executed. This service makes available significant liquidity to the client. Additionally, on some platforms, the use of prime-brokerage services can facilitate more anonymity than that of a market-making bank that deals on a bank-to-bank platform without the use of a prime broker.

In addition to increasing trading on multibank-to-client portals, prime-brokerage services have also enabled some nontraditional market participants to enter the traditional interdealer market through services such as EBS Prime. Some of these clients use autodealing trading systems; others use more traditional manual trading techniques. The use of these services may allow prime-brokerage clients to trade anonymously in the interdealer market. In such a case, the identities of the executing dealer and prime broker are revealed to each other as counterparties to the trade when a trade is matched electronically, but the prime-brokerage client remains anonymous to the executing dealer. Given the separation between a bank's prime-brokerage services unit and its trading desk, the client's identity also remains anonymous to the trading desk of the prime broker's bank in most circumstances. Although the client's traded position is transferred to the prime-broker bank's trading desk, in the absence of an agreement to the contrary, the trading desk is not apprised of the client's identity.

CHAPTER THREE

Currency and Eurocurrency Derivatives

Derivatives are revolutionary financial instruments that have transformed the practice of corporate financial management in the last few decades. While every student of finance should have some knowledge of these instruments, students of international finance in particular need a working knowledge of currency derivatives. This is so because of their widespread use in corporations' control of currency risk.

Derivatives are traded in a multi-trillion-dollar market. This huge market has derivatives in every possible flavor. The varieties might be compared to varieties of candy. Similar to basic categories such as chocolate, hard, and soft candies, derivatives instruments such as forwards, futures, and options are available. Within each basic candy category is a multitude of items varying by texture, flavor, size, and other characteristics. Similarly, within a derivative category such as options, a multitude of contracts varies by underlying asset, size, maturity, and other characteristics. Candy makers can get very creative. So can financial engineers—exchanges, institutions, and MNCs—who help create new types of financial contracts.

The study of derivatives can be challenging and time consuming. It is an ever-changing field with a continuous parade of new actors, new instruments, and new applications. Because our focus is on MNCs and the special issues they face, most of this chapter is devoted to currency derivatives. MNCs do use other types of derivatives and, given the importance of the Euro markets to global finance, we also provide a detailed discussion of Eurocurrency derivatives.

Our objective is to provide students with a working knowledge of key instruments in these markets. We discuss market structure[1] as well as valuation methods for key contracts such as currency forwards, currency futures, and currency options. We then apply this knowledge in subsequent chapters. In Chapter 7—a major focal point for the material on derivatives—we explain how these instruments are used to control currency risk. We also apply derivatives knowledge in other contexts such as capital budgeting (Chapter 9) and, mergers (Chapter 12). We defer discussion of currency swaps to chapter 10, which covers MNC financing, because currency swaps are typically used in the financing context.

Specifically, the topics covered in this chapter are:

- The definition of derivatives and their general characteristics that lend themselves to applications in risk management and speculation.
- Features of currency forward contracts.
- Value of currency forwards.
- Comparison of currency forward and futures contracts.
- Unique features of currency option contracts.
- Factors affecting the value of currency options and a model that uses these factors to price options.

---

[1] A small caveat: Derivatives market structure details are like Saharan dunes; relevant details discernible today are obsolete tomorrow. A knowledge of basic principles such as one generated by this chapter needs to be constantly updated with market developments.

3.1 What Are Derivatives?

Most people are probably aware of stock options used to reward corporate employees, especially top managers. This is a common example of a derivative. In this section, we define derivatives, describe examples of them, and explain why MNCs use them.

Derivatives

Derivatives are financial contracts whose cash flows and value derive from some underlying financial asset or commodity or index.

- **Definition.** **Derivatives** are financial contracts whose cash flows and value derive from some underlying financial asset or commodity or indicator. For example, consider the stock options provided to managers. The value of these options depends on the underlying asset: the firm's stock. Thus, if Intel Corporation provides stock options to its managers, the cash flows or value obtained by the managers directly relates to Intel's share price.

- **Underlying asset.** All derivatives are linked to an underlying asset. While other financial contracts such as a stock or a bond are also linked to an underlying asset—shares of Google are indeed linked to Google's assets—derivatives are more directly tied to specific underlying assets. Cash flows to parties in a derivatives contract are often specified precisely using values of the underlying asset: Mathematical formulas link underlying assets to derivative-related cash flows.

  Underlying assets come in many flavors and include:

  - Financial instruments such as corporate stocks and bonds.
  - Financial assets such as mortgages, loans, and credit card debt.
  - Currencies and Eurocurrencies.
  - Interest rates such as London Interbank Offered Rate (LIBOR).
  - Financial and economic indexes such as the S&P 500 Index and the Consumer Price Index.
  - Indicators of any force that influences business outcomes (e.g., weather).

- **Counterparties.** The term *counterparties* refers to two parties in a derivatives transaction. Typically, these counterparties are known as *long* (buyer) and *short* (seller). Counterparties in a derivatives transaction desire the flexibility of changing their exposures or positions. This led to the creation of many derivatives in a negotiable or tradable form. Derivatives that allow subsequent trading are not just financial contracts; they are also financial instruments. These instruments allow counterparties to trade in and out of positions.

- **Innovation.** If a variable or indicator affecting business outcomes can be identified or measured, a derivative contract likely has been structured around it. Because currencies affect MNCs and other entities, currency derivatives were created. But other more esoteric examples indicate the innovative power of markets. For instance, weather conditions such as temperature and rainfall affect many businesses including retailers, cruise operators, and food processors. This led to the creation of weather derivatives. Creativity also shows in the variety of instruments created around an underlying asset. We explain this next.

Instruments: Basic Building Blocks

Variation in contracting technology or design produces diversity in instruments. Although the market presents an infinite variety of derivatives, key forms are forwards and options. The following list provides a brief general definition of forwards and options; in subsequent sections, we provide more detailed explanations and numerical examples of how these instruments are structured using currencies and Eurocurrencies.

- In a **forward** contract, the long agrees to buy an underlying asset from the short at a future date for a predetermined price known as the *forward price*. Forwards represent preplanned future purchases or sales with locked-in prices. MNCs use forwards to purchase currencies at a future date in order to settle payables and other claims.

options versus forwards
From an MNC's perspective, a long position in a currency call **option** differs from a long position in a currency **forward** because with the option the MNC can simply walk away when the currency is trading in the market for a low value.

- Options come in two forms: calls and puts. With a **call option**, the long has the right but not the obligation to *buy* an underlying asset from the short at a future date for a predetermined price called the *strike price*. In return for this special and flexible right, the long pays the short a premium. Call options are similar to forwards because they represent preplanned future purchases but differ because they provide the long the flexibility to opt out of the purchase. **Put options**, the second category, allow the long the right to *sell* the underlying asset at a predetermined price. MNCs use options for future currency purchase or sales when they also want to retain the flexibility to nullify the contract.

Most derivatives are variants of forwards and options. MNCs use two important variants, futures and swaps. **Futures** are exchange-traded versions of forwards. Swaps represent a series of forwards and are explained in a later chapter.[2]

Risk Management and Demand for Derivatives

Firms face a variety of risk factors. MNCs and other firms routinely face currency risk. We explain this topic in Chapters 6 and 7. In addition to currency risk, firms face interest rate risk and commodity price risk, for example. Rises in interest rates that make it more expensive for consumers to finance their purchases would adversely affect a firm producing durable goods such as appliances. A rise in the price of materials such as grains, beef, and orange juice may affect a restaurant chain. A rise in labor and fuel costs adversely affects a food producer. In each of these cases, derivatives may be employed to *hedge* or mitigate such risks. The fact that risks arise from many sources gives impetus to the development of many kinds of derivatives. Currency derivatives—an important category of derivatives—is hardly the most prevalent: Interest rate derivatives take that honor.

EXAMPLE 3.1

Consider a U.S.-based MNC manufacturing an electronic product in Taiwan. Assume that some of the input components used in this product are sourced from Japan. The MNC would be concerned about the potential appreciation of both the Japanese yen (JPY) and the Taiwanese dollar (TWD). One solution is to lock in the future "purchase" values of JPY and TWD using currency derivatives such as currency forwards or currency options. The MNC would evaluate positions such as (1) long JPY forwards and long TWD forwards and (2) long JPY call options and long TWD call options.

MNCs are not the only entities using derivatives for risk management. Individuals and a host of financial institutions such as banks, pension funds, and insurance companies use derivatives. This demand by multiple sources explains why the derivatives market is a multi-trillion-dollar market today. Because risk factors arise in a multitude of ways, hundreds of varieties of derivatives exist today.

The Wide World of Derivatives

See Exhibit 3.1 for the total size of the derivatives market by categories. The values listed pertain to the "notional" or face value of the contracts; for example, in a forward contract to purchase 2 million Mexican pesos (MXN), notional value equals MXN 2 million. These data note many things. First, the derivatives markets exceed USD 500 trillion. Second, interest rate derivatives form the major category, accounting for at least 75 percent of all derivatives. Third, the organized exchanges are like the tip of the iceberg. Most derivatives are traded in over-the-counter (OTC) markets. These markets may be thought of as "wholesale" markets while exchanges may be thought of as "retail" markets. Because large players dominate the derivatives markets, OTC markets dominate.

---

[2] The following is a brief description of two key swaps used by MNCs. For a fuller explanation and examples, see Chapter 10. In a (basic) *interest rate swap*, periodically and for a certain number of years, counterparty A pays interest to counterparty B calculated using a fixed rate and receives from B interest calculated using a variable (reference) rate such as LIBOR. In a (basic) *cross-currency swap*, periodically and for a certain number of years, A pays interest to B in one currency at a fixed rate and receives interest from B in another currency at a fixed rate.

EXHIBIT 3.1
Notional Value of Derivatives in 2007 (USD billions)

Source: Bank for International Settlements, 2007 statistics.

Exchange-Traded Derivatives	
Interest rate futures	26,787
Currency futures	159
Equity futures	1,133
Interest rate options	44,308
Currency options	133
Equity options	8,103
OTC	
Currency contracts	60,091
Interest rate contracts	346,937
Equity contracts	9,202
Commodity contracts	7,567
Credit-default swaps	42,580

One noteworthy item in the list of derivatives in Exhibit 3.1 is the *credit-default swap (CDS)*. The CDS was once widely acclaimed as an example of financial innovation. CDS contracts trigger payments from one party to another when a reference entity defaults on an obligation. One might say that CDSs are special types of insurance contracts offering protection against default. Because of the sheer complexity of CDSs, however, many large and sophisticated financial institutions have underestimated risks. The tsunami of mortgage defaults in the United States during 2007–2008 triggered massive losses in many financial institutions. A prominent example is leading insurer AIG, which was bankrupted and forced to seek government assistance. One lesson that can be gleaned from the AIG debacle is that derivatives, especially esoteric ones, are dangerous—the famous investor Warren Buffett presciently referred to them "financial weapons of mass destruction" in 2003—and have to be used with a surfeit of caution. (See www.berkshirehathaway.com/letters/2002pdf.pdf for the full text of Buffett's warning.)

Buffett on derivatives
The famous investor Warren Buffett refers to *derivatives* as "financial weapons of mass destruction."

3.2 Currency Forwards

A *currency forward* contract allows the exchange of one currency for another at a future date using a predetermined exchange rate also known as the *forward price*. An MNC that wishes to convert euros (EUR) into JPY in three months' time would enter into a three-month forward contract to buy JPY using EUR. Forward markets enable such contracts.

A currency forward contract has three parameters:

- **Underlying asset.** Units of base currency.
- **Maturity.** Delivery date for the currency.
- **Forward price.** Units of the terms or payment currency per unit of the base currency.

See the following section for an example of these parameters.

Cash Flows and Settlement

Forwards involve cash flows only at maturity. At inception, the two parties—long and short—simply agree on the forward price. At maturity, the short delivers the contracted units of the base currency, and in return, the long makes payment using the terms currency. The payment amount is calculated using the contractual or forward price. See the following example for sample calculations.

EXAMPLE 3.2 Hershey Food Company (commonly known as Hershey's) requires EUR 2 million in 90 days to pay for candy-making equipment purchased from a German firm. The three-month forward rate for EURUSD is 1.40. How can Hershey's protect itself against a rise in the EUR?

Solution: Hershey's takes a long position in the 90-day EUR forward contract for EUR 2 million at a forward rate of EURUSD = 1.40. This means that Hershey's will pay USD 2.8 million in 90 days to obtain EUR 2 million. The following table illustrates the unprotected and hedged scenarios.

Time	Unprotected Scenario	Hedged Scenario
Now ($t = 0$)		Hershey's takes a long position in a 90-day EUR forward contract at the rate of EURUSD = 1.40. No payments are needed at $t = 0$.
Maturity ($t = 90$ days)	Hershey's buys EUR 2 million at spot; if the spot rate is high, Hershey's faces a high cost of purchase.	Hershey's settles the forward contract by taking delivery of EUR 2 million and paying USD 2.8 million. Hershey's is unaffected by a rise in the EUR.

Discussion: By entering into the forward contract, Hershey's eliminates uncertainty and knows exactly how much USD is required to make the EUR purchase.

Certain currency forwards do not entail actual delivery of the foreign currency and are known as **nondeliverable forwards (NDF)**. With an NDF, on the maturity date, an indicator or reference currency exchange rate is used to settle the transaction and mimic the actual delivery of the foreign currency. NDFs are especially prevalent in emerging market currencies. When a currency is illiquid or when government restrictions apply, market participants can still get the benefit of forward contracts by using NDFs. The NDF is the precursor to certain futures transactions (discussed later in this chapter) using similar principles of cash settlement as opposed to outright delivery of the foreign currency.

Market Structure

Currency forwards are traded in the Interbank market where they are also known as *outright forwards:* This is to distinguish forwards from foreign exchange swaps, which are special versions of forwards in which a spot transaction is followed by a forward transaction. Forward markets are private and typically involve contracts between two parties known to each other. In the currency forward markets as in the foreign exchange markets, banks are key players. MNCs participate in these markets through banks. Most transactions are large, exceeding USD 10 million. Most features of currency forward markets—trading systems, participants, clearing—are similar to features of foreign currency markets described in Chapter 2.

An interesting feature of the currency forward markets is the use of proprietary online systems such as Barclay Capital's BARX system. It reduces trading costs for MNCs. More important, for a variety of institutions engaged in arbitraging, online systems allow speedier and synchronized trades with the spot market. The BARX screen in Exhibit 3.2 shows this simultaneous capability.

Forward Price

Notation

Because we focus on only one currency at a time in this chapter, to make our equations more user friendly, we refer to the value of the currency as S. This notation is consistent with the literature on derivatives in which the underlying asset (also called the *spot asset*) is referred to using the same notation. Other notation refers to interest rates (r is the domestic interest rate, and r^* is the foreign interest rate) and the maturity of the contract (t).

Forward Pricing Theory

Suppose you want to obtain a unit of a foreign currency at a future date (t). You have two alternatives:

alternative to forward
Buying a foreign currency at a future date by using a *forward* contract is equivalent to using borrowed funds to purchase the foreign currency itself today and depositing it in an interest-bearing account.

- **Alternative A.** Buy the currency using a forward contract: This implies that you pay the forward price (F) at the future date.

EXHIBIT 3.2
BARX Screen

Source: BARX FX reproduced with
the permission of Barclays Bank
PLC. Copyright © 2008 Barclays
Bank PLC.

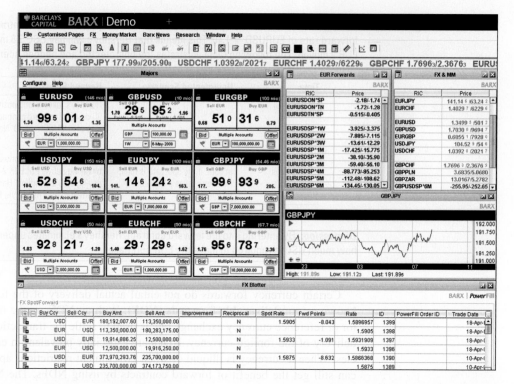

- **Alternative B.** Buy the currency itself today by paying *S*. Because alternative B requires an earlier commitment of capital, you need to reflect the implied financing cost (at the domestic interest rate *r*). But alternative B has an offsetting benefit: Because you do not need the currency until *t*, you can deposit it in a bank and earn interest (at the foreign interest rate r^*).

In equilibrium, A and B should cost the same amount and produce the following pricing equation. Appendix 3A discusses general principles of forward pricing behind the following currency forward pricing equation[3]:

$$F = S \times \left[\frac{1 + r}{1 + r^*} \right]^t$$

If the foreign interest rate is higher (lower) than the domestic interest rate, the forward price is lower (higher) than the spot price of the underlying asset. If the forward price is lower (higher) than the spot price, it is said to contain a **forward discount premium**. The following equation calculates this discount or premium (*FP*):

$$FP = \frac{F}{S} - 1 = \left[\frac{1 + r}{1 + r^*} \right]^t - 1$$

EXAMPLE 3.3

The rupee is quoted as follows: USDINR = 46. The U.S. and Indian interest rates are 5 percent and 10 percent, respectively. Assume annual compounding. What is the two-year forward rate for the rupee? Also calculate the forward premium or discount.

Solution: Before applying the forward pricing formula, calculate *S* (convert to direct quote):

$$S = \frac{1}{46} = 0.02174$$

---

[3] See Chapter 5 for a deeper understanding of the currency forward pricing equation.

Applying the forward pricing formula, we obtain the two-year forward rate as follows:

$$F = 0.02174 \times \left[\frac{1 + 5\%}{1 + 10\%} \right]^2 = 0.01981.$$

The calculated forward price (direct quote) of the rupee is USD 0.01981. The equivalent indirect forward price is INR 50.49.

The forward premium (discount) is calculated as:

$$FP = \frac{F}{S} - 1 = \frac{0.01981}{0.02174} - 1 = -8.88\%$$

Discussion: Because the foreign interest rate is higher than the U.S. interest rate, the forward value of the INR is lower. The INR thus trades at a discount in the forward market.

Counterparty Risk in Forward Contracts

Forward contracts are private contracts between two parties who are known to each other. One problem with these contracts is the presence of **counterparty risk** also known as *default risk*. This risk arises from nonperformance by one of the two parties. During the credit crisis of 2007–2008, numerous defaults occurred in forwards and other derivatives contracts. Even venerable institutions (e.g., Lehman Brothers) defaulted on their commitments. MNCs should be aware of this potential for loss (see the following example).

EXAMPLE 3.4

A U.S.-based MNC with operations in India contracts with an Indian counterparty to convert INR 5 million into USD in a year at the forward rate of USDINR = 50.49. Suppose the rupee weakens to USDINR = 52. Assuming that the Indian counterparty defaults, calculate the MNC's losses.

Solution: The USD cash flows in the two scenarios are calculated as follows:

$$USD \text{ (no default)} = \frac{5,000,000}{50.49} = USD\ 99,030$$

$$USD \text{ (default)} = \frac{5,000,000}{52} = USD\ 96,154$$

The MNC incurs a loss of USD 2,876 in the default scenario.

Discussion: Had the rupee strengthened, the MNC would not have been adversely affected by default.

MNCs conduct due diligence on their counterparties prior to engaging in forward contracts. But they can never be sure that all risk is eliminated. Why then would they conduct forward transactions? Forwards have some compelling advantages. Consider the fact that forwards can be customized in terms of currency, size, and maturity. This customization allows MNCs to obtain more accurate results in their currency hedging.

3.3 Currency Futures

We have seen that forward contracts have an inherent drawback: counterparty risk. This restricts forward market participants to large institutions and MNCs with good credit standing. Other parties desiring to contract future purchases of currencies are potentially left unsatisfied. Futures markets satisfy this need.

futures
Futures contracts are available in a wide variety of underlying assets including grains such as corn, metals such as silver and currencies such as Swiss francs (CHF).

A futures contract is an exchange-traded version of the forward contract. Like the forward contract, the futures contract enables participants to buy or sell an underlying asset at a future date. Because they are traded in exchanges, futures are standardized. For instance, the pound (GBP) futures traded on the **Chicago Mercantile Exchange (CME)** have very specific maturities (every three months) and size (62,500 currency units). The relatively small size of futures

EXHIBIT 3.3
Important Futures Contracts

Contract	Exchange	Size
Corn	CBOT	5,000 bu
Soybean oil	CBOT	60,000 lbs
Hogs—lean	CME	40,000 lbs
Sugar—world	ICE*	112,000 lbs
Crude oil—light sweet	NYMEX†	1,000 bbl
Natural gas	NYMEX	10,000 mmBtu
Treasury bonds	CBOT	USD 100,000
Eurodollar	CME	USD 1,000,000
Euro—Yen	CME	USD 100,000,000
Short sterling	LIFFE‡	GBP 500,000
Three-month Euribor	LIFFE	EUR 1,000,000
Japanese yen	CME	JPY 12,500,000
Canadian dollar	CME	CAD 100,000
British pound	CME	GBP 62,500
Swiss franc	CME	CHF 125,000
Mexican peso	CME	MXN 500,000
Euro FX	CME	EUR 125,000
S&P 500 Index	CME	$250 times S&P 500 Stock Price Index

*Intercontinental Exchange
†New York Mercantile Exchange
‡London International Financial Futures and Options Exchange

compared to forwards allows a wider range of players—including individual investors—to arrange for future purchases and sales of currencies. Exchange trading also offers another advantage: anonymity.

It is useful to look at the evolution of futures as another instance of financial innovation. We can trace the origin of futures to the formation of the Chicago Board of Trade (CBOT) in 1840. Trading commenced in agricultural commodities such as wheat and corn. The first contracts were technically forward contracts. Over time, however, these contracts were standardized to become futures contracts, and other commodities—oil, animal products, and metals—were added to the list of contracts. Another important exchange, the CME, was established in 1898. The second revolution in futures trading occurred in the 1970s with the introduction of financial futures, which are futures contracts on debt instruments (interest rate sensitive), equity indexes, and currencies. See Exhibit 3.3 for a representative list of key futures traded around the world.

Market Structure

Following the Smithsonian agreement of 1971 (see Chapter 4), major Western currencies were allowed to float and values were allowed to respond to market forces. This created a great demand for currency derivatives for risk management as well as speculation purposes. In response to this demand, the CME in 1972 created a subsidiary, the International Monetary Market (IMM), to trade in currency futures. They were among the first of a class of derivatives known as *financial futures* that now dominate futures trading. Today, although futures are traded in other exchanges such as the London International Financial Futures and Options Exchange (LIFFE), CME is the market leader in currency futures. Exchanges such as the CME provide not only the infrastructure for trading but also vital clearing functions such as clearing trades, settling accounting, and keeping track of collateral posted by counterparties.[4]

Chicago Mercantile Exchange

The CME lists more than 20 futures contracts in various currencies, cross-currencies, and currency indexes. This list includes the major currencies—JPY, GBP, EUR, and CHF—as

---

[4] Clearing fees are an important component of an exchange's revenues. CME, for instance, charges about USD 1 in fees for each currency futures contract traded. This may appear to be a small amount, but successful exchanges such as CME trade millions of contracts each year.

EXHIBIT 3.4
Selected CME Currency Futures

Source: *www.cme.com* (accessed April 19, 2008).

Currency	Country	Size	Maturities	Initial Margin (maintenance)
AUD	Australia	100,000	6 in qtr cycle	USD 2,430 (1,800)
BRL	Brazil	100,000	12 consec. months	USD 2,800 (2,000)
GBP	United Kingdom	62,500	6 in qtr cycle	USD 2,430 (1,800)
CAD	Canada	100,000	6 in qtr cycle	USD 2,565 (1,900)
CME$Index	United States	Index times 1000	6 in qtr cycle	USD 1,958 (1,450)
CNY	China	1,000,000	13 consec. months +	USD 1,350 (1,000)
CZK	Czech Republic	4,000,000	6 in qtr cycle	USD 4,995 (3,700)
ILS	Israel	1,000,000	6 in qtr cycle	USD 6,750 (5,000)
JPY	Japan	12,500,000	6 in qtr cycle	USD 3,780 (2,800)
RUB	Russia	2,500,000	4 in qtr cycle	USD 3,000 (2,000)
CHF	Switzerland	125,000	6 in qtr cycle	USD 2,970 (2,200)
EUR	Eurozone	125,000	6 in qtr cycle	USD 3,510 (2,600)
Cross EUR/CAD	Eurozone/Canada	125,000	6 in qtr cycle	CAD 4,860 (3,600)

Contract maturities vary. Typical maturities for a currency include the next six months in the quarterly cycle of Mar/Jun/Sep/Dec. Also, margins are revised according to market conditions.

well as emerging markets currencies such as the Chinese renminbi (or yuan), South African rand, and the Russian ruble (CNY, ZAR, and RUB, respectively). Trading may occur on the trading floor of the exchange in Chicago as well as electronically in the **Globex** system. In some currencies, electronic trading is conducted virtually around the clock: With CNY futures, trading is solely on the Globex around the clock from Sunday afternoon to Friday afternoon. Settlement procedures vary: GBP futures require actual delivery of pounds while CNY contracts use cash settlement.[5] CME futures are typically settled on the third Wednesday of the stated month. The characteristics of key CME currency futures contracts are provided in Exhibit 3.4.

Globex
Mirroring 24-hour trading in currencies, many currency futures are traded around-the-clock in electronic platforms such as *Globex*.

Daily Settlement

Margin Account

Recall that in a forward contract, both parties are subject to default risk. Although default risk can be mitigated by using credit information, the only way to totally avoid it is to require collateral. Especially because futures are traded anonymously, without collateral, or third party guarantees, trading would not occur. Consequently, both the long and the short in a futures transaction are required to set up **margin accounts** (also called *performance bonds*) that serve as collateral. In practice, market participants set up margin accounts at their brokerages. Indeed, margin accounts are not unique to trading in futures contracts. Other investment positions such as short positions in equity also require margin accounts. In general, margin accounts are cash accounts held at the brokerage to protect concerned parties against default. We explain next how margin accounts are used in practice.

margin
Because futures contracts are settled daily, participants need put forth only a modest amount as collateral in *margin* accounts.

Daily Settlement

For margin accounts to be effective as collateral, balances must be more than sufficient to cover any changes in contract value. One problem is that over the life of the contract, value may change by large amounts. For example, consider an investor taking a long position in the CME euro futures contract with a size of EUR 125,000 trading at a futures price of USD 1.45. At maturity, if the ending value of EUR is USD 1.35, the investor loses USD 0.10 per currency unit, which translates to a total loss of USD 12,500. The margin account therefore must have a balance of at least USD 12,500 to cover against this investor's default. Such large balances

---

[5] Cash settlement is a popular method of settling futures. If an MNC takes a long position in a CNY contract, on settlement day, the currency rate published by the People's Bank of China is used to calculate USD equivalent. Cash settlement makes futures contracts such as this one equivalent to nondeliverable forwards (NDF).

in margin accounts would deter futures trading, however. To facilitate trading using smaller accounts, futures exchanges require accounts to be settled every day in a process called *daily settlement*. This is so because price changes in any given day would be significantly less than price changes over contract life. A smaller margin balance would be sufficient to cover risks. The CME euro futures contract that calls for a settlement amount of EUR 125,000 requires only a margin of about USD 3,500, illustrating this important concept.

Initial Margin

The initial deposit is known as the *initial margin*. At the end of each trading day, the change in futures price (current day's close minus previous day's close) is used to calculate the change in value of the futures contract. If the contract value increases, funds are transferred from the short's account to the long's account. If instead the contract value decreases, funds are transferred from the long to the short. The clearing house of the exchange facilitates these transfers, which have the de facto effect of repricing the futures contract. This insight explains an alternate term used to denote daily settlement: *mark to market*.

Maintenance Margin and Margin Call

If margin accounts are allowed to become dangerously low, they may fail to offer adequate protection to counterparties. Thus, a minimum account balance is stipulated. This minimum balance known as the *maintenance margin* is lower than the initial margin. For example, the CME euro futures has a maintenance margin roughly USD 1,000 lower than the initial margin. Should a certain party's account fall below the minimum margin, it triggers a *margin call* that is a request to provide additional funds to replenish the margin account. If a margin call is ignored, perhaps because the party is no longer solvent, the remaining funds in the margin account are used to close out the futures position.

Cash Flows and Settlement

It is important to stress that futures are essentially the same as forwards. Therefore, cash flows in futures contracts are quite similar to cash flows in forward contracts. The main difference, from a cash flow perspective, is that forwards are settled only once at maturity, but futures are settled everyday. However, the sum total of daily settlements in futures must equal the final settlement in an equivalent forward contract.

EXAMPLE 3.5

An MNC enters into a futures contract to buy Canadian dollars (CAD) at a price of USD 0.90. Assume initial and maintenance margins of USD 0.06 and USD 0.03, respectively. Four days of trading are left before contract maturity. Calculate cash flows per unit of the foreign currency.

Solution: See Exhibit 3.5.

EXHIBIT 3.5 Daily Settlement and Delivery in a Futures Contract on CAD

		Long (buyer)			Short (seller)			
Day	Price	Δ	Balance	CF	Δ	Balance	CF	Remarks
0	0.90		0.06	−0.06		0.06	−0.06	Initial margin
1	0.92	+0.02	0.08		−0.02	0.04		
2	0.94	+0.02	0.10		−0.02	0.02*		Margin call
						0.06	−0.04	Call met
3	0.91	−0.03	0.07		+0.03	0.09		
4	0.89	−0.02	0.05	+0.05	+0.02	0.11	+0.11	Close without delivery
				−0.89			+0.89	Delivery
				−0.90			**+0.90**	Total

*Balance is lower than USD 0.03 and triggers a margin call.

Discussion:

A transfer between the long and short occurs at the end of each day. For example on day 1, because the futures price increases from USD 0.90 to USD 0.92, the short pays the long USD 0.02.

A balance lower than USD 0.03 triggers a margin call. For instance, on day 2, the settlement of USD 0.02 drops the short's balance to USD 0.02. Thus, the short is required to add USD 0.04 to the account to bring it back to the initial balance.

Settlement takes place not at the original futures price of USD 0.90 but at the most recently "marked" price of USD 0.89.

The sum of cash flows for the long is + USD 0.90. The sum of cash flows for the short is the negative of this amount.

Futures Prices

Currency futures prices are widely disseminated. Because CME currency futures are fairly liquid, one can use prices from the CME as reference prices. It publishes daily bulletins summarizing market activity and prices (See Exhibit 3.6 for an April 17, 2008, example).

Important metrics (with values for the June 2008 GBP contract) are:

Settlement price (1.9837).

Volume in trading floor and Globex (866, 128,139).

Open interest or number of contracts outstanding (108,883).

Interbank spot rate (1.9910).

How does one benchmark the futures settlement price? We can apply futures pricing formulas. Recall that futures contracts are essentially the same as forward contracts. This means that the currency forward pricing formula introduced earlier in this section also serves as the futures pricing formula. Key inputs are the spot currency rate, interest rates (usually LIBOR), and the contract maturity expressed as a number of days. See the following example.

EXAMPLE 3.6

Today is April 17. An MNC wishes to buy GBP in June. The CME June futures contract quoted at 1.9837 is a possible vehicle for the purchase. The contract is expected to settle on June 20. Make the following additional assumptions: (1) the number of days to maturity is 64; (2) applicable LIBOR rates for the USD and GBP are 2.92 percent and 5.04 percent, respectively; the quotes use the actual/360 convention; (3) spot GBPUSD = 1.9910. What is the theoretical futures price? Redo the problem assuming that the given interest rates are annual compounding rates.

Solution: To solve the problem, we need to modify the pricing formula to accommodate LIBOR conventions, insert given values of spot currency and interest rates, and calculate futures price F as follows:

$$F = S \times \frac{1 + r \times t}{1 + r^* \times t}$$

$$= 1.9910 \times \frac{1 + 2.92\% \times \frac{64}{360}}{1 + 5.04\% \times \frac{64}{360}}$$

$$= 1.9836$$

Using the annual compounding convention:

$$F = S \times \left[\frac{1 + r}{1 + r^*}\right]^t$$

$$= 1.9910 \times \left[\frac{1 + 2.92\%}{1 + 5.04\%}\right]^{64/365}$$

$$= 1.9839$$

Discussion: It is important to understand interest rate conventions. In money markets, most rate quotes use LIBOR conventions.

EXHIBIT 3.6 CME Daily Bulletin Futures Prices, April 17, 2008

CURRENCY FUTURES

2008 DAILY INFORMATION BULLETIN - http://www.cmegroup.com/tools-information/build-a-report.html?
report=dailybulletin CME Group Inc. A CME/Board of Trade Company. 20 South Wacker Drive, Chicago,
Illinois 60606-7499. Statistics: (312) 930-8280 Fax: (312) 930-8203 E-Mail: marketdataops@cmegroup.com

FINAL

CURRENCY FUTURES

Thu, Apr 17, 2008 PG07

PG07 BULLETIN # 74@

FOR PRODUCTS THAT ARE TRADED IN BOTH REGULAR TRADING HOURS (RTH) AND ELECTRONIC TRADING HOURS (ETH) THE INFORMATION REPRESENTED ON THIS PAGE FOR OPENING RANGE, HIGH, LOW, CLOSING RANGE, SETTLEMENT PRICE AND VOLUME REPRESENTS RTH ACTIVITY ONLY. NOTE: LIFE OF CONTRACT HIGH AND LOW REPRESENTS BOTH RTH AND ETH. RTH VOLUME REFLECTS PIT TRADING, BLOCK TRADES AND CASH-FOR-FUTURES ONLY. ETH REPRESENTS GLOBEX VOLUME TRANSACTIONS FROM THE GLOBEX® ELECTRONIC SESSION ONLY. VOLUME OR OPEN INTEREST (BOTH BEFORE AND AFTER THE LAST DAY OF TRADING) MAY BE AFFECTED BY: CASH FOR FUTURES, SPREADS, AND PRIOR DAYS' CLEARED TRADES (OUT-TRADES), POSITION ADJUSTMENTS, OPTION EXERCISES, POSITIONS IN DELIVERY, OR POSITIONS IN A CASH SETTLEMENT CYCLE. PRODUCT LISTINGS REPRESENT CONTRACTS WITH PRICE/VOLUME ACTIVITY AND/OR HAVE ESTABLISHED OPEN INTEREST. PRODUCTS THAT ARE ELIGIBLE TO TRADE, BUT ARE INACTIVE, DO NOT APPEAR IN THIS REPORT. LEGEND: B=BID, A=ASK, N=NOMINAL, P=POST SETTLEMENT SESSION, *=NEW CONTRACT HIGH PRICE, #=NEW CONTRACT LOW PRICE, R=RECORD VOLUME OR OPEN INTEREST. SETTLEMENT PRICES ARE DETERMINED BY CME RULE 813.

Contract	OPEN RANGE	HIGH	LOW	CLOSING RANGE	SETT. PRICE	RECIPROCAL	CHGE	RTH VOL	GLOBEX VOL	OPEN INTEREST	OI CHG	CONTRACT HIGH	CONTRACT LOW
BRIT PND FUT													
JUN08	1.9718	1.9850B	1.9710A	1.9840A@1.9838	1.9837	(.5041)	+214	866	128139	108883	- 2608	2.0977B	1.9153A
SEP08	----	----	----	1.9494N	1.9714	(.5073)	+220	200	18	1314	+ 199	2.0906B	1.9106A
DEC08	----	----	----	1.9354N	1.9583	(.5106)	+229	----	6	150	+ 6	2.0831B	1.9002A
MAR09	----	----	----	1.9243N	1.9476	(.5135)	+233	----	----	48	UNCH	2.0405B	1.8915A
JUN09	----	----	----	1.9149N	1.9382	(.5159)	+233	----	----	132	-	1.9676B	1.8840A
TOTAL BRIT PND FUT								1066	128163	110527	- 2403		
BP INTERBANK SPOT:		1.9923	1.9693		1.9910		+190						
CANADA DLR FUT													
JUN08	0.9950	.9950	.9855A	.9875A	.9870	(1.0132)	-107	4927	57380	95459	+ 10	1.1022B	.8542A
SEP08	----	----	----	.9963N	.9860	(1.0142)	-103	----	175	6554	+ 20	1.1008B	.8918A
DEC08	----	----	----	.9949N	.9848	(1.0154)	-101	----	97	2641	+ 8	1.0999B	.9282A
MAR09	----	----	----	.9934N	.9837	(1.0166)	-97	----	3	506	+ 1	1.0927	.9601A
JUN09	----	----	----	.9916N	.9825	(1.0178)	-91	----	1	1017	+ 61	1.0173B	.9581A
SEP09	----	----	----	.9898N	.9813	(1.0191)	-85	----	1	61	UNCH	.9880	.9683A
TOTAL CANADA DLR FUT								4927	57657	106238	+ 4		
CD INTERBANK SPOT:	1.0010		.9860		.9902	(1.0098)	-95						
EMINI EURFX FUT													
JUN08	1.59010	#1.59440	1.58060	----	1.58490	(.6310)	-64	3874	3874	2483	-	1.59440	1.43180
SEP08	1.58310	#1.58570B	1.57490A	----	1.57800	(.6337)	-57	2	2	16	UNCH	1.58570B	1.52130A
TOTAL EMINI EURFX								3876	3876	2499	- 181		
EURO FX FUT													
JUN08	1.58440	1.59030	1.58350	1.58470@1.58490	1.58490	(.6310)	-64	545	219984	173287	- 5824	1.59460	1.30920
SEP08	----	1.58150B	1.57850A	1.57900A	1.57900	(.6337)	-57	200	644	2953	+ 282	1.58700B	1.34470A
DEC08	----	----	----	1.57650N	1.57650	(.6364)	-51	201	1	788	+ 198	1.57850	1.34740A
MAR09	----	----	----	1.57200N	1.57140	(.6387)	-47	1	----	111	+ 3	1.57200B	1.41190A
JUN09	----	----	----	1.56550N	1.56120	(.6405)	-43	----	----	35	UNCH	1.56630B	1.42570A
TOTAL EURO FX FUT								947	220629	177174	- 5347		
EURO/FX INTERBANK SPOT:		1.5983	1.5848		1.5896		-56						
EMINI J YEN FUT													
JUN08	0.009840	.009865B	.009771A	----	.009792	(102.1242)	-74	109	109	183	+ 4	.010470B	.009231A
SEP08	----	----	.009825A	----	.009838	(101.6467)	-70	----	----	1	UNCH	.010205B	.009812A
TOTAL EMINI J YEN FUT								109	109	184	+ 4		
JAPAN YEN FUT													
JUN08	0.009797@0.009795	.009860B	.009775A	0.009791@0.009794B	.009792	(102.12)	-74	3816	124905	172194	- 431	.010493	.008415A
SEP08	----	----	----	0.009908N	.009838	(101.65)	-70	----	5	3035	UNCH	.010508B	.008505A
DEC08	----	----	----	0.009952N	.009886	(101.15)	-66	----	----	546	- 1	.010465	.008617A
MAR09	----	----	----	0.009996N	.009935	(100.65)	-61	----	----	33	UNCH	.010385	.008961A
JUN09	----	----	----	0.010044N	.009986	(100.14)	-58	----	----	20	UNCH	.010274B	.009461A
TOTAL JAPAN YEN FUT								3816	124910	175828	- 432		
JY INTERBANK SPOT:		.009832	.009736		.009747	(102.59)	-71						

MEX PESO FUT

Month				Settle	(Inverse)				Vol	OI / Chg			Month High	Month Low
MAY08	0.09475	.09475	0.09522N	.09507	(10.52)	---	---	---	15	13898	---	3	.09395	.09040
JUN08	0.09475	#.09365	.09472	.09475	(10.55)	---	13899	136193 +	100	13898	2456	---	.09505	.08750A
SEP08	---	.09365	.09365	.09367	(10.68)	---	---	1191 -	1	---	1191	1	.09420	.08675
DEC08	---	---	.09262	(10.80)		---	---	400	1	---	UNCH	---	.09183	.08660
MAR09	---	.09130A	.09180N	.09165	(10.91)	---	---	89	15	---	UNCH	---	.09110B	.08780
JUN09	---	---	.09092N	.09077	(11.02)	---	---	---	15	---	2455	2	.08850	.08710
TOTAL MEX PESO FUT			.09547			101	13899	137878 +			2455			
TOTAL MEX PESO FUT			.09547			101	13899	137878 +			2455			

MP INTERBANK SPOT: 0.09562   .09531   .09547   (10.4744)

SWISS FRNC FUT

Month				Settle	(Inverse)				Vol	OI / Chg			Month High	Month Low
JUN08	0.9939	.9999B	0.9960	.9944	(1.0056)	---	72104	67508 +	1267	72104	5840	---	1.0400	1.0400
SEP08	---	.9933A	1.0005N	.9943	(1.0057)	---	7	1328 +	66	---	---	7	1.0349B	.8274A
DEC08	---	.9946A	.9996N	.9941	(1.0059)	---	9	60 +	62	---	3	9	1.0159B	.8442A
MAR09	---	---	.9991N	.9940	(1.0060)	---	4		55	---	UNCH	4	1.0111B	.8646A
TOTAL SWISS FRNC FUT			.9929			1267	72120	68900 +			5845			
TOTAL SWISS FRNC FUT			.9929			1267	72120	68900 +			5845			

SF INTERBANK SPOT: 1.0040   0.9908   .9908   (1.0071)

CASH-FOR-FUTURES (EFP'S), ALL OR NONE, DELIVERIES/EXERCISES, BLOCK TRADING

	DELIVERY		OPTION		BLOCK TRADING — FUTURES		OPTIONS		CASH-FOR-FUTURES (EFP'S)					AON'S	
	CASH SETTLED	MONTH-TO-DATE	EXER-CISES	MONTH-TO-DATE	TOTAL	MONTH-TO-DATE	TOTAL	MONTH-TO-DATE	APR08	MAY08	JUN08	TOTAL	MONTH-TO-DATE	TOTAL	MONTH-TO-DATE
AD	---	---	---	142	---	---	---	---	---	---	1648	1648	17374	---	146
BP	---	---	---	3817	---	---	---	---	---	---	616	616	35063	---	---
BR	---	---	---	75	---	---	---	---	---	---	---	---	1753	---	---
CD	---	---	---	3870	---	---	---	---	---	---	4923	4923	25379	---	---
E7	---	---	---	---	---	---	---	---	---	---	---	---	6	---	---
EC	---	---	---	15496	---	---	---	---	---	---	421	421	19996	---	---
JY	---	---	---	5246	---	---	---	---	---	---	3803	3803	32947	---	---
MP	---	---	---	---	---	---	---	---	---	---	30	30	21238	---	---
NE	---	---	---	---	---	---	---	---	---	---	264	264	7105	---	---
UN	---	---	---	---	---	---	---	---	---	---	---	---	15	---	---
RU	---	---	---	---	---	---	---	---	---	---	6	6	1284	---	---
RA	---	---	---	2514	---	---	---	---	---	---	78	78	1205	---	---
SF	---	---	---	---	---	---	---	---	---	---	1219	1219	20507	---	---
AC	---	---	---	---	---	---	---	---	---	---	---	---	2	---	---
AJ	---	---	---	---	---	---	---	---	---	---	---	---	3	---	---
RP	---	---	---	---	---	---	---	---	---	---	---	---	31	---	200
CN	---	---	---	---	---	---	---	---	---	---	53	53	233	---	---
RY	---	---	---	---	---	---	---	---	---	---	1	1	---	---	---
RF	---	---	---	---	---	---	---	---	---	---	50	50	249	---	---
PZ	---	---	---	---	---	---	---	---	---	---	---	---	511	---	---
Z	---	---	---	---	---	---	---	---	---	---	25	25	51	---	---
ILS	---	---	---	---	---	---	---	---	---	---	---	---	88	---	---
RMB	---	---	---	---	---	---	---	---	---	---	---	---	---	---	---
BPEU	---	---	---	1938	---	---	---	---	---	---	---	---	---	---	---
CDEU	---	---	---	2020	---	---	---	---	---	---	---	---	---	---	---
JYEU	---	---	---	901	---	---	---	---	---	---	---	---	---	---	---
SFEU	---	---	---	2800	---	---	---	---	---	---	---	---	---	---	---
ECEU	---	---	---	2967	---	---	---	---	---	---	---	---	---	---	---
TOTAL:	0		0		0		0		0	0	13136	13136	185041		

INCLUDES ALL OPTIONS

COMMODITY ABBREVIATION TABLE

AD = AUSTRALIAN DOLLAR	BP = BRITISH POUND	BR = BRAZIL REAL	CD = CANADIAN DOLLAR	E7 = E-MINI EURO FX
EC = EURO FX	JY = JAPANESE YEN	MP = MEXICAN PESO	NE = NEW ZEALND DOLLAR	UN = NKR/USD CROSS RATE
RU = RUSSIAN RUBLE	RA = S.AFRICAN RAND	SF = SWISS FRANC	AC = AD/CD CROSS RATES	AJ = AD/JY CROSS RATES
RP = EFX/BP CROSS RATES	CN = EC/NOK CROSS RATES	RY = EFX/JY CROSS RATES	RF = EFX/SF CROSS RATES	PZ = POLISH ZLOTY (US)
Z = POLISH ZLOTY (EC)	ILS = SHEKEL	RMB = RMB USD	BPEU = BRITISH POUND (EU)	CDEU = CANADIAN DOLLAR (EU)
JYEU = JAPANESE YEN (EU)	SFEU = SWISS FRANC (EU)	ECEU = EURO FX (EU)		

Currency markets are among the few markets to offer simultaneous forward and futures trading. Forwards are traded in the Interbank market; futures are traded in the CME and other exchanges. A divergence between futures and forwards prices offers opportunities to buy in the cheap market and sell in the expensive market. Because of electronic trading systems such as BARX and Globex and resulting capabilities for computerized program trading, institutions are able to exploit such price discrepancies. In equilibrium, however, futures prices equal forward prices.

3.4 Currency Options

A *currency option* is defined as an instrument that provides the long with the right but not the obligation to purchase (or sell) the underlying or base currency at a future date at a prespecified strike price denominated in the terms currency. In European-style options, exercise can take place only at maturity. In American-style options, exercise can also take place prior to maturity.

Options are broadly divided in two categories, those that allow the holder to buy the underlying asset and those that allow the holder to sell the underlying asset. These two categories of options are called *call options* and *put options,* respectively. We mostly discuss call options because they are easier to explain but later extend concepts to put options.

Options share more similarities than dissimilarities with forwards and futures. A key similarity is that options allow an entity to arrange for the future purchase or sale of an underlying asset. A key dissimilarity is that options allow the holder to opt out of the future purchase or sale if the situation so demands. This distinction—the ability for the holder to exercise the option or not—makes options a flexible and useful tool.

Options Parameters and Terminology

Options are more complex than futures and have their own terminology. We discuss key terms concerning options next.

Financial versus Real Options

Many assets and situations exhibit features of options. Earlier we discussed that the main feature of an option is its flexibility; it affords the holder the flexibility of taking one of two actions as appropriate. **Financial options** are financial instruments that offer flexibility in the future purchase or sale of underlying assets such as currencies while **real options** are business situations that provide flexibility and, hence, the ability for firms to increase cash flows. We discuss real options in Chapter 9. The focus in the current chapter is financial options, especially currency options. Financial options, as is the case with forwards and futures, come in many different flavors including on debt instruments, equity indexes, commodities, and currencies.

Underlying Asset

An underlying asset is the commodity, instrument, index, or currency that is bought or sold using the option. For example, in a call option on the stock of Microsoft, the underlying asset is shares of Microsoft; in a put option on the JPY, the JPY is the underlying asset.

Strike Price

option parameters
The key parameters defining a currency option are *maturity* and *strike price.*

The strike price (also called the *exercise price)* of the option is the contractual price at which the underlying asset is bought or sold. This price is one of the key parameters defining the option contact and is predetermined. For example, if a person buys a call option designated as a "25 Microsoft" call, the strike price of the option is USD 25; this enables the person to use the option to purchase shares of Microsoft at the fixed price of USD 25.

Maturity

Another important option parameter is the maturity of the option. Options, unlike equities, have finite lives, with the vast majority expiring within six months. One interesting consequence of the finite maturity of options is the fact that an option's value diminishes with each passing day; this leads many market participants to refer to options as *wasting assets.*

European versus American Options

Option exercise involves the purchase or sale of the underlying asset at the specified strike price. Options that allow exercise at any point in time prior to maturity are known as *American options.* In contrast, *European options* permit exercise only on the maturity date.

Option Premium

Because the option holder is able to choose whether or not to exercise the option, the holder cannot lose money from option exercise. In contrast, the counterparty—the seller of the option—loses whenever exercise occurs. As compensation, the option holder pays a premium to the option seller at contract inception.

Market Structure

The Philadelphia Stock Exchange (PHLX) pioneered trading in foreign currency options in 1982. Today, it and the CME are the main exchanges for trading currency options. Other exchanges trading currency options include the International Securities Exchange (a subsidiary of Eurex that is partly owned by Deutsche Bourse) and LIFFE (a subsidiary of NYSE/Euronext). Trading volume statistics indicate that exchange-traded currency options are not as popular as currency futures. There are indications, however, that OTC options have much more trading volume.

Philadelphia Stock Exchange

Although a pioneer, the PHLX is fighting for market share in currency options with other exchanges such as the CME. PHLX launched second-generation currency options in 2007. See Exhibit 3.7 for the main parameters for these second-generation options. Catering to retail investors, the PHLX offers the smallest contract sizes: Most currency contracts contain only 10,000 units.

Chicago Mercantile Exchange

Although the CME specializes in futures contracts, it has leveraged its success in currency futures with corresponding currency options contracts. A common template is used for

EXHIBIT 3.7
Currency Options Traded on the Philadelphia Stock Exchange (PHLX)

Source: *www.phlx.com* (accessed November 15, 2008).

	Australia	United Kingdom	Canada	Europe	Japan	Switzerland
Currency	AUD	GBP	CAD	EUR	JPY	CHF
Ticker	XDA	XDB	XDC	XDE	XDN	XDS
Type	European style, expires third Friday of settlement month.					
Quote	Displayed quotes are in cents/unit. Per contract price is determined by multiplying the quoted price by the contract size.					
Strike price	Mostly vary by 0.5 to 2.0 cents. Most liquid contracts have strike prices near the foreign currency's current value.					
Maturity	Quarterly on the March cycle plus two near-term months.					
Settlement	USD settlement, no foreign exchange is used.					
Minimum price change	Premiums quoted in USD cents. Minimum change is 1/100 of a cent, translating to USD 1.					

denominations, maturity, and settlement. Compared to the PHLX, contract sizes are larger. For example, the GBP and EUR options contracts have sizes of 62,500 and 125,000 units, respectively. The CME lists European-style and American-style options. The last trading day is the second Friday of the contract month. Physical delivery of the foreign currency occurs on the third Wednesday. As with currency futures, most trading occurs in the around-the-clock Globex electronic system.

Option Exercise and Cash flows

In this section, we develop examples to demonstrate cash flows in call and put currency option positions. We determine payoffs and profits. *Payoff* equals cash flow at maturity. *Profit* equals payoff net of premium.[6] To facilitate our discussion, we use the following notation:

S_t = Price of underlying asset (currency value) at maturity

X = Option stick or exercise price

C = Call premium

P = Put premium

Call Option

Suppose A purchases from B a currency call option by paying a premium of 0.06 (all values in USD). The option expires in three months, is of European style, and has a strike price of 1.25. The underlying asset is 1 unit of EUR (results can be scaled to other contract sizes easily). At maturity, A exercises the option if $S_t > 1.25$. What if $S_t = 1.34$? For this scenario, the consequences are:

- **Inception.** A pays B 0.06.
- **Maturity.** A pays 1.25 to B on delivery of EUR 1. Because the value of the currency is 1.34, payoff to A is $1.34 - 1.25 = 0.09$. Instead, B delivers currency worth 1.34 and receives only 1.25 in return, so payoff to B is $1.25 - 1.34 = -0.09$.
- **Summary.** A makes a profit of 0.03. B makes a loss of 0.03.

In Exhibit 3.8, we calculate payoff and profit to A under various scenarios to demonstrate the overall pattern: The long gains when currency value rises.

Put Option

Suppose P purchases from Q a currency put option by paying a premium of 0.03 (all values in USD). The option expires in three months, is of European style, and has a strike price of 1.25. The underlying asset is 1 unit of EUR (results can be scaled to other contract sizes easily). At maturity, P exercises the option if $S_t < 1.25$. What if $S_t = 1.16$? For this scenario, the consequences are:

- **Inception.** P pays Q 0.03.
- **Maturity.** P receives 1.25 from Q on delivery of EUR 1. Because the EUR is worth only 1.16, payoff to P is $1.25 - 1.16 = 0.09$. Instead, because Q pays 1.25 and receives currency worth only 1.16, payoff to Q is $1.16 - 1.25 = -0.09$.
- **Summary,** P makes a profit of 0.06. Q has a loss of 0.06.

In Exhibit 3.9, we calculate payoff and profit to P under various scenarios to demonstrate the overall pattern: The long gains when currency value falls.

---

[6] Alternate terms for (payoff, profit) are (gross profit, net profit) and (maturity cash flow, net cash flow). One limitation of the profit equations used in this chapter is that they do not properly account for the time value of money. We need to calculate the future value of the option premium to correct this problem. We take this additional step in Chapter 7 when we discuss MNC applications involving options.

EXHIBIT 3.8
Call Option: Payoff and Profit to Long (buyer)
Call Parameters: $C = 0.06$, $X = 1.25$ *(all values in USD)*

Currency Value at Maturity	At Contract Inception	Cash Flows at Maturity		Overall Result	
	Premium Paid	Exercise Price Paid	Value Received	Payoff	Profit
1.16	0.06	No exercise	No exercise	0	−0.06
1.19	0.06	No exercise	No exercise	0	−0.06
1.22	0.06	No exercise	No exercise	0	−0.06
1.25	0.06	No exercise	No exercise	0	−0.06
1.28	0.06	1.25	1.28	0.03	−0.03
1.31	0.06	1.25	1.31	0.06	0.00
1.34	0.06	1.25	1.34	0.09	0.03
1.37	0.06	1.25	1.37	0.12	0.06

Payoff and profit to short (seller) is the exact opposite (that is, positive values are negative, and negative values are positive).

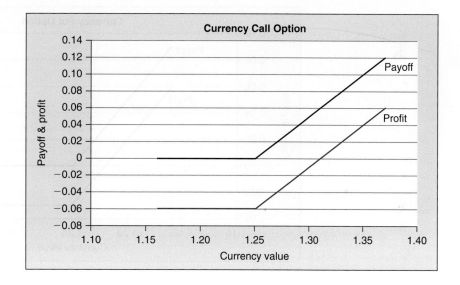

Summary of Option Payoffs and Profits

In this section, we summarize four possible positions in options. We also summarize key elements of these positions as well as payoff and profit equations. In the previous section, sample calculations were made using an understanding of when option exercise occurs.

- In calls, exercise occurs when $S_t > X$.
- In puts, exercise occurs when $S_t < X$.

The logic behind our earlier calculations is succinctly captured in a series of equations displayed in Exhibit 3.10. The key idea in these equations is that a call buyer benefits when $(S_t - X)$ is positive and a put buyer benefits when $(X - S_t)$ is positive. The Max(.) operator indicates that the option is not exercised when these values are negative. These equations are helpful in performing calculations efficiently and are used in Chapter 7 when options are employed to hedge currency risk.

Factors Affecting Call Option Prices

Unlike futures and forwards, options require an up-front *premium*. The long pays this premium to the short as compensation for the liability imposed on the short. Option premiums are also referred to as *option prices* or *option values*. In this section, we discuss factors affecting option prices.

EXHIBIT 3.9
Put Option: Payoff & Profit to Long (Buyer)
Put Parameters: $P = 0.03$, $X = 1.25$ *(all values in USD)*

	At Contract Inception	Cash Flows at Maturity			Overall Result	
Currency Value at Maturity	Premium Paid	Exercise Price Received	Value Given Up	Payoff		Profit
1.16	0.03	1.25	1.16	0.09		0.06
1.19	0.03	1.25	1.19	0.06		0.03
1.22	0.03	1.25	1.22	0.03		0.00
1.25	0.03	No exercise	No exercise	0		−0.03
1.28	0.03	No exercise	No exercise	0		−0.03
1.31	0.03	No exercise	No exercise	0		−0.03
1.34	0.03	No exercise	No exercise	0		−0.03
1.37	0.03	No exercise	No Exercise	0		−0.03

Payoff and profit to short (seller) is the exact opposite (that is, positive values are negative, and negative values are positive).

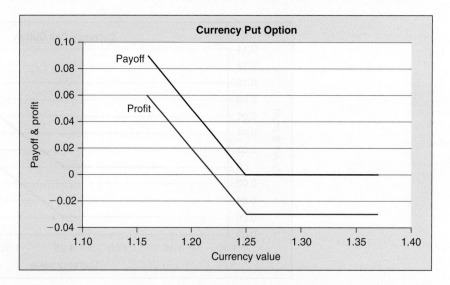

EXHIBIT 3.10
Summary of Option Payoff and Profits

	Call Option	Put Option
Long (buyer)	Long pays premium up front. Long exercises by buying currency.	Long pays premium up front. Long exercises by selling currency.
	Payoff $= Max(0, S_t - X)$	Payoff $= Max(0, X - S_t)$
	Profit $= Max(0, S_t - X) - C$	Payoff $= Max(0, X - S_t) - P$
	Long gains when currency rises.	Long gains when currency falls.
Short (seller)	Short receives premium up front. Short responds to exercise by selling currency.	Short receives premium up front. Short responds to exercise by buying currency.
	Payoff $= -Max(0, S_t - X)$	Payoff $= -Max(0, X - S_t)$
	Profit $= -Max(0, S_t - X) + C$	Profit $= -Max(0, X - S_t) + P$
	Short gains when currency falls.	Short gains when currency rises.

Underlying Asset

Because a call option gives the long the ability to buy the underlying asset at a prespecified strike price, the price of the underlying asset and call price are positively related. Put prices are negatively related to the price of the underlying asset.

Strike Price

Because the long pays the strike price on exercise, strike and call prices are negatively related. In contrast, strike and put prices are positively related. One may consider the difference between the price of the underlying asset and the strike price as a single compound factor. Call prices are positively related to the difference while puts are negatively related.

Maturity

Maturity and call prices are positively related because of time value. Consider a long position in the EUR call option with $X = 1.55$. Suppose the spot value EURUSD = 1.57. We could say that the option is "in the money" because if exercised today, it would produce a positive payoff (USD 0.02). The *intrinsic value* of this option is USD 0.02. The market price is usually higher than intrinsic value. Consider a plausible market price of USD 0.05. The comparison of the market price with intrinsic value indicates a time value of USD 0.03. *Time value* is the component of option value that reflects the possibility that over time, a better outcome could be obtained. The longer the maturity, the higher is the time value, and the higher is the option price. This is true for puts as well as calls.

intrinsic value and time value

An option's value equals the sum of its *intrinsic value* (the amount that can be obtained today itself through exercise) and its *time value* (the extra value that is potentially available by waiting).

Volatility

Options are unusual instruments because of their asymmetric payoff. Consider a long position in a currency call option. We learned that this position provides a positive payoff when the currency rises and $(S_t - X)$ is positive. Instead, when the currency falls and $(S_t - X)$ is negative, the long does not lose because exercise does not take place. When currencies are volatile, large values of $(S_t - X)$—positive or negative—are possible. This means that the long reaps more rewards in a volatile scenario. Thus, call prices are higher when volatility is higher. A similar argument may be made regarding put options: A long position in puts benefits from large values of $(X - S_t)$, and this again is made more likely by volatility. Thus, put prices are also positively related to volatility.

Interest Rates

Because a currency call option may be used to make a deferred purchase of the underlying currency (pay premium now, but pay strike price later to effect purchase), a high domestic rate of interest makes the call attractive for this purpose. Hence, call prices are positively related to domestic interest rates. On the flip side, however, not having the foreign currency on hand (because we defer purchase), we incur the opportunity cost of not earning interest on the foreign currency. Hence, call prices are negatively related to foreign interest rates. Puts—because they enable the deferred sale of a foreign currency—are related in the opposite way to domestic and foreign interest rates.

Currency Call Option Pricing Formula

We had earlier discussed the six factors influencing call option prices. These six factors and the symbols used to represent them are:

1. The value of the underlying currency (S).
2. The strike price (X).
3. The time to maturity (t).
4. The volatility (σ).
5. The domestic currency interest rate (r).
6. The foreign currency interest rate (r^*).

Option pricing models use these six inputs to calculate call option premiums. The option pricing model was originally developed by Fisher Black and Myron Scholes in 1973 principally to price options on stocks. This model is still used today to price options on stocks as well as other assets. One version of the Black-Scholes model allows for dividends on the underlying stock. Others (notably two sets of authors, (1) Garman and Kohlhagen and (2) Biger and Hull, both in 1983[7]) have observed that options on currencies are similar to options on stocks

[7] For the specific version of the currency option pricing model we use in this section, see N. Biger and J. Hull, "The Valuation of Currency Options," *Financial Management* (1983), pp. 24–28.

paying dividends because currencies "pay interest." The following currency option formula is therefore fundamentally the same as the formula originally developed by Black-Scholes for stocks paying dividends.

$$C = Se^{-r^*t}N(d_1) - Xe^{-rt}N(d_2)$$

where

$$d_1 = \frac{\ln\left(\frac{S}{X}\right) + \left(r - r^* + \frac{\sigma^2}{2}\right)t}{\sigma\sqrt{t}}, \text{ and}$$

$$d_2 = d_1 - \sigma\sqrt{t}$$

EXAMPLE 3.7

Using the option pricing model, determine the value of a 90-day EUR call option with a strike price of 1.55. Assume that the U.S. and Eurozone interest rates (continuous compounding) are 2.9 percent and 3.8 percent, respectively. You are provided with past weekly values of EURUSD rates in this example including the spot value of 1.5992.

Solution: The option pricing model requires six inputs (S, X, r, r^*, t, σ). Five of the six are readily inferred from the narrative provided previously; the remaining input (σ) must be calculated using the time series of EURUSD as demonstrated next. Once all six inputs are available, the option pricing model can be applied. See calculations below:

Option Pricing Model

Use Past Data to Calculate σ

Date in 2008	EURUSD	Percent Change
January 8	1.4708	N/A
January 15	1.4804	0.65%
January 22	1.4631	−1.17%
January 29	1.4775	0.99%
February 5	1.4648	−0.86%
February 12	1.4584	−0.44%
February 19	1.4725	0.97%
February 26	1.4975	1.69%
March 4	1.5216	1.61%
March 11	1.5344	0.84%
March 18	1.5731	2.52%
March 25	1.5423	−1.96%
March 1	1.5615	1.25%
March 8	1.5711	0.61%
March 15	1.5790	0.51%
March 22	1.5992	1.28%
Weekly σ		1.1959
Annual σ	*SQRT(52)	8.62

Obtain Option Parameters

90-Day Option on EUR

$X = 1.55$	Strike price
$t = 90/365$	Maturity

Obtain Currency Spot

$S = 1.5992$	Spot currency

Continuously Compounded Rates

$r(\text{USD}) = 2.9\%$

$r^*(\text{EUR}) = 3.8\%$

$$d_1 = \frac{\ln\left(\frac{S}{X}\right) + \left(r - r^* + \frac{\sigma^2}{2}\right)t}{\sigma\sqrt{t}}$$

$$= \frac{\ln\left(\frac{1.5992}{1.55}\right) + \left(0.029 - 0.038 + \frac{0.0862^2}{2}\right) \times \frac{90}{365}}{0.0862\sqrt{90/365}}$$

$$= 0.6996$$

$$d_2 = d_1 \, \sigma\sqrt{t}$$
$$= 0.6996 - 0.0862 \times \sqrt{90/365}$$
$$= 0.6568$$
$$N(d_1) = 0.7579$$
$$N(d_2) = 0.7443$$
$$C = Se^{-r^*t}N(d_1) - Xe^{-rt}N(d_2)$$
$$= 1.5992e^{-0.038(90/365)} \times 0.7579 - 1.55e^{-0.029(90/365)} \times 0.7443$$
$$= 0.0552$$

These calculations are best performed using a spreadsheet. Some details include these:

- Convert weekly EURUSD values into weekly returns. Calculate the standard deviation of weekly returns (use Excel function STDEV). Annualize the standard deviation by multiplying with $\sqrt{52}$. (If weekly values are independent, annual variance is 52 times weekly variance.)
- Perform the $N(.)$ calculation using the Excel function NORMSDIST.

The option pricing formula is useful in two ways. First, managers can calculate the "fair" value of an option before its purchase or sale. Second, the formula allows managers to predict how option prices will change if inputs change. In particular, managers are interested in how option prices change relative to the underlying currency. This sensitivity is known as *delta* and is explained in Appendix 3B.

Pricing Put Options

Although explicit put pricing formulas are available, the easiest way to price puts is to follow a two-step process. First, use the call-pricing formula explained previously to value a call with similar parameters. Next, use the *put-call parity* formula that links put prices to call prices.

$$P = C + Xe^{-rt} - Se^{-r^*t}$$

See the following example for a sample calculation.

EXAMPLE 3.8

Consider the call option described in Example 3.7. Recall: $t = 90/365$, $X = 1.55$, $S = 1.5992$, $r = 2.9\%$ and $r^* = 3.8\%$. The call pricing formula produced a call value of 0.0552. What is the value of the corresponding put?

Solution:
Using the put-call parity equation:

$$P = 0.0552 + 1.55 \times e^{-0.029 \times (90/365)} - 1.5992 \times e^{-0.038 \times (90/365)} = 0.0099$$

3.5 Eurocurrency Derivatives

Currencies trading outside their borders are known as *Eurocurrencies*. Chapter 2 explained the Eurocurrency markets in detail. Here we briefly discuss two important derivatives based on Eurocurrencies.

Eurodollar Futures

Eurodollar futures
The prices of *Eurodollar futures* convey the market's estimates of interest rates expected to prevail in future time periods.

Recall that Eurodollars are U.SD deposits outside of the U.S. The LIBOR rates compiled by the British Bankers' Association provide information about this important market. Because of the importance of LIBOR rates in financial contracting, the CME introduced the Eurodollar futures contract in 1981. Today, this contract is the most widely traded futures contract in the world. See Exhibit 3.11.

EXHIBIT 3.11 CME Eurodollar Futures Quotes from April 17, 2008

09

09

PG09

INTEREST RATE FUTURES

2008 DAILY INFORMATION BULLETIN - http://www.cmegroup.com/tools-information/build-a-report.html?
report=dailybulletin CME Group Inc. A CME/Board of Trade Company. 20 South Wacker Drive, Chicago,
Illinois 60606-7499. Statistics: (312) 930-8280 Fax: (312) 930-8203 E-Mail: marketdataops@cmegroup.com

FINAL

INTEREST RATE FUTURES

Thu, Apr 17, 2008 PG09

PG09 BULLETIN # 74@

FOR PRODUCTS THAT ARE TRADED IN BOTH REGULAR TRADING HOURS (RTH) AND ELECTRONIC TRADING HOURS (ETH) THE INFORMATION REPRESENTED ON THIS PAGE FOR OPENING RANGE,
HIGH, LOW, CLOSING RANGE, SETTLEMENT PRICE AND VOLUME REPRESENTS RTH ACTIVITY ONLY. NOTE: LIFE OF CONTRACT HIGH AND LOW REPRESENTS BOTH RTH AND ETH. RTH
VOLUME REFLECTS PIT TRADING, BLOCK TRADES AND CASH-FOR-FUTURES ONLY. ETH REPRESENTS GLOBEX VOLUME TRANSACTIONS FROM THE GLOBEX® ELECTRONIC SESSION ONLY.
VOLUME OR OPEN INTEREST (BOTH BEFORE AND AFTER THE LAST DAY OF TRADING) MAY BE AFFECTED BY: CASH FOR FUTURES, SPREADS, AND PRIOR DAYS' CLEARED TRADES
(OUT-TRADES), POSITION ADJUSTMENTS, OPTION EXERCISES, POSITIONS IN DELIVERY, OR POSITIONS IN A CASH SETTLEMENT CYCLE. PRODUCT LISTINGS REPRESENT CONTRACTS
WITH PRICE/VOLUME ACTIVITY AND/OR HAVE ESTABLISHED OPEN INTEREST. PRODUCTS THAT ARE ELIGIBLE TO TRADE, BUT ARE INACTIVE, DO NOT APPEAR IN THIS REPORT.
LEGEND: B=BID, A=ASK, N=NOMINAL, P=POST SETTLEMENT SESSION, #=NEW CONTRACT HIGH PRICE, *=NEW CONTRACT LOW, R=RECORD VOLUME OR OPEN INTEREST. SETTLEMENT
PRICES ARE DETERMINED BY CME RULE 813.

	OPEN RANGE	HIGH	LOW	CLOSING RANGE	SETT. PRICE	IMM INDEX DISCOUNT %	PT.CHGE. ##	GLOBEX® VOLUME	RTH VOLUME	OPEN INTEREST	CONTRACT HIGH	CONTRACT LOW
EURO DLR FUT												
MAY08	97.1300	97.1450B	97.0500A	97.0700A	97.0700	2.93 ( ) – 14.0	23570	40	72101 +	7926	98.0100B	95.9300A
JUL08	----	----	*97.1100A	97.1850A	97.1650	2.83 ( ) – 19.5	117	----	2599 –	43	97.9200	97.1050A
AUG08	----	----	*97.1800A	97.2250A	97.2050	2.79 ( ) – 19.0		----	275	UNCH	97.2200B	97.1300A
OCT08	----	----		97.3350N	97.1600	2.84 ( ) – 17.5	21	----	121 +	21	97.5850B	97.0700A
JUN08	97.1950	97.2350B	97.0650A	97.1150 @97.1200	97.1200	2.88 ( ) – 17.0	584454	22684	1405462 +	14680	98.2550	93.5000A
SEP08	97.3100 @97.3200	97.3500B	97.1300A	97.2250A@97.2200	97.2250	2.77 ( ) – 18.5	655232	23457	1378681 +	52692	98.3350	93.4550A
DEC08	97.1800	97.2500B	97.0350	97.1400	97.1350	2.86 ( ) – 18.5	625942	22381	1339946 +	26252	98.3650	93.3450A
MAR09	97.1500	97.2400B	97.0300A	97.1400	97.1350	2.86 ( ) – 12.5	594665	18320	1072007 +	24347	98.1850	93.3250A
JUN09	96.9650	97.0900B	96.8650A	96.9800	96.9800	3.02 ( ) – 11.0	603855	20632	851720 +	25790	98.0000	93.2600A
SEP09	96.7950	96.9200B	96.6800A	96.8000A	96.7950	3.20 ( ) – 10.0	432844	19283	757201 +	24583	97.7700	93.2050A
DEC09	96.6450	96.6900B	96.4500A	96.5600	96.5600	3.44 ( ) – 10.5	294064	11269	549808 +	6001	97.5050	93.1200A
MAR10	96.4650	96.5250B	96.3100A	96.4000	96.4050	3.59 ( ) – 9.5	223587	6364	355672	11517	97.2750	93.1150A
JUN10	96.2150	96.3150B	96.1350A	96.2250	96.2250	3.77 ( ) – 7.5	78911	9233	240105 +	2686	97.0600	93.0600A
SEP10	96.0800	96.1250B	95.9750A	96.0500	96.0550	3.94 ( ) – 5.5	58738	3640	185578 +	1456	96.8950	92.9500A
DEC10	95.8950	95.9400B	95.8250A	95.8800	95.8850	4.10 ( ) – 5.0	37198	4207	159438 +	826	96.7450	92.8850A
MAR11	95.7900	95.8050B	95.6900A	95.7600	95.7750	4.22 ( ) – 1.5	30143	4525	108727 +	3590	96.6100	92.8250A
JUN11	95.5650	95.6850B	95.5650	95.6500	95.6500	4.35 ( ) – 0.5	11787	2986	109630 +	68	96.4700	92.7900A
SEP11	95.4450	95.5450B	95.4450	95.5350	95.5400	4.46 ( ) + 0.5	10520	1532	70306 +	735	96.3150B	92.7500A
DEC11	95.3900	95.4400B	95.3300A	95.4150	95.4200	4.58 ( ) + 1.5	7572	1608	73372 +	61	96.1950	92.7100A
MAR12	95.3100	95.3700B	95.2500A	95.3400	95.3450	4.65 ( ) + 1.5	7248	2360	91223 +	851	96.0800	92.6700A
JUN12	95.2500	95.2800B	95.1900A	95.2700	95.2600	4.74 ( ) + 2.0	5911	2391	47035 +	19	95.9750B	92.6350A
SEP12	95.1650	95.1950B	95.1050A	95.1900	95.1800	4.82 ( ) + 3.0	5781	1088	55148 +	241	95.8650B	92.6250A
DEC12	95.0600	95.0950B	95.0000A	95.0850	95.0800	4.92 ( ) + 3.0	5016	1184	36145 +	84	95.7500B	92.6000A
MAR13	94.9950	95.0300B	94.9350A	95.0250	95.0200	4.98 ( ) + 3.5	3890	1197	20313 +	286	95.6200B	92.5650A
JUN13	94.9400	94.9700B	94.8800A	94.9700B	94.9600	5.04 ( ) + 4.0	209	273	8186 +	239	95.5250B	92.5450A
SEP13	94.8600	94.9000B	94.8100A	94.9000B	94.8950	5.10 ( ) + 4.5	558	277	11567 +	113	95.4300B	92.6250A
DEC13		94.8150B	94.7250A	94.8150B	94.8100	5.19 ( ) + 4.5	34	350	8844 –	148	95.3300B	92.6900A
MAR14	94.7250	94.7650B	94.6750A	94.7650B	94.7650	5.23 ( ) + 4.5		429	13535 –	118	95.2250B	92.7800A
JUN14	94.7150	94.7250B	94.6250A	94.7250B	94.7150	5.28 ( ) + 5.0	----		7657 +	UNCH	95.1500B	93.1250A
SEP14	94.6600	94.6700B	94.5700A	94.6700B	94.6650	5.33 ( ) + 5.5	----	2	4873 –	1	95.0800B	93.5600A
DEC14	94.5950	94.6050B	94.5050A	94.6050B	94.6000	5.40 ( ) + 5.5	----	2	2445 –		95.0000B	93.6450A
MAR15	94.5650	94.5750B	94.4750A	94.5750B	94.5750	5.42 ( ) + 6.0	----	1	4918 –	UNCH	94.9400B	93.6650A
JUN15	----	94.5350B	94.4200A	94.5200B	94.5300	5.47 ( ) + 6.0	----	30	952 +	30	94.8950B	93.6400A
SEP15	----	94.4900B	94.3750A	94.4750B	94.4900	5.51 ( ) + 6.5	----	20	2754 +	20	94.8500B	93.6200A
DEC15	----	94.4450B	94.3300A	94.4300B	94.4450	5.55 ( ) + 6.5	----	30	1130 +	30	94.8050B	93.5900A
MAR16	94.3600	94.4250B	94.3100A	94.4100B	94.4250	5.57 ( ) + 6.5	----	630	2647 +	605	94.7900B	93.5700A
JUN16	----	94.3850B	94.2800A	94.3700B	94.3850	5.61 ( ) + 6.5	----		1474 +	UNCH	94.7600B	93.5450A
SEP16	----	94.3450B	94.2400A	94.3300B	94.3500	5.65 ( ) + 7.0	----		1245 +	UNCH	94.7300B	93.5250A
DEC16	----	94.3000B	94.1950A	94.2850B	94.3050	5.69 ( ) + 7.0	----		814 +	UNCH	94.6950B	93.4950A
MAR17	----	94.2850B	94.1800A	94.2700B	94.2950	5.70 ( ) + 7.5	----		680 +	UNCH	94.6900B	93.4800A
JUN17	----	94.2750B	94.1600A	94.2500B	94.2750	5.72 ( ) + 7.5	----		814 +	UNCH	94.6700B	93.5800A
SEP17	----	94.2500B	94.1350A	94.2250B	94.2550	5.74 ( ) + 8.0	----		481 +	UNCH	94.6550B	93.6050A
DEC17	----	94.2100B	94.0950A	94.1850B	94.2150	5.78 ( ) + 8.0	----		304 +	UNCH	94.6200B	93.5650A
MAR18	----	94.2000B	*94.0850A	94.1750B	94.2100	5.79 ( ) + 8.5	----		270 +	UNCH	94.6150B	94.0850A
TOTAL	EURO DLR FUT							4301867	182435	9061203 - 185241			

U.S. 3-MTH DLR: BBA FIX: 2.81750

Contract	OPEN RANGE	HIGH	LOW	CLOSING RANGE	SETT. PRICE	PT.CHGE	RTH VOLUME	GLOBEX VOLUME	OPEN INTEREST	CONTRACT HIGH	CONTRACT LOW
10Y NOTE FUT											
JUN08	116'140	116'250	116'030A	116'115 @116'110	116'115	- 0'075	63048	922206	2065493 - 33348	119'305	108'160
SEP08	114'295	114'295	*114'295	114'295	114'250	- 0'090	2071	9066	13600 + 8777	115'270	114'295
TOTAL 10Y NOTE FUT							65119	931272	2079093 - 24571		
5Y NOTE FUT											
JUN08	112'230	112'300	112'140	112'147	112'147	- 0'125	28168	640146	1815908 + 17773	115'152	104'190
SEP08	----	----	----	112'067N	111'262	- 0'125	----	1	7302 UNCH	112'100	112'100
DEC08	----	----	----	112'067N	111'262	- 0'125	1955	----		----	----
TOTAL 5Y NOTE FUT							30123	640147	1823210 + 17773		
2Y NOTE FUT											
JUN08	106'207 @106'205	106'207	106'135	106'165	106'165	- 0'082	62536	335232	1107923 - 5263	107'275	105'235
SEP08	----	----	----	106'172N	106'090	- 0'082	----	----	5 UNCH	----	----
TOTAL 2Y NOTE FUT							62536	335232	1107928 - 5263		
30Y BOND FUT											
JUN08	116'310 @116'315	117'105	'145	116'225 @116'210	116'220	- 0'100	12662	257331	889244 - 8832	121'130	113'110
SEP08	----	----	----	115'280N	115'180	- 0'100	----	23	2116 + 5	119'020	114'210
DEC08	----	----	----	114'160N	114'060	- 0'100	----	----	49 UNCH	118'090	117'150
MAR09	----	----	----	113'100N	113'000	- 0'100	----	----	14 UNCH	----	----
TOTAL 30Y BOND FUT							12662	257354	891423 - 8827		

EURODOLLAR GLOBEX VOLUME AS PERCENT OF TOTAL VOLUME

CONTRACT	GBX VOL	TOTAL VOL	GBX% OF TOTAL		CONTRACT	GBX VOL	TOTAL VOL	GBX% OF TOTAL
Jun08	584454	607138	96.26		Jun11	11787	14773	79.79
Sep08	655232	678689	96.54		Sep11	10520	12052	87.29
Dec08	625942	648323	96.55		Dec11	7572	9180	82.48
Mar09	594665	612985	97.01		Mar12	7248	9608	75.44
Jun09	603855	624487	96.70		Jun12	5911	8302	71.20
Sep09	432844	452127	95.74		Sep12	5781	6869	84.16
Dec09	294064	305333	96.31		Dec12	5016	6200	80.90
Mar10	223587	229951	97.23		Mar13	3890	5087	76.47
Jun10	78911	88144	89.53					
Sep10	58738	62378	94.16					
Dec10	37198	41405	89.84					
Mar11	30143	34668	86.95		EURODOLLAR FUT TOTAL	4301867	4484302	95.93

Settlement and Profit

The CME Eurodollar futures contract uses an innovative design. It has a notional value of USD 1 million and shows the March quarterly cycle for almost 10 years. Its key feature concerns delivery. Rather than requiring the delivery of an actual 90-day money market instrument with a face value of USD 1 million—as its precursor the CME Treasury bill futures contract did—the Eurodollar futures contract uses a cash settlement based on changes in market interest rates. The 90-day LIBOR prevailing on the last day of the contract determines the profit or loss to the counterparties. Assuming a person takes a long position at an initial price of F, the profit at maturity per contract is given by:

$$\text{Profit} = \underbrace{\left(\frac{100-F}{100} - LIBOR\right)}_{\substack{\text{Initial} - \text{Ending} \\ \text{LIBOR Interest Rate}}} \times \underbrace{\frac{90}{360} \times 1{,}000{,}000}_{\substack{\text{Adjustment for} \\ \text{Maturity and Contract Size}}}$$

The value $(100 - F)$ is the implicit interest rate in the futures contract; division by 100 makes it a percent value. At contract inception, the long locks in its future investment at this interest rate. Therefore, the long gains (loses) if the actual LIBOR is lower (higher) than this initial assessment. The ratio 90/360 adjusts the interest calculation to reflect a 90-day maturity. Finally, the size of the contract (USD 1 million) is factored in the last term. For multiple contracts, simply multiply the result with number of contracts.

EXAMPLE 3.9

A Eurodollar futures contact expired today. The London fixing of the three-month LIBOR rate on USD deposits is 4.2 percent. Calculate the final Eurodollar futures price used for settlement. Also calculate the profit to an investor who entered into a long position in eight contracts at a price of 95.63. Recall that contract size is USD 1 million.

Solution:

$$\text{Profit} = \left[\frac{100 - F}{100} - \text{LIBOR}\right] \times \frac{90}{360} \times 1{,}000{,}000 \times \text{Number of contracts}$$

$$= \left[\frac{100 - 95.63}{100} - 4.2\%\right] \times \frac{90}{360} \times 1{,}000{,}000 \times 8$$

$$= 3{,}400$$

Discussion: The contractual rate equals the difference between 100 and 95.63, or 4.37 percent. At maturity, LIBOR equals 4.2 percent. The long benefits from the 0.17 percent fall in interest rate because it has locked in a higher interest rate for the implied purchase of the Eurodollar instrument. Recall from basic financial principles that a higher rate implies a lower purchase price for a debt instrument. Thus, the long gains from the long's commitment to a higher interest rate (lower purchase price).

Implied LIBOR

What information do Eurodollar prices contain? Recall that $(100 - F)$ represents the market's expectation of forward interest rates. We refer to this as the *implied LIBOR*. Suppose a financial manager wants to estimate funding costs for a future project. The implied LIBOR could provide the answer to this manager as demonstrated by the following example.

EXAMPLE 3.10

An MNC manager who is engaged in making projections for funding a future project wishes to estimate the interest rate for the year 2011. She obtains the following Eurodollar futures quotes: 95.895, 95.775, 95.650, and 95.540 for the 2010 December, 2011 March, 2011 June, and 2011 September contracts respectively. (Assume 90 days in each quarter.)

Solution: See calculations below.

2011 Rate Calculations

	January–March	April–June	July–September	October–December
F (given values)	95.895	95.775	95.650	95.540
Implied LIBOR = 100 − *F*	4.105	4.225	4.350	4.460
1 + *LIBOR*% × (90/360)	1.01026	1.01056	1.01088	1.0115
FV of USD 1	1.0103	1.0209	1.0320	1.0435
2011 rate forecast				**4.35%**

"FV of USD 1" equals the cumulative compounded value of USD 1. For example, the FV at the end of June equals 1.01026 × 1.01056 = 1.0209.

Discussion: Note that the 2010 December futures convey information about rates during 2011 January–March, and so on. Based on the implied LIBOR rates, future value factors are calculated and compounded to determine the ending value of a deposit of USD 1. Futures markets indicate rising quarterly rates during 2011: from 4.105 percent in quarter 1 to 4.460 percent in quarter.

Short-Term Interest Rate Futures

A more recent introduction that is also highly successful is the *short-term interest rate (STIR)* futures traded in LIFFE (now a part of NYSE/Euronext). STIR seeks to replicate the Eurodollar contract using the EUR, GBP, CHF, and JPY as underlying currencies. LIBOR rates are used as reference for GBP and CHF. The EURIBOR—published by a consortium of banks in Brussels—is used for the EUR contract, and TIBOR—published by banks in Tokyo—is used for the JPY contract.

Some features of STIR futures contracts follow:

- In keeping with recent trends, trading is conducted electronically using the LIFFE CONNECT platform.
- It uses a quarterly cycle as in CME Eurodollar futures: expiration on third Wednesdays.
- Notional values vary. The EUR contract size is EUR 1 million.
- Quotes are based on 100 minus reference interest rate.

MNCs are major users of Eurocurrency futures. The major exchanges—CME and LIFFE—have a variety of educational material that explains various applications involving interest rate forecasting as well as risk mitigation. One major benefit of these markets is that they make interest rate dynamics in various currencies transparent and easily observable. MNC applications of currency-related interest rate information are explained further in Chapters 5, 8, and 10.

Summary

- Derivatives are financial instruments whose cash flows and values flow directly from an underlying security, currency, or commodity. Firms use derivatives to manage various risks such as currency risk and interest rate risk.
- Important categories of currency-related derivatives are currency forwards, currency futures, and currency options.
- Currency forwards are private contracts used to lock in the future purchase or sale price of a currency.
- Currency futures are fundamentally the same as currency forwards but differ because they are public contracts requiring the use of collateral to protect the parties involved.
- Currency forwards and futures are valued with a simple equation that requires as input the current spot rate as well as the interest rates in the two currencies.
- Currency options are more complex instruments compared to currency forwards because they allow the option holder the flexibility of backing out of the transaction. Currency call

options allow the option holder to buy currencies at a fixed price, and currency put options allow the option holder to sell currencies at a fixed price.

- Because options are asymmetric or flexible instruments, their valuation formula is more complex and requires currency volatility as an input. A modified Black-Scholes formula is used to value currency call options.

- By using the put-call parity equation, a currency put option can be valued by using the corresponding currency call option's price as an input.

Questions

1. **Derivatives Definition.** What are derivatives? Give examples of several currency derivative products.

2. **Derivatives Market.** How large is the market for derivatives? What entities are creating the demand for derivatives products?

3. **Uses of Derivatives.** Contrast the speculative and hedging motives for derivatives.

4. **Derivatives Categories.** Which category of derivatives is more prevalent in markets, interest rate, and foreign exchange? Why?

5. **Currency Forward Definition.** Explain how a currency forward contract works. In particular, explain the cash flows in this contract.

6. **Forward Pricing.** A colleague of yours at work makes the following assertion: "A forward contract is always priced higher than the spot contract. This is because the forward price is made up of the spot price plus the interest cost of holding the spot asset over the horizon of the forward contract. The interest cost is a positive item. Hence, the forward price is higher." Your colleague's statements appear to make sense, but you cannot help but notice that a 90-day forward price for a particular currency is quoted in *The Wall Street Journal* at a value lower than that of the spot price. Could this be a misprint, or is it possible that the forward price of a currency be lower than the spot price? Explain.

7. **Forward Markets.** Who are the participants in the currency forward markets?

8. **Forward Markets.** Why is it difficult for retail investors to transact in the currency forward markets?

9. **Currency Futures Definition.** What are currency futures? How do they differ from currency forwards?

10. **Futures Markets.** In the United States, when and where did trading in currency futures originate?

11. **Futures Cash Flows.** Explain how daily settlement works with currency futures.

12. **Real versus Financial Options.** What are real and financial options? In what category do currency options fall?

13. **Option Valuation.** Explain how the value of the underlying asset and the strike price affect option values.

14. **Option Time Value.** What is time value in an option?

15. **Option Exercise.** Comment on the following statement: "One should exercise a call option on a currency only if the spot rate exceeds the sum of the strike price and option premium."

16. **Comparison of Options Positions.** You are the financial analyst for the firm Sixties Wine that distributes California wine in Italy. Your firm routinely hedges its exposure to the EUR. In the past, the firm has used long positions in EUR put options to accomplish its hedging objectives. Due to a change in market liquidity conditions, the firm finds that it is no longer possible to use EUR put options. One of your colleagues is responsible for responding to this problem. In a report, your colleague recommends that the firm use short positions in call options on the EUR and makes the claim that "short positions in call options on the EUR are identical to long positions on put options. . . ." Critically examine this statement.

Problems

1. **Forward Pricing.** The U.S.-based firm Fishing Well is negotiating with its bankers to enter into a three-month EUR forward contract. The firm has hired a financial analyst to provide a second opinion on the forward quote. The bank is currently quoting the three-month forward rate at USD 1.5642. How would the analyst go about evaluating this quote? You may consider the following information to answer this question. The spot rate is USD 1.5591. The interest rates in the United States and the Eurozone are 5 percent and 3 percent, respectively. Assume annual compounding.

2. **Forward Default Losses.** Duerbo Corporation entered into a forward contract to purchase CHF 10 million in six months at a rate of USD 0.60. Two months later, CHF is trading at USD 0.65, and a four-month CHF forward contract (maturing at the same time as the original six-month contract) is trading at USD 0.63. At this time, what is the potential loss from default on the forward position?

3. **Forward Default Losses.** Pimco Corporation entered into a forward contract to purchase EUR 100 million in six months at a rate of USD 1.40. Two months later, EUR is trading at USD 1.45, and a four-month EUR forward contract (maturing at the same time as the original six-month contract) is trading at USD 1.46. At this time, what is the potential loss from default on the forward position?

4. **Futures Daily Settlement.** Consider the following sequence of prices for a currency futures contract. Each contact involves 10,000 units of the foreign currency. The initial and maintenance margin requirements are USD 800 and USD 500, respectively. Calculate the daily margin account balances for the long and the short. Assume that the long bought the futures at a price of 1.67 and that the futures contract is held to expiration, which is in day 6.

Day	Futures Price
1	1.72
2	1.68
3	1.61
4	1.55
5	1.60
6	1.62

5. **Forward Premium.** Skeeter Corporation wishes to purchase JPY in the forward market. Assume that contract maturity is two years. USDJPY spot equals 100, and interest rates (annual compounding) in USD and JPY are 3 percent and 1 percent, respectively. Calculate forward price and forward premium.

6. **Futures Pricing.** Roland Enterprises has exposure to GBP because of its U.K. sales. It is considering the use of GBP futures to mitigate its risk. The company's CFO is not confident that GBP futures are priced accurately in markets and assigns the task of futures pricing to his assistant, Mary Snead. Assume that LIBOR rates based on USD and GBP for six-month maturities are 3.14 percent and 5.76 percent, respectively. LIBOR conventions for these currencies are actual/360 and actual/365, respectively. Spot GBPUSD equals 1.90. Calculate the benchmark rate for the six-month GBPUSD futures contract.

7. **Futures Pricing.** Consider a nine-month futures contact on EUR that settled at USD 1.6014 yesterday. LIBOR (USD) and EURIBOR (EUR) rates for nine-month matures at close of trading yesterday were 4 percent and 6 percent, respectively. At today's open, EURIBOR rates are unchanged, but LIBOR has increased to 4.20 percent. Because of increased inflows into USD assets, EURUSD falls by 1 percent. What is the new futures price? What is the percent change in the futures price? (For simplicity, assume that maturity both for calculations based on yesterday's close and today's open equals nine months, or 0.75 years)

8. **Long Call Cash Flows.** Rixon Corporation purchases CHF call options with a strike price of USD 0.90. The option premium is USD 0.04 per currency unit. A financial analyst at Rixon forecasts the following possible values for spot CHFUSD at maturity. Calculate option payoff and profit (per currency unit) for each of these spot values.

Possible Value of CHFUSD	Option Exercise (Y/N)	Payoff	Profit
0.92			
0.96			
1.02			

9. **Short Call Cash Flows.** Rider Corporation sells EUR call options with a strike price of USD 1.50. The option premium is USD 0.03 per currency unit. A financial analyst at Rider forecasts the following possible values for spot EURUSD at maturity. Calculate option payoff and profit (per currency unit) for each of these spot values.

Possible Value of EURUSD	Option Exercise (Y/N)	Payoff	Profit
1.38			
1.46			
1.52			

10. **Long Put Cash Flows.** Shale Corporation purchases BRL put options with a strike price of USD 0.50. The option premium is USD 0.02 per currency unit. A financial analyst at Shale forecasts the following possible values for spot BRLUSD at maturity. Calculate option payoff and profit (per currency unit) for each of these spot values.

Possible Value of BRLUSD	Option Exercise (Y/N)	Payoff	Profit
0.42			
0.47			
0.52			

11. **Short Put Cash Flows.** Sheila Corporation sells MXN put options with a strike price of USD 0.10. The option premium is USD 0.005 per currency unit. A financial analyst at Sheila forecasts the following possible values for spot MXNUSD at maturity. Calculate option payoff and profit (per currency unit) for each of these spot values.

Possible Value of MXNUSD	Option Exercise (Y/N)	Payoff	Profit
0.09			
0.11			
0.13			

12. **Option Contract Size and Cash Flows.** Options on GBP trade on the Philadelphia Stock Exchange. A call expiring in three months with a strike price of USD 1.50 is trading at a price of USD 0.05. Consider an investor who buys five contracts and holds the options to maturity. At maturity, GBP is trading at USD 1.63. What is the net profit obtained by this investor? Assume contract size is 10,000 currency units.

13. **Option Contract Size and Cash Flows.** In question 12, what is the net profit for the person who sold the five contracts?

14. **Option Contract Size and Cash Flows.** Options on GBP are traded on the Philadelphia Stock Exchange. A put expiring in three months with a strike price of USD 1.60 is trading at a price of USD 0.04. Consider an investor who buys three contracts and holds the options to maturity. At maturity, GBP is trading at USD 1.57. What net profit does this investor obtain? Assume contract size is 10,000 currency units.

15. **Call Option Valuation.** Determine the value of a call option on the CAD that has the following characteristics: (a) is a European type, (b) matures in six months, and (c) has the

strike price of USD 0.95. In the spot market, the CAD is trading at USD 0.92. The U.S. and Canadian interest rates are 4 percent and 6 percent, respectively (continuous compounding). The CAD has an annual standard deviation of 12 percent.

16. **Call Option Valuation.** Determine the value of a call option on the JPY that has the following characteristics: (a) is a European type, (b) matures in nine months, and (c) has the strike price of USD 0.010. In the spot market, the JPY is trading at USD 0.008. The U.S. and Japanese interest rates are 4 percent and 1 percent, respectively (continuous compounding). The JPY has an annual standard deviation of 15 percent.

17. **Put Option Valuation.** Given the information in question 16, what is the value of a put option with similar parameters?

Extensions

1. **Forward versus Futures Pricing.** The following are six-month forward and futures quotes on the GBP: forward = USD 1.60 and futures = USD 1.61. If you are a currency arbitrager, what action would you take, and what would your profit be? What are some constraints in undertaking this action?

2. **Option Combination.** A speculator believes that the EUR—currently trading at 1.60—will be trading in the range 1.70–1.80 in six months. She wishes to buy a EUR call option with a strike price of 1.70 so that at any value above 1.70, the option will have a positive payoff. However, because she does not believe that the EUR will trade above 1.80, she sells a EUR call option with a strike price of 1.80. Evaluate the consequences of the speculator's actions. Show potential consequences by constructing a spreadsheet. Discuss pros and cons of this strategy. Also assess whether this option combination is a better strategy than simply buying a EUR call with a strike price of 1.70.

3. **Call Option Delta.** Consider European-type call options on BRL traded in OTC markets with a maturity of one year and a strike price of USD 0.62. You have the following additional information: BRLUSD spot = 0.65; risk-free interest rates (continuously compounded) denominated in the USD and BRL are 2 percent and 12 percent, respectively. During the recent month, spot rates of BRLUSD have indicated a standard deviation (annualized) of 11 percent. Calculate delta. Explain the importance of this concept. Do you think that this option has high or low sensitivity to the underlying currency?

4. **Comparison of Call Option Delta.** Redo problem 3 using (a) BRLUSD spot = 0.55 and (b) BRLUSD spot = 0.62. Compare resulting deltas. What is your inference? Can you explain your results?

5. **Put Options Delta.** Consider European-type put options on INR traded in OTC markets with a maturity of one year and a strike price of USD 0.02. You have the following additional information: INRUSD spot = 0.018; risk-free interest rates (continuously compounded) denominated in the USD and INR are 3 percent and 9 percent, respectively. During the recent month, spot rates of INRUSD have indicated a standard deviation (annualized) of 13 percent. Calculate put option price and delta. What is your judgment about this option's sensitivity to the underlying currency? Using delta, estimate the change in the value of the put if the INR decreases in value by USD 0.001.

6. **Option Combination.** Call options enable holders to make money when the underlying currency rises in value. Put options enable holders to make money when the underlying currency falls in value. An investor holding both calls and puts can therefore make money under both conditions (rising or falling markets). Evaluate the preceding statements by using the following two options: (a) EUR call with strike price of USD 1.50 and a premium of USD 0.02 and (b) a EUR put with a strike price of USD 1.50 and a premium of USD 0.03. Construct a spreadsheet, and use values of EURUSD ranging from 1.20 to 1.80 in 0.05 increments. Calculate profits and graph results (profit versus spot rate).

7. **Option Delta.** Bill Wicker, a financial analyst with an MNC, obtains the following time-series data on a currency and an option on that currency (see table on the next page). Fill in the blanks to determine the daily delta and average delta. Note that the change column represents the difference between current day and previous day values. Delta is the ratio of the two changes as explained in Appendix 3B. Based on your results, can you determine

whether the option is a call or a put? What is the approximate strike price? Input these data in a spreadsheet. Use regression analysis (or the slope function) to calculate the sensitivity between option price changes and currency value changes, and comment on your result.

Time-Series Data

| Day | Currency | | Option | | Delta |
	FX Spot	Change	Option Premium	Change	
1	1.515	N/A	0.052	N/A	N/A
2	1.517	?	0.053	?	?
3	1.522	?	0.055	?	?
4	1.515	?	0.051	?	?
5	1.502	?	0.045	?	?
6	1.492	?	0.041	?	?
Average					?

Case

Clover Machines: *Building Derivatives Capability*

Brian Bent, CFO of Clover Machines, expects that when foreign revenues reach 20 percent of all revenues, Clover would be exposed to significant currency risk. It is well known that currency derivatives are important to manage currency risk. Therefore, he wishes to develop organizational capacity to work with derivatives.

Based on Clover's expansion plans, currencies of interest include EUR, BRL, RUB, INR, and CNY representing the currencies of the Eurozone, Brazil, Russia, India, and China, respectively. Internally, Mr. Bent refers to these currencies collectively as the *EBRIC currencies.*

Three instruments are of particular interest to Mr. Bent: currency puts, currency calls, and currency futures. When the firm receives revenues in foreign currencies, currency options (puts in particular) as well as currency futures may be used to unload currencies at favorable rates. This would allow Clover to focus on its core competency of producing and selling the finest agricultural and construction machines.

Based on cursory evidence (CME statistics, for instance), most of the volume of option trading is concentrated in the major currencies of EUR, GBP, CAD, CHF, and JPY. Mr. Bent is concerned that options on BRIC currencies are not widely traded. Thin trading causes many problems, one of which is the unreliability of quoted prices. This problem in particular requires firms to build competencies in pricing derivatives because market prices cannot be trusted.

Just that day—July 1, 2008—Mr. Bent had observed market quotes on BRL options (see Case Exhibit 3.1) traded on the CME. Volume stats published by the CME (see http://www.cmegroup.com/tools-information/build-a-report.html?report=dailybulletin) indicate a much lower volume for these options. He wondered about the validity of these quotes.

Mr. Bent meets with a financial analyst, Julia Neat, and poses the following questions to her:

1. Which exchanges list BRIC currency options? How does their trading volume compare against major currency option volume? What are trends? (This requires Web-based research.)
2. What is the pricing formula for currency call options? What are the inputs? What are the difficulties in determining inputs? What are the sources of information one can use?

CASE EXHIBIT 3.1
Market Quotes on BRL Options, July 1, 2008

Currency (spot = 0.6282)	August Options (60 days)	Strike	Settlement Price
BRL	Call	6100	0.0164
BRL	Call	6200	0.0112
BRL	Put	6100	0.0100
BRL	Put	6200	0.0124

3. What is the pricing formula for currency put options? What are the implementation issues?

4. Estimate model prices for calls and puts indicated in Case Exhibit 3.1. Assume that the options are for 60 days, the spot is 0.6282, and options are European type. Assume that interest rates (continuous compounding) for USD and BRL are 2.5 percent and 13 percent, respectively. Use historical currency data in Case Exhibit 3.2 to calculate currency sigma.

5. Clover would likely use put options with a strike price of 0.6100 to help protect future revenues denominated in BRL. Explain the pros and cons of using 0.6100 puts rather than 0.6100 calls to achieve the same purpose.

6. What is the volatility estimate implicit in the 6100 call option? [*Hint:* Use the goal seek feature in Excel.] What is a possible rationale? [*Hint:* Estimate volatility using different data subsets such as most recent 12 months or most recent 6 months to see whether markets are focused on short-term or long-term volatility effects or whether any trends exist.]

7. Estimate the futures price for the same maturity. Explain the pros and cons of using put options compared to futures in protecting future BRL revenues.

8. Explain the effect of high Brazilian interest rates on both option and futures prices.

Ms. Neat sets out to answer these questions and produce a brief report (see Case Exhibit 3.2). Please help her in this task.

CASE EXHIBIT 3.2
BRLUSD Spot

Source: *oanda.com.*

Date	Interbank Rate
2007	
January 1	0.4689
February 1	0.4708
March 1	0.4709
April 1	0.4866
May 1	0.4926
June 1	0.5174
July 1	0.5188
August 1	0.5350
September 1	0.5091
October 1	0.5449
November 1	0.5739
December 1	0.5615
2008	
January 1	0.5724
February 1	0.5684
March 1	0.5968
April 1	0.5735
May 1	0.5890
June 1	0.6158
July 1	0.6282

Appendix 3A

Forward Pricing Theory

In this appendix, we explain general principles for pricing forwards. The basic idea is that forward prices are simply future values of the current value of the underlying asset (spot price). This simple relationship assumes no frictions (taxes, transaction costs, storage costs, insurance fees) and that the underlying asset itself does not have any special cash flows (interest payments, dividends) associated with it.

Suppose gold trades in the spot market for USD 1,000. Assume that a trader can finance the purchase of an ounce of gold at a rate of 10 percent. Thus, the total cost of this purchase over an interval of one year is USD 1,000 × (1 + 10%), or USD 1,100. If the forward price is USD 1,120, the trader can use the forward contract to sell the gold for USD 1,120 while incurring a total cost of only USD 1,100. Thus, the trader's profit equals USD 20. If the symbols F, S, and r are used to denote the forward price, spot price, and interest rate, respectively, the profit to this strategy is given by:

$$\text{Profit} = F - S \times (1 + r)^t$$
$$= 1,120 - 1,000 \times (1 + 10\%)^1$$
$$= \text{USD } 20$$

In well-functioning markets, this profit potential should not exist because it is obtained without any risk or investment. A profit obtained in this way is known as *arbitrage profits*. Should this arbitrage profit potential exist, traders will conduct this transaction enough times so that ultimately, the spot price will increase and the forward price will decrease to squeeze out the profit potential. To what level must the forward price fall to eliminate this profit? From the preceding calculation, we note that if the forward price falls to USD 1,100, the arbitrage profit is eliminated. Thus, in equilibrium, the forward price should equal the spot price plus the interest cost. Mathematically,

$$F = S \times (1 + r)^t$$

This formula readily applies to most forward contracts. A minor adjustment has to be made in the case of currency forwards. A trader who obtains a certain amount of a foreign currency today, unlike gold, can deposit the currency to earn interest. The interest earned on the foreign currency will offset the interest cost of funding the purchase of the foreign currency. Thus, the net interest cost must be used to determine the forward price of a currency. If the interest rate on the local currency is higher than the interest rate on the foreign currency, the interest cost will be higher than the interest earned. This results in the forward price being higher than the spot price. However, if the foreign interest rate is higher than the domestic interest rate, the opposite result occurs, and the forward price is lower than the spot price.

The formula to calculate the forward price of a currency is:

$$F = S \times \left[\frac{1 + r}{1 + r^*}\right]^t$$

Here r^* is the interest rate in the currency bought using the forward contract.

The forward premium or discount FP is the percent by which F differs from S. It is calculated by dividing the preceding equation with S and subtracting 1:

$$FP = \frac{F}{S} - 1 = \left[\frac{1 + r}{1 + r^*}\right]^t - 1$$

The derivation of the currency forward price is explained in greater detail in Chapter 5 where we discuss the *interest rate parity* theory.

Appendix 3B

Option Delta

An option's delta is a measure of its sensitivity relative to the underlying asset. Formally,

$$\text{Option delta} = \frac{\text{Change in option price}}{\text{Change in currency value}} = \frac{\Delta C}{\Delta S}$$

EXAMPLE 3.11

Consider the example of three EUR call options with varying strike prices. One is in the money ($X = 1.50$), one is at the money ($X = 1.55$) and the other is out of the money ($X = 1.60$). A manager wishes to determine the delta of the options and uses the following values on the currency and the options as inputs. Calculate deltas for the three options.

Instrument	Price at Beginning of Week	Price at End of Week
EURUSD	1.55	1.60
EUR call option ($X = 1.50$)	0.07	0.11
EUR call option ($X = 1.55$)	0.03	0.06
EUR call option ($X = 1.60$)	0.01	0.02

Solution: The delta calculation for the first call option ($X = 1.50$) is given by

$$\text{Call option delta} = \frac{0.11 - 0.07}{1.60 - 1.55} = 0.80$$

Similarly, the deltas for the remaining two options are calculated to equal 0.60 and 0.20, respectively.

Discussion: Call option deltas range in value from zero to 1. In-the-money call options ($S > X$) have high deltas because of the high probability of exercise, and, therefore, changes in currency values matter a good deal. Out of-the-money call options ($S < X$) have low deltas because changes in currency values may not matter at all as long as the option is out of the money (*underwater*). At-the-money option deltas are moderately high.

There are two important implications:

1. Hedging requires high levels of sensitivity. This precludes the use of out-of-the-money options.
2. Hedging requires a careful assessment of the number of options required to offset a currency position. Deltas are key inputs to this calculation.

In practice, deltas for calls and puts are calculated directly from the currency option pricing formula as follows:

$$\text{Call option delta} = \frac{\Delta C}{\Delta S} = e^{-r^{*}t} \times N(d_1)$$

$$\text{Put option delta} = \frac{\Delta P}{\Delta S} = e^{-r^{*}t} \times (N(d_1) - 1)$$

CHAPTER FOUR

Currency Systems and Valuation

The global market for large commercial airplanes is dominated by U.S.-based Boeing and Europe-based EADS (parent of Airbus). During 2006–2007, the EUR appreciated against the USD by more than 25 percent. Airbus—with costs denominated in EUR and revenues in USD—faced adverse financial consequences. In contrast, Boeing profited from this situation. Why did the EUR rise in value against the USD? And why did the Chinese yuan (CNY) during the same time period remain virtually unchanged against the USD, increasing competitive pressure on U.S. and European firms? MNC financial managers need answers to these and other questions related to currency valuation. Knowledge of currency systems and valuation will help managers predict and manage cash flows more effectively.

In this book, we follow a two-step approach to currency valuation and cover various aspects of it in Chapters 4 and 5. As a first step, in this chapter, we explain currency systems and their history and provide a general discussion of how macroeconomic factors and other factors affect currency values. This discussion will help students understand answers to the two questions just posed: The rise of the EUR against the USD is best explained by macroeconomic factors, while the unchanged value of CNY against the USD is best explained by the currency system designed and enforced by the Chinese government. Later, in Chapter 5, we show formulas explicitly linking currency values to macroeconomic factors such as interest rates and inflation and demonstrate the use of these formulas in currency forecasting.

The modern history of currency systems offers insight into many defining moments such as the development of the European Union and the emerging markets crisis of 1997–1998. This insight enables MNC managers to better understand the global environment and prepare for challenges ahead. To this end, in this chapter, we start with the history of currency systems and proceed to discuss factors affecting currency values. We discuss market forces as well government intervention as influencers of currency values. This chapter provides a global perspective of all factors affecting currencies.

More specifically, we discuss the following topics in this chapter:

- A brief history of the international monetary system, highlighting the move toward floating currency systems.
- A description of currency systems belonging to the continuum of fixed to floating.
- A discussion of how currency values are determined in general followed by a description of specific factors affecting currency values.
- The reasons for governments to intervene in currency markets and the mechanisms governments use to raise or lower currency values.
- The importance of currency stability for global economic health.

4.1 A Brief History of Monetary Regimes

Today we live in a world in which most currencies that we commonly encounter—the U.S. dollar (USD), the British pound (GBP), the euro (EUR), the Swiss franc (CHF), and the Canadian dollar (CAD)—are freely floating with market forces determining their values. Furthermore, we have systems in place including national central banks such as the U.S. Federal Reserve and international organizations such as the **International Monetary Fund (IMF)** to oversee the health of the global monetary system. How did we arrive at such arrangements for currencies and systems to oversee the currency markets? What social, economic, and political forces led us in this direction? To provide a partial answer to these questions, in this section, we sketch a brief history of the International Monetary System.

Gold Standard

Humankind had valued gold since ancient times—principally because of its beauty and rarity—and used the metal for economic contracting. The ultimate use of gold was as a currency. The use of gold as currency, known as the **gold standard**, simply follows the age-old tradition of using valuable commodities as money. Gold simply lent itself very well to such use because of its compactness, rarity, and value. The use of gold as currency changed over time from its initial use as the material for coins (enabling easy conversion to value by melting) and later to use as collateral to support the value of coins made of other material.

While the history of gold as money is interesting and fascinating, we confine our attention to the emergence of the so-called *classical gold standard* in the 1870s when major nations such as United States, Germany, and France adopted the use of gold to back their currencies. Prior to this era, nations were almost equally divided into three monetary regimes: gold, silver, and bimetallism (gold as well as silver). Various difficulties in the use of silver (volatility, rising production, transportation, and storage costs) as well as the need to harmonize for the sake of trade led to the classical gold standard. See Exhibit 4.1 showing the pattern of gold standard adoption. Most nations had adopted it by 1905.

This classical gold standard era of 1870–1910 coincided with the emergence of monetary unions such as the Scandinavian and Latin monetary unions in Europe. Scholars believe that these developments are related and perhaps are causes of the dramatic increase in trade in the latter half of the 19th century.[1] Events during this time are interesting parallels to events in Europe a century later that led to the European Monetary Union.

How are currency exchange rates obtained under the gold standard? Countries assess the value of their currencies in terms of gold per currency unit. By comparing the amount of gold that can be purchased by two currencies, the implied exchange rate known as the *mint parity rate* is determined.

EXAMPLE 4.1

The Bank of England equates a GBP at 112.982 grams.[2] The United States equates a USD at 23.22 grams. What is the mint parity rate from the Bank of England's perspective?

Solution: The *mint parity rate* is the implied exchange rate between the two currencies. By comparing the amount of gold that can be purchased by the two currencies—GBP and USD—the exchange rate GBPUSD can be determined. This procedure is similar to finding a cross-rate.

$$\text{Mint parity rate GBPUSD} = \frac{112.982}{23.22} = 4.87$$

---

gold standard
Under the *gold standard*, countries can maintain currency values by importing and exporting gold.

How are currency rates enforced? Under the gold standard, central banks define gold points—a pair of threshold values that trigger export or import of gold. The gold points bracket the mint parity rate. The dispersion around the mint parity rate is usually determined

---

[1] J. Lopez-Cordova and C. Meissner, "Exchange Rate Regimes and International Trade: Evidence from the Classical Gold Standard Era," *American Economic Review* 93, no. 1 (2003), pp. 344–353.

[2] Michael Bordo, Owen Humpage, and Anna Schwartz, "The Historical Origins of US Exchange Market Intervention Policy," *International Journal of Finance and Economics* 12 (2007), pp. 109–132. See footnote 2 for the numerical example discussed here.

EXHIBIT 4.1   **Classical Gold Standard (1870–1910)**

Source: J. Lopez-Cordova and C. Meissner, "Exchange Rate Regimes and International Trade: Evidence from the Classical Gold Standard Era,"
American Economic Review 93, no. 1 (2003), pp. 344–353.

Country	Monetary Union Country (MU)	1870	1875	1880	1885	1890	1895	1900	1905	1910
							Year			
United Kingdom	Sterling union	Gold	Gold	Gold	Gold	Gold	Gold	Gold	Gold	Gold
Australia	Sterling union	Gold	Gold	Gold	Gold	Gold	Gold	Gold	Gold	Gold
New Zealand	Sterling union	Gold	Gold	Gold	Gold	Gold	Gold	Gold	Gold	Gold
Canada	Sterling, U.S./Canada	Gold	Gold	Gold	Gold	Gold	Gold	Gold	Gold	Gold
United States	U.S./Canada	Paper	Paper	Gold	Gold	Gold	Gold	Gold	Gold	Gold
France	Latin MU	Bimetal	Bimetal	Gold	Gold	Gold	Gold	Gold	Gold	Gold
Belgium	Latin MU	Bimetal	Bimetal	Gold	Gold	Gold	Gold	Gold	Gold	Gold
Switzerland	Latin MU	—	—	—	—	—	—	Gold	Gold	Gold
Italy	Latin MU	Paper	Paper	Paper	Paper	Paper	Paper	Paper	Paper	Paper
Denmark	Scandinavian MU	Silver	Gold	Gold	Gold	Gold	Gold	Gold	Gold	Gold
Norway	Scandinavian MU	Silver	Gold	Gold	Gold	Gold	Gold	Gold	Gold	Gold
Sweden	Scandinavian MU	Silver	Gold	Gold	Gold	Gold	Gold	Gold	Gold	Gold
Germany		Silver	Gold	Gold	Gold	Gold	Gold	Gold	Gold	Gold
Netherlands		Silver	Gold	Gold	Gold	Gold	Gold	Gold	Gold	Gold
Finland		Silver	Silver	Gold	—	—	—	—	Gold	Gold
Austria		Paper	—	—	—	—	—	Paper	—	—
Russia		Paper	—	—	—	Paper	—	Gold	—	—
Spain		Bimetal	—	—	—	Paper	—	Paper	Paper	Paper
Portugal		Gold	—	—	—	Gold	—	Paper	—	—
Japan		Silver	—	—	Paper	Silver	Silver	Gold	Gold	Gold
Brazil		Paper	—	—	—	Paper	—	Paper	Paper	Gold
Mexico		Silver	—	—	—	Silver	—	Silver	Gold	Gold
Chile		—	—	—	—	—	—	Paper	Paper	Paper
Argentina		—	—	—	—	Paper	—	Paper	Gold	Gold
Egypt		—	—	—	—	—	—	Gold	—	—
India		Silver	—	—	—	—	Silver	Gold	Gold	Gold
China		Silver	—	—	—	—	—	Silver	—	—
Indonesia		—	—	—	—	Silver	—	Silver	Silver	Silver
Philippines		—	—	—	—	—	—	Silver	—	—

by shipping costs. If the market exchange rate dips below the export point, a country exports gold. If the market exchange rate exceeds the import point, the country imports gold. Consider the previous example in which we estimated a mint parity rate of GBPUSD 4.87. Suppose the Bank of England estimates shipping costs of gold to be 1 percent of 1 USD. This implies a gold export point of 4.82 (fewer USD per GBP, or weak-pound scenario) and a gold import point of 4.92 (more USD per GBP or strong-pound scenario). When a currency strengthens, gold is bought to counter this appreciation. When a currency weakens, gold is sold to counter the weakness. Thus, cross-border gold flows discipline exchange rates.[3]

World War I brought about the collapse of the gold standard system in 1915. European countries, in particular, experienced very high rates of inflation, making it impossible to maintain the fixed currency values necessary for the gold standard. Furthermore, this war marked

---

[3] Cross-border gold flows also serve to correct balance of payments imbalances. Countries running deficits would lose gold and countries with surpluses would gain gold. In surplus countries, gold inflows increase money supply. In turn, inflation rises and stymies exports. The opposite occurs in the case of deficit countries that have an outflow of gold; consequently, money supply shrinks, rates increase, and capital flows in from deficit countries. See Bordo, Humpage, and Schwartz (2007), footnote 1.

a turning point in the fortunes of England. The preeminence of England and its currency, the GBP, was lost. The United States emerged as the most important global power. Oversight of the USD was entrusted to a brand-new institution created by the 1913 Federal Reserve Act: the Federal Reserve Bank.

Bretton Woods Agreement

Following the uncertainty during the years between the two World Wars and the calamity brought about by World War II, the major powers started the task of rebuilding the international monetary system. The **Bretton Woods** conference of 1944 had two important objectives. First, it was important that countries cooperate with one another and make their currencies freely convertible. Second, it was vital that currency values have some stability. To meet these goals, the gold standard was in effect reintroduced along with a system to maintain orderly currency markets.

The key provisions of the Bretton Woods agreement of 1944 are as follows:

- The U.S. currency became the key international currency, and its value was linked to gold at a price of USD 35 per ounce.
- The U.S. central bank held gold reserves to protect the value of the USD and to permit the conversion of USD into gold by any entity.
- Other central banks held gold along with key currencies such as the USD and GBP with the objective of maintaining the value of their currencies.
- A new institution called the *International Monetary Fund (IMF)* was created with the objective of overseeing the world monetary markets. The IMF was expected to provide financing to countries experiencing temporary balance of payments difficulties as a result of imbalances between exports and imports of goods and services.
- Provisions were made for periodic assessment of currency values and for making adjustments to keep the global monetary system in balance.

Bretton Woods
The *Bretton Woods* agreement achieved current account convertibility and facilitated trade among major western nations.

The Bretton Woods system was successful. It paved the way for the economic development of many countries during the 1950s and 1960s. One of the major objectives of Bretton Woods was **current account convertibility**—the convertibility of currencies for conducting trade. This step was perceived as essential to the reconstruction of postwar economies. For major industrial nations—United States, United Kingdom, France, and Germany—convertibility was accomplished by 1958. The 1944–1958 era is viewed as an important milestone in the development of the modern global economy. As discussed in Chapter 1, trade is often the first step in globalization.

The second major objective of the Bretton Woods conference was the stability of currency rates revolving around the USD, which in turn was pegged to gold. This objective was largely realized by the 1960s. By this time, another fortuitous development was the elimination of most forms of **capital controls**—taxes and other impediments to flows of capital—by industrial nations. The resulting cross-border movement of capital (foreign direct investment (FDI) or portfolio investments) include (1) cross-border investments in financial securities such as stocks and bonds, (2) the cross-border expansion of business activity by investments in assets such as plant and equipment, and (3) cross-border acquisitions of real assets such as land and mineral rights. The free movement of capital is now recognized as the most important fuel for global economic growth. For instance, in countries such as China, economic activity has been fueled in recent years by inbound FDI.

One black cloud, however, emerged in the 1960s. At that time, the United States was running large balance of payments deficits.[4] This was mainly due to an overvalued USD. The price of gold—fixed at USD 35 per ounce—was too low. The overvalued USD dampened U.S. exports and increased U.S. imports. This led to increased holdings of USD by external entities to a level far exceeding U.S. gold holdings (see Exhibit 4.2). The United States was no longer in a position to fulfill its promise of selling gold at the official price. This ultimately led to the collapse of the Bretton Woods system.

---

[4] Chapter 13 discusses trade issues, including trade statistics such as balance of payments.

EXHIBIT 4.2
External Dollar Liabilities and Gold Stock

Source: Michael Bordo, Owen Humpage, and Anna Schwartz, "The Historical Origins of US Exchange Market Intervention Policy," *International Journal of Finance and Economics* 12 (2007), pp. 109–132.

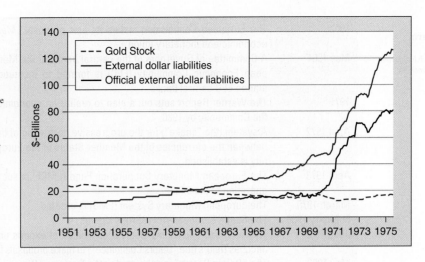

Smithsonian Agreement

Events during 1969–1973 resulted in the dismantling of the Bretton Woods agreement.[5] During this period, the United States, France, and the United Kingdom had weaker economies compared to Germany and Japan. The weaker economies were characterized by lower economic growth, lower exports, higher imports, higher inflation, and outflow of the national currency. Although a whole host of nations were affected by this crisis, the two principal actors were the United States and Germany. These nations were troubled by the excessive flow of USD into Germany; this was caused by trade imbalance between these two nations (the United States imported more than it exported) as well as speculation that the German currency eventually would have to be revalued higher.

Germany and the United States both took unilateral actions to alleviate the crisis. Germany—much to the chagrin of its European partners—experimented with floating its currency in 1969 and again in 1971. The United States arguably took the most precipitous action: In April 1971, it announced the closing of the "gold window" (USD would no longer be converted into gold) as well as a 10 percent tax on imports. The U.S. steps in particular deepened the crisis. In an attempt to resolve it, 10 leading nations (the largest contributors to the IMF) came together and signed the **Smithsonian agreement** in December 1971. The Smithsonian agreement essentially resurrected the gold standard but revised the exchange rates (mint parities). To relieve pressure on the USD, the currency-gold ratio was set at USD 38 per ounce (compared to the earlier rate of USD 35). The values of certain currencies such as the German mark also were reset against the USD. Finally, the United States eliminated the import tax that was essentially used as a bargaining chip.

Smithsonian agreement
Signed in 1971 in response to a currency crisis faced by the United States and other nations. The Smithsonian agreement attempted to resurrect the gold standard, but the rapid breakdown of the agreement ultimately paved the way for major western nations to float their currencies.

The Smithsonian agreement was essentially a quick fix. It did not address the fundamental economic problems arising from fixed currency values in a fast-changing world. It did not take long for other crises to erupt (e.g., the GBP crisis in June 1972). Fixed currency regimes fell like dominoes, and by the end of 1973, most major western currencies were floating.

The post-Smithsonian era was an exciting time for globalization. This period was characterized by the following:

- Explosive growth in global trade and the emergence of global trading agreements. The WTO and NAFTA are examples of this trend.

- The emergence of the USD as the preeminent currency. This parallels the eminence the British pound had enjoyed in the last century. Most global contracts today are in terms of the USD.

- The increasing integration of developing countries in the global economy.

- Current account convertibility between all industrial nations and most developing nations.

- The dismantling of capital controls, especially between the major industrial nations.

[5] William Gray, "Floating the System: Germany, the United States, and the Breakdown of Bretton Woods, 1969–1973," *Diplomatic History* 31, no. 2 (2007), pp. 295–323.

EXHIBIT 4.3
Road to the Euro

Source: *http://www.ecb.int/pub/pdf/
other/ecbhistoryrolefunctions
.2006en.pdf*

1962	The European Commission makes its first proposal (*Marjolin Memorandum*) for economic and monetary union.
May 1964	A Committee of Governors of the central banks of the Member States of the European Economic Community (EEC) is formed to institutionalize the cooperation among EEC central banks.
1971	The Werner Report sets out a plan to realize an economic and monetary union in the Community by 1980.
April 1972	A system (the "snake") for the progressive narrowing of the margins of fluctuation between the currencies of the Member States of the European Economic Community is established.
April 1973	The European Monetary Cooperation Fund (EMCF) is set up to ensure the proper operation of the snake.
March 1979	The European Monetary System (EMS) is created.
February 1986	The Single European Act (SEA) is signed.
June 1988	The European Council mandates a committee of experts under the chairmanship of Jacques Delors (the "Delors Committee") to make proposals for the realization of EMU.
May 1989	The "Delors Report" is submitted to the European Council.
June 1989	The European Council agrees on the realization of EMU in three stages.
July 1990	Stage One of EMU begins.
December 1990	An Intergovernmental Conference to prepare for Stages Two and Three of EMU is launched.
February 1992	The Treaty on European Union (the "Maastricht Treaty") is signed.
October 1993	Frankfurt am Main is chosen as the seat of the EMI and of the ECB and a President of the EMI is nominated.
November 1993	The Treaty on European Union enters into force.
December 1993	Alexandre Lamfalussy is appointed as President of the EMI, to be established on 1 January 1994.
January 1994	Stage Two of EMU begins and the EMI is established.
December 1995	The Madrid European Council decides on the name of the single currency and sets out the scenario for its adoption and the cash changeover.
December 1996	The EMI presents specimen euro banknotes to the European Council.
June 1997	The European Council agrees on the Stability and Growth Pact.
May 1998	Belgium, Germany, Spain, France, Ireland, Italy, Luxembourg, the Netherlands, Austria, Portugal and Finland are considered to fulfill the necessary conditions for the adoption of the euro as their single currency; the Members of the Executive Board of the ECB are appointed.
June 1998	The ECB and the ESCB are established.
October 1998	The ECB announces the strategy and the operational framework for the single monetary policy it will conduct from 1 January 1999.
January 1999	Stage Three of EMU begins; the euro becomes the single currency of the euro area; conversion rates are fixed irrevocably for the former national currencies of the participating Member States; a single monetary policy is conducted for the euro area.

The European Monetary Union

In the tradition of the monetary unions of the 19th century such as the Latin and Scandinavian monetary unions, but on a much larger scale, the European Monetary Union (EMU) of the 20th century brought together most nations in Europe. This is one of the most significant economic events of recent times. We next focus on one particular aspect of this union: the EUR.

Origins

EUR
Starting with the 1957 Treaty of Rome, European nations took steps to integrate their monetary systems, and this ultimately led to the creation of the single currency (*EUR*) in 1999.

The origins of the **European Monetary Union (EMU)** lie in the Treaty of Rome in 1957 and the creation of the European Commission in 1967. EMU refers to the integration of the monetary systems of nations comprising the European Commission. Initially, EMU had limited objectives such as coordination of exchange rates. For instance, in order to attain objectives of economic and monetary union, in 1971 member states created as a first step a "snake" mechanism to link the exchange rates of various currency pairs. The snake turned out to be a limited success linking successfully only a few currencies. The subsequent push came about with the creation of the *European Monetary System (EMS)* in 1979 (see Exhibit 4.3). This revitalized the snake system. Also, a new pseudocurrency, the European currency unit (ECU), was created. Initially, the ECU was to be used in official transactions including those between various central banks. The ECU was the precursor to the EUR.

Monetary Integration

The broader objective of the EMS was to coordinate monetary policies. Exchange rate stability thus was only one of many objectives. Inflation abatement and convergence of economic performance among member states was perhaps a more important objective. These steps produced the conditions for the EUR (See Exhibit 4.4 for a famous theory concerning the use of a single currency for a region). Along the way, in 1987, the Single European Act unified European markets. Thus, European integration was being achieved at many different levels with monetary union being one of many components.

Maastricht Treaty

The Delors Report of 1989 was the impetus for renegotiating and strengthening the treaty between member states. Among other things, this report provided a roadmap for achieving monetary union. It called for irrevocably locking exchange rates and creating institutions to oversee monetary policies. The recommendations of the Delors Report were embedded in the Maastricht Treaty of 1992. This treaty—in effect since November 1993—formally created the **European Union (EU)**. A component of overall union is the *European Monetary Union (EMU)*. The **European Central Bank (ECB)** was created as an oversight authority.[6]

EXHIBIT 4.4
Robert Mundell and the Optimum Currency Area

Given the obvious fixed costs of managing a currency (that is, the country needs an infrastructure for maintaining monetary policy) and the transaction costs incurred for cross-border transactions, it might make sense for a collection of countries to adopt a single currency. What are preconditions for such adoption? Economist Robert Mundell won the 1999 Nobel Prize in part for his answer to this question. In a famous paper published in 1961, Mundell[7] stated the fundamental condition as follows: "If the world can be divided into regions within each of which there is factor mobility and between which there is factor immobility, then each of these regions should have a separate currency which fluctuates relative to all other currencies." Among other things, this means that if labor is free to move about in an area, it might make sense to have a common currency for that area. It is debatable whether the EU satisfied this condition when it adopted the EUR as its single currency.

In later works, Mundell deepened his analysis to provide other insights about having a common currency. One interesting insight is that a larger currency area could mitigate the effects of "shocks" in a particular region because of the pooling of reserves and the resulting risk mitigation. According to Mundell[8]: "A harvest failure, strikes, or war, in one of the countries causes a loss of real income, but the use of a common currency (or foreign exchange reserves) allows the country to run down its currency holdings and cushion the impact of the loss, drawing on the resources of the other country until the cost of the adjustment has been efficiently spread over the future. If, on the other hand, the two countries use separate monies with flexible exchange rates, the whole loss has to be borne alone; the common currency cannot serve as a shock absorber for the nation as a whole except insofar as the dumping of inconvertible currencies on foreign markets attracts a speculative capital inflow in favor of the depreciating currency."

---

[6] For a complete discussion of this history, see *European Central Bank: History, Role and Functions* available from http://www.ecb.int/pub/pdf/other/ecbhistoryrolefunctions2006en.pdf.

[7] R.A. Mundell, "A Theory of Optimum Currency Areas." *American Economic Review* 51 (1961), pp. 509–517.

[8] R.A. Mundell, "Uncommon Arguments for Common Currencies." *The Economics of Common Currencies*, ed. H.G. Johnson and A.K. Swoboda (London: Allen and Unwin, 1973), pp. 114–132.

Birth of the EUR

One may consider the EUR to be the logical consequence of this chain of events. EMU was planned to take place in three steps. Step 1 included preparatory items such as freeing capital flows between member states. Step 2 focused on economic convergence in order to create a level playing field. Step 3 concluded with the introduction of a single currency and conduct of monetary policy by a single entity (ECB). In fact, the EUR was introduced as a currency for settling accounts in January 1, 1999. At this time, the exchange rate between the EUR and national currencies such as the lira and mark was irrevocably fixed. Notes and coins were later issued on January 1, 2002.

Implications for MNCs

EUR and MNCs
The introduction of the *EUR* profoundly impacted MNCs with operations in Europe by reducing transaction costs and by making their pricing policies transparent.

The introduction of the EUR changed the landscape for MNCs operating in Europe. There were positive as well as negative effects. One major positive effect was the reduction in transaction costs. A negative effect on MNCs—arguably a positive for European consumers—was the increase in price transparency: Firms could no longer blatantly use different prices in different markets. But the implications of the EUR go far beyond these initial "conduct-of-business" or operating effects. One notable effect was the increasing role of the EUR in financial contracting, such as the trend to denominate corporate debt instruments in the EUR. Thus, the EUR's introduction has financing as well as operating consequences for MNCs.

4.2 Contemporary Currency Systems

Nations manage their currencies using various systems that form a continuum. At one extreme, a currency can be fixed and invariable in value. This is known as the **fixed currency system**. However, the term *fixed* can be a little confusing because value is itself a relative concept. When a person places a value on an asset, not only is the value explicitly linked to another asset such as a currency but also the value is implicitly benchmarked or *anchored* to other assets. Thus, fixing the value of a currency requires the selection of an *anchor*. Commonly used anchors include commodities such as gold or even other currencies. The key feature of an anchor is its stability. Gold is perceived as a good anchor because it is a precious metal and its supply is constrained. While countries no longer use gold or other commodities as anchors, they sometimes *peg* their currencies to leading currencies such the USD and EUR. The so-called *pegged currency systems* are the modern day versions of fixed systems.

At the other extreme, a currency can be allowed to float in accordance with market forces of supply and demand. This is known as the **floating currency system**. A pure floating system—with zero management by governments—is perhaps not encountered in the world today. Instead, floating currency systems tend to fall in two categories based on whether "management activities" are occasional or frequent. In a later section, we describe how governments manage currency values through intervention.

IMF Classification of Currency Systems

In its publications describing global currency systems, the IMF uses the following classifications (see Exhibit 4.5).

Currency Board Arrangements

The currency board arrangements represent the highest level of rigidity. The country passes legislation that forces monetary authorities to issue currency only against reserves of a foreign currency. Thus, the two currencies maintained a fixed rate of exchange. Traditional central banking functions are de facto outsourced to the country of the peg. Few countries follow this system today, a prominent example being Hong Kong.

Conventional Fixed Peg Arrangements

While not as rigid as currency board arrangements, conventional fixed pegs are almost as rigid, requiring a country to maintain its currency relative to an anchor currency or composite (e.g., trade weight mix of currencies) and only allow a narrow band of ±1 percent. In most

fixed systems
Variations of the *fixed currency system* (currency boards, pegs) tend to be used by smaller or weaker economies.

cases, the anchor is either the USD or EUR. The conventional fixed peg is a popular system. Most Caribbean, African, and Middle Eastern countries as well as some Asian countries use a conventional fixed peg arrangement. Prominent examples are Saudi Arabia and China.

Pegged Exchange Rates within Horizontal Bands

This represents a slightly looser peg, and the band is often in the range of 1 to 2 percent. Not too many countries follow this system, possibly because it is best not to have a peg if it cannot be adhered to. Denmark, Hungary, and the Slovak Republic, for example, follow it.

Crawling Pegs

The currency value is adjusted in small amounts at a fixed rate. The adjustments may be preset or triggered by macroindicators such as inflation. This is not a popular system. Iran and Costa Rica are examples of users.

Managed Floating

In this system, monetary authorities manage currencies actively. Indicators for managing the exchange rate are broadly judgmental (e.g., balance of payments position, international reserves, parallel market developments), and adjustments may not be automatic. Direct and indirect methods of intervention are employed. This is a popular method. Countries that use it include Russia, Argentina, Thailand, Malaysia, and Singapore.

Independent Floating

Market forces primarily set the exchange rate. Any official foreign exchange market intervention is aimed at moderating the rate of change and preventing undue fluctuations in the exchange rate rather than at establishing a level for it. Major currencies such as the USD, EUR, JPY, GBP, and CHF belong to this category. We increasingly find currencies of emerging economies such as Turkey and Brazil in this list.

We next explain these systems in more detail by focusing on two broad categories: floating and fixed.

Floating Currency Systems

Floating currency systems—managed or independent—require the highest level of investments as well as confidence in the monetary and market infrastructures. An independent central bank such as the U.S. Federal Reserve is required to monitor the market situation and intervene if necessary. The currency market should be large and liquid. The country should also have an open economy with a set of "shock absorbers." Flexibility in labor markets, mobility of capital, and other elements of flexibility are essential. Most industrialized nations such as the United States, United Kingdom, and Japan adopt floating currency systems because they have this infrastructure in place.

One interesting development is the enlargement in the list of countries with floating currency systems (see Exhibit 4.5). The IMF classification in 2006 indicates 51 countries with managed floating currencies and 25 countries with independent floating currencies. Although placed by the IMF in a separate category, the 12 Euro area nations should also be counted in the "floating" category. This adds to a total of 88 nations with floating currencies. This compares to a total of 70 countries with a pegged currency system (7 countries with currency boards, 52 with a fixed peg, and another 11 with other types of pegs).

floating currency systems
A *floating currency system* allows a country to flexibly manage its monetary system as well as its economy.

One reason the world is moving toward floating systems is that it allows countries to pursue independent macroeconomic policies. Thus, countries can optimize their monetary (money) supply and fiscal (government spending and taxation) policies to meet national priorities. A nation's central bank often conducts monetary policies, manipulates the money supply, and benchmarks interest rates. For example, a country facing sluggish economic growth may want to decrease its interest rates by increasing the money supply. An alternate solution is to use fiscal policy measures such as tax rebates. Both monetary and fiscal policies affect currencies, although a case can be made for the stronger effect of monetary policies because of their directness. A floating system accommodates such currency shifts, while a fixed system allows currency pressures to build up and potentially faces collapse.

EXHIBIT 4.5   **IMF Classification of Currency Systems**

Source: *http://www.imf.org/external/np/mfd/er/2006/eng/0706.htm.*

De Facto Exchange Rate Arrangements and Anchors of Monetary Policy as of July 31, 2006 1/

Exchange Rate Regime (Number of countries)	Monetary Policy Framework								
	Exchange rate anchor					Monetary aggregate target	Inflation targeting framework	IMF-supported or other monetary program	Other
Exchange arrangements with no separate legal tender (41)	Another currency as legal tender (9)	ECCU (6)	CFA franc zone (14)						Euro area (12)
			WAEMU	CAEMC					Austria
	Ecuador El Salvador Kiribati Marshall Islands Micronesia, Fed. States of Palau Panama San Marino Timor-Leste, Dem. Rep. of	Antigua and Barbuda Dominica Grenada St. Kitts and Nevis St. Lucia St. Vincent and the Grenadines	Benin Burkina Faso Côte d'Ivoire Guinea-Bissau Mali Niger Senegal Togo	Cameroon Central African Rep. Chad Congo, Rep. of Equatorial Guinea Gabon					Belgium Finland France Germany Greece Ireland Italy Luxembourg Netherlands Portugal Spain
Currency board arrangements (7)	Bosnia and Herzegovina Brunei Darussalam Bulgaria Hong Kong SAR Djibouti Estonia Lithuania								
Other conventional fixed peg arrangements (52)	Against a single currency (47)					China Guyana Sierra Leone Suriname			Pakistan
	Aruba Bahamas, The Bahrain, Kingdom of Barbados Belarus Belize Bhutan Bolivia Cape Verde China Comoros Egypt Eritrea Ethiopia Guyana Honduras Iraq Jordan Kuwait Latvia Lebanon Lesotho Macedonia, FYR Maldives		Malta Mauritania Namibia Nepal Netherlands Antilles Oman Pakistan Qatar Rwanda Saudi Arabia Seychelles Sierra Leone Solomon Islands Suriname Swaziland Syrian Arab Rep. Trinidad and Tobago Turkmenistan Ukraine United Arab Emirates Venezuela, Rep. Bolivariana de Vietnam Zimbabwe						

	Against a composite (5)					
	Fiji Libyan Arab Jamahiriya Morocco	Samoa Vanuatu				
Pegged exchange rates within horizontal bands (6)	**Within a cooperative arrangement (4)** Cyprus Denmark Slovak Rep. Slovenia	**Other band arrangements (2)** Hungary Tonga		Hungary Slovak Rep.		
Crawling pegs (5)	Azerbaijan Botswana Costa Rica Iran, I.R. of Nicaragua		Iran, I.R. of			
Managed floating with no pre-determined path for the exchange rate (51)			Argentina Bangladesh Cambodia Gambia, The Ghana Haiti Jamaica Lao P.D.R. Madagascar Malawi Mauritius Moldova Mongolia Sri Lanka Sudan Tajikistan Tunisia Uruguay Yemen, Rep. of Zambia	Colombia Czech Rep. Guatemala Peru Romania Serbia, Rep. of Thailand	Afghanistan, I.R. of Armenia Georgia Kenya Kyrgyz Rep. Mozambique	Algeria Angola Burundi Croatia Dominican Rep. Guinea India Kazakhstan Liberia Malaysia Myanmar Nigeria Papua New Guinea Paraguay Russian Federation São Tomé and Príncipe Singapore Uzbekistan
Independently floating (25)			Albania Congo, Dem. Rep. of Indonesia Uganda	Australia Brazil Canada Chile Iceland Israel Korea Mexico New Zealand Norway Philippines Poland South Africa Sweden Turkey United Kingdom	Tanzania	Japan Somalia Switzerland United States

ECCU: Eastern Caribbean Currency Union
WAEMU: West African Economic & Monetary Union
CAEMC: Central African Economic & Monetary Union

In general, floating currency systems offer several benefits:

- They allow monetary authorities to flexibly respond to the environment. Currency values can be used as tools to further national goals such as employment and inflation. This benefit is not available in fixed systems.
- An economy with multiple shock absorbers can weather economic storms better. For example, during the early part of the credit crisis of 2007–2008, the USD declined significantly against currencies such as the EUR, and this helped moderate the economic downturn. Later, the USD rose in value after the economy hit bottom and showed signs of upspring.
- A floating currency system avoids currency meltdowns experienced by countries such as Argentina. Fixed systems can sometimes be put under so much pressure that they break down.

Floating currency systems do have disadvantages. As mentioned earlier, nations have to invest in the requisite infrastructure. Also, firms incur transaction costs and risks from fluctuating currencies, a topic we cover in detail in Chapters 6 and 7. We note from the behavior of the USD against other floating currencies that there is considerable variation. Firms need to find mechanisms to cope with risks posed by currency changes.

In floating currency systems, investors and institutions may take currency positions in anticipation of future changes in the value of the currency. When such "front running" becomes widespread, currency volatility rises. In fact, some fear that speculation based on ill-informed expectations runs the risk of creating a self-fulfilling prophecy. Thus, if speculators attack a currency and expect it to fall in value, the speculators' very actions may cause the currency to crash. In extreme cases, excessive currency speculation has the potential to totally undermine a country's economy by discouraging economic activity. For example, if a country were to depend on loans from foreign sources, excessive currency volatility may discourage international investors. This is perhaps what happened to some countries during the emerging markets crisis of 1997–1998.

Pegged Currency Systems

Pegged currency systems are the modern version of fixed currency regimes. Under this system, countries link their currencies firmly to either a single currency or a portfolio of foreign currencies. The IMF identifies 70 countries that peg their currencies to other currencies, making pegged systems the most popular of currency systems. When using a typical pegged system, a country would fix its currency's value in relation to another currency, usually a stable currency such as the USD. A narrow band is established around this fixed value. Steps are then taken to ensure that the currency rate stays within this narrow band. (See Exhibit 4.6 for an extreme scenario where a country simply adopts another country's currency)

Advantages

Pegged systems are attractive because they offer a measure of discipline to countries with a historical track record of high inflation and governmental mismanagement of the economy. By pegging their currencies to a key currency, these countries are also forced to follow the macroeconomic policies of the other nation. It is important that inflation rates are controlled. A country that pegs its currency to the USD will have to control its inflation to a level close to U.S. inflation. Such economic discipline may ultimately offer economic as well as political stability to nations. There is another advantage. Pegged currency systems simplify the currency management problem. The institutional support required for pegged systems is less than that required for floating systems. Also, these countries do not need liquidity in their capital and currency markets, a prerequisite for a successful floating system.

EXHIBIT 4.6
Dollarization

Dollarization occurs when a country predominantly uses another country's currency (usually the USD but not always) as the medium of exchange in domestic transactions as well as the unit of measurement for various accounts. One might consider dollarization to be an extreme case of pegging one's currency to another currency. A country that pegs its currency to another currency maintains reserves of the foreign currency to support and define the value of its own currency. In contrast, a country that dollarizes simply uses the other currency in lieu of its own currency. Dollarization can occur with or without official sanction. In either case, it leads to large holdings of assets denominated in a foreign currency by a country's citizens. Dollarization is viewed as a panacea for the boom-bust cycles and overall instability suffered by small developing economies. It offers a more permanent solution compared to pegging. Recent examples of dollarized economies are Cambodia, Panama, Ecuador, and Zimbabwe. Most countries that dollarize are small and economically vulnerable, and in some cases (e.g., Zimbabwe) are failed states. Dollarization can provide these countries stability to attract foreign investment and to impact trade favorably. All of these benefits must be weighed against the opportunity cost of relinquishing the ability to print one's own money and to set one's own macroeconomic policy. These are conventional costs of dollarization, but recently in Zimbabwe, a fairly bizarre cost of dollarization was identified: Armed gangs of robbers residing in neighboring South Africa were lured to Zimbabwe by the hard currency to execute cross-border sallies!

Disadvantages

The disadvantage is that the country needs to maintain stable economic policies that mirror that of the peg country. Another disadvantage is that the peg has to be maintained through intervention from time to time. The strongest measure a country might adopt is a currency board that requires large reserves and the highest level of discipline. In a currency board scenario, the country is virtually unable to use monetary tools such as money supply and discount rate lending to control the economy.

Conditions Fostering the Use of a Pegged Currency System

According to the IMF, the following conditions support the adoption of a pegged currency system by a country:

- Low involvement with international capital markets.
- High level of trading with the country of the key currency.
- The two countries involved face similar shocks
- Willingness to give up monetary policy and rely on the monetary credibility of the other country.
- Current reliance of the economic and financial system on the key currency.
- High current inflation in the country, making exchange-rate-based stabilization attractive.
- Flexible labor markets.
- Flexible fiscal policy.
- Considerable international reserves held by the country

   This list suggests the following types of countries are most suitable for pegged systems:

- Small economies with a dominant trading partner that maintains a stable monetary policy.
- Developing countries facing considerable inflationary problems.
- Countries with transition economies aspiring for partnership/membership in unions such as the EU.

4.3 Currency Valuation Basics

A foreign currency is similar to any other asset. Its value or price is given by its exchange rate. Thus, when a U.S.-based MNC considers the purchase of EUR from a bank, a banker's quote of EURUSD 1.45 is a measure of the value the banker attaches to the currency. Keeping in mind that exchange rates are nothing but prices for currencies, we can start our analysis of the demand and supply for currencies. Like any other asset, the value of a currency is determined by its demand and supply. In this section, we provide an overview of how currency values are determined and how changes in values are calculated.

Currency Demand

MNCs and other entities that require a foreign currency for trade, investment, travel, or other purposes generate currency demand. In the aggregate, demand depends on the currency's value. Some entities may demand a currency regardless of its value, while others modify their demand based on value. Overall, currency demand is inversely related to currency values.

EXAMPLE 4.2

This example shows how exchange rates affect currency demand by MNCs. A U.S.-based firm (an MNC) sources footwear from Italy. Payables are denominated in EUR, and the firm has to exchange USD into EUR to meet its obligations. Thus, the MNC contributes to overall market demand for the EUR. If the EUR rises in value significantly, the MNC may decide to source similar products from Brazil.

Demand for a currency may arise from many sources. In general, the demand for a country's currency is determined by the demand for the purchase of that country's goods, services, and financial assets. Thus, entities not holding the country's currency but desiring to purchase its goods, services, and financial assets would demand its currency. In the EUR example, demand would arise typically from non-Europeans who do not currently hold the EUR; these persons create the demand for the EUR by wishing to purchase European goods, services, and assets.

Demand for a currency such as the EUR can be visualized in graphical form as in Exhibit 4.7. On the horizontal, or *X* axis, is the price or the exchange rate of the EUR in terms of the USD. On the vertical, or *Y* axis, is the amount of EUR demanded by entities holding USD. Note that the demand line is downward sloping, indicating that at higher values of the EUR, the demand

EXHIBIT 4.7
Demand for EUR

Note: Demand for EUR falls as the currency rises in value.

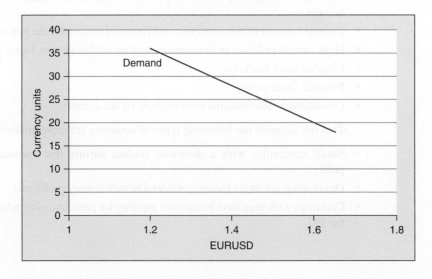

is lower. Likewise, at lower values of the EUR, the demand is higher. This reflects the normal behavior of markets.

One important concept related to the demand of a product is demand *elasticity*. This measures the percentage of change in demand relative to a percentage change in price. High demand elasticity in the context of currency demand indicates that entities are very sensitive to the currency rate. Thus, a small change in currency values causes big changes in the demand for products and services denominated in that currency. The elasticity of a demand curve is displayed in its slope. A steep demand curve indicates high demand elasticity.

Currency Supply

When MNCs and other entities demand a foreign currency for trade, investment, travel, or other purposes, they are simultaneously creating currency supply. This happens because they offer their holdings of the domestic currency to purchase a foreign currency. They are more likely to offer their currency as payment if they can obtain a higher amount of the foreign currency in return. Thus, supply depends on the value of the currency. Some entities may supply a currency regardless of its value; others modify their supply based on value. Overall, currency supply is directly related to currency values.

EXAMPLE 4.3	A U.S.-based hedge fund holds EUR 6 billion of European financial assets. The fund liquidates EUR 2 billion of its holdings. The proceeds from this sale are converted from EUR into USD. This transaction results in a supply of EUR. The hedge fund will find this transaction more attractive if the value of the EUR is high.

Supply for a currency may arise from many sources. In general, the need to purchase goods, services, and financial assets from a foreign country determines the currency supply. Thus, entities holding a particular currency but wishing to purchase items denominated in another currency will produce a supply schedule. Supply is the flip side of demand. Supply of a particular currency is associated with demand for another currency. This is so because of the obvious fact that a currency transaction involves two currencies.

Supply for a currency such as the EUR can be visualized in graphical form as in Exhibit 4.8. On the horizontal or *X* axis, we have the price or the exchange rate of the EUR in terms of the USD. On the vertical or *Y* axis, we have the quantity of EUR supplied by entities holding the currency. Note that the supply line is upward sloping, reflecting the fact that at higher values of the EUR, the supply is higher. Likewise, at lower values of the EUR, the supply is lower.

EXHIBIT 4.8
Supply of EUR

Note: The supply of EUR rises as the value of the currency rises.

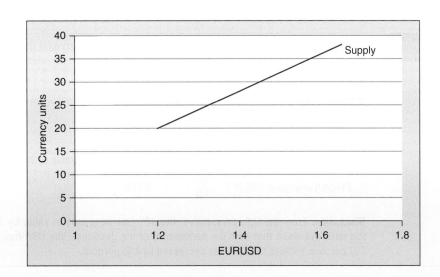

EXHIBIT 4.9
Equilibrium Value
of EUR

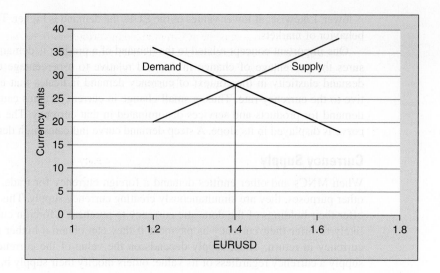

Currency Equilibrium

The intersection of demand and supply, as shown in Exhibit 4.9, will determine the equilibrium value of a currency as well as the amount transacted. The equilibrium EURUSD exchange rate is indicated on the X axis as the point aligned with the intersection of demand and supply. The equilibrium transaction amount involving the EUR and the USD is shown on the Y axis as the point aligned with the intersection of demand and supply. Exhibit 4.9 indicates an equilibrium value of EURUSD = 1.4.

In practice, demand and supply schedules are dynamic. As the environment and needs of various contracting entities change, these curves shift, leading to changes in the exchange rate. For example, consider the effect of the U.S. Federal Reserve Bank selling a considerable quantity of EUR for USD. This will shift the supply curve for the EUR to the left. The new equilibrium value for the EUR will be lower. Such transactions occur frequently.

Calculating the Change in a Currency's Value

Currency values change when demand and supply change. Because of the duality in a currency transaction, there are two perspectives on how a currency changes in value. This discussion relates to the two ways—direct and indirect—a currency is quoted. In the following example, we show calculations and interpret results. Surprisingly, the answers from the two methods do not match.

EXAMPLE 4.4

The JPY is trading at JPY 102 per USD. Suppose the demand curve for the JPY shifts to the right. The new equilibrium value of JPY is JPY 95 per USD. Calculate the currency changes from the U.S. and Japanese perspectives.

Solution: From the U.S. perspective, the percentage change in the value of JPY is:

$$\text{Percent change in JPYUSD} = \frac{1/95}{1/102} - 1 = 7.37\%$$

From the Japanese perspective, the percentage change in the value of the USD is:

$$\text{Percent change in USDJPY} = \frac{95}{102} - 1 = -6.86\%$$

Discussion: From the U.S. perspective, the JPY has increased in value by 7.37 percent. However, this does not mean that from the perspective of the Japanese, the USD has decreased in value by 7.37 percent. Instead, the USD has decreased by 6.86 percent.

The differential view of an exchange rate—the home (that is, direct) and foreign (that is, indirect) perspectives—must be acknowledged in various analyses. For example, in Chapter 6 we discuss that MNCs sometimes use risk-sharing contracts with foreign partners by which payments are adjusted for currency price changes. If the currency change is not carefully specified in the contract, disputes will arise.

4.4 Factors Affecting Currency Values

In this section, we deepen our understanding of currency valuation by studying specific factors that affect currency demand and supply. We do so in two steps. We first consider how trade affects currency demand and supply. This analysis is known as the *current account analysis*. Next, we look at the investment motive for currency demand and supply. This is known as the *financial account analysis* (see Chapter 13 for a detailed discussion of these accounts).

Current Account Analysis

The traditional analysis of currency rates focuses on demand and supply in the cross-border goods market. Thus, focus is on the current account. This trade-centric view focuses on the following factors as determinants of currency rates.

Inflation

Inflation measures changes in prices. Inflation in a country has the potential to change consumption patterns. If the U.S. price level increases faster than foreign price levels, U.S. goods become more expensive than foreign goods. U.S. residents, in response, will import more foreign goods. This increases the supply of USD as well as the demand for foreign currencies. At the same time, foreign residents will import fewer U.S. goods, decreasing the demand for USD and decreasing the supply of foreign currencies. These two simultaneous effects (illustrated in Exhibit 4.10) are consistent with one another and will decrease the value of USD relative to foreign currencies. If one plots these effects, the demand curve for the foreign currency will shift to the right, and the supply curve for the foreign currency will shift to the left.

One problem is that broad measures of inflation may be misleading. For example, the main measure of inflation, the Consumer Price Index (CPI), is constructed to reflect price changes in a bundle of goods that the average citizen is assumed to consume. In recent years, this inflation rate in the United States has been 2–4 percent annually. But inflation is not constant across product categories: Inflation in ultra-premium wines (costing more than USD 10 a bottle) has been running at more than 5 percent annually, while inflation in computers has been negative. The extent to which the basket of goods reflected in the CPI has a global market will ultimately determine the link between inflation and currency rates.

National Income

National income is a measure of goods and services produced, and, therefore, income earned, in a country. National income is also a measure of economic activity, and it is measured

EXHIBIT 4.10
Effect of Inflation on Currency Value

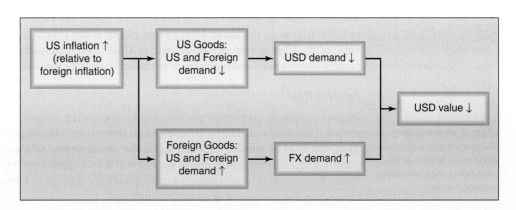

effect of trade
Factors such as *inflation* and *national income* affect currency values through their impact on imports and exports.

annually as gross national product (GNP). Typically, GNP is expressed as a percentage change of national income by comparing current year's income to the previous year's income. When GNP rises, the national consumption of goods also rises. This often has the collateral effect of increasing consumption of foreign goods, which in turn increases demand for foreign currencies. This means that demand for foreign currencies shifts to the right, thereby increasing the value of foreign currencies.

Following the emerging markets crisis of 1997–1998 and up to the credit crisis of 2007–2008, the U.S. economy has performed well, especially relative to most European economies. Consequently, U.S. consumption of foreign goods increased significantly. Has this led to a fall in the value of the USD against the EUR? For the first part of this time period until the middle of 2001, contrary to indications, the USD remained strong. But in later years, the USD did decrease significantly. One lesson from this episode is that one should not rely on a single currency factor. Often multiple factors are simultaneously at work affecting currencies.

Productivity

A country's productivity has implications for the quantity of goods produced as well as the cost of production. A country with higher productivity can expect a greater demand for its products. This results in a greater demand for its currency. Thus, increased productivity will result in a lower demand for a foreign currency, shifting the demand curve to the left, resulting in a lower value for the foreign currency.

In recent decades, the JPY has increased in value against the USD. One possible explanation is high Japanese productivity in industries such as automobiles. This translated into increased automobile exports from Japan to the United States. In turn, this increased the supply of USD and the demand for JPY and led to the appreciation of the JPY.

Preferences for Domestic versus Foreign Goods

Residents of a country can also display preferences for foreign relative to domestic goods. For example, in the United States today, consumers appear to show a greater preference for foreign automobiles relative to domestic autos, increasing the market share of Japanese and German automakers. A higher preference for foreign goods will produce greater demand for foreign currencies, therefore shifting the demand curve to the right and increasing the equilibrium value of the currency. Instead, when residents prefer domestic goods, the demand curve will be shifted to the left, lowering the value of the foreign currency.

How well does this factor predict currency values? Over the last two decades, U.S. consumers have shown a strong preference for Japanese automobile and electronic products. This preference is also evident in the large trade deficit that the United States runs against Japan. Over this time period, the USD has decreased significantly in value against the JPY.

Financial Account Analysis

Modern approaches to understanding currency values tend to increasingly focus on capital (or financial) flows across borders. Capital flows could be FDI or investment flows. If U.S. investors were to demand purchases of shares of firms listed in the Mumbai Stock Exchange, this would increase the demand for the Indian rupee (INR) and increase the value of INR relative to USD. Likewise, if Korean MNCs build plants in the United States, this will decrease the value of the Korean won (KRW) relative to USD. Two important factors guide capital flows, namely interest rates and preferences regarding corporate management and governance.

Interest Rate

effect of investments
Because *interest rates* affect cross-border investment flows, they also affect currency values.

Investors evaluate investment possibilities by comparing reward to risk. A key indicator of reward is the return offered by an investment. Returns are often highly related to interest rates. Thus, the level of interest rates can signal the attractiveness of a country for investments. A country with a relatively high rate of interest will draw capital from foreign sources. This cross-border investment flow will require a corresponding exchange of currencies, strengthening the currency of the investment destination country.

EXAMPLE 4.5

During the 1990s, Japanese and U.S. interest rates fluctuated around 1 percent and 5 percent, respectively. This led Japanese investors to purchase U.S. financial assets. In fact, during certain years, Japanese investors were the largest purchasers of U.S. Treasury investments. Did this result in the weakening of the JPY relative to the USD? The answer is not so clear cut. Unfortunately, at the same time, the United States was running large trade deficits against Japan, putting downward pressure on the USD. A clearer example is the EUR during 2002–2005. During this period, there were large capital flows from the Eurozone into the United States. The USD did strengthen against the EUR as a consequence.

Because of inflation, observed interest rates may not reflect true underlying returns for investors. To adjust for inflation, we need to subtract inflation from observed rates—known as *nominal rates*—to obtain inflation-adjusted rates known as *real rates*. Suppose nominal returns are 9 percent and 5 percent in India and Germany, respectively. If the 9 percent nominal rate in India is accompanied by a 7 percent inflation rate, the real rate is 2 percent. In Germany, if the 5 percent nominal rate is accompanied by a 2 percent inflation rate, the real rate is 3 percent. Under these conditions, Indian investors would be drawn to the Eurozone capital markets despite a lower nominal rate. The distinction between nominal rates and real rates is more fully explained in Chapter 5.

Corporate Management and Governance Preferences

Just as consumer tastes and preferences dictate the purchase of foreign versus domestic products, investors may also indicate tastes relative to investments in domestic and foreign markets. For example, if German investors consider the U.S. management system to be more efficient than the German management system, equity investments would flow toward U.S. markets. A similar argument can be made for corporate governance systems.

4.5 How Governments Intervene in Currency Markets

Governments typically seek high economic growth and low inflation. One determinant of these macroeconomic outcomes is the currency value. For example, a country that desires to increase its economic growth may want to increase exports. A lower value of the country's currency will facilitate this goal. Here is another example concerning inflation: A country with a high rate of inflation may want to cool down its economy by decreasing the production of goods and services as well as their exports. This can be accomplished by increasing the value of its currency.

Sterilized and Nonsterilized Intervention

Governments change currency values by intervening in currency spot markets. **Currency intervention** refers to the act of buying and selling foreign currencies using the domestic currency. As such, intervention involves changing the amount and composition of a country's *international reserves,* assets that are denominated in a foreign currency.

These transactions are typically conducted by the central banks, which in the case of the United States is the *Federal Reserve Bank.* A side effect of intervention is change in the money supply or *monetary base.* Consider an intervention by the Federal Reserve to lower the value of the USD against the JPY. Because the Federal Reserve pays for JPY purchases using its holdings of USD, more USD will enter into circulation. Thus, the USD money supply increases. Similarly, when the Federal Reserve sells foreign currencies, the collateral effect is a smaller monetary base. A transaction in which the monetary base is altered is known as *nonsterilized currency intervention.*

There are reasons that a central bank may not want to alter its monetary base while pursuing currency intervention. For example, an increase in the monetary base may have the side effect of increasing inflation: When a larger amount of money chases the same amount of goods, inflation occurs. Thus, central banks may desire to conduct *sterilized currency intervention,* requiring two simultaneous transactions to be conducted. First, there is a currency transaction that affects currencies as well as the monetary base. Second, there is an offsetting monetary base transaction.

EXAMPLE 4.6	The Federal Reserve wishes to increase the value of the CAD relative to the USD. The Fed executes a currency market transaction to purchase USD 2 billion worth of assets denominated in CAD. How can this intervention be sterilized?

Solution: The primary transaction involves an outflow of USD 2 billion resulting in a holding of CAD denominated assets. This outflow increases the USD monetary base by USD 2 billion. Therefore, an offsetting transaction that reduces the monetary base by USD 2 billion is required. The Federal Reserve sells securities in the market for USD 2 billion to achieve this purpose.

Other Methods of Intervention

Central banks use the following methods in addition to spot market intervention[9]:

- **Forward market intervention.** We learned in Chapter 3 of the link between spot and forward markets. Consequently, by intervening in forward markets, corresponding results may be achieved in spot markets. For example, long currency forwards may be used to increase the value of a currency in the forward market. This, in turn, will increase spot prices. Forward market intervention has the advantage of not requiring an upfront cash outlay.

- **Foreign exchange swap intervention.** Not to be confused with cross-currency swaps, foreign exchange swaps involve reversing spot and forward transactions. These swaps are often used in conjunction with spot market intervention to sterilize the spot transaction. The net effect of such a combination is the same as using outright forwards.

- **Option market intervention.** Central banks also use call and put options to meet intervention objectives. One advantage is that options require a smaller upfront premium compared to outlays in the spot market. Also, because of the smaller amounts involved in terms of the premium, there is perhaps no need to sterilize the transaction.

- **Indirect intervention.** These are methods involving transactions in foreign currency-denominated instruments as well as various forms of controls. Capital controls—taxes or restriction in security market transactions—and currency controls—restrictions on exchange of currencies—are indirect tools of intervention.

See Exhibit 4.11 for intervention details as reported by central bankers.

Challenges in Implementing Intervention

Foreign exchange intervention is difficult to implement in practice. The main difficulty is that the size of most central banks' international reserves is a small fraction of daily volume in currency markets. For example, even a large central bank such as the U.S. Federal Reserve has international reserves amounting to only tens of billions of USD.[10] This compares to daily trading volume in the spot currency markets exceeding half a trillion USD.

Nevertheless, economists note that G7 nations (Canada, France, Germany, Italy, Japan, United Kingdom, and United States) have intervened many times over the last decade. The assessment of the consequences of such intervention is controversial. Some economists believe that many of these interventions are successful while others dispute such claims. Most market watchers agree on one thing, however: Currency interventions per se may not influence prices, but when coupled with credible signals from governments about monetary and fiscal policies, they are effective in changing the equilibrium value of currencies. The U.S. markets, for instance, look for signals from leaders such as the chairman of the Federal Reserve and the Treasury Secretary.

[9] C. Neely, "The Practice of Central Bank Intervention: Looking Under the Hood," *Federal Reserve Bank of St. Louis Review* (May/June 2001), pp. 1–10.

[10] For data about various forms of reserves and the monetary base, visit http://research.stlouisfed.org/fred2/.

EXHIBIT 4.11
Survey of Central Bankers

Source: C. Neely, The Practice of Central Bank Intervention: Looking Under the Hood," *Federal Reserve Bank of St. Louis Review* (May/June 2001), pp. 1–10.

	Responses (N)	Never (%)	Sometimes (%)	Always (%)
Foreign exchange intervention changes the domestic monetary base	20	40	30	30
Intervention transactions are conducted with the following counterparties:				
Major domestic banks	21	0	28.6	71.4
Major foreign banks	18	16.7	72.2	11.1
Other central banks	17	76.5	23.5	0
Investment banks	16	68.8	25.0	6.3
Intervention transactions are conducted in the following markets:				
Spot	21	0	4.8	95.2
Forward	17	47.1	52.9	0
Future	16	93.8	6.3	0
Other (please specify in margin)	15	93.3	6.7	0
Intervention transactions are conducted by:				
Direct dealing with counterparties via telephone	20	0	30.0	70.0
Direct dealing via electronic communication	16	56.3	31.3	12.5
Live FX brokers	19	36.8	52.6	10.5
Electronic brokers (e.g., EBS, Reuters 2002)	16	87.5	0	12.5
The following are factors in intervention decisions:				
Resisting short-term trends in exchange rates	19	10.5	42.1	47.4
Correcting long-run misalignments of exchange rates	18	33.3	44.4	22.2
Profiting from speculative trades	17	100	0	0
Other	16	62.5	25.0	12.5
In your opinion, how long does it take to observe the full effect of intervention on exchange rates?				
A few minutes	18	38.9		
A few hours	18	22.2		
One day	18	0		
A few days	18	27.8		
More than a few days	18	11.1		
Intervention has no effect on exchange rates	18	0		

4.6 Currency Crises in Emerging Markets

Past experience suggests that the world endures a calamitous economic experience once every 10 years. Some of these are caused by wars (e.g., world wars of the 20th century) and some are caused by supply shocks (e.g., oil crisis of the 1970s). Yet others are caused by bubbles in asset prices (e.g., tech stocks in 2000 and the credit crisis of 2007–2008). While all countries are in turn affected by economic crises, emerging markets are arguably affected the most. Also, when emerging markets are affected, their currencies are affected to a far greater extent. In the next sections, we explain the causes and consequences of such crises and actions governments take to remedy the situation.

Causes

Emerging economies are vulnerable to external and internal forces. This is so for a variety of reasons.

- *They typically do not have a variety of industries and are deeply affected when specific industries are affected.* For example, Taiwan depends on its electronics industry, and most of it customers are in the United States. A slowdown in the United States would affect Taiwan to a considerable extent.

- *Their financial markets lack depth.* In thin markets, a small disturbance can have a large impact on prices. For example, one frequently finds large daily changes (2 percent or more) in the Brazilian stock market index.

- *Many emerging economies are characterized by imbalances such as trade deficits or budget deficits.* For example, prior to the emerging markets crisis of 1997–1998, the budget deficit of many Asian countries, as a percent of GDP, exceeded 4 percent.
- *Many emerging economies rely on short-term external debt.* When things go wrong, refinancing becomes difficult, leading to bankruptcies. This was particularly true in Asian countries such as Thailand during 1997–1998.
- *Many emerging economies have weak economic institutions.* Central banks lack credibility; legal systems are not fully developed; enforcement of financial contracts is weak. Of these problems, the lack of credible monetary authorities is perhaps a key weakness.

Consequences

The emerging markets crisis of 1997–1998 (see Exhibit 4.12 for a chronology) offers perhaps an extreme example of what can go wrong.

- *Rating agencies such as Standard & Poor's downgrade the overall country risk rating as well as the rating of debt issued by governments.* Rating changes have great consequences.
- *Stock markets collapse.* For instance, the Malaysian stock market index dropped about 50 percent during this crisis.
- *Financial systems collapse.* Banks become bankrupt. For instance, many Indonesian banks failed in 1997.
- *Currency values plunge.* For instance, the Korean won (KRW) dropped in value by 50 percent against the USD in 1997.
- *Global asset prices collapse because of contagion.* Risk aversion increases and there is a flight to safety, perhaps boosting values of CHF and gold.

EXHIBIT 4.12
Causes of Emerging Markets Crisis of 1997–1998

July 2, 1997	After weeks of speculators selling its currency, Thai central bank announces a managed float of the baht and asks for technical assistance from IMF.
July 11	Indonesia widens trading range for the rupiah.
July 14	Malaysia abandons defense of the ringitt.
July 24	Malaysian Prime Minister Mahathir Mohamad launches bitter attack on "rogue speculators."
July 28	Thailand seeks IMF rescue package.
August 5	Thailand unveils austerity plan as part of deal with IMF.
August 10	Financial scandal in Japan involving loans to a racketeer widens with Yamaichi Securities forcing some board members to resign.
August 20	IMF approves USD 3.9 billion credit facility for Thailand.
August 24	Malaysian Prime Minister blames George Soros with statement "All these countries have spent 40 years trying to build up their economies and a moron like Soros comes along."
August 27	Japan announces it will keep rates low to facilitate recovery.
September 4	Several multi-billion-dollar projects delayed or canceled in Malaysia.
September 17	Standard and Poor's downgrades 7 financial institutions in Thailand.
September 24	Former and current officials of Daiwa and Yamaichi in Japan are arrested or resigned.
October 1	Malaysia calls for total ban on Forex trading.
October 8	Indonesia to ask for assistance from IMF.
October 16	Thailand revises its growth forecast for 1997 to 1% from 2.5%.
October 22	Indonesian central bank prepares bailout plan that will liquidate many troubled banks.
October 29	Political turmoil in Thailand, dissension in cabinet.
October 31	IMF announces USD 23 billion package for Indonesia.
November 17	South Korea abandons defense of the won.
November 21	South Korea to seek rescue package from IMF.
December 1	Several South Korean banks on the brink of collapse.
December 4	IMF to provide USD 57 billion assistance to South Korea.

- *At the human level, untold misery unfolds as a consequence of lost jobs and livelihood.* The associated political turmoil does not help matters.

Response

IMF and global crises
Global crises occur infrequently but have a strong impact. The *IMF* assists individual nations during these events.

The International Monetary Fund (IMF) is the main institution in charge of the global monetary system. If a country is experiencing problems such as currency devaluations and the resulting outflow of capital, the IMF often arranges *rescue packages*. These take the form of loans and guarantees to the beleaguered nation. The hope is that, through these actions, the nation will regain trust and favor in the global marketplace. Because of IMF and other actions, the world did recover quickly from the 1997–1998 crisis.

4.7 Currency Trends

The trends discussed here were obtained from the 77th annual report of the Bank of International Settlements issued in June 2007. It is best to view them as short- to medium-term trends. Currency markets do change in character every so often. Participants need to monitor developments on a continual basis.

- **Low volatilities.** Despite high trading volumes, major currencies exhibited lower volatilities in recent years. This trend runs counter to trends in stock markets. The BIS report shows that while stock market volatility has trended upward, currency volatility both for G7 and emerging markets has trended downward (see Exhibit 4.13). MNCs generally prefer low currency volatilities, although an argument may be made that they are entities best positioned to capitalize on high currency volatilities.[11]
- **Carry trades.** Carry trade is an important phenomenon influencing currency values in recent years. *Carry trades* are simultaneous transactions in two currencies. Hedge funds and other speculators short low-interest currencies (also called the *funding currency*) and long high-interest currencies[12] (also called the *target currency*). Currency derivatives are typically

EXHIBIT 4.13
Currency and Stock Market Volatility

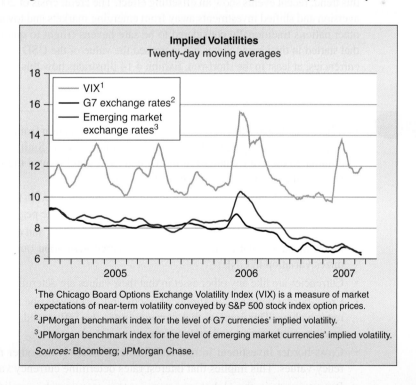

[1]The Chicago Board Options Exchange Volatility Index (VIX) is a measure of market expectations of near-term volatility conveyed by S&P 500 stock index option prices.
[2]JPMorgan benchmark index for the level of G7 currencies' implied volatility.
[3]JPMorgan benchmark index for the level of emerging market currencies' implied volatility.
Sources: Bloomberg; JPMorgan Chase.

[11] Chapter 9 introduces the concept of real options. MNCs may create real options by virtue of their global presence. These real options may rise in value as currency volatility rises.

[12] Carry trades generally involve transactions in the money market securities of the two currencies as well as in currency derivatives (forwards or futures). Chapter 5 explains these types of transactions in more detail.

EXHIBIT 4.14
BRLUSD and the Credit Crisis of 2007–2008

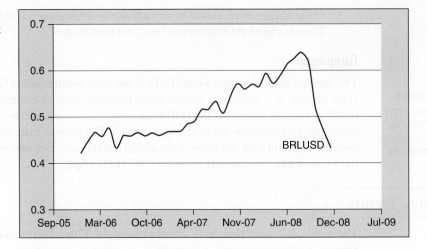

used. Recent examples of funding (low-interest) currencies are JPY and CHF; examples of target currencies are AUD, NZD, BRL, and the South African rand (ZAR). Carry trades typically increase the value of target currencies although one must also remember that these trades have to be reversed at some future point, and this reversal may strengthen the financing currency. How does one detect the presence of carry trade? Answer: Observe trading volumes and open interest in the currency futures markets.

• **Strength in emerging market currencies.** Independent of carry trades, there appears to be secular strengthening of emerging market currencies against the USD. One explanation is that these economies are experiencing high rates of growth; this in turn attracts FDI and portfolio investments. Another explanation is that countries such as Brazil are resource rich, and their currencies are riding the commodities boom of recent years. Although the BIS report identifies this trend, recent events show an offsetting effect. The credit crisis of 2007–2008 heightened risk aversion and shifted investments away from emerging markets and toward the United States and other nations traditionally considered to be safe havens (flight to quality). Ironically, the crisis that started in the United States has increased the value of the USD relative to emerging market currencies, at least in the short-run. Exhibit 4.14 illustrates how this crisis affected the BRL.

Summary

- The International Monetary system has made the transition from fixed currency systems to floating currency systems. In particular, the failure of the Smithsonian agreement of 1971 eliminated the gold standard in the United States and moved the United States as well as other countries toward variations of the floating system.

- Currency systems tend to fall within the continuum of fixed to floating. Two systems commonly used today are the managed floating system and the pegged currency system.

- Floating currency systems infuse the discipline of markets and enable countries to use their monetary and fiscal policies to achieve desired economic outcomes. This system minimizes variation in GNP.

- Currencies are like any other asset in that their values are determined by supply and demand.

- Cross-border demand and supply of goods and services is one important influence on currency values. This implies that currency rates are influenced by inflation rates, national income, productivity, and preferences.

- Cross-border investment in real and financial assets is the other major influence on currency values. This implies that interest rates determine currency values.

- Recent trends in the global monetary system are toward consolidation. The adoption of the EUR as a single currency by European nations and the dollarization movement are evidence of this consolidation.

Questions

1. **Gold Standard Description.** Explain the functioning of the gold standard. What are the benefits and disadvantages of such a system?

2. **Gold Standard in United States.** When did the United States abandon the gold standard? What were the circumstances? Why?

3. **Pegged System Description.** What is a pegged currency system? Give examples of some countries on this system today. Can you generalize characteristics of these countries in terms of size, location, and so forth?

4. **Types of Pegged Systems.** Distinguish between pegged systems with a crawling band and pegged systems with a tight band.

5. **Pegged System and Country Characteristics.** What are reasons that a small Caribbean nation might consider pegging its currency to the USD? Discuss pros and cons.

6. **Pegged System and Country Characteristics.** For what reasons might an Eastern European country consider pegging its currency to the EUR? Discuss the pros and cons.

7. **Pegged System and Country Characteristics.** What are reasons that a large Latin American country such as Argentina might consider pegging its currency to the USD? Discuss the pros and cons.

8. **Floating System Description.** What are the benefits of a floating currency system? Is the role of the central bank smaller or larger with this system, and why? What institutions are necessary to support this system?

9. **Demand for Currencies.** Explain the various ways in which the demand for a foreign currency arises. Your answer may focus on the demand for the EUR in the United States.

10. **Supply of Currencies.** Explain various ways in which the supply of a foreign currency arises. Your answer may focus on the supply of the INR.

11. **Currency Valuation.** Explain how the value of the USD relative to the GBP will change in response to the following events:

    a. U.K. investors become interested in the run up of the NASDAQ index and start investing more in the U.S. equity markets.

    b. U.S. investors seek to diversify away from the high levels of the U.S. markets by investing in British equities.

    c. The U.S. central bank tries to cool growth in the U.S. economy by raising short-term interest rates.

    d. U.S. exports of computers and telecommunications equipment to the UK rise.

    e. More Americans travel to the UK.

12. **Central Bank Action and Currency Valuation.** Suppose the U.S. Federal Reserve bank recently lowered interest rates to stimulate domestic economic activity. How will this action affect the value of the USD relative to foreign currencies such as the EUR?

13. **Trade War and Currency Valuation.** Canada is a major lumber exporter to the United States. Suppose frictions develop because the United States perceives that Canadian lumber is subsidized by low access rates charged by the Canadian government for obtaining lumber from Crown-owned lands. Assume that the crisis escalates and the volume of trade diminishes dramatically. Prior to this crisis, assume Canada had a trade surplus with the United States. Assess the effects of this trade war on CADUSD.

14. **Commodity Prices and Currency Valuation.** The recent boom in commodities has assisted the Canadian economy. Suppose this resulted in a change in value of the CADUSD from 0.85 to 0.90. What is the percentage change in the value of the CAD? Explain how economic boom can change the value of a nation's currency. What are immediate and long-term effects?

15. **Currency Change Percent.** The EUR rises in value from EUR 0.65 per USD to EUR 0.60. From a U.S. investor's perspective, what is the percentage change in the value of the EUR? What is the percentage change in the value of the USD from a European investor's perspective?

16. **Inflation and Currency Valuation.** Assume that the inflation rate in the United States rises sharply relative to the rate in Canada. How would this affect the value of the CAD from the U.S. perspective?

17. **Currency Crises.** Economists speculate that the emerging markets crisis of 1997–1998 was made worse because of the pegged currency systems employed by many emerging economies. What is the reasoning behind this position?

18. **Central Bank Intervention.** Explain how central banks intervene in currency markets. Do the effects of intervention upset the money supply balance of a country and have collateral effects? How can policy makers protect against such collateral effects?

19. **Central Bank Intervention.** Assume that the U.S. Federal Reserve desires to raise the value of the USD against the EUR by engaging in USD 5 billion worth of transactions. The EUR is currently trading at USD 1.60. Explain actions that the Federal Reserve needs to take.

20. **Euro Description.** What is the EUR? When was it introduced? What are the reasons for its introduction? What are challenges in managing the EUR? What are future prospects?

Extensions

1. **Characteristics of Emerging Market Currencies.** The INR is not considered a volatile currency, especially when compared to other emerging market currencies such as the Russian ruble (RUB), South African rand (ZAR), and BRL. Speculate on reasons for low volatility of the INR. Also speculate on correlation between INR and major currencies.

2. **Consequences of Dollarization.** Assume that a major South American country is seriously considering dollarization. The country's currency is already pegged to the USD. Critics contend that with dollarization, many businesses will migrate to a neighboring nation whose currency is not linked to the USD at all. What is your reaction to the proposal and the critics? Explain.

3. **Effects of Capital Controls.** Assume that the Indian government restricts foreign investments in this country. In particular, foreign institutional investors (FIIs) are required to register and gain approval for their investments. The government also restricts the maximum percent of a firm that a foreign entity can own. Once investments were made, FIIs found it difficult to transfer ownership because of various other restrictions. One reason the Indian government imposed restrictions—broadly known as *capital controls*—on FIIs is the popular belief that FII fund flows induced volatility in equity prices. Evaluate effects on the INR of new regulations that either (a) enhance or (b) remove FII restrictions.

4. **Effects of Private Funds.** Hedge funds and private equity funds are privately owned funds usually with a large pool of funds available for investments. Assume that most of these funds are located in the United States and funded by U.S. investors. Assume that these funds are collectively sitting on cash balances of half a trillion dollars that are slated toward potential foreign investments. Investments typically targeted by these funds include the purchase of private businesses, large infrastructure projects, and real estate. Estimate short-term, medium-term, and long-term currency effects.

Case

Clover Machines: *Effects of Emerging Market Currencies*

Clover Machines continues its operational push abroad. Following revisions to its strategic plan, it has set up subsidiaries in South America and Asia to add to its subsidiaries in Europe. Consequently, Clover expects its foreign revenues to rise from a current level of 12 percent of total revenues to 15 percent in the coming year. A long-term goal is to increase this ratio to 40 percent.

Expansion also means that Clover is exposed to emerging market currencies. Although derivatives—options, futures, and swaps—can be used to reduce currency effects somewhat, it would be prudent to understand currency fundamentals as an aid to long-term business planning. Emerging market currencies in particular appear to follow different dynamics. Brian Bent, Clover's CFO, reviews conventional wisdom on emerging currencies that is summarized as follows:

- Low correlation with the USD and high standard deviations.
- Highly sensitive to capital account flows, especially with respect to activities of foreign institutional investors (FII).
- Highly sensitive to macroeconomic conditions.
- Highly sensitive to political conditions.

Mr. Bent is concerned about the firm's plan to expand in India. Both in construction and agricultural machines, a low current market size deterred potential market entrants in the past. However, Clover is willing to take a long-term perspective. In the construction industry, booming end-user demand and rising labor rates can mean only exponential growth in demand for Clover and other providers of machines. The agricultural sector in India is also large but fairly unproductive compared to other countries: This again could lead to great demand for machinery in the future. Many factors are countering this potential demand. First, a small handful of local producers are making (low-horsepower) low-quality machines but sell them at correspondingly low prices; Clover will have to make the case for its higher quality and higher cost machines. Second, and more germane to this case, the Indian rupee (INR) has showed recent signs of volatility. Mr. Bent is concerned about how changes in INR can impact Clover's business, especially in India. Of particular concern is unexpected depreciation of the INR.

A financial analyst at Clover reporting to Mr. Bent has collected the following salient details pertaining to the INR.

- History of the INR in the 1990s: After being range bound for much of the decade, INRUSD rose more than 15 percent in the period August 2006 to October 2007. More than half of these gains were given up in 2008.
- A strong recent correlation appears to exist between INRUSD and the SENSEX (main stock market indicator; in Yahoo! use symbol ^BSESN). The SENSEX had a very strong year in 2007: It touched 20,000 for the first time that December. In 2008, however, the SENSEX lost more than 30 percent from its peak, breaching the 13,000 mark in July.

CASE EXHIBIT 4.1
Indian Rupee

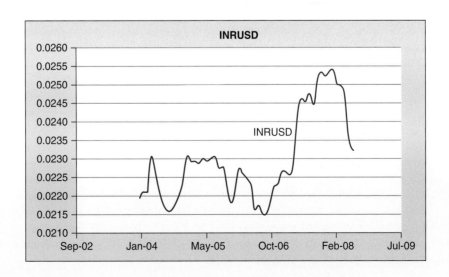

- The Indian economy continues to do well despite high oil prices (India is a net importer of oil). Growth is pegged at 8 to 9 percent. However, inflation is running at around 10 percent. Severe labor shortages in certain sectors (e.g., textiles, IT) have pushed up wages more than 10 percent a year in the last two years. Transportation costs have also risen significantly. Short-term interest rates are more than 10 percent.

- India follows the parliamentary system. Because it could not gather a majority on its own, the governing party has put together a coalition of various parties with seemingly different ideologies. Recently, the coalition was threatened over a nuclear treaty that India signed with the United States. A major partner withdrew from the coalition and made a no-confidence motion. The ruling party won the resulting vote by a slim margin: 275 for versus 256 against. The stock market rose more than 10 percent in response, but the INR did not respond to these developments.

Based on these facts, evaluate the currency and its prospects. Indicate theoretical models and ideas that you have used in determining this assessment. Extend your analysis to a second BRIC currency by collecting similar data from Internet and other sources.

Currency Parity Conditions

The Japanese central bank has just raised short-term rates by 50 basis points. An MNC wishes to provide a cash infusion to its Japanese subsidiary in three months. How can managers—using this information about interest rates in Japan—estimate the Japanese yen's (JPY) value in three months to estimate funding requirements? This chapter presents material that allows you to answer such questions. We build on material presented in Chapter 4—factors affecting currency values—and develop the so-called parity conditions relating currency values—spot and forward—with interest and inflation rates.

This chapter further develops the theme of globalization. Currency-related parity conditions arise from forces of globalization that result in relationships or parities between currency rates and economic variables such as interest rates and inflation. The two forms of globalization discussed in this chapter are international trade (cross-border movement of goods) and financial globalization (cross-border movement of money). These flows are powerful mechanisms for harmonizing currency values with national levels of interest and inflation rates. Thus, currency markets, product markets, and financial markets are inextricably linked. We derive parity conditions, discuss limitations and evidence, and show examples. This material therefore builds on the previous chapter that discussed current and capital account–related factors affecting currencies.

This chapter also discusses currency forecasting. MNC managers often require currency forecasts for budgeting, planning, and contracting purposes. We demonstrate various methods of forecasting currencies including the use of parity conditions. Some methods of forecasting involve the selection of appropriate "signals" from markets while others require elaborate data collection and processing. This chapter shows how MNC managers can construct, use, and evaluate forecasting methods.

Specific topics are the following:

- Simple forms of currency arbitrage such as locational arbitrage and triangular arbitrage.
- More complex currency strategies such as covered interest arbitrage involving currency and debt market.
- Derivation and explanation of the interest rate parity theory.
- Derivation and explanation of the purchasing power parity theory.
- Derivation and explanation of the international Fisher effect.
- The use of the preceding parity conditions in forecasting future currency values.
- Other approaches to forecasting currency values such as the fundamental or technical approaches.

5.1 Basic Arbitrage in Currency Markets

In Chapter 2, you learned that major currencies are traded in global around-the-clock markets. A special feature of currency markets is simultaneous trading in multiple locations such as New York, London, Singapore, and Tokyo. When trading takes place in multiple locations, one possibility is that prices differ for a particular currency depending on location. Currency trading also has another unusual feature that lends itself to price discrepancies. Currencies—at least the major ones—trade in all possible pairs. This means that a person can purchase or sell a certain currency by indirectly trading in and out of other intermediary currencies. Thus, executing the purchase or sale of a currency can be done in multiple ways. This situation also lends itself to potential price discrepancies.

Market participants respond in two ways to discrepancies in currency prices. For entities focused on currencies as a vehicle for other business purposes—MNCs are in this category—it is important to compare and diligently analyze prices from various markets. For other entities whose focus and expertise are on trading nimbly in currency markets, discrepancies offer the potential for profits. These entities—principally financial institutions such as banks and hedge funds—conduct complex synchronized trades known as *arbitrage*.

What is **arbitrage**? Arbitrage is the process of exploiting price differentials in markets. In some cases, price differentials are easy to detect when, for instance, an asset trades simultaneously in two different markets. For example, quotes for JPYUSD (Japanese yen in terms of the U.S. dollar) may differ in two different markets. In other cases, the detection of a price differential requires decision makers to evaluate an asset with its synthetic equivalent. Consider the availability of trading in the following currency pairs: JPYCHF (Japanese yen in terms of the Swiss franc) and CHFUSD. By trading through the CHF, a person can de facto create a JPYUSD trade (because JPYCHF × CHFUSD = JPYUSD). One needs to compare the implied JPYUSD quote with other explicit JPYUSD quotes. Consequently, arbitrage occurs not just between two identical assets but also between an asset and its implied or synthetic equivalent.

arbitrage
In an *arbitrage* transaction, an investor buys an asset trading at a low price and sells an equivalent asset trading at a high price.

Arbitrage is based on the intuitive "buy-low, sell-high" rule. When trading an asset or its synthetic equivalent (a combination of other assets producing equivalent cash flows) at differential prices, the arbitrager buys at the low price and sells at the high price. An arbitrage transaction must satisfy two conditions. First, profit must be ensured and there should be no possibility of a loss. Second, it must be self-financing. The latter condition prevents confusion of arbitrage with risk-free investment. In a risk-free investment, a person earns a guaranteed return or profit by investing a net amount of money. In arbitrage, guaranteed profits are earned without a capital outlay. Arbitrage profits are the proverbial free lunch.

In the following section, we describe two basic forms of arbitrage involving currencies known as *locational* and *triangular arbitrage*, respectively.

Locational Arbitrage

Consider the situation in which a currency is quoted at different prices in two locations. An arbitrager can simultaneously buy at the less expensive location and sell at the more expensive location. This is known as **locational arbitrage**.

Because of the size and liquidity of global currency markets, transactions of this nature are easy to execute. Transaction costs, however, can offset the profitability of arbitrage.

EXAMPLE 5.1

Suppose EURUSD (euro in terms of the U.S. dollar) is quoted at 1.584 in New York and 1.589 in Paris. An arbitrager will buy EUR in New York and simultaneously sell it in Paris to exploit the price discrepancy. With a transaction involving EUR 1 million, the arbitrager will net a profit of USD 5,000. Does this example satisfy the two arbitrage conditions? There is no risk of loss because both transactions occur simultaneously and at prevailing spot prices. Also, there is no net investment because the two transactions (to buy and to sell the EUR) are offsetting transactions and, at worst, may require the arbitrager to obtain financing for a day. Because both conditions are satisfied, this is an arbitrage transaction. See calculations below.

Locational Arbitrage

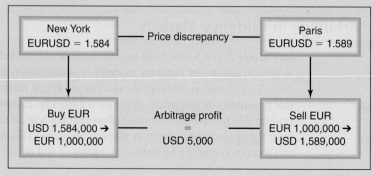

The process of arbitrage is critical to the functioning of currency markets. It is precisely because of arbitragers that currencies are priced rationally. In efficient markets, one does not expect to find many arbitrage opportunities. In particular, in the liquid currency markets with daily trading volume exceeding USD 0.5 trillion a day, it is inconceivable that arbitrage opportunities would present themselves frequently. Even the potential for a few opportunities provides incentives for arbitragers to monitor markets closely. Today, arbitraging activities are conducted with computers using software to track markets and to automatically trigger trades.

Triangular Arbitrage

Triangular arbitrage is a more sophisticated version of locational arbitrage. Triangular arbitrage, as the name implies, involves three currencies. With three currencies, three exchange rates are possible with the third rate implicitly determined by the two other rates. When the third currency rate (the explicit rate) is not equal to implied rate, arbitrage is possible.

EXAMPLE 5.2

Consider quotes on three currencies as follows: (1) EURUSD = 1.50, (2) USDJPY = 100, and (3) EURJPY = 155. Is there a price discrepancy? If so, show how arbitrage can take place. Assume that USD 15,000 is employed to conduct arbitrage.

Solution: Considering quotes (1) and (2), we calculate the implied EURJPY rate as follows:

Implied EURJPY = EURUSD × USDJPY = 1.50 × 100 = 150

But (3) indicates that the market quote for EURJPY is 155 (>150). Thus, EUR is overpriced relative to JPY. So, the arbitrage strategy would involve selling EUR at JPY 155. The following steps are part of this arbitrage:

- Convert USD 15,000 into EUR (@EURUSD = 1.50) to obtain EUR 10,000.
- Convert EUR 10,000 into JPY (@EURJPY = 155) to obtain JPY 1,550,000.
- Convert JPY 1,550,000 into USD (@USDJPY = 100) to obtain USD 15,500.

Discussion: Triangular arbitrage involves three transactions. You start with one currency and end with more of the same currency. The three transactions just identified are conducted simultaneously to produce an arbitrage profit of USD 500. The two conditions of arbitrage are satisfied: There is zero risk; although capital of USD 15,000 is committed, there are no financing costs because all transactions are completed instantaneously. Note that triangular arbitrage can also be conducted starting with another currency. But regardless of the starting currency, any strategy would involve shorting EUR @ EURJPY = 155. In this example, one could start with, say, EUR 10,000; convert to JPY 1,550,000 @EURJPY = 155; convert to USD 15,500 @USDJPY = 100; convert to EUR 10,333 @EURUSD = 1.50; and realize arbitrage profits of EUR 333. See calculations below.

Triangular Arbitrage

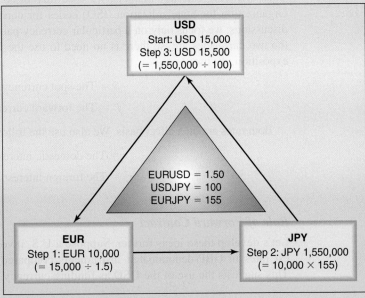

5.2 Money Markets and Currency Markets

The previous section discussed basic arbitrage in currency markets. However, currency markets also interact with other markets leading to other, more complex forms of arbitrage. In this section, we discuss the interaction between currency markets and money markets. A *money market* is a subset of financial markets that trades bills and other short-term instruments issued by governments, banks, corporations, and other entities.

Currency markets interact with money markets in the following sense. Market participants are no longer restricted to purely domestic money market instruments denominated in their own currency. Financial globalization provides access to not only various other national money markets but also global markets such as the Eurocurrency markets. Because of currency markets—spot and forward—participants are able not only to invest in instruments denominated in foreign currencies but also to convert back to the original currency at prespecified rates. By assuming no difference in risk and other characteristics, these foreign currency investments are substitutes to domestic investments, and, hence, returns must be identical. If returns differ, arbitrage spanning currency and money markets occurs. We discuss such arbitrage next.

Covered Interest Arbitrage

CIA versus carry trade
Both *carry trade* and *covered interest arbitrage* (CIA) are strategies to exploit interest rate differences between currencies.

Depending on the denomination currency, money market instruments offer differential rates of interest. In Chapter 2, we discussed how investors use carry trades to borrow in the low-interest currency and invest in the high-interest currency. **Covered interest arbitrage** (also known as **CIA**) is a similar concept and involves borrowing in one currency (known as the *funding currency*) and lending in another (known as the *target currency*). There are key differences, however. An entity conducting carry trade is vulnerable to currency volatility in the target currency. Declines in the target currency can reduce or overwhelm the interest differential. In CIA, forward contracts are used to insulate the investor from declines in target currency value. Another difference is that **carry trade** always involves borrowing the low-interest currency. Sometimes, in CIA, the investor may have to borrow the high-interest currency. The choice of which currency to borrow depends on not just interest rates but also the currency forward premium or discount.

Notation

A quick word about notations that we use in this and subsequent sections. Earlier, in discussions involving currency markets, we used market conventions that spell out International Organization for Standardization (ISO) codes for currency pairs. In most of the following discussions, we focus only on a particular currency pair, and the context makes it clear what the two currencies are, so there is no need to use the ISO notation. For ease and clarity of exposition, we use:

$$S = \text{The spot currency rate}$$

$$F = \text{The forward currency rate}$$

Both rates are on a direct basis. We also use the following symbols for interest rates:

$$r = \text{The domestic interest rate}$$

$$r^* = \text{The foreign interest rate}$$

Role of Forward Contract

Let's develop these ideas further. Suppose a U.S. investor is confronted with higher interest rates in GBP-denominated instruments compared to USD-denominated instruments. This suggests the use of the USD as funding currency and the GBP as the target currency:

The investor borrows USD, converts them into GBP, and invests them in a one-year GBP-denominated instrument. Suppose this investment is not protected with a forward contract (i.e., unhedged). If the GBP trades unchanged in one year, the investor profits from the interest differential. Instead, if the GBP declines, the profit can be smaller or even eliminated. In certain cases, the currency loss can be more than the interest differential, producing overall losses. This is why a forward contract is used in covered interest arbitrage to protect the reconversion value. The investor would short the GBP using a forward contract. Without this "forward cover," the strategy would be called *uncovered interest arbitrage (UCIA)*; we introduced this concept earlier and called it a *carry trade*. We explain CIA with an example.

EXAMPLE 5.3

Suppose interest rates are 4 percent and 8 percent in the U.S. and U.K. money markets, respectively. How can an arbitrager exploit this rate differential? Assume that spot and one-year forward rates (GBPUSD) are 1.50 and 1.46, respectively. Use a borrowing level of USD 1,500 to calculate the arbitrage profit.

Solution: CIA involves borrowing USD 1,500 at 4 percent for one year, immediately converting USD into GBP at the spot rate, earning 8 percent interest over the period of one year, reconverting into USD at the forward rate and repaying the USD loan. The cash that remains equals arbitrage profit. The calculations are as follows:

- Borrow USD 1,500 (@ r = 4 percent).
- Convert USD 1,500 (@ S = 1.50) into GBP 1,500/1.50 = GBP 1,000
- Earn interest (@ r^* = 8%) to produce future value (FV) of GBP 1,080.
- Reconvert (@ F = 1.46) into USD 1,080 × 1.46 = USD 1,576.80
- Repay loan (@ r = 4%) with USD 1,500 × (1 + 4%) = USD 1,560.

Thus, arbitrage profit equals USD 16.80. See the following graphical explanation.

Covered Interest Arbitrage

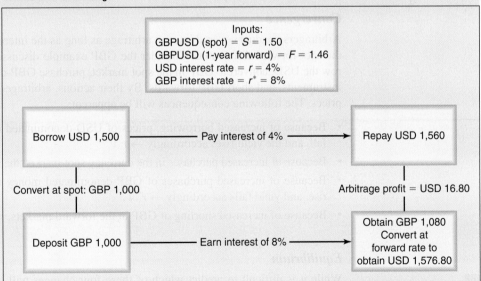

Discussion: This strategy satisfies the two arbitrage conditions. There is no risk because all cash flows are calculated using predetermined parameters. The interest on the USD loan is contractually set at 4 percent. The interest on the GBP deposit is contractually set at 8 percent. The reconversion uses a forward contract: The forward price of 1.46 is set at inception. Thus, the condition of no risk is satisfied. There is also no investment because the entire amount of USD 1,500 is borrowed and the financing cost of USD 60 is factored into the cash flow calculations.

Arbitrage Profit Equation: The profit from borrowing 1 unit of the domestic currency and deploying it in a CIA strategy can be written as:

$$\text{CIA Profit} = \frac{1}{S} \times (1 + r^*) \times F - (1 + r)$$

This equation has four inputs: S, F, r, and r^*. Using values from the previous example:

$$\text{CIA profit} = \frac{1}{1.50} \times (1 + 8\%) \times 1.46 - (1 + 4\%) = 0.0112$$

To obtain total profit, multiply per unit profit and the size of the (gross) investment. Multiplying 0.0112 and 1,500, we obtain a total arbitrage profit of USD 16.80.

If the direction of the CIA is reversed (borrowing 1 unit of the foreign currency), the equation becomes:

$$\text{CIA profit} = S \times (1 + r) \times \frac{1}{F} - (1 + r^*)$$

EXAMPLE 5.4

This example illustrates CIA when borrowing occurs in the high-interest currency. Assume $S = 0.75$, $F = 0.70$, $r = 6$ percent, and $r^* = 10$ percent. Calculate profit per unit of currency borrowed.

Solution: Using the CIA arbitrage equation,

$$\text{CIA profit} = 0.75 \times (1 + 6\%) \times \frac{1}{0.70} - (1 + 10\%) = 0.0357$$

Discussion: The reason for borrowing the high-interest currency is that the rate of that currency's depreciation ($FP = -6.67\%$) exceeds the interest differential (4 percent).

Interest Rate Parity

Convergence

Arbitragers conduct covered interest arbitrage as long as the interest differential is more than the spot-forward differential. Consider the GBP example discussed earlier. Arbitragers borrow the USD, convert to GBP in the spot market, purchase GBP-denominated money market instruments, and short GBP forwards. By their actions, arbitragers will eventually influence prices. The following consequences will be apparent:

- Because of increased borrowing, prices of USD-denominated money market instruments fall, and the yield rises accordingly $\rightarrow r \uparrow$.
- Because of increased purchases in the currency spot market, the GBP rises in value $\rightarrow S \uparrow$.
- Because of increased purchases of GBP-denominated money market instruments, prices rise, and yield falls accordingly $\rightarrow r^* \downarrow$.
- Because of increased shorting of GBP in the forward markets, prices fall $\rightarrow F \downarrow$

Equilibrium

IRP

IRP is the equilibrium condition where the profit to covered interest arbitrage equals zero.

While it is difficult to predict which of these four changes will occur more speedily, some combination of them eventually occurs in such a way that arbitrage profit is eliminated. In equilibrium, arbitrage profit equals zero. Mathematically,

$$\text{Profit} = \frac{1}{S} \times (1 + r^*) \times F - (1 + r) = 0$$

This equilibrium condition is known as **interest rate parity (IRP)**.

There are many ways to write the IRP equation. One convenient way is to equate the ratio of interest rates to the ratio of the currency rates as follows:

$$\underbrace{\frac{1 + r}{1 + r^*}}_{\substack{\text{Ratio of Interest} \\ \text{Rate Factor}}} = \underbrace{\frac{F}{S}}_{\substack{\text{Ratio of Forward} \\ \text{to Spot}}}$$

Another way is to equate the difference between the two rates of interest on one hand and the expected percentage change of the value of the currency on the other. This is accomplished by subtracting 1 from each side of the preceding equation and simplifying. The approximate equation is:

$$r - r^* = \frac{F}{S} - 1$$

Implications

If $r < r^*$, then $F < S$. When a foreign interest rate is higher than the domestic rate, the corresponding foreign currency's forward rate will be less than the spot rate. Thus, higher interest rates are associated with depreciating currencies. This result appears counterintuitive and contrary to the interest rate effect discussed in Chapter 4 where we discussed that a high rate of interest attracts capital flows into a country and strengthens its currency. The two ideas are only apparently inconsistent. The explanation to the riddle lies in the timing of the currency value change. When capital flows into a country because of a higher interest, that country's currency value rises immediately. Over time, however, as investors exit the currency, its value decreases.

Interest Rate Conventions

So far our calculations assumed a horizon of one year. The IRP equation may be adapted quite easily for different time periods and for different interest rate conventions. Assuming that t equals the number of years or fraction of a year, the usual annual compounding convention would imply the following equation:

$$\left(\frac{1 + r}{1 + r^*}\right)^t = \frac{F}{S}$$

However, most money market instruments—especially Eurocurrency instruments—use the actual/360 simply interest system discussed in Chapter 2. The ubiquitous LIBOR rates use this interest rate convention. Assumption of a horizon of t days suggests the following (LIBOR) version of the IRP:

$$\frac{1 + r \times \dfrac{t}{360}}{1 + r^* \times \dfrac{t}{360}} = \frac{F}{S}$$

In practice, the majority of covered interest arbitrage involves the use of Eurocurrency instruments. Thus, the preceding LIBOR version of CIA is more useful than the annual compounding version of CIA. This is true for both detection of parity violations and arbitraging.

Implied Forward Rate

A key application of the IRP concerns calculation of the implied forward rate based on inputs of spot exchange and domestic and foreign interest rates. The following example uses LIBOR rates to determine the forward rate for a currency.

EXAMPLE 5.5

The 180-day LIBOR rates for USD and JPY are 4 percent and 1 percent, respectively (actual/360 convention). The spot rate is as follows: USDJPY = 110. Estimate the 180-day forward rate for JPY.

Solution: The LIBOR version of IRP is:

$$\frac{1 + r \times \frac{t}{360}}{1 + r^* \times \frac{t}{360}} = \frac{F}{S}$$

Rearranging and solving for *F*,

$$F = S \times \frac{1 + r \times \frac{t}{360}}{1 + r^* \times \frac{t}{360}}$$

$$= \frac{1}{110} \times \frac{1 + 4\% \times \frac{180}{360}}{1 + 1\% \times \frac{180}{360}}$$

$$= 0.00923$$

Discussion: In this example, JPY strengthens because of its lower interest rate. This is best understood by expressing the forward rate just obtained as a USDJPY rate. The inverse of 0.00923 indicates a forward rate of USDJPY = 108.34. Thus, the forward value of the JPY is higher than its spot value.

Impediments to Interest Rate Parity (IRP)

IRP may not hold for the following reasons:

1. When default risk varies, the interest levels in various countries may reflect not only the forward premium but also differential levels of default risk.
2. Transaction costs for conducting covered interest arbitrage may be high enough to prevent arbitrage from occurring even when there are deviations from parity.
3. Political risk or country risk would also cause deviations from IRP.
4. Taxations and other market imperfections hinder the free movement of capital across borders.

Interest Rate Parity (IRP) Evidence

Does the IRP hold?
Empirical tests of the IRP show that the theory works well in the case of major currencies.

The empirical evidence indicates that the IRP theory works quite well, especially with major currencies. But how do researchers determine whether IRP holds? MacDonald and Taylor,[1] in a summary article, explain two ways in which IRP tests are conducted:

- **Simulation tests.** The actual arbitrage strategy is simulated with available data to determine whether profits are available. Profits are typically calculated net of the costs of the following transactions: (1) selling a domestic security or borrowing money, (2) purchasing a spot foreign exchange, (3) entering a forward contract, and (4) buying a foreign security.
- **Regression tests.** The dependent variable *(Y* variable) is the ratio of forward-to-spot (or equivalently, the natural log of forward minus the natural log of spot). The independent variable *(X)* is the interest differential (specification differs depending on whether logs are used for the *Y* variable). IRP requires an intercept of 1.

Structuring appropriate tests has numerous difficulties. For instance, one has to make sure that the interest rates are essentially risk free and do not contain premiums relating to factors such as country risk. Another difficulty is that the data should be synchronized. Finally, the presence of capital controls can also bias the interest rate differential: A currency affected by capital controls may have a higher interest rate unrelated to the forward premium.

The Euro markets offer perhaps the best data to test IRP. Studies using these data show that the IRP holds, especially with major currencies. One particularly striking result involves

[1] Ronald MacDonald and Mark Taylor, "Interest Rate Parity: Some New Evidence," *Bulletin of Economic Research* 41, no. 3 (1989), pp. 255–274.

real-time and highly synchronized data obtained from the London currency markets in 1985[2]: Thousands of possible arbitrage transactions are calculated, and none showed a profit. Recent evidence also shows that emerging markets currencies are by and large consistent with IRP.

5.3 Product Markets and Currency Markets

One key aspect of globalization is international trade—the movement of goods across borders. Although many impediments to the movement of goods still exist, the success of global trade agreements such as the World Trade Organization (WTO) agreements indicates that goods move relatively freely across borders. Does this then influence price levels and currency values? We address this important point in this section.

Law of One Price

The ability of goods to move freely across borders would mean that their prices in various locations should be similar. This is known as **the law of one price (LOP)**. Note that this concept is the same as the one underlying locational arbitrage. One important difference is that forces behind locational arbitrage arise in financial markets while those behind the law of one price arise in product markets.

Let's assume that the price of sugar conforms to the law of one price. What does this mean in practical terms? Imagine that 5 lbs of sugar sells for USD 3.00 in the United States and GBP 1.50 in the United Kingdom. The law of one price relies on the currency rate to make these prices equal. This implies that the spot rate GBPUSD = 2.00. Using the symbol *P* to denote price levels, we can depict this relationship using the following equation:

$$P^{USD} = P^{GBP} \times S$$

Are national prices for goods equal? *The Economist* takes a tongue-in-cheek look at this issue and publishes prices for McDonald's Big Mac in various currencies. As Exhibit 5.1 shows, there is considerable variation in prices. The law of one price is violated with this product.

EXHIBIT 5.1
Food for Thought about Exchange Rate Controversies: *The Big Mac Index: Sizzling*

Source: *The Economist* print edition, July 5, 2007.

AMERICAN politicians bash China for its policy of keeping the yuan weak. France blames a strong euro for its sluggish economy. The Swiss are worried about a falling franc. New Zealanders fret that their currency has risen too far.

All these anxieties rest on a belief that exchange rates are out of whack. Is this justified? *The Economist*'s Big Mac Index, a light-hearted guide to how far currencies are from fair value, provides some answers. It is based on the theory of purchasing-power parity (PPP), which says that exchange rates should equalise the price of a basket of goods in any two countries. Our basket contains just a single representative purchase, but one that is available in 120 countries: a Big Mac hamburger. The implied PPP, our hamburger standard, is the exchange rate that makes the dollar price of a burger the same in each country.

Most currencies are trading a long way from that yardstick. China's currency is the lowest. A Big Mac in China costs 11 yuan, equivalent to just $1.45 at today's exchange rate, which means China's currency is undervalued by 58 percent. But before China's critics start warming up for a fight, they should bear in mind that PPP points to where currencies ought to go in the long run. The price of a burger depends heavily on local inputs such as rent and wages, which are not easily arbitraged across borders and tend to be lower in poorer countries. For this reason PPP is a better guide to currency misalignments between countries at a similar stage of development.

The most overvalued currencies are found on the rich fringes of the European Union: in Iceland, Norway and Switzerland. Indeed, nearly all rich-world currencies are expensive compared with the dollar. The exception is the yen, undervalued by 33 percent. This anomaly seems to justify fears that speculative carry trades, where funds from low-interest countries such as Japan are used to buy high-yield currencies, have pushed the yen too low. But broader measures of PPP suggest the yen is close to fair value. A New Yorker visiting Tokyo would find that although Big Macs were cheap, other goods and services seemed pricey. A trip to Europe would certainly pinch the pocket of an American tourist: the euro is 22 percent above its fair value.

The Swiss franc, like the yen a source of low-yielding funds for foreign-exchange punters, is 53 percent overvalued. The franc's recent fall is a rare example of carry traders moving a currency

---

[2] Mark Taylor, "Covered Interest Parity: A High-Frequency, High-Quality Data," *Economica* 54 (1987), pp. 429–438.

towards its burger standard. That is because it is borrowed and sold to buy high-yielding investments in rich countries such as New Zealand and Britain, whose currencies look dear against their burger benchmarks. Brazil and Turkey, two emerging economies favoured by speculators, have also been pushed around. Burgernomics hints that their currencies are a little overcooked.

Cash and carry
The hamburger standard

	Big Mac prices		Implied PPP[†] of the July 2nd	Actual dollar of exchange rate	Under (−)/over (+) valuation against the dollar, %
	in local currency	in dollars			
United States[‡]	$3.41	3.41			
Argentina	Peso 8.25	2.67	2.42	3.09	−22
Australia	A$3.45	2.95	1.01	1.17	−14
Brazil	Real 6.90	3.61	2.02	1.91	+6
Britain	£1.99	4.01	1.71§	2.01§	+18
Canada	C$3.88	3.68	1.14	1.05	+8
Chile	Peso 1,565	2.97	459	527	−13
China	Yuan 11.0	1.45	3.23	7.60	−58
Czech Republic	Koruna 52.9	2.51	15.5	21.1	−27
Denmark	Dkr 27.75	5.08	8.14	5.46	+49
Egypt	Pound 9.54	1.68	2.80	5.69	−51
Euro area**	C3.06	4.17	1.12††	1.36††	+22
Hong Kong	HK$12.0	1.54	3.52	7.82	−55
Hungary	Forint 600	3.33	176	180	−2
Indonesia	Rupiah 15,900	1.76	4,663	9,015	−48
Japan	¥280	2.29	82.1	122	−33
Malaysia	Ringgit 5.50	1.60	1.61	3.43	−53
Mexico	Peso 29.0	2.69	8.50	10.8	−21
New Zealand	NZ$4.60	3.59	1.35	1.28	+5
Peru	New Sol 9.50	3.00	2.79	3.17	−12
Philippines	Peso 85.0	1.85	24.9	45.9	−46
Poland	Zloty 6.90	2.51	2.02	2.75	−26
Russia	Rouble 52.0	2.03	15.2	25.6	−41
Singapore	S$3.95	2.59	1.16	1.52	−24
South Africa	Rand 15.5	2.22	4.55	6.97	−35
South Korea	Won 2,900	3.14	850	923	−8
Sweden	SKr 33.0	4.86	9.68	6.79	+42
Switzerland	SFr 6.30	5.20	1.85	1.21	+53
Taiwan	NT$75.0	2.29	22.0	32.8	−33
Thailand	Baht 62.0	1.80	18.2	34.5	−47
Turkey	Lire 4.75	3.66	1.39	1.30	+7
Venezuela	Bolivar 7,400	3.45	2,170	2,147	+1
Colombia	Peso 6,900	3.53	2,023	1,956	+3
Costa Rica	Colon 1,130	2.18	331	519	−36
Estonia	Kroon 30.0	2.61	8.80	11.5	−23
Iceland	Kronur 469	7.61	138	61.7	+123
Latvia	Lats 1.39	2.72	0.41	0.51	−20
Lithuania	Litas 6.60	2.61	1.94	2.53	−24
Norway	Kroner 40.0	6.88	11.7	5.81	+102
Pakistan	Rupee 140	2.32	41.1	60.4	−32
Paraguay	Guarani 10,500	2.04	3,079	5,145	−40
Saudi Arabia	Riyal 9.00	2.40	2.64	3.75	−30
Slovakia	Koruna 61.3	2.49	18.0	24.6	−27
Sri Lanka	Rupee 210	1.89	61.6	111	−45
UAE	Dirhams 10.0	2.72	2.93	3.67	−20
Ukraine	Hryvnia 9.25	1.84	2.71	5.03	−46
Uruguay	Peso 62.0	2.59	18.2	23.9	−24

[†]Purchasing-power parity; local price divided by price in United States   [‡] Average of New York, Chicago, Atlanta and San Francisco   §Dollars per pound   **Weighted average of prices in euro area   ††Dollars per euro

Sources: McDonald's; *The Economist*

Purchasing Power Parity (PPP)

The law of one price, when applied to national price indexes, is known as **purchasing power parity theory (PPP)**. The rationale for using a price index is that it is easily obtained and analyzed. Typically, the consumer price index (CPI) is used to measure prices for a standardized basket of goods. PPP would indicate that differences in the level of the CPI in two nations should be explained by the relative value of the two currencies. Mathematically, the equation for PPP is the same as the equation for the law of one price if one assumes that the variable *P* equals the overall price level in a country.

PPP comes in two versions: absolute and relative. The relative version of PPP is a less restrictive and perhaps more useful version of the theory. Although the absolute version of PPP requires equivalent prices, relative PPP requires only that price changes be harmonized with currency changes. Thus, while absolute PPP focuses on price levels, relative PPP focuses on price changes or inflation. If absolute PPP holds, relative PPP holds automatically. Instead, absolute PPP is not necessary for relative PPP to hold. In practice, most references to PPP signify the relative version of the theory.

absolute versus relative PPP
Absolute PPP requires LOP to hold. *Relative PPP* requires only that price-level *changes* are harmonized with currency.

Derivation

The idea of relative PPP can be mathematically developed to show the role played by inflation. The steps are fairly straightforward. We compare PPP equations at two points—*t* and *t* + 1—by taking the ratio of the two. The resulting equation expresses the relationship between inflation and currency value changes. For simplicity, we use domestic prices without the USD indicator. Foreign prices use the superscript*. See the following:

$$P_t = P_t^* \times S_t$$
$$P_{t+1} = P_{t+1}^* \times S_{t+1}$$

Dividing the latter by the former and recognizing that the ratio of prices represents 1 + inflation—denoted as 1 + *i*—and that the ratio of spot rates represents 1 + currency change percent—denoted as 1 + *s*—we have the *relative PPP* equation:

$$(1 + i) = (1 + i^*) \times (1 + s)$$

An equivalent way of writing the relative PPP equation expresses the relationship between inflation rates and the expected value of the spot rate at the future time point. This version of the relative PPP equation is:

$$\underbrace{\frac{1 + i}{1 + i^*}}_{\substack{\text{Ratio of Inflation} \\ \text{Rate Factor}}} = \underbrace{\frac{E(S)}{S}}_{\substack{\text{Ratio of Expected Spot} \\ \text{to Spot}}}$$

EXAMPLE 5.6

Consider the following starting values for CPI: US CPI = 300 and Canadian (CAD) CPI = 250. Spot CADUSD = 1.10. Suppose that a year later CPI levels are expected to rise to 309 and 255 in the United States and Canada, respectively. Assume relative PPP holds. What are inflation rates in the United States and Canada? What is expected ending value of CADUSD? What is its change?

Solution: We can determine inflation rates as follows:

$$i = \frac{309}{300} - 1 = 3\%$$

$$i^* = \frac{255}{250} - 1 = 2\%$$

Next, we use the relative PPP equation to solve for *E(S)*:

$$E(S) = S \times \frac{1 + i}{1 + i^*} = 1.10 \times \frac{1 + 3\%}{1 + 2\%} = 1.1108$$

This implies that:

$$s = \frac{1.1108}{1.10} - 1 = 0.98\%$$

Discussion: CAD appreciates by approximately 1 percent because CAD inflation rate is 1 percent lower than USD inflation rate. Also note that absolute PPP is violated in this example: 250 × 1.10 ≠ 300.

EXHIBIT 5.2
Real Exchange Rates

Source: For a comprehensive review of the PPP literature, see Alan Taylor and Mark Taylor, "The Purchasing Power Parity Debate," *Journal of Economic Perspectives* 18, no. 4 (2004), pp. 135–158.

	A. PPP Holds (real exchange rate q is constant)					
	S	P	i	P^*	i^*	q
Time	$= S_{-1}\dfrac{1+i}{1+i^*}$	Given	$= (P/P_{-1}) - 1$	Given	$= (P^*/P^*_{-1}) - 1$	$= S \times \dfrac{P^*}{P}$
0	1.0000	100		100		1.0000
1	0.9810	103	3.00%	105	5.00%	1.0000
2	0.9633	105	1.94%	109	3.81%	1.0000
3	0.9727	107	1.90%	110	0.92%	1.0000

	B. PPP Does Not Hold (real exchange rate q fluctuates)					
	S	P	i	P^*	i^*	q
Time	Given	Given	$= (P/P_{-1}) - 1$	Given	$= (P^*/P^*_{-1}) - 1$	$= S \times \dfrac{P^*}{P}$
0	1.0000	100		100		1.0000
1	0.9720	103	3.00%	105	5.00%	0.9909
2	0.9750	105	1.94%	109	3.81%	1.0121
3	0.9640	107	1.90%	110	0.92%	0.9910

Real Exchange Rate

A manager who wishes to assess whether PPP holds for a certain foreign country can analyze a time series of inflation rates and exchange rates to determine whether changes are indeed off-setting. Managers (and especially researchers) use real exchange rates to determine whether PPP is valid. **Real exchange rates** are defined as exchange rates that have been adjusted for relative inflation. According to PPP, because exchange rate changes are offset by differences in inflation, real exchange rates must be constant.

Mathematically, we define a real exchange rate as follows:

$$q = S \times \frac{P^*}{P}$$

Exhibit 5.2 demonstrates its calculation and shows how deviations from PPP can induce volatility in q.

Impediments to PPP

PPP arises from goods market arbitrage. This involves one or both of the following "arbitrage" activities: (1) the purchase of goods from a low-priced country for sale in a high-priced country (trading) and/or (2) capital investments in a low-priced country to produce goods for sale in other countries (manufacturing). These are not true arbitrage transactions, however, because of numerous difficulties in their execution and inability to eliminate risk. Anything that blocks, hinders, or penalizes cross-border trading and manufacturing activity can lead to a violation of PPP. The following impediments are commonly found today:

- Taxes differ between countries and can cause major deviations in prices between countries. For example, value-added taxes often lead to higher prices in Germany compared to the United States.

- Transportation costs can be prohibitive and can discourage cross-border transactions. For example, durable goods such as cars and washing machines can sometimes incur transportation costs of more than 5 percent of value.

- National consumption preferences can differ. Because even similar products are no longer substitutes in the minds of consumers, they may trade at different prices.

Purchasing Power Parity (PPP) Evidence

Most tests of the PPP involve the calculation of the real exchange rate.[3] As stated earlier, if PPP holds, real exchange rates remain constant. But there are difficulties in constructing these tests properly.

[3] For a comprehensive review of the PPP literature, see Alan Taylor and Mark Taylor, "The Purchasing Power Parity Debate," *Journal of Economic Perspectives* 18, no. 4 (2004), pp. 135–158.

- Differences in the construction of price indexes occur. The components of the U.S. CPI differ from that of most other countries. Even when the components coincide, as is the case with the U.S. and German indices, the weights may differ dramatically.
- The presence of nontradable components in goods will cause violations. For example, the price of a Big Mac contains traded components such as grain and meat. In addition, the price may contain nontraded components such as rent for the restaurant and labor. This would explain why wealthier nations have higher prices.
- Prices are "sticky." When currency values change because of monetary or other shocks, prices may not change correspondingly because of real-world considerations such as supplier contracts and retail strategies.[4]

Numerous efforts have been made to test whether PPP works. Tests of the absolute form check whether prices for particular goods or overall price levels such as the U.S. CPI or the U.S. producer price index (PPI) are in harmony with currency rates. Most tests reject absolute PPP. The Big Mac results are quite representative of the academic studies of this genre.

Tests also reject relative PPP. Most tests calculate the series of real exchange rates to check for constancy. Evidence shows that real exchange rates vary over time; this is a violation of PPP because real exchange rates are expected to be constant. Furthermore, the variation in real exchange rates appears to be equal to the variation in unadjusted exchange rates; PPP would indicate that the variation in raw exchange rates would be offset by the variation in inflation rates.[5]

Does the PPP hold?
Empirical tests of the PPP show that deviations from PPP diminish by about 15% annually. This empirical fact aids currency forecasting.

Do we reject PPP theory on the basis of these empirical results? One viewpoint is that PPP provides information about long-term currency movements. In the short term, PPP is not descriptive because of factors such as portfolio preferences, short-term asset price bubbles, and monetary shocks: These factors cause deviations from PPP. Research shows that there is better news when the long-run picture is evaluated. Over the long term (>10 years), price changes are somewhat consistent with currency values as demonstrated by Exhibit 5.3. In the long term, currency values do appear to converge toward PPP. Deviations from PPP appear to decrease at a rate of about 15 percent a year. This result suggests that MNC managers interested in forecasting long-term currency values should consider using the PPP.

5.4 Eurocurrency Futures Markets and Currency Markets

Earlier, we discussed how the interaction between currency markets and money markets produces interest rate parity. In this section, we develop this theme further and discuss how currency markets are related to Eurocurrency markets. MNCs increasingly use Eurocurrency futures not only as signals of future interest rates (as explained in Chapter 3) but also as complements to their financing activities. Furthermore, arbitragers use these markets to conduct more complex forms of covered interest arbitrage.

Eurocurrency futures are short-term interest rate derivatives based on LIBOR, Tokyo Interbank Offered Rate (TIBOR), and EURIBOR rates. The most famous example is the Chicago Mercantile Exchange (CME) Eurodollar futures contract: This is a short-term USD-denominated forward rate contract. Equivalent contracts in other major currencies are traded in the London International Financial Futures and Options Exchange (LIFFE). For example, the LIFFE short term interest rate (STIR) contracts provide forward rate contracts in major currencies such as the EUR, CHF, GBP, and JPY. The essence of these futures contracts is that users can lock-in a rate of interest for a future loan or deposit. This feature of Eurocurrency futures was discussed with examples in Chapter 3. Next we discuss how Eurocurrency futures can be used in covered interest arbitrage.

[4] Rudiger Dornbusch, "Expectations and Exchange Rate Dynamics," *Journal of Political Economy* 84, no. 6 (1976), pp. 1161–1176.

[5] Keneth Rogoff, "The Purchasing Power Parity Puzzle," *Journal of Economic Literature* 34, no. 2 (1996), 647–668.

EXHIBIT 5.3
Dollar-Sterling PPP over Two Centuries

Source: Alan Taylor and Mark Taylor, "The Purchasing Power Parity Debate," *Journal of Economic Perspectives* 18, no. 4 (2004), pp. 135–158.

(a) U.S. and UK CPIs in dollar terms

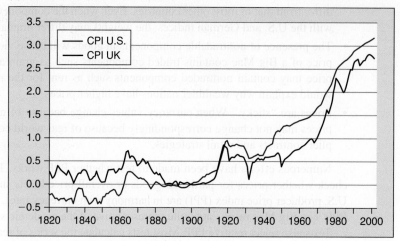

(b) U.S. and UK PPIs in dollar terms

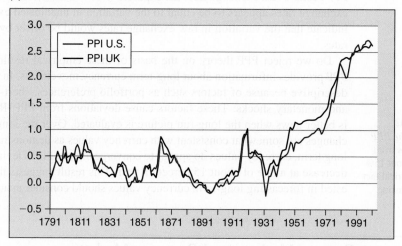

Recall that covered interest arbitrage entails borrowing in currency A, converting to currency B, making a deposit or investment in currency B, reconverting to currency A at a future date, repaying the loan in currency A, and pocketing a profit. Suppose an arbitrager can borrow in currency A for 180 days and deploy it in a money market instrument denominated in currency B. Assume that only a 90-day maturity instrument is available in currency B. The arbitrager thus needs to roll over the currency B investment in 90 days. This creates uncertainty about the eventual outcome. But what if Eurocurrency futures are available in currency B that allows the arbitrager to lock-in an interest rate between 90 and 180 days? A long position in such a contract would remove uncertainty. The futures price settlement at maturity will provide an offset for any interest rate changes. Using a combination of the 90-day money market instrument and the 90-day Eurocurrency futures contract, the arbitrager can replicate the effects of a 180-day money market instrument. The following is an example of this approach to covered interest arbitrage.

EXAMPLE 5.7

The 180-day USD LIBOR rate is 4.5 percent. The 90-day GBP LIBOR rate is 6 percent. The LIFFE GBP futures contract maturing in 90 days trades at 94.21. Spot GBPUSD equals 1.90. A 180-day forward GBPUSD equals 1.89. Calculate the per unit profit from covered interest arbitrage. What is the equilibrium forward rate that precludes arbitrage? Assume the actual/360 convention for interest calculations.

Solution: Understanding that a futures quote of 94.21 implies a locked-in rate of 5.79 percent (the difference between 100 and the futures quote of 94.21) and applying LIBOR conventions of interest calculations, we apply a modified covered interest arbitrage equation as follows:

$$\text{Profit} = \frac{1}{S} \times \left(1 + r^* \times \frac{t}{360}\right) \times F - \left(1 + r \times \frac{t}{360}\right)$$

$$= \frac{1}{1.90} \times \left(1 + 6\% \times \frac{90}{360}\right) \times \left(1 + 5.79\% \times \frac{90}{360}\right) \times 1.89 - \left(1 + 4.5\% \times \frac{180}{360}\right)$$

$$= 0.001773$$

To calculate the equilibrium rate *F*, set profit equal to zero, and solve for *F*. The answer is 1.8867. Alternatively:

$$F = S \times \frac{1 + r \times \dfrac{t}{360}}{1 + r^* \times \dfrac{t}{360}}$$

$$= 1.90 \times \frac{1 + 4.5\% \times \dfrac{180}{360}}{\left(1 + 6\% \times \dfrac{90}{360}\right) \times \left(1 + 5.79\% \times \dfrac{90}{360}\right)}$$

$$= 1.8867$$

Discussion: The per unit arbitrage profit is 0.001773. If USD 10 million is employed in this strategy, profit equals USD 1,173. A quick word about how the basic arbitrage equation is used. The first part of the equation reflects the target currency interest calculations. Because the horizon of 180-days is split into two 90-day periods earning 6 percent and 5.79 percent, respectively, we use two terms instead of one. The second half of the equation reflects the funding currency calculation and is more straightforward.

Covered interest arbitrage can also use instruments in long-term debt markets such as Eurobonds. Long-term forward contracts offer reduced levels of liquidity. Nevertheless, they are available for at least the major currencies. Currency swaps are increasingly used in interest arbitrage transactions. This is an advanced topic, and we refer the reader to Fletcher and Taylor (1996).[6]

5.5 International Fisher Effect: Real Rates of Return and Inflation

We know that the underlying value of a future cash flow is diminished by inflation. Suppose an investor is considering a one-year investment that promises a return of 8 percent. If the investor invests USD 100, the cash flow at year-end equals USD 108. However, measured in actual buying power, the investor has not enhanced his buying power by 8 percent. If the inflation rate is, say, 5 percent, USD 108 in one-year's time will purchase only the equivalent of approximately USD 103 today (inflation eats away 5 percent of value). This fundamental and intuitively obvious idea is known as the Fisher effect. In the following section, we discuss this idea and then extend it internationally to derive the **international Fisher effect (IFE)**.

Nominal Rates

Nominal rates (interest rates, returns, and yields) are observed or contractual rates. These are examples for different types of nominal rates: a 2 percent interest rate offered in a bank savings account; a 4.2 percent yield on a Treasury bill; a 12 percent return offered by a project. Thus, depending on the context, we may have an interest rate, return, or yield expressed in nominal terms.

---

[6] Donna Fletcher and Larry Taylor, "'Swap' Covered Interest Parity in Long-Date Capital Markets," *Review of Economics and Statistics* 78, no. 3 (1996), pp. 530–538.

Real Rates

Real rates (interest rates, returns, yields) are not directly observed but represent the underlying increase in buying power. Because of inflation, real rates are lower than nominal rates. A real rate is approximately equal to the nominal rate minus the rate of inflation. In the discussion in the preceding example, the real rate is calculated as 8 percent minus 5 percent and equals 3 percent. Alternatively, the real rate is 3 percent because buying power increases from USD 100 to USD 103. Investors ultimately care about real rates, not nominal rates.

National Fisher Effect

Denoting the nominal rate, the real rate, and the rate of inflation as r, rr, and i, respectively, the precise version of the **Fisher effect (FE)** is given by:

$$(1 + r) = (1 + rr) \times (1 + i)$$

This implies that the nominal rate contains two components: the real rate of return and inflation. Alternatively, when inflation is removed from a nominal return, one determines the real return.

EXAMPLE 5.8

Consider again the earlier example in which an investment of USD 100 produces a nominal return of 8 percent. The inflation rate is 5 percent. What is the real return?

Solution: Rearranging the FE equation to solve for *rr*:

$$rr = \frac{1 + r}{1 + i} - 1$$

$$= \frac{1 + 8\%}{1 + 5\%} - 1$$

$$= 2.857\%$$

Discussion: The investor is able to consume 2.857 percent more as a consequence of this investment. The approximate answer is 3 percent (=8 percent − 5 percent) but neglects the interacting effects of inflation and interest rates.

International Fisher Effect

international Fisher effect (IFE)
According to the IFE, national differences in interest rates are explained by differences in inflation rates.

An essential idea behind the Fisher effect is that investors "gross-up" nominal rates to compensate for the loss of purchasing power due to inflation. This concept can be extended globally. If capital is able to flow easily across borders, investors will gross-up national nominal rates to reflect national inflation rates. Consequently, differences between national nominal rates will be attributable only to differences in inflation. Equivalently, cross-border capital flows will be directed at countries with higher levels of real returns; in equilibrium, there will be no international differences in real returns. This concept is known as the *Fisher open hypothesis (FOH)* in the economics literature, or more commonly as the *international Fisher effect (IFE)*.

In equation form, the idea that national differences in nominal rates reflect differential inflation is given by:

$$\frac{(1 + r)}{(1 + r^*)} = \frac{(1 + i)}{(1 + i^*)}$$

This is one particular version of the IFE.

Noting from the PPP equation that the ratio of the inflation rate factor equals the ratio of expected spot rate to current spot rate, we can rewrite the IFE as follows:

$$\underbrace{\frac{1 + r}{1 + r^*}}_{\substack{\text{Ratio of Interest} \\ \text{Rate Factor}}} = \underbrace{\frac{E(S)}{S}}_{\substack{\text{Ratio of Expected Spot} \\ \text{to Spot}}}$$

EXHIBIT 5.4
The Overall View of
Parity Conditions

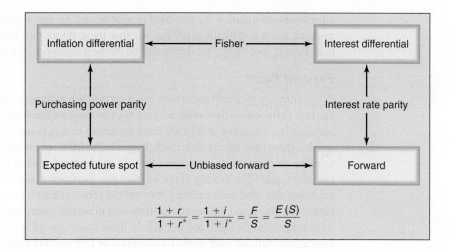

The IFE equation appears to be very similar to the IRP equation. However, important differences exist. First, the IRP is based on capital market arbitraging, and the IFE is based on overall investor behavior. Thus, while the IRP can be expected to hold every time, the IFE can be expected to hold only on average. Second, because the IRP relies on hedging, it involves the currency forward rate, and the IFE involves the futures spot rate. Because the IFE is similar to the IRP yet different because of its reference to the future spot rather than the forward rate, it is also known as *uncovered interest rate parity (UIRP)*. Thus FOH, IFE, and UIRP refer to the same concept.

In market equilibrium, parity conditions connect the currency, debt, and product markets. This overall view is presented in Exhibit 5.4. The IRP shows the equivalence between interest rate differential and the forward-spot differential. The PPP shows the equivalence between the inflation rate differential and the future spot–spot differential. The IFE shows the equivalence between the interest rate differential and the inflation rate differential. If these three parity conditions hold simultaneously, we would also have the equivalence of the forward rate and expected future spot rate; this parity, known as the *unbiased forward* (or *forward parity*), is explored in the next section on currency forecasting.

5.6 Currency Forecasting

MNCs and financial institutions often engage in currency forecasting. Various business decisions—budgeting, financing, working capital management—hinge on currency forecasts. As an example, consider an MNC selling products in Japan. JPY forecasts are necessary to plan cash inflows. In this section, we discuss various approaches to forecasting currency values. A word of caution: Currency forecasting is notoriously difficult. Prevalent models do not offer consistent performance. Therefore, decision makers need to know the limitations of each model and be willing to use multiple models as well as appropriate business judgment.

Using the Spot or Forward Rates

Because complex models often fail, sometimes participants use simple market "signals" such as the spot rate or the forward rate. Next we discuss issues related to this approach.

Spot Rate

This is the simplest forecasting method and involves the use of the spot rate as a forecast of future currency value. When great uncertainties make modeling the relationship between exchange rates and other variables difficult, this is a viable option. One possible scenario is when an MNC is forecasting currency values for highly volatile emerging market currencies. This method actually has some theoretical justification. The underlying idea is that currency rates follow a random walk—a well-known assumption for many types of financial assets including stocks. Market participants are assumed to use all available information in their trading, implying that all relevant information is embedded in spot prices. As new information arrives, currency rates respond, but it is difficult to predict whether these future movements will be positive or negative. Hence, spot values are deemed to be the best estimates of future values.

Forward Rates

When currency forwards are available—as is the case with major currencies and many emerging markets currencies—they offer an easy way to forecast the future spot value. Because entities are already contracting at forward rates for future transactions—voting with their wallets, so to speak—these rates are credible market signals. An MNC considering forwards as forecasts needs to make one important assessment first. Is the forward market for the currency at the desired maturity liquid? The validity of the forward rate increases as liquidity increases. In Chapter 2, we explained that short-term currency forward markets—at least for major currencies—are extremely liquid. We also noted, however, that forwards in certain emerging markets' currencies as well as most long-dated forwards are illiquid. In these cases, the MNC would be advised to seek other forecasting methods such as the fundamental or PPP method discussed later in this section.

Are forward rates unbiased?
While it appears a good idea to use forward rates as forecasts, *empirical tests of forward parity* suggest this not to be true.

What are the theory and evidence related to the use of forward rates as predictors for future spot rates? The equality of forward rate to the expected spot rate is known as **forward parity** or *unbiased forward rates*. A similar concept in term structure theory relates forward interest rates to the expected interest rate. In both cases, the validity of the theory requires two conditions: (1) markets are efficient and (2) there are no risk premiums (or discounts) for forward contracts. Unfortunately, most studies of the forward parity conclude that it does not work well as a forecasting method. In a famous study, Fama[7] relates spot currency changes (*Y* variable) to the difference between the forward and spot rate (*X* variable): Forward parity requires a slope of 1, but Fama reports a negative slope. This remains one of the great unsolved puzzles in finance.[8] Research continues, and a recent study[9] claims that this anomaly is not as pervasive as previously believed and reports the surprising result that emerging markets' currencies are fairly consistent with forward parity.

How does an MNC manager proceed? Given the simplicity of using the forward rate to predict currency values and the general support for the idea, MNCs should always use this as their first and quick step in forecasting currencies—especially emerging markets' currencies—and search for other more reliable but costlier methods.

Forecasting Future Spot Rates Using Parity Conditions

If forward prices are unavailable or unreliable when available because of low liquidity, a viable alternative is to use implicit forward prices. This can be achieved by using the IRP model. Recall that according to IRP, interest rate differentials are reflected in the forward price relative to the spot price. This model can be applied easily for any desired interval as long as we can identify the domestic and foreign interest rates over the same interval.

EXAMPLE 5.9

A U.K.-based MNC wishes to forecast the value of JPY in seven years' time. GBP- and JPY-denominated risk-free (government) debt instruments have yields of 6 percent and 3 percent, respectively. If JPYGBP = 0.0075 now, what is the expected future spot?

Solution: Using IRP,

$$\text{JPYGBP (year 7)} = 0.0075 \times \left(\frac{1 + 6\%}{1 + 3\%}\right)^7 = 0.00917$$

Because JPY has lower interest rates, JPYGBP rises in value.

---

[7] Eugene Fama, "Forward and Spot Exchange Rates," *Journal of Monetary Economics* 14 (1984), pp. 319–338.

[8] For surveys, see Keneth Froot and Richard Taylor, "Anomalies: Foreign Exchange," *Journal of Economic Perspectives* 4 (1990), pp. 179–192; and C. Engel, "The Forward Discount Anomaly and the Risk Premium: A Survey of Recent Evidence," *Journal of Empirical Finance* 3 (1996), pp. 123–192.

[9] Ravi Bansal and Magnus Dahlquist, "The Forward Premium Puzzle: Different Tales from Developed and Emerging Economies," *Journal of International Economics* 51 (2000), pp. 115–144.

Discussion: To improve precision, we need to make sure that differences in yields are not related to risk factors such as country risk. Nor should the instruments differ in terms of features such as coupon, callability, and convertibility. Finally, we need to ensure that the conventions used for quoting yields are similar and compatible with annual compounding.

The efficiency of IRP forecasts is determined by the validity of the underlying theory. We discussed earlier that the IRP works well over short- and medium-term horizons and for the major currencies. Therefore, under these conditions, IRP forecasts work well. What about forecasting over the long term or for currencies of developing countries? The PPP may be better suited in these situations.

Using the PPP in forecasting is very similar to using the IRP in forecasting. Instead of using interest rates, we use inflation rates. However, implementation issues differ significantly. Ex ante inflation rates are more difficult to obtain than ex ante interest rates. This is so because interest rates for various maturities are reflected in publicly traded debt securities and widely disseminated. There is no analogous way to assess inflation. So, decision makers routinely use current inflation as a proxy for future inflation.

Forward Interest Rates and Currency Forecasting

MNCs are often interested in the future path of currency values. For instance, an Indian firm evaluating a long-term project in Canada would be interested in forecasting the value of the CAD each year over the project's life. Assuming that the firm uses IRP for forecasting, the use of a *single* long-term interest rate to calculate a series of annual currency values may provide erroneous answers if the term structure is not flat. A better method is to use forward rates signaled by debt futures markets such as Eurocurrency futures markets. The following example demonstrates this approach.

EXAMPLE 5.10

Consider the following term structure information in two countries:

Country	Year 1 Rate	Year 2 Forward Rate
Canada	4%	6%
India	6%	10%

Assume CADINR = 30. Use IRP to forecast one- and two-year currency rates.

Solution:

$$\text{CADINR (year 1)} = 30 \times \frac{1 + 6\%}{1 + 4\%} = 30.577$$

and

$$\text{CADINR (year 2)} = 30.577 \times \frac{1 + 10\%}{1 + 6\%} = 31.73$$

Discussion: Because Indian rates are higher, the CAD strengthens against the INR. The rate at which it strengthens is not constant, however, because the interest rate differential changes in value from year 1 to year 2.

Fundamental Forecasting

Fundamental currency forecasting refers to the construction and use of models that link currency values with a set of variables advocated in economic theory. Data are used first to build the model and later to forecast currency values using estimated model parameters. Here is one simple way to understand fundamental forecasting. In Chapter 4, we discussed current account and financial account factors that determine exchange rates. This suggests the use of these variables in forecasting future currency values. Thus, one might construct a model using variables such as inflation, interest rates, money supply, and national income.[10]

In general, fundamental forecasting models require the following steps:

- **The identification of factors affecting the demand and supply of currencies.** These factors could include conventional factors such as interest rates, money supply, and productivity as well as currency-specific factors such as market sentiment and commodity prices.
- **The estimation of the relationship between the factors and the currency.** This is done using statistical models such as regression models.
- **The forecast of the factors themselves over the period studied.**
- **The forecast of the currency value is performed using the forecast of the factors.**

Of these steps, the most difficult is forecasting the factors. The quality of the currency forecast depends on the quality of the forecast of the factors themselves.

EXAMPLE 5.11

A U.S.- based MNC with operations in the United Kingdom is interested in forecasting the value of the GBP in a year's time. The GBP is currently trading at GBPUSD = 1.50. A financial analyst in the firm determines the explanatory variables governing the value of the GBP to be relative inflation and European-originated capital flows into the U.S. equity markets. She obtains quarterly data on the following variables: S (currency spot), i (inflation), and *capflow* (capital flow). These raw data are translated into the following variables: s (percent change in currency value), INF (relative change in inflation), and FL (change in capital flow).

$$s_t = \left(S_t^{GBP} / S_{t-1}^{GBP} \right) - 1$$

$$INF_t = \left(i_t^{GBP} - i_t^{USD} \right) / \left(i_{t-1}^{GBP} - i_{t-1}^{USD} \right) - 1$$

and

$$FL_t = \left(capflow_t / capflow_{t-1} \right) - 1$$

How can the analyst use these data to develop a currency forecast? Assume that the analyst has available sufficient data to run the econometric model. She also has access to forecasts of inflation and capital flows.

Solution: The solution is found in multiple steps. The initial step of variable identification has already been completed. The remaining steps are model building, factor forecasting, and currency forecasting.

Model Building

To assess the effects of relative inflation and fund flows on the GBP, the analyst runs the following regression:

$$s_t = a + b \times INF_t + c \times FL_t + error$$

The following results are obtained from the regression analysis[11]:

$$R\text{-squared} = 40\%$$

$$a = 0.005$$

$$b = -0.06$$

$$c = 0.05$$

---

[10] For example, see the real interest differential (RID) model in Jeffrey Frankel, "On the Mark: A Theory of Floating Exchange Rates Based on Real Interest Differentials," *American Economic Review* 69, no. 4 (1979), pp. 610–622.

[11] Financial models have varying levels of precision. The level of precision directly determines the level of trust to place in a model. Thus, diagnostic statistics are necessary. In regression analysis, two levels of diagnostics are commonly used. First, the user determines whether the overall model merits consideration by estimating the fit of the model; *R*-squared is the statistic used for this purpose. Second, the user determines whether the explanatory variables individually have power; the *t*-statistics for the coefficients are used for this purpose.

Forecast of Input Factors

Next, the analyst obtains current values of the explanatory variables as well as forecasts for the next year as follows:

Variable	Current Value ($t = 0$)	Forecast ($t = +1$)
i^{GBP}	4%	6%
i^{USD}	2%	3%
capflow	3 billion	3.3 billion

Forecast of Currency Rate

Using these values, the analyst can generate the forecast for the GBP for the next year (denoted as +1) as follows:

$$INF_{+1} = \frac{(6\% - 3\%)}{(4\% - 2\%)} - 1 = 0.50$$

$$FL_{+1} = \frac{3.3}{3.0} - 1 = 0.10$$

$$s_{+1} = 0.005 + (-0.06) \times 0.50 + 0.05 \times 0.10 = -0.02 \text{ or } -2\%$$

$$S_{+1}^{GBP} = S_0^{GBP} \times \left(1 + s_{+1}^{GBP}\right) = 1.50 \times (1 - 2\%) = 1.47$$

Discussion: The forecast of 1.47 reflects a 2 percent decrease. From the preceding analysis, we can also infer that the inflation factor is the most influential factor causing the currency decrease. The *R*-squared and the *t*-statistics of slopes *b* and *c* together indicate the confidence one can place in the model. Once again, a key step is obtaining inflation and capital-flow forecasts. Of the two, forecast of inflation is perhaps the easiest; it is often inferred from interest rates using the Fisher effect equation. Capital flows are much more volatile and may be a function of stock market levels and interest rates.

Technical Forecasting

Unlike fundamental forecasting, technical forecasting relies solely on the time series of currency values. Thus, time itself instead of economic factors such as interest rates and inflation becomes the determining factor. As with stock price forecasting using technical analysis, hundreds of approaches are available. One strategy is to identify seasonality and long-term trends in currency values. This can be accomplished by using low-tech approaches such as chart gazing and sophisticated statistical approaches such as Box-Jenkins time-series analysis. Technical forecasting hinges on detecting systematic patterns in data and is thus a refutation of the well-known efficient markets hypothesis, which states that future price changes depend on new information only and are independent of past prices.

One simple technical approach is *moving averages*. Financial market participants widely use this method not only to forecast currencies but also to forecast other financial factors/assets such as interest rates and stock prices. For example, www.finance.yahoo.com provides moving averages and more than 10 other technical indicators for currencies, stocks, and other financial assets.

Assessing Forecast Accuracy

MNCs often derive currency forecasts from multiple sources. How can MNCs determine which of these sources provides the best forecasts? We discuss four ways to assess a forecasting system.

Absolute Forecast Error

One simple method to assess forecast accuracy is to calculate the *absolute forecast error (AFE)*, which equals the absolute value of actual currency value minus forecast value.

Denoting currency forecasts as $\hat{S}$ and ignoring time subscripts for convenience, we define:

$$AFE = |S - \hat{S}|$$

By working with absolute values, we avoid canceling out positive and negative forecast errors. This is necessary because both types of forecast error have negative consequences for MNCs. A good forecasting system will have a small average AFE. The *mean absolute forecast error (MAFE)* is given by:

$$MAFE = \frac{1}{N} \sum AFE$$

Root Mean Square Error

An alternate method consistent with the AFE is *root mean square error (RMSE)*. Here errors are squared to avoid canceling out positive and negative errors. The equation is:

$$RMSE = \sqrt{\frac{1}{N} \sum (S - \hat{S})^2} = \sqrt{\frac{1}{N} \sum AFE^2}$$

Success Ratio

This method, known as the *success ratio (SR)*, assesses the percentage of times a forecasting system correctly predicts the direction of currency change.

EXAMPLE 5.12

A manager is evaluating two competing forecasting systems A and B and produces four forecasts from each system. The following table lists these forecasts and the current spot and the actual future spot.

Current spot	Actual future spot	Forecast A	Forecast B
1.44	1.49	1.52	1.55
1.31	1.29	1.33	1.26
1.52	1.53	1.51	1.54
1.41	1.40	1.38	1.44

Solution:

			A				B		
S_0	S_1	$\hat{S}$	AFE	AFE^2	Success	$\hat{S}$	AFE	AFE^2	Success
1.44	1.49	1.52	0.03	0.0009	Y	1.55	0.06	0.0036	Y
1.31	1.29	1.33	0.04	0.0016	N	1.26	0.03	0.0009	Y
1.52	1.53	1.51	0.02	0.0004	N	1.54	0.01	0.0001	Y
1.41	1.40	1.38	0.02	0.0004	Y	1.44	0.04	0.0016	N
MAFE			0.028				0.035		
RMSE				0.0287				0.0394	
SR					50%				75%

Discussion: It is difficult to choose between A and B. On the one hand, A has lower MAFE and RMSE. On the other hand, B has a higher SR. The choice depends on consequences (financial losses) of mistakes in forecasting. If losses are constant and do not depend on the magnitude of the mistake, B is better. If instead losses depend on the magnitude of the mistake, A is better.

Regression Method

One final method of evaluating forecasts uses regressions. It has the advantage of automatically providing several statistics of interest including some not supplied by previous methods.

$$S_t = a + b \times \hat{S}_t + e_t$$

Ideally, a forecasting system exhibits the following characteristics:

- A high regression *R*-squared, indicating precision
- $a = 0$, indicating lack of bias
- $b = 1$, indicating one-to-one mapping

The intercept *a* denotes bias in the forecasting model. A known bias, however, can be easily corrected. For example, a positive intercept value of 0.02 requires the decision maker to gross-up forecast values by 0.02. Similarly, the firm can incorporate a value other than 1 for *b*. Consider a forecasting service whose regression values are *a* equals 0.02 and *b* equals 0.8. If the forecast for next period is 0.40, the firm can adjust this forecast as follows:

$$\text{Revised forecast} = 0.02 + 0.8 \times 0.40 = 0.34$$

Because we can adjust for *a* and *b*, *R*-squared is the main assessment criterion. But practical problems remain. Of interest to decision makers is the consequence of forecast errors. In some situations, underestimation of currency values might be more problematic than overestimation; in other situations, overestimation might be more problematic. Also, effects may be nonlinear: A forecast error of 10 percent might be more than twice as problematic as a forecast error of 5 percent. To understand these issues fully, one needs to look at the context in which MNCs use currency forecasts. A context-sensitive evaluation model could then be developed.

Summary

- Currency values are shaped by the actions of investors, producers, and consumers in financial and real markets.
- An important force in financial markets is arbitrage. Investors exploit price discrepancies by simultaneously buying currencies at lower prices and selling at higher prices.
- A complex form of arbitrage—covered interest arbitrage—involves the exploitation of interest rate differentials in national money markets. Currency transactions—spot and forward—are used to generate arbitrage profits.
- Covered interest arbitrage helps maintain a strict relationship between interest rate differentials and forward/spot differentials. This relationship is known as *interest rate parity,* or *IRP.* IRP predicts that the currencies of countries with high interest rates will trade at lower forward prices relative to spot prices.
- Currency values are also affected by inflation rates because of the interaction between currency and goods markets. A high rate of inflation will lead a country's citizens to purchase foreign goods. In addition, foreigners purchase fewer goods from the high-inflation country. These actions lead to eventual currency devaluation. This theory is known as *purchasing power parity,* or *PPP.*
- Firms use IRP and PPP to forecast currency values. Other forecasting methods include technical and fundamental analyses as well as the use of spot and forward prices.
- Fundamental forecasting is a general approach by which users specify theoretical variables, determine the relationship of these variables to currency value, and, using this relationship, predict future currency values.
- MNCs can evaluate the efficacy of a forecast method using many methods including the absolute forecast error approach and regression methods. The latter involves regressing actual currency values on forecasts; the efficiency of the forecasting method is denoted by *R*-squared.

Questions

1. **Law of One Price.** Explain the law of one price (LOP). What economic forces enable this law?

2. **Law of One Price.** Assume you are comparing prices between the United States and Afghanistan. Do you expect the LOP to hold? Explain.

3. **Locational Arbitrage.** What is locational arbitrage? How many currencies are involved in it? What are its constraints?

4. **Locational Arbitrage.** Explain how large bid-ask spreads can prevent locational arbitrage even if a particular currency appears to be quoted inexpensively in one location.

5. **Triangular Arbitrage.** What is triangular arbitrage? How many currencies are involved in it? How many locations are involved? Who are the entities conducting this type of arbitrage?

6. **Covered Interest Arbitrage.** What is a covered interest rate arbitrage? How important is the presence of the currency forward contract for this type of arbitrage?

7. **Interest Rate Parity.** What is interest rate parity (IRP)? What is the connection between covered interest arbitrage (CIA) and IRP? What are impediments to IRP?

8. **Interest Rate Parity.** Under which conditions is the IRP is more likely to hold?

9. **Purchasing Power Parity.** Compare and contrast the absolute and relative forms of PPP. What are impediments to it? What are conditions under which the PPP is likely to hold?

10. **Purchasing Power Parity.** What is the difference between LOP and PPP?

11. **Real Exchange Rates.** What are real exchange rates? What do they signify? What is their use?

12. **Fisher Effect.** Explain the national and international versions of the Fisher effect. What is the main use of the international Fisher effect?

13. **Forecasting Using Parities.** Compare and contrast the forecasting of currencies using IRP and PPP. What factors enable a person to choose one theory versus the other?

14. **Fundamental Forecasting.** Explain the idea behind fundamental forecasting. Assume that you are trying to forecast the exchange rate between the USD and the CNY (Chinese yuan). What factors would you use and why?

15. **Bias and Efficiency in Forecasting.** Explain the concepts of bias and efficiency in forecasting. Between the two, which is the more serious concern? As a decision maker, how would you respond to bias in your forecasting method?

Problems

1. **Law of One Price.** The law of one price (LOP) is assumed to hold between the United States and Canada. The CAD is trading in the spot market at CADUSD = 0.90. If half a gallon of orange juice costs USD 2.50 in the United States, what is its cost in Canada?

2. **Law of One Price.** The law of one price (LOP) is assumed to hold between the United States and Mexico. A bottle of white tequila sells for USD 15 in the United States. The same bottle sells for MXN 120 in Mexico. What is the spot rate for the MXNUSD?

3. **Locational Arbitrage.** In New York, the Japanese yen is quoted at JPYUSD = 0.009. In Tokyo, the USD is quoted at USDJPY = 105. What type of arbitrage is possible in this situation? How is it executed? What are potential risk factors?

4. **Locational Arbitrage.** In New York, the EUR is quoted at EURUSD = 1.505 – 1.508 (bid-ask). In Paris, the EUR is quoted at EURUSD = 1.507 – 1.509 (bid-ask). Is locational arbitrage possible? Explain.

5. **Locational Arbitrage.** In the Tokyo currency markets, a foreign exchange dealer provides the following quotes: USDJPY is quoted at a bid of 101 and ask of 103. In the New York currency markets, the same currency, USDJPY, is quoted at a bid of 104 and ask of 105. Is there a way for an arbitrager to exploit this situation? Explain with calculations.

6. **Triangular Arbitrage.** In the London currency markets, the following quotes are available: EURUSD = 1.50 and EURCAD = 1.6. In the New York currency markets, we find the CAD trading at CADUSD = 0.9. Explain how an arbitrager can exploit this situation. If the arbitrager can employ USD 1,000 (or its equivalent in another currency) toward this strategy, how much would the arbitrager end with?

7. **Interest Rate Parity.** Two countries, Cambria and Nubira, have nominal interest rates of 5 percent and 10 percent, respectively. (Assume annual compounding.) These interest rates are inferred from the yields of government debt instruments and are applicable over the next four years. The currencies of these two countries, the Cab and the Nub (ISO codes are CAB and NUB) are freely traded in markets without any governmental restrictions. The current exchange rate is CABNUB = 2.

    a. Estimate the path of CABNUB over the next four years.

    b. What is the annual rate of change of CABNUB?

    c. What is the annual rate of change of NUBCAB?

8. **Covered Interest Arbitrage.** Interest rates on one-year instruments denominated in JPY and USD are 1 percent and 5 percent, respectively. The JPY is currently trading at a rate of USDJPY = 100. The one-year forward rate is USDJPY = 98. Explain how an arbitrager can exploit this situation. What is the net profit for USD 1,000 (or its equivalent in another currency) committed to this strategy?

9. **Covered Interest Arbitrage.** From an investor's perspective, the one-year borrowing and lending rates for GBP are 7 percent and 6 percent, respectively. In contrast, the one-year borrowing and lending rates for JPY are 3 percent and 1 percent, respectively. The spot rate is GBPJPY = 150, and the one-year forward rate is GBPJPY = 140. Use calculations to explain how an arbitrager can exploit this situation.

10. **Purchasing Power Parity.** During the past year, the consumer price indexes (CPI) of the United States and the Eurozone rose by 2 percent and 5 percent, respectively. If PPP holds, what is the percentage change in the value of the EUR over the same time period?

11. **Purchasing Power Parity.** The EUR is currently traded at a level of EURUSD = 1.35. Economists estimate the inflation rates to be 2 percent in the United States and 3 percent in Europe. Using the PPP, estimate the value of EURUSD in two years. Explain why the EUR is expected to appreciate or depreciate against the USD.

12. **Real Exchange Rate.** Consider the following data on USDMXN and price levels in the United States and Mexico. Calculate the sequence of real exchange rates and comment on your results.

		Price Level (P)		
Year	USDMXN	Mexico	United States	Real Exchange (q)
−3	10.00	100	100	?
−2	10.50	106	102	?
−1	10.70	110	105	?
0	10.90	114	108	?

13. **Domestic Fisher Equation.** Economists estimate the one-year inflation rate to be 3 percent in the United States. The one-year Treasury bill with a face value of USD 100 is quoted at a discount of USD 4.5 from face value. Estimate the nominal and real interest rates.

14. **Interest Rate Parity.** You are a financial analyst with the U.S.-based MNC Prod & Push, which sells consumer products around the world. You report directly to the CFO. You have been assigned the task of negotiating with bankers on certain forward contracts involving the USD and CHF. Reports from corporate economists indicate interest rates of 6 percent and 3 percent in the U.S. and Switzerland, respectively, over the next five years. Assuming a flat term structure (that is, rates do not vary from year to year) and a spot rate of CHFUSD = 0.60, for purposes of negotiations with the banker, construct estimates of forward rates for year one and year four contracts. Assume annual compounding.

15. **International Fisher Equation.** The United Kingdom and Chinese interest rates are 5 percent and 10 percent, respectively. If the rate of inflation in the United Kingdom is 3 percent, use the IFE to determine the inflation in China.

16. **International Fisher Equation.** The U.S.-based MNC Fairwon is contemplating a major corporate investment in Mexico to construct turbines. The level of long-term interest rates is about 5 percent higher in Mexico at 11 percent. Fairwon estimates that its USD cost of capital (for domestic projects) is about 12 percent. You have been given the task of estimating the MXN cost of capital for the project. Assume that the IFE holds and that the interest rate differential equals the inflation rate differential. Assume that this differential also helps to explain the difference in cost of capital in two currencies for a firm.

17. **Comparing Currency Forecasts.** Grotex is a small engineering firm exporting to European markets. Over the last four quarters, Grotex has obtained forecasts for the value of the EUR (in USD) from two different sources. A financial analyst in the firm is assigned the task of selecting one of these two sources for future business. Given the following data, what various conclusions can be derived?

Data	Year −4	Year −3	Year −2	Year −1
Forecast I	1.10	1.15	1.05	0.90
Forecast II	1.15	1.25	1.05	0.95
Actual	1.20	1.15	1.10	0.95

18. **Interest Rate Parity and Forward Interest Rates.** The U.S. and Mexican spot and forward interest rates are provided in the following table. If the MXN is currently trading at MXNUSD = 0.12, estimate the values at the end of the first and the second years. What is the (average) appreciation or depreciation rate of the MXNUSD during the two years?

Country	Year 0–1 (spot rate)	Year 1–2 (forward rate)
United States	6%	9%
Mexico	2%	4%

19. **Covered Interest Arbitrage and Money Market Futures.** The 180-day USD LIBOR rate is 2.5 percent. The 90-day EURIBOR rate is 4 percent. (Assume actual/360 convention for interest.) Exchange-traded futures contract on a EUR-denominated money market contract (reference rate is EURIBOR) maturing in 90-days trades at 96.20. (Assume pricing convention of Eurodollar futures.) Spot EURUSD equals 1.40, and 180-day forward EURUSD equals 1.39. Calculate the per unit profit from covered interest arbitrage. What is the equilibrium forward rate?

20. **Fundamental Forecasting.** Rosemont, Inc., a U.S. firm with business interests in Australia, has assigned the job of predicting the future value of the AUD to Kristina Jacobs, a financial analyst. Ms. Jacobs believes that the value of AUDUSD is explained by two factors as follows:

$$INT = \frac{\text{Australian interest rate}}{\text{U.S. interest rate}} - 1$$

and

$$COM = \frac{\text{Global commodity prices at year end}}{\text{Global commodity prices at year beginning}} - 1$$

Using 10 years of data, Ms. Jacobs regresses the percentage change in the value of AUDUSD on these two factors and finds the following results:

Percent change in AUDUSD $= -0.02 - 0.15 \times INT + 0.90 \times COM$

The *R*-squares are adequately high and the coefficient *t*-statistics are significant. Ms. Jacobs also obtains the current and forecasted values of her explanatory variables. The global commodity price index is expected to increase from its current value of 140 to 145 in a year. The financial markets in the United States and Australia indicate interest rates of 5 percent and 10 percent, respectively, in one-year risk-free instruments.

a. If spot AUDUSD = 0.78, what is Ms. Jacobs' estimate of AUDUSD in one-year's time?

b. Using your general knowledge concerning Australia, what other factors would you consider in the equation?

21. **Forecasting Efficiency.** Mike Myers, a junior financial analyst in a U.S.-based MNC, has been assigned the task of evaluating currency forecasts provided by a bank. Using forecasts and the following actual values, answer the following questions.

a. What is the mean absolute forecast error?

b. Using the regression feature of a spreadsheet, estimate the bias and efficiency of the forecasts. Comment on these results.

c. Calculate revised forecasts by incorporating the bias determined in (b). What is the mean absolute forecast error for the revised forecasts? Compare your answers with (a) and comment.

Quarter	Actual	Bank Forecast
−6	0.67	0.65
−5	0.69	0.68
−4	0.65	0.67
−3	0.62	0.60
−2	0.66	0.66
−1	0.70	0.69

Extensions

1. **Term Structure and Currency Forecasting.** The term structure for USD- and CAD-denominated instruments is provided in the following table. Assume CADUSD = 0.88. Use annual compounding.

Years	USD	CAD
0.5	2.1%	3.5%
1.0	2.6%	3.6%
1.5	3.0%	4.1%
2.0	3.2%	4.3%

Perform the following calculations:

a. Generate forecasts of CADUSD over this interval.

b. Calculate the forward rate for the second year for the two currencies and show the relationship between these forward rates and the currency change during the same interval.

2. **Real Exchange Rates and Currency Forecasting.** Surya Enterprises is an Indian firm sourcing Ayurvedic medicines and therapeutics from India for sale in the United States. Surya's CEO, Krishna Swamy, is concerned about its pricing policy as well as cash flow from U.S. sales. Both concerns directly relate to currency values. Mr. Swamy's immediate concern is to forecast the USD for the coming year. This will help him devise an appropriate pricing policy for the firm's products.

Suppose you are reporting to Mr. Swamy. Consider the following data on USDINR and price levels in the United States and India. Assume the following additional information. One-year interest rates in India and the United States are 8.5 percent and 3.1 percent, respectively. Assume that long-term real rates of interest are approximately 2 percent in both countries.

| Year | USDINR | Price Level (P) | | Real Exchange (q) |
		India	United States	
–5	40.00	100	100	40.00
–4	41.30	107	102	?
–3	42.21	115	105	?
–2	43.44	122	108	?
–1	44.60	127	110	?
0	45.20	135	113	?

a. Calculate the sequence of real exchange rates.
b. Can you demonstrate multiple ways of forecasting USDINR using these data?

Case

Clover Machines: *Currency Arbitrage*

Clover Machines continues its operational push in South America and Asia. Its initial foray in these regions is in Brazil and India. Laura Brooks, Clover's CEO, is pleased with progress to date. With expertise in agricultural machines, Clover has been able to quickly custom config-ure and offer machines needed by these markets. Brazil is one of the world's leading produc-ers of ethanol. Unlike the United States, Brazil makes ethanol from sugarcane. Clover devised machines for harvesting sugarcane and has made inroads in the market. In India, where farms tend to be small, Clover has introduced low-cost, low-horsepower tractors and tilling acces-sories; it also worked hard to build relationships with leading banks to offer credit to small farmers to purchase its equipment.

In keeping with operational progress, Clover Machines has made progress in setting up operational structures in Brazil and India. Looking into the future and anticipating financial transactions in these countries, Brian Bent, Clover's CFO, has cultivated relationships with leading banks. Mr. Bent also notes that the economic situation in these countries is quite dif-ferent from that in the United States. Currency markets appear more volatile, and the bank-ing sector not as efficient. Currency forward markets in particular do not have the depth and efficiency of markets for major currencies. Also credit markets—for both borrowing and lending—appear highly volatile.

Mr. Bent is aware of the potential of currency arbitrage. Volatile markets sometimes provide arbitrage opportunities to investors because of mispricing. Low-liquidity and high-volatility markets offer more arbitrage opportunities than do stable and high-liquidity markets such as in the United States. As he sets up financial shop in these emerging markets, Mr. Bent is wondering whether Clover can exploit market conditions. He requests a junior analyst, Adao Ronaldinho, to obtain currency and interest rate quotations from a few banks. This information is as follows:

| BRLUSD Spot Quotes | | |
Bank	Bid	Ask
Banco do Brasil	0.6152	0.6171
Itau	0.6149	0.6166
Bradesco	0.6172	0.6185
Unibanco	0.6167	0.6178

BRLUSD Six-Month Forward Quotes

Bank	Bid	Ask
HSBC	0.5943	0.5972
Itau	0.5889	0.5911

Interest Rates (simple interest basis)

Bank: Currency	Bank Borrows	Bank Lends
BNP Paribas: USD	2.4%	3.0%
Unibanco: BRL	12.2%	13.1%

Mr. Bent requests answers to the following questions:

1. There appears to be a wide disparity between the spot quotes. If Clover wishes to simply use these markets to short BRL—unload BRL revenues, for instance—it would choose to transact with Bradesco. But is there opportunity for currency arbitrage contained in these spot rates? Assume that USD 1 million is directed toward this activity.

2. How would bank commissions for currency transactions affect arbitrage? Assume a round-trip (for buying and selling) transaction fee of USD 175 (same fee in all banks; half of this amount for a single trip). Is the transaction identified in (1) profitable after commissions? Next, assume round-trip commissions are a percentage fee of transaction size: What is the break-even percent commission?

3. Mr. Bent notes high interest rates in Brazil. How can Clover deploy USD 1 million to exploit these rates? A possible strategy is to invest in a foreign currency and lock-in USD returns by using forward rates. Calculate the annualized return of such an investment. Note that quoted rates apply to six-month transactions but have been annualized. Ignore bank commission and fees. Compare your strategy with covered interest arbitrage. What are the similarities and differences?

4. Employ an investment strategy opposite to that discussed in (3). That is, evaluate opportunities for deploying BRL 1 million in a USD-denominated interest-bearing deposit. Apply the method used in answering (3).

5. Discuss the prevalence of currency arbitrage. Which entities are best positioned to exploit them? What should be the optimal strategy of firms such as Clover?

CHAPTER SIX

Currency Risk Exposure Measurement

Daimler's Mercedes-Benz car division is in a battle with Toyota's Lexus division in the global luxury car market. Recent years have been difficult for Daimler not only because of Lexus's sterling products but also because of the strength of the euro (EUR). During 2006–2007, for instance, while the Japanese yen (JPY) advanced against the U.S. dollar (USD) by about 10 percent, the EUR advanced against the USD by more than 30 percent. Mercedes as well as Lexus cars are made in their respective home markets with costs denominated in EUR and JPY, respectively, and shipped to the important U.S. market. No wonder then that Daimler's margins shrank while Toyota's expanded. What are short-term and long-term ramifications for both firms?

Daimler and Toyota are not unique in their exposure to currency fluctuations. All MNCs— and surprisingly even many domestic firms—are subject to currency risk. Many firms that are affected devote significant efforts to measure and to manage this risk. Especially for MNCs, currency risk is a direct consequence of global operations and cannot be easily avoided. How can MNCs measure and manage this risk factor effectively?

In this chapter, we define currency risk and explain the conditions under which it affects firms. A major emphasis is on quantifying currency risk. We discuss various ways to measure the two main categories of currency risk: transaction exposure and operating exposure. As with risk analyses in other contexts, important elements of currency risk analysis are (1) identification of the way currency changes affect financial results and (2) measurement of variation in performance and an assessment of its significance. This chapter is the first of a two-chapter sequence on currency risk. Chapter 6 shows how currency risk is measured and Chapter 7 shows how currency risk is managed.

In particular, in this chapter we discuss the following:

- Measurement of variation in currencies and empirical evidence on current levels of currency variation in both major and emerging market currencies.
- Definition of transaction exposure and description of situations producing this type of exposure.
- Measurement of currency risk using techniques such as best- and worst-case scenarios as well as portfolio risk models.
- Netting of transaction exposure by aggregating transactions at a point in time as well as over time.
- The use of value-at-risk (VaR) methods to assess transaction exposure.
- Definition of operating exposure and explanation of how currency changes induce variation in price and quantity of goods and services sold by a firm.
- The use of regression analysis in assessing operating exposure.
- An evaluation of the currency exposure of various types of firms including purely domestic firms.
- Description of accounting or translation exposure.

6.1 Variation in Foreign Exchange

Currency risk reflects the impact of currency values on MNCs' financial performance. Thus, an understanding of currency risk starts with an understanding of currency variation. You learned earlier that most of the developed countries and even some of the developing countries have floating exchange rates. Thus, the value of these currencies may change as economic conditions and market sentiment changes (see Exhibit 6.1). For instance, in 2000, the newly launched currency, the EUR, declined in value because of capital flows from Europe into the United States. Yet the same currency rose dramatically in value in 2006–2007 because of economic weakness in the United States and strength in the Eurozone.

Currency value changes are not unique to freely floating currency systems. Other systems such as the managed floating system and even the fixed currency systems such as the pegged currency are subject to change. In fact, history shows that the discrete changes in the value of the fixed currencies are often very large: Radical declines in Asian currencies during the crisis of 1997–1998 bear this out. We note that in recent times, pegged currencies such as the Hong Kong dollar (HKD) and the Chinese yuan (CNY) are successfully maintained at fairly constant values. But history indicates that the appearance of stability may be misleading and the threat of radical changes can never be assumed away.

The Standard Deviation of a Currency

How do we quantify the variation in currency values? As in the analysis of financial instruments such as stocks and bonds, we use measures of dispersion such as the standard deviation. We discuss methods to estimate the standard deviation of currencies next.

Currency Input

The input to a standard deviation calculation is a time series of (direct) currency values. The currency values are converted into currency returns (percent changes in currency values) to avoid magnitude (scale) differences between various currencies; this ensures comparability between high-value and low-value currencies. Using notation introduced in Chapter 4:

$$s_t = \frac{S_t}{S_{t-1}} - 1$$

EXHIBIT 6.1
Currency Volatility in the 2000s

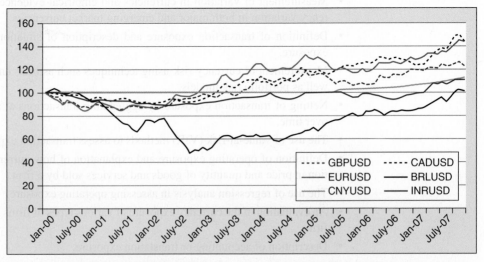

Note: Currencies depicted are the British pound (GBP), the Canadian dollar (CAD), the Euro (EUR), the Brazilian real (BRL), the Chinese yuan (CNY), and the Indian rupee (INR). Currency values are set to 100 in January 2000 to facilitate comparison. For much of this period, the CNY was controlled at a fixed value and is therefore the least volatile currency. The BRL appears to be the most volatile currency.

EXAMPLE 6.1

If the GBP changes in value from USD 1.80 to USD 1.90 in a certain period, calculate the GBP's percent of change in value.

Solution:

$$s_t = \frac{S_t}{S_{t-1}} - 1$$

$$= \frac{1.90}{1.80} - 1$$

$$= 5.56\%$$

Formula for Standard Deviation

The variance of a currency (σ^2) is the average of squared deviations from the mean. The standard deviation of a currency (σ) is the square root of the variance. Especially if N is small (<30), one needs to use the formula for sample data (use $N-1$ in the denominator). Mathematically,

$$\sigma = \sqrt{\frac{1}{N-1} \sum_{t=1}^{N} (s_t - \bar{s})^2}$$

EXAMPLE 6.2

An MNC manager wishes to calculate the risk of positions in two currencies: the British pound and the Singapore dollar. She collects values of the two currencies at the beginning of each year for 10 years (see below). Calculate the standard deviation using these data and determine which currency is riskier.

Solution:

Calculation of Currency Standard Deviation

	GBP				SGD			
	GBPUSD	s	s − s̄	(s − s̄)²	SGDUSD	s	s − s̄	(s − s̄)²
1998	1.6335	N/A	N/A	N/A	0.5685	N/A	N/A	N/A
1999	1.6566	0.0141	0.0103	0.00011	0.5984	0.0526	0.0361	0.00130
2000	1.6370	−0.0118	−0.0363	0.00132	0.6048	0.0107	−0.0058	0.00003
2001	1.4977	−0.0851	−0.1096	0.01200	0.5757	−0.0481	−0.0646	0.00417
2002	1.4426	−0.0368	−0.0612	0.00375	0.5411	−0.0601	−0.0766	0.00587
2003	1.6055	0.1129	0.0885	0.00783	0.5737	0.0602	0.0438	0.00191
2004	1.8245	0.1364	0.1120	0.01253	0.5888	0.0263	0.0098	0.00010
2005	1.8834	0.0323	0.0078	0.00006	0.6076	0.0319	0.0154	0.00024
2006	1.7404	−0.0759	−0.1004	0.01008	0.6053	−0.0038	−0.0203	0.00041
2007	1.9736	0.1340	0.1095	0.01200	0.6529	0.0786	0.0621	0.00386
s̄		0.0245				0.0165		
σ²				0.00746				0.00224
σ				8.64 %				4.73%

Discussion: The standard deviations for the GBP and the Singapore dollar (SGD) are 8.64 percent and 4.73 percent, respectively. The SGD is less risky because it is tightly pegged to the USD. Note that because annual data are used, the resulting standard deviation is the annual standard deviation. Finally, note the use of direct quotes as input (indirect quotes will produce slightly different but erroneous answers).

Some Thoughts on Decimals and Precision

Students (and decision makers) routinely face questions concerning precision in their analyses. For example, when using currency quotes as inputs in the preceding calculation, how many decimals are appropriate? Also, when answers are obtained, such as those concerning currency standard deviation, how many decimals should be displayed? Throughout this text, we try to portray actual practice (e.g., 4–5 decimals for currency quotes). Precision also depends on tools used for calculation. For instance, the preceding calculation was performed using a spreadsheet. If a student uses a calculator, small differences may occur.

In most MNC applications involving standard deviations—demonstrated later in this chapter—the annualized standard deviation is required. If annual data are used to calculate the standard deviation, no further adjustment is needed. Sometimes one uses monthly, weekly, or even daily data to "extract more information" from a time series. If the unit of measurement is not annual, a correction is necessary. For example, if weekly data are used, the following adjustment is necessary:

$$\text{Annual } \sigma = \text{Weekly } \sigma \times \sqrt{52}$$

This adjustment assumes that weekly percent changes in currency values are independent, implying that annual $\sigma^2 =$ weekly $\sigma^2 \times 52$. Because the standard deviation is the square root of the variance, the annual standard deviation is equal to weekly standard deviation times the square root of 52.

Exhibit 6.2 presents the standard deviations of 11 currencies relative to the USD. Weekly data are used, allowing us to focus on a shorter and more recent time period (2005–2007).

The annual standard deviations range from a low of 1.54 percent (CNY) to a high of 12.87 percent (BRL). As indicated by the Bank of International Settlements in its recent annual reports and discussed in Chapter 2, in recent years, currency volatility has diminished . Making allowances for this empirical fact, we can make the following general observations:

standard deviations

Most *currency standard deviations* are between 5 and 10 percent.

- Heavily managed currencies of smaller or closed economies have the lowest standard deviations, often less than 5 percent. CNY falls in this category.
- The currencies of most industrial nations such as Canada, the United Kingdom, and Japan have standard deviations around 10 percent.
- The highest standard deviations are found in the emerging markets when currencies are allowed to float freely. For example, the standard deviation of the Brazilian real is generally more than 10 percent and in certain periods has even exceeded 20 percent.

Currency standard deviations are used as measures of currency risk. As with risk measures in other settings (for instance, stock market risk), there are key statistical considerations/limitations. The following sections summarize these limitations.

EXHIBIT 6.2
Currency Standard Deviation: 2005–2007

Source: Federal Reserve Bank of NY website. Calculations based on weekly returns using Tuesday values. To obtain annual from weekly, multiply by square-root of 52. To obtain monthly from annual, divide by square-root of 12.

	Weekly	Monthly	Annual
Major Currencies:			
EUR	1.0208%	2.12%	7.36%
JPY	1.1913%	2.48%	8.59%
GBP	1.0864%	2.26%	7.83%
CAD	1.0558%	2.20%	7.61%
CHF	1.1472%	2.39%	8.27%
Emerging Market Currencies:			
BRL	1.7842%	3.71%	12.87%
CNY	0.2131%	0.44%	1.54%
INR	0.7046%	1.47%	5.08%
MXN	0.8914%	1.86%	6.43%
SGD	0.5326%	1.11%	3.84%
KRW	0.8141%	1.69%	5.87%

Normality Assumption

The use of the standard deviation as a risk measure is based on the implicit assumption that currency changes are normally distributed. Consider the following example of a currency's movement in a certain time period that violates this assumption: During a majority of the period, the currency is relatively steady in value, but big movements occur in a few periods. This scenario may occur, for instance, when periods of stable cross-border capital flows are punctuated by periods when these flows change dramatically. This pattern was recently observed with emerging market currencies such as the INR; capital flows related to foreign institutional investors (FII) occur in fits and starts and severely affect stock market levels as well as the currency.

Independence Assumption

By making the mathematical adjustment (i.e., multiplying with the square root of the number of weeks or months in a year) to obtain annual standard deviations from weekly or monthly data, one assumes that currency changes are independent. This assumption may not hold true. For example, currency movements in the month of December may not be independent of currency movements in the month of November. Such a relationship between November and December changes would give rise to serial correlation (that is, correlation over time) violating the independence assumption.

History Repeats Assumption

By estimating standard deviations from past data, we are assuming that historical levels of volatility will prevail in the future. Again, this assumption is questionable. The EUR, for instance, was volatile in its first year of existence and then settled down. More generally, currency markets respond to various shocks. In recent years, the USD was sensitive to oil price shocks. How can one predict future volatility by using historical volatility? There are some innovative alternatives to using historical data as discussed in the earlier section, The Standard Deviation of a Currency. One method is to infer currency volatility from currency option prices; this estimates current volatility rather than past volatility. Additionally, one can apply statistical models of volatility that assess changes in volatility over time; this method has the advantage of inferring future volatility.

Currency Volatility and Firm Performance: Overview

currency exposure
Currency changes affect a firm in many ways. Obvious effects are felt in receivables and payables. Subtle effects are felt in the firm's competitive position.

How does currency volatility affect firms? MNCs are subject to currency **exposure** in obvious as well as subtle ways. For an example of obvious effects, consider near-term contractual flows denominated in foreign currencies. MNCs routinely exhibit this type of exposure either in their accounting books (e.g., receivables and payables in foreign currencies) or in formal contracts with other parties not reflected in accounting books (e.g., an agreement to buy equipment from a foreign supplier). For an example of subtle—and equally important—effects, consider how currency changes affect a firm's competitive position.

EXAMPLE 6.3

Consider a U.S. firm conducting business in Mexico: It has receivables (resulting from sales) of MXN 50 million. At the spot rate of MXNUSD = 0.097, the value of these receivables is USD 4,850,000. But the U.S. firm is not assured of obtaining this value because the exchange rate is likely to vary. Calculate the range of values and extent of possible losses.

Solution: Based on information in Exhibit 6.2, we know that the annual standard deviation of the MXN is around 7 percent. If this receivable is due in a year, we can estimate a range of values for MXN based on its standard deviation. Using $\pm 1\sigma$, we forecast the MXN as follows:

$0.097 \pm (0.097 \times 7\%) = \{0.09021 \text{ to } 0.10379\}$

In turn, this produces a range of USD values for receivables as follows:

$\{50,000,000 \times 0.09021 \text{ to } 50,000,000 \times 0.10379\}$

At the lower end of this range, the receivables are worth USD 4,510,500. This implies a potential loss of USD 339,500.

> *Discussion:* The use of $\pm 1\sigma$ provides a range covering 68 percent of all possible outcomes in a normal distribution. A more risk-averse manager may want to use the $\pm 2\sigma$ range that covers 95 percent of possible outcomes.

Financial analysts assess three types of exposures to currency risk: transaction, economic, and translation. A brief explanation follows. **Transaction exposure** refers to currency impacts on a firm's currency holdings as well as its near-term contractual cash flows in other currencies. **Economic exposure** refers to the impact on all of a firm's cash flows. A major component of economic exposure is the effect of currency changes on the firm's operating cash flows; this component is known as **operating exposure**. **Translation exposure** refers to the effects on the firm's financial statements and, in particular, the effects on net income and book value of assets.

How does currency risk compare with other risks firms face? Experts generally agree that among macroeconomic risk factors, interest rate risk is the most important because of the many ways in which interest rate affects firms (for instance, the impact on customers and suppliers, impact on financing costs, impact on costs borne by customers and suppliers). This conclusion is supported by the fact that in derivatives markets, the largest category is interest rate derivatives. Commodity price risk is another risk factor. Airlines face the risk that rising oil prices will increase costs; restaurants face risks of rising prices of meat, coffee, and other food items; and consumer durable manufacturers face the risk that an economic downturn will diminish demand and hurt top-line growth. Does currency risk compare in magnitude with these risks? Absolutely! Currency values routinely change by 10 percent or more in a year. This has the potential to seriously disrupt a firm's financial performance.

6.2 Transaction Exposure

Transaction exposure is the most identifiable form of currency exposure. Research indicates that most MNCs estimate their transaction exposure and take steps to hedge and control it. In this section, we discuss how transaction exposure occurs and how firms can calculate exposure.

Definition of Transaction Exposure

Transaction exposure measures the following impacts of currency changes:

- Impact on the value of liquid financial assets.
- Impact on the value of contractual cash flows.

The term *transaction* loosely refers either to liquid financial assets or imminent contractual cash flows. From the perspective of a U.S.-based MNC, transaction exposure is the currency effect on the "USD equivalent cash flows" of a position or asset. We model these effects in examples later in this section.

MNCs may have liquid assets such as cash holdings in various currencies and investments in short-term instruments such as the Eurocurrency instruments. These are balance sheet items that are fairly easy to ascertain. The home currency value of these holdings depends on exchange rates.

transaction exposure
Transaction exposure typically concerns an MNC's foreign currency receivables and payables.

In addition to these liquid assets, firms have near-term (0–1 year) contractual inflows and outflows in foreign currencies. These contractual flows generally occur in the context of the firm's daily operations. It may have sourced raw materials abroad and may owe payments in a foreign currency. Likewise, the firm may have sold products to a foreign entity and expects to receive payments in a foreign currency. Typical MNCs such as Procter and Gamble and John Deere have thousands of these positions at any point in time.

Contractual flows may also occur in the context of a firm's purchases of capital equipment. These transactions do not occur as frequently as those involving suppliers and customers.

Finally, contractual flows may arise in the context of financing flows such as dividend and interest payments as well as changes in the level of debt and equity. Other examples include payment and receipt of licenses, foreign taxes, and international travel by employees.

For each transaction—asset or contractual cash flow—three aspects are relevant: amount, timing, and volatility. *Amount* and *timing* refer to the units of a foreign currency (negative indicating payables and positive indicating receivables) and the expected cash flow date, respectively. *Volatility* refers to the potential range of (home-currency-equivalent) values resulting from currency changes. Transaction exposure—and currency exposure, more generally—is a summary of amount, timing, and volatility. Difficulties occur in summarizing transaction exposure across a range of transactions (different currencies and different time periods). We discuss these issues with examples next.

Scenario Analysis

MNCs typically have multiple currency positions. In the following example, we show a simple way to aggregate amounts and calculate the resulting volatility. We use the so-called scenario approach.

EXAMPLE 6.4

Eastman Kodak purchases components for its digital cameras from Japan and is required to make a payment of JPY 80 million in 60 days. In addition, the firm has cash balances totaling MXN 100 million that it expects to transfer from Mexico in 60 days. Let's assume that the best and worst cases for USDJPY are 120 and 90, respectively. For USDMXN, the best and worst cases are 6 and 8, respectively. Estimate currency exposure (that is, indicate exposure amounts and currency portfolio volatility). Note that the currency quotes supplied earlier are of the indirect type.

Solution:

Currency Exposure Using Best- and Worst-Case Scenarios

Currency Positions					
JPY	−80,000,000				
MXN	10,000,000				

		Value in USD			
		Best Scenario		Worst Scenario	
		Currency Spot	USD Value	Currency Spot	USD Value
JPY	−80,000,000	1/120	−666,667	1/90	−888,889
MXN	10,000,000	1/6	1,666,667	1/8	1,250,000
Total			**1,000,000**		**361,111**

Discussion: We find that the best- and worst-case results are USD 1,000,000 and USD 361,111, respectively. This indicates a wide range, and, consequently, a high degree of transaction exposure. How are exchange rate inputs obtained to perform these calculations? One method is to obtain currency values over a period of time and determine the lowest and highest values over this interval; another method would be to construct some kind of confidence interval, one or two standard deviations around current or expected exchange values; another method is to obtain forecasts from bankers or consultants.

The use of scenario analysis to estimate currency exposure is a useful yet limited approach. This method works well either if there is only one currency or if the scenarios are constructed carefully taking into consideration the relationship between various currency pairs. By lining up low values for currencies in one scenario and high values in another, we are implicitly assuming that the currencies are perfectly correlated. Equivalently, we are assuming away any potential benefits of diversification stemming from exposure to multiple currencies. This approach, therefore, is not realistic: Estimates of currency volatility resulting from this method are subject to a positive bias. The next section offers an improved method without this bias.

EXHIBIT 6.3
Currency Correlations (2005–2007)

Source: *http://www.oanda.com/ convert/fxhistory* (accessed June 30, 2008). Calculations are based on weekly returns using Tuesday values of currencies (we used direct quotes: values of currencies expressed in USD).

	EUR	JPY	GBP	CAD	CHF	BRL	CNY	INR	MXP	SGD
JPY	0.53									
GBP	0.79	0.49								
CAD	0.36	0.04	0.38							
CHF	0.92	0.65	0.78	0.30						
BRL	0.21	−0.08	0.20	0.19	0.12					
CNY	0.18	0.15	0.19	0.00	0.17	−0.04				
INR	0.21	0.20	0.22	0.15	0.16	0.20	0.12			
MXN	0.25	0.02	0.31	0.21	0.19	0.54	0.01	0.18		
SGD	0.70	0.53	0.64	0.24	0.64	0.22	0.29	0.29	0.36	
KRW	0.57	0.30	0.54	0.23	0.51	0.35	0.21	0.35	0.32	0.64

Markowitz Portfolio Approach

One of the breakthroughs in modern finance is the portfolio model of Markowitz. This model, first developed in the 1950s, has so revolutionized the practice of finance that Professor Markowitz was awarded the 1990 Nobel Prize in Economic Sciences for this particular work. Although the model was primarily developed and used for equity portfolios, it finds good use in analyzing currency portfolios.

The Markowitz model considers the interaction between assets in determining risk. This interaction—the so-called diversification effect—serves to diminish risk. A key indicator of the diversification potential is the correlation between assets. In statistical terms, we use the Pearson correlation coefficient (CORR) to measure this relationship. The lower the correlation coefficient is, the higher is the diversification potential. Other variables that affect risk include the respective weights of the items in the portfolio (w) and the respective standard deviations of the items (σ). The objective of the decision maker is to estimate the portfolio's risk (or standard deviation). The Markowitz model applies the following equation for two-asset portfolios:

effect of correlation on risk
MNCs determine the *standard deviation of currency portfolios* to assess risk. Low correlation among currencies reduces portfolio risk.

$$\text{Variance of portfolio} = \underbrace{w_1^2\sigma_1^2}_{\substack{\text{Risk of}\\\text{Asset 1}}} + \underbrace{w_2^2\sigma_2^2}_{\substack{\text{Risk of}\\\text{Asset 2}}} + \underbrace{2w_1w_2\,\text{CORR}\,\sigma_1\sigma_2}_{\substack{\text{Interaction Effect of}\\\text{Asset 1 and Asset 2}}}$$

To determine portfolio standard deviation, we find the square root of the portfolio variance.

The Markowitz model is useful in the context of currency portfolios because of imperfect correlation between currencies. Exhibit 6.3 displays correlations between the 11 currencies we studied earlier. Note that most correlations are fairly low. The highest correlation (0.92) is between EUR and CHF, illustrating the fact that geographically near and economically integrated countries show high correlation. The lowest (–0.08) is between JPY and BRL, illustrating the fact that when economies differ in character (Brazil is resource based and Japan is manufacturing based), and when they are not integrated, low correlations are found. The most important result, however, is that currency correlations tend to be low. A majority of the correlations (29 of 55 possible pairs) are less than or equal to 0.25. Under these conditions, portfolio theory would indicate the opportunity for significant diversification benefits.

EXAMPLE 6.5

A U.S. firm has receivables in two currencies: BRL 150 million and GBP 50 million. The time frame is six months. Estimate currency exposure using the Markowitz model. The following additional inputs are available (from Exhibits 6.2 and 6.3):

- The (annual) currency standard deviations are 13 percent for BRL and 8 percent for GBP.
- The correlation between the BRL and GBP is 0.20.
- BRLUSD = 0.6 and GBPUSD = 2.0.

Solution:

Markowitz Model Calculations

Currency Portfolio Composition and Current Value

Currency	Amount	S	USD Value	w
BRL	150,000	0.6	90,000	47.37%
GBP	50,000	2.0	100,000	52.63%
			190,000	

Other Information

	Sigma	Correlation
BRL	13%	0.2
GBP	8	

Portfolio Standard Deviation

$$\sigma^2 = w_1^2\sigma_1^2 + w_2^2\sigma_2^2 + 2w_1w_2\,CORR\,\sigma_1\sigma_2$$

$$= (0.4737)^2(0.13)^2 + (0.5263)^2(0.08)^2 + 2(0.4737)(0.5263)(.2)(.13)(.08)$$

$$= 0.006602$$

$$\sigma = \sqrt{0.006602}$$

$$= 8.1252\%$$

Six-Month Portfolio Standard Deviation

$$\sigma = \frac{8.1252\%}{\sqrt{2}} = 5.7454\%$$

Discussion: Diversification reduces currency risk. The individual currency standard deviations are 13 percent and 8 percent, respectively. Despite a weight of 47.37 percent in the high-risk currency (BRL), the resulting portfolio standard deviation is only 8.1252 percent. (Without diversification, portfolio standard deviation would have been higher than 10 percent). The estimated value of 8.1252 percent uses annual inputs. However, the currency positions are only for six months. The adjusted six-month standard deviation is 5.7454 percent.

Confidence Interval

In certain situations, managers need to convert the risk metric from a standard deviation to a range of values. Carrying forward the assumption of a normal distribution, one can calculate a 68 percent confidence interval ($\pm 1\sigma$) or a 95 percent confidence interval ($\pm 2\sigma$).

EXAMPLE 6.6

Calculate the 95 percent confidence interval (range of portfolio values) for the previous problem involving BRL and GBP exposures. Recall that:

- Mean portfolio value = USD 190,000
- Standard deviation = 5.7454 percent.

Solution: 95% confidence interval: USD 190,000 $\pm$ (2 $\times$ 5.7454% $\times$ 190,000)

Low value = USD 168,167

High value = USD 211,833

Discussion: Of the two figures, the low value of USD 168,167 is critical. The decision maker can make contingency plans based on this risky outcome. The choice between 68 percent and 95 percent confidence intervals depends on the decision maker's risk aversion. In this example, we probably have a highly risk-averse decision maker who wishes to exclude only 5 percent of all outcomes. More significantly, by focusing on the low value of USD 168,167 (as a measure of currency risk), the decision maker excludes only the lowest 2.5 percent of outcomes in the left tail of the normal distribution.

Mean Portfolio Value

In the preceding calculations, we assume that the future outcomes (the distributions) are centered on the current portfolio value. How realistic is the assumption that the future spot rate is approximated by the current spot rate? From discussions in Chapter 5, we know that this assumption is probably not justified because interest rates and inflation rates are rarely the same between two countries. Therefore, a potential solution is to use parity conditions (IRP or PPP) to forecast future spot values; these forecasts can then be used to calculate the mean portfolio value.

EXAMPLE 6.7

Consider again the previous example involving the BRL and GBP. The portfolio contains BRL 150,000 and GBP 50,000. The six-month standard deviation is 5.7454 percent. The spot rates are BRLUSD = 0.60 and GBPUSD = 2.00. Assume that interest rates for instruments denominated in USD, BRL, and GBP are 4 percent, 8 percent, and 6 percent, respectively (use annual compounding). Calculate a revised 95 percent confidence interval based on forecasted portfolio mean value.

Solution: We apply the IRP to solve for forward currency values:

$$\text{Forecasted BRLUSD} = 0.60 \times \left[\frac{1 + 4\%}{1 + 8\%}\right]^{0.5} = 0.58878$$

$$\text{Forecasted GBPUSD} = 2.00 \times \left[\frac{1 + 4\%}{1 + 6\%}\right]^{0.5} = 1.98104$$

$$\text{Mean portfolio value} = 150,000 \times 0.58878 + 50,000 \times 1.98104$$
$$= \text{USD } 187,369$$

95% Confidence interval: $187,369 \pm (2 \times 5.7454\% \times 187,369)$

Low portfolio value = USD 165,839

Discussion: The low end of the confidence interval indicates a portfolio value of USD 165,839. This represents a loss of USD 21,530 from expected portfolio value of USD 187,369. The loss relative to current portfolio value of USD 190,000 is higher because of higher interest rates in the two foreign currencies and associated depreciation (that is, from 0.60 to 0.58878 for BRLUSD and from 2.00 to 1.98104 for GBPUSD).

Netting Currency Flows

Netting

In a real-world setting, currency exposure is difficult to estimate because of multiple transactions occurring at different times. The first step is to sort transactions by date and currency. This step—known as *netting*—allows MNCs to recognize offsetting transactions and focus on only net amounts.

EXAMPLE 6.8

Consider the following information on a firm's receivables and payables:

- In three months, the firm expects to receive EUR 50,000 and GBP 30,000.
- In six months, the firm expects to receive EUR 20,000 and GBP 60,000.
- In three months, the firm expects to pay EUR 15,000 and GBP 5,000.
- In six months, the firm expects to pay EUR 5,000 and GBP 35,000.

Use the process of netting to determine the amounts and timing of currency exposure.

Solution: In three months, the firm expects to receive EUR 50,000 and expects to pay EUR 15,000. On a net basis, therefore, the firm expects to receive EUR 35,000 in three months. Similarly, in three months, the firm expects to receive GBP 25,000, which is the difference between receivables of GBP 30,000 and payables of GBP 5,000. Use the same procedure to calculate the net amounts for the six-month period. In six months, the firm may expect to receive EUR 15,000 and GBP 25,000. The following table summarizes this information.

	Three Months	Six Months
EUR	+EUR 35,000 (=50,000 − 15,000)	+EUR 15,000 (=20,000 − 5,000)
GBP	+GBP 25,000 (=30,000 − 5,000)	+GBP 25,000 (=60,000 − 35,000)

Discussion: Netting is applied on eight original positions to determine four "net" exposures. From the firm's perspective, this summary has the potential to save substantial transaction costs. If the management of each position costs a certain sum of money, say USD 100, then the firm would save USD 400 because of netting.

Netting across Time

But how do we net currency flows occurring at different time points? Suppose the firm expects to receive EUR 35,000 in three months and EUR 15,000 in six months as in the previous example. How can these two amounts be consolidated so that there is a single EUR amount the firm can manage? From finance basics, we understand that the comparison or consolidation of cash flows occurring at different times is accomplished by using time value principles. Let us examine three scenarios for using time value concepts to consolidate currency amounts over time.

Scenario I: The Interest Rate Is Zero This is the easiest of all scenarios. While it is quite unlikely, it does occur in some situations. For example, during recent years, interest rates in Japan have been about 1 percent; for all practical purposes, this rate is quite close to zero. The reason this scenario is easy to analyze is that we can simply sum currency amounts occurring at different points in time.

EXAMPLE 6.9

Consider the previous problem. We had identified the following exposures:

	Three Months	Six Months
EUR	+EUR 35,000	+EUR 15,000
GBP	+GBP 25,000	+GBP 25,000

Consolidate EUR and GBP exposures. Assume that interest rates in the EUR and GBP are zero.

Solution: Because interest rates are zero in both the EUR and GBP, we would have identical answers whether we identify the exposure at three months or six months. Consolidated exposure: EUR 50,000 and GBP 50,000.

	Three Months	Six Months	Consolidated Exposure
EUR	+EUR 35,000	+EUR 15,000	+EUR 50,000
GBP	+GBP 25,000	+GBP 25,000	+GBP 50,000

Discussion: The consolidated exposures of EUR 50,000 and GBP 50,000 may be interpreted either as exposures at three months (assuming a borrowing rate of zero) or at six months (assuming a lending rate of zero).

Scenario II: The Interest Rate Is Known with Certainty This scenario is also fairly easy to analyze because we can directly apply time value concepts to transfer currency values from one period to another.

EXAMPLE 6.10

Consider the previous example in which the following flows occur:

	Three Months	Six Months
EUR	+EUR 35,000	+EUR 15,000
GBP	+GBP 25,000	+GBP 25,000

Consolidate EUR and GBP exposures (use six months as common horizon). Assume that (forward) interest rates in the EUR and GBP for the three- to six-month interval are 7 percent and 9 percent, respectively. Use annual compounding.

Solution:

$$\text{EUR in 6 months} = \text{EUR } 15{,}000 + \text{EUR } 35{,}000 \times (1 + 7\%)^{3/12}$$
$$= \text{EUR } 50{,}597$$

$$\text{GBP in six months} = \text{GBP } 25{,}000 + \text{GBP } 25{,}000 \times (1 + 9\%)^{3/12}$$
$$= \text{GBP } 50{,}544.45$$

	Three Months	Six Months	Consolidated Exporsure
EUR	+EUR 35,000	+EUR 15,000	+EUR 50,597
GBP	+GBP 25,000	+GBP 25,000	+GBP 50,544

Discussion: If we are asked to consolidate exposure at three months, we simply discount the six-month flows using the given interest rates.

Scenario III: The Interest Rate Is Uncertain   This is the more likely scenario. Netting across time is more complex in this setting. The implication is that firms face currency and interest rate risk. To summarize and consolidate currency risk in this scenario, firms need first to predict future interest rates (so-called forward rates). One source of information of forward rates is the yield curve. London Interbank Offered Rate (LIBOR) and Treasury yield curves are well publicized. Another way to infer forward rates is to use derivatives markets. In Chapters 3 and 5, we demonstrated the use of Eurocurrency futures to infer forward interest rates. Equivalently, the firm can use price quotes from an over-the-counter (OTC) derivatives instrument known as the **forward rate agreement (FRA)**; market participants use the FRA to lock in interest rates for a future loan. The FRA is the OTC equivalent of Eurocurrency futures.

Value at Risk

VaR
VaR provides a quick way to understand potential losses in a risky situation.

Sometimes decision makers want an answer to a simple question: What are potential losses because of a particular risk factor? Using an approach similar to the Markowitz approach, **value at risk (VaR)** provides a direct answer to this important question. Formally, VaR is defined as the maximum likely losses in a given asset or situation or business. For example, if an MNC has a currency portfolio worth CAD 10 million with likely losses of CAD 1.5 million, then VaR equals CAD 1.5 million.

Because a firm faces many risk factors including currency risks, the decision maker may be interested in assessing the VaR of each position individually as well as collectively. This information can then be used in the corporate planning and budgeting process as well as in risk management initiatives. But investors in firms are also interested in this information. Microsoft, for instance, responds to this demand and discloses VaR estimates in its annual reports (see Exhibit 6.4). Note the significance of these values: one-day currency related VaR is about USD 50 million.

EXHIBIT 6.4
Microsoft's VaR (excerpt from 2007 annual report)

The following table sets forth the one-day VaR for substantially all of our positions as of and for the years ended June 30, 2007 and 2006:

(In millions)

Risk Categories	June 30, 2007	June 30, 2006	Year ended June 30, 2007		
			Average	High	Low
Interest rates	$34	$66	$43	$67	$32
Currency rates	55	91	52	101	15
Equity prices	60	88	59	89	49
Commodity prices	7	12	7	12	4

How is VaR estimated? The decision maker considers a position or an asset whose value is at risk and specifies a probability estimate for unlikely and likely outcomes. A commonly assumed probability for unlikely outcomes is 5 percent. This implies that 95 percent of the outcomes are deemed likely. Given this assumption, a decision maker will calculate all possible outcomes, order them according to their value, and identify the 5 percent VaR using the outcome that has a 95 percent chance of being exceeded (see Exhibit 6.5).

EXAMPLE 6.11

Consider the following potential values of a currency portfolio worth USD 30 million today:

Value	Probability	Cumulative Probability
25.1–26.0 million	5%	5%
26.1–27.0 million	10%	15%
27.1–28.0 million	10%	25%
28.1–29.0 million	15%	40%
29.1–30.0 million	10%	50%
30.1–31.0 million	15%	65%
31.1–32.0 million	25%	90%
>32.0 million	10%	100%

Solution: There is a 95 percent chance that the future portfolio value exceeds USD 26 million. Equivalently, there is a 5 percent chance that the portfolio value will be USD 26 million or lower. Comparing this value with the current portfolio value of USD 30 million, we conclude that the 5 percent VaR is USD 4 million.

Discussion: In this calculation, we implicitly assume that the expected portfolio value equals its current value. The commonly used delta-normal approach (see the section Delta-Normal Approach) relaxes this assumption.

Delta-Normal Approach

This approach is based on the assumption that changes in value are normally distributed (see Exhibit 6.5) and is closely related to the Markowitz model described earlier. The manager assesses the standard deviation of the currency portfolio and calculates:

5% VaR = −Portfolio value × [Expected change − 1.65 × Portfolio standard deviation].

If the expected change in the portfolio is positive, it offsets the risk somewhat. On the other hand, a negative expected change could add to VaR. The coefficient of the portfolio standard deviation of 1.65 is a parameter from the normal distribution curve associated with a probability of 5 percent.

EXHIBIT 6.5
VaR

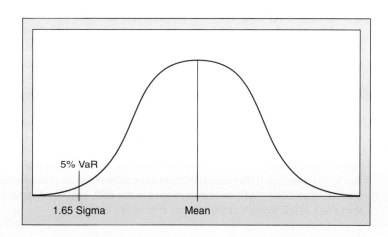

EXAMPLE 6.12

Consider the following information regarding a currency portfolio:

- The currency portfolio is worth USD 10,000.
- The annual portfolio standard deviation is 12 percent.
- The firm is expecting to unwind the position in three months.
- The firm estimates the portfolio to lose 2 percent of its value during the three months.

These estimates are indicated by the parity conditions.
Calculate the 5 percent VaR using the delta-normal approach.

Solution:

$$5\% \text{ VaR} = -10,000 \times \left[-2\% - 1.65 \times \frac{12\%}{\sqrt{4}} \right] = \text{USD } 1,190$$

Discussion: In this example, we explicitly consider the expected change in the value of the position. The portfolio is expected to decline by 2 percent, or USD 200. This amount is added to the "delta-spread" of USD 990—the second term in the preceding equation—to produce a VaR of USD 1,190.

Historical Simulation Approach

This alternative approach is based on a time series of value (percent) changes in the components of the portfolio. For instance, if the portfolio contains positions in the BRL and GBP, then N time-series observations are obtained on these currencies. These N percent changes are used to generate N potential portfolio values. Using the approach outlined in Example 6.11, these values are ordered, and the 5 percent VaR is identified. For example, if $N = 40$, the third lowest value would be identified as the minimum portfolio value. VaR is then calculated as the current portfolio value minus the third lowest value.

JP Morgan (now JP Morgan Chase) popularized VaR in the 1990s. Initially, it was designed as a service to its banking clients. VaR was used to summarize an entity's portfolio risk in one easy-to-understand number. Software was developed to facilitate VaR computations. JP Morgan's RiskMetrics division, which was later spun out as a separate company, provided these services.

6.3 Economic and Operating Exposure

Economic exposure is the currency-related exposure the firm faces in regard to all of its cash flows, both in the near term and in the future. Economic exposure includes but is not limited to transaction exposure. A critical component of economic exposure is *operating exposure:* the effect of currencies on the firm's risky operating cash flows. Exposure may also arise from asset values, but ultimately they are dictated by cash flow potential. We show the decomposition of economic exposure in equation form:

$$\text{Economic exposure} = \text{Transaction exposure} + \text{Operating exposure}$$

One interesting thing to note is that even purely domestic firms experience currency exposure: Although they have zero transaction exposure (by definition), they may have operating exposure. If a domestic firm has competitors from other countries or domestic competitors with a cost base in a foreign currency because of foreign production, then currency changes can affect operating cash flows. For example, a devaluation of the competitor's currency leads it to cut prices and lower market share for the domestic firm.

EXAMPLE 6.13

Gallo Wines—one of the largest wine producers in the world—mostly operates in the United States and may be considered a domestic firm. Gallo faces significant competition from Australian, French, Italian, New Zealand, and Chilean firms. An important wine category (varietal) for the firm is Chardonnay. In this category, Gallo faces significant competition from Australian producers. In the late 1990s, the Australian dollar (AUD) weakened relative to the USD, enabling Australian producers to enhance their share in U.S. markets at the expense of firms like Gallo.

Operating Exposure: Overview

Operating exposure is formally defined as the impact of currency changes on operating cash flows. We first provide an overview of operating exposure by presenting two ways in which currencies affect operating cash flows:

- **Conversion impact.** This represents the currency impact that occurs when an MNC's foreign cash flows are converted back to USD. For example, Apple generates revenues in EUR by selling its products in Europe. If EURUSD decreases, Apple obtains fewer USD. This particular component of operating exposure—in which foreign cash flows are fixed but home currency cash flows vary due to currency changes—appears similar to transaction exposure. But this appearance is deceiving. Recall the two features of transaction exposure: the focus on (1) short-term cash flows and (2) contractual cash flows. Operating exposure differs because it considers short-term as well as long-term cash flows and, more important, operating exposure focuses on risky (noncontractual) cash flows.

- **Price and unit impact.** Second, the foreign cash flows themselves could change as a result of currency changes. For example, if EURUSD decreases, Apple could potentially increase the EUR selling price for its iPods. This, in turn, could potentially decrease unit sales. This type of currency effect forms the core of operating exposure. Operating exposure analysis focuses on how currency changes affect unit sales and selling prices. As the ensuing discussion demonstrates, operating exposure is more challenging to estimate than transaction exposure.

Operating Exposure: A Closer Look at Contributing Factors

Operating exposure for a firm is determined by the currencies in which it incurs costs and earns revenues. To understand exposure at a deeper level, however, it is important to understand industry conditions: the pricing policy of the MNC, the nature of the product (differentiated or not), the intensity of competition, and the cost basis for competitors. These industry conditions are captured in the three effects we discuss next: (1) pricing policy effect, (2) market structure effect, and (3) cost structure effect.[1] Exhibit 6.6 also illustrates these effects.

EXHIBIT 6.6 Operating Exposure

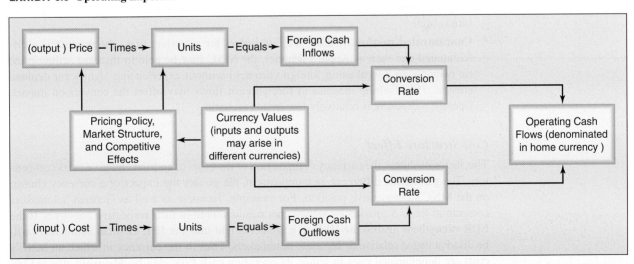

---

[1] This analysis is adapted from Robert Grant and Luc Soenen, "Strategic Management of Operating Exposure," *European Management Journal* 22, no. 1 (2004), pp. 53–62.

Pricing Policy Effect

An MNC's pricing policy potentially determines the price at which it sells. One of the following scenarios may unfold:

operating exposure and pricing policy
Operating exposure is lower for firms that are price leaders.

- **Price follower.** If the MNC is a price follower in a foreign market and prices are set by domestic firms in that foreign market, a currency change has no effect on prices or units. Cash flows denominated in the foreign currency do not change, but because of currency changes, the converted value of the foreign cash flows is affected. Operating exposure is generally considered high in this scenario.

- **Price leader.** If the MNC is a price leader, it may change prices in response to currency changes for reasons such as (1) to maintain its gross margins or (2) to synchronize global prices for a product. First, consider the issue of gross margins. If the MNC sources and sells in the same foreign country, a currency change does not change gross margins, so there is no need to change prices. Instead, if the MNC sources from a different country, the currency change can change gross margins and necessitate a change in prices. Firms such as Apple usually have only a few global sources to service numerous national markets. Apple therefore would probably change local prices in response to currency changes. Second, consider the need for synchronizing global prices. Unsynchronized prices could lead to re-shipment of Apple products from weak-currency countries to strong-currency countries. Taken together, these two points suggest that firms such as Apple may change prices in response to currency changes. What are the ultimate effects of these price changes? It depends on the elasticity of demand for the MNC's products. If the elasticity is low, units sold may not change. Instead, if elasticity is high, units may change significantly. Thus, firms selling products with a higher elasticity of demand face increased operating exposure. Overall, operating exposure is lower for the price leader scenario compared to the price follower scenario.

Market Structure Effect

This factor reflects the market power of the MNC in the foreign country.

operating exposure and market structure
Operating exposure is higher in competitive markets.

- **Competitive market.** Suppose there are many sellers for a product in a foreign market and the MNC increases its price in response to a weakening foreign currency. The consequences in terms of unit sales may be severe. For example, if the INR weakens and Hewlett Packard increases its selling price for notebook computers in India, it may lose sales to competitors such as Lenovo (China) and Acer (Taiwan). Given these circumstances, it is likely the MNC will not raise its price. As in the price follower scenario, operating exposure is high.

- **Concentrated market.** If there are few sellers for a product (e.g., the product is a differentiated one such as Apple's iPhone), the MNC may be able to increase selling price (in response to a weakening foreign currency) without experiencing significant demand erosion. The resulting increase in foreign cash flows may offset the conversion impact. Operating exposure is relatively low in this scenario.

Cost Structure Effect

This factor evaluates the currency composition of the costs of an MNC relative to its competitors. The greater the difference in composition, the greater the impact of a currency change on the MNC's competitive position. For example, Japanese as well as German automakers compete in the U.S. market by selling cars manufactured in their respective countries. If the EUR strengthens against the USD to a greater extent than the JPY, German automakers will be disadvantaged relative to Japanese automakers. Thus, if the currency in which an MNC's costs are denominated rises in value, its operating cash flow may be adversely affected not only because of the rise in costs but also because of deterioration in the MNC's competitive position. Because of its focus on how currency changes affect competition, this type of exposure is known as *competitive exposure*.

To summarize, operating exposure, at its heart, is about price and quantity effects of currency changes. Crucial factors shaping this exposure are:

- Nature of the product sold by the MNC (commodity-like or differentiated).
- Extent of competition (high or low).
- Pricing policy of the MNC (leader or follower).
- Cost base of MNC relative to its competitors (similar or dissimilar).

EXAMPLE 6.14

A U.S.-based MNC is selling products in Mexico. In the status quo (current year), it sells 10,000 units @ MXN 5. Mexico is a high inflation country. Over the following year, inflation is expected to run at 9 percent compared to a U.S. rate of 0 percent: MXNUSD = 0.18. The inflation differential predicts a future MXNUSD of 0.16514. Consider the following scenarios and calculate cash flows in USD:

Scenario I. Unit price conforms to PPP (Price = MXN 5.45) and units are unchanged.

Scenario II. Unit price as well as number of units sold is unchanged.

Scenario III. Unit price trends partially toward PPP (Price = MXN 5.25) and units sold falls to 8,000.

Solution:

Illustration of Price and Quantity Effects

	Status Quo	Scenario I	Scenario II	Scenario III
Units	10,000	10,000	10,000	8,000
× Price per unit (MXN)	5.00	5.45	5.00	5.25
= Cash flows in MXN	50,000	54,500	50,000	42,000
× MXNUSD	0.18	0.16514	0.16514	0.16514
= Cash flows in USD	9,000	9,000	8,257	6,936

Discussion: Scenario I assumes that the unit price increase is consistent with overall inflation. The firm is not affected in this scenario. But scenario I is not very realistic. Even though Mexican inflation is 9 percent, the firm may be unable to raise its price. Scenario II offers a counterpoint to Scenario I: The selling price is quite sticky. The MNC is unable to pass on its loss of buying power caused by inflation to its Mexican customers. This leads to reduced USD cash flows. Scenario III is perhaps a more realistic scenario because it considers sticky prices as well as competitive effects. As prices rise, it is plausible that competitors with a cost base in MXN or other depreciating currencies are able to steal market share from the U.S. firm. Scenario III is the most realistic and the worst-case scenario. USD cash flows are the lowest in this scenario. The firm experiences the proverbial "double whammy" from sticky prices and low-cost competitors. (We did not consider the fact that the MXNUSD adjusts partially to inflation because our focus is on prices and quantity).

Estimating Operating Exposure

Consider a U.S.-based auto manufacturer such as Ford Motors. Ford faces substantial transaction exposure by virtue of its liquid assets in foreign currencies, debt denominated in foreign currencies, and contractual obligations in foreign currencies. However, its most significant exposure is operating exposure (especially competitive exposure). The key element of concern is the difference in the cost basis of Ford and its Japanese and Korean competitors in the U.S. market. Thus, Ford's cash flows are affected by the JPYUSD and KRWUSD rates.

Consider the effect of JPY and KRW devaluation. Among the cash flows affected by currency changes, perhaps the most important is Ford's revenue. Revenues depend on prices as well as quantities of goods sold. Both these variables—price and quantity—are affected by currency values. Because of intensified competition from Japanese and Korean manufacturers, Ford can be expected to lose market share. Furthermore, this competition decreases prices. Thus, both prices and quantities are lower for Ford. This is an example of the double whammy caused by operating exposure.

operating exposure

Operating exposure is *estimated* by linking currency changes to revenue changes.

How might an analyst estimate Ford Motor's exposure to currency risk in the United States? One approach is to look at the past and estimate the relationship between currency changes and revenues for Ford. Let's assume that quarterly data on Ford revenues (denoted as R) and the values of JPY and KRW are available for the past 10 years (40 observations). First calculate the time series of percent changes for revenues ($\Delta R\%$) and currency rates (s_{JPY}, s_{KRW}). Estimate the following regression:

$$\Delta R\% = a + b \times s_{JPY} + c \times s_{KRW} + e$$

If one considers variation in revenues as a proxy for total risk faced by the company, we can determine the impact of currency risk by taking the ratio of the variance explained by currencies (s_{JPY}, s_{KRW}) to revenue variance. The regression R-squared readily provides this ratio.

The regression approach also allows an MNC manager to plan for adverse currency effects on revenues. By using estimated coefficients and using a forecast of currency changes, one can calculate revenue effects

---

EXAMPLE 6.15

Suppose an MNC identifies two currencies—JPY and KRW—as impacting its revenues. The following regression is run: $\Delta R\% = a + b \times s_{JPY} + c \times s_{KRW} + e$. The manager finds that $a = 0.02$, $b = 0$, and $c = 0.6$; a and c are also statistically significant. Regression R-squared is 40 percent. Calculate the revenue consequence of a 10 percent depreciation in both the JPY and KRW.

Solution:

$$\Delta R\% = 0.02 + 0 \times (-0.10) + 0.6 \times (-0.10)$$
$$= -0.04$$

Discussion: Revenues will decrease by 4 percent. Only the weakening of KRW affects the MNC adversely. Because 40 percent of the variability in revenues is explained by the regression equation and because the coefficient for one of the two currencies is significant, we deem currency exposure as significant.

What are the assumptions behind this analysis? First, we assume that the historical relationship is valid in today's environment. This assumption is true when production technology, consumer behavior, and the competitive landscape are static; these conditions may not always be true. Furthermore, this assumption is questionable when firms are truly global players with production in various parts of the globe. The second assumption is that the relationship between revenue changes and currency value changes is linear. This may not be true if there are some ranges of currency values in which the revenue effects are magnified and ranges in which the effects are muted. This happens, for instance, when customers show brand loyalty and only reluctantly shift to alternative products if price differentials cross a high threshold. Finally, contemporaneous effects are assumed. In a real setting, many effects are lagged in nature and require adjustments to statistical models.

This type of regression analysis can be conducted at aggregated or disaggregated levels. At an aggregate-level, one might focus on net income or operating cash flows or even stock returns.[2] A disaggregate-level analysis would focus on components of net income or cash flows such as units and prices; the analysis could also focus on cost components such as labor and raw material costs.

---

[2] This type of regression method is routinely used in research studies to determine the presence of economic exposure. Because economic exposure is overall exposure, the *Y*-variable is stock returns. For an example, see Luke Lin, David So-De Shyu, and Chau-Jung Kuo, "The Exchange Rate Exposure of Chinese and Taiwanese Multinational Corporations," *Journal of American Academy of Business* 12, no. 1 (2007), pp. 173–179.

6.4 Translation Exposure

The third type of exposure is translation exposure. Also called *accounting exposure,* this type of exposure measures the impact of currency values on the accounting statements of the firm. In particular, translation exposure concerns the currency impact on net income. By definition, translation exposure does not affect purely domestic firms and is of relevance only to MNCs.

FAS-52
In the United States, *FAS-52* governs currency translation procedures.

- **Translation procedure.** To understand translation exposure, one has to first understand how MNCs account for foreign revenues, expenses, assets, and liabilities. In the United States, the **Financial Accounting Standard No. 52 (FAS-52)** governs these procedures. A key step is translating (or converting) values arising in foreign (functional) currencies into the home (reporting) currency of the MNC. This accounting regulation distinguishes between revenues and expenses on one hand and assets and liabilities on the other. Revenues and expenses are translated using average exchange rates for the period. Assets and liabilities are translated using the exchange rate on the reporting date. Using this process, the MNC is able to report its financial position in the reporting (home) currency. We explain this procedure using numerical examples in Chapter 14.

- **Ex post versus ex ante exposure.** In previous sections concerning transaction and operation exposures, our approach was to estimate exposure before the fact (ex ante). For instance, recall how we estimated how currency values would potentially affect receivables or payables. The purpose of ex ante measurement is to enable a judgment of whether a particular exposure needs control or not. In contrast, most analyses of translation exposure are ex post. After currencies have changed, firms calculate effects using FAS-52 and other accounting regulations and report results to the public. In general, ex ante analyses are more useful than ex post analyses. This does not automatically mean that translation exposure is an irrelevant concept. Assuming that translation exposure is persistent, estimating it ex ante may make sense. That is, one may want to estimate how much future net income will be affected by assumed changes in currency values.

- **Real effects of translation exposure.** There is some controversy whether translation exposure is relevant. One position is that it is irrelevant once a firm identifies its transaction and economic exposures. However, this may be an extreme position because many internal contracts within a firm such as executive compensation contracts depend on accounting numbers. Thus, it is possible that translation exposure has secondary effects on how a firm is run. The accounting literature has also considered whether translation adjustments provide relevant information to market participants. Conceivably, even if translation exposure does not help with hedging and other within-firm decision making, it could provide valuable information to investors. The evidence, however, does not clearly indicate a value for reporting translation adjustments in financial statements. One prominent study[3] concludes that translations do not provide meaningful information. A recent study[4] actually finds that translations provide misleading information about firms with foreign manufacturing operations. For example, if a U.S. firm has manufacturing facilities in Malaysia and if the Malaysian ringgit (MYR) depreciates, the translation adjustment would be negative while the economic effect would be positive (that is, costs are lower).

- **Accounting flows versus cash flows.** Translation exposure focuses on accounting flows rather than cash flows. An important element in translation exposure is net income, which contains many noncash elements such as depreciation, bad debt provisions, asset write-offs, and deferred taxes. Also, translation exposure focuses on book values of assets rather than market value or the present value of cash flows. Foreign assets may have changed in value, dramatically making their translated book values irrelevant. For instance, if PPP

---

[3] Dan Dhaliwal, K.R. Subramanyam, and Robert Trezevant, "Is Comprehensive Income Superior to Net Income as a Measure of Firm Performance," *Journal of Accounting and Economics* 26 (1999), pp. 43–67.

[4] Henock Louis, "The Value Relevance of Foreign Translation Adjustment," *Accounting Review* 78, no. 4 (2003), pp. 1027–1047.

holds, book values translated at current exchange rates may grossly misrepresent asset values. If the foreign currency depreciates because of inflation, the book value translated into the domestic currency would undervalue assets.

6.5 Firm Type and the Nature of Currency Exposure

In previous sections, we described various types of currency exposures and estimation methods. But are there some general patterns? Do certain types of firms experience transaction exposure and others experience operating exposure? Do certain firms have lower levels of currency exposure compared to others? To answer these questions, we categorize firms and describe how operating characteristics affect transaction and operating exposures.

- **Purely domestic firms.** By definition, purely domestic firms do not have any transaction exposure. However, domestic firms may have some operating exposure because they may be competing with firms having a cost basis in other currencies. These competitors may be foreign firms as well as domestic firms with foreign outsourcing. Consider wineries in the Finger Lakes region of New York State (e.g., Glenora). These firms have zero transaction exposure (no foreign sourcing or sales), but they compete with foreign producers as well as domestic firms (e.g., Constellation Brands) with foreign sourcing. Purely domestic firms, especially in the United States, are predominantly small firms. This implies that even small firms may face currency exposure.

- **International production/sourcing and domestic sales.** These are also largely domestic firms but firms that obtain inputs (components and products) from international sources. Most retailers in the United States fall in this category, with Walmart serving as a prime example. Walmart, despite having an international presence, predominantly serves U.S. customers. Most goods that Walmart sells are purchased from foreign sources. Although Walmart primarily pays USD-denominated prices for these foreign goods, input prices would respond to currency changes. Because Walmart has payables in USD, it faces no transaction exposure. But, because in the long run the prices it pays are influenced by currency changes, Walmart is subject to operating exposure. One can conduct a similar analysis to extend to other firms with overseas production and domestic sales.

- **Domestic production and international sales.** If firms produce domestically and sell internationally, they naturally face transaction exposure. Transaction exposure components include foreign receivables and currency balances in foreign accounts. The firm may also owe taxes in a foreign currency. In addition to transaction exposure, the firm is subject to price and quantity risk because of competition from foreign firms. Consider Italian textile machinery manufacturers in centers such as Biella, Brescia, and Prato. Locally produced machines are exported to Asian markets where they compete with Asian producers from China and Japan. These Italian firms face transaction as well as operating exposure. Examples in this category are often medium-size firms but may also include large firms from smaller countries.

- **International production and international sales.** If firms both produce and sell in multiple foreign countries, they may face a very low level of transaction exposure because of netting. A counterintuitive result is that these firms—the most international of the three categories—probably also face a low amount of operating exposure. This is especially true when firms operate in multiple countries and are able to shift production to low-cost countries without incurring high transaction costs. Overall currency exposure may be related to the number of countries in which a firm has subsidiaries: The higher the number of countries, the lower the exposure level. Apple—and, practically, any of the major MNCs—is a good example. Apple produces its iPods, iPhones, and other products in a variety of foreign locations (often using specialized manufacturing firms known as *contract manufacturers*) and sells these products in global markets.

Summary

- Currency exposure is caused by variation in currency values. One measure of currency variation is the standard deviation of percentage currency value changes. Typical figures are in the 5–10 percent range.
- Firms face three types of currency exposure: transaction, operating, and translation (economic exposure is an all-encompassing concept).
- Transaction exposure is the effect of currency value changes on a firm's liquid foreign exchange positions as well as near-term contractual flows such as receivables and payables denominated in foreign currencies.
- Transactions in a particular currency can be netted to provide a summary of transaction exposure.
- Transactions in multiple currencies can be aggregated using portfolio methods that consider the correlation between various currencies.
- Value-at-risk methods can be used to assess the likely downside of currency positions. The delta-normal method uses the currency portfolio standard deviation as an input. The historical simulation method overlays historical changes in currencies on current positions to understand the likely downside.
- Operating exposure measures the risk of currency value changes on a firm's future uncertain operating cash flows and resulting effects on its value. Key impacts relate to price per unit and the number of units.
- Translation exposure refers to changes in accounting values (incomes and asset values) in financial reports in response to currency value changes.

Questions

1. **Currency Standard Deviation.** Conventional wisdom holds that emerging market currencies are much more volatile than major currencies. Consider recent evidence on currency standard deviations in light of this statement. Do you agree with the statement? Why or why not?

2. **Transaction Exposure Application.** What is transaction exposure? Consider the U.S.-based firm Dell that sells computers worldwide. Using your general knowledge about this firm (failing which, check out the profile of the firm on finance.yahoo.com), explain ways in which transaction exposure occurs for Dell.

3. **Transaction Exposure Application.** Consider the U.S.-based firm Boeing Corporation that is the world's leading aircraft producer. Unlike many other industries—especially in consumer products—Boeing signs contracts with its customers before beginning production. Delivery is often one to three years after signing the contract. Assume that contracts call for payments to Boeing denominated in USD. In light of these details and general knowledge you may possess about this firm, assess its transaction exposure.

4. **Scenario versus Markowitz Approaches.** Consider the two common methods used to assess transaction exposure in firms—the scenario approach and Markowitz approach. Compare the two approaches and indicate their advantages and disadvantages.

5. **Netting.** What is netting? How do firms use it to consolidate and assess currency risk? What type of exposure is best measured by netting? What types of information systems are required for firms to use netting as a method of assessing exposure?

6. **Economic Exposure.** Define *economic exposure*. Consider a U.S.-based software services firm such as IBM or Accenture. Using your general business knowledge, assess the economic exposure these firms face.

7. **Operating Exposure.** Define *operating exposure* and its various components. How can one measure operating exposure?

8. **Operating Exposure.** React to the statement "a purely domestic firm without any foreign operations cannot experience operating exposure."

9. **Operating Exposure.** Consider again Boeing Corporation and recognize that Boeing's chief competitor is the European firm EADS (Airbus). Evaluate operating exposure for Boeing.

10. **Operating Exposure.** Consider the continuum of operating exposure. What types of firms/industries face the least and most amounts of operating exposure?

11. **VaR.** Value at risk is a common method in various financial fields such as corporate finance, investments, and banking. Explain what *VaR* means. What are various methods to calculate VaR? What does VaR indicate to a decision maker?

12. **Translation Exposure.** What is translation exposure? Evaluate its importance relative to other types of exposure.

Problems

1. **Consolidating Exposure.** The Northern Truck Company is expecting the following cash flows (see the following table) in a foreign currency. If the interest rate is 6 percent, estimate the company's consolidated exposure at the ninth month. Assume a flat term structure (no change between rates for varying maturity) and annual compounding.

Time	Three Months	Six Months	Nine Months
Cash flow (CAD millions)	2	3	1

2. **Consolidating Exposure.** The Eastern Truck Company is expecting the following cash flows (see the following table) in a foreign currency. If the interest rate is 8 percent, estimate the consolidated exposure of the company at the sixth month. Assume a flat term structure (no change between rates for varying maturity) and annual compounding.

Time	Three Months	Six Months	Nine Months
Cash flow (CAD millions)	5	3	8

3. **Consolidating Exposure.** The Southern Truck Company is expecting the following cash flows (see the following table) in a foreign currency. In Mexico, one- and two-year interest rates are 10 percent and 8 percent. respectively. These rates apply to deposits of MXN in banks. Assume annual compounding. Estimate the consolidated exposure of the company in year 2. [*Hint:* Because the term structure is not flat, calculate the relevant forward rate.]

Time	Year 1	Year 2
Cash flow (MXN millions)	20	40

4. **Scenario Analysis.** A U.S.-based MNC has receivables of JPY 100 million and AUD 2 million in three months. USDJPY is expected to trade in a range between 110 and 130. AUDUSD is expected to trade in a range between 0.78 and 0.82. Estimate best- and worst-case scenarios.

5. **Scenario Analysis.** Maplesoft, a U.S.-based software firm, has receivables of CHF 1 million and payables of EUR 2 million in six months. CHFUSD is expected to trade in a range between 0.85 and 0.90. EURUSD is expected to trade in a range between 1.40 and 1.50. Estimate best- and worst-case scenarios.

6. **Currency Portfolio Risk.** A financial analyst working for a U.S.-based MNC is contemplating the following currency portfolio comprising positions in INR and SGD (see the following table). If the correlation between INR and SGD is 0.25, estimate the standard deviation of the currency portfolio.

Currency	Weight	Standard Deviation
INR	40%	20%
SGD	60%	10%

7. **Standard Deviation Conversion.** The (annual) standard deviation of the currency portfolio of your firm is estimated to be 12 percent. You are in the process of assessing currency risk over the next quarter. What is the appropriate quarterly standard deviation? Explain the assumption behind the conversion from annual to quarterly standard deviation.

8. **Currency Confidence Interval.** Economists indicate that the value of the MXN relative to the USD is behaving very erratically with an annual standard deviation of 18 percent. Your firm, a U.S.-based MNC, has receivables of MXN 1 million in three months. Estimate the risk on this position by estimating the 68 percent confidence interval. The spot rate for MXN is USD 0.12 and the three-month forward rate is USD 0.11.

9. **Standard Deviation Calculation.** During its first six months, the EUR traded successively lower against the dollar as follows: 1.17, 1.15, 1.06, 0.99, 0.92, and 0.86. Estimate the euro's annual standard deviation. Discuss possible biases in your estimate.

10. **Scenario Analysis.** An Italian home appliance manufacturer Miele SPA has the following receivables and payables in 30 days: (a) receivables of USD 80,000 and (b) payables of CHF 25,000. USDEUR is expected to trade in the range of 0.65 to 0.70. CHFEUR is expected to trade in the range 0.55 to 0.60. Estimate the best- and worst-case outcomes for this Italian firm.

11. **Portfolio Confidence Interval.** Beringer Wines, a U.S.-based firm, has the following receivables in three months: (a) CAD 230,000 and (b) EUR 120,000. The spot rates are CADUSD = 0.90 and EURUSD = 1.30. The standard deviations of CAD and EUR are 6 percent and 10 percent, respectively; these are annual figures. The two currencies have a correlation of 0.20. Estimate the risk of the currency portfolio and derive the 68 percent confidence interval.

12. **Portfolio Confidence Interval.** Dell, a U.S.-based firm, has the following positions: (a) receivables of EUR 20 million in six months and (b) payables of JPY 200 million in six months. The spot rates are USD 1.40 and USD 0.01, respectively, for the EUR and JPY. The annual standard deviations are 10 percent and 8 percent for the EUR and JPY, respectively; the two currencies have a correlation of 0.3. The market interest rates are 4 percent, 6 percent, and 1 percent, respectively for the United States, Eurozone, and Japan. Assume annual compounding. Estimate the risk of the currency portfolio and derive the 68 percent confidence interval.

13. **Currency VaR.** Victor Corporation has payables of BRL 5,000 in 30 days. The BRL spot is USD 0.50. The forecast of the BRL in 30 days is as follows:

Value	Probability
0.42–0.43	5%
0.44–0.45	20%
0.46–0.49	25%
0.50–0.53	25%
0.54–0.55	20%
0.56–0.58	5%

   a. Estimate 5 percent VaR. (Calculate VaR based on current, not expected, value.)

   b. Estimate 25 percent VaR. (Calculate VaR based on current, not expected, value.)

14. **Currency VaR.** Victor Corporation has receivables of SGD 500,000 in 90 days. The SGDUSD spot is 0.80. The forecast of the SGD in 90 days is provided in the following table.

Value	Probability
0.77–0.79	5%
0.80–0.82	5%
0.83–0.85	25%
0.86–0.88	25%
0.89–0.93	30%
0.94–0.96	5%
0.97–0.99	5%

a. Estimate the 5 percent VaR. (Calculate VaR based on current, not expected, value.)

b. Estimate the 10 percent VaR. (Calculate VaR based on current, not expected, value.)

15. **Currency Portfolio VaR.** Verbena is a U.S. corporation with a currency portfolio worth USD 2 million. The firm expects to liquidate this portfolio in three months. A financial analyst in the firm estimates that the annual standard deviation of the portfolio is 12 percent.

a. Using the delta-normal approach, determine the 5 percent VaR for this portfolio.

b. Next, recalculate the 5 percent VaR, assuming that the expected *depreciation* of this portfolio during the next three months is 4 percent.

16. **Operating Exposure.** A U.S.-based MNC Floating Point sells computers in India. Annual sales are 10,000 units at a price of INR 50,000 each. INR is currently at USDINR = 50. Because of market shocks, the INR depreciates to USDINR = 54. Consequently, the firm is forced to raise prices to INR 52,000 per computer.

a. Examine the exposure faced by this firm assuming that units do not change.

b. Next assume that because of increased prices, unit volume declines by 10 percent, and reestimate exposure.

17. **Operating Exposure.** The Krisco Corporation is based in the United Kingdom and competes globally with U.S.-based corporations. As such, the firm is exposed to changes in the value of the USD. A financial analyst in the firm used information on the past 24 quarters and estimates the following regression:

$$\text{Percent change in Revenues} = 0.1 + 1.2 \times s_{USD}$$

The USD is currently trading at USDGBP = 0.75. The current level of revenues is GBP 1.4 billion. Estimate the revenues for the next year assuming the USD falls to USDGBP = 0.70.

Extensions

1. **Operating Exposure.** The Jacek Corporation is based in the United States and sources components from Japan. As such, the firm is exposed to changes in the JPY's value. The exposure is only on expenses, not on revenues. A financial analyst in the firm used information on the past eight years and estimates the following regression:

$$\text{Percent change in Expenses} = -0.02 + 0.6 \times s_{JPY}$$

The JPY is currently trading at USD 0.009. In the current year, the firm has a net margin (profits divided by revenues) of 10 percent and profits of USD 30 million. The firm's direct expenses involving components from Japan is 20 percent of revenues. In answering the following questions, assume that the JPYUSD rises to 0.01.

a. Calculate s_{JPY}.

b. Forecast expenses. Compare the forecast with the status quo and explain why the change is expected.

c. Forecast profits.

2. **Three-Currency Portfolio.** Consider the following information on currency spot, correlations, and standard deviations. Consider a three-currency portfolio that contains JPY 100 million, GBP 1 million, and CAD 1 million.

Currency	Spot XXXUSD	Standard Deviations	Correlations with JPY	GBP
JPY	0.01	8.59%		
GBP	2.00	7.83%	0.49	
CAD	1.00	7.62%	0.04	0.38

a. What is portfolio standard deviation? Compare to individual standard deviations and explain the difference. [*Note:* The formula for currency portfolio standard deviation has to be modified to accommodate three currencies. Each currency will have a variance term and each currency pair will have a covariance term; the terms themselves are similar to those in the two-currency equation.]

b. If a Brazilian entity (firm) were to have an identical portfolio of JPY/GBP/CAD, would your conclusions remain valid? Explain.

c. Assume the investment in JPY as well as total investment is fixed. Can you solve for investment amounts in the other two currencies that will minimize portfolio risk? [*Hint:* Use Solver function in Excel.]

Case

Clover Machines: *Estimating Currency Risk*

Clover Machines already has an established subsidiary in Europe selling advanced farming and construction machinery such as combines (with attachment for wheat harvest) and dozers (hilly terrain capability). Last year, sales came in at EUR 1 billion. Sales have been increasing at the rate of 4 percent a year for the past five years, and Clover expects the momentum to continue. The European subsidiary performs significant assembly prior to sales. Costs incurred at the subsidiary level for assembly are roughly 12 percent of list price. Assume no other local expenses.

In its newly formed subsidiary in Brazil, Clover expects the following sales for two key products:

Product	Sales (units) Range: Low End	Sales (units) Range: High End	List Price	Discount
250 hp dozer (land clearing)	520	640	BRL 500,000	10%
Harvester with sugarcane attachment	800	1,000	BRL 400,000	15%

Also, in the newly formed subsidiary in India, the following sales are expected:

Product	Sales (units) Range: Low End	Sales (units) Range: High End	List Price	Discount
30 hp tractor (with tilling attachments)	15,000	20,000	INR 600,000	10%
Excavators	100	120	INR 2,500,000	5%
Back hoe loaders	200	250	INR 1,800,000	5%

Both in Brazil and India, the initial mode of penetration for Clover is to take orders from third-party distributors and fulfill orders using fully assembled machines shipped from the United States. Minor expenses are incurred locally to the tune of 3 percent of list price.

Clover is thus exposed to the three following currencies: EUR, BRL, and INR. As noted, the amounts exposed are substantial. Mr. Bent is wondering about the exact nature of Clover's exposure. Certain of his colleagues insist that Clover is adequately diversified in terms of currencies and that their movements should offset each other at least in the medium term. Others have the opinion that the USD moves unilaterally against emerging market currencies, so there is no real diversification between currency pairs such as BRL and INR.

Also, Mr. Bent has the nagging concern that the issue at hand is more than the converted value of sales revenues. He wonders whether economic conditions in foreign countries affect units sold (and perhaps prices) and whether the same conditions influence currency values. Anecdotal evidence suggests that these effects are heightened in emerging economies.

Most market watchers expect the BRL and INR to strengthen by 5 percent against the USD from their current levels of 0.6208 and 0.02350, respectively. In contrast, the EUR is expected to depreciate by 2 percent from its current high level of 1.6055. Mr. Bent wishes to factor in these expectations in a thorough analysis of Clover's currency risk.

With a view to sorting out these issues, Mr. Bent assigns the task of conducting the exposure analysis to his assistant Amy McDonough. The overall objective of the assignment is to understand and quantify exposure so that adequate steps can be taken to control risks if necessary. Specific questions posed by Mr. Bent include these:

1. What types of exposure—transaction, operating, or translation—does Clover face? Explain.

2. What are amounts facing transaction exposure? Produce high, low, and mean estimates.

3. What are the characteristics of the currencies at play? Use the data in Case Exhibit 6.1 to produce means, standard deviations, and correlations. Provide a written explanation of your numerical results.

CASE EXHIBIT 6.1
Monthly Data, FX Rates

Source: *https://research.stlouisfed.org.*

Date	EURUSD	USDBRL	USDINR
2006-01-03	1.1980	2.3320	44.9200
2006-02-01	1.2092	2.2170	44.1300
2006-03-01	1.1899	2.1200	44.3500
2006-04-03	1.2124	2.1430	44.3900
2006-05-01	1.2607	2.0785	44.7700
2006-06-01	1.2824	2.2697	46.1900
2006-07-03	1.2793	2.1595	45.9200
2006-08-01	1.2778	2.1875	46.5100
2006-09-01	1.2833	2.1397	46.3800
2006-10-02	1.2744	2.1570	45.9700
2006-11-01	1.2771	2.1388	44.7900
2006-12-01	1.3316	2.1610	44.5000
2007-01-02	1.3286	2.1340	44.1300
2007-02-01	1.3021	2.1052	44.0100
2007-03-01	1.3173	2.1230	44.1100
2007-04-02	1.3374	2.0465	43.0500
2007-05-01	1.3600	2.0330	41.0000
2007-06-01	1.3440	1.9010	40.2700
2007-07-02	1.3627	1.9160	40.4200
2007-08-01	1.3682	1.8810	40.2500
2007-09-03	1.3641	1.9672	40.6300
2007-10-01	1.4229	1.8179	39.7000
2007-11-01	1.4435	1.7473	39.2200
2007-12-03	1.4657	1.7840	39.3900
2008-01-02	1.4738	1.7681	39.4100
2008-02-01	1.4851	1.7438	39.1200
2008-03-03	1.5195	1.6779	40.3300
2008-04-01	1.5615	1.7410	39.8800
2008-05-01	1.5458	1.6618	40.5800
2008-06-02	1.5550	1.6305	42.3800
2008-07-01	1.5778	1.6090	43.2300

4. Assuming that exposure to the three currencies forms a currency portfolio, what is the risk of this portfolio? [*Hint:* There are alternate methods to assess variability. The quickest method is to use the Markowitz equation adequately expanded to cover three portfolio components. Alternatively, the time series of currency values can be used to form a sales index; the standard deviation of the percent changes in the sales index equals portfolio risk. Also, the sales index can be used to infer the 5 percent VaR.]

Appendix 6

Sales Index

The Sales Index method is a very simple and practical idea to assess transaction and direct operation exposures.[5] The foreign sales of a firm are viewed as a currency portfolio. Once this portfolio is defined using either current values or some form of a sales forecast, the variability of the portfolio is determined by using historical currency rates.

Suppose a firm operates in three markets: the UK, Japan and Singapore. Its sales for the forthcoming year (say, 2010) are forecasted to be 40% in the UK, 30% in Japan and 30% in Singapore. If the beginning value of the sales index is USD 100 in January 1996 and if the currency values are 1.5096 (GBP), 0.0094 (JPY) and 0.7092 (SGD):

$$\text{GBP units} = \frac{40}{1.5096} = \text{GBP } 26.50,$$

$$\text{JPY units} = \frac{30}{0.0094} = \text{JPY } 3191.49, \text{ and}$$

$$\text{SGD units} = \frac{30}{0.7092} = \text{SGD } 42.30.$$

These values define the Sales Index equation as follows:

$$\text{Sales Index} = 26.50 \times S_{GBP} + 3{,}191.49 \times S_{JPY} + 42.30 \times S_{SGD}$$

This equation is used to generate the Sales Index in the exhibit on the next page. Although generally constructed over a longer period, we show the index over a 2-year period as a sample.

Alternate Methods of Calculating the Sales Index

In the method used in Exhibit 6.7, we fixed currency units, not currency weights. As currency values change over time because units are fixed, currency weights (proportions) change. An alternate method therefore is to fix the currency weights at the initial level of 40 percent (GBP), 30 percent (JPY), and 30 percent (SGD). To apply this alternate method, we need to calculate the weighted average percent change in currency values for each time period and to cumulate the changes over time to construct the index. (Equity portfolio managers often encounter these issues as they seek to benchmark returns against indices constructed with various weighting schemes.)

VaR

The sales index idea is similar in spirit to the historical simulation VaR methodology. Current portfolio composition is coupled with historical exchange rates to determine likely outcomes. The only difference is that the VaR method uses historical changes in currency values, while the sales index uses historical levels of currency values. Because of the similarity, the principles

---

[5] Lewent and Kearney, "Identifying, Measuring and Hedging Currency Risk at Merck," *Journal of Applied Corporate Finance* 2 (1990), pp. 19–28.

EXHIBIT 6.7
Sales Index

$$\text{Sales Index} = 26.50 \times S_{GBP} + 3{,}191.49 \times S_{JPY} + 42.30 \times S_{SGD}$$

Date	GBPUSD	JPYUSD	SGDUSD	Sales Index
1996: Jan	1.5096	0.0094	0.7092	100.00
Feb	1.5320	0.0095	0.7092	100.92
Mar	1.5262	0.0093	0.7092	100.12
Apr	1.5050	0.0096	0.7092	100.52
May	1.5495	0.0093	0.7092	100.74
Jun	1.5529	0.0091	0.7092	100.19
Jul	1.5556	0.0094	0.7092	101.22
Aug	1.5612	0.0092	0.7092	100.73
Sep	1.5653	0.0090	0.7092	100.20
Oct	1.6278	0.0088	0.7092	101.22
Nov	1.6820	0.0088	0.7092	102.66
Dec	1.7123	0.0086	0.7143	103.04
1997: Jan	1.6012	0.0082	0.7143	98.82
Feb	1.6287	0.0083	0.7092	99.65
Mar	1.6448	0.0081	0.6993	99.02
Apr	1.6200	0.0079	0.6944	97.52
May	1.6360	0.0086	0.6897	99.98
Jun	1.6650	0.0087	0.6993	101.47
Jul	1.6388	0.0084	0.6993	99.82
Aug	1.6203	0.0083	0.6803	98.20
Sep	1.6117	0.0083	0.6623	97.21
Oct	1.6786	0.0083	0.6536	98.62
Nov	1.6885	0.0078	0.6329	96.41
Dec	1.6427	0.0077	0.5917	93.13

of VaR can be applied in the sales index analysis. One could sort the sales index values and identify the 5 percent VaR directly.

Transaction versus Economic Exposure

As calculated in Exhibit 6.7, because we fix the amount of the foreign sales revenues at forecasted levels and vary only the currency values, we derive inferences about transaction exposure. The sales index method can be modified to provide a rough estimate of economic exposure by using actual sales data from prior years instead of a fixed level of forecasted sales; thus, both foreign sales revenues and currency values will change and provide an overview of economic exposure.

CHAPTER SEVEN

Currency Exposure Management

Although it is impossible to hedge against all currency or interest risk, Honda uses derivative financial instruments to reduce the substantial effects of currency fluctuations and interest rate exposure on its cash flow and financial condition. These instruments include foreign currency forward contracts, currency swap agreements and currency option contracts, as well as interest rate swap agreements. Honda has entered into, and expects to continue to enter into, such hedging arrangements (Honda Motors Annual Report, 2006).

This chapter helps explain how firms such as Honda use derivatives and other methods to manage currency risk. Key takeaways are hedging methods using currency forwards and options.

In the previous chapter, you learned to estimate various forms of MNC currency exposure, principally transaction and operating exposure. Having determined that a manager's firm faces significant exposure, what are the next steps? In this chapter, we provide answers to this important question. We explain how managers, as a first step, decide whether the estimated level of currency risk warrants mitigation efforts. If currency risk requires mitigation, managers, as a second step, select and apply appropriate methods of alleviating currency risk. We discuss both issues in this chapter. MNCs overwhelmingly use derivatives to control currency exposure. This activity—known as *hedging*—involves the use of forwards, options, and money markets to directly reduce currency exposure and is a key focus of this chapter. Building on your knowledge of derivatives from Chapter 3, we show how hedges can be established and evaluated. Because MNCs' real-world hedging primarily concerns mitigation of transaction exposure, we focus our discussion of hedging on payables and receivables. But MNCs are also concerned about operating exposure. To mitigate it, certain operating strategies are more relevant than hedging: We list and describe these strategies with examples.

More specifically, we discuss the following issues:

- Firm-specific factors that influence an MNC's decision to hedge. We present data on the types of firms that hedge and the procedures they use.
- Use of derivatives to manage currency exposure. The focus is the use of forward, money market, and options hedges. We derive cash flows and compare them for hedging alternatives.
- The use of delta hedges. This is required in most real-world scenarios because of currency or asset mismatches.
- Operating strategies commonly used to alleviate currency risk because hedging has limitations in controlling certain kinds of exposure.

7.1 Why Manage Currency Risk?

Risk management—in the context of corporate finance—is defined as the set of activities that reduces the variance of cash flows. This chapter focuses on one particular aspect of risk management: controlling currency exposure. Surveys show that most MNCs pursue a variety of strategies to reduce currency exposure. In this section, we consider the benefits of currency risk management. By understanding the benefits, we hope you understand why certain firms pursue aggressive risk management strategies while others are less involved.

The two main benefits of reducing currency risk are:

- The successful management of currency risk enables firms to focus more on their strategic plan without undue distractions.
- The reduction of currency risks reduces the volatility of income. This in turn allows firms to maximize the use of tax shields and to pay taxes at a lower marginal rate.

These reasons for risk management are general and apply equally to the mitigation of risk factors such as commodity risk and interest rate risk. We discuss these and other reasons for managing currency risk next.

The Need to Execute the Firm's Strategic Plan

strategic plan and hedging
Firms hedge to prevent any currency-related disruptions to the execution of their *strategic plans*.

Many firms consider their strategic plan and ask the critical question: Does currency exposure have the potential to disrupt the successful execution of the strategic plan? For instance, are there large capital outlays that would potentially be jeopardized by adverse swings in currency values? An airline would be concerned about the constant need to upgrade its fleet. A semiconductor firm would be concerned about the need to build new fabrication facilities. A pharmaceutical firm would be concerned about funding research and development (R&D) expenditures. For these firms, a hiatus in such investments could seriously threaten long-term viability.

EXAMPLE 7.1

Consider a Korean-based MNC producing LCD panels for consumer electronics. The firm markets its products globally but has two main markets, the United States and Brazil. Assume that from the Korean perspective, the two respective currencies are risky. The firm expects operating cash flows of U.S. dollar (USD) 1 billion of which it expects to invest half in R&D. Assume that adverse currency movements could cause cash flows to be either USD 1.8 billion or USD 0.2 billion. Evaluate strategic alternatives considering adverse currency movement.

Solution:

	Alternative I	**Alternative II**	**Alternative III**
Action	Issue stocks, bonds; raise private equity or debt	Combine with another firm (e.g., joint venture, merger)	Forgo R&D expense
Advantage	Invites external monitoring; ensures continued operations	Obtain expertise and financing from another entity	None
Disadvantage	Costly financing because of financial problems	Must share benefits; relinquish partial control of firm	Miss product cycle and head toward long-term failure

Discussion: Very few firms in financial difficulty are able to tap private or public markets effectively. This rules out alternative I for many firms. Alternative II is also problematic: Firms in distress rarely get good terms in combinations. Alternative III will reduce going concern value drastically. In conclusion, none of these options is particularly attractive. This firm needs to take steps (e.g., hedging) to avoid this situation in the first place.

The preceding example may appear extreme to some. However, research shows that investment opportunities in many industries are negatively correlated with industry cash flows.[1] This means that opportunities abound when cash flow is low. Firms that are prepared through hedging and other means are able to act opportunistically and generate wealth for their shareholders.

[1] Kenneth A. Froot, David S. Scharfstein, and Jeremy C. Stein, "Risk Management: Coordinating Corporate Investment and Financing Policies," *Journal of Finance* 48 (December 1993), pp. 1629–1658.

Tax Advantages to Reducing Currency Exposure

taxes and hedging
Hedging reduces volatility in taxable income, and this reduces *total taxes* over a period of time.

Firms can reduce their total taxes over time by smoothing taxable income. This happens for two reasons. First, the tax code incorporates a progressive scheme of taxation that taxes higher levels of income at marginally higher rates. Second, firms need taxable income to offset tax shields such as deprecation and interest tax shields.

EXAMPLE 7.2

A firm expects taxable incomes of $10 million and $100 million over a period of two years. Assume that the variation in incomes occurs because of currency exposure and that the firm can eliminate this risk substantially through hedging and producing incomes of USD 50 million and USD 60 million over this two-year period. Assume that the tax code indicates rates of 20 percent for incomes up to USD 50 million and 30 percent for incomes above USD 50 million. Calculate taxes in the two scenarios and identify the benefit of hedging.

Solution: Unhedged scenario tax calculations (all values in USD million):

Year 1 taxes = 20% (10) = 2
Year 2 taxes = 20% (50) + 30% (100 − 50) = 25

We make similar calculations for the hedged scenario and complete the following table.

	Year 1		Year 2		
Scenario	Income	Taxes	Income	Taxes	Total Taxes
Unhedged	10	2	100	25	27
Hedged	50	10	60	13	23

Discussion: Hedging reduces total taxes from USD 27 to 23 million. The benefit of hedging equals USD 4 million.

Commonly used tax shields (that is, deductions or expenses that reduce taxable income) such as those for depreciation and interest (expense) produce a similar effect. They provide maximum benefits to the firm that can use them promptly. If firms are unable to use these tax shields in the year in which they occur (because of lack of taxable income), they either expire or are used in later periods providing lower present value (PV) of benefits. The volatility of taxable income caused by currency exposure can be a detriment to a firm's ability to efficiently use these tax shields.

Other Managerial Reasons for Reducing Currency Exposure

Management Compensation

Accounting and cash flow values are frequently used as inputs in calculating management compensation. Bonuses earned by top managers in the United States, for instance, are usually based on accounting metrics such as net income or operating cash flows. This U.S. practice is spreading globally. Managers of firms with bonuses determined in this manner would prefer a steady stream of income and would therefore prefer to hedge currency and other risks. Managers compensated with stock options may, however, actually prefer corporate volatility. The structure of compensation and, more specifically, the mix of bonus and options will determine whether managers wish to hedge currency risk.

EXAMPLE 7.3

Consider managers allocated one-year stock options with a strike price of 30 (all values in USD). The current stock price is 30, so the options are at the money. Assume that in the absence of hedging, the stock price at year-end is equally as likely to be 28 or 38. Hedging shrinks the distribution of prices; outcomes are 30 and 36. Calculate the manager's expected cash flow under the unhedged and hedged scenarios.

Solution:

E(Cash flow: Unhedged) = 50% $\times$ Max(0,28−30) + 50% $\times$ Max(0,38 − 30) = 4

E(Cash flow: Hedged) = 50% $\times$ Max(0,30−30) + 50% $\times$ Max(0,36 − 30) = 3

Notes:

Unhedged. The stock price could be either 28 or 38. If it is 28, the option is not exercised, so payoff is zero. If the stock price is 38, the option is exercised, and payoff is 8 (= 38 − 30). Because these are equally likely outcomes, the expected cash flow is 4.

Hedged. The stock price could be either 30 or 36. If the stock price is 30, the option is not exercised, so payoff is zero. If the stock price is 36, the option is exercised, and payoff is 6 (= 36 − 30). Because these are equally likely outcomes, the expected cash flow is 3.

Discussion: Options are asymmetric instruments. Option value increases when outcomes are dispersed (volatility is higher). This happens because there is no downside loss and only upside gain.

Managerial Risk Aversion

Managers are typically ill-diversified and have a disproportionate amount of their wealth invested in the firm. This happens for two reasons. First, because of incentive compensation, many managers hold shares of the firm as well as options. Second, a manager's future compensation is of significant value. This lack of diversification presents a conflict of interest between managers and shareholders. Agency theory predicts that managers seek self-interest and will adopt a risk-averse posture and a desire to reduce risk levels through hedging. In other words, for totally selfish reasons, managers may want to reduce the volatility of the firm's cash flows.

Debt Contracting

Creditors prefer a stable pattern of net income and cash flows because it allows trouble-free interest and principal repayments. If cash flow volatility is high, creditors lose because they bear downside costs and do not share upside potential. If cash flows are high, benefits accrue to shareholders; if cash flows are low, creditors lose.[2]

Customer and Supplier Concerns

Like creditors, customers and suppliers also want the company on a firm and stable footing. This is especially true when customers and suppliers have long-term contracts. Those with customers typically occur when the firm provides support services for capital or durable goods. Long-term contracts with suppliers occur when specialized (noncommodity) inputs are outsourced. When a firm faces a significant probability of bankruptcy, even if it is not likely, customers and suppliers are concerned and wish to contract using terms disadvantageous to the firm. For instance, customers demand warranties, and suppliers demand prepayments.

Market Inefficiencies

Firms sometimes hedge because of opportunities provided by inefficiencies in various financial and currency markets. Unlike other reasons for hedging that result from within the corporation, this reason for hedging is motivated by mispricing in markets. For example, a firm may buy certain currencies—to which it is exposed via payables—in the forward

---

[2] One can use option theory to understand creditors' point of view. A debt contact may be viewed as equivalent to a call option on the firm's assets: Bondholders have sold this call to shareholders. If the firm does not perform well, shareholders walk away without exercising the call, and bondholders claim the assets; if the firm does well, shareholders pay bondholders the exercise price (equal to debt face value) and claim the assets. Option theory indicates that as σ increases, the call value increases. Thus, a rise in volatility hurts bondholders and benefits stockholders because they hold short and long positions, respectively.

markets principally because they are priced lower than indicated by parity conditions. In many respects, this is similar to conducting currency arbitrage. Risk reduction is a collateral benefit, not the main motive.

Comparison of Currency Risk with Other Risks

Firms face a wide variety of risks. Currency risk is only one of these risks. Others include interest rate, commodity price, regulatory, economic downturn, technology, and governance risk. Two perspectives explains how currency risk compares to these other risk factors. First, at a superficial level, currency risk appears less threatening than other risk factors such as commodity price risk. Earlier, we learned that individual currency standard deviation is around 5–10 percent. In comparison, the standard deviation of many commodities important to corporations (e.g., steel, oil) is much higher. This suggests that currency risk is not as important as other risks such as commodity price risk. An alternate point of view asserts that currency risk is more significant than this superficial analysis reveals because this risk affects firms within an industry differentially. Unlike input price risk that affects all firms in an industry uniformly, currency risk affects firms differentially and may change an industry's competitive landscape. For example, steel prices may affect Hyundai and Ford in the same way. But if the Korean won (KRW) declines against the USD, Hyundai may obtain a competitive leg up on Ford.

A key method of managing risks is the use of derivatives, a major topic in this chapter. A review of derivative markets reveals that currency derivatives are quite popular with MNCs. This confirms our view that currency risk is important. However, we must also acknowledge that MNC usage of interest rate derivatives far surpasses MNC usage of currency derivatives.

7.2 Actual Hedging Behavior by Firms

Hedging is the main way in which MNCs reduce currency exposure. In this section, we offer some evidence on hedging activities of firms in general followed by a discussion of the specific forms of currency risks hedged.

General Hedging Activity

Studies find that an increasing number of U.S. firms hedge against commodity, currency, and interest rate risks. This is not a surprising result. In an earlier chapter, you learned that the derivatives markets have grown significantly. Exhibit 7.1 provides results from a survey conducted by the Wharton School of the University of Pennsylvania. Two results emerge. First, large firms are more likely to hedge; MNCs are clearly in this category. Second, firms producing primary products (e.g., oil, lumber) hedge to a greater extent, although firms in other industries also hedge significantly.

EXHIBIT 7.1
Hedging Activity by U.S. Nonfinancial Firms

Source: Gordon Bodnar, Gregory Hayt, and Richard Marston, "1998 Wharton Survey of Financial Risk Management by U.S. Nonfinancial Firms," *Financial Management* 27, no. 4 (1998), pp. 70–91.

Category	Percent of Firms Hedging
Size	
Large	83%
Medium	45%
Small	12%
Type of Firm	
Primary products	68%
Manufacturing	48%
Services	42%

EXHIBIT 7.2
What Types of Currency Exposure Are Hedged?

Source: Gordon Bodnar, Gregory Hayt, and Richard Marston, "1998 Wharton Survey of Financial Risk Management by U.S. Nonfinancial Firms," *Financial Management* 27, no. 4 (1998), pp. 70–91.

	Percent of Firms Responding in the Following Ranges for Percent of Exposure Hedged				
Exposure	**0–25 Percent**	**26–50 Percent**	**51–75 Percent**	**76–100 Percent**	**Average Proportion Hedged**
On-balance-sheet commitments	40%	13%	12%	35%	49%
Off-balance-sheet commitments	72%	11%	5%	13%	23%
Anticipated transactions < 1 year	42%	22%	9%	27%	42%
Anticipated transactions > 1 year	78%	11%	4%	6%	16%
Competitive exposure	90%	6%	2%	3%	7%
Translation	84%	6%	3%	8%	12%
Repatriation	50%	14%	5%	31%	40%

Why do large firms hedge more? Hedging generally requires a centralized department staffed by professionals to oversee and coordinate its activities. Such systems have the potential to cost millions of dollars on an annual basis. Furthermore, risk management activities require investments in hedging instruments. These investments can entail substantial transaction costs. Thus, only firms of sufficient size and with a sophisticated treasury department can undertake risk management activities. Most MNCs are large firms and conduct hedging.

Currency Hedging

The Wharton survey discussed earlier also provides evidence on currency hedging. Exhibit 7.2 indicates the types of exposure that are hedged.

From Exhibit 7.2, we conclude that the following types of exposure are hedged:

- **On-balance-sheet commitments.** These are items such as receivables and payables. In Chapter 6, you learned that these items constitute a significant proportion of transaction exposure.

- **Anticipated transactions in < one year.** These cash flows are based on transactions such as the sale of goods, completion of service agreements, sourcing of components, and purchases of capital equipment.

- **Repatriation**. These are cash flows between subsidiaries and parent involving dividends, interest, royalties, and licensing fees.

While Exhibit 7.2 provides an overall look at hedging by firms, Exhibit 7.3 affords a close look at hedging conducted by one firm and how this hedging contributed to its financial success.

7.3 Hedging Techniques

Hedging is a financial remedy to currency exposure. In a **hedge**, firms take a position in derivative instruments that are opposite to their currency position. When currency positions produce losses, the derivative positions compensate by producing offsetting gains. The goal of hedging is to reduce variation in cash flows. In this section, we first discuss some general issues about implementing hedges followed by numerical examples. Because firms predominantly focus on hedging on-balance-sheet commitments, our examples are primarily on receivables and payables.

In Exhibit 7.4, we show Honda Motor's currency derivatives positions. Honda has a total of Japanese yen (JPY) 899 billion of forwards and JPY 177 billion of options outstanding in 2006. Honda primarily has short positions (that is, contracts to sell) in currencies such as the USD, EUR (euro), and GBP (pound). In this section, we explain the hedging techniques that result in such positions.

EXHIBIT 7.3

A Currency Player in the Heartland, Industrial Stalwart Nordson, Credit Swaps, Foreign Hedges in International Success

Excerpted from Christopher O'Leary (christopher.oleary@ thomsonmedia.com), *The Investment Dealers' Digest: IDD*. New York: February 23, 2004, p. 1. Copyright Thomson Media Inc. All rights reserved. http://www.thomsonmedia .com, http://www.iddmagazine.com.

How can chief financial officers protect their companies from a U.S. dollar in full swoon? Consider the lessons learned by a 50-year-old industrial company in Ohio's heartland. Granted, Nordson Corp. seems an unlikely candidate for the leading edge of international currency hedging, but its growing expertise in that area has helped it not only withstand the past recession, but also handle the whipsaw volatility of the U.S. dollar with some dexterity.

For Nordson, located in Westlake, Ohio, the solution has been to increase its use of a variety of international currency hedging tools, using strategies like short-term borrowing in local currencies to hedge international sales, and purchasing longer-term foreign-denominated debt.

At first glance, Nordson seems as homegrown as they come. It manufactures systems that dispense adhesives, sealants and coatings for a host of industrial processes, including bookbinding operations and medical supply manufacturing. "We glue, we solder, we paint, we put down anything—even the sugar on Frosted Flakes," says Peter Hellman, executive VP and chief administrative and financial officer for the company.

More and more, however, Nordson is working for international clients. In fact, the manufacturer increasingly owes its livelihood to its expanding international operations. Nordson's non-U.S. sales were 63 percent of its total sales of $667.3 million last year, compared with 57 percent in 2002. These international sales, in particular the 17 percent jump in its Japanese and South Pacific markets last year, have offset a sales contraction in the U.S. of 11 percent in 2003.

In addition, Nordson also runs a bevy of international manufacturing and distribution operations, including plants and offices located in Germany, the Netherlands, Japan, Italy, France, China, India and the United Kingdom. "We are an international company disproportionate to our size," Hellman says.

That also creates a disproportionately large currency problem. With so many operations in foreign countries, with most of its revenue derived from foreign markets, and with the dollar at its weakest point in a decade, Nordson needed every bit of its skill in currency hedging. For starters, it needed to make sure that it didn't wind up at a competitive disadvantage to local overseas competitors whose operations are all transacted in euros.

Hedging

Nordson has a number of ongoing forward exchange contracts in various currencies, with the greatest number denominated in euros. In addition, it uses foreign denominated fixed-rate debt and foreign currency deals to hedge the value of its investments in its wholly-owned international subsidiaries. Those deals have worked out well for Nordson, which, as of November 2003, had recorded a net gain of $2.3 million from hedging its exposure in foreign operations.

The company also has entered into several interest-rate swaps, including most recently a roughly $73,000 swap that converts a Japanese 200 million leasehold improvement note from fixed- to floating-rate debt.

Hellman said Nordson uses a wide variety of international banks to handle these transactions, often relying on banks whose major market presences are in Europe or Asia, for example, to handle euro or yen hedges. Nordson is under far less pressure to include their lenders as underwriters, a problem many companies face these days, as Nordson has not had to take on any debt obligations in recent years—its last bond deal was issued in May 2001, and it has not closed any new bank loan facilities since then, either.

Operational Issues

Firms face the following issues in implementing a risk management program:

- The percentage of the exposure to hedge.
- The desirable instruments and levels of hedging sensitivities.
- The hedging horizon.

We now discuss these three operational issues in detail.

Partial versus Full Hedging

Once an exposure is identified, firms determine the proportion of exposure that needs to be eliminated. Actual firm behavior suggests that firms engage only in partial hedging. There are two explanations for this behavior. First, hedging is a costly activity. Consequently, firms optimize the hedged position to exploit the trade-off between hedging benefits and costs.

EXHIBIT 7.4
Honda's Currency
Derivatives Positions
(2006)

	Notional Principal JPY billions	Average Contractual Rate
Forward Exchange Contracts		
To sell USD	270	115.88
To sell EUR	133	138.57
To sell CAD (Canadian dollar)	19	100.59
To sell GBP	83	201.67
To sell other FX	83	
To buy USD	6	115.78
To buy other FX	1	
Cross-Currencies	304	
TOTAL	**899**	
Currency Options		
Purchased to sell	58	
Written to sell USD	105	
Purchased to sell other FX	5	
Written to sell other FX	9	
TOTAL	**177**	

Second, hedging is an imprecise science. Precision errors can occur in setting up hedges. Consequently, firms are tentative in their hedging strategy. This also helps explain why firms rarely hedge their operating exposure and other long-term exposures. The precision errors are much larger in these hedges when compared to transaction exposure.

Hedging Instrument

Firms select instruments based on their sensitivities to the underlying currency. This advanced issue is best understood after studying basic hedging techniques. But matching and symmetry are two initial considerations.

- **Matching.** As far as possible, hedging instruments must closely match the exposure in terms of currency as well as maturity. Thus, if a firm has EUR receivables in three months, the derivative instrument should ideally be a three-month EUR derivative such as a three-month EUR option.
- **Symmetry.** Symmetric hedges are fixed hedges and lock in currency values for future transactions regardless of whether currencies rise or fall. Asymmetric hedges are flexible hedges and lock in currency values only when it is advantageous to the MNC. Symmetric hedges are typically executed using forwards or futures; asymmetric hedges are typically executed using options. For example, if an MNC has currency payables, a forward hedge would lock in an exchange rate; this protects against a rising foreign currency but also removes any benefits of a falling currency. An option hedge would preserve some of the benefits of a falling currency. The advantages and disadvantages of symmetric versus asymmetric hedges are explained using numerical examples later in this chapter.

Hedging Horizon

Given the short maturity of the exposure, when hedging transaction exposure, most firms choose to match the maturity of the hedging instrument with the maturity of the primary position. Instead, when hedging operating exposure, firms often plan on a hedging maturity shorter than the primary position's maturity. This is so because, by its very nature, the maturity of operating exposure is long term—often more than 10 years—and it is very expensive and risky to set up long-term hedges. Long-term derivatives can easily backfire on the firm. Moreover, firms cannot predict how their operating environment will change in the long term.

Forward Hedge

The **forward hedge** is the simplest hedging method and involves the purchase or sale of a foreign currency using a forward contract. As long as the maturity is reasonably short and

forward hedge

A *forward hedge* is the simplest hedge to execute and locks in the future value of receivables or payables.

the currency is a major one, forward hedges can be tailored precisely. Forward hedges can eliminate cash flow variability completely. Matching can be a problem, however, in certain emerging market currencies (for example, Sri Lankan rupee) and when the horizon is more than two years.

In equation form, a forward hedge produces the following expected cash flow:

$$E(CF) = \text{Amount} \times F$$

The cash flow equals the amount of the foreign currency times the forward rate.

EXAMPLE 7.4

A Brazilian exporter to Europe invoices goods in EUR and expects to receive EUR 4 million in three months. A three-month forward contract is available at a EURBRL (EUR in terms of Brazilian real) rate of 2.7513. Explain the hedging strategy and show its result.

Solution: The exporter takes a short position in the forward contract with a notional value of EUR 4 million. At maturity, she delivers EUR 4 and receives:

$$E(CF) = \text{BRL } 4,000,000 \times 2.7513$$
$$= \text{BRL } 11,005,200$$

Discussion: The exporter receives EUR 4 million from European sales. She simply uses this EUR cash flow to settle the forward contract. Because EUR cash inflows (from sale) equal EUR cash outflows (settlement of forward), net EUR cash flow at maturity is zero. The forward contract uses a prespecified rate of BRL 2.7513 and enables the exporter to convert EUR into BRL at a prespecified rate.

How do firms benchmark forward hedges? One method is to compare the cash flow of a forward hedge to the expected cash flow of remaining unhedged. If the forward hedge cash flow is higher than the expected unhedged cash flow, the forward hedge is preferred. The decision becomes complex, however, if the unhedged cash flow is higher than the hedged cash flow. Firms may still prefer the hedge because of reduced risks.

EXAMPLE 7.5

An Indian garment exporter to the United States is concerned about the weakening dollar and is considering a six-month currency forward at a rate (USDINR[USD in terms of Indian rupees]) of 42. The firm internally forecasts USD values as follows: USDINR equals 40 (probability = 50 percent) and USDINR equals 45 (probability = 50 percent). Evaluate the hedging decision. Assume that the firm has receivables of USD 2 million.

Solution:

Scenario	USDINR	Probability	Cash Flows (INR) Unhedged	Cash Flows (INR) Hedged
I	40	50%	80,000,000	84,000,000
II	45	50%	90,000,000	84,000,000
E(CF)			85,000,000	84,000,000
σ(CF)			5,000,000	0

Note: E(CF) and σ(CF) are the mean and standard deviation of cash flows respectively.

These values are calculated using probability-weighted equations explained in Chapter 6.[3]

Discussion: By hedging, the firm eliminates all risk, but the expected cash flow is lower. The hedging decision hinges on the firm's risk aversion and its motivation for hedging. A key question would concern the scenario I unhedged outcome of INR 80 million. Does this create unfavorable outcomes in firm strategy, taxes, supplier contracts, or so forth?

---

[3] As a quick review, calculations for the unhedged position are:

$$E(CF) = 50\% \times 80,000,000 + 50\% \times 90,000,000 = 85,000,000$$
$$\sigma(CF) = \sqrt{50\%(80,000,000 - 85,000,000)^2 + 50\%(90,000,000 - 85,000,000)^2} = 5,000,000$$

Futures contracts are practically identical to forward contracts. The preceding discussion of forwards applies equally to futures. Futures have one drawback, however. Because exchanges standardize them, their maturity may not always match the currency position's maturity. This requires a special type of hedging known as *delta hedging*. We discuss it in a later section.

Money Market Hedge

money market hedge
A *money market hedge* requires a preemptive currency transaction and can eliminate currency risk completely like a forward hedge.

The money market hedge involves the preemptive purchase or sale of a foreign currency in anticipation of a future transaction. For instance, if a U.S.-based firm has EUR receivables in a year requiring a conversion from EUR to USD, the firm would borrow EUR and make the conversion today. The repayment of the EUR loan would be made using the receivables. Preemptive conversion fixes the exchange rate and eliminates risk. This hedging procedure is called the **money market hedge** because it involves money market transactions (e.g., borrowing EUR). Like the forward hedge, its close sibling, the money market hedge can eliminate cash flow variability completely.

EXAMPLE 7.6

A U.S. firm has receivables of EUR 5 million in nine months. The spot and forward (EURUSD) rates are 1.55 and 1.52, respectively. Assume that the firm can borrow as well as lend at the following Eurocurrency rates (actual/360 simple interest): 2 percent (USD) and 4 percent (EUR). Show details of the money market hedge.

Solution: The money market hedge requires a preemptive conversion of EUR into USD. So, the steps are:

- Borrow EUR (set borrowing amount at PV of 5,000,000).
- Convert EUR into USD and lend this amount (FV is the net cash flow from receivables).
- Repay EUR loan (loan repayment cancels receivables).

$$\text{EUR to be borrowed} = \frac{5,000,000}{1 + 4\% \times (9/12)} = 4,854,369$$

$$\text{USD to be deposited} = 4,854,369 \times 1.55 = 7,524,272$$

$$E(CF) = 7,524,272 \times (1 + 2\% \times (9/12)) = \text{USD } 7,637,136$$

Alternatively, we can use an all-in equation to calculate the expected cash flow:

$$E(CF) = 5,000,000 \times \frac{1}{\left(1 + 4\% \times \frac{9}{12}\right)} \times 1.55 \times \left(1 + 2\% \times \frac{9}{12}\right) = 7,637,136$$

Discussion: The EUR loan repayment of 5 million is an exact offset to receivables. The remaining item is the USD deposit; the cash flow from this deposit is USD 7,637,136. Note that the calculations use three inputs: EUR interest rate, spot rate, and USD interest rate. Because these inputs are prespecified, there is no variability. So, $\sigma(CF)$ is zero.

Consider the structure of the all-in equation for the money market hedge for receivables in the preceding example. Using notation developed in Chapter 5 and rearranging slightly, we can write this as:

$$E(CF) = \text{Amount} \times S \times \frac{1 + r}{1 + r^*}$$

IRP states that:

$$F = S \times \frac{1 + r}{1 + r^*}$$

Therefore, under parity, the forward and money market hedges provide identical outcomes. Because of this feature of money market hedges, they are also known as *synthetic forward hedges.*

EXAMPLE 7.7

USD and BRL 180-day interest rates are 3 percent and 12 percent, respectively. Calculate the forward rate using IRP. Show equivalence of forward and money market hedges for a U.S. firm with BRL 10 million receivables. Assume spot USDBRL = 1.9152. Assume that interest rates use London Interbank Offered Rate (LIBOR) conventions of actual/360 simple interest.

Solution: According to IRP, the BRLUSD forward rate is:

$$F = S \times \frac{1+r}{1+r^*} = (1/1.9152) \times \frac{1 + 3\% \times (180/360)}{1 + 12\% \times (180/360)} = 0.4999724$$

The forward hedge produces:

$$E(CF) = Amount \times F$$
$$= 10,000,000 \times 0.4999724$$
$$= 4,999,724$$

The money market hedge produces:

$$E(CF) = Amount \times S \times \frac{1+r}{1+r^*}$$
$$= 10,000,000 \times (1/1.9152) \times \frac{1 + 3\% \times (180/360)}{1 + 12\% \times (180/360)}$$
$$= 4,999,724$$

Although forward and money market hedges are identical from a theoretical standpoint, practical differences exist. At certain times, because of deviation from parity, one or the other offers a better solution. More generally, the money market hedge is more difficult to implement because of higher transaction costs. Critically, the bid-ask spread (borrowing rate > lending rate) in Eurocurrency markets may deter MNCs from implementing the money market hedge.

EXAMPLE 7.8

This is a payables hedging example. A U.S. firm has payables of JPY 500,000 in 270 days. USD and JPY 270-day interest rates are 3 percent and 1 percent, respectively (actual/360 simple interest). Spot JPYUSD is 0.01. Apply the money market hedge for this payables position.

Solution: The firm has to borrow USD, convert them into JPY, deposit in a JPY interest-bearing account, and use the FV of this deposit to meet the payables. These steps are implicit in the following all-in equation (same as the equation used for receivables):

$$E(CF) = Amount \times S \times \frac{1+r}{1+r^*}$$
$$= -500,000 \times 0.01 \times \frac{1 + 3\% \times (270/360)}{1 + 1\% \times (270/360)}$$
$$= -5,074$$

Note: Because it represents payables, the amount is negative. Consequently, $E(CF)$ also is negative and represents the cash flow required to repay the USD debt.

option hedge
An *option hedge* is the most complex of hedges. The upfront option premium is the price paid for flexibility down the road.

Option Hedge

The **option hedge** involves the purchase or sale of an option (call or put). Unlike the forward hedge, upfront cash flows are related to the option premium. If the firm purchases an option, cash flow is negative. In evaluating the hedge, the premium has to be netted against other cash flows. Firms typically purchase call options to hedge against payables and put options to hedge against receivables. Option hedges are asymmetric and do not eliminate cash flow variability completely.

We next derive equations for evaluating option hedges. For simplicity, we assume that the maturities of options and currency positions match. We relax these assumptions later in the chapter.

Call Option Payables Hedge

Recall the following option notation: C equals call option premium, X equals strike price, S equals currency value. If a firm uses a call option to hedge a payables position, the cash flow per currency unit equals:

$$CF = -S - FV(C) + Max(0, S - X)$$

The currency value represents a negative flow because of payables. The future value (FV) of the call premium is another negative cash flow. The $Max(.)$ term captures the effects of exercise: Exercising the option produces a positive cash flow; cash flow is zero otherwise.

EXAMPLE 7.9

A U.S. firm has EUR payables that mature in 180 days. It hedges using a call option on EUR with a strike price of USD 1.50 and a premium of USD 0.04. Suppose the maturity value of EURUSD is 1.60. Assume that the USD-denominated LIBOR rate is 4 percent (actual/360 simple interest). Calculate the (net) cash flow to the payables hedge.

Solution:

$$CF = -S - FV(C) + Max(0, S - X)$$
$$= -1.60 - 0.04 \times \left(1 + 4\% \times \frac{180}{360}\right) + Max(0, 1.60 - 1.50)$$
$$= -1.60 - 0.0408 + 0.10$$
$$= -1.5408$$

When a firm forecasts multiple currency values and attaches associated probabilities, we can derive the following equation for a call option payables hedge:

$$E(CF) = \sum_i p_i \times \text{Amount} \times \underbrace{[-S - FV(C) + Max(0, S - X)]}_{\text{CF per Currency Unit}}$$

$$\underbrace{\phantom{E(CF) = \sum_i p_i \times \text{Amount} \times [-S - FV(C) + Max(0, S - X)]}}_{\text{CF (total)}}$$

The amount within square brackets—the cash flow per currency unit—varies as S varies. The total cash flow is obtained by multiplying the cash flows per currency unit by the number of units of the currency. The expected cash flow equals the weighted average of these cash flow values (using probabilities as weights). See the following example for an explanation.

EXAMPLE 7.10

Reconsider the preceding example involving an option hedge by a U.S. firm. The call option is on EUR with a strike price of USD 1.50 and a premium of USD 0.04. The firm forecasts that the EURUSD is equally likely to be 1.45 or 1.60 at maturity. Assume payables of EUR 25,000. Assume that the USD-denominated LIBOR rate is 4 percent (actual/360 simple interest). Calculate the cash flow of the call option hedge in the two scenarios. What are the expected value and standard deviation?

Solution: We use this equation:

$$E(CF) = \sum_i p_i \times Amount \times [-S - FV(C) + Max(0, S - X)]$$

The solution is best understood in the following spreadsheet format.

◇	A	B	C	D	E	F	G	H
1				Call Option / Payables Hedge				
2		(1)	(2)	(3)	(4)	(5)	(6)	(7)
3							CF / Unit	CF
4						Max(0,	=	=
5	Scenario	Amount	p_i	S	FV(C)	S − X)	−(3)−(4)+(5)	(1) × (6)
6	I	25,000	50%	1.45	0.0408	0	−1.4908	−37,270
7	II	25,000	50%	1.60	0.0408	0.10	−1.5408	−38,520
8								
9	E(CF)							−37,895
10	σ(CF)							625

Excel Hint: Array formulas are used to calculate $E(CF)$ and $\sigma(CF)$. For the former, use the sum of column (2) times column (7). For the latter, use SQRT of the sum of column (2) times the squared value of "column (7) minus $E(CF)$."

Discussion: The call option puts a ceiling on the cash outflow and reduces risk. The strike price (USD 1.50) net of the FV or the premium (USD 0.0408) is the maximum amount the firm would pay per currency unit. This truncates the distribution of cash flows and reduces the standard deviation.

Put Option Receivables Hedge

Because they provide holders with the right to sell the underlying currency, puts are typically used in hedging receivables. The mechanics of a put option hedge is very similar to a call option hedge. Recall that P equals put option premium. If a firm uses a put option to hedge a receivables position, the per currency unit cash flow is:

$$CF = S - FV(P) + Max(0, X - S)$$

The currency value represents a positive flow because of receivables. The future value of the put premium is a negative cash flow. If the option is exercised, it produces a positive cash flow.

EXAMPLE 7.11

A U.S. firm has Canadian dollar (CAD) receivables that mature in 270 days. It hedges using a put option on CAD with a strike price of USD 1.00 and a premium of USD 0.05. Suppose the maturity value of CADUSD is 0.90. Assume that the USD-denominated LIBOR rate is 6 percent (actual/360 simple interest). Calculate the (net) cash flow to the receivables hedge.

Solution:

$$CF = S - FV(P) + Max(0, X - S)$$
$$= 0.90 - 0.05 \times \left(1 + 6\% \times \frac{270}{360}\right) + Max(0, 1.00 - 0.90)$$
$$= 0.94775$$

When a firm forecasts multiple currency values and attaches associated probabilities, we can derive the following cash flow equation for a put option receivables hedge:

$$E(CF) = \sum_i p_i \times Amount \times [S - FV(P) + Max(0, X - S)]$$

This equation is analogous to the call option payables equation derived earlier. See the next example for a detailed explanation.

EXAMPLE 7.12

Reconsider the previous example involving a put option receivables hedge. A U.S. firm's CAD receivables mature in 270 days. It hedges using a put option receivables hedge on CAD with a strike price of USD 1.00 and a premium of USD 0.05. The firm forecasts that the CADUSD will be worth 0.85 (probability = 60 percent), or 1.10 (probability = 40 percent) in 270 days. Assume receivables of CAD 500,000 and that the USD-denominated LIBOR interest rate is 6 percent (actual/360 simple interest). Calculate the cash flow of the put option hedge in the two scenarios. Evaluate the hedge.

Solution: We use the equation

$$E(CF) = \sum_i p_i \times Amount \times [S - FV(P) + Max(0, X - S)]$$

$$FV(P) = 0.05 \times \left(1 + 6\% \times \frac{270}{360}\right) = 0.05225$$

◇	A	B	C	D	E	F	G	H
1				Put Option / Receivables Hedge				
2		(1)	(2)	(3)	(4)	(5)	(6)	(7)
3							CF / Unit	CF
4						Max(0,	=	=
5	Scenario	Amount	p_i	S	FV(P)	X – S)	(3) – (4) + (5)	(1) × (6)
6	I	500,000	60%	0.85	0.05225	0.15	0.94775	473,875
7	II	500,000	40%	1.10	0.05225	0	1.04775	523,875
8								
9	E(CF)							493,875
10	σ(CF)							24,495

Discussion: The put option acts like insurance and sets a floor on the value of the receivables. The exercise price (USD 1.00) net of the future value of the premium (USD 0.05225) is the floor per currency unit. This truncates the distribution of cash flows and reduces the standard deviation.

EXAMPLE 7.13

COMPARING HEDGES: A COMPREHENSIVE RECEIVABLES EXAMPLE

Input Data

Hatori, a Japanese MNC, is expecting receivables of EUR 300,000 in 90 days. The chief financial officer (CFO) collects the following information from currency, interest rate, and derivatives markets.

- Currency markets: Spot EURJPY = 160.
- Eurocurrency markets: EUR rate = 4 percent, JPY rate = 1 percent (actual/360 simple interest).
- Options: Put options on EURJPY maturing in three months and with a strike price of JPY 155 are priced at JPY 3.
- Forwards: 90-day forwards trade at EURJPY = 158

The CFO also obtains the following forecast of EURJPY (90 days):

EURJPY	Probability
140	20%
155	30%
165	30%
175	20%

Using this information, evaluate Hatori's hedging alternatives.

Solution: See calculations on next page.

Hatori: Comparison of Hedging Alternatives

Situation: EUR 300,000 receivables in three months

A. Unhedged

Amount	p	S	CF
300,000	20%	140	42,000,000
300,000	30%	155	46,500,000
300,000	30%	165	49,500,000
300,000	20%	175	52,500,000
$E(CF)$			47,700,000
$\sigma(CF)$			3,536,948

Note: For details on mean and standard deviation calculations, please refer to examples in Chapter 6.

B. Forward Hedge

$$E(CF) = \text{Amount} \times F$$

F	158
$E(CF)$	47,400,000

C. Money Market Hedge

$$E(CF) = \text{Amount} \times S \times \frac{1 + r}{1 + r^*}$$

Rate JPY	1%
Rate EUR	4%
S	160
$E(CF)$	47,643,564

$= 300{,}000 \times 160 \times [1 + 1\% \times (90/360)]/[1 + 4\% \times (90/360)]$

Note: We use the Eurocurrency interest convention.

D. Option Hedge

$$E(CF) = \sum_i p_i \times \text{Amount} \times [S - FV(P) + Max(0, X - S)]$$

Scenario	Amount	P	S	FV(P)	Max(.)	CF/unit	CF
I	300,000	20%	140	3.0075	15	151.9925	45,597,750
II	300,000	30%	155	3.0075	0	151.9925	45,597,750
III	300,000	30%	165	3.0075	0	161.9925	48,597,750
IV	300,000	20%	175	3.0075	0	171.9925	51,597,750
$E(CF)$							47,697,750
$\sigma(CF)$							2,343,075

E. Summary of Alternatives

	E(CF)	s(CF)
Unhedged	47,700,000	3,536,948
Forward	47,400,000	0
Money Market	47,643,564	0
Option	47,697,750	2,343,075

Comparison of Hedging Alternatives

A decision maker should compare the results of various hedging strategies against the unhedged position. Financial theory informs us that one financial alternative (X) dominates another (Y) when one of the following two conditions is satisfied:

- Alternative X provides a higher value or cash flow for the same or lower level of risk.
- Alternative X has a lower level of risk while providing the same or a higher value or cash flow.

Using these criteria, we note that the money market hedge dominates the forward hedge. Hence, we eliminate the forward hedge as a viable alternative. The option hedge and the unhedged situation

forward versus option
A *forward hedge* completely eliminates the variability of outcomes while an *options hedge* eliminates only variability in the unfavorable scenario.

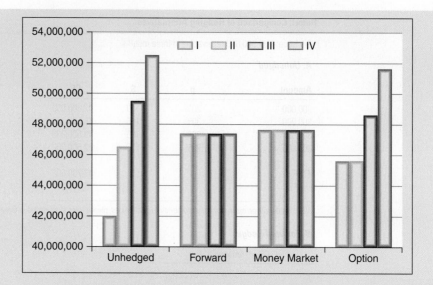

provide marginally higher expected cash flows compared to the money market hedge. But this is consistent with theory. These three alternatives are comparable in the sense that higher expected cash flows accompany higher risk. The decision maker needs to exercise judgment to decide between these three alternatives. A key consideration is the decision maker's level of risk aversion. For example, although the option hedge offers only a small reduction in standard deviation compared to the unhedged position, it offers valuable downside protection by ensuring a minimum value of JPY 45,597,750, which is considerably higher than the minimum value of JPY 42,000,000 in the unhedged alternative.

7.4 Maturity Mismatches

Earlier we considered scenarios in which the horizon of the currency position is identical to the maturity of the hedging instrument. These are ideal scenarios in which the mechanics of hedging are easy. In particular, the hedge ratio—the amount of derivatives relative to the amount of currencies in the underlying position—is one. Recall examples in which receivables or payables of X are hedged using forwards and options of the same quantity X.

In real-world scenarios, maturities are mismatched more often than not. This is almost always the case when hedging with exchange-traded futures and options. Because the maturity of these instruments is standardized and set by exchanges, they rarely match the maturity of the currency exposure. When maturities are mismatched, hedges do not work properly. This is demonstrated in the following example.

EXAMPLE 7.14

Consider a U.S. firm that has receivables of CAD 1 million. This is a 69-day position. The hedging instrument is the Chicago Mercantile Exchange (CME) CAD futures contract with a maturity of 90 days. The size of each contract is 100,000 currency units. Assume that the firm takes a short position in 10 futures contracts (equaling CAD 1 million). The beginning and ending values of CADUSD (the spot rate) and CAD futures follow:

	Begin ($t = 0$)	End ($t = 69$)
CADUSD spot	0.68	0.66
CAD futures	0.70	0.69

Evaluate the effectiveness of hedging.

Solution: We compare the per currency unit consequences of (a) unhedged and (b) hedged positions.

a. Net cash flow per unit $= -0.68 + 0.66 = -0.02$

b. Net cash flow per unit $= (\text{CADUSD}_{69} - \text{CADUSD}_0) - (\text{CAD futures}_{69} - \text{CAD futures}_0)$

$$= (0.66 - 0.68) - (0.69 - 0.70) = -0.01$$

Discussion: Hedging only partially reduces risk. This is because the changes in the spot and futures prices are not equal. From the data provided, we note that the futures price changes by 0.01 in response to a 0.02 change in spot. This means that 10 futures contracts will only partially hedge CAD 1 million receivables.

• **Delta hedging.** How do managers construct hedges with futures when maturities are mismatched? They construct a delta hedge, which uses as its input the *delta,* or the sensitivity between the hedging instrument and the underlying currency. Consider the previous example in which the CAD futures contract changes by 0.01 relative to a 0.02 change in CADUSD. The ratio between these values $(0.01/0.02 = 0.5)$ is the delta of the futures contract. Because the futures contract is only half as sensitive as the currency, we need twice as many futures for our hedge. This idea is captured in the following formula for the number of futures contracts for a hedge:

delta hedge
The *number of futures contracts* required for a hedge is inversely related to its sensitivity or delta.

$$\text{Number of futures contracts} = -\frac{1}{\text{Delta}} \times \frac{\text{Spot position}}{\text{Size of each futures contract}}$$

The first term—one over delta—adjusts for the sensitivity of the futures relative to the spot position. In other words, the first term reflects the risk factor. The second term—the ratio of spot to size of futures contract—adjusts for differences in contract size. In other words, the second term reflects the scale factor. The number of futures equals the negative of the product of the risk and scale factors. Note that the value for the spot position is positive for receivables and negative for payables. We demonstrate the use of this formula with an example. We refer the reader to Appendix 7 for a discussion of delta hedging using options using a similar equation. Readers will find a more advanced treatment of the topic in standard texts in the field of derivatives or risk management.

EXAMPLE 7.15

Consider a firm with payables of JPY 250 million in 44 days. It hedges this position using the CME JPY futures contract maturing in 90 days. The futures contract size is JPY 12.5 million. A financial analyst notes that the JPY futures contract tends to change by USD 0.0008 in response to a USD 0.0010 change in JPY. Calculate the number of futures contracts required for a hedge.

Solution:

Step 1. Calculate the hedge ratio. S refers to the currency and F to the futures contract)

$$\text{Delta} = \frac{\Delta F}{\Delta S} = \frac{0.0008}{0.0010} = 0.80$$

Step 2. Calculate the number of contracts and identify whether the position is long or short.

$$\text{Number of futures contracts} = -\frac{1}{\text{Delta}} \times \frac{\text{Spot position}}{\text{Size of each futures contract}}$$

$$= -\frac{1}{0.80} \times \frac{(-250,000,000)}{12,500,000} = 25$$

Because the currency position is a short position (i.e., payables) and to hedge against currency value changes, the firm has to long 25 CME JPY futures contracts. Here is a way to understand why the futures position is a long one. Suppose the JPY rises in value. The firm will incur losses in its payables (JPY is more expensive to buy). As an offset, the long futures position generates gains when JPY rises.

Discussion: Delta hedges must be used with caution. The main problem is that deltas do not remain constant. They depend on factors such as the structure of the derivatives contract, the time remaining to maturity, and market factors such as interest rates. This is why delta hedges must be carefully monitored and fine-tuned.

The preceding methodology is important because it can also be applied to conduct *cross-hedging*. This occurs when the underlying currency in the derivatives position is different from the currency being hedged. An example of such a situation is when a firm hedges a Czech koruna (CZK) payables position using EUR options. This type of hedging, although complex, is fairly prevalent.

7.5 Operating Decisions to Mitigate Transaction Exposure

MNCs rely primarily on currency hedging to reduce transaction exposure. But they also use operational remedies. In this section, we discuss some of the operating strategies for risk reduction with examples. The advantage of operational solutions is that they are repeatable and become part of the corporate DNA. Thus, they have the potential to save transaction costs. Moreover, an MNC facing heightened currency risk must find multiple solutions to the problem: Operational solutions are complements to hedging.

The operating strategies that mitigate transaction exposure include:

- Specifying the appropriate invoice currency.
- Leading and lagging contractual cash flows.
- Netting currency cash flows across corporate subsidiaries and affiliates.
- Risk-sharing contracts with customers and suppliers.

Invoice Currency

Many of the long positions in foreign currencies are on-balance-sheet items such as receivables. As an alternative to hedging this risk, the firm can try to change the invoice currency. The simplest solution is for the MNC to use its home currency for invoicing. In fact, when U.S.-based MNCs sell products in Asia, they often use the USD as the invoice currency.

It would be appropriate to invoice in the home currency in the following situations:

- The foreign currency has a record of depreciating against the home currency.
- The foreign currency exhibits a great deal of variation. For example, high standard deviation currencies such as the BRL cause concern.
- The MNC is making industrial sales in which each transaction is large and enables the foreign entity to efficiently make the necessary currency conversion.
- The foreign counterparty either has reduced negotiating leverage or has opposite positions in the invoice currency.

EXAMPLE 7.16

Economists have studied patterns of currency invoicing across the world. U.S. and European firms primarily invoice in their home currency. In contrast, Japanese firms do so in the USD. The data on Honda's derivatives presented earlier support this evidence. Why do we see these discrepancies? In part, tradition explains this situation. But another factor is the relative importance and economic power of countries and regions.

In some cases, the MNC may want to invoice in a third currency. For example, an Indian exporter of engineering goods to Egypt may want to use the USD as the invoice currency. It may be easier for the Egyptian counterparty to arrange a payment in USD than a payment in INR. More important, both parties may perceive the USD as a stable currency for contracting.

Leading and Lagging Contractual Cash Flows

Leading refers to the advancement of the timing of the cash flow, and **lagging** refers to deferring the timing of the cash flow. Cash flows under consideration may be payments to suppliers, receipts from customers, or payments to and receipts from subsidiaries and affiliates. By modifying the timing of these cash flows, the firms can synchronize inflows and outflows in the same currency.

EXAMPLE 7.17

Suppose a U.S. firm has receivables of EUR 2 million from a customer in Germany in 45 days and a payment to the German subsidiary of EUR 3 million in 60 days. If the EUR decreases in value during the 45–60 day period, the firm faces losses. Explain the use of leading and lagging in this context.

Solution: The firm can lag its day 45 cash flow and lead its day 60 cash flow. Lagging of the 45-day cash flow can be accomplished either by negotiating with the customer to receive the money later (who would not like that!) or simply by receiving the EUR cash flow and not converting to USD. Leading the 60-day cash flow is accomplished more easily because it concerns a transaction with a subsidiary.

Discussion: The net effect of leading and lagging is to reduce the exposure of these two items to a net exposure of negative (payables) EUR 1 million. The advantage of using leading and lagging is that it does not disrupt the firm's operations. These transactions can easily be accomplished at the corporate rather than the divisional level. The firm, however, needs good information systems in place and effective cash management practices.

Netting

MNCs conduct a large number of foreign currency transactions with subsidiaries, affiliates, and third parties (suppliers and customers). **Netting** is the process by which these cash flows are summed or aggregated to provide a single sum in each currency. Netting can be viewed from the following three perspectives:

- As a calculation/analytical tool to aggregate and therefore estimate currency exposure (discussed in Chapter 6).
- As an efficient method to manage cash transactions between an MNC parent and its subsidiaries and affiliates (discussed in Chapter 11).
- As an integral part of a firm's currency risk management initiatives (current chapter).

Naturally, all three perspectives are connected. The following example explains the role of netting in currency risk management.

EXAMPLE 7.18

Alstom, a global energy and transport firm with more than 800 subsidiaries, uses a proprietary system from the Swiss firm Coprocess to net it tens of thousands of transactions with subsidiaries. Subsidiaries and the parent electronically upload data onto a central system. The netting center's manager claims that a key benefit of the system is to provide and enable hedging of currency risk. One interesting feature of Alstom's netting system is that it asks subsidiaries to input information about any currency hedges (e.g., forwards) in place. Payments and currency denominations are adjusted and synchronized to minimize risk.

[For an explanation of netting, see http://www.coprocess.com/experts_explained.html]

Risk-Sharing Contracts

In their contracts with suppliers and customers, MNCs can insert clauses that enable currency risk sharing. The need for risk sharing occurs in long-term contracts because currency values can change significantly from the time of the signing of the contract to its settlement. The typical structure of a risk-sharing contract is as follows. As in a normal invoice, a price is stipulated in a particular currency, usually the home currency of one of the contracting parties. This automatically induces risk for the other party. To mitigate this risk, however, a clause would call for an ex post adjustment of this invoice price. The size of the adjustment would reflect the movement of the invoice currency against the home currency of the counterparty and result in sharing the currency effect.

EXAMPLE 7.19

A U.S.-based MNC sourcing garments from the Dominican Republic has to pay DOP (the Dominican peso) 60,000 in 30 days. The DOP is currently trading at USDDOP = 30. If USDDOP decreases in value, the exporter gains and the U.S. firm loses. Consider a scenario in which in 30 days USDDOP equals 23. Suppose the risk-sharing contract calls for equally sharing the change in the USDDOP rate. Calculate the DOP payment for the U.S. firm.

Solution:

$$\text{Change in USDDOP} = \frac{23}{30} - 1 = -23.33\%$$

$$\text{Payment in DOP} = 60,000 \times (1 - 50\% \times 23.33\%) = 53,000$$

$$\text{Payment in USD} = 53,000/23 = 2,304.35$$

Discussion: The payment is adjusted for half of the currency change, so both parties share the currency impact. If there had been no risk-sharing clause, the U.S. firm would have paid USD 2,608.70 (=60,000/23). Assuming that USDDOP is unchanged at 30, the payment would have been only USD 2,000 (=60,000/30). Without a risk-sharing clause that revises the invoice price, therefore, the U.S. firm would have incurred losses of USD 608.70. The risk-sharing clause halves this loss.

We used the USDDOP as the unit of analysis as specified in the contract. Had we calculated the change based on DOPUSD, our answer would be different:

$$\text{Change in DOPUSD} = \frac{1/23}{1/30} - 1 = 30.43\%$$

This demonstrates the importance of explicitly specifying risk sharing in the form of an equation in the contract.

7.6 Operating Decisions to Mitigate Operating Exposure

Chapter 6 explains that operating exposure is high in situations in which the firm:

- Sells commodity-like products that have many substitutes.
- Faces intense competition from firms with cost bases in other currencies.
- Is a follower in the marketplace and is forced to comply with prices set by competitors.

By its very nature, operating exposure represents long-term currency effects. Hedging is typically not the preferred tool to tackle such long-term problems. We next discuss the following operational and contractual solutions[4]:

- Geographical dispersion of suppliers.
- Geographical dispersion of customers.
- Achievement of product differentiation.

Geographically Dispersed Suppliers

MNCs frequently source materials and supplies from many countries. Assuming that MNCs can switch easily between suppliers, adverse foreign exchange movements can be countered with a change in sourcing. Thus, operating exposure is mitigated. This practice also has many advantages beyond reducing currency exposure. For example, with multiple suppliers, a firm has the necessary negotiating leverage to reduce its costs.

EXAMPLE 7.20

During 2000, U.S. firms with suppliers in Japan and Germany would have found that German suppliers became relatively less expensive due to currency movements: The JPY appreciated against the USD while the EUR depreciated. Similarly, a Japanese airline buying aircraft would have found a European source (Airbus) relatively less expensive than a U.S. source (Boeing). Although the JPY appreciated against both the USD and the EUR, the appreciation against the EUR was higher. With multiple suppliers, firms have the ability to switch to low-cost suppliers based on currency movements.

[4] See the following article for a survey of 289 U.K. firms regarding the use of methods presented in this section: Katrina Bradley and Peter Moles, "Managing Strategic Exchange Rate Exposures: Evidence from UK Firms," *Managerial Finance* 28 (2002), pp. 28–42. In particular, see Table 2 (p. 32) to see how frequently various methods are used.

Diversifying suppliers across countries has another advantage for a firm. It reduces its exposure to country risk (political and economic risk in foreign countries). For example, in 2000, transportation workers in India went on strike, shutting down ports. Goods that required shipping were stranded in Indian ports. Such an event can have grievous consequences for an importer of Indian goods or components. Such problems can be mitigated, however, by using a diversified and flexible sourcing strategy. One financial theory that models such flexibility in operations is real options theory (discussed in Chapter 9).

Geographically Dispersed Customers

global operations and currency risk
By operating in many countries and *dispersing customers and suppliers,* MNCs can reduce currency risk.

Firms can reduce the currency-related variability of revenue flows by selling their products in multiple countries. By using this strategy, firms obtain currency diversification in their receivables, thereby reducing transaction exposure. But geographically dispersed customers can also reduce operating exposure. Increasing foreign sales revenues (because of an increase in units or price, or both) in a country with a stronger currency could potentially make up for a shortfall in a country with a weaker currency.

EXAMPLE 7.21

Dell, initially a predominantly U.S.-centric firm, has aggressively pursued global markets in recent years. In 2008, Dell derived nearly half of its revenues from foreign markets, recording the strongest growth in the Asia-Pacific region. Dell sells in a wide variety of currencies. For example, two currencies to which it has exposure are the Chinese yuan (CNY) and INR. Because the CNY and INR do not always move in tandem, Dell is able to diversify currency risk from its revenues.

Selling in multiple countries has many advantages unrelated to the currency exposure issue. For example, by selling in many countries, the firm can achieve economies of scale: Auto companies are able to design cars for multiple markets to recoup the billions of dollars in developmental costs. Furthermore, operating in many countries also mitigates country risk.

Product Differentiation

One important reason for operating exposure is the substitutability of products. An MNC that differentiates its products is less vulnerable to price competition when its domestic currency appreciates or when the competitor's currency depreciates. Product differentiation may be achieved by investments in R&D as well as marketing. Even with similar products, an effective marketing campaign can create a brand image for the product that can protect it from price competition.

EXAMPLE 7.22

The Parma ham—the real prosciutto—from the Emilia-Romagna region of Italy is a unique product. If the EUR appreciates and makes this product more expensive, it may have only a slight impact on U.S. sales of this product. Similarly, a first-growth wine (or a second-growth wine for that matter, classifications established in 1855) from the Bordeaux region of France is another example of a differentiated product.

Summary

- Currency exposure increases the variability of cash flows. By using risk management methods, MNCs can reduce this variability. Two benefits of reduced variability are (1) a better ability to allocate investments necessary for achieving strategic goals and (2) a greater ability to capture tax shields. Additionally, there are benefits such as improved contracting with suppliers and customers.
- Currency hedging is the use of derivatives to reduce currency risk. Firms need to balance the various benefits of hedging currency risk against the transaction costs of setting up hedging systems and managing such systems. Evidence shows that most large firms use currency hedges.

- The three important ways to hedge currency exposure are the use of (1) forwards or futures, (2) synthetic forwards constructed using loans and deposits, and (3) put and call options. We demonstrate these methods in the context of foreign currency receivables and payables.
- Firms evaluate hedging methods by calculating the mean and standard deviation of future cash flows. The mean and standard deviation of each hedging alternative can be compared with the mean and standard deviation of the unhedged position.
- Firms can also reduce currency risk by restructuring their operations. Decisions regarding the foreign sourcing of materials, the choice of the currency to invoice customers, and leading and lagging currency flows all contribute to effective management of currency exposure.

Questions

1. **Rationale for Hedging.** Explain the tax rationale for hedging. What kinds of firms are more likely to obtain tax benefits of hedging? Explain.

2. **Rationale for Hedging.** Explain how hedging can help a firm execute its strategic plan. What kinds of firms are likely to obtain this type of benefit? Explain.

3. **Rationale for Hedging.** A Taiwanese consumer electronics firm has fallen on hard times. Its net income in the current year has fallen 60 percent from the previous year's income of TWD 100 million. The CFO estimates difficult prospects during the next two to three years. One difficulty the firm experienced is the weakening value of USD. The firm has most of its costs denominated in the domestic currency TWD and earns revenues in USD. Can you reason with the firm's chief executive officer (CEO) to help him understand how the firm can benefit from hedging?

4. **Rationale for Hedging.** Explain benefits of hedging to a firm's various stakeholders.

5. **Money Market Hedge.** A colleague at work is confused by the term *money market hedge*. Can you explain what this method of hedging entails and how it compares with a forward hedge?

6. **Forward versus Futures Hedge.** The CFO of your firm—a USD 2 billion technology firm—has asked you to evaluate prospects for using futures for hedging. Your firm has been hedging using forwards in the past. What are your likely conclusions? Why?

7. **Forward versus Options Hedge.** The CFO of your firm—a USD 40 billion MNC—has asked you to evaluate prospects for using options for hedging. Your firm has been hedging using forwards in the past. Outline the advantages and disadvantages of options compared to forwards.

8. **Real-World Hedging Behavior.** Review research on real-world hedging behavior and indicate the kinds of firms that hedge frequently as well as the types of exposures that are hedged.

9. **Operating Techniques for Transaction Exposure.** What kinds of firms are likely to use invoicing techniques to mitigate currency risk? Provide actual names of several firms likely using this method.

10. **Operating Techniques for Transaction Exposure.** Explain how leading and lagging foreign currency cash flows can mitigate currency risk. What are limitations to this method?

11. **Operating Techniques for Transaction Exposure.** Explain how netting can mitigate currency risk. In what settings does this method work, and what are its organizational and structural requirements?

12. **Operating Techniques for Operating Exposure.** Explain various operational methods to mitigate operating exposure. In your opinion, should a firm focus on hedging or operational solutions, or both? Explain your position.

Problems

1. **Tax Rationale for Hedging.** A firm is projecting that because of currency variability, its pretax income during the next two years will vary: Taxable incomes of USD 50,000 and USD 200,000 are expected during year 1 and year 2, respectively. Assume that the firm can eliminate this risk totally through hedging and that hedging produces taxable incomes of

USD 125,000 each year. (Total income is invariant at USD 250,000). On incomes up to USD 100,000, the firm pays taxes at a rate of 15 percent; on incomes above USD 100,000, the tax rate is 25 percent. Over the two-year period, what are the potential tax savings from hedging?

2. **Tax Rationale for Hedging.** A firm is expected to earn an income of USD 100,000 before depreciation and taxes during the next year. (Deduct depreciation to calculate taxable income.) However, because of currency risk, the actual income before depreciation and taxes could be either USD 30,000 or USD 170,000 with equal probability (the expected value is maintained at USD 100,000). The firm depreciates its assets by USD 50,000 annually, an amount not affected by currency movements. The tax rate is 40 percent, and there is no tax credit associated with losses. Assume that hedging reduces volatility to zero and guarantees an income before depreciation and taxes of USD 100,000. Calculate taxes in the unhedged and hedged scenarios. What is the expected saving in taxes resulting from hedging?

3. **Forward Hedge.** The Dominican Republic peso (DOP) is forecasted to change from its current value of USDDOP = 35 against the USD to either 32 or 40 in three months. These two possibilities are equally likely. A U.S. importer of goods from the Dominican Republic has payables of DOP 500,000 in three months.

   a. Estimate the mean and standard deviation of this position.

   b. How would you characterize currency risk in this situation? Use a 68 percent confidence interval.

   c. Consider the availability of a three-month forward on the DOP at a rate of USDDOP = 36.5. How does the hedged position compare with the unhedged position? If you were a decision maker, how would you respond?

4. **Option Hedge of Payables.** A U.S.-based MNC wishes to make a payment of EUR 10,000 to an affiliate in 30 days. The MNC purchases EUR call options maturing in 30 days to mitigate currency risk. The option strike price is USD 1.30 and its premium is USD 0.04. At maturity, assume that EURUSD equals 1.43.

   a. Are the EUR call options exercised? Estimate the payoff and profit.

   b. Assuming options are not used, what is the USD payment?

   c. With options, what is the net USD payment?

5. **Option Hedge of Receivables:** A U.S.-based MNC expects to receive GBP 5,000 from an affiliate in 30 days. The MNC purchases GBP put options maturing in 30 days to mitigate currency risk. The option strike price is USD 1.80, and its premium is USD 0.03. At maturity, assume that GBPUSD = 1.66.

   a. Are the GBP put options exercised? Estimate the payoff and profit.

   b. Assuming options are not used, what is the USD receipt?

   c. With options, what is the net USD receipt?

6. **Option Hedge of Payables without Financing Costs.** Jason Pharmaceuticals sources materials from a British affiliate and is to make a payment of GBP 50,000 in three months. Jason's treasurer is considering the use of GBP call options to protect the payables. GBP calls with three months to maturity and a strike price of USD 1.40 are available with a premium of USD 0.05. Disregard financing costs for the option premium.

   a. You are requested to assist the treasurer by assessing the net cash flow of payables (including the option premium) assuming possible values of GBP in three months. Fill in the following table to answer this question.

Possible Value of GBPUSD	Net Cash Flow of Payables
1.35	
1.40	
1.45	
1.50	
1.55	

b. Estimate the mean and standard deviation of the net cash flow of payables assuming (i) no hedging and (ii) hedging with options. Assume that the five outcomes for the GBP are equally likely. What is the percentage decrease in standard deviation as a result of hedging?

7. **Option Hedge of Receivables without Financing Costs.** Winston Cigars, a U.S-based firm, distributes cigars in the UK and expects receivables of GBP 75,000 in three months. GBP puts with three months maturity and a strike price of USD 1.30 are available with a premium of USD 0.04. Disregard financing costs for the option premium.

a. You are requested to assist the treasurer by assessing the net cash flow from receivables (including the option premium) for the following values of GBP in three months. Fill in the following table to answer this question.

Possible Value of GBPUSD	Net Cash Flow of Receivables
1.25	
1.30	
1.35	
1.40	
1.45	

b. Estimate the mean and standard deviation of the net cash flow of receivables assuming (i) no hedging and (ii) hedging with options. Assume that the five outcomes for the GBP are equally likely. What is the percentage decrease in standard deviation as a result of hedging?

8. **Option Hedge of Payables with Financing Costs.** A Japanese electronics firm purchases capital equipment from a U.S. firm for USD 5,000. Payment is due in 120 days. Spot USDJPY equals 105. The Japanese firm fears that the USD will strengthen in the near future and wishes to insure against this by purchasing USD call options with a strike price of JPY 105. The premium is JPY 3. Analysts' forecasts of USD calls for a USDJPY rate of either 100 or 120 in 120 days. Assume equal probability. Use a JPY TIBOR rate of 2.4 percent (actual/360) to factor in the financing cost of options in your calculations. Compare the unhedged and hedged positions by calculating the mean and standard deviation of resulting cash flows. Make a recommendation to the firm's CFO using your analysis.

9. **Option Hedge of Receivables with Financing Costs.** An Italian ceramics producer sells USD 30,000 worth of goods to a U.S. affiliate and expects payment in 60 days. The USD has been weakening lately, and the Italian firm is concerned about giving up its margins to currency fluctuation. The firm's CFO is considering the purchase of 60-day USD put options with a strike price of EUR 0.75 and a premium of EUR 0.03. Analysts' forecasts of USD calls for a USDEUR rate of either 0.65 or 0.80 in 60 days. Assume equal probability. Use a EURIBOR rate of 3.6 percent (actual/360) to factor in the financing cost of options in your calculations. Compare the unhedged and hedged positions by calculating the mean and standard deviation of resulting cash flows. Make a recommendation to the firm's CFO using your analysis.

10. **Money Market Hedge of Payables.** Hawkes Imports, a U.S. firm, imports sauvignon blanc wines from New Zealand. It has payables of New Zealand dollars (NZD) 1,000,000 in six months. The treasurer of Hawkes is considering a money market hedge and is faced with the following data:

NZD spot	USD 0.62
NZD 6-month forward	USD 0.60
USD rate, lending	4%
USD rate, borrowing	4.3%
NZD rate, lending	5%
NZD rate, borrowing	6.2%

Show the steps involved in this hedge and the net cash flow (cost) of meeting the payables. Assume annual compounding.

11. **Money Market Hedge of Receivables.** Tom Turbines, a U.S. firm, exports windmills to New Zealand and expects receivables of New Zealand dollar (NZD) 2,500,000 in six months. Using the information from problem 10, demonstrate how the firm can use the money market hedge to protect its receivables position.

12. **Comparison of Multiple Hedging Methods.** Burgess, a U.S.-based MNC, has receivables of EUR 10,000 in 90 days. Spot EURUSD equals 1.43. The firm's economist forecasts that the EURUSD could end the period with a value of either 1.40 (probability of 50 percent) or 1.50 (50 percent). The firm is concerned about the resulting currency risk. It has also assessed some hedging alternatives. Forward contracts of 90-day EURUSD are traded at 1.42. The 90-day interest rates (actual/360) in the United States and Europe are 5 percent and 7 percent, respectively. Put options with 90-day expiration and a strike price of USD 1.45 are available for a premium of USD 0.02. You are requested to advise the firm about the alternatives available and recommend the best approach.

13. **Comparison of Multiple Hedging Methods.** The U.S-based MNC Conte has receivables of JPY 1.5 million in six months. The spot JPYUSD is 0.0095. The firm's economist forecasts that the JPYUSD could end the period with a value of either 0.0091 (probability of 40 percent) or 0.0101 (60 percent). The firm is concerned about its currency risk. It has also assessed some hedging alternatives. Six-month JPY forward contracts are traded at USD 0.0096. The six-month interest rates (annual compounding) in the United States and Japan are 5 percent and 2 percent, respectively. Put options with six-month expiration and a strike price of USD 0.0098 are available for a premium of USD 0.0004. Your job is to advise the firm about the alternatives available and the best approach.

14. **Comparison of Multiple Hedging Methods.** The U.S-based MNC Kline has payables of CHF 40,000 in six months. The firm's economist forecasts that the CHFUSD could end the period with a value of either 0.55 (probability of 60 percent) or 0.65 (40 percent). The firm is concerned about its currency risk. It has also assessed some hedging alternatives. Six-month CHFUSD forward contracts are traded at 0.60. The six-month interest rates (annual compounding) in the United States and Switzerland are 5 percent and 4 percent, respectively. Call options with six-month expiration and a strike price of USD 0.60 are available for a premium of USD 0.01. Your job is to advise the firm about the alternatives available and the best approach. Assume that the spot rate is USD 0.62.

15. **Delta Hedge with Futures (Payables).** Consider a U.S. firm with payables of GBP 500,000 in 53 days. It hedges this position using a CME GBP futures contract maturing in 90 days. The futures contract size is GBP 62,500. A financial analyst notes that the GBP futures contract tends to change by USD 0.01 in response to a USD 0.02 change in GBP. Calculate the number of futures contracts required for a hedge. Indicate whether the futures position is long or short.

16. **Delta Hedge with Futures (Receivables).** Consider a U.S. firm with receivables of BRL 800,000 in 25 days. It hedges this position using a CME BRL futures contract maturing in 60 days. The futures contract size is BRL 100,000. A financial analyst notes that the BRL futures contract tends to change by USD 0.004 in response to a USD 0.010 change in BRL. Calculate the number of futures contracts required for a hedge. Indicate whether the futures position is long or short.

17. **Risk-Sharing Contract.** Buyex, a U.S. firm, has an agreement with a firm in Singapore to buy components for a total of Singapore dollars (SGD) 60,000. Buyex is concerned about the appreciation of the SGD and enters into a risk-sharing contract. According to this contact, the Singapore firm will allow a discount in the invoice price equivalent to 30 percent of the depreciation of USDSGD. The USDSGD trades at 1.28 at the time of signing the contract. Suppose, on settlement date, USDSGD equals 1.17. Estimate the payment made by the U.S. firm.

Extensions

1. **Hedging with Option Combination.** The Blackstone Group is a U.S.-based conglomerate with extensive European operations. Through its operations, Blackstone has a net short exposure to EUR (i.e., similar to payables) amounting to about EUR 1 million a year. Spot EURUSD equals 1.50. The CFO asks the financial analyst with Blackstone, Chip Henderson, to make currency projections. Mr. Henderson conducts Monte Carlo simulations to determine the probability distribution for EURUSD values. The results of Mr. Henderson's investigations lead him to believe that probable values of EURUSD are in the range of 1.45–1.60, possibly concentrated in the smaller range of 1.50–1.55. In other words, there is a slight upward bias that may prove detrimental to Blackstone. One possible way to hedge is to purchase call options on EUR with a strike price of 1.50. Because of high volatility, these options are expensive. Mr. Henderson notes that the premium is USD 0.05, implying that net purchase cost using the option is USD 1.55. On thinking more deeply about the problem at hand, he has a bright idea: offsetting the cost of the 1.50 calls with short positions in 1.55 calls that have a premium of USD 0.02.

   a. Calculate outcomes related to using the option with the strike price of 1.50. Explain why this is a costly way to hedge.

   b. Assume that Blackstone simultaneously longs the 1.50 call and shorts the 1.55 call. Demonstrate costs and benefits of this approach. In outlining your calculations, focus on the highly likely range of 1.50–1.55.

2. **Delta Hedge with Options.** Arkan Corp has receivables of EUR 100,000 in three months. A financial analyst in the firm has identified a EUR put option as a hedging instrument. This put option has a delta of −0.4. If the size of a put option contract is EUR 50,000, estimate the number of put option contracts necessary to provide total protection to the firm.

3. **Delta Hedge with Options.** Erikan Plastics has considerable exposure to the EUR. A financial analyst in the firm is assessing the use of options on the EUR as a hedging device. To assist in implementing the hedging, the analyst has gathered data on the EUR and an option on it. These data show prices on the two items over a period of four weeks as follows:

Week	EUR spot	EUR option spot
−4	1.41	0.031
−3	1.42	0.035
−2	1.38	0.018
−1	1.35	0.006

   Estimate the sensitivity (i.e., delta) of the option to the underlying currency. If the firm is planning to protect a position involving EUR 1 million and if each option contract contains 10,000 currency units, estimate the number of option contracts necessary to protect the EUR position.

4. **Delta Hedge with Options.** A U.S. networking firm enters into a merger agreement with a small Dutch firm. This is an all-cash deal worth EUR 250,000. At the EURUSD spot rate of 1.50, it is worth USD 37.5 million. The payment is expected in 12 days. The U.S. firm's CFO wishes to hedge against currency risk in this transaction by taking a long position in EUR call options. An available call option has the following characteristics: strike price equals USD 1.50, maturity equals 45 days, and EURUSD standard deviation equals 10 percent. The continuously compounded risk-free rates in USD and EUR are 4 percent and 5 percent, respectively.

   a. Using the currency pricing formula, estimate the delta for this option. (See Appendix 3B for the formula.)

   b. Assuming that contract size is 10,000, how many contracts are necessary for the hedge?

c. Assume that on the day of the payment (12th day) spot EURUSD equals 1.55. The call position is liquidated, and payment for the deal is made. Calculate cash flows and demonstrate the protection obtained from the call hedge. You may assume that the beginning (date of agreement) and ending (date of settlement) option prices are USD 0.020 and USD 0.052, respectively.

Case

Clover Machines: *Hedging Currency Risk*

Recall information about Clover Machine's expected sales in Europe from the case in the previous chapter. The information is repeated here:

> Clover Machines already has an established subsidiary in Europe selling advanced farming and construction machinery such as combines (with attachment for wheat harvest) and dozers (hilly terrain capability). Last year, sales came in at EUR 1 billion. Sales have been increasing at the rate of 4 percent a year for the past five years, and Clover expects the momentum to continue. The European subsidiary performs significant assembly prior to sales. Costs incurred at the subsidiary level for assembly are roughly 12 percent of list price. Assume no other local expenses.

Assume that net sales revenues minus local expenses are repatriated at the end of the year. Brian Bent, Clover's CFO, is concerned about preserving the USD value of this cash flow. Of particular concern is the widely expected depreciation of the EUR. During the past year, the EUR had appreciated significantly against the USD and reached a current level of 1.6055. Many market watchers consider the EUR overvalued and expect a modest pullback of 2 percent in the coming year. Mr. Bent fears a larger reversal in the EUR value—perhaps in the neighborhood of 10 percent—and wishes to protect USD cash flows.

The macroeconomic backdrop is as follows. The EUR had appreciated significantly in recent months Because of moderate growth in the Eurozone coupled with a financial crisis in the U.S. There are some tentative signs that the U.S. financial crisis is winding down. Also, global strains related to rising oil prices have stressed Eurozone economies. Furthermore, high EUR levels have severely compromised the competitiveness of Eurozone businesses, especially those in northern Europe that depend on export markets, primarily in the United States.

The CFO has asked you to evaluate various hedging alternatives available to Clover. To that end, you collected the following information on options and interest rates. You also find that one-year futures contracts (contract size = 100,000 currency units) are trading at 1.5902.

Option Quotations

Option Type	Contract Size	Maturity (in years)	Strike Price	Premium per Currency Unit
Call	125,000	1 year	1.60	0.051
Call	125,000	1 year	1.55	0.075
Put	125,000	1 year	1.60	0.071
Put	125,000	1 year	1.55	0.045

Money Market Rates

Reference Rate	Maturity (in years)	Currency	Rate (percent)
LIBOR	1 year	USD	2.9%
EURIBOR	1 year	EUR	4.2%
LIBOR	1 year	CHF	2.3%

Note: Clover can deposit or lend at these rates. To obtain its borrowing rates, add 25 basis points.

Mr. Bent is interested in the following, which you are to provide:

1. A calculation of value at risk in the receivables position. Use information from previous cases to calculate the currency standard deviation. Considering your result as well as information in the case about prospects for the EUR, in your opinion, should Clover hedge its EUR receivables?

2. A comparison of the futures and money market hedges.

3. Currency scenarios constructed using information provided in the case. Compare all hedging alternatives (unhedged, futures, money market, and option hedge), and make a final recommendation. Discuss how alternative currency scenarios may change your conclusions.

Appendix 7

Delta Hedging Using Options

As with futures, delta hedging with options uses the following equation:

$$\text{Number of option contracts} = -\frac{1}{\text{Delta}} \times \frac{\text{Spot position}}{\text{Size of each option contract}}$$

EXAMPLE 7.23

An MNC has payables of EUR 5 million in three months. The CFO wishes to hedge this exposure using EUR options. Assume that these are options traded on the Philadelphia Stock Exchange with a contract size of 125,000 currency units. Calculate the number of call option contracts required for hedging. Assume that the following options are available:

Instrument	Option Premium	Delta (see Appendix 3B for procedures to calculate delta)
EUR call option (X = 1.50)	0.12	0.80
EUR call option (X = 1.55)	0.08	0.60
EUR call option (X = 1.60)	0.04	0.20

Solution: Assume that the in-the-money option (X = 1.50) is used in hedging. Its delta is 0.80.

$$\text{Number of option contracts} = -\frac{1}{0.80} \times \frac{(-5,000,000)}{125,000} = 50 \text{ contracts (long position)}$$

Because delta equals 0.80, we need 1.25 options for each EUR in payables (1/0.80 = 1.25). The ratio of the spot position to the option contract size indicates a scale factor of negative 40 (= −5,000,000/125,000). The negative of the product of risk and scale factors is positive 50.
Alternatively, we can use the at-the-money option (X = 1.55) to hedge. Its delta is 0.60.

$$\text{Number of option contracts} = -\frac{1}{0.60} \times \frac{(-5,000,000)}{125,000} = 67 \text{ contracts (long position)}$$

Because the sensitivity is lower, more option contracts are required.

Discussion: One typically uses at- or in-the-money options for hedging. Out-of-the-money options are rarely used because their deltas are low. The lower the delta, the higher the number of options required for hedging.

CHAPTER EIGHT

Capital Budgeting

Honda Motors—in its 2007 annual report—revealed plans for 2008 capital expenditures of Japanese yen (JPY) 710 billion. Among future projects, Honda identifies an engine plant in Canada, an assembly plant in Indiana (United States), and increases in capacity in various plants including a passenger car plant in the United Kingdom and a motorcycle plant in India. Honda may be an exceptional automobile manufacturer but is certainly not unusual among MNCs in the number and scope of international projects. How do firms identify, evaluate, and select foreign projects? This activity, known as *capital budgeting,* is our focus in this chapter.

International projects are often high-profile projects and crucial elements in corporate strategy. As part of its global strategy of competing with General Motors and Toyota, Hyundai Motor Company built a plant in Chennai, India, to manufacture small cars. Projects such as this are usually more complex than domestic projects because they involve a wide array of risk factors (for example, currency risk, repatriation risk, execution risk). Because cross-border projects also are closely tied to corporate strategy, they cannot be viewed in isolation; their evaluation often requires innovative approaches to capital budgeting.

In this chapter, we discuss various types of international projects and their importance to firms and ways in which MNCs can conduct capital budgeting analysis. In particular, we discuss the following:

- The capital budgeting process in MNCs and how it generates stockholder value.
- The general conditions under which cross-border projects are valuable.
- How cash flows are estimated for international projects and how this process differs from the process for domestic projects.
- Two ways of calculating the net present value (NPV) of international projects: the domestic (or home) currency cash flow and foreign (or local) currency cash flow methods.
- Sensitivity analysis and a demonstration of how to apply scenario or break-even analyses using variations in currency values.
- Country risk in international projects and methods for incorporating country risk effects in project NPV.

8.1 The MNC Capital Budgeting Process

Capital budgeting is the comprehensive set of activities in which firms:

- Define their long-term strategy and goals.
- Identify and define activities (projects) that will help achieve goals.
- Determine the cash flows for the proposed projects.
- Determine NPV or other value indicators.
- Choose the optimal mix of projects.
- Execute projects.
- Track the performance of ongoing projects.

• **Overall goal and capital budgeting.** The overall goal of financial management is to maximize shareholder wealth. Firms choose various strategies and business models to achieve this overall goal. International projects are often integral parts of corporate strategy. For example, Intel Corporation maximizes shareholder wealth by adopting the long-term strategy of supplying semiconductor chips for computer and communications equipment. Its business model in turn hinges on its ability to rapidly improve its chip design and frequently introduce newer and better chips. A key component of this business model is the establishment of international research and development (R&D) centers to develop new generations of chips and international fabrication centers to manufacture chips. These global initiatives are reflected in Intel's capital budget.

cash flow analysis
Among various steps in capital budgeting, *cash flow analysis* is the most important.

- **Cash flow analysis.** Among the various components of the capital budgeting process, cash flow analysis is arguably the most important. This analysis requires firms to conceptualize the project and forecast future cash flows. Consider the following example. A leading U.S.-based manufacturer of personal computers (PCs) evaluates an assembly/manufacturing facility in Malaysia with a capacity of 5 million units a year. To determine the project's viability, the firm assesses the types of PCs it expects to assemble in this factory and respective target geographical markets. A key input is expected market demand and prices. Revenues are calculated based on these forecasted numbers. Cost estimates are derived next. In the PC industry, a challenge might involve cost estimates of hard drives and other key electronic components. To complete the cost of goods sold calculations, other inputs relating to production and supply chain are needed.

- **Decentralization and teamwork.** Who makes cash flow projections? Who proposes projects and how? As technology makes information transfer easier within firms and as incentive contracts are given even to middle- and lower-level managers, the modern firm has become more decentralized. While the Malaysian project discussed earlier is an example of a large project proposed at the corporate level, many projects originate at the divisional level. For instance, a divisional-level manager may propose to source a component from a certain vendor by arguing that the component specifications are superior or that the cost is lower. A successful capital budgeting system encourages well-informed and well-structured proposals that can be acted upon at lower levels (when appropriate) without expending costly upper level managerial time. Another aspect of successful capital budgeting is cross-functional teamwork. To determine the value of the Malaysian project, input is needed from various parts of the firm. Engineers in manufacturing provide information on the project's cost. Marketing managers provide information on demand and pricing. Sometimes teams in two or more countries provide joint input.

- **Role of the chief financial officer.** The input of the chief financial officer (CFO) is critical in the project selection process. Empowered managers in various levels of the firm as well as in various functions such as production and marketing propose projects that make sense from their perspective. By virtue of focusing on the firm as whole, the CFO has increased ability to understand how proposed projects interact with the rest of the firm and to evaluate whether they will generate firm value. Such scrutiny by the CFO is especially valuable in larger projects in which the cost of top management analysis is justified by potential value generation. Smaller projects are more optimally processed at lower levels.

8.2 Competitive Advantage Offered by International Projects

Project analysis is costly in terms of managerial time. Consequently, firms often weed out unsuitable projects by using a more general qualitative assessment. This prescreening involves analyzing the rationale for the project. Typical aspects addressed are (1) project feasibility, (2) fit with the strategic and business plans of the firm, (3) whether the project takes advantage of the firm's core competency, and (4) whether the project involves some competitive advantage. Some of the important ways in which cross-border projects offer advantages are discussed next.

Why invest in international projects?
International projects offer various *advantages* that decrease costs and raise revenues.

- **Foreign labor.** A wide disparity exists between labor costs in western countries such as the United States and Germany and developing countries such as India and China. But different industries require different types of labor. An automobile assembly plant requires skilled labor, but an automobile R&D center requires engineers, programmers, and mathematicians. MNCs short-list countries based on their requirements and choose the locations with the lowest cost. Sometimes the sourcing of foreign labor is motivated not because of costs but because of unique capabilities. Computer software companies look to talent in countries such as India and Israel for writing sophisticated computer codes. In India, the southern cities of Chennai, Hyderabad, and Bangalore have become major software centers. Microsoft has set up a software development center at Hyderabad, its first outside the United States. The German software firm SAP has similar operations in Bangalore.

EXAMPLE 8.1

Many electronic component firms manufacture their goods in Asian countries such as China and Taiwan. Automakers also follow a similar strategy by setting up plants in low-cost countries such as the Czech Republic, Mexico, China, and India. One important constraint is shipment time and cost of transportation. This explains why in the case of inexpensively air transportable products such as disk drives, distance from production site to eventual market is unimportant, but in the case of a bulky product such as an automobile, the production site is likely to be closer to the eventual market or at least close to a major port.

- **Revenue enhancement.** By tapping new markets for their products, firms can increase revenues. A producer may find that the domestic market alone cannot support sales at a desired price point or simply not have enough consumers for the firm's products. A collateral benefit of foreign expansion is that firms obtain economies of scale and become more competitive.

EXAMPLE 8.2

The legendary Italian wine producer Angelo Gaja produces and sells about 500,000 bottles annually. With a typical bottle priced above USD 150, it would be virtually impossible for this producer to solely target the Italian market. Aggressively distributing the wine in the U.S. market and more recently in Asian markets has increased overall sales revenue. While scale may not be a motivating factor in this example, in others, especially in cases involving manufactured consumer goods, global sales can provide a firm the necessary scale to be profitable and successful.

- **Diversification of cash flows.** Firms may want to adopt foreign projects to stabilize cash flows. As discussed in an earlier chapter, firm-level diversification can enhance value under certain conditions. More generally, global diversification helps firms to weather adversity in domestic markets. One subtle benefit of diversification is that firms can opportunistically shift their revenue or cost streams to more advantageous locations. Thus, a firm may direct its products to the most lucrative markets and maximize its revenues. Similarly, production can be concentrated in the most cost-efficient locations.

EXAMPLE 8.3

During the 1990s, Japanese electronic manufacturers such as Sony and Matsushita were insulated from the recession in that country by virtue of their overseas operations, especially in the booming U.S. market. But diversification is not always a panacea. During the same period, Walmart—the giant U.S. retailer—made a foray into European markets, principally Germany. After losing hundreds of millions of dollars and seeing its stock price fall, Walmart finally pulled out of Germany in 2006.

- **Counter threat of adverse regulation.** Although more than 100 countries are signatories to the World Trade Organization (WTO), foreign governments do have the power to impose costs on MNCs through onerous regulation. Faced with this problem, firms can preemptively employ the "political hedge" of investing (not just selling) in foreign countries. A firm that has a production facility employing local citizens in a foreign country reduces the probability of adverse government action in that country. This is so because of the lobbying clout of the local beneficiaries (for example, labor).

EXAMPLE 8.4	Japanese auto manufacturers Toyota and Honda set up production facilities in the United States in the 1980s to counter protectionist sentiment. Rather than face the threat of adverse action—a quota was widely expected—these firms started U.S. production. This, to a large extent, defused the power of U.S. regulators and politicians to act against them.

- **Create flexibility for future actions.** International projects are often strategic in nature. A certain project is often a small piece in the larger puzzle of global operations. An initial foray into a market may enable a firm to learn about a foreign market and help generate profitable opportunities in the future.

EXAMPLE 8.5	An interesting phenomenon in recent years is western firms' investment in China and India. By 2008, almost all MNCs had at least one subsidiary in these countries. A firm often makes an initial investment with the understanding that profits are not immediately forthcoming. Anecdotal evidence indicates that some MNCs have "empty offices" in China. But these initial investments are learning experiences that create organizational capacity for executing future projects.

8.3 Types of Overseas Projects

The following are examples of various kinds of international projects and associated capital budgeting issues.

- **International outsourcing.** Also known as *offshoring,* international **outsourcing** involves short- to medium-term contracts with overseas firms to obtain raw materials, components, or products. For example, U.S. computer firms source LCD panels from suppliers in Taiwan, Korea, and Japan. In recent years, the scope of outsourcing has increased. In the manufacturing context, firms sometimes outsource design and development as well as production, as Microsoft did with its Xbox game console. Also, we increasingly see outsourcing contacts for services (e.g., processing insurance claims). Outsourcing differs from overseas production in that the sourcing firm does not own foreign assets. This reduces risk. The key issues in an outsourcing decision are the (1) amount of cost savings, (2) supplier's reliability, (3) supplier's ability to produce according to specifications, and (4) supplier's ability to be flexible and to meet shifting demand. Cost saving is a key driver of most outsourcing decisions. However, in some cases, cost may not be the key issue: Outsourcing can simplify operations and allow firms to focus on more promising links in the value chain.

outsourcing
Foreign projects of MNCs range in complexity from low (*outsourcing*) to high (produce and sell abroad).

- **Global production.** A firm may use a foreign location for its manufacturing operations. U.S.-based electronics and toy firms routinely use Asian countries such as China as production centers. Cross-border production projects and outsourcing decisions are often relatively easy to analyze. A key component in these decisions is cost saving, which is usually easier to assess than project revenues. If the foreign location is less expensive, it justifies the investment in the overseas production. This investing has some interesting and complex issues, however. While a foreign location may appear to be less expensive based on labor costs, the firm may lose some flexibility because of restrictive labor laws in foreign countries, for example, in European Union (EU) countries. Also, product quality and timeliness are issues of concern.

- **Global sales.** Firms may pursue global sales using various strategies. The simplest method is to export goods. A more robust approach is to establish a global sales and distribution infrastructure. For example, firms can hire a sales force and create a supply chain. With certain products, it may also be necessary to create an after-sales service infrastructure. These types of projects are more challenging to analyze than production-only projects because estimates of sales revenues are typically subject to significant precision errors. To estimate revenues, one needs to analyze the macroeconomic factors affecting aggregate demand in the country, the industry factors affecting product demand, and the firm's competitive position.

University of Chester, Queen's Park Library

Title: International corporate finance / J. Ashok Robin.
ID: 36134808
Due: 09-01-19

Total items: 1
29/11/2018 16:49

Renew online at:
http://libcat.chester.ac.uk/patroninfo

Thank you for using Self Check

248

• **Producing and selling abroad.** After gaining experience in selling products in a foreign country, firms often explore the possibility of starting production in that country. This analysis can be quite complex. Firms need to forecast product demand as well as prices. Often, in foreign markets, these variables show more volatility than they do in the United States. For example, during the emerging markets crisis of 1997–1998, Japanese auto firms' revenues from some affected countries dropped by more than 50 percent. In addition to the uncertainty surrounding demand and revenues, firms must estimate risk factors associated with production. These risk factors include inflation in the prices of input materials, uncertainty over contracting with suppliers, losses arising from poor quality or not being able to complete tasks on time, labor unrest, and so on.

• **International joint venture.** MNCs set up **joint ventures (JVs)** in various countries with local partners. Joint venture agreements can be quite complex. They often involve complicated financing and risk-sharing arrangements. They often involve the production and sales of products. In fact, many joint ventures can be thought of as separate firms with their own organization. The financial analysis of a joint venture can be as complicated as calculating a firm's enterprise value.

8.4 Overview of International Capital Budgeting

Project NPV

Modern corporations apply the discounted cash flow (DCF) approach to valuing projects. The chief metric is net present value (NPV), which is defined as:

$$\text{NPV} = \sum_{t=0}^{N} \frac{\text{CF}_t}{(1 + \text{WACC})^t}$$

The key input for an NPV calculation is project cash flows (*CF*) over the period "0" to "*N*." These cash flows are discounted at the opportunity cost of capital; a typical proxy is the overall financing costs, also known as the **weighted average cost of capital (WACC)**. The initial cash flow is CF_0 which is generally negative and reflects the capital investments necessary for the project. The final cash flow CF_N typically includes the salvage value obtained by selling the remaining assets of the project.

A project's NPV represents its wealth effect. When a firm in an efficient market embarks on a project, the firm's value increases by an amount equal to project NPV. Because firms seek to maximize shareholder wealth, they accept projects only with NPV > 0.

Special Considerations in International Projects

Next we list and briefly explain special considerations. We explain these issues in depth (with numerical examples when possible) later in this chapter as well as in the next chapter.

• **Organizational form.** Because of host-country business regulations and because of tax laws of both the host and home countries, more variation in organizational form occurs in foreign projects compared to domestic projects. Two commonly encountered settings are a (1) foreign branch of an MNC and (2) foreign subsidiary or joint venture in which the MNC has a stake of less than 100 percent. Projects implemented by a foreign branch are more straightforward to analyze. In the case of the latter, cash flows to the MNC may not coincide with project cash flows because the repatriation schedule—the timing of cash flows transmitted to the MNC—may be affected by regulations as well as contracts with the joint venture partner.

EXAMPLE 8.6   Many countries, including China, regulate repatriation of profits or cash flows. MNCs need to follow stipulated procedures. Often cash flows are classified as deriving from profits or capital, and regulations differ for these two categories. Funds can be transferred only after approval. It is not unusual that countries permit only one transfer of subsidiary profits per year.

challenges in evaluating international projects
An analysis of international projects contains *challenges* such as cash flows in foreign currencies.

- **Currency translation.** Regardless of organization form, foreign projects produce cash flows denominated in foreign currencies. Sometimes foreign projects produce cash flows in multiple currencies that may also include the home currency. The involvement of foreign currencies is an important and obvious difference between foreign and domestic projects. To calculate a project's NPV, currency forecasts are necessary. As discussed in an earlier chapter, this may be challenging if the currency in question is volatile (e.g., emerging markets currencies) or if the horizon is long (more than five years).

- **Country risk.** This risk includes components such as political risk, regulatory risk, and economic risk. Different counties have different components, but all foreign countries have a unique set of economic risks. In some cases, all three elements are present, adding to the complexity of the analysis. In addition to normal difficulties in estimating cash flows and risk, with foreign projects, one needs to give explicit consideration to country risk both in the structure of the project as well as its evaluation.

EXAMPLE 8.7

In 2008, Argentina's government imposed a tax on agricultural exports. The resulting dispute between farmers and the government derailed the economy. Inflation rose, national output fell, currency value fell, and the country was in political turmoil. Consequently, a U.S. importer of wine from Argentina faced risks including the risk of nonshipment of previously ordered merchandise. This is an example of a country-specific risk factor uncorrelated with global economic factors. Country-specific risks also occur because of natural calamities and political upheaval.

- **Taxes.** MNCs face taxes in multiple jurisdictions. This is a complex topic that we tackle more fully in later chapters. However, we need a basic understanding of taxes in the context of capital budgeting. A foreign project conducted through a subsidiary typically faces three types of taxes. First, based on operating results, the subsidiary pays income taxes each year. Second, when funds are repatriated as dividends to the parent, it must pay dividend taxes (known as *withholding taxes*) in certain countries. Third, when the parent receives funds, depending on tax laws and on agreements between the two countries, it must also pay home country income taxes (known as *repatriation taxes*). We address the issue of local income taxes in this chapter. We leave the discussion of the other taxes to later chapters.

- **Discount rate.** In theory, the **discount rate** should be set equal to the firm's *opportunity cost of capital* reflected in the returns the firm can obtain in the next best project of equivalent risk. Imagine a firm considering a certain project. If an alternate or benchmark project (similar risk, similar assets, etc.) offers a 10 percent return, then the discount rate should be 10 percent. In practice, however, this approach is difficult to implement. For instance, how can an MNC identify an alternative of equal risk for a project in a foreign country? An alternate approach, the WACC approach, is to infer the discount rate from capital markets by understanding the risk—and therefore the cost—of the firm's equity and debt. The WACC approach is more common in practice, and we explain how it is calculated in a later chapter. In this chapter, we take the home country WACC as a given input and show how to transform it into a rate appropriate for discounting foreign cash flows.

- **Real options.** Almost all corporate projects involve some sort of flexibility regarding future action. For instance, an oil and gas firm would make decisions on amounts based on the output's market prices. A consumer products firm would learn about customer needs by selling one product and apply the knowledge in launching a different product. Essentially, firms respond to market conditions and decide accordingly. Flexible parameters in projects are known as *real options.* Just as a currency option allows exercise when rates are advantageous, real options allow certain corporate actions when conditions are advantageous. Firms value the possession of real options. International projects are often strategic projects and therefore often have embedded real options. For example, firms initiate penetration of a foreign market with a tentative project and, later, based on market conditions, make further investments. Also, international projects contain flexibility related to future currency values. We discuss real options in the next chapter.

Project Cash Flow Equation

Cash flows (CF) are calculated for each year using the following equation:

$$CF = (R - E - D) \times (1 - T) + D - \Delta NWC - \Delta FA$$

Inputs for cash flows are

R = Revenues (price × quantity)

E = Expenses (direct expenses + overheads and other fixed expenses)

D = Depreciation

T = Tax rate

ΔNWC = Change (or investment) in working capital

ΔFA = Change in fixed assets or capital expenditure (net out taxes if any)

All items must be in the same currency. The first term $(R - E - D) \times (1 - T)$ is also known as *net operating profit after tax (NOPAT)* and is similar to net income. The addition of depreciation (or other nontax deductions such as deferred taxes) to NOPAT produces operating cash flows. Total cash flows (CF) are obtained by netting out investing-related flows such as changes in working capital and capital expenditure.

EXAMPLE 8.8

During a particular year, a firm records the following transactions in its subsidiary in Taiwan:

- Produced 5,000 units of a product at a direct (labor, raw materials, and other variable) cost of (Taiwanese dollar) TWD 80 per unit.
- Incurred fixed costs of TWD 100,000.
- Depreciated fixed assets for TWD 50,000.
- Sold all units at a unit price of TWD 150.
- Paid taxes at a rate of 20 percent.
- Increased working capital from TWD 250,000 to TWD 275,000.
- Invested TWD 75,000 in fixed assets.

Solution:

$R = 5,000 \times 150 = 750,000$

$E = 5,000 \times 80 + 100,000 = 500,000$

$\Delta NWC = 275,000 - 250,000 = 25,000$

Other values are $(D, T, \Delta FA)$ explicitly stated.
Applying the formula for cash flows:

$CF = (R - E - D) \times (1 - T) + D - \Delta NWC - \Delta FA$

$\quad = (750,000 - 500,000 - 50,000) \times (1 - 20\%) + 50,000 - 25,000 - 75,000$

$\quad = TWD\ 110,000$

Alternatively,

Operating cash flows = $(750,000 - 500,000 - 50,000) \times (1 - 20\%) + 50,000 = 210,000$

Investing cash flows = $-25,000 - 75,000 = -100,000$

CF = Operating cash flows + Investing cash flows = $210,000 - 100,000 = 110,000$

Discussion: This calculation is straightforward and similar to a cash flow calculation for a domestic project. If two or more currencies are involved, we are required to make conversions in such a way that all cash flows are expressed either in the foreign currency (TWD in this example) or the home currency.

Cash Flow Inputs

Various inputs are required to calculate project cash flows. Some specific considerations relative to calculating cash flows for a foreign project are discussed next.

Number of Units Sold

Of all variables, the number of units sold is perhaps the most critical. It is also the most important because it influences most other cash flow variables. Unit demand is difficult to estimate in a foreign setting. A typical two-step method (1) generates an industry-level forecast over a period of about five years and (2) analyzes the firm's competitive position to forecast a pattern of market share over the same period. Unit demand equals (1) times (2). But both inputs are difficult to assess in a foreign setting principally because environmental factors—consumer demand, gross national product (GNP), inflation, and so on—may induce a high level of uncertainty regarding unit demand. Furthermore, the MNC is handicapped in not having local expertise and knowledge.

Price

cash flow inputs
Among cash flow inputs, *units* and *prices* are often the most difficult to estimate.

Next to number of units in terms of difficulty in estimation, prices depend on macro factors such as inflation and GNP as well as industry-level factors such as overall demand, innovation, and competition. Some countries have high and volatile levels of inflation (e.g., Latin American countries), making price estimation difficult. Also, if the MNC does not have market power, prices will be more volatile. Finally, prices of high technology outputs (e.g., LCD screens, DRAM chips) are difficult to predict.

Direct Expenses

For mature products in competitive industries—usually sold on a cost-plus basis—direct expenses are probably highly correlated to prices. In other cases, however, direct expenses may follow a different path. Different factors may affect input and output factor prices. For instance, input factors may be commodity-like and follow global prices, while output could be a specialized product with prices tracking consumer utility and satisfaction. Input and output prices also may be in different currencies and face different inflation rates.

EXAMPLE 8.9

In recent decades, inflation has rarely been a concern for domestic U.S. firms. However, it is a key consideration for U.S.-based MNCs considering foreign projects, especially in emerging markets. Either because of weak macro policies (e.g., budget deficits) or because of booming economies, inflation is high in many emerging economies. In recent years, wage inflation has been 10 percent or higher in China and India. In some extreme cases—salaries of software engineers in India is a frequently cited example—wage inflation was around 15 percent during certain years.

Investment Flows

Investment flows have multiple components. The initial investment comprises fixed assets as well as investments in working capital. This is probably the least problematic of all cash flow inputs. However, if an initial investment includes building infrastructure (e.g., a factory), it is not unusual to see cost overruns. During the project's life, the firm makes secondary and tertiary investments as well as continuing investments in working capital. Toward the end of the project, some of these investments are recovered: Working capital is recovered fully (at least from an accounting standpoint) while fixed assets typically result in lower salvage values. Because they arise at a future date, salvage values are prone to estimation errors, especially in a foreign setting.

8.5 Net Present Value of an International Project

Consider Sunbeam Corp, a U.S. firm, setting up a project in Mexico to produce and sell a product. Related data are available in the following section.

Forecasted Data

Capital Requirement

Sunbeam's project is for five years and requires an initial investment of MXN 25 million for equipment. On completion of the project, the equipment's salvage value is expected to be MXN 8 million. Sunbeam's working capital requirement is 25 percent of the following year's sales (equivalently, the firm's cash cycle—the days between incurring production costs and receiving cash from customers—is approximately 90 days).

Sales of Units/Production Forecast

Units follow the typical inverted U shape—rising initially and falling toward project end. Units are expected to be 200,000 each year for the first two years, rising to 300,000 in the following two, and falling to 200,000 in the final year.

Margins

The product's selling price is expected to be constant at MXN 200 per unit. Direct costs, labor, and raw materials are expected to be MXN 120 per unit. Overhead costs are MXN 10 million annually.

Discount Rate

The firm's policy requires a return equal to its WACC of 9 percent on projects involving the production and sale of a product.

Other Information

The tax rate in Mexico is 30 percent. Mexico allows straight-line depreciation for tax purposes. The spot rate is MXNUSD = 0.10.

Foreign Currency Cash Flows

Using forecasted data, we perform a standard cash flow analysis to determine MXN cash flows (see Exhibit 8.1). These results are subsequently processed using specific models of global finance to determine project NPV.

Domestic Currency Cash Flows and NPV (Approach I)

Earlier, we calculated the project's foreign currency cash flows. These values represent cash flows derived at the subsidiary level. We now assume that these cash flows are repatriated to the parent immediately and without any leakage due to withholding or other taxes. This allows us to estimate the home currency (USD) cash flows and resulting NPV.

EXHIBIT 8.1
Sunbeam's Mexican Project: Calculation of Foreign Currency Cash Flows

Item		MXN Cash Flows (000s)					
		$t = 0$	$t = 1$	$t = 2$	$t = 3$	$t = 4$	$t = 5$
Units and NWC							
1	Units 000s		200	200	300	300	200
2	Revenues = Units × 200		40,000	40,000	60,000	60,000	40,000
3	NWC	10,000	10,000	15,000	15,000	10,000	0
Investment CF							
4	Capital expenditure	25,000					
5	Salvage						8,000
6	Taxes (salvage)						2,400
7	Change in NWC	10,000	0	5,000	0	−5,000	−10,000
8	Investment	−35,000	0	−5,000	0	5,000	15,600
	$CF = -4 + 5 - 6 - 7$						
Operating CF							
9	Revenues		40,000	40,000	60,000	60,000	40,000
10	Direct Expenses = Units × 120		24,000	24,000	36,000	36,000	24,000
11	Fixed Expenses		10,000	10,000	10,000	10,000	10,000
12	Depreciation		5,000	5,000	5,000	5,000	5,000
13	Pretax income		1,000	1,000	9,000	9,000	1,000
14	Taxes		300	300	2,700	2,700	300
15	NOPAT		700	700	6,300	6,300	700
16	Operating $CF = 15 + 12$		5,700	5,700	11,300	11,300	5,700
	$CF = 8 + 16$	−35,000	5,700	700	11,300	16,300	21,300

Constant Currency Assumption

The MXNUSD rate is 0.10. As we learned earlier, one possible forecast of future currency values is the spot value. Making this assumption, we can derive USD cash flows and calculate NPV using the WACC of 9 percent (see Exhibit 8.2).

The project appears to be a profitable one from the U.S. parent's perspective because NPV is USD 493,510. But how valid is the assumption of a constant value for MXN? Are inflation and interest rates equal in the two countries? Are there any disturbances in currency markets (e.g., foreign institutional investor—FII— flows) that may change currency values?

Changing Currency Assumption

Suppose that the U.S. inflation rate is 2 percent and the Mexican inflation rate is 4 percent. If parity conditions hold, the MXN would be expected to lose value over time relative to the USD. By ignoring this expected depreciation, the assumption of a constant MXN value would overstate the project's NPV. Our answer of NPV = USD 493,510 under this assumption overstates true project value.

How can we factor the expected depreciation of the MXN in our calculations? First, we need to calculate estimates of future MXNUSD using the inflation differential. Using purchasing power parity (PPP):

$$\text{MXN value in 1 year} = 0.10 \times \frac{1.02}{1.04} = 0.09808$$

$$\text{MXN value in 2 years} = 0.10 \times \left(\frac{1.02}{1.04}\right)^2 = 0.09619$$

Similarly, we calculate values of MXNUSD in years 3, 4, and 5. We find these values to be 0.09434, 0.09253, and 0.09075, respectively. MXNUSD depreciates annually at the rate of 1.9231 percent. Using these forecasts, we recalculate USD cash flows (see Exhibit 8.3).

As expected, NPV (USD) is lower at 217,440. However, the project remains profitable.

Foreign Currency Cash Flows and Net Present Value (Approach II)

We retain the assumption of differential inflation. Recall that U.S. and Mexican inflation rates are 2 percent and 4 percent, respectively. In the alternate approach considered here, we calculate project NPV by directly discounting MXN cash flows without converting them to USD. The main requirement for this approach is a discount rate or WACC appropriate for MXN cash flows. Because Mexico has a higher inflation rate, the discount rate for MXN cash flows should be

EXHIBIT 8.2
Sunbeam's Mexican Project USD Cash Flows and NPV (constant MXNUSD assumption)

	$t = 0$	$t = 1$	$t = 2$	$t = 3$	$t = 4$	$t = 5$
CF (MXN 000s)	−35,000	5,700	700	11,300	16,300	21,300
× MXNUSD	0.10	0.10	0.10	0.10	0.10	0.10
= CF (USD 000s)	−3,500	570	70	1,130	1,630	2,130
NPV@ 9% (USD 000s)	493.51					

EXHIBIT 8.3
Sunbeam's Mexican Project USD Cash Flows and NPV (declining MXNUSD assumption)

	$t = 0$	$t = 1$	$t = 2$	$t = 3$	$t = 4$	$t = 5$
CF (MXN 000s)		−35,000	5,700	700	11,300	16,300	21,300

Assumption: USD inflation = 2%, MXN inflation = 4%

Using PPP, MXNUSD forecast $= S \times \left(\dfrac{1 + 2\%}{1 + 4\%}\right)^t$

	$t = 0$	$t = 1$	$t = 2$	$t = 3$	$t = 4$	$t = 5$
× MXNUSD	0.10000	0.09808	0.09619	0.09434	0.09253	0.09075
= CF (USD 000s)	−3,500.00	559.04	67.33	1,066.05	1,508.19	1,932.92
NPV@ 9% (USD 000s)	217.44					

EXHIBIT 8.4

Sunbeam's Mexican Project MXN Cash Flows and NPV (differential inflation assumption)

	$t = 0$	$t = 1$	$t = 2$	$t = 3$	$t = 4$	$t = 5$
CF (MXN 000s)	−35,000	5,700	700	11,300	16,300	21,300

Assumption: USD inflation = 2%, MXN inflation = 4%

Using IFE, MXN discount rate = $(1 + 9\%) \times \dfrac{1 + 4\%}{1 + 2\%} - 1 = 11.1373\%$

NPV@ 11.1373% (MXN 000s)   2174.40

commensurately higher. See Exhibit 8.4. The international Fisher effect, discussed in Chapter 5, indicates that nominal returns differ among countries because of inflation. Use this theory to adjust the USD-based discount rate of 12 percent and produce the MXN discount rate as follows:

$$\text{MXN discount rate} = (1 + 9\%) \times \frac{(1 + 4\%)}{(1 + 2\%)} - 1 = 11.1373\%$$

WACC

The international Fisher effect (IFE) is used to convert an MNC's *WACC* for discounting foreign cash flows.

The foreign currency NPV is MXN 2,174,400. Note that this value equals the home currency NPV of USD 217,440 at the spot rate of MXNUSD = 0.10. We explain this equivalence in the next section.

Comparing Approach I and Approach II

Approaches I and II—the home currency and foreign currency approaches—are symmetrical methods. In the former, we recognize the devaluation of the MXN *explicitly* by using lower rates to convert future MXN cash flows into USD cash flows. In the latter, we recognize the devaluation of the MXN *implicitly* by applying a higher discount rate. In both cases, the underlying factor is differential inflation: The higher Mexican inflation rate translates to lower cash flows in one method and a higher discount rate in the other. Because both cases address the same fundamental issue (inflation), the answers are identical.

We now demonstrate the mathematical equivalence of the two methods. For generality and following the convention used in earlier chapters, we use the superscript * to refer to MXN-denominated cash flows, interest rates, and WACC; values without a superscript are in USD.

Approach I (domestic currency NPV) uses the following equation:

$$\text{NPV} = \sum_{t=0}^{N} \frac{\text{CF}_t}{(1 + \text{WACC})^t}$$

To implement this equation, cash flows in MXN are converted to cash flows in USD. Because inflation rates are available, the PPP is used to generate the estimate of future spot rates for MXN. Thus,

$$\text{CF}_t = \text{CF}_t^* \times S \times \left(\frac{1 + i}{1 + i^*}\right)^t$$

Furthermore, according to the international Fisher effect,

$$1 + \text{WACC} = (1 + \text{WACC}^*) \times \frac{1 + i}{1 + i^*}$$

Substituting the expressions for CF_t and $1 + WACC$ in NPV,

$$\text{NPV} = \sum \frac{\text{CF}_t^* \times S \times \left(\frac{1 + i}{1 + i^*}\right)^t}{(1 + \text{WACC}^*)^t \times \left(\frac{1 + i}{1 + i^*}\right)^t}$$

$$= S \times \sum \frac{\text{CF}_t^*}{(1 + \text{WACC}^*)^t}$$

The right-hand side of the equation discounts foreign currency cash flows with the foreign currency WACC. This is approach II. Thus, approach I provides an answer equal to the spot rate times the answer from approach II. In the Sunbeam example, approaches I and II provided answers of USD 217,440 and MXN 2,174,400, respectively; the numerical difference is explained by the spot rate of MXNUSD = 0.10. Under parity conditions, the two approaches are equivalent.

Sensitivity Analysis

sensitivity analysis

MNCs use *sensitivity analysis* to identify risks in foreign projects.

When decision makers expect model inputs to vary, they conduct sensitivity analyses to understand how input volatility affects output volatility. NPV calculations use volatile inputs, especially in cross-border projects, and call for sensitivity analyses. In the context of project NPV, **sensitivity analysis** is the analysis of how the output (i.e., NPV) responds to changes in input values such as exchange rates, margins, and investment levels. One form of sensitivity analysis is **break-even analysis**, which is the attempt to identify threshold values of inputs that produce positive NPV. We show a sample calculation next.

EXAMPLE 8.10

Recall Sunbeam's Mexican project. Earlier, by using a selling price of MXN 200 per unit, we found a project NPV of USD 217, 440. Determine the break-even selling price.

Solution: There are multiple ways to solve the problem. An intuitive method is to set up a spreadsheet and redo calculations using various values for the selling price. The table and chart below reflect a series of calculations performed using this approach.

Sunbeam's Mexican Project (declining MXNUSD assumption)

Unit Price in MXN	NPV (USD 000s)
150	−2,723.35
175	−1,252.95
190	−370.71
195	*− 76.64*
200	217.44
205	511.55
225	1,687.84
250	3,158.23

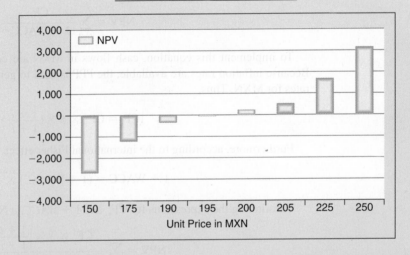

The break-even selling price is one that produces a project NPV closest to zero. The chart indicates a break-even selling price of approximately MXN 195.

Discussion: Sensitivity analysis may also focus on other input variables such as direct expenses and units sold per year. One could also calculate the break-even Mexican inflation rate; however, this requires us to make assumptions about the effect of Mexican inflation on prices and units.

A limitation of most sensitivity analyses such as break-even analysis is that input factors are varied one at a time. The problem with this approach is similar to the problem of assessing the risk of individual currency positions in isolation (Chapter 6). An interesting technique that allows multiple inputs to vary is Monte Carlo simulation. A firm concerned about the effects of inflation as well as unit sales may consider simulating both of these effects simultaneously. To do so, the firm must assess not only the variability in the two input factors but also the correlation between them. These statistical values are then used to construct thousands of scenarios. Each scenario determines the project's NPV. This produces a probability distribution for the project's NPV and offers a better assessment of project risk.

8.6 Currency Risk

International projects differ from domestic projects because the former are subject to unique risk factors such as currency risk and country risk. In this section, we discuss the incorporation of currency risk in capital budgeting and suggest a method for integrating capital budgeting and risk management.

Currency Risk Break-Even Analysis

Chapters 6 and 7 discussed issues relating to currency risk measurement and management. One way to evaluate currency risk in the context of capital budgeting is to assess break-even currency values. The following example illustrates this approach.

EXAMPLE 8.11

A U.S. firm considers an investment of USD 16,000 in Canada. This is a four-year investment to produce and sell a new product. The firm expects to sell 1,000 units of the product each year at a price of CAD 20. On an annual basis, direct expenses are expected to be CAD 10 per unit and indirect expenses are expected to be CAD 1,200. Depreciation is straight line to zero. Canadian taxes are 40 percent, and there are no additional taxes (withholding or repatriation) when cash flows are repatriated. The firm's WACC is 12 percent. The CADUSD spot rate is 0.80. The firm expects the CAD to depreciate against the USD and is interested in determining the break-even rate of depreciation.

Solution: The initial investment of USD 16,000 is equivalent to CAD 20,000 at the spot rate, implying a depreciation of CAD 5,000 a year.

We can use principles learned earlier to calculate the annual cash flows in CAD as follows:

$$CF = (1,000 \times (20 - 10) - 1,200 - 5,000) \times (1 - 40\%) + 5,000 = CAD\ 7,280$$

At the spot rate of USD 0.80, this annual cash flow is equivalent to USD 5,824. However, the CAD is assumed to change in value each year at a rate equal to g. Using the capital budgeting approach I discussed earlier,

$$NPV = -16,000 + \frac{5,824 \times (1 + g)}{(1.12)} + \frac{5,824 \times (1 + g)^2}{(1.12)^2} + \frac{5,824 \times (1 + g)^3}{(1.12)^3} + \frac{5,824 \times (1 + g)^4}{(1.12)^4}.$$

By setting the preceding value to zero, we determine the break-even value of g to equal negative 4.213 percent. There are two ways to perform this calculation. The simplest way is to use a spreadsheet to solve the problem: In Microsoft Excel, use the goal-seek function to solve for break even. Alternatively, use the formula for growing annuities.

Discussion: Break-even analysis allows firms to understand thresholds. As a follow-up, the firm might obtain the probability distribution of CADUSD to currency values to calculate the probability of $(g < -4.213\%)$. If this probability is low, say 10 percent or less, the currency risk is manageable. If, on the other hand, the probability is high, the firm needs to take steps to mitigate risk.

One can also employ scenario analysis to understand the impact of currency values on a project NPV. This requires the decision maker to construct scenarios containing values of CAD and associated probabilities to calculate NPV. One way to construct scenarios for CAD values is to use estimates of the standard deviation. For example, if the forecast for CAD is 0.80 and if the standard deviation of changes in CAD is 10 percent, two plausible scenarios are 0.72 and 0.88.

Integrating Capital Budgeting and Exposure Management

How can firms integrate their capital budgeting and risk management practices? By determining break-even currency values, a firm can buy options with strike prices approximately equal to the break-even values.

EXAMPLE 8.12

Reconsider the previous example of the Canadian project. Recall that we calculated a break-even growth rate of negative 4.213 percent for CADUSD, whose spot value is 0.80. Suggest an option strategy to control currency exposure and discuss advantages and disadvantages.

Solution: We calculate the future path of CADUSD as follows:

Year (t)	Break-Even *CADUSD* *CADUSD* = 0.80 × (1 − 4.213%)^t
1	0.7663
2	0.7340
3	0.7031
4	0.6735

break-even analysis and options

A *break-even analysis* can identify strike prices for an options hedge.

One strategy would be to purchase CAD put options with strike prices approximately equal to the break-even values. So, one-year puts will be purchased with a strike price of 0.76, two-year with 0.73, and so on.

Discussion: Use of this strategy would guarantee that annual project cash flows are at least equal to break-even values (that is, we establish a "floor" of zero). Hopefully, in most years, the firm obtains market values that are higher than break-even values. The downside to the strategy is its cost. Options premiums may be prohibitively high. In an extreme scenario, if rates fall below break even in all years, the firm would be able to offset currency losses against option payoffs but would bear the net cost of premiums. In a real-world setting, firms may set strike prices for puts at lower than break-even levels to control costs.

8.7 Country Risk

Country risk may be defined as the variation or risk in firm performance induced by a country's environmental factors such as economic policies and conditions, political institutions, geography, and currency values. The two main components of country risk are political risk and economic risk.

$$\text{Country risk} = \text{Economic risk} + \text{Political risk}$$

- **Economic risk.** This risk occurs because of changes in the macroeconomic environment and manifests itself in factors such as national growth, inflation, and interest rates. History shows that these factors are much more variable in developing countries and impose significant risks on MNCs. Because enterprise profitability is often the result of proper execution against realistic budgets, a high level of economic risk can engender losses. Thus, in an environment that is constantly shifting, firms are unable to properly calibrate their operations and, hence, are unable to generate much profit.

political risk

Political risk—changes in regime, law and order problems, war—is often an important component of country risk.

- **Political risk.** Political risk arises from a country's sociopolitical environment. Political risk manifests itself in many ways. In certain countries, political turmoil can lead a firm's potential market to deteriorate and can increase its cost of operations. Examples of countries experiencing political turmoil in recent years include Colombia, where the government battled leftist guerillas, and Sri Lanka, where the government engaged in a long-running war with a minority ethnic group. In both countries, the respective government's war efforts adversely affected economic growth.

EXHIBIT 8.5
Fitch Sovereign Risk Ratings: Examples in Various Categories

Source: *www.fitchratings.com* (accessed March 2008).

AAA	AA	A
Canada	Australia	China
Germany	Hong Kong	Chile
Singapore	Japan	Czech Republic
United Kingdom	Italy	Taiwan
United States	Kuwait	Malaysia
BBB	**BB**	**B/C/D**
Mexico	Brazil	Iran
Russia	Colombia	Dominican Republic
S. Africa	Sri Lanka	Bolivia
Kazakhstan	Turkey	Ecuador
India	Vietnam	Argentina

Political risk may also arise from adverse actions the foreign government undertakes. These may include regulatory actions that impose costs on the firm as well as outright expropriation of assets. Adverse regulatory action is a common occurrence and is feared by MNCs. The European Commission, for instance, has imposed significant costs on mergers of MNCs by demanding divestiture of significant assets: A high-profile recent case was the unsuccessful merger of General Electric and Honeywell. Regulations may extend beyond antitrust and pertain to issues such as pollution, taxes, and labor.

Country risk for an MNC must be estimated at the micro as well as at the macro levels. *Macrolevel country risk* is defined as overall country risk more or less affecting all MNCs. In contrast, *microlevel country risk* is industry-specific or firm-specific country risk that MNCs face. For example, consumer electronics firms and oil companies may face differential levels of county risk in developing countries, with the latter facing significantly higher levels of risk.

A variety of sources provide information on country risk. Some of these sources are freely available, often from business journals such as *Euromoney*. Country risk information is available in the form of overall country ratings as well as ratings for subcomponents such as political risk, credit risk, and access to capital markets. One specialized risk measure pertains to the default risk of sovereign bonds (bonds issued by the government); Fitch issues the long-term foreign currency (LTFC) default issuer risk rating that is widely disseminated (see Exhibit 8.5). All of the ratings are "macro" ratings. Microlevel country risk ratings—reflecting industry-specific or firm-specific conditions—are much more difficult to obtain: Many firms use consultants and bankers or develop the capability to make the ratings in-house.

Incorporating Country Risk in the Project NPV: Two Approaches

Country risk can be incorporated in a project NPV. There are two approaches:

- Adjustments to the discount rate.
- Adjustments to cash flows.

Of these, the latter is commonly used in practice.

Adjustments to Discount Rate

Recognizing that country risk increases the volatility of a firm's cash flows, the first approach makes adjustments to the discount rate. The higher the level of country risk, the higher is the discount rate. MNCs can look to markets for guidance on making this adjustment. For example, if an MNC is considering an investment in a country whose sovereign debt has a yield of 8 percent compared to a home government bond yield of 6 percent (assume that the denomination currency is the same), the discount rate for the foreign project could be adjusted by 2 percent. The problem with this approach is that it is ad hoc and not well supported by theory. There is no accepted model such as the capital asset pricing model (CAPM) that provides guidance on risk premiums for country risk. Furthermore, there is considerable

country risk

To incorporate *country risk* in an NPV analysis, it is better to adjust cash flows than it is to adjust the discount rate.

debate on whether country risk is a diversifiable risk factor and whether it should be associated with a risk premium.

Adjustments to Cash Flows

The second approach is to specifically identify the scenarios in which the project cash flows will be affected and the associated probabilities. The NPV of the project can then be calculated for the various scenarios, and the expected NPV can be derived using the scenario probabilities. We demonstrate this method in the following example.

EXAMPLE 8.13

A U.S.-based firm considers an investment in a developing country (India) that has some level of political risk. The project parameters are as follows:

- The capital expenditure is INR 100 million.
- The project is a three-year project producing annual operating cash flows of INR 40 million.
- At the end of three years, the firm's assets will be sold (salvage) for INR 60 million to a foreign (i.e., local) firm.
- The WACC of 12 percent is used as the discount rate in NPV computations involving the domestic currency (i.e., USD).
- USDINR = 50. Assume constant currency value.

Assume that because of political risk, a 60 percent probability of expropriation of assets in year 3 exists (i.e., salvage value is expropriated). Assume zero taxes. Calculate the project NPV.

Solution: The firm considers two scenarios: no expropriation (40 percent) and expropriation (60 percent). Using the home currency NPV method discussed earlier in this chapter, we calculate the project NPV for these two scenarios (see below). These computations follow. The NPV without expropriation is USD 775,600; the NPV with expropriation is USD −78,530. Using probabilities for these two states, we find:

$$\text{Expected NPV} = 40\% \times 775,600 + 60\% \times (-78,530) = \text{USD } 263,120$$

NPV of Project Facing Expropriation of Assets

	Cash Flows (000s)			
	$t = 0$	$t = 1$	$t = 2$	$t = 3$
Scenario I: No Expropriation (probability = 40%)				
Capital expenditure	−100,000			
Salvage				60,000
Operating cash flows		40,000	40,000	40,000
CF (INR)	−100,000	40,000	40,000	100,000
÷ USDINR	50	50	50	50
= CF (USD)	−2,000	800	800	2000
NPV @ 12%	775.60			
Scenario II: Expropriation (probability = 60%)				
Capital expenditure	−100,000			
Salvage				60,000 or 0
Operating cash flows		40,000	40,000	40,000
CF (INR)	−100,000	40,000	40,000	40,000
÷ USDINR	50	50	50	50
= CF (USD)	−2,000	800	800	800
NPV @ 12%	−78.53			
Summary and Expected NPV				
No expropriation	40%	775.60		
Expropriation	60%	−78.53		
Expected NPV		263.12		

Discussion: The expected project NPV equals USD 263,120. However, there is a 60 percent chance that the NPV is negative. This is a substantial risk factor. However, the use of insurance can mitigate this risk.

Political Risk Insurance

One solution to the problem of political risk is insurance. Political risk coverage, especially for long-term projects, is widely available. Insurance firms in London and New York specialize in offering this type of coverage. The Chubb group, for instance, offers "expropriation insurance" policies providing coverage against confiscation, expropriation, or nationalization of assets by a foreign government as well as willful damage of property. In addition to private insurers such as Chubb, multinational organizations such as the World Bank Group's Multilateral Investment Guarantee Agency (MIGA) offer political risk insurance.

EXAMPLE 8.14

Consider the problem presented in Example 8.13 concerning the Indian project of a U.S. firm. Assume that the firm can obtain insurance at an upfront cost of INR 12 million and enjoy 100 percent protection. Calculate the (1) project NPV and (2) break-even insurance premium.

Solution: See below for calculation of the project NPV using this additional information, which shows that the NPV is USD 535,601. This compares to an NPV of USD 263,120 without purchase of the insurance contract.

Insurance Coverage for Expropriation

	Cash Flows (000s)			
	t = 0	*t* = 1	*t* = 2	*t* = 3
Capital expenditure	−100,000			
Salvage				60,000
Operating cash flows		40,000	40,000	40,000
Insurance premium	−12,000			
CF (INR)	−112,000	40,000	40,000	100,000
÷ USDINR	50	50	50	50
= CF (USD)	−2,240	800	800	2,000
NPV @ 12%	535.601			

Next we calculate the break-even insurance premium. This equals the expected NPV of savings as follows (i.e., avoiding expropriation):

$$\text{Premium} = \frac{60\% \times 60{,}000{,}000 \times (1/50)}{(1 + 12\%)^3} = \text{USD } 512{,}482$$

Discussion: Even if the firm does not purchase insurance, using estimates of insurance premiums in NPV calculation is a useful method and is superior to the use of ad hoc expropriation probabilities and may offer a more market-oriented estimate of project NPV.

Also note that firms are prepared to pay an even higher amount for insurance coverage than the break-even amount indicated above (USD 512,482). This happens because of the risk reduction that insurance offers and resulting benefits in areas such as taxes, bankruptcy costs, and strategic planning. Similar ideas were discussed earlier in chapter 7.

Summary

- Capital budgeting is the process by which firms define, choose, implement, and monitor projects.
- Cross-border or international projects may take different forms and can offer many advantages to the MNC.
- International projects pose unique difficulties for the decision maker. Among the many differences between international and domestic projects, the most important is the presence of foreign currency-denominated cash flows.
- There are two alternative methods for calculating a cross-border project's NPV. The first approach requires the decision maker to convert the foreign currency cash flows into

domestic currency cash flows by using currency forecasts; these cash flows are discounted to provide the project NPV in the domestic currency. The second approach preserves foreign currency cash flows and calculates foreign currency NPV by adjusting the discount rate to more appropriately reflect the foreign currency.

- International projects expose firms to currency risk. This requires firms to conduct sensitivity analyses to determine the extent of the risk. One method is to calculate break-even values of a currency's appreciation or depreciation.

- International projects often contain country risk. It has two components: political risk and economic risk. Political risk is the chance that political changes will affect the project cash flows and NPV. Likewise, economic risk is the risk posed by macroeconomic factors such as inflation, growth, and interest rates in foreign countries. We demonstrate simple methods to incorporate country risk in project analysis.

Questions

1. **Organizational Structure.** What type of organizational structure—centralized or decentralized—facilitates the analysis of international projects? Explain.

2. **Work Process.** Explain the role of teamwork in assessing international projects. Do international projects demand more challenging teamwork than domestic projects? Explain.

3. **Organizational Structure and Work Process.** After years of selling computers in India that have been shipped from its plant in Malaysia, Dell wishes to set up an assembly plant in India in partnership with a local firm. Explain the challenges in analyzing such a project. How do you go about obtaining relevant cash flow inputs? In your answer, be sure to explain the role of organizational structure and work processes.

4. **Advantages of International Projects.** In recent years, leading MNCs based in the United States and western Europe have set up projects in Brazil, Russia, India, and China (BRIC countries). Explain this phenomenon by discussing the advantages offered by international projects. Give examples.

5. **Types of International Projects.** What are the simplest types of international projects? What are the most complex? Provide examples. Consider a U.S.-based firm producing routers and other networking hardware. If this firm wishes to conduct business in Asia, what types of projects should it consider?

6. **Discount Rate for Foreign Cash Flows.** Almost by definition, overseas projects generate cash flows denominated in a foreign currency. How do firms estimate the appropriate discount rate for these cash flows? What theory is generally applied?

7. **Country Risk.** Define *country risk*. What are its components? How does country risk impact a project's cash flows?

8. **Expropriation.** What are two methods to factor in expropriation of assets in NPV calculations? Which of these methods is more sensible? Why?

9. **Country Risk Insurance.** What are various ways to mitigate country risk? Is insurance a viable alternative?

10. **Currency Risk.** How does currency risk affect international projects? Explain one analytical method to evaluate its thresholds.

Problems

1. **Basic NPV Calculation.** Lawson is a U.K.-based wine and spirits company. It seeks to create a fine wine division to enhance its portfolio of global properties. The CFO is scrutinizing a proposal to make an investment in a vineyard in Chile. It requires the purchase of 20 acres of vineyards in the Maipo valley and setting up the requisite infrastructure for processing grapes and bottling wine. The project is expected to last five years, after which

an exit through its sale to a local affiliate is assumed. The following table lists the cash flows denominated in the Chilean peso (CLP). Assume spot GBPCLP = 600.

Time	Cash Flow (CLP millions)
0	−200
1	100
2	80
3	160
4	140
5	240

a. The appropriate CLP discount rate for projects of this nature is 15 percent. What is project NPV in CLP?

b. Assume that GBPCLP remains constant at 600. Convert project cash flows into GBP (pounds). Using Lawson's GBP WACC of 10 percent, calculate the project NPV in GBP.

2. **Calculation of Foreign Cash Flows and NPV.** Edgar Enterprises, a U.S.-based firm, is considering a project in Mexico to produce and sell automobile components. It is a five-year project with an initial investment of USD 100,000. Each year, the project will produce 1,000 units of the product at a direct cost of MXN 200 and selling price of MXN 500. Indirect expenses, not including depreciation, are expected to be MXN 100,000. Depreciation is straight line to zero. Taxes are 30 percent. Calculate cash flows and the NPV assuming an MXN discount rate of 20 percent. The current spot rate is MXNUSD = 0.20. Assume that salvage is zero and there is no working capital requirement.

3. **Calculation of Domestic Cash Flows and NPV.** Romig Enterprises, a U.S.-based firm, is considering a project in China to produce and sell compressors. It is a four-year project with an initial investment of USD 500,000. Each year, it would produce 800 units of the product at a direct cost of CNY 600 and sales price of CNY 2,000. Indirect expenses, not including depreciation, are expected to be CNY 120,000. Depreciation is straight line to zero. Taxes are 30 percent. Calculate USD cash flows and the NPV assuming a USD discount rate of 10 percent. The current spot rate is USDCNY = 6.50. Assume that currency values do not change during the life of the project, salvage is zero, and no working capital requirement exists.

4. **Use of Inflation Data in NPV.** A project in Hong Kong costs Hong Kong dollar (HKD) 100,000 and produces cash flows of HKD 40,000 per year for four years. Gruner, a Swiss firm using the Swiss franc (CHF), is interested in adopting this project. If this had been a domestic project, the discount rate would have been 14 percent. Forecasts of inflation rates over the next four years indicate inflation of 2.5 percent in Switzerland and 5 percent in Hong Kong. Spot CHFHKD is 6.2.

a. What is the appropriate discount rate for HKD cash flows? Using this discount rate, calculate the project NPV in HKD.

b. Making appropriate assumptions and using data given in the problem, forecast future values of CHFHKD.

c. Estimate CHF cash flows, and calculate the project NPV in CHF. Are HKD and CHF project NPVs different? Explain.

5. **Use of Interest Rate Data to Convert Project Cash Flows.** Otter Mills, a U.S.-based sawmill, is considering a project to export lumber products to Europe. A project analysis identifies that during the third year of the project, revenues would be euro (EUR) 5 million. Direct expenses are expected to be 40 percent, and indirect project-related expenses are EUR 1 million for that year. Assume that depreciation equals EUR 0.5 million and taxes are 25 percent. Otter wishes to calculate project USD-denominated cash flows for

the third year. You are given the following additional information: spot EURUSD equals 1.22, USD interest rate equals 3 percent, and EUR interest rate equals 5 percent. Use annual compounding.

6. **Use of Interest Rate Data to Convert Project Cash Flows.** Schwarz, a German firm, is considering a five-year project in China that requires an investment (capital expenditure) of EUR 400,000. The following additional information is presented:

R_t = CNY 1,300,000 $\times$ 1.2^{t-1} (i.e., annual growth rate of revenue is 20 percent)

Direct expenses are 20 percent of revenues.

Fixed expenses are CNY 200,000 annually.

Net working capital for each year equals 20 percent of revenues for the following year.

Taxes are 30 percent.

Assume straight-line depreciation for tax purposes.

After-tax salvage value is CNY 3 million.

Spot EURCNY equals 10.5.

a. Calculate CNY-denominated cash flows.

b. Assume that interest rates in Europe and China are 3 percent and 7 percent, respectively, and annual compounding. Making appropriate assumptions, calculate EUR-denominated cash flows.

7. **Comprehensive Cash Flows and Break-Even Units.** Brady, a U.S.-based firm, is considering a four-year project in Turkey. The following information is available about the project:

Initial investment. The initial investment of USD 500,000 is used to purchase capital equipment. This equipment will be depreciated straight line to zero. At the end of four years, the remaining equipment will be sold for Turkish lira (TRY) 200,000.

Working capital. The investment in working capital is TRY 100,000. There are no changes in working capital until the end of the project when the full amount is recovered.

Units, price, and costs. The firm will produce 1,000 units of a product annually. The selling price is expected to be TRY 400 in the first year. This price is expected to increase at a rate of 5 percent annually. The direct expense per unit is expected to be TRY 200 in the first year. This is expected to increase at a rate of 6 percent annually. Indirect expenses are expected to be TRY 50,000 annually.

Taxes and miscellaneous. Turkish taxes on income and capital gains are 30 percent. There are no additional withholding taxes. All cash flows are repatriated when generated, and there are no additional U.S. taxes. The parity conditions are assumed to hold between Turkey and the United States. The relevant inflation indexes indicate a rate of 2 percent for the United States and 8 percent for Turkey. Spot USDTRY equals 1.2. Brady's USD denominated WACC is 13 percent.

a. Calculate TRY cash flows.

b. What is the appropriate TRY discount rate? Calculate the project NPV.

c. Use parity conditions to generate future spot rates. Calculate the project NPV in USD.

d. Calculate break-even units.

8. **Break-Even Currency Depreciation.** A U.S. firm is considering an investment of USD 20 million in India. This is a five-year investment to produce and sell domestic appliances. The firm expects to sell 100,000 units of the product each year at a price of INR 5,000. Direct expenses are expected to be INR 2,000 per unit, and indirect expenses are expected to be INR 25 million a year. Depreciation is straight line to zero. Indian taxes are 30 percent, and there are no additional taxes (withholding or repatriation) when cash

flows are repatriated. Assume zero salvage value. The WACC of the firm is 10 percent. Spot USDINR equals 40.

   a. Assume that INR values are constant. Calculate cash flows in USD and the project NPV.

   b. Assume that the INR depreciates. What is the break-even rate of depreciation?

9. **Break-Even Currency Depreciation.** Saint, a U.S.-based firm, is considering a three-year project in Kuwait. The details follow:

   Initial investment. The initial investment is USD 20,000, which is used to purchase capital equipment that will be depreciated straight line to zero. At the end of three years, the remaining equipment is expected to be sold for Kuwaiti dinar (KWD) 5,000.

   Working capital. The investment in working capital is KWD 2,000. There are no changes in working capital until the end of the project when the full amount is to be recovered.

   Units, price, and costs. The firm will produce 200 units of a product annually. Its selling price is expected to be KWD 50 per unit, and the direct expense per unit is expected to be KWD 20. Indirect expenses are expected to be KWD 2,000.

   Taxes and miscellaneous. Kuwait taxes on income and capital gains are 30 percent. There are no additional withholding taxes. All cash flows are repatriated when generated, and there are no additional U.S. taxes. Parity conditions are assumed to hold between Kuwait and the United States. The relevant inflation indexes indicate a rate of 4 percent for the United States and 10 percent for Kuwait. Spot KWDUSD equals 3.2. The firm's domestic (USD) WACC is 10 percent.

   a. Calculate cash flows in KWD.

   b. Using parity conditions, determine the future path of KWDUSD.

   c. Based on the preceding information, determine annual cash flows in USD, and calculate the NPV.

   d. Assuming that Kuwaiti inflation has no effect on the project cash flows in KWD, calculate the break-even depreciation in KWD. Assuming the USD inflation is unchanged, what is the KWD inflation rate consistent with this break-even depreciation?

10. **Expropriation and Project NPV.** Redy Tody, an Indian-based pharmaceutical firm, is considering a project in Canada. The following table lists foreign currency (CAD) cash flows. The CAD is currently trading at CADINR equals 30. Assume that future spot rates are equal to the current spot rate. The WACC of the firm is 16 percent.

Year	Cash Flows (CAD)
0	−120,000
1–3	40,000
4	90,000

   a. Calculate the project cash flows in INR, and determine the NPV.

   b. If the year 4 cash flows contain a terminal/salvage value of assets of CAD 50,000 and if there is a 15 percent probability of expropriation, calculate the project NPV.

11. **Break-Even Expropriation Probability.** Brunello, an Italian firm, is considering a project in Pakistan. The following table lists Pakistani rupee (PKR) cash flows. The PKR is currently trading at PKREUR equals 0.0082. Assume that future spot rates are equal to the current spot rate. The WACC of the firm is 12 percent.

Year	Cash Flows (PKR million)
0	−10
1–4	3
5	8

   a. Calculate the project cash flows in EUR, and determine NPV.

b. If the year 5 cash flow contains a terminal/salvage value of assets of PKR 5 million and if this value is subject to a 30 percent probability of expropriation, what is the project NPV?

c Based on information in (b), assess the break-even probability of expropriation.

12. **Country Risk and Value of Insurance.** Saltex, a U.S.-based firm, is considering a project in Israel. Its exit policy depends on selling its assets to a local firm for Israeli shekel (ILS) 50 million in six years. The firm analyzes the political situation in Israel and assesses a 20 percent probability of not realizing this value because of expropriation or war. The ILS trades for USD 0.25 currently and is not expected to change in value over the next six years. If the firm's USD-based WACC is 13 percent, estimate the value of insurance coverage for country risk.

Extensions

1. **Use of Options in Project Analysis.** A U.S. firm has a three-year project to set up a food processing plant in Argentina. Analysts predict that the Argentinean peso (ARS) will depreciate against the USD by 5 percent a year. The firm duly incorporates this prediction in estimating the project NPV. The firm's CFO, however, is concerned that the resulting project NPV of USD 1.2 million may evaporate if the ARS depreciates more than expected. Based on further analysis, the CFO determines that the break-even rate of ARS depreciation is 8 percent. As long as the ARS depreciates at less than 8 percent, the project remains profitable. The following table shows these critical values. One financial analyst at the firm had the bright idea to buy put options with strike prices set at break-even rates. Spot ARSUSD equals 0.80.

Year	Forecasted Spot (5% depreciation)	Break-Even Spot (8% depreciation)
1	0.76000	0.73600
2	0.72200	0.67712
3	0.68590	0.62295

a. Evaluate the advantages and disadvantages of purchasing puts with strike prices set at break-even rates as recommended by the analyst.

b. What are practical difficulties in implementing this approach? What is your recommendation to the CFO?

c. What are similarities between the use of puts to mitigate currency risk in (a) and the use of country risk insurance?

2. **Country Risk and Value of Insurance.** Shell Oil is considering a project in Nigeria to extract offshore oil. The Nigerian government is offering Shell the possibility to drill in the Bonga deep-sea oil field. Shell has the appropriate capabilities to drill for oil there at depths exceeding 1,000 meters. It finds the Nigerian project very attractive for the cash flows it offers. It assesses the NPV of this five-year project to be EUR 2 billion. The CFO reviews this calculation and deems the analysis to be flawed because the probability of expropriation or loss due to war is not adequately reflected in the NPV. In particular, the CFO notes that the NPV depends heavily on the assumed salvage value of EUR 12 billion. Nigeria has a volatile political situation. The government is highly unstable, and in the past has not shied away from expropriating assets of foreign MNCs. Furthermore, the government is battling with a militant group that appears to be fond of blowing up oil lines. Suppose the probability of losing this salvage value is 25 percent.

a. Estimate the desirability of obtaining country risk insurance that provides 100 percent protection but requires annual premiums of EUR 200 million (paid at the beginning of the year). Assume that annual premiums are required even if the only cash flow of concern to Shell pertains to salvage value. Assume that the discount rate is 10 percent.

b. Estimate the break-even probability of expropriation considering the premiums quoted.

Clover Machines: *Evaluating a Foreign Project*

Recall that Clover already has robust sales in Europe, primarily in the southern countries of Spain, France, and Italy. Because of the growth of eastern economies, including Russia, Clover is interested in pursuing a project in the Czech Republic (CR). In fact, Clover is thinking of using a new strategy for this CR project. Instead of the usual policy of setting up only sales subsidiaries, Clover is envisioning the use of a production and sales subsidiary. CR is known for its engineering prowess and heavy machinery. Clover could set up an assembly line there to service the eastern Europe markets with emphasis on CR and Russia.

The eastern Europe farm equipment market is comparable in size to the Latin American market that Clover is also pursuing. During the past year, the total size of that market exceeded USD 4 billion. No single firm has a market share exceeding 20 percent. Market penetration of farm equipment is low and is expected to increase. Consequently, growth rates for farm equipment are expected at least to double the rate of productivity, which is pegged at 4 percent. The Russian market in particular offers great promise. Although the Russian farm sector has contracted in recent years, recent high output prices have renewed interest in corporate farming. With the average corporate farm in Russia many times larger than the average one in the United States, it is inevitable that demand for machinery will increase.

Clover wishes to initially assemble and sell only one product, a combine with various attachments. Its research shows that there is a market for 2,000 combines annually. Clover expects a 15 percent penetration of this market during the project's life. Clover will export at cost required inputs worth USD 50,000 per unit including transportation. Assembly costs are Czech koruna (CZK) 200,000 per unit. Clover expects to employ several employees at its CR subsidiary covering areas such as assembly oversight, marketing, and accounting. The cost of these employees and other expenses is included in selling, general and administrative (overhead) costs of CZK 20 million a year.

Pricing information is as follows. The market is evenly divided between CR and Russia. Invoicing for both the CR and Russian markets is in CZK. List prices are fixed at CZK 3,000,000. Dealer incentives and discounts are expected to be 10 percent of list.

Capital requirements follow. The initial infrastructure costs are USD 35 million. This includes the setup of an assembly line and other related investments. For tax purposes, this entire amount is depreciated using straight-line (to zero) depreciation over the project life of five years. Because all transactions are conducted on a cash basis, the only working capital item is inventory. Assume an investment of CZK 100 million toward inventory; this investment stays constant and is recovered at the end of five years when the project is completed. The salvage value is expected to be CZK 200 million.

Regarding taxes and discount rate, the CR imposes an income tax of 20 percent. Assume no withholding taxes and no further U.S. taxes. Clover has a USD (domestic) WACC or discount rate of 10 percent.

Please use the following information to translate cash flows into USD for discounting:

- USDCZK spot rate is 25.
- USD and CZK term structure is reflected in the following table. All rates are on an annual compounding basis.

Maturity (years)	USD	CZK
1	2.5%	4.5%
2	3.0%	5.2%
3	3.1%	6.0%
4	3.5%	7.0%
5	4.0%	7.0%

Note: These are yields on zero-coupon treasury instruments.

In your analysis, please address the following:

1. Without a numerical analysis, does this appear to be a reasonable project for Clover? Evaluate its strategy and the market scenario.

2. Using information provided in the case, produce forward estimates of CZKUSD (years 1–5). What theory did you use to produce these forecasts? What are this theory's limitations in this particular setting?

3. What are project cash flows? Convert all CZK cash flows into USD. Calculate the project NPV in USD. Should Clover pursue this project?

4. Conduct sensitivity analyses based on two key inputs: market share and list price. Calculate break-even points.

5. The case assumes a market share of 15 percent. Assume that the standard deviation of the market share is 4 percent. Evaluate project risk.

CHAPTER NINE

Advanced Capital Budgeting

Ireland—also known as the Celtic Tiger—not only has low corporate taxes but also vigorously offers tax breaks and other incentives to high-tech industries. How do MNC managers evaluate projects when offered an asymmetric situation between their home countries and foreign countries such as Ireland? How do capital budgeting methods incorporate home versus foreign country differences in taxes, regulations, and other factors? In the previous chapter, we focused on two key issues: the analysis of foreign currency cash flows and the incorporation of country risk in project value. Here we focus on advanced capital budgeting issues such as differential taxes, blocked currencies, foreign financing subsidies, and international parity breakdown. These factors create asymmetries between parents and subsidiaries with respect to cash flows as well as cost of capital. How do MNC managers reconcile and manage these differences?

We also tackle another complex issue in capital budgeting: project flexibility. We previously discussed that projects in foreign countries contain various risks such as currency, political, demand, inflation, and regulatory risk. While standard finance theory tells us that risk destroys value, newer theory takes a proactive view and suggests that risk can actually be exploited to add value to corporations. The key is to design projects with flexible parameters. For example, when a global consumer products firm invests in a country with a volatile demand and risky currency, it can design flexible production and marketing strategies to respond to market changes. Project flexibility creates real options for firms. In this chapter, we show ways to define and value real options embedded in international projects.

Specifically, in this chapter, we discuss:

- The scenarios under which the parent and subsidiary have different views of the project's cash flows or cost of capital.
- How a decision maker can analyze these asymmetries and calculate the true value of projects.
- How asymmetries influence corporate strategies of entry and exit in foreign projects.
- The various types of real options embedded in international projects.
- How to understand the various parameters of real options such as underlying asset, maturity, volatility, and strike price.
- A simple way to value real options using probabilities of option exercise. A more advanced method using option pricing theory is detailed in Appendix 9B.

9.1 Parent versus Subsidiary Asymmetry: Main Reasons

MNC projects may be analyzed at either the subsidiary or the parent level. Sometimes the two analyses provide dissimilar estimates of the project net present value (NPV). We refer to such a situation as the *parent-subsidiary asymmetry*. In this section, we explore parent-subsidiary asymmetries related to cash flows.

Why would cash flows to a parent differ from cash flows to a subsidiary? Consider the case of a project undertaken by a 100 percent owned subsidiary of an MNC in a foreign country. Three reasons can cause cash flow asymmetries to occur:

1. The parent and subsidiary may have different taxes.
2. The subsidiary may not be able to immediately repatriate the cash flows it generates.
3. The subsidiary obtains local financing to partially or fully fund the project. The cost of financing deviates from parity conditions.

We discuss these asymmetries in detail.[1]

taxes
An MNC parent usually pays additional *taxes* on cash flows derived from a subsidiary, *decreasing* project NPV.

• **Taxes.** Typical capital budgeting practices require the estimation of after-tax project cash flows. However, MNCs potentially are taxed at three levels. First, the foreign country taxes the subsidiary' earnings. Second, when after-tax subsidiary earnings are repatriated to the parent, the foreign country may impose another tax such as the withholding tax. Third, the remittance to the parent triggers remittance taxes by the parent country. Thus, after-tax cash flows at the subsidiary level often overestimate true after-tax cash flows to the parent. In recent years, various tax treaties between countries have addressed the taxation issue to avoid double taxation of corporate income. This is achieved by allowing the parent to use taxes paid by its subsidiary as a **foreign tax credit (FTC)**. Nevertheless, because national corporate tax rates differ, after-tax cash flows of the parent and the subsidiary may differ.

EXAMPLE 9.1

MNCs sometimes go to extraordinary lengths to save on taxes. And why shouldn't they? Taxes are higher than payroll expenses for many firms. In a celebrated case in the 2000s, Microsoft created two subsidiaries in Ireland called Flat Island and Round Island, respectively. It funneled its European sales through these corporations and shielded itself from high European taxes. Analysts estimate that Microsoft saved hundreds of millions of USD each year because of this scheme. An interesting side result is that Microsoft, despite having almost no employees in Ireland, was the Emerald Isle's largest taxpayer at one point of time!

---

remittances
Remittances from subsidiaries to MNC parents may be held back, *decreasing* project NPV.

• **Remittance constraints.** Restrictions on **remittances** (cash flows from subsidiaries) represent the second reason for asymmetry in cash flows. Such restrictions alter the timing as well as the amount of cash remitted to the parent. For example, consider the scenario in which the host country allows repatriation of profits only after a period of five years. Assuming that the blocked funds earn no interest, the sum of the cash flows to the parent will remain unchanged, but the value will decrease because of the delay in receiving cash. Even if the cash were to be deposited in interest-bearing accounts, the parent often experiences a loss in value because such interest is typically lower than the return the firm can normally obtain with its funds.

EXAMPLE 9.2

Remittance constraints are common in controlled economies. For example, in China, the agency State Administration of Foreign Exchange administers foreign exchange controls. Nontrade-related outward bound remittances are closely regulated.

---

financing subsidies
In an international finance setting, *financing subsidy* refers to cash flows remitted by subsidiaries to MNC parents.

• **Local financing.** MNCs may obtain local financing for various reasons including low cost, mitigation of currency risk, and mitigation of expropriation risk. Normal rules of capital budgeting allow considering only operating and investing flows when calculating the project NPV; financing flows are ignored because the discount rate captures the effects of such flows. But local financing may be at rates that deviate from parity either because parity conditions do not hold or because special deals are offered to the firm. A common approach to handle these situations is to deviate from normal capital budgeting practice and to include the NPV of financing flows in the project NPV. If there are any financing subsidies, for

---

[1] An additional tax-related issue concerns the effect of inflation on the depreciation tax shield. This issue is explained in Appendix 9C.

instance, their values would be added to the project NPV to provide a more accurate picture of project value.

EXAMPLE 9.3   When ThyssenKrupp, the German steel producer, wanted to set up a plant in the United States, it went shopping for tax breaks. Louisiana was initially the frontrunner; its governor, Kathleen Blanco, waged a public campaign to offer USD 300 million of tax and other subsidies. Alabama upped the ante and offered subsidies of more than USD 400 million; among other items, it set up tax-free financing (investors get tax breaks and, hence, lend money less expensively to the corporation) under the Gulf Opportunity Zone program. In 2008, ThyssenKrupp started constructing a state-of-the-art USD 3.7 billion stainless steel-processing facility in Mobile, Alabama.

For all three problems concerning cash flow asymmetry—taxes, remittance constraints, and local financing—the solution involves calculating cash flows from the perspective of the parent, not the subsidiary. For example, with tax asymmetry, managers should focus on the after-tax cash flows to the parent; depending on the countries involved, the parent may have at the subsidiary level single taxation, double taxation, or taxation plus incremental taxation at the parent level. Regardless of the technicalities of the tax laws, the fact remains that we need to assess the cash flows the parent can obtain. Similarly, with restricted remittances, managers should focus on the timing and amount of cash flows actually remitted to the parent. Finally, with local financing, managers should consider normal project cash flows as well as flows related to local financing.

Cash flow estimates may also differ for the parent and the subsidiary because of informational asymmetries: the parent and the subsidiary may have differences of opinion about cash flow components (e.g., unit sales, unit price, cost per unit). For example, estimates at the subsidiary level could be higher because of unrealistic optimism regarding demand for the firm's products. Differences may also occur because one of the entities may have superior forecasting abilities. Ideally, the corporate capital budgeting process should consider these issues and reconcile cash flow estimates. A serious problem, however, is positive bias at the subsidiary level: Local managers may "tweak" numbers to encourage adoption of projects. Requester bias is a well-known problem in capital budgeting and is perhaps exacerbated in the global context because of distance. As with most agency problems, the solution lies in using incentive contracts and efficient monitoring mechanisms.

Example of Cash Flow Asymmetry: Taxes

The tax and other parent-subsidiary asymmetries produce the following condition (CF represents cash flow):

$$\text{Parent-level CF} \neq \text{Subsidiary-level CF}$$

No Tax Treaty Scenario

Recall the three types of taxes on MNCs: foreign corporate and withholding as well as home country corporate taxes. Ignoring withholding taxes for the moment, we focus on home and foreign country corporate taxes labeled as T and T^*, respectively. If the two countries involved have no tax treaty, then:

$$\text{Subsidiary-level CF} = \text{Taxable CF} \times (1 - T^*)$$

$$\text{Parent-level CF} = \text{Taxable CF} \times (1 - T^*) \times (1 - T)$$

MNC parents pay double taxes in this scenario and obtain lower cash flows than subsidiaries.

EXAMPLE 9.4

An MNC generates income of 100 units of a foreign currency. The foreign tax rate is 20 percent, and the home tax rate is 35 percent. Assume no withholding taxes and that the two countries do not have a tax treaty. Calculate after-tax cash flow and the effective tax rate for the parent.

Solution:

$$\text{Parent-level CF} = \text{Taxable CF} \times (1 - T^*) \times (1 - T)$$
$$= 100 \times (1 - 20\%) \times (1 - 35\%)$$
$$= 52$$

Note: The terms $\times (1 - T^*)$ and $(1 - T)$ reflect what is left after having paid the respective taxes. The effective tax rate—the difference between pre- and after-tax cash flows is 48 percent.

Tax Treaty Scenario

Double taxation is eliminated by tax treaties. If $T < T^*$, the foreign tax credit is higher than home taxes, so the MNC does not face additional home taxes. If $T > T^*$, the foreign tax credit falls short, and the MNC has home taxes in addition to foreign taxes paid by its subsidiary; the total of foreign and home taxes paid in this scenario equals taxable income times the home tax rate. The following equation concisely depicts these two scenarios:

$$\text{Subsidiary-level CF} = \text{Taxable CF} \times (1 - T^*)$$
$$\text{Parent-level CF} = Minimum\{\text{Taxable CF} \times (1 - T^*), \text{Taxable CF} \times (1 - T)\}$$

The following is an example of cash flow and NPV calculations in the presence of a tax treaty and where $T > T^*$.

EXAMPLE 9.5

Eastland, a U.S.-based MNC, invests USD 14 million in a project in Singapore. At a spot rate using Singapore dollars (SGD) in terms of USD of USDSGD = 1.7, this investment equals SGD 23.8 million. This is a four-year project generating revenues of SGD 15 million during the first year and increasing at 25 percent thereafter. Direct expenses are assumed to be 40 percent of revenues, and fixed costs are SGD 3 million. The initial investment is depreciated straight line to zero for tax purposes. The salvage value is assumed to be SGD 500,000. The corporate income tax rates in Singapore and the United States are 25 percent and 35 percent, respectively; a tax treaty allows Singapore taxes to be used as a foreign tax credit. The Singapore subsidiary estimates a discount rate of 15 percent. Calculate cash flows (CF) and NPV from the subsidiary and MNC perspectives.

Solution: See below (values generated by spreadsheet and rounded for display).

Eastland's Singapore Project: Tax Asymmetry

	$t = 0$	$t = 1$	$t = 2$	$t = 3$	$t = 4$
A. Subsidiary Perspective (SGD 000s)					
Investment CF					
1 Capital expenditure	23,800				
2 Salvage					500
3 Taxes on salvage = 2 × 25%					125
4 Investment CF = −1 + 2 − 3	−23,800	0	0	0	375
Operating CF					
5 Revenues (g = 25%)		15,000	18,750	23,438	29,297
6 Direct expenses = 5 × 40%		6,000	7,500	9,375	11,719
7 Fixed costs		3,000	3,000	3,000	3,000
8 Depreciation		5,950	5,950	5,950	5,950
9 Pretax income		50	2,300	5,113	8,628
10 Taxes = 9 × 25%		13	575	1,278	2,157
11 Net operating profit after tax (NOPAT)		38	1,725	3,834	6,471
12 Operating CF = 11 + 8		5,988	7,675	9,784	12,421
13 CF = 4 + 12	−23,800	5,988	7,675	9,784	12,796
Net present value (NPV) at 15%	960				

(Continued)

		$t = 0$	$t = 1$	$t = 2$	$t = 3$	$t = 4$
B. Parent Perspective (SGD 000s)						
14	CF repatriated = 13	−23,800	5,988	7,675	9,784	12,796
15	Taxable income = 2 + 9		50	2,300	5,113	9,128
16	U.S. taxes (35%)		18	805	1,789	3,195
17	Foreign tax credit = 3 + 10		13	575	1,278	2,282
18	U.S. tax payment = 16 − 17		5	230	511	913
19	CF = 14 − 18	−23,800	5,983	7,445	9,273	11,883
	NPV at 15%	−76				

Notes:

- The procedure for calculating cash flows is explained in Chapter 8. Total CF equals operating CF plus investment CF.
- At the subsidiary level, the parent pays 25 percent taxes. After-tax CF is repatriated to the U.S. parent, triggering additional U.S. taxes. Taxes paid in Singapore are considered to be a foreign tax credit, thereby offsetting U.S. tax liabilities. The tax treaty between the United States and Singapore enables this system. (For a discussion of tax treaties, see Chapter 14.)

Discussion: At the SGD discount rate of 15 percent, the subsidiary cash flows produce a NPV of SGD 960 (all values are 000s). Based on this estimate, the project should be adopted. However, we arrive at a different conclusion if we scrutinize this project from the parent's perspective. The NPV is negative SGD 76; therefore, the project should be rejected. We now discuss the reason for this asymmetry in detail.

The parent pays additional taxes in the United States. In the first year, for example, the firm pays taxes of SGD 5 in the United States.[2] The additional U.S. tax results from the higher tax rate of 35 percent in the United States. For example, in year 1:

Additional U.S. taxes for year 1 = Taxable income $\times$ (35% − 25%) = 50 $\times$ 10% = 5.

We can calculate the NPV of additional taxes as:

$$\text{NPV of additional taxes} = -\frac{5}{(1 + 15\%)^1} - \frac{230}{(1 + 15\%)^2} - \frac{511}{(1 + 15\%)^3} - \frac{913}{(1 + 15\%)^4}$$

$$= -\text{SGD } 1,036$$

Because cash flows repatriated minus additional U.S. taxes equals cash flows realized by the U.S. parent,

NPV to parent = NPV to subsidiary + NPV of additional taxes

= SGD 960 − SGD 1,036

= −SGD 76

The parent rejects the proposed project.

Example of Cash Flow Asymmetry: Restricted Remittances

Restrictions on subsidiaries' remittances to parents lead to blocked currencies and impose opportunity and other costs on MNCs. Because of local regulations, a foreign subsidiary may be unable to repatriate cash flows to the MNC parent. These cash flows are usually deposited in local banks and earn below market rates of interest. Potentially multiple concerns from the MNC perspective include:

- Earning below market rates of interest.
- Holding cash amounts in a weakening currency.
- Having idle cash when the firm needs financing for other projects.
- Inducing a lack of discipline in local managers (agency costs).

We next develop an example that focuses on the first issue identified (earning below market interest).

---

[2] In reality, U.S. taxes are paid in USD but are the equivalent to SGD 5 at the currency rate in effect at the time of the Singapore tax payment. For our calculations, it is convenient to compile all cash flows including taxes in SGD, so we make no USD conversion for U.S. taxes.

EXAMPLE 9.6

Lancer, a U.S. MNC, is considering an investment in India to set up a software center. The initial investment is USD 1,000. At the spot rate for the Indian rupee (INR) of INR 43, this initial investment equals INR 43,000. The project is expected to generate incremental after-tax cash flows of INR 30,000 a year for five years. The investment's after-tax salvage value is INR 20,000. Projects of this nature tend to be discounted at 18 percent in India. Finally, assume that, because of governmental restrictions, the earnings from the project cannot be repatriated until the conclusion of the project; the blocked funds are invested locally in INR-denominated Indian bank accounts to yield 5 percent. Estimate NPV from the perspective of the parent and the subsidiary.

Solution: See below.

Lancer's Indian Project NPV: Blocked Currency Effects

		t = 0	t = 1	t = 2	t = 3	t = 4	t = 5
A. Subsidiary Perspective							
1	Capital expenditure	43,000					
2	Salvage						20,000
3	Operating CF		30,000	30,000	30,000	30,000	30,000
4	CF	−43,000	30,000	30,000	30,000	30,000	50,000
	NPV at 18%	59,557					
B. Parent Perspective							
5	Local bank account (rate = 5%)		30,000	61,500	94,575	129,304	185,769
6	Repatriation						185,769
7	CF to MNC	−43,000					185,769
	NPV at 18%	38,201					
C. Direct Estimate of Blocked Currency Effects							
8	CF blocked		−30,000	−30,000	−30,000	−30,000	
9	CF repaid						135,769
	NPV at 18%	−21,356					

Discussion: NPVs from the subsidiary and parent perspectives are both positive. However, the two entities value the project differently because of blocked currency effects. The subsidiary views annual amounts of INR 30,000 as essential components of project cash flows (along with capital expenditure and salvage). Instead, the parent, because it cannot access these flows, considers only the aggregate cash flow at the end of the project (INR 185,769) as the benefit for investing INR 43,000.

The effect of blocked currencies can be calculated by comparing the NPVs derived from the parent and subsidiary perspectives. Alternatively, a manager can directly calculate this value as follows (also see panel C in the above table):

$$\text{NPV of blocked currency} = -\frac{30{,}000}{1.18^1} - \frac{30{,}000}{1.18^2} - \frac{30{,}000}{1.18^3} - \frac{30{,}000}{1.18^4} + \frac{135{,}769}{1.18^5}$$

$$= -21{,}356$$

Thus, from the parent's perspective, blocked funds reduce value by INR 21,356.[3]

NPV to parent = NPV to subsidiary + NPV of blocked currency

= INR 59,557 − INR 21,356

= INR 38,201

---

[3] Some may view the risk of blocked currencies as lower than the risk of other cash flows (revenues, etc.) and argue for a lower discount rate. There is one caveat, however. The currency amounts blocked are not known with certainty and derive from other cash flows such as revenues, so the risk of blocked currencies and the risk of these other cash flows arguably are equivalent. In this text, therefore, we use the WACC to also determine the NPV of blocked currency.

MNCs encounter the blocked currency problem to varying degrees in almost all countries. For example, in China, subsidiaries are generally allowed to repatriate cash flows only once a year and that only after jumping through some bureaucratic hoops. Although this situation is not as severe as the one depicted in the preceding example, when large sums of money are involved, the impact can be significant. For this reason, MNCs seek ways to offset subsidiary operating cash flows against recurring capital expenditure. This offset works, however, only during a project's growth phase. Blocked currency effects in cash cow projects cannot be mitigated in this manner.

Example of Cash Flow Asymmetry: Local Financing

Under parity conditions (or, equivalently, efficient markets without cross-border constraints on capital flow), the location of financing should not impact the project NPV. Whether a firm obtains local financing or home country financing should be irrelevant to project valuation. In a later section, we explore how parity breakdown can result in parent-subsidiary asymmetry. In this section, we assume that parity holds but that local financing contains a subsidy. Next we develop an example explaining how to value projects in the presence of local financing subsidies; we disregard any currency-related effects in this example to solely focus on the subsidy.

EXAMPLE 9.7

Assume that Tokay, a U.S.-based MNC, is considering a five-year project in Hungary with an initial investment of USD 5,000 and annual after-tax cash flows of USD 2,000. There is no salvage value. The appropriate discount rate is 15 percent. The Hungarian government is providing loan guarantees that enable the firm to obtain financing of USD 3,000 at a rate of 6 percent instead of the usual 9 percent. Calculate the NPV of the financing subsidy as well as the project NPV.

Solution: See below.

Tokay's Hungarian Project: Financing Subsidy

		USD					
		$t = 0$	$t = 1$	$t = 2$	$t = 3$	$t = 4$	$t = 5$
	A. Subsidiary Perspective						
1	Capital expenditure	5,000					
2	Operating CF		2,000	2,000	2,000	2,000	2,000
3	CF	−5,000	2,000	2,000	2,000	2,000	2,000
	NPV at 15%	1,704					
	B. Financing Subsidy						
	Financing at 6%						
4	Borrowing	3,000					
5	Interest payments (rate = 6%)		180	180	180	180	180
6	Principal repayment						3,000
7	Financing CF	3,000	−180	−180	−180	−180	−3,180
	NPV at 9%	350					
	C. Parent Perspective: Summary of NPV						
8	NPV to subsidiary	1,704					
	+	+					
9	NPV of subsidy	350					
	=	=					
	NPV to parent	2,054					

Discussion: We determine an NPV to subsidiary of USD 1,704. However, the NPV to the parent is higher because of lower foreign debt financing costs; the below market interest rate of 6 percent adds value to the project.

The value of the subsidy and the NPV to the parent is calculated as follows:

$$\text{NPV of financing subsidy} = +3{,}000 - \sum_{t=1}^{5} \frac{3{,}000 \times 6\%}{(1 + 9\%)^t} - \frac{3{,}000}{(1 + 9\%)^5} = \text{USD } 350$$

NPV to parent = NPV to subsidiary + NPV of financing subsidy

= USD 1,704 + USD 350

= USD 2,054

An alternate way to determine NPV to the parent is to reestimate cash flows by netting outflows related to subsidiary financing. This would indicate that the initial investment is USD 2,000; annual after-tax cash flows are USD 2,000 minus USD 3,000 times 6 percent; final cash flow is reduced by the USD 3,000 repayment. Given the complications in understanding the appropriate discount rate with this approach, we do not recommend it.

Identifying the Various Components of Value

In the previous section, we discussed why the parent view of cash flows may differ from the subsidiary view. In these situations, the recommended solution is to focus solely on cash flows to the parent. This was seen as a foolproof way to handle difficulties such as incremental taxation at the parent level and blocked currencies or partial financing at the subsidiary level. When multiple asymmetries exist, the firm may wish to separate overall NPV into various components as follows:

NPV to parent = NPV to subsidiary + NPV of blocked currency

+ NPV of additional taxes + NPV of financing subsidy . . .

These additional components of value may be viewed as project *side effects*. Thus, the value of a project is:

NPV to parent = NPV to subsidiary + NPV of side effects

Side effects may be financial or operational in nature. We have already discussed financial side effects such as additional remittance taxes, constraints on remittances, and local financing subsidies. There may be other effects such as withholding taxes and tax holidays (i.e., deferment or exemption) offered by the local government. Operational side effects usually involve the effect of the project on sales/performance of related projects; this is typically present in multiproduct firms.

Separating out various side effects has two advantages:

- The firm can optimize the structure of its project and negotiate better contracts. For example, when trying to locate in a foreign country, a firm is able to negotiate better terms from the local government if it is able to separately calculate the NPV of local financing and recognize its marginal impact on overall NPV. With certain types of projects (e.g., manufacturing projects that generate local jobs), the firm may have strong leverage in its negotiations. In the United States, localities (counties and states) routinely provide tax breaks and financial guarantees to lure investments.

- The firm can apply appropriate discount rates to various cash flow streams. Recall that in the blocked currency studied earlier, the NPV of blocked funds was determined using a discount rate of 18 percent. Assuming that blocked funds are kept in bank accounts, a lower discount rate (perhaps the cost of debt, not the overall cost of capital) might be more appropriate. By valuing components separately, a decision maker is able to make such judgments and apply appropriate rates to each component of value.

9.2 Differing Real Cost of Capital for Parent and Subsidiary

Parity conditions imply identical NPV estimates for the subsidiary (foreign cash flows discounted at foreign discount rate) and the parent (foreign cash flows converted to domestic currency and discounted using the domestic discount rate). Parity violations therefore imply an asymmetry in parent-subsidiary value. We explain this issue next.

Parity Violation and Parent Financing

Real-world conditions need not be consistent with the international Fisher effect. For instance, consider the typical situation that MNCs operating in developing countries face. The local cost of capital is often prohibitively high because of underdeveloped capital markets. This has the effect of lowering the subsidiary estimate of NPV. In contrast, because of lower real cost of capital in home markets, the parent estimate of NPV is higher.

When the NPV to the parent is higher than the NPV to the subsidiary due to differing real costs, we may view a foreign investment as containing two value components:

- NPV from investments in value-producing assets.
- NPV from arbitrage profits in a high return currency.

In other words, the project NPV arises from real as well as financial components. The following example explains this.

EXAMPLE 9.8

Let's revisit the Lancer example from the section Example of Cash Flow Asymmetry: Restricted Remittances. The local currency (INR) cash flows follow:

Lancer's Indian Project NPV

	t = 0	t = 1	t = 2	t = 3	t = 4	t = 5
CF (INR)	−43,000	30,000	30,000	30,000	30,000	50,000

The INR (subsidiary level) cost of capital is 18 percent. Assume the following additional information:

- The firm's home (USD) cost of capital (WACC) is 12 percent.
- The U.S. and Indian inflation rates are 2 percent and 5 percent, respectively.

Using these inputs, calculate the (revised) project NPV and the value gained because of parent financing.

Solution: With these inputs, one quickly notes that parity conditions do not hold. This happens because the differential in the cost of capital (18% − 12% = 6%) is much higher than the inflation rate differential (5% − 2% = 3%). If parity conditions hold, the Indian cost of capital should equal:

$$WACC^* = (1 + 12\%) \times \frac{(1 + 5\%)}{(1 + 2\%)} - 1 = 15.294\% < 18\%$$

We apply the discount rate of 15.294 percent to calculate NPV to the parent. See below.

Lancer's Indian Project NPV: Cost of Capital Asymmetry

	t = 0	t = 1	t = 2	t = 3	t = 4	t = 5
A. Subsidiary Perspective						
CF	−43,000	30,000	30,000	30,000	30,000	50,000
NPV at 18%	59,557					
B. Parent Perspective						
CF	−43,000	30,000	30,000	30,000	30,000	50,000
NPV at 15.294%	66,686					
C. NPV of Parent Financing						
NPV to parent	66,686					
−	−					
NPV to subsidiary	59,557					
=	=					
NPV of parent financing	7,129					

Discussion: Because the MNC faces a lower cost of capital, the investment in India generates value partly as a currency investment above and beyond the project's fundamentals. This additional value of INR 7,129 may also be viewed as value generated by currency arbitrage involving inexpensive borrowing in the United States and lending in India. We discuss this in Appendix 9A.

9.3 Managerial Response to Value Differences between Parents and Subsidiaries

We know that value differences can result from cash flow or cost-of-capital asymmetries. These differences in NPV trouble decision makers, especially when one of the two parties views the project as an NPV < 0 project. In this section, we consider how firms respond to such value differences. The overall message is that firms should not focus solely on NPV. The overall business environment and conditions in financial markets are additional inputs in project analysis. Together, these inputs allow firms to develop strategies regarding project search, partner search, and project exit/entry.

Scenario I: NPV > 0 for parent and NPV < 0 for subsidiary. Ideally, a project should have a positive NPV from the perspective of both the parent and the subsidiary. But what if a project has a positive NPV only from the parent's perspective? Although this project can potentially add to its value, the firm may be wise to consider the following:

- Do the cash flow computations ensure consistency of assumptions between the parent and the subsidiary? If the subsidiary uses more conservative or pessimistic assumptions, should the parent consider using the same?

- Are the parity conditions violated? Comparing the cost of capital differential with the inflation differential can reveal parity violations. One possibility is that the subsidiary WACC is higher than expected because of parity violations; this would explain the lower NPV to the subsidiary. In this case, is it possible for the firm to obtain similar or higher value merely by investing in financial assets?

- If foreign rates (interest rates, WACC) are higher than parity-indicated rates, should the firm refrain from obtaining local financing?

- If the subsidiary assessment of NPV is negative, are there other projects with a positive NPV at the subsidiary level? Market equilibrium would be consistent with better projects being available for the MNC, affording the chance for even higher NPV.

- Are differences in the cost of capital attributable to differences in country risk? In this case, has the parent made adequate adjustments to cash flows? For instance, is the possibility of expropriation reflected in expected cash flows?

A likely scenario encountered by MNCs in developing countries is higher than parity-indicated WACC. Therefore, a foreign project may be considered equivalent to an investment in real assets as well as an investment in financial assets.

Scenario II: NPV < 0 for parent and NPV > 0 for subsidiary. Next let's consider the situation in which project NPV is positive at the subsidiary level but negative at the parent level. In general, firms should shun such opportunities. This situation could occur when the foreign discount rate is lower than that indicated by parity conditions. The MNC would be incurring currency-related losses in such projects. Exceptions should be made only when the MNC can monetize the higher subsidiary-level NPV by selling it to a third party. Mechanisms for selling off the subsidiary may include:

- **The sale of assets to a third party.** Given the fact that the NPV at the subsidiary level is positive, it is likely that local parties are interested.

- **A spin-off that creates a new public firm.** Local investors might find the shares of the spin-off attractive.

9.4 International Projects and Real Options

real options
An MNC creates *real options*—to alter scale, to abandon, to grow, to alter inputs—by structuring its operations in a *flexible* manner.

Corporate projects, especially those that are cross-border, are rarely static. Over time, decisions on the continuation of projects or their modification are required. The more flexible the project, the higher the number and greater the scope of future decisions. Project flexibility may be defined as the ability to fine tune a project's parameters. This ability to change project parameters creates real options.

Traditional capital budgeting approaches overlook real options and undervalue most international projects. In fact, many international projects, especially ones that involve entry into a country, would appear to be money-losing projects by traditional metrics. Consider the move by many MNCs to invest in China in the 1990s. It is not clear whether many of these projects made money for their respective parents during their initial years. But the opportunity this large nation offers may be thought of as a real option.

Overview of Real Options

Real options come in many flavors. Four options especially important in international projects are presented next.

Option to Alter Operating Scale

The **option to alter operating scale** allows the firm to change the project's scale. Projects can be scaled up or down. For instance, if demand for the firm's products decreases, the project can be scaled down; in extreme cases, it can even be abandoned. When establishing production facilities abroad, for example, firms such as Dell Computer Corporation create excess capacity to scale up production when demand increases. Similarly, firms may use operating strategies such as outsourcing components and temporary labor to quickly scale down operations when market conditions deteriorate.

EXAMPLE 9.9	The U.S. market share of leading Italian pasta maker Barilla has grown in recent years. In 1998, Barilla set up a U.S. subsidiary and built a plant in Ames, Iowa. With a foot in the door and as consumer demand picked up, Barilla set up a new plant near Rochester, New York, with an annual capacity of 100,000 tons. In this example, the option to expand was not enabled by excess capacity in its Ames plant but by its organization (or capabilities) in the United States that allowed it to find another location for a second plant. Barilla also set up the new plant in Rochester in such a way that it could be upgraded to a higher capacity.

Option to Abandon

The **option to abandon** is available to firms if they can set up projects in such a way that it is possible to abandon them (if conditions so dictate) and realize salvage value. MNCs, for instance, seek countries with flexible labor laws from which a quick exit is possible. This is often cited as one reason that MNCs prefer to set up manufacturing facilities in Asian countries compared to European countries such as Germany and France where labor laws are more restrictive. A key determinant of this option's value is salvage value. In capital-intensive industries in which substantial salvage value may be realized, the option to abandon is valuable. In contrast, the option may be irrelevant in industries involving higher levels of human capital and correspondingly lower levels of physical capital.

EXAMPLE 9.10	Fiat (Italy) entered into a series of agreements and joint ventures with General Motors (United States) in the late 1990s. Fiat designed a particularly novel exit strategy: As part of its agreement, Fiat obtained put options (written by GM) that allowed Fiat to sell its automobile division to General Motors at a predetermined price. When this appeared likely, in 2005, General Motors paid out nearly USD 2 billion to Fiat to negate the deal.

Option to Grow

The **option to grow** refers to the firm's ability to initiate a project, to learn from it, and to find opportunities for other related investments. Thus, an appliance manufacturer, having invested in a project overseas to manufacture washing machines, can later ponder the possibility of manufacturing ovens. In the international context, complexity of regulations and diversity of consumers form barriers to entry. Once a firm gathers knowledge of this environment, it can profitably pursue other related business opportunities.

EXAMPLE 9.11

Apple Inc. (United States) is a remarkable firm that finds new ways to leverage its product design and customer interface strengths. Following on the heels of the revolutionary iPod, Apple introduced the iPhone in 2007. This is a classic story of an MNC that makes an initial investment in a product (iPod) and based on capabilities gleaned from that project, launches a related but different product (iPhone). It launched both products in most major global markets to resounding success. In 2008, Apple readied its launch of a new product, the iPhone 3G. Thus, by making an initial investment in an entirely new product (iPod), Apple gained expertise and exercised its option to grow by introducing other distinct yet related products.

Option to Alter Inputs

The option to alter inputs is especially relevant to manufacturing projects in which alternative inputs to production can be used. Major automobile manufacturers set up plants in multiple countries and have production costs denominated in a variety of currencies. They can minimize production costs by shifting production to weak currency countries. Other examples of options to alter inputs include the option to shift between various suppliers for components and the ability to shift between alternate energy sources.

EXAMPLE 9.12

BMW, with most of its production in Germany, recently started U.S. production. It might, for instance, allocate the production of 1 million cars between its German and U.S. plants, depending on EURUSD rate. There are opportunities for hundreds of millions of EUR in savings. See the following calculations.

Plant Location	Cost per Unit	Production Strategies	
		Mix I	Mix II
Germany	EUR 20,000	400,000 units	600,000 units
United States	USD 25,000	600,000 units	400,000 units

Scenario	EURUSD	Total Cost (EUR)		Low Cost?
		Mix I	Mix II	
Weak EUR	1.00	23,000,000,000	22,000,000,000	Mix II
Strong EUR	1.50	18,000,000,000	18,666,666,667	Mix I

Note: A sample calculation for the strong EUR and Mix II scenario follows:

$$\text{Total cost (EUR)} = 600{,}000 \times 20{,}000 + (400{,}000 \times 25{,}000)/1.5 = 18{,}666{,}667$$

Valuation of Option to Expand

Earlier we discussed the strategic nature of international projects. Firms often make an initial investment in a foreign country that on a stand-alone basis does not appear valuable. Over time, when they have resolved uncertainty and gained capabilities, the firms make additional investments to capture value. This type of option—known as *option to alter operating scale* or, more simply, the option to expand—is perhaps the most common option in international projects. We explain the steps necessary to analyze this option in global projects.

Option Premium

Firms have the choice to structure investments in such a way that the option to expand is available. For instance, if a firm sets up a production facility in a foreign country to support local sales, it may decide to set up adequate infrastructure for future expansion. This may mean, for example, that it buys a larger parcel of land and constructs a factory with extra square footage. It may also obtain licenses from the local government for large-scale operations, obtain extra power (electricity) facilities, and so on. These extra investments that enable future expansion may be thought of as the *option premium*.

Option Exercise

The firm builds up its infrastructure and commences production and sales. It has many uncertainties to resolve and capabilities to build. Are initial estimates of margins valid? Does demand meet expectations, and is there future demand for more units? Has the subsidiary built up capacity to manage labor and produce quality products on a timely basis? Is the physical infrastructure capable of meeting future needs? Based on positive answers to these questions, the firm may decide to make additional investments and commit to a higher level of production. This step may be thought of as *exercising the option*. Sometimes one overwhelming factor such as a significant rise in the price of the product triggers the option exercise.

Valuation Method

decision tree method
The *decision tree method* is a simple but effective way to value real options in projects.

A simple method for valuing an option to expand is to consider the value from the expansion and the associated probability. The expected value approximates the value of the option that can then be added to the base case project value. This method—also known as the decision tree method—is explained in the following example. See Appendix 9B for the way to apply option pricing theory (Black-Scholes model) directly to value real options.

EXAMPLE 9.13

Sterling Corp. is considering a project in China to manufacture and sell a consumer product. The project life is five years, but a critical juncture arises in two years when Sterling assesses the success of its project and decides whether to increase capacity. Assume that there is a 40 percent chance that Sterling will succeed and exercise the option to expand. Using the information in the table below, decide whether Sterling should proceed with this project. Estimate the project NPV and the NPV of the option to expand. Assume all cash flows are denominated in the Chinese yuan (CNY).

Sterling: Inputs to Value the Option to Expand

Item	Base Case (years 0–5)	Expansion (years 2–5)
Investment life or horizon	5	3
Capital expenditure	200,000	30,000
Salvage value at end of life	100,000	20,000
NWC as % of next year's sales*	30%	30%
Variable cost per unit	1	1
Price per unit	2	2
Overheads per year	4,000	0
Units per year	45,000	25,000
Tax rate (Chinese)	15%	15%
Discount rate	10%	10%
Other taxes	None	None

*NWC refers to net working capital.

Solution:

Step 1. Calculate NPV of base case investment.

Sterling: Base Case NPV

		t = 0	*t* = 1	*t* = 2	*t* = 3	*t* = 4	*t* = 5
Units and NWC							
1	Units (Q)		45,000	45,000	45,000	45,000	45,000
2	Revenues (2Q)		90,000	90,000	90,000	90,000	90,000
3	NWC (30% of next year's revenue)	27,000	27,000	27,000	27,000	27,000	0
Investment CF							
4	Capital expenditure	200,000					
5	Salvage						100,000
6	Taxes on salvage (15%)						15,000
7	Change in NWC	27,000	0	0	0	0	−27000
8	Investment CF	−227,000	0	0	0	0	112,000
Operating CF							
9	Revenues (2Q)		90,000	90,000	90,000	90,000	90,000
10	Direct expenses (1Q)		45,000	45,000	45,000	45,000	45,000

(Continued)

		t = 0	t = 1	t = 2	t = 3	t = 4	t = 5
11	Fixed costs		4,000	4,000	4,000	4,000	4,000
12	Depreciation		40,000	40,000	40,000	40,000	40,000
13	Pretax income		1,000	1,000	1,000	1,000	1,000
14	Taxes (15%)		150	150	150	150	150
15	NOPAT		850	850	850	850	850
16	Operating CF		40,850	40,850	40,850	40,850	40,850
17	CF	−227,000	40,850	40,850	40,850	40,850	152,850
	NPV at 10%	−2,603					

Step 2. Calculate the payoff to the option to expand.

Sterling: Option to Expand Payoff at t = 2

		t = 0	t = 1	t = 2	t = 3	t = 4	t = 5
Units and NWC							
1	Units (Q)				25,000	25,000	25,000
2	Revenues (2Q)		0	0	50,000	50,000	50,000
3	NWC (30% of next year's revenue)	0	0	15,000	15,000	15,000	0
Investment CF							
4	Capital expenditure			30,000			
5	Salvage						20,000
6	Taxes (salvage)						3,000
7	Change in NWC	0	0	15,000	0	0	−15,000
8	Investment CF	0	0	−45,000	0	0	32,000
Operating CF							
9	Revenues (2Q)		0	0	50,000	50,000	50,000
10	Direct expenses (1Q)		0	0	25,000	25,000	25,000
11	Fixed costs		0	0	0	0	0
12	Depreciation				10,000	10,000	10,000
13	Pretax income		0	0	15,000	15,000	15,000
14	Taxes (15%)		0	0	2,250	2,250	2,250
15	NOPAT		0	0	12,750	12,750	12,750
16	Operating CF		0	0	22,750	22,750	22,750
17	CF	0	0	−45,000	22,750	22,750	54,750
	Payoff = NPV at 10%			35,618			

Step 3. Calculate the NPV of option to expand and the project NPV.

Sterling: NPV of Option to Expand and Project NPV

	t = 0	t = 1	t = 2	t = 3	t = 4	t = 5
Option payoff			35,618			
Probability of exercise			40%			
E (payoff)			14,247			
PV (payoff) at 10%	11,775					
Summary						
NPV of option to expand	11,775					
+	+					
NPV of base case	−2,603					
=	=					
Project NPV	9,172					

Discussion: Without the option to expand, the project is not acceptable. Note that the inputs used for the expansion option are not guaranteed. They are available with only a probability of 40 percent. Using option terminology, there is a 40 percent chance that $S > X$ (that is, value exceeds strike price).

EXHIBIT 9.1
**Modeling the Option
to Abandon**

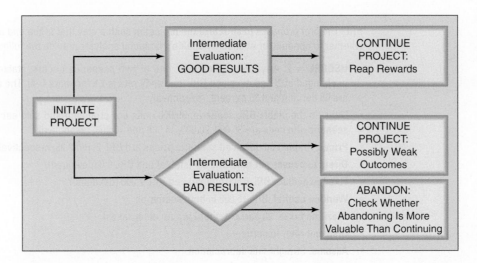

Valuation of Option to Abandon

Foreign corporate investments sometimes do go awry. Firms can prepare for these eventualities by obtaining an option to abandon. It can be obtained in a variety of ways. In jurisdictions without constraints on corporate exit such as the United States, the firm can simply fulfill its existing contracts with various stakeholders and sell remaining assets to third parties. Despite low prices for asset sales (unless assets are mismanaged, asset market value and cash flows are positively correlated) and exit costs, it may be preferable in certain occasions to exit than to continue a money-losing business. Firms can also proactively structure their projects to allow the sale of assets to third parties or joint venture partners.

Option Premium

Firms have the choice to structure investments in such a way that the option to abandon is available. For instance, if a firm sets up a production facility in a foreign country to support local sales, it may (1) use leases for building and equipment rather than outright purchases and, furthermore, insert clauses allowing early return of property or assets, (2) use temporary rather than permanent labor, or (3) cultivate local investors who may purchase assets. The additional expenses (or investments) involved in these steps constitute the option premium.

Option Exercise

Exit involves many explicit and implicit costs including (1) payouts for lease terminations, (2) payouts to terminate employees, and (3) any taxes or regulatory or financing penalties. These expenses and costs may be considered the exercise price of the option. In return, the firm obtains the market value of the liquated assets (if the project really did not go well) or perhaps the market value of the going concern (subsidiary) if it sells the entire business to a third party.

Valuation Method

One can visualize the option to abandon in a decision tree (see Exhibit 9.1). After initiating a project whose cash flows are inadequate, the firm faces the abandonment decision. Should it continue or abandon? To decide, the firm compares cash flows associated with either alternative. The overall project NPV depends on this conditional decision: The probability of abandoning the project is a key determinant of the project NPV. The following example demonstrates this valuation method.

EXAMPLE 9.14

Ronaldo Inc. (the United States) is considering a project in Brazil to manufacture and sell industrial components. The four-year project faces considerable currency and economic uncertainty. The principal concern is that after project initiation, the Brazilian dollar (BRL) will fall because of economic problems. Consequently, the firm faces a double set of problems: (1) poorer operating results in BRL because of lower units and other reasons and (2) lower USD cash flows because of a lower value of

BRL. The firm proposes to structure the project in such a way that at the end of year 1, it will evaluate whether to continue or abandon. Ronaldo's financial analysts provide the following data:

- **USDBRL = 2.** At year-end, however, one of two scenarios occurs: stable BRL (currency rate is unchanged at 2) and devalued BRL (currency rate is 2.5 for years 1–4). The associated probabilities are 65 percent and 35 percent, respectively.
- **Units.** In the stable BRL scenario, 35,000 units are produced and sold each year. In the devalued scenario, the units are 30,000, 20,000, 15,000 and 10,000, respectively.
- **Prices.** Stable and devalued scenario prices are BRL 2 and 2.25, respectively.
- **Direct expenses per unit.** BRL 0.8 (stable) and BRL 0.9 (devalued).
- **Fixed expenses.** BRL 6,500 (stable) and BRL 7,000 (devalued).
- **Working capital.** BRL 15,000 in both scenarios.
- **Brazilian taxes.** 20 percent (there are no other taxes).
- **Discount rate.** 10 percent.
- **Assume.** Straight-line depreciation.

The project's capital expenditure is BRL 80,000. If the firm abandons the project in year 1, it obtains an after-tax amount of BRL 75,000. If the project continues, there is no salvage value at year 4. Estimate the project's NPV.

Solution: Use the following steps to solve the problem:

Step 1. Calculate cash flows and NPV for the stable BRL scenario.
Step 2. Calculate cash flows and NPV for the devalued BRL scenario.
Step 3. Evaluate the decision at $t = 1$: abandon or continue.
Step 4. Calculate the project NPV.

Step 1.

Calculate the project NPV for the stable BRL scenario.

Ronaldo, Project NPV, Stable BRL Scenario

		$t = 0$	$t = 1$	$t = 2$	$t = 3$	$t = 4$
Units and NWC						
1	Units (Q)		35,000	35,000	35,000	35,000
2	Revenues (2Q)		70,000	70,000	70,000	70,000
3	NWC	15,000	15,000	15,000	15,000	0
Investment CF						
4	Capital expenditure	80,000				
5	Salvage					0
6	Taxes (salvage)					0
7	Change in NWC	15,000	0	0	0	−15,000
8	Investment CF	−95,000	0	0	0	15,000
Operating CF						
9	Revenues (2Q)		70,000	70,000	70,000	70,000
10	Direct expenses (.8Q)		28,000	28,000	28,000	28,000
11	Fixed costs		6,500	6,500	6,500	6,500
12	Depreciation		20,000	20,000	20,000	20,000
13	Pretax income		15,500	15,500	15,500	15,500
14	Taxes (20%)		3,100	3,100	3,100	3,100
15	NOPAT		12,400	12,400	12,400	12,400
16	Operating CF		32,400	32,400	32,400	32,400
17	CF (BRL)	−95,000	32,400	32,400	32,400	47,400
18	USDBRL	2	2	2	2	2
19	CF (USD)	−47,500	16,200	16,200	16,200	23,700
	NPV (USD) at 10%	**8,974**				

Step 2.

Calculate the project NPV for the devalued BRL scenario.

Ronaldo, Project NPV, Devalued BRL Scenario

		$t = 0$	$t = 1$	$t = 2$	$t = 3$	$t = 4$
Units and NWC						
1	Units (Q)		30,000	20,000	15,000	10,000
2	Revenues (2.25Q)		67,500	45,000	33,750	22,500
3	NWC	15,000	15,000	15,000	15,000	0
Investment CF						
4	Capital expenditure	80,000				
5	Salvage					0
6	Taxes (salvage)					0
7	Change in NWC	15,000	0	0	0	−15,000
8	Investment CF	−95,000	0	0	0	15,000
Operating CF						
9	Revenues (2.25Q)		67,500	45,000	33,750	22,500
10	Direct expenses (.9Q)		27,000	18,000	13,500	9,000
11	Fixed costs		7,000	7,000	7,000	7,000
12	Depreciation		20,000	20,000	20,000	20,000
13	Pretax income*		13,500	0	−6,750	−13,500
14	Taxes (20%)		2,700	0	−1,350	−2,700
15	NOPAT		10,800	0	−5,400	−10,800
16	Operating CF		30,800	20,000	14,600	9,200
17	CF (BRL)	−95,000	30,800	20,000	14,600	24,200
18	USDBRL	2.0	*2.5*	*2.5*	*2.5*	*2.5*
19	CF (USD)	−47,500	12,320	8,000	5,840	9,680
	NPV (USD) at 10%	**−18,689**				

*Assume that negative pretax income produces immediately available tax credits.

Note: This calculation assumes that Ronaldo does not exercise the option to abandon.

Step 3.

Determine Ronaldo's decision when faced with the abandonment decision at $t = 1$.

Ronaldo, Abandon or Continue Decision at $t = 1$

	$t = 0$	$t = 1$	$t = 2$	$t = 3$	$t = 4$
Abandonment decision $t = 1$					
CF (USD): Continue			8,000	5,840	9,680
PV at $t = 1$ (USD): Continue		19,372			
CF (BRL): Abandon		75,000			
USDBRL		2.5			
CF (USD): Abandon		30,000			

Note: If the project is continued, cash flows are {8,000; 5,840; 9,680}; PV at $t = 1$ is USD 19,372. Compare this PV to the abandonment value of USD 30,000.

Step 4.

Summarize cash flows, use probabilities, and determine overall project NPV.

Ronaldo, Summary and Project NPV

	$t = 0$	$t = 1$	$t = 2$	$t = 3$	$t = 4$
Summary of Cash Flows					
Stable BRL	−47,500	16,200	16,200	16,200	23,700
Devalued BRL	−47,500	42,320			
Summary of NPV	NPV	Prob.			
Stable BRL	8,974	65%			
Devalued BRL	−9,027	35%			
NPV	**2,674**				

Note: Stable BRL cash flows are as in step 1; NPV equals 8,974. Devalued BRL cash flow for year 1 is from step 2; year 2 cash flow equals operating cash flows of 12,320 (step 2) plus abandonment value of 30,000 (step 3); together, this implies an NPV of −9,027. Overall, NPV is a weighted average of NPV for the two scenarios.

Discussion: If a standard NPV analysis is applied, the following calculation would be made:

NPV = 65% × 8,974 + 35% × (−18,689)

With the real options method, the calculation is:

NPV = 65% × 8,974 + 35% × (−9,027)

In the former, the firm follows a fixed strategy and anticipates no future changes in the project. In the latter, the firm follows the flexible strategy of responding appropriately to the environment (that is, abandoning the project when it makes sense to do so).

Volatility and the Valuation of Real Options

Recall the real options example concerning BMW's global production discussed in the section Overview of Real Options. Depending on the EURUSD rate, BMW opportunistically shifts production between its U.S. and German factories. Most global auto firms (e.g., General Motors, Toyota, Honda, and Hyundai) use this method today. A key factor determining the value of such options is currency volatility. Consider two extreme scenarios: (1) EURUSD is constant and (2) EURUSD fluctuates significantly. In scenario (1), BMW would shift production between the factories for reasons unrelated to currency (e.g., increase in demand for a certain model relative to others). In scenario (2), BMW would actively shift production in response to currency changes. Thus, the option comes into play (equivalently, the option is exercised) when currency rates are volatile. The greater the volatility of the EURUSD, the more valuable is the option.

The link between volatility and option value may appear counterintuitive. In traditional asset pricing theories, volatility is consistent with risk and has a negative connotation. With real options, the volatility of the underlying asset encourages flexibility in decision making and can potentially be value enhancing.

Summary

- MNC parents and subsidiaries may view projects differently because of asymmetries in cash flows and cost of capital.
- Cash flow asymmetries are created in three situations. First, parents may face more layers of taxation than subsidiaries. Second, foreign countries may impose restrictions on remittances from subsidiary to parent, thereby changing the timing of cash flows to the parent. Third, local financing may contain subsidies and increase the value of a project to a parent firm.
- Cost of capital asymmetries can occur in situations that violate international parity conditions. This occurs when capital markets are segmented or when temporary changes move markets out of alignment.
- International projects often contain real options. Four types of real options prevalent in international projects are the option to grow, to alter operating scale, to abandon, and to alter inputs.
- Real options may be valued using the decision tree method. A project is mapped out as a series of sequential decisions. To calculate project NPV, one must first understand how the firm will react in the future conditional on its own performance or environmental variables such as currency values. We explain an alternative method using option pricing theory in Appendix 9B.

Questions

1. **Tax Asymmetry.** What are the various taxes an MNC pays? Why would taxes make cash flows at the parent level appear different from cash flows at the subsidiary level?

2. **Blocked Funds.** Evaluate the problem of blocked remittances for MNCs. Explain the prevalence of the problem and the circumstances in which the negative impact is greatest on the MNC.

3. **Responding to Asymmetries.** Consider a situation in which a foreign project is worth *less* from the perspective of the subsidiary than of the parent. Why might this situation occur? What are ways in which the MNC parent can respond to this situation?

4. **Responding to Asymmetries.** Consider a situation in which a foreign project is worth *more* from the perspective of the subsidiary than of the parent. Why might this situation occur? What are ways in which the MNC parent can respond to this situation?

5. **Parity Conditions and Asymmetries.** Consider a situation in which parity does not hold. Explain how this leads to parent-subsidiary asymmetry. Provide one example, and explain how a parent should respond to this situation.

6. **Parity Conditions and Asymmetries.** Kippers, a U.K.-based firm, is interested in pursuing a project in Egypt to assemble industrial equipment for the Middle Eastern market. Kippers has assigned one of its managers, Darla Moffet, to write a proposal working with Casbah, a local partner. Ms. Moffet's initial evaluation—from a subsidiary perspective—indicates a negative NPV for the project. Explain mitigating factors that might make the NPV positive.

7. **Real Options in International Projects.** What are real options? How do they compare to financial options? Is the prevalence of real options greater in international projects? Explain.

8. **Valuation of Real Options.** What are two methods to value real options? Explain the advantages and disadvantages.

9. **Real Options and Market Penetration.** A common method of penetrating a new "geography" is to start a subsidiary with limited objectives. The MNC then gauges progress in its business capability and assesses local business conditions to decide on subsequent steps. What types of real options are available with this strategy? Give examples.

10. **Global Production Strategy.** Leading MNCs—from Toyota Motors to Hewlett Packard—have global production strategies often involving plants in multiple countries. What types of real options are embedded in these strategies? What are "triggers" for exercising these options?

Problems

1. **No Tax Treaty.** Corporate income taxes are 25 percent and 35 percent in Sri Lanka and Germany, respectively. Assume there is no tax treaty between these nations.

   a. What is the effective tax rate for a German firm doing business in Sri Lanka?

   b. What is the effective tax rate for a Sri Lankan firm doing business in Germany?

2. **Tax Treaty.** Corporate income taxes are 20 percent and 40 percent in Singapore and India, respectively. Assume the nations have a tax treaty that eliminates double taxation by allowing a tax credit for foreign taxes.

   a. What is the effective tax rate for a Singaporean firm doing business in India?

   b. What is the effective tax rate for an Indian firm doing business in Singapore?

3. **Foreign Tax Credit.** Tekmex, a U.S.-based MNC, is investigating a project in Pakistan. The cash flow components are as follows (denominated in the local currency, Pakistani rupee, or PKR, thousands):

Year	Earnings before Taxes	Depreciation
1	10,000	5,000
2	20,000	5,000

The initial investment in plant and equipment is PKR 10,000, and the pretax salvage value is PKR 4,000. Because the investment is fully depreciated in year 2, the liquidation of plant and equipment generates taxable capital gains. The Pakistani tax rate on income and capital gains is 20 percent. Assume that cash flows are repatriated as they occur and trigger no withholding taxes. Assume that the tax treaty between the United States and Pakistan allows for taxes in Pakistan to be claimed as a tax credit against U.S. taxes of 30 percent.

a. Calculate after-tax cash flows to the subsidiary and to the parent.

b. If the appropriate discount rate is 12 percent, calculate the NPV to the subsidiary and the parent.

c. What is the NPV of additional U.S. corporate taxes?

4. **Blocked Remittances.** Mylox, a U.S.-based pharmaceutical firm, is proposing a project in a developing country. The project's after-tax cash flows in the foreign currency are as follows:

Year	After-Tax Cash Flows
1	300
2	500
3	800
4	400

The initial investment in the project is USD 200. The spot rate for the foreign currency is USD 0.75. The appropriate discount rate for foreign currency cash flows is 15 percent.

a. Assume that all cash flows are repatriated when earned. What is the project NPV?

b. Next, assume that the foreign government forces the firm to place all cash flows in a bank account earning 2 percent until the end of the project. What is the NPV of the project to the parent and to the subsidiary? What is the NPV of blocked funds?

5. **Blocked Remittances and Parity Conditions.** Xomo, a U.S.-based firm, is proposing a project in a developing country. The project's after-tax cash flows in the foreign currency are as follows:

Year	After-Tax Cash Flows
1	300
2	400

The initial investment in the project is USD 1,000. The spot rate for the foreign currency is USD 2.00. The appropriate discount rate for foreign currency cash flows is 20 percent.

a. Assume that all cash flows are repatriated when earned. What is the project NPV?

b. Next, assume that the foreign government forces the firm to place all cash flows in a bank account earning 4 percent until the end of the project. What is the NPV of the project to the parent and to the subsidiary? What is the NPV of blocked funds?

c. Consider the following additional information. Interest rates in the United States and foreign country (annual compounding) basis are 5 percent and 8 percent, respectively. Assuming that parity conditions hold, estimate domestic currency cash flows and NPV to the parent under the two scenarios, unblocked and blocked. Comment on the NPV obtained in this manner.

6. **Blocked Remittances and Break-Even Probability.** Atherton Corporation, a U.K. firm, is conducting a project in Sri Lanka. Its cash flows over the project life of three years are projected to be as follows in Sri Lankan rupees:

Year	Cash Flow
0	−25 million
1	10 million
2	15 million
3	11 million

Atherton is working with government officials to ensure that funds are not blocked. The firm is not confident, however, that it will succeed in its negotiations. If currencies are blocked, they are deposited in local accounts earning 1 percent and repatriated only at the end of the project. Assume the appropriate cost of capital (for foreign cash flows) is 18 percent. What is the break-even probability of blocked currency?

7. **Financing Subsidy.** Arcos Corporation, a U.S. firm, is trying to fund a project in Mexico. The Mexican government has offered Arcos a loan guarantee that will enable it to borrow MXN 10 million for five years at an annual interest cost of 5 percent. Without this guarantee, Arcos would have paid a rate of 8 percent. What is the NPV of the loan guarantee?

8. **Financing Subsidy.** Needles Corporation, a Dutch MNC, is considering a project in the United States. The initial investment is EUR 35,000. The firm raises 60 percent of this funding in the United States through its subsidiary. This funding is through a term loan at a cost of 7 percent. Needles uses a cost of capital of 16 percent to discount the cash flows of its projects in the United States. This is a five-year project with annual revenues of USD 25,000. Direct expenses are 30 percent, and fixed expenses excluding depreciation are USD 2,000 annually. The spot rate EURUSD equals 1.30. U.S. taxes are 30 percent.

   a. What are the project cash flows from the parent's perspective? What is NPV? Exclude information about local financing in answering this question.

   b. You have additional information that the local financing was obtained at a cost of 7 percent because of certain governmental guarantee programs; otherwise, the interest cost would have been 10 percent. What is the NPV of local financing? What is the project's NPV?

9. **Parity Violation and Parent Financing.** A Canadian MNC is considering a mining project in Brazil with the following cash flows:

Year	Cash Flow (BRL million)
0	−100
1	30
2	55
3	55

The subsidiary-level cost of capital for this project is 20 percent. The subsidiary obtained this rate by conducting a benchmark study of cost of capital for Brazilian firms for similar projects. The firm's CFO notes that this cost is artificially high due to parity violation. In particular, the CFO notes that three-year interest rates in Canadian dollar- (CAD) and BRL-denominated risk-free debt are 4 percent and 10 percent, respectively, and that the company's CAD-denominated WACC is 9 percent.

   a. What is the NPV from the subsidiary's perspective?

   b. What is the NPV from the parent's perspective?

   c. What is the NPV of the parent's financing?

10. **Option to Abandon.** Skyfu, a U.S.-based firm, is interested in setting up a project in the Dominican Republic. The initial investment is Dominican peso (DOP) 10,000 (this and subsequent DOP figures are in thousands). The firm is concerned about business conditions in the country. Recently, the government enacted reforms of the financial sector and reduced a host of business taxes. Skyfu believes that its own chance of success in the project depends on the success of the government's initiatives. If the firm succeeds, it expects cash flows of DOP 20,000 each year for two years. If the firm fails, it expects cash flows of DOP 2,000 each year for two years. The probability of failure is 40 percent. However, if the project is a failure, in year 1, Skyfu has the option to liquidate its capital assets for DOP 4,000. Spot DOPUSD equals 0.023. The USD discount rate is 10 percent.

   a. Draw a decision tree to illustrate the project and estimate the NPV of the project in USD. Also estimate the NPV of the option to abandon in USD. Assume that the exchange rate stays constant.

b. You have the following additional information. Failure of Skyfu (and the government's initiatives) also means a one-time devaluation of the DOP by 25% at $t = 1$. Recalculate NPV in USD for the project as well as for the option to abandon.

11. **Option to Expand.** Slater Corporation, a U.S. firm, is interested in initiating operations in Mexico. It is interested in making an initial investment of USD 40,000 to start an office in Mexico and to distribute one of its products. It estimates that it can generate after-tax cash flows of USD 4,000 a year over the next two years. Slater's biggest fear is the collapse of the Mexican economy because of a global credit crisis. The situation is expected to resolve in two years. If the Mexican economy collapses, Slater's business in Mexico would also collapse and produce zero cash flows after year 2. If the economy survives the global crisis, however, Slater would reap the benefits by obtaining cash flows of USD 4,000 for years 3–10. Slater also plans to set up its Mexican business flexibly to exploit good economic conditions: If the economic situation is resolved satisfactorily, Slater expects to expand its operation to sell a broader range of products. At year 2, after resolving uncertainty, the firm plans an additional investment of USD 25,000 that will produce additional annual cash flows of USD 20,000 during years 3–10. The probability of a crisis in two years is 25 percent. The probability of maintaining the status quo is 75 percent. The appropriate discount rate is 12 percent. Estimate the NPV of initiating operations in Mexico. Also estimate the NPV of the option to expand.

12. **Option to Expand.** Elastic Corporation, a Canadian firm, is evaluating a project in the United States. This project involves the establishment of a lumber mill in Wisconsin to process Canadian timber. The factory expects to service clients in the construction industry. All cash flow figures are in thousands.

Initial Investment. The initial investment is CAD 20,000. The project is over a period of two years. This investment will be depreciated straight line to zero.

Operating Results. The firm expects two equally likely scenarios for the first year of operations. Under the favorable scenario, the firm expects to produce and sell 1,000 units of a product. Under the unfavorable scenario, it expects to produce and sell only 400 units. The selling price is expected to be CAD 20; the variable expense is expected to be CAD 6, and fixed costs excluding depreciation are expected to be CAD 3,000.

Additional Investment. If the firm encounters the favorable scenario during year 1, it could make an investment of CAD 5,000 to enable it to produce and sell a total of 4,000 units (additional units is 3,000) in the second year. The cost parameters remain unchanged with the exception of depreciation. This secondary investment will be totally depreciated in year 2. If the firm chooses not to make the investment in year 1, the results of year 1 will be repeated during year 2.

Discount Rate and Miscellaneous. Assume a discount rate of 10 percent and zero taxes.

a. Estimate the NPV of the project.

b. Estimate the NPV of the option to expand.

Extensions

1. **Withholding Taxes.** An Irish firm is considering the following project in Singapore:

Investment: The project spans four years and requires an investment of SGD 400 (this and other SGD values are in thousands). The investment is depreciated straight line to zero.

Revenues and Expenses. The project's revenues during the four years are as follows: SGD 300, 400, 600, and 400. Direct expenses are 20 percent of revenues and fixed expenses are SGD 60 each year.

Taxes. Singapore corporate taxes are 20 percent. An additional 10 percent withholding tax is imposed on remittances to the parent. Assume the Irish firm pays no taxes in Ireland.

a. Calculate after-tax cash flows to the subsidiary and to the parent.

   b. If the appropriate discount rate for SGD cash flows is 12 percent, calculate the NPV to the subsidiary and the parent.

   c. What is the NPV of withholding taxes?

2. **Option to Switch Production Location.** A leading computer manufacturer sets up two plants in Malaysia and India. The plants have an annual capacity of 5 million units each. The outputs of both plants are sold in global markets, and the firm invoices these computers in USD. However, costs in the Malaysian and Indian plants are denominated in the two local currencies: Malaysian ringgit (MYR) and Indian rupee (INR), respectively. History shows that the correlation between MYRUSD and INRUSD is low or negative. Assume that current manufacturing costs in the two plants are approximately equal, at USD 200 per unit. Assume that the firm is servicing current market needs of 6 million by using both plants at 60 percent capacity. Assume that a cost saving of 10 percent per unit—the difference in the status quo and revised costs if a switch in production location is made—is the trigger that will lead to production shifts between the plants. Study the forecasted currency scenarios and then answer the related questions.

Scenario	Probability	S_{MYR}	S_{INR}
I	20%	−5%	0%
II	40%	6%	−5%
III	40%	5%	7%

   a. Evaluate each scenario and state whether a shift in production will occur.

   b. If the shift occurs, how many units will each plant produce? What savings are realized from the shift?

   c. What is the ex ante (that is, forecasted) expected cost saving in a year? Assume that once a shift in currency rates takes place at the beginning of the year, no further shifts occur for that year.

   d. Can you think of reasons why the firm uses the 10 percent threshold for shifting production? What is the implication of your explanation for your answer in (c)?

   e. Based on the data provided in the scenario table, how would you characterize the correlation between the two currencies? (You may want to perform an actual calculation of the correlation coefficient.)

3. **Multiple Asymmetries.** A U.S. firm, Magenta, is evaluating a project in Sri Lanka that involves the construction and operation of a beachfront resort. The initial investment in the project is USD 500. Magenta projects a construction period of two years followed by a partial occupancy period of three years (cash flows for years 3–5) and a full occupancy period of three years (cash flows for years 6–8). Magenta expects to sell its stake in the venture for Sri Lankan rupee (LKR) 20,000 at the end of eight years. The partial occupancy period is expected to generate annual revenues of LKR 20,000 while incurring direct expenses at the rate of 30 percent and fixed costs of LKR 5,000. The full occupancy period is expected to generate annual revenues of LKR 30,000 while incurring direct expenses at the rate of 25 percent and fixed costs of LKR 8,000. Sri Lankan taxes are 20 percent, and U.S. taxes are 30 percent. A tax treaty between the two countries allows Magenta to use Sri Lankan taxes as a credit against U.S. taxes. You may assume that the investment is depreciated straight line to zero during the six years (3–8) following construction; the LKR trades at LKR 60 per USD; Magenta's WACC (LKR) for the project is 12 percent. For simplicity, assume that the LKR is projected to be unchanged during the project's life.

   a. Calculate the cash flows in LKR to the parent and determine NPV. What is the project NPV in USD? What is the internal rate of return?

   b. Assume that Sri Lanka prohibits the transfer of monies during the life of the project and that the blocked funds are kept in bank accounts earning 2 percent. What is the NPV of blocked funds? Determine your answer in USD terms. (Please disregard effects of potential changes in the timing and amounts of U.S. taxes.)

   c. Suppose Magenta obtains partial financing (say 40 percent of project) in Sri Lanka at a rate of 4 percent. Assume that the market rate for such financing is 8 percent. What is the NPV in USD of this financing subsidy?

   d. Consider the additional information in both (b) and (c). Assume that local regulators allow Magenta to use blocked funds to service the local loan. What is the NPV in USD of savings arising from the offset?

   e. Using your answers from (a)–(d), summarize project NPV in USD.

   f. What are some benefits of obtaining local financing?

Case

Clover Machines: *Advanced Project Analysis*

Recall Clover's initiatives in emerging markets. India is a market of strategic importance to Clover, especially for agricultural machines in the near future and perhaps for constructing them in a few years. Along with other BRIC (Brazil, Russia, and China) countries, India is currently an engine of global growth zipping along at an annual growth rate (GDP) of almost 10 percent while industrialized nations are languishing at rates below 2 percent. An important factor is that, from Clover's perspective, agriculture is the dominant sector in India with 60 percent of its population engaged in some form. India remains a poor country, however, and most of its farmers engage in subsistence agriculture. This is reflected in the fact that agriculture produces only one-fifth of national income. Government officials realize that the situation must change if India is to join the ranks of developed countries. Clover can capitalize on the urgent need for machines to facilitate efficient farming.

One problem Clover faces in penetrating Indian markets—besides obvious ones related to unique local business conditions—is the nature of local demand for farm equipment. Because most farms are small and financial resources are scarce, India has little demand for high-end equipment. Most of the demand is for small and inexpensive tractors, but this demand is growing at exponential rates. Prior to 1990, a total of only 150,000 tractors were sold there each year. In comparison, current year sales are projected at more than 300,000 units. A few local firms—Mahindra & Mahindra (M&M) being a prominent example—specialize in such tractors. Indeed, M&M is a top-5 global producer of tractors and presents formidable competition. Indian tractor producers have great cost advantages especially in low-end products. To counter this competitive threat, Clover plans to introduce innovative machines relying on its experience of servicing its demanding global clients and to produce them inexpensively using Indian labor. Noting that market penetration is lowest in South India and that the city of Chennai already has an excellent infrastructure for automobile production (and a port in case imports of parts or exports of finished goods are desired), Clover develops the following proposal to locate a plant and office in that city. The product and market characteristics follow.

- **Product.** 50 hp tractor with specialized accessories.
- **Potential market.** 300,000 tractors per year initially, increasing at 10 percent annually.
- **Clover's market share.** 10 percent a year for three years, 15 percent for the remaining years.
- **Project life.** 6 years.
- **Price.** INR 800,000 initially, growing at 6 percent a year. Assume sales are at list prices.

The cost structure is as follows. Direct expenses are 40 percent of sales (i.e., gross margins are 60 percent). Overheads are INR 4 billion. The capital investment in (nondepreciable) land (depreciable), plant, and equipment is INR 3 billion and INR 18 billion, respectively. At the end of the project, the land can be sold for INR 5 billion if INR 0.5 billion (tax deductible) can be spent in cleaning up the industrial waste. Salvage value of plant and equipment is INR 8 billion. Working capital needs are a constant INR 8 billion.

Clover faces two levels of taxes: 20 percent corporate income taxes in India and 34 percent corporate income taxes in the United States (allowing for full foreign tax credit because of a tax treaty between the United States and India). Assume that capital transactions (sale of land, plant and equipment) are taxed at ordinary income rates.

All financing is obtained from the parent, whose overall cost of capital (WACC) is 10 percent. The risk-free rates of interest in USD and INR are 5 percent and 9 percent, respectively (annual compounding basis). The USDINR spot is 42.

Brian Bent, Clover's CFO, poses the following questions pertaining to this project:

1. What are subsidiary-level after-tax cash flows? What are NPVs in INR and in USD?

2. What are the parent's after-tax cash flows? What is NPV in USD at the parent's level? Explain the discrepancy between subsidiary- and parent-level NPV.

3. Assume that local financing is available in the amount of INR 10 billion. Market rates would have been 10 percent for this financing, but because of government guarantees and subsidies, Clover pays only 7 percent. What additional value is generated by using this financing opportunity? For simplicity, ignore the tax impact on subsidy value.

4. Based on Appendix 9B, assume that Clover has adequate infrastructure (principally land) for a follow-up project to produce construction machinery. At the moment, Clover faces many uncertainties, which is why it has not yet invested in the construction project. If it is entered into immediately, the project requires a capital expenditure of INR 30 billion and produces a PV of future cash flows of INR 25 billion (NPV is negative). However, if risks are resolved and demand for construction equipment rises, Clover can capitalize quickly. These risk factors have a standard deviation of 30 percent. Assume that Clover has this "real option" in play for a period of four years. What is its value? In words, explain the nature and benefit of this real option. Elaborate on factors that make this real option valuable in the Indian setting.

Appendix 9A

Currency Arbitrage

We can view the issue of less expensive parent financing (differing real cost of capital that results in the firm's cost of capital expressed in the foreign currency being lower than the subsidiary cost of capital; see the section Parity Violation and Parent Financing) through the prism of currency arbitrage. Each project cash flow may be considered the end result of currency arbitrage in which an initial amount had been borrowed at a lower home rate of financing and deposited at a higher foreign rate (recall interest rate arbitrage principles from Chapter 5). Thus, there are as many currency investments as there are cash flows in a project. The sum of the value from these investments equals the NPV of currency arbitrage.

Each currency investment provides a rate of return reflecting the difference between the subsidiary cost of capital ($WACC^S$) and the firm's actual cost of capital for foreign currency cash flows ($WACC^*$). This return—denoted as FX return per currency unit—represents the present value (PV) of arbitrage profit earned per unit of currency invested. It is calculated as:

$$\text{FX return per currency unit} = \left[\frac{(1 + WACC^S)}{(1 + WACC^*)}\right]^t - 1$$

The return is positive when $WACC^S > WACC^*$. Also, this value is in PV terms because of the denominator, which serves the purpose of discounting at $WACC^*$.

The total amount of FX return per investment is:

$$\text{FX return} = \text{Cash flow invested} \times \text{FX return per currency unit}$$
$$= [\text{PV of cash flow @ } WACC^*] \times \text{FX return per currency unit}$$

These values can be summed over multiple investments to produce the NPV of currency arbitrage.

$$\text{NPV of currency arbitrage} = \sum \text{FX return}$$

EXAMPLE 9.15

Considering again the Lancer example (see Example 9.8), the NPV of currency arbitrage of 7,129 arises from a series of currency investments implicit in the project cash flows.

Lancer's Indian Project NPV

	$t = 0$	$t = 1$	$t = 2$	$t = 3$	$t = 4$	$t = 5$
CF (INR)	−43,000	30,000	30,000	30,000	30,000	50,000

Recall that $WACC^* = 15.294\%$, $WACC^S = 18$ percent. Calculate the NPV of currency arbitrage by using the FX return method.

Solution: To demonstrate steps in this method, consider the first cash flow of INR 30,000 at $t = 1$. This results from a currency investment of INR 25,424 (= PV @ 18%). We can apply the equations concerning FX returns as follows:

$$\text{FX return per currency unit} = \left[\frac{(1 + WACC^S)}{(1 + WACC^*)}\right]^t - 1$$
$$= \left[\frac{1 + 18\%}{1 + 15.294\%}\right]^1 - 1$$
$$= 2.347\%$$

$$\text{FX return} = \text{Cash flow invested} \times \text{FX return per currency unit}$$
$$= 25,254 \times 2.347\%$$
$$= 597$$

Repeating this calculation for all five currency investments implicit in this project, we find a total value of INR 7,129.

NPV of Currency Arbitrage

		$t = 0$	$t = 1$	$t = 2$	$t = 3$	$t = 4$	$t = 5$
1	FV of FX investment = Foreign currency CF		30,000	30,000	30,000	30,000	50,000
2	(Implied) FX investment = PV of (1) at 18%		25,424	21,546	18,259	15,474	21,855
3	FX return per currency unit = $(1.18/1.15294)^{t-1}$		2.347%	4.749%	7.208%	9.724%	12.299%
4	FX return = (2) × (3)		597	1,023	1,316	1,505	2,688
5	NPV of currency arbitrage = Sum of (4)	7,129					

Note: The FX return values (597, 1,023, etc.) are already in PV terms, so there is no need for further discounting to calculate the NPV of currency arbitrage.

Appendix 9B

Using Option Pricing Theory to Value Projects

A more rigorous approach to valuing projects with real options explicitly uses option pricing theory. Real options embedded in projects can be viewed as call options or as put options. By identifying the parameters of these options, one can determine value by directly applying option pricing models.

Consider the Black-Scholes call option pricing model:

$$C = SN(d_1) - Xe^{-rt} N(d_2)$$

where

C = Call option value

S = Value of the underlying asset

X = Exercise price

r = Risk-free rate

t = Maturity of the option

σ = Standard deviation of the underlying asset

$$d_1 = \frac{\ln\left(\frac{S}{X}\right) + \left(r + \frac{\sigma^2}{2}\right)t}{\sigma\sqrt{t}}$$

and

$$d_2 = d_1 - \sigma\sqrt{t}$$

To value a real option using Black-Scholes, we need to determine the five inputs identified in the preceding equation. See the following example for a calculation.

EXAMPLE 9.16

Honda Motors sets up a small production facility in India as a prelude to establishing a larger manufacturing operation. Assume that Honda is proposing to review this possibility over the next five years by monitoring the performance of its initial investment. If it succeeds, Honda plans to invest USD 300 million in a new plant. The output of this plant is expected to be 500,000 cars a year, and Honda estimates the present value of net cash flows (excluding the investment) derived to be USD 400 million. Assume that the annual variability (standard deviation) of automobile demand is 20 percent. The interest rate is 6 percent.

Solution:

Using Black-Scholes to Value a Real Option		
S	400	Value of asset
X	300	Investment required
σ	20%	Standard deviation of demand
t	5	Time frame for decision
r	6%	Risk-free interest rate
d_1	1.5377	
d_2	1.0905	
$N(d_1)$	0.9379	
$N(d_2)$	0.8623	
C	**183.54**	

Note: See Chapter 3 for computational details concerning option models.

Discussion: Determination of real option inputs is not an exact science. Considerable judgment is necessary.

- *t* represents the time period during which the firm can exercise the option. In the Honda example, the firm may decide, depending on its prospects, whether to construct a larger plant sometime in the next five years. Hence, $t = 5$.
- *S* represents the present value or benefits acquired by investing in the new plant. We must exclude the investment required for the new plant in this calculation. Using the framework of capital budgeting, *S* equals NPV plus investment. Equivalently, *S* equals the PV of future cash flows.
- *X* is the investment necessary in the new plant.
- σ is the input most difficult to determine. Recall our discussion in the section Volatility and the Valuation of Real Options about volatility and real options. For Honda, we need to assess environmental variables that will trigger the option. As identified in the example's narrative, this variable is market demand. Hence, the standard deviation of market demand is used as an input. But this may be imprecise. Honda's exercise of the real option may depend on other subjective factors such as its ability to resolve operational difficulties in running a plant in India.

The Black-Scholes calculation indicates a project value of USD 183.54 million. How does this differ from a traditional NPV calculation? Note that traditional NPV $= S - X =$ USD 100 million. The extra value of USD 83.54 is the result of the project flexibility Honda has in determining the right time (and conditions) for building the new plant. Black-Scholes incorporates this flexibility; traditional NPV does not.[4]

Appendix 9C

Inflation and the Depreciation Tax Shield

An MNC is considering a foreign project. What happens when inflation estimates for the foreign country change? Generally speaking, changes in inflation should not affect value for the parent. This results from the offsetting effects of inflation and currency values. Normally, project cash flows increase as inflation increases; however, this increase is offset by the higher local currency discount rate or by the lower value of the local currency when converted to the parent currency. If parity conditions hold, these are equally offsetting effects.

In reality, however, inflation does affect project NPV because it does not affect all cash flows equally. For example, inflation has no effect on the depreciation tax shields generated by the firm's investments. Thus, in an inflationary environment, the present values of the tax shields decrease. This happens because the amount of the tax shields does not vary, but the discount rates increase with inflation. This effect of inflation is especially important in a capital-intensive project.

EXAMPLE 9.17

A U.S.-based MNC considers a project in Switzerland involving the production and sale of a product. The product's current price is Swiss franc (CHF) 100; the Swiss inflation rate of 2 percent is expected to raise the product price annually by 2 percent. Expenses also track the inflation rate because they are expected to be 40 percent of revenues. Depreciation, however, is fixed because it is related to the historical cost of the investment. Cash flows in CHF are derived for each year and converted to USD using the purchasing power parity (PPP) forecasted values of CHF. Assume that USD and CHF inflation rates are 3 percent and 2 percent, respectively. The Swiss inflation rate means that revenues and expenses in CHF are affected.

---

[4] Using option terminology, traditional NPV determines project value as equal to Max $(0, S - X)$. This is also referred to as the *intrinsic* or *exercise value of an option*. But the market value of an option includes intrinsic as well as time value. Thus, traditional NPV has a negative bias.

1. Calculate base NPV.
2. Assume CHF inflation increases to 4 percent. Recalculate NPV.

Solution: See below (values generated by spreadsheet and rounded for display).

Inflation and Project NPV

Scenario I: Status Quo

Tax rate	30%				
WACC (USD)	12%				
CHFUSD	0.70				
USD inflation	3%				
CHF inflation	2%				
Price in CHF ($t = 0$)	100				
Expense ratio	40%				

		$t = 0$	$t = 1$	$t = 2$	$t = 3$
Investment CF		−12,000			
Units sold (Q)			100	200	200
Revenues $= Q \times 100 \times 1.02^t$			10,200	20,808	21,224
Expenses (40%)			4,080	8,323	8,490
Depreciation			4,000	4,000	4,000
Taxable income			2,120	8,485	8,734
NOPAT			1,484	5,939	6,114
CF (CHF) = Inv. CF + NOPAT + Depreciation		−12,000	5,484	9,939	10,114
CHFUSD=0.70(1.03/1.02)^t		0.7000	0.7069	0.7138	0.7208
CF (USD)		−8,400	3,876	7,095	7,290
NPV (USD) of project at 12%		**5,906**			
Tax shield of depreciation. (CHF)			1,200	1,200	1,200
USD equivalent of the tax shield of depreciation			848	857	865
NPV of tax shield (USD)		**2,056**			

Scenario II: Increase in CHF Inflation to 4%

		$t = 0$	$t = 1$	$t = 2$	$t = 3$
CHF inflation	4%				
Investment CF		−12,000			
Units sold (Q)			100	200	200
Revenues $= Q \times 100 \times 1.04^t$			10,400	21,632	22,497
Expenses (40%)			4,160	8,653	8,999
Depreciation (no change)			4,000	4,000	4,000
Taxable income			2,240	8,979	9,498
NOPAT			1,568	6,285	6,649
CF (CHF) = Inv. CF + NOPAT + Depreciation		−12,000	5,568	10,285	10,649
CHFUSD = 0.70(1.03/1.04)^t		0.7000	0.6933	0.6866	0.6800
CF (USD)		−8,400	3,860	7,062	7,241
NPV (USD) of project at 12%		5,831			
Decrease in NPV		75			
Tax shield of depreciation (CHF)			1,200	1,200	1,200
USD equivalent of the tax shield of depreciation			832	824	816
NPV of Tax Shield (USD)		1,980			
Decrease in NPV of Tax Shield		76			

Discussion: Note that both revenues and expenses are higher, but depreciation stays constant. The project's NPV is consequently lower. See calculations at the bottom of each panel in the above scenarios that isolate the value of depreciation tax shield. Note that the change in project NPV of 75 is entirely explained by the change in the value of the depreciation tax shield. (There is a small discrepancy due to rounding).

- Tax Factor
- Transfer Pricing
- Reinvoicing Centers
- Fees & Royalties
- Leading & Lagging
- Shifting Liquidity
- Intercompany loans
- Dividends
- Equity Versus Debt

Cashflow - Ch.8
- 203 Int Corp fin.
- CF Manual.

CHAPTER TEN

Long-Term Financing

MNCs such as Vodafone and Nokia need large amounts of capital to conduct their global businesses. These MNCs obtain financing in a variety of ways and tap global as well as domestic capital markets. Global markets are especially attractive because they offer funding denominated in various currencies and, depending on market conditions, global funding can be less costly than domestic funding. This chapter offers an overview of MNC financing with specific details about how these firms obtain equity and debt financing in international markets and how the cost of capital is calculated.

Our emphasis is on global financing issues. Why do U.S. MNCs such as Xerox and IBM issue bonds in Japan? Why do Korean firms such as Samsung and Hyundai list their shares on U.S. and European markets? How do firms from emerging nations such as China and Brazil—which are increasingly active in global mergers and acquisition (M&A) markets—finance their multibillion-dollar acquisitions in the United States and Europe? These and other interesting global issues of financing are discussed.

MNC financing must be considered holistically. MNCs tend to take an integrated look at their operating, financial, and currency risk factors and try to structure the optimal package of financing. While **cost of capital** is a key consideration, other considerations in a financing foray may exist. What are optimal financing methods in light of these multiple considerations? Why are derivatives sometimes used in conjunction with financing? MNCs, for instance, use currency swaps as well as interest rate swaps to restructure and mitigate risks. These are some of the advanced concepts studied in this chapter.

Specific topics covered in this chapter include:

- How MNCs differ from domestic firms in regard to their financing needs and concerns.
- Debt and equity financing procedures and alternatives for MNCs.
- How to calculate cost of debt, cost of equity, and WACC.
- Strategic issues in MNC financing such as mitigation of agency costs and risks such as currency and country risk.
- Integrating derivatives transactions (principally swaps) with financing transactions.
- Financing for joint ventures (JV) and mergers and acquisitions (M&A).
- How non-U.S.-based MNCs can use depository receipts to tap U.S. equity markets.

10.1 Financing MNCs' Activities

MNCs, by virtue of their larger size, greater product and geographical diversity, and organizational knowledge, may approach financing differently than do purely domestic firms. While the general theory of capital structure also applies to MNCs, it is useful to learn why and how the financing of MNCs differs. We identify the advantages and disadvantages that MNCs have in their financing activities.

MNCs Need Continuous Access to Capital Markets

MNCs are larger than purely domestic firms. This implies more opportunities for investments as well as a greater need for capital. Consider global giants such as Boeing, Philips Electronics, and Honda Motors. How do these MNCs achieve and sustain large revenues as well as large profits? They do so by investing billions of dollars in diverse global activities. These investments are supported by external financing. Even if an MNC generates large operating cash flows, it may have to resort to external funding to meet its investment needs. The following Honda example illustrates the point that MNCs require large infusions of capital and source global markets to satisfy this need.

EXAMPLE 10.1

Honda's 2006 annual report indicates the following capital expenditures.

Honda's Capital Expenditure (JPY millions)

	2005	2006
Motorcycle business	41,845	52,246
Automobile business	317,271	392,934
Financial services	1,941	1,316
Power products and other businesses	12,923	11,345
Total	*373,980*	*457,841*

Source: Honda 2006 Annual Report.

How does Honda finance 2006 investments of JPY 457,841 million? The annual report indicates that Honda is an active user of debt markets (proceeds from long-term debt is Japanese yen, JPY, 865,677 million). Honda uses a mixture of bank loans, long-term bonds, and medium-term notes to obtain this debt financing. The denomination currency for debt is predominantly JPY.

Advantages Enjoyed by MNCs

By virtue of their ongoing need for large amounts of capital, MNCs are well known for their skills in accessing public markets. But this ability does not just arise from their regular and close contact with capital markets. MNCs also have structural advantages in accessing capital. These advantages are described next.

Large Firm Size

MNCs tend to be large firms with significant amounts of fixed assets in their balance sheets. MNCs are large because they serve multiple national markets with a variety of products and services. This influences financing activities in two ways. A large firm size and resulting large financing requirement provides advantages such as economies of scale in accessing financial markets. Size also helps by providing a sufficient base of fixed assets to serve as collateral. This helps to mitigate the risk of investors and helps reduce the cost of financing.

High Profile and Name Recognition

MNCs are often high-profile firms (e.g., Boeing, McDonalds) with global name recognition. This is a great asset in accessing international capital markets. In the Eurobond markets, for instance, individual investors—principally European citizens—gravitate toward issues of firms with which they are familiar. MNCs also enjoy advantages in having corporate infrastructures in many countries and being able to respond to market conditions rapidly.

Diversification

The diversification of MNCs proves to be another asset in the context of financing. Because an MNC receives cash flows from multiple businesses spread across the globe, the portfolio of cash flows is diversified with respect to (1) currency risk, (2) business risk, and (3) country risk. This profile makes MNCs attractive to prospective creditors. In fact, many MNCs have high-quality debt ratings issued by agencies such as Moody's and Standard & Poor's (S&P). This enables them to obtain both debt and equity capital at preferential terms.

Constraints That MNCs Face

MNCs also face difficulties in financing by virtue of their operations in foreign markets. This is especially true for MNCs operating in only a few countries and that are therefore vulnerable to problems in a particular country. These problems affect operating cash flows and in turn

---

MNC advantages
Because they are large, diversified, and well-known, MNCs have inherent *advantages* in obtaining financing.

affect the ability of firms to obtain financing. Examples of problems encountered by MNCs in foreign countries include (1) the emergence of a strong competitor and (2) the deterioration of economic fundamentals. Earlier, we considered concepts of country and currency risk. These are all unique risks faced by MNCs that make their operating cash flows vulnerable and deter potential financiers.

EXAMPLE 10.2

Xerox, a U.S.-based MNC, has a worldwide presence today. However, in the past, Xerox focused on sales in Latin American countries. In the late 1990s, because of adverse market conditions, Xerox suffered massive losses in Mexico. The weakness in the U.S. market at that time also did not help. Consequently, the firm's stock price plunged by more than 80 percent and its credit rating fell to levels prohibiting new issuance of debt. At that time, investors began to question the firm's going concern viability. It took many years before Xerox was able to recover from this crisis.

10.2 MNC Debt Financing

MNCs can obtain long-term debt financing through bank loans and the issue of bonds. In this section, we discuss each of these two approaches in detail.

Bank Loans

bank loans
Bank loans offer advantages such as privacy, flexibility, and low renegotiation costs.

Bank loans have traditionally been the main way in which firms obtained financing. The United States is perhaps an exception because most U.S. firms prefer public debt markets to bank financing. In contrast, in Germany and Japan, banks have traditionally been important sources of capital. Moreover, in these countries, banks often have multifaceted relations with firms. In Japan, industrial groups known as *keiretsus* have large banks such as the Mitsubishi Bank at their center; these banks perform both financing and monitoring functions.

Syndicated Loans

MNCs' credit needs are large and routinely involve tens or hundreds of millions of dollars. To accommodate such large loan requests, consortiums of banks pool resources to offer syndicated loans. Each bank in the syndicate suffers only moderate credit exposure; by participating in multiple syndicates, banks are able to diversify their credit risk. This ability of banks to reduce risk has a salutary effect for MNCs: lower interest costs.

EXAMPLE 10.3

The credit crisis of 2007–2008 severely dented global banks. Weak economies and spiraling defaults meant that banks were cautious in their lending activities. While U.S. banks such as Citibank were hard hit, Japanese banks were relatively less affected and have provided loans to MNCs and global financial institutions. A popular vehicle is the so-called ninja loan. This is a cross-border syndicated loan denominated in JPY. In 2007, a record USD 17 billion was advanced in the ninja market. As an interesting aside, in the popular lexicon, the term *ninja loans*—as part of the black humor originating from the credit crisis—refers to loans advanced to individuals with "no income, no job and no assets."

Advantages

Bank loans are attractive financing vehicles for the following reasons:

• **Privacy.** Because of private contracting, firms do not have to divulge sensitive information to their competitors. Also, the role of accounting information is diminished—a boon to firms operating in jurisdictions where accounting information is not timely or reliable—because in private negotiations, high-quality information can be transmitted to counterparties without the burden of following cumbersome external standards. It is no surprise that in countries where bank loans are prevalent, accounting systems are often not well developed.

• **Flexibility.** Banks can structure flexible and timely financing. A typical loan takes the form of either a term loan or a line of credit. The latter, in particular, offers flexibility to firms—similar to the flexibility offered by credit cards—to access only the required amounts at specific points in time. Because firms can repeatedly tap into such lines of credit, they are also known as *revolving credits* or simply as *revolver.*

• **Low renegotiation costs.** If firms gets into difficulty repaying their debts, it is far simpler and cheaper (because of lower transaction costs) to renegotiate bank loans.

EXAMPLE 10.4

Tata Motors funded its USD 2 billion purchase of Land Rover and Jaguar (from Ford Motors) in 2008 with a bank loan from Citigroup and JP Morgan Chase. The loan amount was actually for USD 3 billion, helping Tata to also set up production facilities for its revolutionary USD 2,500 model, the Nano. This loan was expected to be repaid shortly with proceeds from long-term debt or equity. MNCs value this type of bank loan—known as *bridge loans*—for their immediacy and flexibility and support for mergers and acquisitions. (Later, Tata announced plans to issue equity through a rights offering.)

Limitations

Bank loans have two major limitations: transaction size and cost. The Tata example is an extreme one: Few bank loans exceed USD 100 million. What if MNCs require larger amounts? Also, bank loans cost more than public funding via bonds. The extra cost of bank loans compensates banks for their intermediary services and is reflected in the spread between the prime rate (bank lending rates to their best customers) and the rate on government instruments (such as the U.S. Treasury rate); this spread routinely exceeds 2 percent. To avoid these limitations, MNCs may want to directly tap investors through a public issue rather than going through a banking intermediary.

Bond Financing

Types of Bonds

bond financing

Choices in international *bond financing* include Eurobonds and floating rate notes.

A U.S.-based MNC has the option to issue a domestic bond, a foreign bond, or a Eurobond. Recall the following definitions. A *domestic bond* is a USD-denominated bond issued in the United States. A *foreign bond* is issued in a non-U.S. country in its local currency. A *Eurobond* is similar to the foreign bond except that it is issued in a currency other than the currency of the country in which it is issued. The last option is becoming increasingly more important to MNCs because of the potentially wider pool of investors that can be attracted.

Eurobonds

Unlike the diversity of firms tapping the U.S. domestic bond markets, firms tapping the Eurobond markets are fairly homogenous. They tend to be MNCs, large in size, and have wide name recognition. These firms also tend to have very high bond quality ratings, often AAA; this perhaps explains why Eurobond issues are rarely rated by ratings agencies such as Moody's and S & P. The Eurobond market is huge and supports USD 1 trillion of new issues each year.

One reason firms find the Eurobond market attractive is that it supports flexibility in the structure of the issue. One or more currencies can be used: For example, a dual-currency bond can stipulate one currency for coupon payments and another for the principal repayment. Optionlike features can be built into the contract; these include callability and convertibility. Variable coupon payments based on interest rate indexes can also be stipulated. When the Eurobond market started in the 1960s because of various regulations that closed off U.S. markets to global investors, yields on Eurobonds were less than the yields on comparable U.S. bonds. This yield differential was a powerful draw to U.S. firms. Over time, however, liberalization in U.S. markets has led to a closing of the gap with the Eurobond market, with the result that yields are roughly the same. In today's environment, the main draw of the Eurobond market is that it is a flexible and unregulated market.

Floating Rate Instruments

Floating rate instruments typically take the form of medium-term notes known as *floating rate notes (FRNs)* with coupon payments tied to the London Inter Bank Offered Rate (LIBOR).

Firms wishing to exploit future interest rate declines find FRNs attractive. FRNs are complex instruments with numerous defining parameters (e.g., the reference interest rate, formula for the coupon rate relative to this benchmark, timing for resetting the coupon interest, frequency of interest payment). Most FRNs use the six-month LIBOR rate known as *LIBOR6*. The coupon frequency, often four in a year, allows for multiple rates of interest during a particular year. Coupon payments are determined using benchmark rates at the beginning of the coupon period.

EXAMPLE 10.5

In 2008, Coca-Cola Enterprises issued USD 275 million in three-year FRNs with coupon equal to three-month LIBOR plus 60 basis points (bp = 0.01%). The proceeds were used to refinance maturing commercial paper. The firm's total debt was USD 9.7 billion: Coca-Cola is a veteran user of bond markets.

Reverse Floater

This is an interesting innovation. The *reverse floater* type of bond is used to benefit the issuer when market rates increase. The typical coupon rate of a reverse floater is "X percent − LIBOR"; this produces an inverse relationship between the market rate and the coupon interest the firm pays. Consider a reverse floater with a coupon of 6 percent − LIBOR. If LIBOR exceeds 6 percent, the issuer will actually receive coupon payments instead of paying them.

EXAMPLE 10.6

In 1993, Chase Manhattan and Chemical Banking Corp. underwrote a reverse floater for Grupo Televisa of Mexico for a face value of USD 100 million. This was a three-year note with a coupon rate of 12.25 percent minus LIBOR and with a minimum payment of 3 percent. Grupo Televisa thus took a bet that USD interest rates would increase. On the other hand, investors bet that interest rates would decline.

Foreign Bonds

Foreign bond markets are mostly concentrated in the United States, Japan, and Switzerland. In recent years, the Japanese foreign bond market perked up with some large issues of *Samurai bonds*. In 2008, AFLAC, a U.S. insurance firm, made a JPY 30 billion issue under its JPY 100 billion shelf registration.[1] AFLAC pays interest at the rate of 1.87 percent. Such low rates attract issuers to the Japanese market.

10.3 MNC Equity Financing

MNCs are with few exceptions established firms that have already gone through the initial public offering (IPO) process. For the sake of completeness, however, we also consider equity financing during a firm's start-up phase when it is not yet considered an MNC.

Venture Capital and IPO Financing

Many famous MNCs such as Google, Apple, and Microsoft received **venture capital (VC)** financing during their start-up stage. A special type of financial intermediary, the *VC firm*, provides VC financing. The unique feature of VC financing is bundling money along with business guidance. The general partners of VC firms are usually industry veterans. Some of these partners or their associates are installed as directors in start-up companies that receive funding. Through these directors, VC firms provide "value-added services." For example, VC firms often help start-ups with corporate strategy, staffing decisions, human resource infrastructure, and contacts with customers/suppliers.

---

[1] *Shelf registration* provides blanket approval for a series of financing forays. Because of its single step, it saves transaction costs and also allows firms to move quickly when market conditions permit a security issue.

VC financing is an innovation that originated in the United States after World War II and is now a global phenomenon. In 2007, USD 35 billion of VC financing was provided to start-ups. Although the lion's share (USD 25 billion) represents funding to U.S. firms, global activity is increasing. For example, approximately USD 2 billion was provided to Chinese start-ups. Well-known U.S.-based VC firms such as Sequoia Capital are expanding operations to hot locations such as India and China.

VC firms are able to absorb the high risk of investing in start-ups by robustly monitoring their investments and by providing funding in stages based on the start-up's meeting certain milestones. When the start-up matures, the VC firm seeks to exit its investment, usually by arranging an IPO. At this stage, the start-up has matured enough to run its business without help from the VC firm.

Internal Equity

For MNCs as well as domestic firms, a major source of funding is internal equity: the use of operating cash flows to fund investments. An advantage of internal equity is its low transaction cost. Moreover, regulatory permission is not required. The advantages of internal equity explain why growth firms such as Google and Apple rarely pay dividends. Rather than return the money to stockholders, these firms find it advantageous to deploy their resources internally in the firm.

| EXAMPLE 10.7 | Two common financial metrics allow us to quantify the use of internal equity: net income and the dividend payment. The following table illustrates the use of internal equity by growth firms. |

Net Income and Dividend Payment (2007, USD million)

Firm	Growth	Net Income	Dividend	Internal Equity = Net Income − Dividend
Apple	High	3,496	0	3,496
Google	High	4,204	0	4,204
Sony	Low	1,074	212	862
Pfizer	Low	8,144	7,975	169

Source: *www.finance.yahoo.com* (accessed September 15, 2008).

External Equity

Firms with existing public equity (i.e., post-IPO) can conduct a seasoned offering and issue additional shares. This process is generally considered problematic because it dilutes profits (earnings per share decreases) and may be a signal to investors that company shares are overpriced. For this reason, announcements of seasoned equity offerings are invariably accompanied by share price declines. Despite these concerns, seasoned offerings for growth firms with insufficient operating cash flows may be the only viable financing alternative.

| EXAMPLE 10.8 | Recall that Tata Motors used bridge loan financing to support its 2008 acquisition of Land Rover and Jaguar. Later, Tata announced plans to raise permanent capital through a rights offering by which it offered new shares to existing shareholders. Firms use this method to keep control in the hands of existing shareholders. Financial analysts, however, were concerned about dilution of earnings per share. As a result of a series of negative analyst notes published following this announcement, shares of Tata fell significantly. |

Dual Listing

MNCs may also consider sourcing equity from a foreign market. This can be achieved by **dual listing**, or cross-listing. For example, shares of Toyota Motors are listed on the Tokyo and New York stock exchanges. Dual listing may raise capital either explicitly or implicitly.

dual listing

Non-U.S. firms such as Toyota Motors (Japan) and Companhia Vale (Brazil) list their shares on the NYSE as well as on their respective national exchanges.

In most cases, firms merely list their already issued shares in a foreign exchange. This does not provide fresh financing for the firm, but it does broaden the financing pool by attracting shareholders from another country. In other cases, firms explicitly issue new shares in another country and raise money.

Dual listing has the following potential advantages:

- **Increased liquidity.** The resulting enlarged shareholder base supports greater liquidity. This in turn serves to decrease transaction costs for investors.

- **Increased visibility and prestige for the firm.** This may have a payoff in terms of increased operating cash flows. MNC managers often say that certain transactions in a foreign country such as building factories and obtaining new accounts are made possible by listing in that country.

- **Access to foreign sources of capital.** The firm can leverage the listing by issuing bonds or obtaining bank financing in the foreign country, or a listing can pave the way for a seasoned equity offering that raises new equity. Listing may also make a firm eligible for government-subsidized financing in certain countries.

- **Reduction in political risk.** Countries are more reluctant to impose costs on foreign firms in which their own citizens are investors. Listing can decrease the probability of expropriation.

When markets are segmented, firms can use dual listing as a tool to increase value and lower the cost of capital. Market segmentation can result from direct barriers such as tax or ownership restrictions as well as indirect barriers such as information availability and differences in accounting standards. Dual listing circumvents these barriers by allowing foreign shareholders to invest in the firm's equity. For example, many U.S. pension funds are prohibited from investing in nondollar-denominated issues. This rule is circumvented by the purchase of foreign equity listed on the U.S. stock markets. Research[2] shows that foreign firms that list their shares on the National Association of Security Dealers Automated Quotations (NASDAQ) or New York Stock Exchange (NYSE) increase their firm values.

10.4 Cost of Capital and Optimal Financing

A CFO's job is to obtain financial resources to support the firm's operations. Firms seek two related objectives in their financing activities: access and cost. First, the firm needs access to sufficient pools of capital for current as well as future financing. Second, financing should be obtained at the best rates possible. We address the latter point in this section. We explain how to calculate or infer the cost of capital for an MNC and discuss ways in which it can be minimized. A lower cost of capital leads to higher firm value. Before proceeding to the specifics of cost of capital calculations, we list two related general propositions.

- **Discount rate.** The cost of capital—the return demanded by a firm's investors—serves as the firm's discount rate in NPV calculations. Although different labels are used, the meaning is the same. What differs is the perspective. Cost of capital represents the return demanded by investors from firms. The discount rate is the benchmark rate used internally by managers to value projects. Firm value is generated when projects generate returns higher than the cost of capital.

- **Risk.** In general, cost of capital represents the characteristics not of investors but of the firm. If a firm is engaged in risky enterprises, its cost of capital will be high. Instead, if a firm is engaged in safe ventures, its cost of capital will be low.

[2] Miller, "The Market Reaction to International Cross-Listings: Evidence from Depository Receipts," *Journal of Financial Economics* 51 (1999), pp. 103–123.

Cost of Debt

Cost of debt for a firm is the return its creditors demand. Debt contracts (e.g., bonds) stipulate interest payments and principal repayments. By comparing the money raised by the firm with the sums promised to creditors as interest and principal repayments, one can determine the implied cost of debt. Firms can compare costs of alternate debt financing arrangements to determine the lowest cost alternative.

Time value concepts—principally, the internal rate of return method—are used to determine the cost of debt. What is known as the cost of debt from the firm's perspective can also be called the *yield from the investor's perspective.*

$$r_B = \text{Cost of debt}$$
$$= \text{Yield of debt (or implied return)}$$

Transaction Costs

cost of debt
The (pretax) cost of debt equals the bond yield or the IRR of the bond's cash flows. The *all-in cost of debt* also considers any issue costs.

As a practical matter, in cost of debt calculations, one needs to incorporate debt issuance costs. This produces an **all-in cost of debt**. Debt issuance costs are typically quite low, especially for MNCs.

Coupon Frequency

U.S. domestic bonds pay coupon interest twice a year. Other bonds (including Eurobonds) pay annual coupons. This creates practical difficulties in comparing yields. In the case of U.S. domestic bonds, the yield calculated using semiannual cash flows is simply doubled to produce the annual **bond equivalent yield (BEY)**. This cannot be compared directly with Eurobond yields. We need to determine the domestic bond's effective yield to facilitate the comparison.

EXAMPLE 10.9

A U.S. firm is considering a debt issue. Two alternatives are available. A domestic bond issue is available at a BEY of 7 percent after incorporating transaction costs. A second alternative is a Eurobond issue with the following parameters:

- Face value = 200, Issue price = 190.
- Transaction costs = 2.
- Maturity = 8 years.
- Coupon = 6 percent (annual).

Solution: Recall that U.S. domestic bonds offer semiannual coupons.

Domestic bond: Effective yield $= \left(1 + \dfrac{7\%}{2}\right)^2 - 1 = 7.12\%$

The Eurobond yield is 7.01%. See calculations below.

All-in Cost of Debt Calculation

Coupon	6%
Years	8
Face	200
Issue price	190
Issuance costs	2

Year	Cash Flow
0	188
1	−12
2	−12
3	−12
4	−12
5	−12
6	−12
7	−12
8	−212
Internal rate of return (IRR)	**7.01%**

Calculator Keystrokes

PV	188
PMT	−12
FV	−200
N	8
I ?	

Discussion: The Eurobond yield is lower; hence, the Eurobond is less expensive.

Taxes

The tax laws of most nations allow firms to deduct interest expense before calculating taxes (recall cash flow calculations in the capital budgeting chapters). Consider U.S. firms that typically pay taxes at a rate of 35 percent. Every USD of interest expense has the associated benefit of decreasing the tax bill by USD 0.35. Thus, if the firm has a before-tax cost of debt of 10 percent, the after-tax cost is only 6.5 percent.

Challenges in Calculating the Cost of Debt

Cost of debt calculations are rarely straightforward because of various features such as callability (firm can retire the bond by paying a prespecified price to investors) and convertibility (investors can exchange bonds for shares at a predetermined ratio). A feature that is advantageous to the issuer (e.g., callability) increases the cost of debt. In contrast, a feature that is advantageous to the investor (e.g., convertibility) decreases the cost of debt.

Cost of Equity

cost of equity
The CAPM is used to calculate the *cost of equity*. A key input is equity beta.

The **cost of equity** (r_S) is usually more challenging to determine than is the cost of debt. This is so because cash flows to stockholders are not contractually specified. This in turn means we must infer the cost of equity from market prices. Financial theories such as the **capital asset pricing model (CAPM)** are used to infer the cost of equity. These theories specify the relationship between risk and return. The higher the risk of a firm's equity, the higher is the cost of equity. The following are alternatives used by managers to estimate the cost of equity.

Domestic CAPM

Despite more modern developments, the domestic or local market version of the CAPM (DCAPM) is the most commonly used model. The corporate cost of equity is provided by:

$$r_S = r_F + \beta_S (r_M - r_F)$$

$$\beta_S = \frac{\sigma_{SM}}{\sigma_M^2}$$

The first component (r_F) is the risk-free rate of interest: In the U.S. setting, managers use the yield on Treasury bonds as proxy. The second component, $\beta_S(r_M - r_F)$, represents the risk premium. The risk premium is in turn determined by the product of the market risk of equity (β_S) and expected returns in the overall market net of the risk-free rate ($r_M - r_F$); the former is known as *beta* and the latter is known as the *market risk premium*. Key decisions regarding implementation include (1) choice of market index for calculating beta and (2) determination of expected market returns.

EXAMPLE 10.10

An MNC's equity has a correlation of 0.4 with the market index and a standard deviation of 40 percent compared to a market standard deviation of 12 percent. The risk-free rate is 6 percent, and the expected return on the market index is 15 percent. Use DCAPM to estimate the cost of equity.

Solution:

$$\beta_S = \frac{\sigma_{SM}}{\sigma_M^2}$$

$$= \frac{.4 \times 40\% \times 12\%}{(12\%)^2}$$

$$= 1.33$$

$$r_S = 6\% + 1.33\,(15\% - 6\%) = 18\%$$

Discussion: Despite having a much higher standard deviation than the market, the cost of equity is only slightly higher than the expected market return. A key determinant of this relationship is correlation between the MNC's equity and the market index.

International CAPM

A fundamental assumption of the **international version of the CAPM (ICAPM)** is that financial markets are integrated. This means that investors optimize their portfolios (that is, increase returns and lower risks) by investing globally. Thus, the relevant benchmark portfolio is not the domestic index but a global index. The risk of equity or the equity beta (β_S) is defined relative to this global benchmark. Similarly, the market risk premium ($r_M - r_F$) is based on this global benchmark. Because of its assumption of financial market integration, the use of the ICAPM is particularly appropriate for MNCs that have a global investor base.

The ICAPM is used to calculate the cost of equity by following these steps[3]:

- The *numeraire* (unit of measurement) is defined as the firm's domestic currency.
- A global benchmark is identified. The Morgan Stanley All Country World Index (ACWI) is a common choice. Index values are converted to the numeraire currency. Returns are then calculated. (This parallels the calculation of the S&P 500 index or Dow Jones Industrial Average—DJIA—index returns in the U.S. setting for applying the DCAPM.)
- β_S is calculated relative to the global benchmark.
- r_M is defined as the long-term return on the global benchmark.
- r_F is defined as the yield on long-term government bonds denominated in the numeraire currency.

The cost of capital is calculated based on these inputs. The following example demonstrates these calculations. (For a more detailed explanation concerning conversion of the index and calculation of the ICAPM beta, see Appendix 10.)

EXAMPLE 10.11

The chief financial officer (CFO) of a global mining firm based in Brazil notes that Brazil is increasingly globally integrated and that her firm has many foreign investors. Accordingly, she wishes to use the ICAPM to calculate the cost of equity. The numeraire currency is the Brazilian currency denomination (BRL). The CFO identifies the Morgan Stanley ACWI as the benchmark portfolio and converts index values to BRL values. Refer to this converted index as ACWI-BRL. Other information follows:

- Long-term Brazilian government bond yield = 13.4 percent.
- Expected market return (based on past returns of ACWI-BRL) = 18 percent.
- Beta (against ACWI-BRL) = 0.2.

Using these inputs, calculate the cost of equity.

---

[3] For a detailed discussion of these steps see, Rene Stulz, "Globalization of Capital Markets and the Cost of Capital: The Case of Nestle," *Journal of Applied Corporate Finance* 8, no. 3 (1995), pp. 30–38.

Solution:

$$r_S = 13.4\% + 0.2\,(18\% - 13.4\%) = 14.32\%$$

Discussion: We need to ensure that all inputs are consistent and reflect the same currency. Most global benchmarks such as the ACWI are measured in USD terms and hence need conversion for non-U.S. firms. This conversion explains why the past return on the ACWI may appear to be high from the perspective of countries such as Brazil with high inflation. A high rate of inflation causes erosion in currency values (recall purchasing power parity, or PPP) and amplifies returns on the global index.

What are potential advantages of using the ICAPM relative to the DCAPM in estimating the cost of equity for an MNC? Because the shareholders of many MNCs hold globally diversified portfolios, the ICAPM, which assumes such global diversification, can potentially provide a lower, more realistic estimate of the cost of equity. Unfortunately, research fails to validate this theoretical expectation. One recent study[4] analyzes firms most likely to benefit from using the ICAPM (firms that list their shares on foreign exchanges, thereby having a global base of shareholders) and finds that the ICAPM cost of capital estimates differ from DCAPM estimates in only 12 percent of the firms studied. A possible explanation is that national benchmarks are correlated with the global benchmark, so the DCAPM largely coincides with the ICAPM. One interesting version of the ICAPM has exchange rate factors in addition to the market index.

Factor Models

Factor models explain asset returns by using macroeconomic variables such as interest rates, inflation rates, and exchange rates in lieu of the market index. The hope is that by using a set of factors, more precision can be obtained than by simply using the market index as in the CAPM. However, two issues prevent the widespread usage of factor models. First, studies find that in many cases, information contained in factors such as exchange rates are adequately captured by the market index. Second, implementation difficulties exist: Factor models are more challenging to estimate than the CAPM.

Other Models

One author[5] identifies 12 methods of calculating the cost of equity! Existing research does not offer clear guidance on model selection. Until new research shows us the way, it probably makes sense for MNC managers to use multiple methods and to exercise judgment. For example, if the ICAPM is used by emerging market firms, because of low correlation between these firms and global benchmarks, unusually low cost of equity values are obtained. A "smell test" will probably identify that these low costs are erroneous. A possible correction for this downward bias is to use sovereign yield premiums (yield on a country's government bonds compared to yields on other countries' government bonds) as an additional component of cost of equity. These premiums are large for emerging markets and may serve to offset the downward bias imparted by the ICAPM.

Weighted Average Cost of Capital

The weighted average cost of capital (WACC) calculates an overall capital cost by weighting costs of debt and equity with their respective proportions (w_B, w_S) in the capital structure. The tax rate (T) is used to calculate the after-tax cost of debt; this calculation recognizes the tax deduction offered by interest expense. WACC is formally defined as:

$$WACC = w_B \times r_B \times (1 - T) + w_S \times r_S$$

WACC
The *WACC*—the overall cost of capital for the firm—is used as the discount rate for valuing projects.

[4] K. Koedijk and M. Dijk, "The Cost of Capital of Cross-Listed Firms," *European Management Journal* 10 (2004), pp. 465–486.

[5] Campbell Harvey, "12 Ways to Calculate the International Cost of Capital," Working Paper, Duke University, 2005.

EXAMPLE 10.12

A firm has a cost of equity of 15 percent and a cost of debt of 9 percent. If this firm is financed by one-third equity and two-thirds debt and if the tax rate is 30 percent, calculate WACC.

Solution:

$$WACC = w_B \times r_B \times (1 - T) + w_S \times r_S$$
$$= \frac{2}{3} \times 9\% \times (1 - 30\%) + \frac{1}{3} \times 15\%$$
$$= 9.2\%$$

Discussion: The WACC equals 9.2 percent. This means that the hurdle/discount rate for projects of risk similar to the rest of the firm is 9.2 percent. The WACC is an after-tax discount rate. This is why, in capital budgeting exercises, one discounts after-tax cash flows.

Implementation Issues

How is a manager to calculate the costs of debt and equity that are used as inputs in the WACC equation? The cost of debt is set equal to the yield to maturity (YTM) of the bonds issued by the firm. The cost of equity is estimated using the CAPM; the equity beta is estimated and inputted in the CAPM equation.[6]

Optimal Capital Structure

Firms manage their debt and equity levels to minimize their overall cost of capital. In general, as a firm increases its debt, because of the tax advantage of debt, its WACC declines. But at some point, excessive debt creates difficulties such as the possibility of bankruptcy and other incentive problems; this reverses the decline in the WACC. See Exhibit 10.1.

10.5 Strategic Issues in Financing MNCs

Financing decisions are multidimensional. Corporate objectives in financing are not limited to obtaining low-cost capital. In this section, we explore the interaction of financing policies with strategies to:

- Reduce agency costs.
- Mitigate country risk.
- Exploit market inefficiencies.
- Mitigate currency risk.

EXHIBIT 10.1
WACC

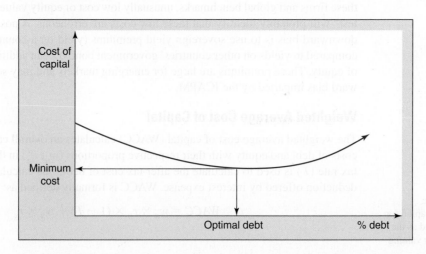

[6] An alternative is the Gordon constant growth model: The cost of equity equals dividend yield plus long-term growth rate $\left(r_S = \dfrac{D_1}{P} + g \right)$.

Mitigation of Agency Costs

MNCs may face agency costs arising from decentralization of activities in foreign countries. In general, equity holders provide a keener level of monitoring because of their exposure to the firm's residual risk. Creditors also provide valuable monitoring, although their vigilance relaxes once it becomes clear to them that the firm will meet its interest and principal repayment obligations. Agency costs can be mitigated through an appropriate capital structure. The geographical source of financing can also be important. For example, raising debt or equity capital for a subsidiary directly in a foreign country can improve the monitoring of the subsidiary's activities.

> **EXAMPLE 10.13**
>
> Cairn Energy is a U.K.-based MNC with a majority stake in a JV in India known as Cairn India. In 2008, Cairn India made a private placement of equity for USD 625 million. This issue dilutes Cairn Energy's stake in the JV from 69 percent to 65 percent. However, it brings in new large external investors who may provide valuable monitoring benefits.

Raising equity capital in the foreign country can help decrease agency costs in another important way. This equity can be used in incentive contracts for managers. Thus, if a U.S.-based MNC operates a subsidiary in Singapore, it might make sense to partially fund this subsidiary with equity capital in Singapore. This equity can then be used in incentive contracts, especially for top- and middle-tier management. The advantage of using subsidiary equity rather than parent equity is that it offers relatively more sensitivity to the performance of the subsidiary managers. This is especially true when the subsidiary is only a small part of the parent and the correlation between the performance of the subsidiary and the parent's stock price is very low.

agency costs and country risk
By raising financing in countries in which it operates, an MNC can reduce *agency costs* as well as *country risk*.

The issue of agency costs is a relevant and important one. We earlier considered differences between corporate governance practices in various countries and argued that the U.S. model is generally considered superior to others. This would indicate that U.S. firms in particular face situations in other countries that are more challenging. A smarter financing strategy may be one part of an overall strategy to mitigate the agency problem. U.S. as well as non-U.S. firms can benefit from this approach.

Mitigation of Country Risk

Country risk has two components, economic and political. Even in countries without political risk, MNCs face risks from volatility in macroeconomic variables such as inflation and interest rates. To some extent, by designing appropriate financing policies, a firm can mitigate these economic risks.

> **EXAMPLE 10.14**
>
> Consider the operation of MNCs in a Latin American country such as Brazil or Argentina. In the past, one source of risk in these countries was hyperinflation and resulting high rates of interest. A high rate of interest can stifle business activity. This risk can be mitigated somewhat if the MNC sources local debt financing at a fixed rate of interest. Even if this debt initially appears unattractive because of high rates, it can potentially provide the firm an insurance against a rise in interest rates. If the interest rate rises and affects the firm's business, some of the losses can be offset by the advantage of having fixed the interest payment at lower levels. This strategy, therefore, provides a natural hedge against interest rate risk.

Local financing can also mitigate political risk to a certain extent. MNCs face political risk especially in emerging economies. Political risk can take many forms including regulations affecting labor, restrictions on import of input materials, regulations on the domestic sale of goods and services, impositions of various kinds of taxes, and environmental regulations. By sourcing local capital, firms create local stakeholders who may have political influence. For example, a firm that borrows funds from banks that the government partially owns can pre-empt adverse regulation.

Exploiting Lack of Integration in Capital Markets

Interest rates differ globally. MNCs cannot exploit the presence of lower rates if parity conditions hold: A low-interest currency will strengthen and offset the benefits of a lower financing rate. However, parity conditions do not always work. Temporary conditions in a certain foreign market may make it more attractive than others. For example, consider a country with a temporary lull in financing by local entities. This would increase investor demand for securities issued by an MNC, leading to lower yields in the case of debt and higher issue price in the case of equity. Thus, cost of capital would be lower.

To explore these ideas further, we first need to understand the relationship between the home currency and foreign cost of debt. The following equation expresses the home currency cost of debt financing in terms of (1) the foreign cost of debt (r_B^*) and (2) the percent change in the value of the foreign currency (s).

foreign currency debt
If an MNC issues *foreign currency debt*, its cost of debt (r_B) depends on the foreign cost of debt (r_B^*) as well as the change in the value of the foreign currency (s).

$$r_B = (1 + r_B^*) \times (1 + s) - 1$$

If the foreign currency strengthens ($s > 0$), the firm is disadvantaged because it repays its debt by selling holdings of the home currency and purchasing the stronger foreign currency. This implies that the cost of financing (r_B) increases.

An MNC can lower cost of debt through either a lower rate on foreign financing or a weakening currency if capital markets are not integrated.

EXAMPLE 10.15

Consider a U.K.-based pharmaceutical firm conducting business in Japan that requires financing for three years. The choices are as follows (for simplicity, assume zero-coupon instruments):

- GBP denominated instrument: 4 percent.
- JPY denominated instrument: 2 percent.

Spot GBPJPY equals 200. Three-year forwards are available at 190. Compare the two alternatives.

Solution: The GBP-denominated instrument costs 4 percent.

To calculate the cost of JPY-denominated financing, we first infer the annual percent change in JPYGBP (direct quote for JPY from the U.K. point of view) as follows:

$$(1 + s)^3 = \frac{1/190}{1/200}$$

$$s = \left[\frac{200}{190}\right]^{1/3} - 1 = 1.725\%$$

This allows us to calculate the cost of JPY financing in GBP terms as follows:

$$r_B = (1 + 2\%) \times (1 + 1.725\%) - 1 = 3.76\%$$

Discussion: Using the JPY-denominated instrument is cheaper by 24 basis points. This calculation is valid even for coupon instruments as long as the percent change in JPYGBP is the same each year. If there are coupon payments and if the percent change in JPYGBP varies each year, we would have to use one- and two-year currency forward rates in our calculations. Each year's cash flow in JPY is calculated and then converted to GBP using the various forward rates. Finally, the IRR of GBP cash flows is calculated.

Violations of parity can occur for a number of reasons. They may reflect imbalances either in currency markets, interest rate markets, or derivatives markets. The Japanese debt markets in the early 2000s offer an interesting example. Samurai bonds (JPY bonds issued in Japan by non-Japanese issuers) became quite popular with foreign issuers because of (1) the willingness of Japanese investors to buy foreign issues, (2) the willingness of investment bankers to make Samurai issues cheaply, (3) the low interest rates in Japan, and (4) the expected depreciation of JPY.

Mitigating Currency Exposure

Standard financial theory strongly advocates the separation of financing and investment decisions. This implies that when a firm is considering financing alternatives, it should not consider its current and future investment strategies. But this viewpoint is based on assumptions that may not be true. Currency risk is one factor that may force a firm to consider its financing alternatives in light of its investment strategy. A firm may look for ways to mitigate its high level of currency risk for various reasons such as minimization of taxes and the need to focus on the strategic plan. A wise financing decision can help a firm mitigate its currency risk as the following example illustrates.

EXAMPLE 10.16

Consider a Japanese firm selling its products in the United States. By virtue of receiving inflows in USD, the firm is subject to the risk of unfavorable movements in the USD. How can it use financing strategies to control currency risk?

Solution: The firm can denominate its debt in USD. This will enable the firm to make debt payments (interest and principal) in USD. These debt payments can be an offset to the USD receipts from sales in the United States (see below). Thus, the firm is able to reduce its exposure to the USD.

Mitigation of Currency Risk for a Japanese Firm with U.S. Sales

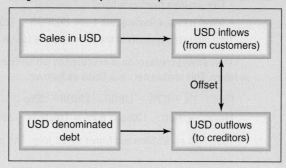

10.6 The Use of Derivatives in Financing Activities

MNCs often combine derivatives positions with their financing instruments. Interest rate and currency swaps are commonly used to tailor the cash flow stream of a bond. Structured notes—less common—are perhaps becoming more frequent. We discuss the use of these derivatives in this section.

MNC Use of Interest Rate Swaps

interest rate swap
MNCs can use *interest rate swaps* to manage interest rate risk in a debt issue.

Swaps are financial contracts that enable firms to exchange cash flows of different types (interest rates, currencies, etc.). The most common type—called *plain vanilla swap*—involves the exchange of interest payments based on a fixed rate of interest (prespecified) for interest payments based on a floating rate (e.g., LIBOR). We now develop an example to show why two firms might want to use an **interest rate swap** in conjunction with a financing transaction.

EXAMPLE 10.17

Two U.S.-based MNCS—Fixit and Movit—are seeking debt financing and are considering a fixed-rate issuance in the U.S. domestic market and a floating rate issuance in the Eurobond market, respectively. Fixit and Movit have relative advantages in the fixed and floating markets respectively. Their financing possibilities follow (for simplicity, assume similar interest rate conventions):

Firm	Domestic Bond	Eurobond
Fixit	7%	LIBOR+50bp
Movit	8%	LIBOR+120bp

bp = basis point (0.01%)

Because of other considerations such as hedging and the structure of existing debt, Fixit wishes a floating rate liability and Movit wishes a fixed liability.

1. In which markets do these firms issue debt? What are interest costs? What is the total interest paid by the two firms?

2. Assume that the firms have access to swap markets. Fixed-to-floating interest rate swaps for the same maturity as the bonds are quoted at 6.7 percent. Demonstrate how the swap market can be used to reduce financing costs for both firms.

Solution:

1. Without use of the interest rate swap, the solution is as follows:

   • Fixit issues a floating rate bond in the Eurobond market at LIBOR + 50bp.

   • Movit issues a fixed-rate bond in the domestic market at 8 percent.

   Total interest payments of the two firms are LIBOR + 8.5 percent.

2. Because of access to swap markets, the two firms engage in the following debt market transactions:

   • Fixit issues a fixed-rate bond at 7 percent.

   • Movit issues a floating rate bond at LIBOR + 120bp.

   Total interest payments of the two firms are LIBOR + 8.2 percent.

   Then a swap transaction is executed by which Fixit receives 6.7 percent from Movit and pays LIBOR in return. This implies net cash flows as follows:

   Fixit: − 7% + 6.7% − LIBOR = LIBOR + 30bp

   Movit: − LIBOR − 120bp − 6.7% + LIBOR = −7.9%

   Thus, Fixit saves 20bp and Movit saves 10bp. See below for a graphic explanation.

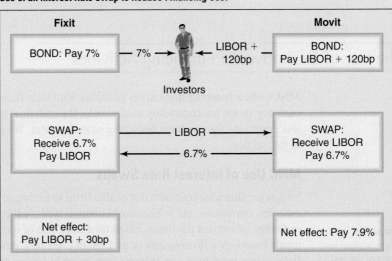

Use of an Interest Rate Swap to Reduce Financing Cost

Discussion: The desirability of the swap follows from the following "comparative advantage" analysis of debt markets:

• Fixit has an absolute advantage in both markets.

• Fixit has a comparative advantage in the fixed markets where it pays 100bp less.

• Movit has a comparative advantage in the floating market where it pays only 70bp more.

This implies that savings are achieved if firms go to their comparative advantage markets: Fixit to fixed markets and Movit to floating markets. Total savings is 30bp, which equals the difference between the total cost for the two firms in the scenario without swaps (8% + LIBOR + 50bp) and the total costs for the two firms in the scenario with swaps (7% + LIBOR + 120bp). Swap markets help unlock these savings for the two firms. Swap market conditions also dictate how these savings are distributed between the two firms.

Generally speaking, firms use interest rate swaps to change the "texture" of their cash flows. Variations of interest rate swaps can, for instance, provide firms with hybrid cash flows such as increasing coupon rates or inversely floating rates. Complex corporate activities involving derivatives to change the texture of cash flows are known as *financial engineering*.

Swaps are complex instruments. Observers may question firms' ability to find counterparties for such transactions. How can a firm find a counterparty for the desired principal amount and time period? How can a firm find a reliable counterparty who would not default on the obligation? Despite these questions, it is interesting to note that the swap market is a thriving market (supported by numerous dealers) and the amount of swap transactions outstanding is in excess of USD 300 trillion!

Two factors explain why the swap market is thriving. First, swaps have become standardized so that the variation in terms is minimized, and it is easy for firms to find counterparties. Second, and more important, swap dealers facilitate the market by assuming counterparty risk and catering to the infinite variations in contracting that are demanded. Consider the following example in which the needs of two firms are roughly consistent but do not match exactly: Firm A desires to swap into receiving fixed payments over a seven-year horizon on a principal of USD 20 million; firm B desires to swap into receiving floating payments over a six-year horizon on a principal of USD 22 million. In such scenarios, the swap dealer can enter into transactions with either party separately. Swap dealers face two kinds of risks: counterparty and basis (that is, the risk from mismatching); but by diversifying across hundreds and thousands of swap transactions, such risks can be mitigated to the benefit of all parties.

MNC Use of Currency Swaps

In a currency swap, an entity exchanges interest payments in one currency for interest payments in another. Unlike the interest rate swap, notional amounts are not equivalent—they are in two different currencies—and are therefore exchanged at inception and at maturity. A currency swap may be viewed as a series of currency forwards.

The first currency swap emerged in response to legislation in the United Kingdom that made it difficult for foreign firms to source capital from U.K. markets. MNCs countered by swapping borrowings in two different markets. Thus, a U.S. firm might borrow in USD in U.S. capital markets and swap its debt with a U.K. firm that borrows in GBP in the U.K. capital markets. Effectively, the U.S. firm would end up assuming the U.K. firm's debt and vice versa. For this reason, this transaction became known as a *parallel loan*. Swaps are modern versions of parallel loans in which swap dealers perform a vital intermediary function.

A typical currency swap allows an MNC to pay a fixed rate of interest in one currency and receive a fixed rate of interest (different rate) in another currency. We explain in the following example how MNCs use such swaps to restructure their financing.

EXAMPLE 10.18

An MNC issues a four-year JPY 200 million bond at par with a coupon of 2 percent (implies that the yield is also 2 percent). It wishes to swap out of the JPY liability into a EUR liability. Explain how a currency swap—2 percent JPY against 6 percent EUR—can help the MNC restructure its liability. What is the resulting interest rate for the MNC? Assume EURJPY equals 125.

Solution: If the MNC is currently servicing a loan of JPY 200 million at a cost of 2 percent, then this currency swap in conjunction with the loan produces the following cash flows:

- **Loan.** MNC pays 2 percent JPY (on par value of bonds) on its JPY debt.
- **Swap.** MNC receives 2 percent JPY (on notional JPY value of swap) as part of the currency swap.
- **Swap.** MNC pays 6 percent EUR (on notional EUR value of swap) as part of the currency swap.

By setting the notional value of the swap at JPY 200 million, the MNC can eliminate its JPY exposure. The resulting financing cost is 6 percent on an EUR-denominated liability of 1.6 million. This result in a tabular format follows.

Cash Flows	Loan	Swap	Net = Loan + Swap
Initial	+ JPY 200 million	− JPY 200 million + EUR 1.6 million	+ EUR 1.6 million
Periodic	− JPY 200 million × 2%	+ JPY 200 million × 2% − EUR 1.6 million × 6%	− EUR 1.6 million × 6%
Final	− JPY 200 million	+ JPY 200 million − EUR 1.6 million	− EUR 1.6 million

Discussion: The swap-related JPY cash flows perfectly offset the loan related to JPY cash flows. The resulting net cash flows (= loan + swap) are EUR denominated. Thus, the swap transformed the currency denomination of debt. In more realistic scenarios, the interest rate on the loan may not match the interest rate on the swap. In such cases, firms need to adjust the notional value of the swap to balance the interest payments.

Over time, hybrid swaps that combined the features of interest rate and currency swaps were developed. Thus, an MNC could swap out of a fixed payment in one currency into a floating payment in another currency.

MNC Use of Structured Notes

Structured notes are straight notes augmented with derivative-like features. Typically, coupon payments are set to reflect interest rates, currency rates, equity indexes, or commodity prices. Structured notes became popular in the 1990s. At that time, certain financial institutions in the United States and United Kingdom were prohibited from making derivatives transactions but were allowed to invest in structured products. Currently, structured notes are principally supplied by investment banks, but MNCs have also become players. MNCs issue structured notes through U.S. shelf-registered medium-term-note (MTN) programs.

EXAMPLE 10.19

In 1997, Toyota Motor Credit Corporation (TMCC), a U.S. subsidiary of the Japanese firm Toyota Motors, issued a two-year USD-denominated zero-coupon note at 75.55 percent of par: a face of USD 100 translated to a price of USD 75.55. The payment at maturity was set equal to the product of the principal amount and the percent change in the value of the Russian ruble (RUB) between the issue and maturity dates. For example, if RUBUSD declines in value by 20 percent, the payment at maturity will be USD 80 for a par value of USD 100. Other complex features of this note include provisions regarding changes in the convertibility status of the RUB. TMCC claimed that this deal not only provided funds at a low cost but also opened up a new investor base for future funding.

10.7 How Foreign MNCs Use U.S. Equity Markets

So far, our emphasis has been on U.S.-based MNCs. In this section, we focus on one particular financing need of non-U.S. MNCs: the desire to source U.S. equity. We discuss this issue and explain the procedure used by foreign firms to list their shares in U.S. markets.

- **Advantages.** Firms with global ambitions eventually consider sourcing equity from the U.S. markets (new shares are issued and these shares trade in U.S. markets). Failing this, these firms consider the intermediate step of listing existing shares on the NASDAQ or NYSE or OTC[7] markets. The following are reasons for these moves by foreign-based MNCs:
  - The U.S. capital markets are the largest and most efficient in the world and have the potential for funding any viable business, however large.

[7] Over-the-counter (OTC) markets are nonexchange markets in which dealers post bid and ask quotes and conduct transactions primarily using electronic networks. The NASDAQ may be thought of as the organized portion of the OTC markets for stocks.

- The standards for transparency and corporate performance are very high in the United States. By listing in U.S. markets, firms offer themselves to the scrutiny of U.S. markets and U.S. investors. While the initial glare of this scrutiny can be unsettling, over time, firms are forced to take organizational steps to create value for their securityholders.

- Firms achieve status by listing on U.S. markets. This status helps them obtain more clients and customers globally. In some sense, this association with U.S. markets can be considered an alternate form of global advertising.

- Firms receive a global currency in their shares. This currency can be used in international deals such as mergers and acquisitions.

- **Costs.** Despite these significant advantages, not all foreign firms wish to list their equity in the United States. They are reluctant for three reasons:

  - The Securities and Exchange Commission (SEC) imposes certain reporting requirements that may prove costly. But these costs have been significantly reduced recently. In the past, foreign firms were expected to comply with U.S. accounting standards. However, recent moves by the SEC indicate that foreign firms will no longer be compelled to convert their financial statements to U.S standards.

  - By listing shares in U.S. markets and by giving voting rights to investors, firms may fear losing control.

  - Firms may also be concerned by the listing fees the exchanges charge. The NYSE—a popular exchange with many non-U.S. firms—charges foreign firms a one-time listing fee that may be as high as USD 250,000 as well as recurring annual fees running into the tens of thousands of USD. These fees may deter smaller foreign firms from listing in the United States.

- **Depository receipt mechanism.** The mechanism used by foreign firms to raise capital or list shares in the United States is known as *American Depository Receipts (ADR)*.[8] This mechanism involves the creation of pseudoshares backed by the actual shares. Financial intermediaries such as Citicorp and the Bank of America create depositories for foreign shares and enable the creation of ADRs. American investors trade these pseudoshares on U.S. exchanges such as the NYSE and the NASDAQ. Well-known ADRs include Sony, Honda, Toyota Motors, Deutsche Telekom, Glaxo SmithKline, and ABN AMRO. For a U.S. investor, trading in these ADRs is as simple as trading in purely U.S. shares such as IBM and Microsoft. For instance, from a brokerage account, the order to buy 100 shares of Sony would take the form of "buy 100 shares of SNE" where SNE is the ticker symbol for the Sony ADR. Payment is in USD but reflects the USD equivalent of the foreign price.

  Depository receipts are listed on exchanges as well as OTC markets in the United States as well as Europe. A wide variety of firms use this facility. Exhibit 10.2 shows a recent sample of issuances.

- **ADR levels.** There are three levels at which firms can issue ADRs. The requirements and benefits of these three levels are discussed next.

  - **ADR Level I.** These shares are traded in the OTC markets (that is, nonexchange traded). Prices are posted electronically in services such as the NASDAQ-operated OTC Bulletin Board. Level I offers the simplest and least onerous listing alternative. Firms need only register with the SEC to establish the program and submit existing public reporting documents.

  - **ADR Level II:** This level allows shares to be traded on an exchange (NASDAQ or the NYSE) but no new financing may be sourced. In addition to the requirement of Level I, firms must provide financial statements annually.

  - **ADR Level III.** This is the most restrictive level because it allows firms to obtain new financing and list their shares on the NYSE or NASDAQ.

- Some foreign firms find these disclosure requirements quite onerous. In particular, regulations imposed by Sarbanes-Oxley in 2002 have diminished Level II and III ADR listings.

---

[8] If the shares are listed in multiple markets—say in the London Stock Exchange as well as the New York Stock Exchange—the issue is known as a *global depository receipt (GDR)* issue.

EXHIBIT 10.2
Depository Receipt Issues—Examples from 2008

Source: *www.adrbny.com* (accessed June 2, 2008).

DR Issue	Symbol	Capital Raised	Exchange	Country	Industry
Air France-KLM	AFLYY	N	OTC	France	Travel & leisure
Akash Optifibre	—	N	LUX	India	Fixed line telecommunication
Avastra Sleep Centres	AVTWY	N	OTC	Australia	Pharmaceuticals & biotechnology
Benetton Group	BNGPY	N	OTC	Italy	Personal goods
ChinaEdu	CEDU	Y	NASDAQ	China	General retailers
Danka Business Systems	DANKY	N	OTC	UK	Technical hardware & equipment
Diamond Bank	DBG	Y	LSE	Nigeria	Banks
Gitanjali Gems	GITG	N	LSE	India	General retailers
Gushan Environmental Energy	GU	Y	NYSE	China	Pharmaceuticals & biotechnology
Hinduja Foundries	—	Y	LUX	India	Industrial metals
Marks and Spencer	MAKSY	N	OTC	UK	General retailers
Nomura Research Institute	NRILY	N	OTC	Japan	Software & Computer Services
VanceInfo Technologies	VIT	Y	NYSE	China	Software & Computer Services
Xinyuan Real Estate	XIN	Y	NYSE	China	Real estate
XSTRATA	XSRAY	N	OTC	UK	Mining
Zhaikmunai	ZKM	Y	LSE	Kazakhstan	Oil & gas producers

Firms concerned about the increased costs of compliance can opt for a Level I listing in the OTC, but this does not allow for new financing. Firms desiring new financing as well as low compliance costs may choose a private placement under SEC Section 144A. This allows the placement of equity or debt instruments directly to qualified institutional buyers (QIB), thereby circumventing regulations regarding publicly traded instruments.

Summary

- Firms obtain debt and equity financing in optimal amounts to minimize their overall cost of capital known as WACC.

- MNCs have certain advantages over domestic firms because of larger firm size, greater expertise in financial matters, and diversification across products and geographies. This allows them access to low-cost funding.

- MNCs have unique risk factors such as country and currency risks that may pose difficulties in obtaining financing, especially debt financing.

- MNCs have access to global debt markets that include national debt markets, foreign bond markets, and Eurobond markets. The Eurobond markets are large and offer MNCs flexibility in bond contracting.

- Strategic concerns often influence financing. Some important strategic concerns are agency cost mitigation and currency risk mitigation. By choosing appropriate financing alternatives, firms can achieve multiple objectives.

- Derivatives, especially swaps, are frequently used in conjunction with debt financing to mitigate currency and interest rate risks.

- Non-U.S.-based MNCs are quite interested in tapping U.S. capital markets. Hundreds of these firms have listed their shares in the NASDAQ, NYSE, and OTC markets using the ADR mechanism.

Questions

1. **Access to Global Markets.** What are reasons MNCs desire access to global debt and equity markets? Are there differences between the needs of U.S.-based and foreign-based MNCs?

2. **MNCs vs. Domestic Firms.** What are some of the advantages and constraints MNCs face in their financing activities?

3. **Bank Loans.** What are the advantages and disadvantages of bank financing? What are typical forms of bank financing, particularly for MNCs?

4. **Bank Loans for Acquisition.** As part of its global strategy, Rio Basta, a Brazilian mining firm, purchased a Canadian mining firm for USD 3 billion. This transaction will increase the Brazilian firm's revenues by 40 percent. Discuss possible ways in which a bank can help finance this acquisition.

5. **Eurobonds.** What are the characteristics of Eurobond markets that are attractive to an MNC? What are alternatives for Eurobond issues for U.S. firms, European firms, and Asian firms?

6. **FRNs.** What are FRNs? Explain circumstances under which an FRN would be attractive to a Taiwanese MNC.

7. **Reverse Floaters.** What are reverse floaters? What are their typical terms? Speculate on the circumstances when a U.S.-based MNC would be interested in this instrument.

8. **Embedded Options.** Give two examples of how options can be embedded in a debt issue. Discuss costs and benefits in these examples to the issuer.

9. **ICAPM.** Discuss differences between the ICAPM and the DCAPM. What are some practical difficulties in applying the DCAPM?

10. **Cost of Equity.** List several non-CAPM methods used to estimate the cost of equity. Explain why these methods may make sense for MNCs.

11. **Agency Costs.** Explain how a careful financing strategy can mitigate agency costs. Provide an example.

12. **Country Risk.** Explain how a careful financing strategy can mitigate country risk. Provide an example.

13. **Interest Rate Swap.** The CFO of a small emerging markets-based MNC has just organized his firm's first foray in the Eurodebt markets. The issue was a fixed-rate medium-term note denominated in the USD. Recent developments, however, indicate that the U.S. economy is slowing down and that rates are probably headed lower. You are a financial analyst reporting to the CFO. Your task is to explain how the firm can use interest rate swaps to exploit this particular market condition. Also note that the CFO may be leery of conducting an exotic transaction. What market data can you use to alleviate the CFO's concerns?

14. **Currency Swaps.** What are currency swaps? What are cash flows related to a currency swap contract? Explain how an MNC can enter into currency swaps to alter its currency exposure.

15. **Swap Markets.** What is the structure of swap markets? What types of firms have access to these instruments? Are transaction costs high? What is the size of the typical transaction? What are benefits of using swap markets for the MNC?

16. **Structured Notes.** What are structured notes? Search the Web and find an example of one.

17. **Depository Receipts.** What are depository receipts? What are key forms? Explain advantages of depository receipts for (a) U.S. firms, (b) European firms, and (c) Asian firms.

Problems

1. **Cost of Debt.** Consider a five-year medium-term note with a par value of CHF 40 million. Annual interest payments of 4 percent are calculated based on par value. If the issue/offer price—the amount obtained by the firm from the issue as a percent of par—is 97 percent, what are CHF cash flows? What is the cost of debt (Swiss francs, or CHF)? [*Hint:* Cost of debt equals the IRR of note-related cash flows.]

2. **FRN Cash Flows.** Danesbury, a U.K.-based drugstore chain, wishes to expand its operations by increasing its number of stores by 50. The firm estimates it requires an investment of GBP 60–80 million to fund this expansion. One possibility was for Danesbury to issue a floating rate note denominated in EUR and paying an interest rate of six-month EURIBOR plus 40 basis points. This note would be issued at par. Assume that this is a two-year note with annual interest payments. Assume that—as with most floating rate instruments—interest payments are determined at the beginning of the period based on the benchmark and contractual formula. Assume the following data: GBPEUR equals 1.34, and six-month EURIBOR equals 4.3 percent. Analysts predict a six-month EURIBOR rate of 4.6 percent at the end of the year. If the amount of the issue is EUR 100 million (issued at par), calculate future EUR-denominated expected cash flows. What is the cost of debt (EUR)?

3. **Reverse Floater Cash Flows.** A U.S. firm wishes to obtain medium-term financing. The firm's CFO estimates that most global rates are on the rise and wishes a financing instrument that provides some protection against rising rates. In discussion with investment bankers, the following alternative was unearthed: a USD 200 million reverse floater with rates set at 9 percent minus three-month LIBOR. This two-year note with annual interest payments would be issued at par. Assume that—as with most floating rate instruments—interest payments are determined at the beginning of the period based on the prevailing benchmark rate. Assume that three-month LIBOR equals 4.8 percent. Analysts predict a three-month LIBOR rate of 5.7 percent at the end of the year. Calculate future expected cash flows (USD). What is the cost of debt (USD)?

4. **Eurobond Cost of Debt.** A firm issues a 10-year Eurobond with a par value of JPY 10 billion. Annual interest payments of 2.2 percent are calculated based on par value. If the issue price is 101 percent, what are cash flows (JPY)? What is the cost of debt (JPY)?

5. **Cost of Debt with Transaction Costs.** A firm issues a 12-year Eurobond with a par value of USD 100 million. Annual interest payments of 3.3 percent are calculated based on par value. The issue price is 96 percent, and the firm pays commissions and fees of USD 750,000 to its investment bankers. What are cash flows related to the bond issue? What is the cost of debt?

6. **DCAPM Beta.** Assume the DCAPM framework. Fill in missing values in the following table.

Firm	Standard Deviation of Firm's Stock Returns	Correlation of Stock with S&P 500	Standard Deviation of S&P 500	Equity Beta
A	40%	0.6	20%	?
B	50%	?	20%	0.5
C	?	0.5	20%	1.2

7. **ICAPM Cost of Equity.** Assume that the ICAPM framework and the relevant benchmark market index is the Morgan Stanley ACWI. The following information pertains to U.S. firms. The U.S. risk-free rate of interest is 4 percent. The expected return on the benchmark market index is 9 percent. Fill in the missing values in the following table.

Firm	Standard Deviation of Firm's Stock Returns	Correlation of Stock with ACWI	Standard Deviation of ACWI	Equity Beta	Cost of Equity
A	50%	0.4	18%	?	?
B	60%	0.2	18%	?	?
C	?	0.5	18%	0.8	?

8. **WACC.** A European MNC is financed with 60 percent equity and 40 percent debt. Assume that the costs of equity and debt are 14 percent and 6 percent, respectively, and that the corporate tax rate is 25 percent. Calculate WACC.

9. **WACC.** The Randall Corporation, a U.S.-based firm, has 400 million shares outstanding. These shares trade on the NYSE, and their most recent market price was USD 21.65. Analysts report that the beta of Randall's equity relative to the world index is 1.3. The firm also has 10-year 6 percent annual coupon debt outstanding with a par value of USD 6 billion. This debt is privately placed. Analysts use other publicly traded debt as benchmarks to determine that the yield on Randall's debt is 5.9 percent. Randall's tax rate is 35 percent. Consider the following additional information. The risk-free rate is 4 percent, and the expected USD-denominated return on the world index is 10 percent.

   a. What is the cost of equity? What model have you used in your calculation?

   b. What is the before- and after-tax cost of debt?

   c. What are market value financing weights?

   d. What is the WACC (USD)?

10. **Home Currency Cost of Debt.** The Hua Xia Corporation, a Chinese mineral extraction firm, wishes to make a Eurobond issue. The terms of the issue are as follows: par value of USD 200 million, annual coupon of 5 percent, maturity of 10 years, and offer price of 102 percent. If analysts expect the USD to depreciate against the Chinese yuan (CNY) by 2 percent annually in the foreseeable future, estimate:

   a. Cost of debt (USD).

   b. Cost of debt (CNY).

11. **Home Currency Cost of Debt.** The Lyons Corporation, a French food processing firm, wishes to make a Euronote issue. The terms of the issue are as follows: par value of USD 200 million, annual coupon of 4.7 percent, maturity of two years, and offer price of 97 percent. Currency markets indicate the following data: spot EURUSD equals 1.50, and two-year forward EURUSD equal 1.45. Making appropriate assumptions, estimate:

   a. Cost of debt (USD).

   b. Cost of debt (EUR).

12. **Interest Rate Swap.** Reeber, a U.S.-based MNC, wishes to transform its liability from fixed to floating in order to exploit what it perceives as a market trend toward lower rates. Its investment banker locates a (USD) fixed to floating swap quoted at 5.3 percent. The reference rate on this swap is six-month LIBOR. Assume that the swap as well as the MNC's liability have the same maturity (10 years) and that both pay coupons once a year. If the firm pays a coupon of 4 percent on its existing liability, what is the net interest cost (in percent) after executing the swap?

13. **Currency Swap Cash Flows:** IBM has substantial operations in Europe. Its services division invoices some of its clients in the local currency. IBM estimates that annual EUR-denominated revenues total EUR 1 billion. IBM wishes to enter into a EURUSD swap to convert these EUR inflows into USD. IBM's investment bankers offer a five-year currency swap that exchanges a 4 percent rate on a EUR-denominated loan against a 3 percent rate on a USD-denominated loan. Assume that EURUSD equals 1.25.

   a. What is the notional value (EUR) of the swap that would enable IBM to convert its receivables into USD? [*Hint:* Set the swap's periodic cash flows in EUR to equal IBM's receivables.]

   b. Using the notional value calculated in (a), calculate IBM's swap-related cash flows. Show initial, periodic, and final cash flows.

14. **Currency Swap Application.** GIA is a large AAA-rated U.S.-based insurance firm that is searching for a good opportunity to issue debt. Its investment bankers suggest that GIA issue a Eurobond denominated in GBP. Specific terms of the issue are GBP 50 million, five years, and fixed-rate annual coupons of 6 percent issued at par. Because GIA has no operations in the United Kingdom, it wishes to transform the GBP liability into a USD liability. Its investment banker offers to swap a 6 percent GBP rate against a 4 percent USD rate. What are GIA's loan- and swap-related cash flows? What is the net effect of entering this swap? Assume that GBPUSD equals 2.

Extensions

1. **Home Currency Cost of Debt.** Tuscania Corporation, an Italian leather goods manufacturer, wishes to make a Kangaroo issue (foreign bond issued in Australia). The terms of the issue are as follows: par value of AUD 100 million, annual coupon of 11 percent, maturity of 10 years, and offer price of 95 percent. If analysts expect rates of inflation in the foreseeable future in Australia and the Eurozone to be 7 percent and 3 percent, respectively, estimate:

   a. Cost of debt (AUD).

   b. Cost of debt (EUR).

2. **Reverse Floater with a Floor.** One-year LIBOR rates are 4 percent. A year from now, this rate is expected to be 2 percent or 5 percent with equal probability. Compare and contrast the cash flows and cost of debt of the following two instruments:

   a. Floating rate note: Par equals USD 100 million; maturity equals 2 years; annual coupons of 7 percent minus one-year LIBOR; offer price is 99 percent.

   b. Floating rate note with floor: Par equals USD 100 million; maturity equals two years; annual coupons of 7 percent minus one-year LIBOR; interest rate floor is 3 percent; offer price is 100 percent.

3. **Currency Swap Application.** Kiefer is a large AAA-rated Swiss-based insurance firm that is searching for a good opportunity to issue debt. Its investment bankers suggest that Kiefer issue a Eurobond denominated in USD. Specific terms of the issue are USD 400 million, six years, fixed-rate annual coupons of 5 percent, issued at par. Because Kiefer has no operations in the United States, it wishes to transform the USD liability into a CHF liability. Its investment banker offers to swap a 4 percent USD rate against a 3 percent CHF rate. Kiefer notes that the USD rate in the swap does not match the Eurobond rate. Hence, Kiefer needs to adjust the notional value of the swap to match the cash flows. Because of this adjustment, Kiefer will have some residual exposure to the USD in year 6 (you will see this clearly if you lay down the cash flows on a time line). This residual exposure is hedged using a forward contract. What are Kiefer's loan- and swap-related cash flows? What is the amount transacted in the forward contract? What is the net effect of entering this swap? Assume spot CHFUSD equals 0.90, and six-year forward in CHFUSD equals 0.98.

Case

Clover Machines: *Global Financing*

Clover Machines is a growing firm. Recall discussions in earlier cases about expansion plans in the Czech Republic, Brazil, and India. Because of these and other initiatives, Clover requires a fresh infusion of capital. Brian Bent, Clover's CFO, argues that Clover must increase its debt ratio from its current level of about 15 percent to an eventual level of 30 percent in five years. Mr. Bent also believes that a more extensive use of global debt markets is warranted.

One financing opportunity arises from years of low and stagnant interest rates in Japan. In fact, hedge funds and arbitragers have recently conducted carry trades to exploit low rates in Japan. These trades are essentially equivalent to covered interest arbitrage and involve borrowing JPY and investing in high interest currencies such as BRL and AUD. Sometimes carry trades are covered using forward contracts, and at other times, they simply represent uncovered interest rate arbitrage. Mr. Bent realizes that Clover cannot conduct activities that make it similar to a hedge fund. However, similar principles may make Clover more profitable. While hedge funds borrow at low rates and invest in *financial* assets of high rate countries, Clover could borrow at low rates and invest in *real* assets of high-rate countries.

Recall from an earlier case the following foreign bond opportunity: Samurai bond with a fixed rate of 1.9 percent. The bond matures in 10 years. This bond will likely not have an active secondary market. Issue price is 97 percent. Samurai bonds are denominated in JPY. Assume the following additional information. Face value is JPY 50 billion. Investment banker fees and commissions are JPY 350 million. Assume USDJPY equals 100.

John Milken, a junior analyst working on Mr. Bent's staff, is asked to provide an analysis of this Samurai bond. The following questions were posed to him:

1. What are Samurai bonds? Based on your general knowledge of global affairs, speculate on reasons for the existence of the Samurai bond market. (Conduct an Internet search to determine this market's current status.)

2. Are there any benefits related to currency risk mitigation in proceeding with the Samurai bond issue? Use your knowledge of Clover's business from previous cases and knowledge of currencies from other discussions in this text to answer this question. If you do not have sufficient data to answer this question, indicate types of data that are required.

3. What is the all-in cost of the Samurai issue? Indicate a cost denominated in JPY.

4. What are potential risks of the Samurai issue? How can Clover mitigate these risks?

5. Assume a flat term structure and risk-free interest rates of 1 percent and 5 percent in Japan and the United States, respectively. Estimate the before-tax cost of debt (equivalently, all-in cost) in USD terms. What are the limitations of this estimate?

6. Calculate Clover's WACC. Assume that the global corporate tax rate is 30 percent and the market risk premium in USD terms is 8 percent. Assume that Clover's capital structure includes the following in addition to this Samurai issue:

   a. 200 million shares with a market price of USD 15. Equity beta is 1.3.

   b. Corporate bonds (U.S. issues) totaling USD 1.2 billion in market value. The before-tax yield is 6.7 percent.

7. Suppose that a few months following the issue, Clover no longer wishes a fixed interest JPY debt. Assume that the desired debt is a floating rate EUR-denominated one. Explain in detail how this can be achieved.

Appendix 10

Calculating the ICAPM Beta

Suppose the manager of a Brazilian mining firm wishes to obtain the cost of equity for the firm. She obtains the following data for the period 2000–2007:

- Company stock price: column (1) in Exhibit 10.3.
- Morgan Stanley ACWI: column (3) in the exhibit.
- Currency values (USDBRL): column (4) in the exhibit.

EXHIBIT 10.3
Cost of Equity Data

	A	B	C	D	E	F	G	H
			Brazilian Stock		ACWI	USDBRL	ACWI-BRL	
1			Brazilian Stock		ACWI	USDBRL	ACWI-BRL	
2			Price	Return	Value	Currency	Value	Return
3		Year	(1)	(2)	(3)	(4)	(5)=(3)×(4)	(6)
4		2000	50		341.626	1.8057	616.87	
5		2001	40	-20.00%	285.721	1.9561	558.90	-9.40%
6		2002	65	62.50%	240.963	2.4242	584.14	4.52%
7		2003	70	7.69%	195.275	3.4375	671.26	14.91%
8		2004	90	28.57%	251.738	2.8533	718.28	7.01%
9		2005	95	5.56%	284.521	2.6895	765.22	6.53%
10		2006	105	10.53%	309.952	2.2666	702.54	-8.19%
11		2007	135	28.57%	370.676	2.1376	792.36	12.78%
12								
13	Mean			17.63%				4.02%
14	Sigma			23.80%				8.78%
15								
16	Covariance							0.0086
17	Beta							1.12

The steps in calculating the beta are as follows:

1. Express the index value in home currency terms. This is performed by multiplying columns (3) and (4) to produce column (5). Label this as ACWI-BRL.

2. Calculate the returns (percentage change) in the stock price and ACWI-BRL. These outputs are in columns (2) and (6).

3. *Beta* for a stock is defined as its covariance with the market divided by the variance of the market. Use returns for these calculations. The covariance—calculated in Excel by using the function COVAR—equals 0.0086. The sigma—calculated in Excel by using the function STEVP—equals 8.78 percent. Variance equals the sigma squared. The beta equals 1.12. Alternatively, use Excel function SLOPE by inputting columns (6) and (2) to directly calculate beta.

CHAPTER ELEVEN

Optimizing and Financing Working Capital

Working capital management concerns day-to-day (short-term) transactions with customers, suppliers, affiliates, and financiers. Because of the broad scope of most MNCs, their geographical reach, and their operations in multiple currencies, MNC working capital management involves complex and interesting issues and questions. These issues and questions are perhaps illustrated by an example. In a recent 10K report, Hewlett Packard (HP) reported the following working capital accounts: a cash balance of about USD 11 billion, an accounts receivable balance of about USD 13 billion, and an accounts payable balance of about USD 12 billion. How do these balances help HP execute its business plan? What factors contribute to the relative size of these accounts? How does HP manage operating cash flows (that is, cash transfers) with its various affiliates? What short-term financing strategies support its current assets?

As noted, the study of working capital can cover a wide variety of topics. This chapter provides an overview of basic principles with an emphasis on issues particularly germane to managing an MNC. Due consideration is given to environmental factors (e.g., currency risk) and to organizational factors (e.g., decentralization). We study topics on both sides of the working capital equation: current assets as well as current liabilities. Regarding current assets, MNCs face challenges managing cash and receivables in multiple countries and in multiple currencies. The challenges include determining optimal balances and transaction mechanics (that is, how to coordinate and execute transactions with suppliers, customers, affiliates). The study of current liabilities is essentially a discussion of short-term financing and is a complement to the previous chapter on long-term financing. In the modern corporation, long-term and short-term financing are connected to form a seamless strategy and common factors affect both. A key decision concerns currency denomination. As with long-term financing, MNCs have multiple objectives in determining the currency denomination of their short-term financing. Currency risk mitigation and a desire to exploit market conditions are common motives. We model these issues and demonstrate cost-of-capital calculations.

Specific topics in this chapter include:

- Issues MNCs face in cash management. What factors determine optimal balances?
- The way firms manage accounts receivable and payables and what the determining factors are.
- The way MNCs use modern tools such as securitization to manage receivables.
- The efficient methods MNCs use to make transfers with suppliers, customers, and affiliates.
- The advantages and disadvantages of various types of short-term bank loans.
- The use of syndicated bank loans.
- The way MNCs tap financial markets to raise short-term debt financing.
- U.S. and Euro commercial paper markets.

11.1 Overview of Working Capital Issues

Corporate (net) working capital is defined by the following equation:

$$\text{Working capital} = \text{Current assets} - \text{Current liabilities}$$

Items in the various working capital accounts—cash, accounts receivable, inventory, accounts payable, short-term debt—reflect a corporation's day-to-day activities. An MNC's working capital is perhaps more complex because it represents these current assets and liabilities consolidated across subsidiaries. Risk factors and currencies vary across subsidiaries.

EXAMPLE 11.1

Honda Motor's 2007 (selected) working capital items follow:

Current Assets	Yen (JPY) (in billions)	Current Liabilities	Yen (JPY) (in billions)
Cash	946	Short-term debt	1,266
Accounts receivable	1,055	Current portion of long-term debt	775
Financing receivables	1,426	Accounts payable	1,167
Inventory	1,183	Accrued expenses	807

Based on the selected items in the table,

$$\text{Working capital} = (946 + 1,055 + 1,426 + 1,183) - (1,266 + 775 + 1,167 + 807)$$

$$= 4,610 - 4,015$$

$$= 595$$

Discussion: Using an approximate currency rate of USDJPY = 100 (USD in terms of Japanese yen), we note that these working capital components represent rather significant amounts. Honda's current assets totaling yen (JPY) 4,610 billion are mostly financed using current items such as short-term debt and accounts payable. The remainder (JPY 595 billion) must be financed by noncurrent items (that is, long-term debt and equity).

Traditional topics in working capital management include cash management, credit policy, and short-term financing. These topics line up with items on the preceding balance sheet. While fundamental corporate issues remain the same, MNCs' practice of working capital management often has a global flair. Cash management seeks to optimize balances across countries. Credit policy is more complex because of unique features of local markets as well as currency considerations. Financing is more global in scope and issues of currency and risk come to the fore. In the following section, we discuss issues pertaining to MNC working capital management. We explain basics that apply to all firms but quickly move on to specific issues of interest to MNCs.

11.2 Cash Management

Cash management in an MNC is inherently more complex than for non-MNCs. A traditional cash analysis evaluates the trade-off between the benefit of holding cash for transactions and liquidity and the opportunity cost of idle cash. MNCs have additional considerations such as the following:

- Balances are held in various currencies. What are currency risk considerations?
- Cash is in the hands of subsidiary managers. What are agency cost considerations?
- MNCs need to be nimble in their transactions. What are real options considerations?

We now discuss traditional as well as these MNC-specific factors affecting cash balances.

Optimal Cash Balances

MNCs need to hold cash balances at the parent as well as subsidiary levels. Cash is the most liquid of current assets and is the fuel needed for day-to-day operations. The following are some factors that MNCs need to consider in determining the overall optimal cash level.

Transaction Costs

Traditional analysis focuses on the transaction cost of moving cash between short-term investments (e.g., money market instruments such as T-bills) and the checking account. Holding a large cash balance allows firms to avoid costly transactions. This factor needs a reinterpretation in modern times because these explicit transaction costs (e.g., bank charges and commissions for transfers) have reduced dramatically because of efficiencies in banking. However, firms also incur implicit transaction costs (e.g., managerial time spent in negotiations) in executing financial contracts with banks and other lenders to finance their cash balances. The larger the cash balance, the smaller is the need for costly recontracting. Thus higher transaction costs call for larger cash balances.

Opportunity Costs

The traditional argument is that cash holdings incur an opportunity cost because they earn below market rates. Over time, this factor has also become less important because today's banks provide facilities to firms allowing them to move in and out of money market accounts when they need cash in the checking account. This avoids holding idle cash. For an MNC, however, this may continue to be an important issue because of banking restrictions in many foreign countries. Higher opportunity costs call for lower cash balances.

EXAMPLE 11.2 — MNCs with subsidiaries in emerging economies such as India and Brazil face a dilemma. Because of underdeveloped financial markets and inefficient banking, MNCs are unable to be nimble and to operate with small cash balances. In other words, transaction costs are high and require MNCs to hold large cash balances often earning low or no interest. Yet market interest rates are high (often exceeding 10 percent), indicating high levels of opportunity costs: This factor suggests that MNCs hold low cash balances. Which factor is more important: transaction costs or opportunity costs?

Agency Costs

Finance theorists such as Jensen have long argued that excess cash balances tempt managers to make unwise decisions. This phenomenon is referred to as the *agency cost* of free cash flows. Examples of unfavorable consequences include loosening fiscal discipline, focusing emphasis away from cost containment and using cash for acquisitions of unrelated businesses. Agency costs may be higher in MNCs because of decentralization. Higher agency costs calls for lower cash balances.

Currency Risk

MNCs need to hold balances of various currencies to support foreign operations. Also, convertibility in many developing nations' currency is restricted, forcing firms to hold local currencies longer than business conditions dictate. Currency risk results from these holdings. One factor that mitigates currency risk is the portfolio effect of holding many different currencies. Nevertheless, considerable risk remains. Higher currency risk calls for lower cash balances.

Real Options

Earlier we discussed real options in the context of capital budgeting. Recall that real options provide firms with flexibility in future actions. A large cash balance may be viewed as either a real option itself or enhancement of other real options the firm holds. For example, a large cash balance may allow the firm to opportunistically (and quickly) purchase components inexpensively or to invest in a new project/asset. Arguably, the real options factor is more important to MNCs than domestic firms and calls for a larger cash balance.

What determines MNC cash balances?
In addition to traditional factors such as transaction and interest costs, *MNC cash balances* are affected by considerations related to agency costs, currency risk, and real options.

In summary, note the following:

$$+ \qquad - \qquad - \qquad - \qquad +$$

Cash $= f$ (transaction costs, opportunity costs, agency costs, currency risk, real options)

The first two are traditional factors and the last three are modern factors relevant to most MNCs.

Short-Term Investment Alternatives

Firms can invest their short-term funds in a wide variety of money market investments that differ in terms of characteristics such as maturity, liquidity, risk, and flexibility. Most money market instruments are liquid with active secondary markets, but some may offer higher rates of interest in exchange for lower liquidity. Unlike long-term debt instruments, money market instruments tend to be issued only by high-quality entities, so there are only minor differences in issuers' default risks; however, other contractual parameters such as maturity and denomination currency can be sources of risk. Some instruments have fixed parameters; others lend themselves to customization to suit MNCs' needs. Overall, MNCs decide based on rates, liquidity, risk, and flexibility.

Treasury Bills

alternatives for short-term investments
MNCs have numerous *alternatives* for parking short-term cash. They must evaluate differences in risk factors and convenience.

The governments of most countries issue short-term bills known as *T-bills* that are widely available. The high liquidity and the low risk level of these instruments make them good candidates for MNCs, which have numerous alternatives for parking short-term money. The interest rate earned on these instruments, however, is generally the lowest among money market instruments. On issue, maturities can range from one month to one year, but securities with only a few days' maturity can be found in secondary markets.

Eurocurrency Instruments

Eurocurrency instruments are obligations of banks and, hence, riskier than T-bills. (Recall our discussion of the TED spread in an earlier chapter.) These instruments come in various currencies and are quite liquid. The most important Eurocurrency instrument is the Eurodollar. In fact, in the United States, the Eurodollar has supplanted the T-bill as the reference money market instrument.

Bank Deposits

All firms have demand deposits (checking accounts) with their banks. These deposits are extremely liquid but offer below market rates. Firms can also choose two other types of bank deposits, savings deposits and time deposits. Each of these is more restrictive but offers higher rates. In particular, time deposits may offer very competitive rates. In some cases, firms may make time deposits in negotiable instruments called *certificates of deposit* (*CD*).

Money Market Mutual Funds

Firms may invest in mutual funds invested in money market instruments. Almost every mutual fund family such as Fidelity and Vanguard offers such a fund. This may be an option for smaller firms unable to transact in high-denomination instruments such as T-bills and Eurodollars. The problem, however, is that these funds restrict the number of transactions in a given period. Most firms find this feature quite unattractive.

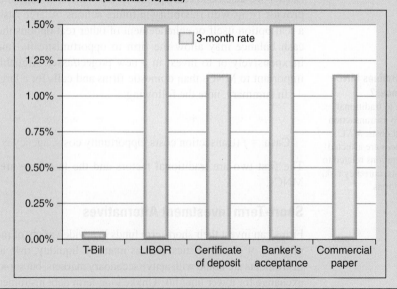

EXAMPLE 11.3

Interest rates on money market instruments are available at *The Wall Street Journal*'s Web page http://online.wsj.com/mdc/public/page/marketsdata.html (click on Bonds, Rates and Credit Markets, Money Rates). See below for a sample.

Money Market Rates (December 19, 2008)

Banker's Acceptances

Large banks issue **banker's acceptances** that are used in the context of international trade transactions. We discuss mechanics in a later chapter. Banker's acceptances are liquid instruments usually offering rates slightly higher than Eurocurrency rates.

Commercial Papers

Commercial papers (CP) are short-term debt instruments issued by large high-quality corporations and financial institutions. These instruments are perceived to be riskier than T-bills and, hence, carry a slight premium. Their liquidity makes them valuable in corporate cash management.

11.3 Receivables

Accounts receivable are created when a firm sells products or services but is to receive cash for the sale in the future. MNCs conduct hundreds of sales transactions every day, creating accounts receivable balances. In this section, we discuss risks related to MNC receivables and ways in which these risks can be mitigated.

Risk Factors

Currency Risk

An obvious risk for an MNC is currency risk. When receivables and payables are denominated in foreign currencies, the MNC is subject to transaction exposure. Recall our discussions in earlier chapters about currency risk in receivables (and payables) and methods of mitigation.

Default Risk

Default risk is a major consideration, especially when an MNC has considerable receivables in foreign countries. History has shown that business conditions in most foreign countries are more volatile than those in the United States. But this risk may be offset by the potential of increased sales and profits. Thus, an MNC must carefully evaluate this trade-off and take appropriate steps to mitigate default risk.

Interest Rate Risk

MNCs are also subject to interest rate risk on their receivables. Because the cash flows occur in the future, MNCs face the risk that interest rates will change in the meantime. Note that for MNCs, receivables are equivalent to advancing loans to customers at a fixed rate of interest (future cash flow is prespecified).

Credit Terms

credit to customers
Offering *credit to customers* in foreign markets may have a high level of risk but may also offer a high level of reward. A quantitative analysis is necessary to understand the trade-off.

MNCs may offer credit to their customers as a way to garner additional sales. This is especially valuable in countries where citizens do not have easy access to consumer credit as they do in the United States or western European countries such as the United Kingdom.

The following issues should be considered in making a credit-granting decision:

- The extent to which existing customers need credit and whether a significant number of them would choose to use credit if offered.
- The extent to which granting credit would induce new customers to buy the firm's products.
- The potential for bad debts.
- The interest cost of extending credit.
- Potential responses from competing firms and the long-run effects on prices and units sold.
- The potential for currency risk by extending credit in foreign currencies.

EXAMPLE 11.4

Assume that an MNC operating in India currently sells 10,000 units of a product at a price of Indian rupee (INR) 300. Direct expenses are INR 180 per unit. Currently, the customers take cash delivery. The firm is considering a new pricing structure that requires customers to choose between cash discounts and credit. The firm wants to offer a revised price of INR 310 with a "5/10 net 60" deal. This means that a customer can pay by the 10th day and take a 5 percent discount, which would bring the price down to INR 294.50. Customers choosing to avail themselves of the credit must pay the full price by the 60th day. The firm estimates that its sales would increase by 20 percent and that half its customers would take the cash discount option. The firm faces a discount rate of 10 percent for INR cash flows. Assume annual compounding.

1. Should the firm proceed with this credit extension? That is, calculate the NPV of the proposed plan and compare it with the status quo.

2. Show how your answers change if you assume a default rate of 15 percent among the 50 percent of customers that do not make use of the discount.

Solution:

$$\text{NPV (current)} = \text{INR } 10{,}000 \times 300 - 10{,}000 \times 180 = \text{INR } 1{,}200{,}000$$

Part 1

To calculate NPV for the proposed plan, we separate the customers into those who will take the discount and pay INR 294.50 and those who will use the 60-day credit and pay the full price of INR 310. See the following equation.

$$\text{NPV (proposed)} = \text{INR } 12{,}000 \times \left[\frac{50\% \times 294.50}{(1 + 10\%)^{10/365}} + \frac{50\% \times 310}{(1 + 10\%)^{60/365}} \right] - 12{,}000 \times 180$$

$$= \text{INR } 1{,}433{,}478.$$

Part 2

To answer part 2, we revise this equation to incorporate the 15 percent default rate among the 60-day credit takers as follows:

$$\text{NPV (proposed)} = \text{INR } 12{,}000 \times \left[\frac{50\% \times 294.50}{(1 + 10\%)^{10/365}} + \frac{50\% \times 310 \times (1 - 15\%)}{(1 + 10\%)^{60/365}} \right] - 12{,}000 \times 180$$

$$= \text{INR } 1{,}158{,}815$$

Discussion: Excluding bad debts, the new pricing structure appears attractive. Key profitability drivers are increased price and increased sales. However, discounts do eat away at profits. In fact, if sales do not rise, NPV would be only INR 1,194,565 (substitute 10,000 units in the NPV equation in part 1). Instead, part 2 indicates that forecasted customer default changes our decision in favor of the status quo.

The firm is also subject to currency risk. If the INR is projected to decline in value and if this projected decline is not factored into the discount rate, the value calculated will be an overly optimistic one. In this case, a wise strategy would be to conduct the analysis in USD by converting the cash flows from INR into USD at projected currency rates.

The MNC's ability to estimate bad debts in a foreign situation may be limited. Bad debts are caused by many factors in addition to economic conditions. Culture may play a role in the willingness of customers to repay the firm. Contract laws may also encourage default and protect the firm's customers from litigation. Nevertheless, MNCs must use their best efforts to forecast the probability of bad debt.

Finally, the cost of administering the credit must be recognized. From an organizational standpoint, MNCs need more staff at the subsidiary level to administer credit sales than they do for cash sales. MNCs with large-scale operations are best able to administer credit policies. This is a chicken-and-egg problem: Credit is often needed to attract new customers and increase the scale of operations.

Monetizing Receivables

Some MNCs may want to avoid all risks associated with receivables in foreign countries. We discuss two ways in which this can be accomplished, both involving the sale of receivables to a third party.

Factoring

Factoring is a fairly common and traditional procedure; it involves selling receivables to third parties known as *factors*. Banks and financing companies serve as factors. Naturally, the MNC would only receive a fraction of the face value of the receivables; this discount compensates the factor for interest as well as default risk. The MNC can then repatriate the funds out of the foreign country to avoid currency risk and repatriation risk also.

EXAMPLE 11.5

U.K. exporters face difficulties collecting monies from customers in other European countries such as Italy, France, and Spain. They increasingly use factors such as Fortis Commercial Finance and Coface to solve collection problems. In fact, exporters can obtain "invoice finance," which means that they receive a discounted value of sales at the moment of invoicing. This helps exporters solve their financing and collection problems.

Securitization

A relatively new phenomenon pioneered in U.S. markets and increasingly imitated in Europe and emerging markets, **securitization** involves the issuance of financial instruments using nontraded assets as collateral. Specifically, pools of homogenous assets are created and financial instruments are issued backed by these assets. Cash flows from securitized assets are used to make interest and principal payments on these financial instruments. As with factoring, securitization bridges a firm's financing and asset management policies and reduces its need for conventional financing. By securitizing receivables, an MNC can simultaneously solve the problem of managing receivables and obtaining financing.

securitization

Securitization is one of the great financial innovations of recent times. MNCs use this method to convert receivables into cash.

Securitization originated in the mortgage industry in the United States with the emergence of firms such as the Federal National Mortgage Association (Fannie Mae). Today, securitization is widely used with automobile lease payments, airline ticket sale proceeds, credit card receivables, equipment leases, and any recurring inflows from customers.

The securitization process is as follows (see Exhibit 11.1). The MNC expects future cash inflows from customers. These inflows result from loans advanced to customers and

EXHIBIT 11.1
The Securitization Process

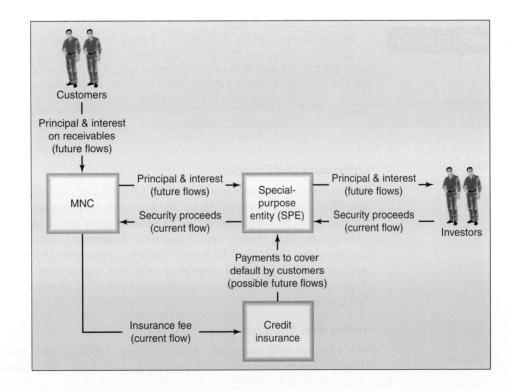

take the form of principal and interest repayments. The MNC creates a special-purpose entity or vehicle (known as *SPE* or *SPV,* respectively) and transfers its assets (receivables) to that entity. In return, the SPE issues debt instruments, raises money from investors, and passes these funds to the firm. Later, as cash flows in from customers, the amounts are transferred to investors through the SPE. To reduce risks and to enhance the offering's credit rating, firms may overcollateralize (that is, issue fewer securities so that payments from customers comfortably exceed promised payments to investors) or purchase credit insurance.

One development in the 1990s is the use of offshore (i.e., Euro) markets to issue asset-backed securities. The growth of asset-backed Euro instruments in recent years has exceeded the growth of the overall Euro markets. This securitization market can be very creative. For example, in 2001, Toys"R"Us collateralized its license fees from its Japanese affiliate into a JPY debt instrument and subsequently swapped out of the JPY into the USD.

Expediting Net Receipts of Cash

With hundreds of transactions per day, a key concern for MNCs is managing payments from customers. How can firms minimize the time it takes for a customer's payment to reach the firm and the time it takes for this payment to be converted into cash in the firm's account? These are important issues, particularly for large firms. Consider the example of an MNC receiving USD 8 billion of payments annually. Assume that it takes the firm 10 days to process customer payments. At an interest rate of 10 percent, this translates to an opportunity cost of more than USD 20 million each year. An efficient payment-processing system can help the firm recover half or more of this lost value.

Lockboxes

A third-party vendor (usually a bank) sets up collection points located near clusters of customers so that payments can be received and processed quickly. This **lockbox** system is especially valuable in cross-border scenarios in which payment transit time (if checks are mailed) is a week or more. The principal objective of a lockbox system is to eliminate mailing as well as processing time. Lockboxes are especially useful for firms that deal with a large volume of checks from retail customers.

EXAMPLE 11.6	Lockboxes have entered the electronic age. A state-of-the-art lockbox contains software as well as hardware components. Remittance documents are scanned and processed not only to convert payments but also to extract information related to the payments. For instance, information in a health care-related payment about a remitter's insurance contract is transmitted to the insurance firm for posting purposes. Specialized vendors such as U.S.-based Wausau sell such software.

Electronic Fund Transfers

By using **electronic funds transfers (EFT)**, MNCs can save on transactions costs and save time. This enables increased speed and precision in managing cash balances. Numerous electronic systems support MNCs. In an earlier chapter, we discussed SWIFT. An important system in the U.S. setting—and bound to be replicated in other countries—is automated clearing house (ACH) in which most financial institutions and the Federal Reserve Bank participate; ACH generated more than 18 billion transactions (USD volume equals tens of trillions) in 2007. Businesses increasingly use ACH to process online payments from their customers.

Netting with Affiliates

MNCs are not only concerned about receiving cash from their customers. They conduct numerous transactions with accompanying payments with their subsidiaries and affiliates.

Netting in this context is the settling of intracompany accounts by offsetting debits and credits. The purpose of netting is to reduce the number of transactions and thereby save transaction costs.

EXAMPLE 11.7	Consider the following USD cash flows between an MNC and its various affiliates: (as an example of reading this matrix: the Mexican subsidiary owes the parent 60 and the parent owes the Mexican subsidiary 25)

	From			
To	**Parent**	**Mexico**	**India**	**Japan**
Parent		60	30	5
Mexico	25		5	0
India	15	20		10
Japan	10	10	5	

bilateral and multilateral netting

Bilateral netting is the settling of accounts between two parties. *Multilateral netting* is the settling of accounts between multiple parties.

Apply (1) bilateral and (2) multilateral netting to settle the accounts.

Solution:

1. To apply bilateral netting, identify each pair (a total of six pairs) and offset the two amounts for the pair. For example, the cash flow for the Mexico-parent pair is 35 in favor of the parent. This produces the following netted amounts:

	From			
To	**Parent**	**Mexico**	**India**	**Japan**
Parent		35	15	
Mexico				
India		15		5
Japan	5	10		

Thus, we reduce the number of transactions from 12 to 6.

2. To apply multilateral netting, identify all cash flows for each entity. First identify all the "to" rows (these are positive cash flows). Next, identify all cash flows in the "from" columns (these are negative cash flows). Subtract "from" values from "to" values for each entity.

Parent = (35 + 15) − (5) = 45
Mexico = (0) − (35 + 15 + 10) = −60
India = (15 + 5) − (15) = 5
Japan = (5 + 10) − (5) = 10

[*Note:* If you have solved the problem correctly, the sum of these values is zero.]

Discussion: Mexico pays the parent, India, and Japan the amounts of 45, 5, and 10 respectively. These three transactions summarize all 12 original cash flows. This example is simplistic in many respects. It importantly assumes away the currency problem. In a real-world setting, MNCs need to conduct netting in multiple currencies. While the complexity of the problem rises with multiple currencies, the principles remain the same.

Prompt settlement of accounts between affiliates requires both the identification of netted amounts as illustrated above and speedy mechanisms such as EFT for transferring funds. One may question why internal transfers are important. After all, on a net basis, overall cash flow is zero. The reason lies in the very nature of decentralization that is important to MNC operations. One needs realistic data on subsidiary performance for monitoring purposes. Prompt settlements lead to more reliable estimates of subsidiary performance.

Netting with External Parties

MNCs also conduct netting in their transactions with customers and suppliers. As in intra-company netting, extracompany netting saves transaction costs. But there are more challenges here. The information systems of various firms need to talk to one another. Standardized enterprise resource planning (ERP) systems are helpful in this regard. Banks and other financial firms also provide solutions for both kinds of netting. (See Appendix 11 for a detailed example of netting.)

11.4 Bank Financing

Bank financing is an important source of short-term capital for MNCs. In this section, we discuss the various forms of financing provided by banks. First, let's consider the range of services offered by banks to MNCs.

Financing is one of many services offered by banks. See Exhibit 11.2 for a list of services. MNCs cultivate relationships with multiple banks and use a variety of these services. Relationships are managed and optimized to minimize total banking costs, improve efficiencies of cash management, improve collections from customers, and obtain valuable advice on various financial matters.

Types of Bank Loans

Bank financing is quite important for most MNCs and can take the forms discussed in this section.

Term Loans

The simplest form of bank financing, **term loans** are unsecured loans made for a specified period of time at a fixed interest rate. By definition, a term loan is fixed and inflexible, so it is not a popular method of financing. Banks may also require firms taking term loans to hold a compensating balance in a low or zero interest-bearing account: This feature adds to the cost of a term loan (r_B). (Recall notation introduced in Chapter 10 where r_B refers to the cost of debt.)

EXHIBIT 11.2
Banking Services Used by MNCs

- Manage various deposits and accounts such as checking, banking, and money market accounts. MNCs also have accounts in multiple locations to maximize the present value of cash disbursements and receipts.
- Facilitate the transfer of funds to and from affiliates. In some cases, this calls for establishing netting facilities.
- Exchange currencies and provide currency forecasting services. Banks also serve as counterparties in derivatives transactions.
- Provide advice on foreign regulations. By operating around the world and having a network of contacts, banks are well positioned to provide this advice.
- Provide various types of financing. This, of course, is the main intermediation function of banks. Financing can take many forms including the traditional term loan, revolving credit agreements, and syndicated loans.
- Facilitate export and import transactions by managing the document trail. Banks help in the creation of documents such as letters of credit.
- Provide lockbox and netting services.
- Provide risk management advice.

EXAMPLE 11.8

A bank offers a term loan for one year at a rate of 8 percent but requires that it hold 12 percent of the loan amount as a compensating balance. Calculate the cost of the loan. Assume that the compensating balance earns zero interest.

Solution: Assume a borrowing of USD 100. The compensating balance of USD 12 implies a net borrowing amount of USD 88. However, repayment requires payment of 8 percent interest on the full amount. Thus, interest plus principal is USD 108. Because the compensating balance is USD 12, the firm needs to repay only USD 96. The cost of the loan is[1]:

$$r_B = \frac{96}{88} - 1 = 9.09\%$$

Alternatively,

$$r_B = \frac{\text{Stated rate}}{1 - \text{Compensating balance \%}}$$

$$= \frac{8\%}{1 - 12\%}$$

$$= 9.09\%$$

Inventory and Accounts Receivable Financing

MNCs with significant amounts of inventory and accounts receivable can use these assets as collateral in their borrowing. There are some constraints, however. Banks may not be willing to accept as collateral (1) inventory that is subject to obsolescence (e.g., computers and high technology products) and (2) accounts receivable in jurisdictions unfriendly to the rights of creditors (e.g., certain emerging markets) and when banks have limited recourse in case of default.

Trade Financing

MNCs engaged in exporting products can obtain funding using mechanisms such as the discounting of banker's acceptances. MNCs engaged in importing products can obtain financing in conjunction with the issuance of letters of credit. These procedures are described in Chapter 13.

Lines of Credit

A **line of credit** is a flexible financing arrangement. In this financing method, firms negotiate parameters such as the maximum amount, interest rates, and fees. As funding needs occur, firms draw on this line of credit. This type of agreement is potentially very valuable to the firm because of its flexibility. The line of credit may also serve as a useful backup for firms as they try to source less expensive capital from the securities markets. Because of these advantages, banks charge commensurately high interest rates. Banks also charge a fee known as a *commitment fee*. Option pricing theory helps us understand the rationale for this fee. The commitment fee may be viewed as the premium for a call option on a loan: Firms exercise this option by borrowing. Assuming that the contractual interest rate is fixed, not floating, option theory indicates both a higher value for the bank's commitment and correspondingly higher fees when interest rates are more volatile.

Eurobank Loans

Eurobanks—banks engaged in cross-border activity—are particularly active in providing loans to MNCs. Because many of the Euro deposits (such as the Eurodollar deposits) are short to medium term, banks are well positioned to make loans over similar maturities. In fact, the high level of lending activity by Eurobanks leads some observers to label this market as a

---

[1] In general with loans involving a single repayment, the cost is given by $(FV/PV)^{1/t} - 1$ where PV is the proceeds from the loan, FV is the repayment of the loan, and t is the maturity of the loan. With multiple payments, the cost equals the IRR of the payments.

wholesale market; one feature of a wholesale market is lower spreads between lending and borrowing rates compared to retail markets such as the U.S. bank markets. Thus, loans in the Euro market may be less costly to firms than loans in their respective domestic markets.

Eurocredits

Loans (or credits) extended by Eurobanks are also known as *Eurocredits*. These loans are often linked to LIBOR; this is analogous to corporate lending by U.S. banks that is linked to the prime rate. The premium over LIBOR may be linked to factors such as flexibility in the terms of the loan, the riskiness of the borrower, and capital market conditions.

EXAMPLE 11.9

A bank offers a firm a 90-day loan for USD 6 million at LIBOR + 60 basis points (bp). If the London Interbank Offered Rate (LIBOR) is currently indicated at 6.2 percent, calculate the loan repayment.

Solution:

$$\text{Loan repayment} = \text{USD } 6{,}000{,}000 \times \left(1 + 6.8\% \times \frac{90}{360}\right) = \text{USD } 6{,}102{,}000$$

Discussion: Interest is calculated using the actual/360 simple interest method. Such a method of interest computation is fairly prevalent in money markets, but other methods may also be used as the loan agreement specifies.

Syndicated Loans from Eurobanks

Banks face elevated levels of default risk when they make a large loan to a customer. A potential solution to this problem is **loan syndication** in which a number of banks collectively bear the risk of a particular loan. The main bank that negotiates the terms of the loan is known as the *lead bank,* or the *lead manager.* This bank will negotiate terms such as the size of the loan, the maturity, the spread or premium over benchmark rates such as LIBOR, and the fees. Once the loan's terms are negotiated, the lead manager will arrange for a consortium of banks to jointly offer this loan. Syndicated loans may be term loans or revolving credit loans. In the latter scenario, the fees would be much larger to reflect the value of the option provided to the borrower.

syndicated loans
MNCs turn to bank *syndicated loans* when they have an urgent need for a large amount of financing.

The syndication process ranges in complexity depending on the loan's size and features. The lead manager can have complex arrangements with other banks. The roles of other banks can vary and can take the form of co-lead manager, manager, or participant bank. Lead managers assume more responsibilities than managers, who in turn assume more responsibilities than participant banks. The loan can be arranged on a *best-efforts basis,* or it can be *underwritten.* A loan obtained under a best-efforts basis is an uncommitted loan; one that is underwritten comes with guarantees from the syndicate. Syndicate banks receive various types of fees including front-end management fees and periodic commitment fees. These fees as well as the spread in the loan contribute to a bank's earnings.

Syndicated loan facilities offer the following advantages to firms:

- **Privacy.** Firms are able to maintain the confidentiality of information they provide to the banker. In a public issue of securities, firms are often put in the awkward position of revealing information that may potentially help a competitor.

- **Flexibility.** Both sides of the transaction can cancel the loan process without the embarrassment and resulting loss of investor confidence that such an event would otherwise entail.

- **Speed.** The negotiations for syndicated loans are typically quicker than those for issuing securities. Even though we find the same intermediaries at work in both markets, loans are processed faster because this is essentially a private transaction involving fewer parties.

- **Contingency.** The market for syndicated loans may be a good alternative source of capital even for firms very active in issuing securities and can be a backup in the event that security market conditions worsen.

EXAMPLE 11.10

A firm obtains a syndicated loan of USD 12 million with front-end management fees and other expenses of 0.8 percent. The loan is for a period of 180 days with a stated rate of 7.2 percent computed as simple interest on an actual/360-day basis. Calculate the all-in cost of financing (the cost of financing that includes fees and other costs).

Solution:

Loan amount $= USD\ 12{,}000{,}000 \times (1 - 0.8\%) = USD\ 11{,}904{,}000$

Interest amount $= USD\ 12{,}000{,}000 \times 7.2\% \times \dfrac{180}{360} = USD\ 432{,}000$

$$r_B = \left(\frac{12{,}000{,}000 + 432{,}000}{11{,}904{,}000}\right)^{365/180} - 1 = 9.20\%$$

Discussion: This procedure produces the loan's effective (i.e., compounded) annual cost. Such an annualizing procedure is customary in cost-of-capital calculations, especially when comparing alternative sources of financing. If a financing alternative is quoted using a different convention, adjustments are necessary before making the comparison.

11.5 Market Financing

MNCs continually search for ways to tap capital directly from investors. Public markets offer MNCs access to a bigger and less expensive pool of capital. We discuss various forms of market-based short-term financing.

Commercial Paper

commercial papers

Commercial paper is the lowest cost form of short-term financing, but only large and low-risk firms may obtain this form of financing.

U.S. commercial papers (USCP) are unsecured short-term instruments issued by large U.S. corporations. The typical issue raises hundreds of millions of dollars. Maturities are very short, about a month, although they can go up to 270 days without the need for registering with the Securities and Exchange Commission (SEC). Because of its unsecured nature, only firms with very high ratings—AAA in a majority of the cases—are able to tap this market. Investment bankers arrange USCP issues and charge fees that are small relative to transaction size.

One problem with USCP is that the funds are obtained on an uncommitted basis. Unlike a line of credit from a bank, the firm cannot be guaranteed that the issue will be subscribed and the funds available. This uncertainty probably deters small firms with fewer financing alternatives; these firms would not want to jeopardize future forays into money and capital markets by developing a bad reputation. Another problem is that firms with even moderately risky ratings cannot tap this market. For example, in 2000, Standard and Poor's cut the short-term debt rating of U.S. telecom firm Lucent Technologies to A-3 from A-2; consequently, Lucent lost access to the USCP market. The USCP market encountered difficulties during the credit crisis of 2007−2008. In fact, the data in Exhibit 11.3 for 2007 imply a decrease in market size from 2006 (only 2007 values are reported below). More decreases were forecasted for 2008.

EXHIBIT 11.3

U.S. Commercial Paper (outstanding year-end 2007 in USD billion)

Source: *www.federalreserve.gov/releases/CP/outstandings.htm* (accessed December 21, 2008).

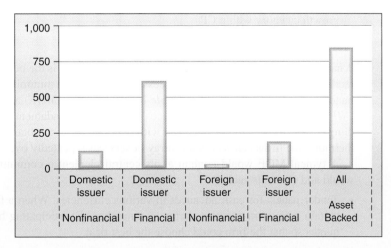

Euro Commercial Paper

Euro commercial paper (ECP) is a viable alternative to USCP. The word *Euro* in this use does not refer to the currency; rather it refers to the cross-border nature of this market. Like the USCP, the ECP is a short-term debt instrument without any coupon payments and maturing in a few months. The ECP is sold at a discount from face, most ECP issues are in USD, and they are generally not underwritten.

While the ECP market has great potential, especially in the asset-backed category, the ECP lags the USCP market. The depth and liquidity of the USCP market has satisfied U.S. firms and prevented them from trying the ECP market. Also, European and Asian firms have chosen to rely more on syndicated loans for short- to medium-term financing. This reliance on bank loans is consistent with the importance of bank relations in the corporate governance and operations of these firms. The ECP market has also lagged because of its fragmented nature and lack of standards for issuance and secondary trading.

EXAMPLE 11.11

An MNC issues a 60-day ECP of face (or par) USD 1,000 at a discount of 6 percent. What is the cost of financing?

Solution:

$$\text{Loan amount} = \text{USD } 1{,}000 - 1{,}000 \times 6\% \times \frac{60}{360} = \text{USD } 990$$

The annualized effective financing cost is calculated as:

$$r_B = \left(\frac{1{,}000}{990}\right)^{365/60} - 1 = 6.30\%$$

Financial calculator inputs: FV = 1,000; PV = −990; N = 60/365. Solve for I.

Discussion: ECP, like U.S. T-bills and USCP, are quoted on a discount basis from face value and based on a 360-day year. Annualized discounts need to be converted to actual discounts based on the instrument's actual maturity. The price is determined by deducting this actual discount from the face value.

Post-2000, the ECP market has shown significant growth (see Exhibit 11.4). Reasons include these:

- Introduction of the EUR and the consolidation of markets and services across Europe. Fragmented domestic CP markets such as the one in Germany are getting integrated into the ECP market.
- Increased demand for debt issuance in response to a wave of mergers and acquisitions (M&A) and restructuring in Europe. Traditional sources of capital such as banks are incapable of meeting this demand fully.
- Adoption of securitization in non-U.S. settings. Asset-backed CP (ABCP) is the highest growth category within CP.

Notes Facilities

A natural evolution in the market for short-term financing is the bundling of diverse financing facilities to provide MNCs ease of access to capital and to minimize transactions costs. These bundled services are known as *multiple-option facilities (MOF)* and *notes-issuance facilities (NIF)*, depending on the type of services bundled. The fundamental concept behind this bundling is that firms negotiate once and with only one agent to obtain an array of services. Furthermore, the firms can access this array of services repeatedly over a long period of time.

A typical MOF would contain as its central element a committed revolving credit and would add elements such as:

- Tender panels for cash advances in various currencies. When a firm indicates need for a certain amount in a certain currency, a number of participating banks would tender their quotes so that the firm could choose the best deal.

EXHIBIT 11.4

ECP Market by Sector

Source: *http://www.icma-group.org/ market_practice/Advocacy/euro_ commercial_paper/euro_ commercial_paper.Par.0002. ParDownLoadFile.tmp/ ECP%20market%20data%20v2.pdf* (accessed June 6, 2008).

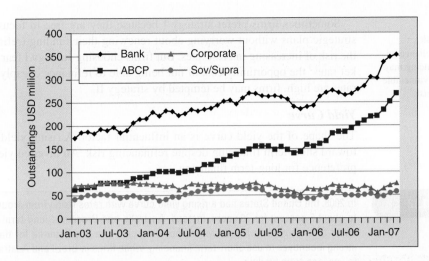

- Facilities for discounting banker's acceptances (explained in a later chapter). This is particularly useful for firms engaged in retail exporting to developing markets in which time drafts are drawn and accepted by banks.
- Uncommitted facilities to issue financial securities such as ECP and Euro notes.

11.6 Financing Strategies to Minimize Cost

In this section, we present some of the strategic issues in MNC short-term financing including:

- The relative use of short-term financing versus long-term financing.
- The choice of currency
- The uses of forwards in conjunction with financing alternatives.

Short-Term versus Long-Term Financing

In this section, we discuss issues influencing the choice between short-term and long-term financing.

Matching Strategy

Firms need financing principally for three reasons: (1) acquisition of long-term assets such as plant, equipment, warehouses and other facilities, (2) day-to-day operations that require funding current assets such as inventory and accounts receivable, and (3) strategic cash reserves. Conventional wisdom requires that firms match the maturities of their financing instruments/ vehicles with the maturities of the assets acquired with these funds. Thus, firms might use stock and bond financing for setting up a plant in a foreign country and to have strategic cash reserves but use short-term bank loans to fund the inventory for this foreign operation. This approach—also called the *duration matching method*—seeks to equate the interest rate risk in financing to the interest rate risk in assets. An implicit assumption is that interest rates affect assets and liabilities equally.

Refinancing Risk

Consider two financing strategies:

- **Strategy I.** Firms obtain only long-term funding that is sufficient to fund long-term as well as operational needs.
- **Strategy II.** Firms obtain long-term funding equal to their long-term needs and repeatedly obtain short-term financing to finance operations.

refinancing risk
An excessive reliance on
short-term financing may
leave an MNC vulnerable
to *refinancing risk*.

Sometimes firms prefer strategy I because they are free to focus on implementing their strategic plans without worrying about renewing their funding (refinancing risk) and facing the risk of increasing interest rates. But firms choosing strategy I fear a rapid decrease in market rates: the opportunity cost of not being able to refinance cheaply may be high. If current rates are high, firms may be tempted by strategy II.

Yield Curve

The shape of the yield curve is an influential factor. A rising yield curve may bias MNCs toward short-term financing despite refinancing risk. An inverted yield curve may indicate a preference for long-term financing.

EXAMPLE 11.12

In 2008, the United States had a rising yield curve with rates rising from around 2 percent for one year to about 5 percent for 30 years. Instead, Australia and Brazil had long-term rates equal to or slightly lower than short-term rates. (www.bloomberg.com is a good source for these data.) U.S. firms had strong incentives to use short-term financing, while firms in Brazil and Australia had strong incentives to use long-term funding.

Currency Considerations

Principally because of both the development of the Euro markets and the increased availability of currency derivatives, MNCs, today are offered considerable choice in currency denomination for their short-term debt. Next we discuss the following considerations related to currencies:

- Calculation of the ex ante and ex post financing cost in a foreign currency debt.
- Parity conditions and the foreign currency financing cost.
- Weak and strong currency financing.
- Financing using a portfolio of currencies.

Ex Ante and Ex Post Financing Costs

Consider short-term financing at a fixed rate of interest. In this scenario, the MNC faces currency risk. If an MNC borrows in a foreign currency and if that currency appreciates in value during the term of the loan, the MNC not only pays interest but also incurs losses related to repayment in a stronger currency. The ex ante financing cost incorporates the MNC's estimate of the future spot value of the foreign currency. The ex post financing cost incorporates the foreign currency's actual spot value; the ex post cost is after the fact. The ex ante cost in particular is important in financial planning.

EXAMPLE 11.13

Consider a U.S.-based MNC that obtained a one-year loan of JPY 30 million at a rate of 3 percent. When it obtains the loan, spot JPYUSD equals 0.0090. At that time, the MNC expected the JPYUSD spot rate to equal 0.0091 in one year. One year hence, at maturity, the actual value of the JPYUSD is 0.0092. Calculate the ex ante and ex post financing costs in USD terms.

Solution:

Ex Ante and Ex Post Financing Costs

	$t = 0$	$t = 1$	
		Predicted (ex ante)	Actual (ex post)
JPY flows	30,000,000	−30,900,000	−30,900,000
Currency			
JPYUSD	0.009	0.0091	0.0092
Percent change		1.11%	2.22%
USD flows	270,000	−281,190	−284,280
Cost (USD)		4.14%	5.29%

Alternatively, we can use the equation introduced in the previous chapter that expresses financing cost as a function of currency change (*s*):

$$r_B = (1 + r_B^*) \times (1 + s) - 1$$

This equation is appropriate for ex post calculations. For ex ante calculations, use the expected value for *s* [or E(*s*)].

In this example:

$$r_B^* = 3\%$$

$$E(s) = \frac{0.0091}{0.0090} - 1 = 1.11\%$$

$$s = \frac{0.0092}{0.0090} - 1 = 2.22\%$$

Ex ante $r_B = (1 + 3\%) \times (1 + 1.11\%) = 4.14\%$

Ex post $r_B = (1 + 3\%) \times (1 + 2.22\%) = 5.29\%$

Discussion: The ex post cost of financing depends on the foreign cost of financing as well as the foreign currency's rate of appreciation or depreciation. In the preceding example, the JPY appreciates and therefore increases financing cost.

Scenario Analysis

To incorporate currency influences in ex ante costs, one needs to produce forecasts of the foreign currency. Instead of generating a point estimate, we can use forecasting methods to generate scenarios and associated probabilities. Using this information, we can calculate the distribution of financing costs.

EXAMPLE 11.14

A U.S.-based MNC is considering taking a one-year 7 percent term loan denominated in the Czech koruna (CZK), which is currently trading at a rate of CZK 36 per USD. Three scenarios are assumed for the CZK as follows:

Scenario	Probability	Outcome
Stable	40%	No change
Weak	40%	$s = -3\%$
Strong	20%	$s = +4\%$

Assuming a loan amount of CZK 10,000, calculate the average and standard deviation of USD financing costs.

Solution: See below.

Currency Scenario Analysis

	$t = 0$	$t = 1$
Stable Currency Scenario		
Cash flow in CZK	10,000	−10,700
CZKUSD ($s = 0\%$)	0.027778	0.027778
Cash flow in USD	277.78	−297.22
Cost (USD)		**7.00%**
Weak Currency Scenario		
Cash flow in CZK	10,000	−10,700
CZKUSD ($s = -3\%$)	0.027778	0.026944
Cash Flow in USD	277.78	−288.31
Cost (USD)		**3.79%**

Continued		
	$t = 0$	$t = 1$
Strong Currency Scenario		
Cash flow in CZK	10,000	−10,700
CZKUSD ($s = +4\%$)	0.027778	0.028889
Cash Flow in USD	277.78	−309.11
Cost (USD)		**11.28%**

Summary of Costs	**Probability**	**Cost**
Stable	40%	7.00%
Weak	40%	3.79%
Strong	20%	11.28%

$$\text{Average} = 40\% \times 7.00\% + 40\% \times 3.79\% + 20\% \times 11.28\%$$
$$= 6.57\%$$

$$\sigma^2 = 40\% \times (7.00\% - 6.57\%)^2 + 40\% \times (3.79\% - 6.57\%)^2$$
$$+ 20\% \times (11.28\% - 6.57\%)^2$$
$$= 0.00076$$

$$\sigma = \sqrt{0.00076} = 2.76\%$$

Discussion: The expected or average cost of financing is 6.57 percent. Because of currency risk, financing cost in the home currency fluctuates. We find a standard deviation of 2.76 percent for this risk factor.

Parity Conditions

choice of currency
If parity conditions hold, the *choice of currency* does not matter. A lower interest cost will be offset by the burden of repayment in a stronger currency.

If parity holds, the choice of currency does not matter on an ex ante basis. For example, if the international Fisher effect (equivalently, the uncovered interest rate parity) holds, a foreign currency appreciates or depreciates relative to the interest rate differential. Financing in a low-interest currency may not offer any benefits because that currency will appreciate.

EXAMPLE 11.15

Consider a U.S.-based MNC that obtains Canadian dollars (CAD) 1,000 for one year at a cost of 6 percent. This produces CAD flows of +1,000 and −1,060 at $t = 0$ and $t = 1$, respectively. The CAD spot rate is USD 0.70. The USD interest rate for similar loans is 4 percent. Assume that IFE holds. What is the expected spot CADUSD in one year? Using this future spot, calculate the financing cost in USD terms.

Solution:

$$E(S_{t+1}) = 0.70 \times \frac{1 + 4\%}{1 + 6\%} = 0.6868$$

Thus, the USD cost of financing is given by:

$$\text{Ex ante } r_B = \frac{1,060 \times 0.6868}{1,000 \times 0.7000} - 1 = 4\%$$

Discussion: Because parity holds, ex ante financing costs in home currency terms are invariant. There is no guarantee, however, that ex post costs will be identical.

Strong and Weak Currency Financing

An important choice in financing is currency denomination. This is important for many reasons including:

- Alignment of financing cash flows with operational cash flows to mitigate currency risk.
- Use of currency forecasts to exploit weakening currencies. If the funding currency weakens, ex post cost of financing decreases.
- To exploit temporary violations of parity.

multiple-currency financing
Financing using a *currency cocktail* can potentially lower cost and/or lower risk.

Portfolio Considerations

MNCs also use multiple-currency financing to achieve diversification benefits. Just as investors achieve benefits by diversifying their portfolios, MNCs lower financing costs and achieve lower risk by diversifying their financing portfolios.

EXAMPLE 11.16

An MNC is considering the following information regarding financing in two currencies. Inputs are financing costs in the Swiss franc (CHF) and the U.K. pound (GBP) as well as forecasts of the two currencies (percent changes from spot) for scenarios I–III. You are asked to evaluate whether an equally weighted CHFGBP financing portfolio will provide superior results.

		CHF	GBP
Financing cost (r_B^*)		3%	5%
Scenario	**Probability**	s_{CHF}	s_{GBP}
I	30%	5%	12%
II	20%	−3%	2%
III	50%	10%	−1%

Solution:

◇	A	B	C	D	E
1					
2			$r_B = (1 + r_B^*) \times (1 + s) - 1$		
3					**50% CHF + 50%**
4	**Scenarios**		**CHF**	**GBP**	**GBP**
5	I	30%	8.15%	17.60%	12.88%
6	II	20%	−0.09%	7.10%	3.51%
7	III	50%	13.30%	3.95%	8.63%
8					
9	Average		9.08%	8.68%	8.88%
10	Variance		0.002598	0.003556	0.001060
11	Sigma		5.10%	5.96%	3.26%

Sample computations follow:

- The cost (USD) for CHF financing in scenario I is given by $(1 + 3\%) \times (1 + 5\%) - 1 = 8.15\%$.
- The cost (USD) for the portfolio (last column) is given by $50\% \times 8.15\% + 50\% \times 17.60\% = 12.88\%$.

The average and standard deviations are calculated using probabilities as weights as shown in the Czech koruna term loan problem.

Discussion: Note the imperfect correlation between the two currencies. For example, in scenario III when the CHF appreciates by 10 percent (increasing financing costs), the GBP decreases by 1 percent (decreasing financing costs). This imperfect correlation implies diversification benefits. The low standard deviation for the portfolio (3.26 percent) compared to individual currency standard deviations is a typical consequence of diversification. Students who have studied portfolio theory may note two features of these results: the portfolio average of 8.88 percent is simply the weighted average of individual costs, and the portfolio standard deviation of 3.26 percent is lower than the weighted average of currency standard deviations.

Use of Forwards

MNCs can use forward contracts in conjunction with short-term financing to (1) satisfy debt-denomination preferences and (2) currency risk mitigation objectives. These two reasons are not mutually exclusive, but MNCs focus on one or the other, depending on their priorities.

EXAMPLE 11.17

A Singapore-based MNC borrows GBP at a rate of 5 percent for one year. The direct (GBPSGD) spot rate (SGD is the Singapore dollar) is 2.6754. The firm notes that the forward rate for the GBP indicates a discount of 3 percent and wants to lock in this discount to decrease financing costs.

1. Calculate finance costs in SGD.
2. If the amount of the loan is GBP 2 million, calculate cash flows related to financing.

Solution:

1. We can explicitly calculate SGD financing costs as follows:

$$r_B = (1 + 5\%) \times (1 - 3\%) - 1 = 1.85\%$$

2. To calculate cash flows, find the forward rate:

$$\frac{F}{2.6754} - 1 = -3\%$$

Solving, we find $F = 2.59514$. Determine cash flows using these currency rates:

	0	1	r_B
Cash flow in GBP	2,000,000	2,100,000	2,100,000/2,000,000 − 1 = 5%
GBPSGD	2.6754	2.59514	
Cash flow in SGD	5,350,800	5,449,794	5,449,794/5,350,800 − 1 = 1.85%

Discussion: The use of the forward effectively transforms the GBP debt into SGD debt. Additionally, note that the use of the forward ensures zero variation (that is, no risk) in the ex post cost of capital.

Financial Slack

Financial slack represents the capacity to source financing—especially short-term financing—as needed. For most firms, short-term financing needs are correlated with operations: Financing requirements increase as operations increase. This implies that short-term financing must be flexible. One way to achieve flexibility is to create "excess capacity" by employing a variety of strategies as follows:

- Using bank lines of credit.
- Shelf registering (using a blanket approval by regulators) short- to medium-term securities such as notes.
- Arranging a commercial paper plan with an investment banker.
- Arranging a plan allowing sale of receivables to third parties.

EXAMPLE 11.18

Hewlett Packard reports financial slack in its 2007 10-K report.

Item	Notes	Available	Used	Remaining
Variety of instruments including notes	2006 shelf registration agreement including long-term items	3,000	1,000	2,000
Lines of credit	Uncommitted	2,455	645	1,810
Euro CP		500	244	256
U.S. CP		6,000	1,821	4,179
Receivables financing	Sale to third parties on nonrecourse basis	N/A	N/A	525

Summary

- MNC cash management requires netting and other sophisticated practices. Because cash occurs in various currencies, cash management must be synchronized with currency hedging.
- Receivables also pose unique challenges. MNCs can exploit their size to securitize receivables.
- Banks are important providers of short-term financing. They are sources of private capital and compete against public markets. Banks distinguish themselves by offering flexibility and confidentiality in their financing relationship with firms. Types of bank loans include term loans, lines of credit, revolving credit arrangements, Eurocredits, and syndicated loans.

- MNCs also obtain financing directly from markets using instruments such as Euro commercial paper. Public financing has the advantage of providing large amounts of capital at low cost.

- MNCs make many strategic decisions in sourcing short-term financing. Issues include the reliance on short-term (versus long-term) alternatives, the choice between private and public markets, and the choice of currency denomination.

- The currency denomination issue is of particular relevance to MNCs. They must calculate cost of capital in terms of their domestic currencies even if financing is sourced in a foreign denomination. Furthermore, the risk of changes in ex post financing costs because of currency fluctuation must be assessed.

Questions

1. **Cash Balances.** Consider an MNC that sells and sources globally. What are some real options available concerning its cash balances?

2. **Cash Balances.** Consider a European MNC with extensive operations in Asia. What might be some concerns this firm faces because of excess cash balances in Asian subsidiaries?

3. **Receivables.** The CFO of a major corporation makes this observation: "Global receivables pose more problems than domestic receivables." What are plausible explanations for this statement?

4. **Credit Policy.** A U.S. appliance manufacturer wishes to penetrate the Indian market. Research shows that Indian middle class customers cannot afford to pay cash but many are willing to buy on credit. What are advantages and disadvantages of offering credit under these circumstances?

5. **Securitization.** What is securitization? How can firms use this process to manage receivables? Can you think of other financial management problems of firms that can be solved by securitization?

6. **Securitization.** Select five MNCs that sell consumer durables. Obtain their annual reports or 10-K reports from the internet (e.g., http.www.sec.gov). Determine the scope of securitization activities of these firms. (You may try a key word search in html or PDF documents.)

7. **Lockboxes.** What are lockboxes? What types of firms use lockbox systems? How has technology improved lockbox efficiency?

8. **Netting.** What is netting? Distinguish intracompany and intercompany netting. Distinguish bilateral and multilateral netting. What are prerequisites for a successful netting system?

9. **Bank Financing.** "You only go to a bank for a loan when you have no capability to source money from markets." So says a CFO of a large MNC. Critically examine this statement. Argue for and against it.

10. **Syndicated Loans.** What is a syndicated loan? What are the characteristics of this market? Why do MNCs use syndicated loans?

11. **Commercial Paper.** What are USCP and ECP? Explain market characteristics and trends. Which of these is more important from the standpoint of MNCs?

12. **Short-Term versus Long-Term Financing.** Lintek, a Taiwanese LCD manufacturer, is currently experiencing a booming market for its products. As with all growing companies, its financing needs have significantly increased. Current as well as fixed assets are increasing each year, triggering financing needs. The CFO is debating with his team about the merits of matching current assets with short-term financing. What are advantages and disadvantages of this approach?

13. **Financial Slack.** Recall the Taiwanese firm Lintek described question 12. Another issue of strategy discussed by the CFO's team is financial slack. What is financial slack? Why would this be an issue of concern to Lintek?

Problems

1. **Net Working Capital.** Using the data on working capital items from a firm's balance sheet in the following table, complete the following:

   a. Calculate net working capital.

   b. Describe the structure of current assets and discuss how they are financed.

   c. Do you believe that all items are actually denominated in the currency stated? For example, do you think that clients settle all receivables by using GBP?

   d. Using knowledge from previous finance classes, calculate financial ratios to characterize the firm's working capital situation.

Current Assets	GBP (millions)	Current Liabilities	GBP (millions)
Cash	247	Short-term debt	444
Accounts receivable	1,220	Current portion of long-term debt	222
Inventory	439	Accounts payable	591

2. **Credit Terms.** Assume that an MNC operating in China currently sells 1,000 units of a product each month at a price in yuans (CNY) of 5,000 and has a profit margin of 25 percent. Currently the customers take cash delivery. The firm is considering a new pricing structure that requires customers to choose between cash discounts and credit. The firm wants to offer a price of CNY 5,200 with a "4/15 net 45" deal. The firm estimates that its sales would increase by 12 percent and that half of its customers would take the cash discount option. The firm faces a discount rate of 12 percent for CNY cash flows (annual compounding).

   a. What is the NPV of selling 1,000 units under the current cash terms?

   b. What is the NPV of selling 1,120 units under the proposed discount/credit terms? Should the firm proceed with this credit extension?

   c. What is the revised answer in (b) if you consider that 6 percent of credit takers default?

3. **Credit Terms in a Weakening Currency.** A French MNC sells luxury goods in Chile. Each month, the firm sells 2,500 handbags at a price of the Chilean peso (CLP) 200,000. Assume a profit margin of 50 percent. The French firm does not sell its products directly to customers but to Chilean retailers. Because of economic difficulties, some retailers have been reluctant to stock the handbags. In addition to uncertainty about generating sales, retailers did not wish to make cash payment for merchandise in advance of actual sales. The French firm's chief financial officer (CFO) estimates that offering credit terms can increase sales. Specifically, it is estimated that offering 2/10, net 60 terms can increase sales by 25 percent. Assume that 40 percent of customers take the discount and an interest rate of 18 percent (annual compounding). Assume no default.

   a. Compare the NPV of the new credit terms with the NPV of the status quo.

   b. Consider the following additional information. The CLP depreciates by 12 percent annually. Does this new information change your answer in (a)? Explain.

   c. Which alternative (proposed or current) exposes the firm to greater currency risk?

4. **Multilateral Netting in Single Currency.** Binck, a Dutch electronics conglomerate, has operations in three foreign countries. Its intra-affiliate transactions during the current week generate payments depicted in the following table. Values represent EUR millions.

To	From			
	Parent	**Brazil**	**China**	**Russia**
Parent		20	50	25
Brazil	30		15	10
China	50	40		20
Russia	15	10	5	

   a. Summarize transactions using bilateral netting.

   b. Summarize transactions using multilateral netting.

5. **Compensating Balance and Loan Cost.** An MNC obtains a one-year bank loan from Mitsubishi Bank. The loan amount is JPY 100 million, and the MNC is required to provide a compensating balance of 8 percent. If the interest rate is 6 percent, calculate the cost of the loan.

6. **Compensating Balance and Loan Cost.** Haidong, a Taiwanese contract manufacturer, has experienced an upsurge in business. High-cost Japanese electronics firms have been outsourcing manufacturing lately, and Haidong has landed some big contracts in recent months. To support its working capital needs, Haidong seeks bank financing of Taiwanese dollar (TWD) 100 million for 120 days. Through its Japanese associates, Haidong is in contact with two Japanese banks offering JPY loans to Asian firms at competitive rates. The two quotes are summarized in the following table.

Bank	Stated Rate	Interest Convention	Compensating Balance
Mizuho	3.3%	actual/360 simple	12%
Shinsei	3.4%	Annual compounding	10%

   a. What are the benefits of a JPY loan for Haidong?

   b. Determine the net and total JPY amounts to be borrowed under the two scenarios (Mizuho and Shinsei). Based on these amounts, calculate the loan repayment amounts and determine the least expensive loan. Assume spot TWDJPY equals 3.54.

7. **LIBOR Rates.** The CFO of a Canadian trucking firm obtains the following quote by telephone from a U.S. banker for a 90-day loan: LIBOR+80 basis points for USD 10 million. The reference rate is three-month LIBOR, which is indicated at 4.1 percent on the day of the offer.

   a. Is this a fixed rate loan or a floating rate loan?

   b. What are the Canadian firm's loan related cash flows? (Recall LIBOR conventions.)

   c. Calculate the (effective) annualized cost of the loan.

8. **Loan Fees.** A Brazilian telecommunications firm obtains a syndicated loan of USD 100 million with front-end management fees and other expenses of 0.5 percent. The loan is for a period of 270 days with a stated rate of 8.4 percent computed as simple interest on an actual/360-day basis. Calculate the all-in cost.

9. **Loan Fees.** A French utility seeks USD financing because it perceives the USD as overbought and because USD rates are lower than EUR rates. A British bank—active in the Eurocurrency market—promises competitive rates and offers a 90-day USD 30 million loan at a rate of 4 percent (LIBOR convention). Loan fees are 0.4 percent. However, another bank, a U.S. one, beat out the British bank's quote by offering the loan at 3.6 percent (LIBOR convention) and fees of 0.4 percent. Assuming the British bank does not wish to change its rate, what fees should it charge to make its quote competitive?

10. **ECP.** An MNC makes a 90-day USD 100 million ECP issue. If the issue was priced at a discount of 5 percent (annualized, simple interest actual/360 convention) and fees totaled USD 250,000, what is the cost of financing?

11. **Ex Ante and Ex Post Financing Cost.** Consider a U.S.-based MNC that obtains a one-year loan of GBP 50 million at a rate of 5 percent. When the loan is obtained, the GBP is trading at GBPUSD equals 1.90. The MNC expects the GBP to strengthen to GBPUSD equals 1.94 at year-end. The MNC obtains the loan in spite of this forecast because it could offset this GBP liability (short position) against its U.K. operations.

   a. What is the ex ante cost of financing in USD?

   b. Suppose the GBP actually strengthens to 1.92. Calculate the ex post financing cost in USD.

12. **Ex Ante Costs with Currency Scenarios.** TVS, an Indian two-wheeler manufacturer, seeks to tap foreign sources for short-term loans. Its motivation is a credit crunch in the Indian market. A Brazilian bank offers a one-year 8 percent term loan denominated in the Brazilian real (BRL). The amount of the loan is BRL 20 million. The BRL is currently trading at a

rate of BRLINR equals 10. Three scenarios are assumed for changes in BRLINR as in the following table.

Scenario	Probability	Outcome
Stable	30%	$s = +2\%$
Weak	40%	$s = -6\%$
Strong	30%	$s = +8\%$

Using this information:

a. Calculate BRL cash flows related to the loan for the three scenarios.

b. Convert BRL cash flows into INR for the three scenarios. What is the home currency financing cost (r_B) in these three scenarios?

c. Calculate the mean and standard deviation of the home currency financing cost.

13. **Financing Costs and Parity Conditions.** A Belgian bank offers a one-year EUR denominated loan at 5.4 percent to a AAA-rated U.S. customer. Assume that this rate is competitive and similar to rates offered by other banks for EUR financing. The U.S. customer also obtains a quote for a USD-denominated loan from a U.S. bank. If the customer is convinced of the competitiveness of the EUR quote but unsure of the USD financing quote, what benchmark can it use to assess the USD financing quote? Assume parity conditions hold and the following market information. Spot EURUSD equals 1.50; one-year forward EURUSD equals 1.48.

14. **Financing with a Currency Portfolio.** Rider, a U.S.-based MNC, embarks on a project to globalize its financing strategy. It has two goals. First, it wants to seek less expensive worldwide sources of capital. Second, independent of costs, it wants to reduce the effects of currency change on its USD cost of financing. To fulfill its second objective, the firm seeks to combine loans denominated in BRL and EUR. See the following table for financing costs as well as forecasts for the two currencies. Assume a one-year loan.

		BRL	EUR
Financing Cost (r_B)		14%	5%
Scenarios	**Probability**	s_{BRL}	s_{EUR}
I	30%	−5%	1%
II	40%	−12%	2%
III	30%	−5%	−1%

a. Calculate home currency (USD) financing costs for each currency for the three scenarios.

b. What is the expected home currency financing cost relative to each currency?

c. What is the standard deviation of home currency financing cost relative to each currency?

d. Assume a 40–60 financing split between the BRL and EUR. Evaluate the characteristics of this financing portfolio and compare with single currency financing options. Recommend how the firm should proceed.

15. **Use of Forwards.** Nintendo, a Japanese game manufacturer, takes out a loan with the following characteristics: loan amount = EUR 120 million, maturity = 180 days, rate = 4.6 percent (actual/360 simple interest). Nintendo does not wish to have exposure to EUR and seeks a forward contract. EURJPY forwards of 180 days are quoted at a discount of 2 percent from the spot value of 160.

a. Construct a table or spreadsheet showing all cash flows related to this financing (EUR and JPY).

b. Calculate the home currency cost of financing assuming the use of the forward.

c. If the forward is used, what is the standard deviation of the home currency cost of financing?

Extensions

1. **Actual Syndicated Loan Announcement.** "The Board of Directors of ECS Holdings Limited (the "Company") is pleased to announce that the Company has obtained a US$55 million three-year Syndicated Loan Facility (the "Facility") comprising a term loan facility of US$45 million and a revolving loan facility of US$10 million. The joint mandated lead arrangers for the Facility are Oversea-Chinese Banking Corporation (OCBC) and Sumitomo Mitsui Banking Corporation, Singapore Branch, and OCBC will be the agent bank for the syndicate of lender banks. The Facility will be used to refinance the Company's existing borrowings under a syndicated loan facility of US$60 million, which is due for repayment on 28 January 2008. The Facility will also be used to finance the Company's general working capital requirements. The Facility is secured by a Deed of Guarantee given by a subsidiary of the Company." (Obtained from a press release of a Singapore-listed IT services corporation that has operations in many Asian countries including China. http://ecs.listedcompany.com/news.html/id/73442, accessed August 2, 2008.)

   a. What are the components of this loan package?

   b. What is the stated objective of this financing?

   c. Speculate why this firm is not tapping markets directly through an ECP issue.

2. **Financing Portfolio and Solving for Minimum Variance.** Consider data presented in the following table on short-term financing options available to a firm. One-year loan rates are provided for loans denominated in two different currencies. Analysts' forecasts of these two currencies are also provided.

		BRL	JPY
Financing cost (r_B^*)		14%	2%
Scenarios	**Probability**	s_{BRL}	s_{JPY}
I	30%	−5%	6%
II	40	−12%	8%
III	30	−5%	−1%

   a. What are characteristics of financing in these two currencies? (Calculate average and standard deviation.)

   b. Conduct a portfolio analysis. Try various portfolio combinations by changing weights in 5 percent increments. Comment on your findings.

   c. Use the Solver function in Excel to determine the minimum variance financing portfolio.

3. **Financing Portfolio and Currency Independence.** Consider data presented in the following table on short-term financing options available to a firm. One-year loan rates are provided for loans denominated in two different currencies. Analysts' forecasts of these two currencies are also provided. Note that the two currencies' changes are independent of one another.

		CAD	JPY
Financing cost (r_B^*)		5%	2%
Scenarios	**Probability**	s_{CAD}	s_{JPY}
CAD I	30%	−5%	
CAD II	40	15%	
CAD III	30	−5%	
JPY I	60		10%
JPY II	40		1%

   a. What are the characteristics of financing in these two currencies? (Calculate average cost and standard deviation of cost.)

b. Assume that you finance in CAD and JPY using proportions of 30 percent and 70 percent, respectively. How many scenarios are there in total for this portfolio? Calculate home currency financing costs in each scenario. Determine the mean and standard deviation of home currency financing costs.

4. **Multilateral Netting in Two Currencies.** Moriba, a Japanese industrial equipment maker, has operations in three foreign countries. Its intra-affiliate transactions during the current week generate payments depicted in the following table. The matrix specifies currency denomination as well as values (millions).

To		From		
	Parent	**United States**	**France**	**India**
Parent		USD 40	EUR 20	USD 30
United States	USD 20		EUR 25	USD 30
France	EUR 10	EUR 50		USD 20
India	USD 20	USD 10	USD 15	

a. Summarize transactions using bilateral netting.
b. Summarize transactions using multilateral netting.
c. Can transactions be further simplified after calculations in (b) if the spot rate at the beginning of the week (EURUSD = 1.50) is used?

Clover Machines: *Credit and Short-Term Financing*

Clover Machines, like most growing firms, experiences large shifts in its liquidity position. These shifts—causing unexpected deficit or surplus cash—result from a variety of reasons. Seasonality is one reason: For instance, sales of construction machinery generally slows down in winter and picks up in spring and early summer. Weather patterns, farm incomes, and a variety of other factors affect the pattern of sales and consequently liquidity. Contracts with suppliers and terms of payment also have an impact. While some of these factors are predictable, others are not; hence, unexpected swings occur. So, it is vital that adequate sources of short-term financing be identified and developed.

In addition to factors discussed after the following table, shifts in the business model can also have ripple effects in liquidity. Consider Clover's nascent operations in Brazil. Recall from an earlier case that Clover introduced two products, a dozer and a harvester, in Brazil. Clover's initial projections are reproduced here:

Product	Sales (units) Range: Low End	Sales (units) Range: High End	List Price	Discount
250 hp dozer (land clearing)	520	640	BRL 500,000	10%
Harvester with sugarcane attachment	800	1,000	BRL 400,000	15%

While projections for the dozer held true (Clover sold 600 units), its harvester sales fell short. Instead of projected sales of 800–1,000 units, Clover sold only 500 units in the previous year. The business manager of Clover's Brazilian subsidiary recommended offering credit coupled with discounts as a means to increase harvester sales. But this would mean a shift in cash flows and create short-term financing needs.

The credit terms proposed were 6/10, net 60. The discount implicit in the credit terms are in addition to the 15 percent discount offered to Clover's sales agent in Brazil; this discount is applied on the net price (85 percent of list). Internal analysis based on market research indicates that sales could grow by 25 percent as a consequence and that sales would be divided equally between discount takers and credit takers.

Because customer payments would occur later under the proposed scheme, Clover would have to obtain short-term financing. Most financing decisions are taken at headquarters. The CFO's staff obtained information on the following two financing possibilities:

- JPY is a low-interest currency. A JPY one-year loan is available with an interest rate of 2 percent. Parity conditions show that the JPY is expected to appreciate by 5.4 percent.
- The Australian dollar (AUD) is a high-interest currency. An AUD one-year loan is available with an interest rate of 10 percent. Offsetting the high rate of interest, analysts note that the AUD is expected to depreciate by 2.8 percent.

Brian Bent, Clover CFO, asks his assistant, Ann Murphy, to evaluate both the credit policy and the resulting financing. He poses the following questions to her:

1. Based on your understanding of the industry and conditions in emerging markets, do you think the credit policy makes sense? What is the policy's NPV? Provide a spreadsheet model of the credit decision. Assume a discount rate of 10 percent and zero bad debts. The cost per unit is BRL 200,000.

2. Estimate financing needs (USD amount) resulting from the credit policy. Assume that USDBRL spot equals 1.6. [*Hint:* Use days of credit sales and discount sales to estimate financing need.

3. What are the financing costs (USD terms) for the two alternatives? Use the information provided below.

4. Speculate why the firm is not considering BRL-denominated financing.

5. Using the information provided below, evaluate the prospects of using a 50−50 currency cocktail for financing.

	JPY	AUD
Spot	0.0100	0.9500

Forecast of Next Year's Spot

Scenario	Probability	JPY	AUD
I	30%	0.0104	0.8740
II	30%	0.0110	0.9120
II	40%	0.0103	0.9690

Appendix 11

Netting in Action: *Alstom Takes Netting to New Level*[2]

Alstom is a global energy and transport company with more than 800 subsidiary companies, an order book of EUR 637.5 million and annual sales in excess of EUR 23 billion. Not surprisingly, the group processes many thousands of inter-subsidiary transactions per month, operates a substantial cash float and has a fairly hefty need for costly foreign exchange services.

[2] Anonymous. *Corporate Finance.* (London). 214. (September 2002), p. 19. Copyright Euromoney Institutional Investor PLC, September 2002.

The company's on-going implementation of a netting solution from Geneva-based Coprocess is aimed at addressing each of these expensive operational issues, and is already paying some interesting, and unexpected, dividends.

Netting, whereby inter-company—and, optionally, third-party—payments and receipts are aggregated into a single amount per currency, is hardly a sexy subject, nor new. It is the kind of back-room operation that rarely garners headlines and yet it generates savings and other benefits that far outweigh the cost of the software or the implementation. "Netting is an unsung hero when it comes to cutting costs and improving efficiency," says Adrian Rogers, director, global risk management solutions at PricewaterhouseCoopers.

Alstom's implementation is not the usual, basic netting system; what distinguishes the project is the capability to manage discrepancies and disputes that the platform enables, which Rick Rohrs, the manager of Alstom's netting centre at the group head office in Paris, believes is unique. The system is also multi-period—subsidiaries can upload all their receivables, not just those due for settlement in the current netting period. Rohrs says that not only is this of tremendous value for early matching and dispute resolution, it is also of value as a source of data for future hedging.

Rohrs is hugely positive about the company's experience. He says the system has easily achieved the project's fundamental aims of improving cash management and ensuring payments get made on time. Although the project is still only about 65% completed, it is already settling in excess of 10,000 invoices per month.

"The netting effect is already an estimated 85% of transactions [or actual payments], a 50% reduction in cash flow [or physical cash movement], leading to annual savings of millions of euros in bank fees and float reduction. The netting project has really improved Alstom's cash flow and liquidity," he says.

But according to PwC's Rogers, it is the less apparent improvements that can be even more beneficial, if more difficult to quantify. "Netting injects discipline into inter-company processes. By establishing a single settlement day for all subsidiaries, and creating one net payment to the netting centre rather than multiple payments to different counterparties, it eliminates leading and lagging when one company decides not to pay an invoice on the due date."

Rohrs agrees. "Netting has eased and simplified the process of settling internal transactions, enforcing a discipline where invoices are settled as per contractual terms. This has reduced internal overdues, the time spent on collecting internal settlements, the accounting cycle time, inter-company mismatches, the cash flow movement and the float on funds."

He says it has improved cash forecasting on internal transactions and has realized savings on banking costs and transfer charges as well as group savings in FX. "The pay-off has been phenomenal. We are already showing savings and we haven't finished the global rollout yet."

Rohrs adds that the unprecedented level of inter-company communication enabled by the Coprocess platform has enabled Alstom to establish a dispute resolution framework, which has reduced the number of disputes to less than 1% of transactions. The savings in time and resources that were in the past required to sort out month-end inter-company disputes at each subsidiary cannot be overstated, says Rohrs.

When Alstom began the system selection process about two years ago, Coprocess had two solutions: the core NT Netting engine and IntraNetting—a web-based desktop application for subsidiaries; both could be configured to be either payables or receivables-driven. Alstom wanted a receivables-led system, but only if it had a communications platform built in to allow flagging and discussion of problem invoices. Coprocess developed the functionality for Alstom and has subsequently incorporated the capability into its product.

"Payment-driven netting solutions are really just fancy payment systems," says Rohrs. "There is no guarantee that the payments will be made on time. Therefore a receivables-led solution is preferable, but you have to provide a way for payers to dispute or question a requested payment because disputes always occur at some point. Our implementation provides for multi-level communications between units and is fully integrated with the company email platform."

For users it could not be simpler. Alongside information about the invoice on the payable and receivables screens of the IntraNetting application, there is a mail icon; if an accounts payable employee thinks there is a discrepancy, they simply click on the icon and a new email message appears already populated with the details for the appropriate contact at the firm to which the payment is due.

"This has been really well received by users," says Rohrs. "To make the communication element work, we have appointed only one payable and one receivable contact in each company, and it ensures that everyone knows who has responsibility for a problem if it occurs."

The Coprocess platform also creates an audit trail. The system records which company has flagged a discrepancy, who has been contacted and when, what comments were made about the payment in question, and who responded and when.

It is not only communication that is integrated into the netting process. The system also interfaces with local Enterprise Resource Planning and accounting systems so that it is able to upload invoices automatically, which Rohrs says saves time and eliminates human error when rekeying invoice information.

The system is useful at a financial strategy level too. If Coprocess' full netting capability is used, where all transactions are converted to the home currency, then users can use its ask-and-offers functionality to manage cash flow. The system allows Alstom to reflect forward contracts during this period—in other words, to use futures bought as part of a hedging strategy. If a subsidiary has forward contracts that are fixed prior to netting, the user either asks (to receive) or offers (to pay) those currencies in the system. This gives the user the flexibility to pay or receive in a currency other than the home currency.

"Currency matching is one of the largest savings because it means we have to purchase less FX and the group doesn't get hit with big spreads. We also gain benefit with the nonmatched FX as it is aggregated to larger volumes resulting in better rates," says Rohrs.

At the subsidiary level, IntraNetting improves financial planning by providing access to real time payment data. Subsidiaries can click on the netting report button to trigger a current calculation of their net position.

Andrew Greenwood, business development manager in the merchant banking division at SEB, says it is the degree that the Coprocess platform is embedded into Alstom's business processes that distinguishes it from other implementations. "Most are like big calculators, but this solution has really dug itself deeper into the company's administration and payment procedures. This level of communication and integration takes netting to the next level."

CHAPTER TWELVE

International Alliances and Acquisitions

Tata Motors—virtually unknown in the West—is a leading automobile producer in India. When cash-strapped Ford Motors solicited bids for its Jaguar and Land Rover divisions, it was quite a surprise to many that the eventual winner was Tata. Why did Tata buy these marquee brands? More generally, what are Tata's global ambitions and what are various ways in which it can achieve these ambitions? In earlier chapters, we discussed the emergence of MNCs and their motivation for engagement in foreign direct investment (FDI) (Chapter 1) and how MNCs evaluate cross-border projects (Chapters 8 and 9). In this chapter, we take this analysis to the next logical step. How do MNCs acquire capabilities in foreign countries through alliances and acquisitions?

Entering a foreign market is inherently a very difficult proposition. Transferring a firm's capabilities to a foreign country to set up a solo "greenfield" project—one started from scratch—is often a time-consuming, costly, and uncertain endeavor. In foreign projects, a firm is not only operating in an unfamiliar environment in the normal operating sense—dealing with employees, customers, and suppliers—but also is dealing with foreign rules and regulations. Capabilities are lower and risks higher in foreign projects. Mergers, acquisitions, and alliances are effective ways to overcome these problems. Empirical evidence supports this position. We know for instance that mergers, acquisitions, and alliances form nearly 80 percent of all FDI. An MNC manager must therefore be well versed in conducting international acquisitions and alliances. What are alternate methods and how do they differ? What are their advantages and disadvantages? And, how are they implemented? These are key topics in this chapter.

More specifically, you will learn:

- Various methods of engaging in international alliances and acquisitions as well as their advantages and disadvantages.
- Why firms seek international alliances and acquisitions.
- Specific ways in which firms can conduct joint ventures with foreign partners.
- How to value a joint venture.
- Issues concerning cross-border mergers: recent history, current trends, and how these mergers are conducted.
- How to value a merger.

12.1 Overview of Alliances and Acquisitions

Alliances and acquisitions[1] come in many different sizes, shapes, and complexity. In this section, we describe these transactions and provide recent cross-border examples. This provides an opportunity to compare and contrast various transactions. In later sections, we provide a more detailed analysis of two of these transactions, joint ventures (JVs) and mergers.

---

[1] A commonly used and generic term in the business world for alliances and acquisitions is *deals*, indicating a contract between two firms.

Licensing Agreements

Licensing agreements are the least complicated of international deals and involve the transfer of technology or intellectual property from one firm to another in return for a fee. The firm granting the rights (or license) is known as the *licensor* and the firm receiving the rights is known as the *licensee.* Licenses are used to obtain proprietary technology and may cover product or process technologies. Occasionally licenses pertain to the use of a brand. Licensing agreements usually involve a stipulation of the number of units of products that can be produced and sold as well as a schedule for licensing fees or royalty fees owed to the owner of the technology. These agreements are typically for the medium term (one to five years).

licenses

Qualcomm *licenses* its wireless technology (e.g., CDMA) worldwide to more than 150 firms.

Licensing agreements are especially prevalent in the high-technology industries. For example, Rambus, a U.S. firm, licenses its technology concerning memory chips to manufacturers all over the world. A similar example is Qualcomm, which owns proprietary cellular phone technologies such as the CDMA. Both firms—Rambus and Qualcomm—sell no products but subsist solely on license fees; this indicates the importance of intellectual property and the validity of licensing as contracting technology. More generally, licenses are vital to transfer know-how from knowledge creators to knowledge users. A well-established legal system is required to support this system. Global institutions such as the World Trade Organization (WTO) and Organisation for Economic Co-operation and Development (OECD) are deeply concerned about harmonizing practices and promoting the effective use of intellectual property.

Some licensing agreements tend to be reciprocal agreements by which two firms exchange complementary technologies. Such deals are known as *cross-licensing agreements.* Eastman Kodak Company entered into a cross-licensing agreement with Olympus Optical Company Ltd. to share digital camera technology; this agreement was part of a larger strategic alliance covering digital imaging.

EXAMPLE 12.1

Microsoft uses licensing as part of its business strategy. Since launching its intellectual property licensing program in December 2003, it has negotiated more than 500 licenses for software, algorithms, and technologies with firms such as LG Electronics (Korea), Nortel Networks (Canada), and Seiko Epson (Japan). A recent licensing agreement concerns Hoya (maker of Pentax cameras); in fact, this is a cross-licensing agreement that covers digital cameras made by Pentax as well as a broad range of other consumer products made by both firms. Microsoft and other large technology firms such as IBM use their licensing strategies to generate diversification benefits—cash flows from licensing fees are correlated with noncore industries and may assume an uncorrelated pattern compared with operating cash flows.

Procurement and Outsourcing Agreements

Firms use procurement contracts to source components and supplies from other firms. These contracts occur for many reasons. Firms may not have the expertise or technology to produce in-house certain components and products. Or firms may simply not have the core competency to produce certain components or products in a cost-effective manner. As with procurement contracts, the term *outsourcing* refers to the use of an external party (often from a foreign country) to source an input. However, outsourcing agreements differ from procurement contracts because of their greater scope. For example, outsourcing may include services (e.g., warranty-related work) and business processes (e.g., accounting, taxation, human resources) in addition to components, raw materials, or products.[2]

EXAMPLE 12.2

U.S.-based technology firms such as Dell and Hewlett Packard regularly outsource manufacture of components to Asian suppliers, principally in China, Taiwan, and Korea. While these U.S. firms could potentially manufacture components such as motherboards, their comparative advantage is to assemble PCs to customer specifications and to provide excellent after-sales service. Even this outsourcing model is currently undergoing a transformation: In 2008, Dell signaled its intention to sell its PC factories and totally outsource PC production.

---

[2] Some writers distinguish between *outsourcing* and *offshoring*. The latter refers to sourcing from a foreign entity.

outsourcing
Outsourcing is more comprehensive than licensing. Firms may even outsource design and/or manufacturing.

Outsourcing agreements are much more complex than licensing agreements. While the time frames are similar—short to medium term—the contractual terms are more complex because of the flow of actual products and services rather than ideas. Apple sourced its popular iPhone from various so-called contract manufacturers including Taiwan's Quanta. In addition to price, parameters such as quality, lead and delivery times, units, and delivery location are stipulated.

Outsourcing—fueled by the Internet and communications technologies—has become a controversial business practice in the United States, especially when it resulted in the displacement of highly skilled workers such as programmers. As a business phenomenon, however, outsourcing is nothing new and is just another face of globalization. Firms in a country focus on what they can do better (theory of comparative advantage). In the modern world, a product may involve numerous inputs and comparative advantage may occur only in some of these inputs. Over time, firms determine what their core competencies are and—to survive and prosper—move noncore elements outside the firm via outsourcing.[3]

EXAMPLE 12.3

Business process outsourcing (BPO) is emerging as a key type of outsourcing. The U.S.-based consulting firm Accenture is a leading firm providing BPO services. Two recent agreements indicate the breadth of expertise as well as the global reach of this firm. First, it entered into a USD 400 million agreement with Thomas Cook (U.K.-based) to provide application management, technology infrastructure management, finance, accounting, and human resource management services. Second, in an agreement with the Japanese pharmaceutical firm Eisai, Accenture provides clinical data management services, using its delivery center in Chennai, India.

Distribution Agreements

Distribution agreements occur when a firm sells another firm's products through its existing distribution channels. These agreements occur when firms build up expertise in certain specific types of distribution procedures. Especially in cases in which it is difficult to organically build up this capability, either because it is expensive or because it requires a lot of time, it makes economic sense for firms to share such capabilities.

EXAMPLE 12.4

Bacardi, USA, a private firm distributing various spirits and liqueurs in the United States, has an agreement to distribute the Amaretto DiSaronno liqueur. Bacardi uses its expertise in marketing a wide range of products, and DiSaronno fits well in this portfolio. An interesting bit of trivia about DiSaronno is that it was apparently concocted in the 16th century in Italy by a beautiful widow who, when romanced by a young artist, sought to create a "rich, smooth almond liqueur" to express her admiration of him.

Firms wishing to quickly penetrate a foreign market commonly use distribution agreements. There are interesting trade-offs, however. On one hand, the firm may benefit from the local knowledge as well as the distributor's existing infrastructure, ensuring a quick start. On the other hand, the firm will be required to share its profits with the distributor and may delay acquisition of capabilities in the foreign country. So, the decision to use a distributor hinges on a cost-benefit analysis. The following example illustrates some of these issues in a simple setting.

EXAMPLE 12.5

A U.S.-based pharmaceutical firm is evaluating the use of a Brazilian distributor for a new product with an estimated three-year life. Use of a distributor ensures annual sales of USD 250,000. The distributor requires an initial payment of USD 15,000 and annual fees of 10 percent of revenue. With its own system, the U.S. firm will have a slower start with year 1 sales of USD 100,000, but in years 2 and 3, sales are expected to be USD 250,000 and USD 300,000, respectively. The initial cost of building its own distribution is USD 20,000; recurring annual fixed costs are USD 30,000. Assume taxes are zero. If the discount rate is 10 percent and if costs excluding distribution expenses are 50 percent of sales, estimate the net present value (NPV) of the two distribution approaches.

---

[3] C. K. Prahalad and Gary Hamel, "The Core Competence of the Corporation," *Harvard Business Review* 68, no. 3 (1990), pp. 79–91.

Solution:

DISTRIBUTION AGREEMENT VALUATION

	Cash Flows (USD)			
	$t = 0$	$t = 1$	$t = 2$	$t = 3$
Scenario I: Distribution Agreement				
Revenues		250,000	250,000	250,000
Costs (excl. distribution) at 50 percent		125,000	125,000	125,000
Initial fees (fixed)	15,000			
Annual fees: 10 percent of revenues		25,000	25,000	25,000
Net cash flows	−15,000	100,000	100,000	100,000
NPV at 10 percent	233,685			
Scenario II: Own System				
Revenues		100,000	250,000	300,000
Costs (excl. distribution) at 50 percent		50,000	125,000	150,000
Distribution costs (fixed)	20,000	30,000	30,000	30,000
Net cash flows	−20,000	20,000	95,000	120,000
NPV at 10 percent	166,852			

Discussion: The use of a distributor often involves a lower up-front cost than setting up one's own system. Also, the distributor ensures a quick start. But a firm's own system may offer long-term benefits because of lower agency costs. Note that year 3 net cash flows are higher with the own system. The longer the horizon, the more likely that an own system offers a better benefit.

Strategic Alliances

strategic alliances
Strategic alliances are usually long-term nonspecific arrangements to share resources and develop or market products.

Strategic alliances are broad agreements between companies to share resources, develop products, or market products. They differ from licensing and distribution agreements in that they are less specific, involve more than one product or issue, and are often for a longer term. Many strategic alliances involve the sharing of technologies and the joint development of products. Some of these agreements can be fairly complicated because they may involve issues such as the sharing of intellectual property rights, the sharing of technical talent, the distribution of products, and formulas for sharing revenues.

Airlines often use this method to share an actual flight using their own flight numbers (code-share), seamlessly serve complex routes, and avoid undue competition in specific markets. Strategic alliances are also quite common in the high-technology arena, in which it involves sharing intellectual property and the coordinating products and services to support unified industry standards. Sometimes a strategic alliance is a prelude to a joint venture or an acquisition.

EXAMPLE 12.6

The Japanese economy and financial markets have been in a state of decline since the mid-1980s. One financial firm, Mitsubishi UFJ securities, wished to expand overseas and to tap into growing foreign markets. It started an investment banking alliance with India's leading private bank, ICICI, in 2006. This was a "loose" agreement with the intent to cooperate in areas such as mergers and acquisitions, corporate finance, and asset management. Mitsubishi executed this agreement to exploit two potential scenarios: (1) to increase cross-border M&A between Japanese and Indian firms and (2) to facilitate Japanese investments in Indian stocks. Although mentioned in the press as a joint venture, this agreement fits the definition of a strategic alliance.

Joint Ventures

Joint ventures (JV) are similar to strategic alliances and involve the partnership of two or more firms. Unlike a strategic alliance, a JV results in a new business entity; partners have equity claims in this entity. JVs can be created by either allocating existing assets to the new entity or obtaining new investments from the partners. JVs are stand-alone businesses and have their own assets, financing, and management. This separation from the businesses of the partners allows an impartial evaluation of the JV's performance, and the results can also be used to motivate JV managers. This reduces agency costs. On the other hand, the independent structure of the JV creates (physical and organizational) distance between JV managers and controllers in partner firms; this JV feature exacerbates agency costs.

joint ventures
Suzuki and Honda have used the *joint venture* method to penetrate the India automobile market.

The JV is a very common method for firms to expand internationally. Auto manufacturers often penetrate markets of developing countries by establishing joint ventures with local partners; for example, Suzuki Motors (Japan) and Honda Motors (Japan) used this method to penetrate the Indian auto market. This method of conducting a cross-border business deal is often the only solution to governmental regulations that discourage outright mergers.

EXAMPLE 12.7	The market for beer in India is poised for significant increase and is attracting international firms. In 2007, Indians consumed less than 1 liter per capita compared to 20 liters in other developing countries. The target market is the 20 to 59 age group. Brewers believe that 10 percent of this age group (nearly 25 million people, upper middle class and higher) forms the potential market. Near term growth is expected at 20 percent. Leading foreign firms have created joint ventures with Indian brewers. Scottish and Newcastle (United Kingdom) started a JV with the leading Indian brewer, United Breweries.

Minority Ownership

A **minority ownership** occurs when one firm purchases less than 50 percent of the (vote-bearing) shares of another firm. In practice, most minority investments involve a 10 percent investment. This level of investment is significant enough to allow the investing firm an active role in the target firm without changing the control of the firm.

Firms often initiate a long-term relationship with another firm by taking a minority equity stake. This type of strategic investment creates flexibility for the acquiring firm. Business ties may be cultivated, and the acquiring firm may even consider an outright purchase of the target firm in the future. Minority investments may be viewed as real options: The initial investment is analogous to an option premium. Networking behemoth Cisco Systems is well known for this particular strategy. Many of its acquisitions—in an annual quota of more than 10 transactions—are initiated with a minority investment.

EXAMPLE 12.8	The Japanese food-processing firm Itochu made a minority investment in the Chinese firm Ting Hsin in 2008. Itochu paid USD 710 for a 20 percent minority stake and installed one of its directors on Ting Hsin's board. Using this investment as a springboard, Itochu wishes to become a major player in the food-processing business in the Asia-Pacific region. Ting Hsin—perhaps affected by high-profile tainted food scandals in China—wished to obtain food safety and other processing technology from the Japanese firm.

Mergers and Acquisitions

A *merger* is said to occur when two firms combine to form a new entity. An *acquisition* is said to occur when one firm acquires another; the target firm loses its identity and becomes part of the acquiring firm. In practice, as the term **mergers and acquisitions (M&A)** indicates, the two terms are used synonymously. A third term—*takeover*—also has an equivalent meaning.

Mergers can be viewed as mechanisms that shift control over assets from existing parties to new parties. A change in control can occur through means such as control over a firm's board of directors—achieved through a proxy contest—but ultimately, it is a merger that changes control permanently. A merger can be beneficial if the new controllers have more expertise and talent. Indeed, under ideal circumstances, such shifts of control could be an ideal driver of global economic growth.

EXHIBIT 12.1
M&A: Top Fifteen Worldwide Announced Deals (2007)

Source: Thomson, *Mergers and Acquisitions Review*, 2007 (4th quarter). http://www.thomsonreuters.com/business_units/financial/league_tables/merger_acquisition.

	Target	Acquirer	Value (USD billion)	Target Industry
1	Rio Tinto (United Kingdom)	BHP Billiton (Australia)	193	Materials
2	ABN-AMRO (Netherlands)	RFS (Netherlands)	99	Financials
3	Kraft Foods (United States)	Shareholders (United States)	61	Consumer Staples
4	BCE (Canada)	Investor Group (Canada)	47	Telecommunications
5	TXU Corp (United States)	Investor Group (United States)	44	Energy & Power
6	Alcan (Canada)	Rio Tinto (United Kingdom)	44	Materials
7	Capitalia (Italy)	Unicredito (Italy)	30	Financials
8	First Data (United States)	KKR (United States)	27	High Technology
9	Alltel (United States)	Atlantis (United States)	27	Telecommunications
10	Hilton Hotels (United States)	Blackstone (United States)	27	Media & Enter.
11	Endesa (Spain)	Investor Group (Italy)	26	Energy & Power
12	Tyco Healthcare (United States)	Shareholders (United States)	26	Healthcare
13	Eiffage (France)	Sacyr Vallehermoso (Spain)	24	Industrials
14	Archstone-Smith (United States)	Investor Group (United States)	22	Real Estate
15	Altadis (Spain)	Imperial Tobacco (United Kingdom)	21	Consumer Staples

Notes: 1, 4, 13, and 15 are either intended or pending as of the date of the report; some are buyouts by investor groups (3, 5, 11, 14) and private equity firms (4, 8, 10).

Aggregate merger activity is related to (1) economic and technological shocks and (2) availability of cheap capital. Economic shocks include disruptions such as high oil prices, inflation, and various economic crises. Technological shocks include innovations that disrupt various industries. The development of the Internet is an example of a technological shock. Because mergers are related to shocks as well as liquidity, they appear in waves. Currently, we are in the midst of a fifth merger wave that started in the 1990s.[4] Other waves have occurred in the 1890s (monopoly wave), 1920s (oligopoly wave), 1960s (conglomerate wave), and 1980s (hostile bust-ups wave). What is interesting about the current wave is its size and internationality. Data in Exhibit 12.1 for the 15 top transactions announced in 2007 support this perspective.

merger wave
Merger waves are triggered by economic/technological shocks and by the availability of cheap financing.

12.2 Motives for International Acquisitions and Alliances

International acquisitions and alliances have become so prevalent that it is difficult to read an issue of *The Wall Street Journal* these days without encountering at least one of these transactions. To understand this phenomenon, one must understand the motivation of firms involved in these deals. We discuss some of these reasons here. Many reasons are common to cross-border as well as domestic transactions. Although we list all important reasons, we emphasize reasons such as penetration of new markets that are particularly relevant for cross-border transactions. Also note that the reasons listed here are typically used to explain international mergers, but most reasons can readily be used to explain other forms of alliances and acquisitions.

Penetrating New Markets

acquisition or alliance
Acquisitions and alliances are the main ways in which firms penetrate foreign markets.

Firms wishing to conduct operations in foreign countries face substantial hurdles. At the operating level, firms transact with employees, suppliers, and customers. These interactions are affected by local norms of contracting, legal systems, culture, and government regulations. For these reasons, new market penetration is often accomplished through a foreign acquisition or alliance. The firm obtains general business capabilities through such a transaction.

[4] Some observers note that the fifth wave was ended by the credit crisis of 2007–2008.

Firms usually plan the penetration of new markets in two steps. As an initial step, firms may want to sell their products in new markets; next, firms may want to produce products in new markets. Even the relatively easier step of selling in a new market may pose great difficulties for the following reasons:

- **Distribution systems.** Firms may not have access to distribution systems. U.S. firms often face great hurdles in selling in Japan because the traditional distribution systems are characterized by old relationships and loyalties.

- **Knowledge of environment.** Firms may also lack knowledge to effectively promote their products in new markets. For instance, what is the best strategy for advertising computer products in a Latin American country such as Argentina? What are Argentinean regulations governing the marketing of the firm's products? What are local norms and culture affecting conduct of business?

EXAMPLE 12.9

U.S. firms wishing to conduct business in emerging markets such as China and India face complex regulations made more difficult by local customs that require firms to interact personally with bureaucrats. Obtaining requisite approvals for starting a business could be a long and torturous process. Local firms already have expertise in starting and running businesses. So, an optimal business method is the use of alliances with local firms. JVs are the vehicle of choice.

Obtaining New Technology

Sometimes appropriate technological inputs are not available in one's own country. This forces firms to transact with foreign firms to obtain technology. If the technology is complex and embedded in corporate processes, the only way to obtain it is to acquire the foreign firm or execute a joint venture. In other cases, the technology may be separable and can be obtained through simpler means such as licensing.

Why are technological inputs dispersed geographically? One reason is that countries have specialized in distinct competencies. This specialization occurs because of tradition, education, and the availability of raw materials. For example, countries such as Japan and Germany have specialized in manufacturing technology and robotics because of the excellence of their engineers. The United States has specialized in computer-related technologies with particular emphasis on operating systems, business software, and networking technologies; this is due in part to the strength of the U.S. higher education system and its emphasis on research. Italy is dominant in textile technologies because of the importance of fashion there. Russia, India, and Israel have specialized in certain types of business and gaming software; this is due to the abundant supply of mathematicians and software engineers in these countries. Thus, MNCs' resource needs will necessitate transactions with entities in various countries.

EXAMPLE 12.10

Oil prices rose dramatically during 2006–2007. This increased demand for deep-sea drilling technology. The British firm Expro possesses such technology. As oil prices hit an all-time high of USD 135 a barrel in May 2007, two deep-pocketed suitors—one the well-known U.S.-firm Halliburton and the other a consortium financed by Goldman Sachs—started a bidding war to acquire Expro.

Overcoming Adverse Regulation

Nations typically regulate sensitive industries such as defense, telecommunication, transportation, media, and energy. In extreme cases, countries simply prohibit foreign firms from entering these markets. But most countries, even the most protectionist ones, have understood the importance of foreign capital to grow these industries. Thus, they allow foreign firms to enter these markets but in a controlled manner that does not allow the firms to dominate local firms or to amass market power. Typically, foreign firms are prevented from obtaining majority control (or total acquisition) of firms in sensitive industries. Therefore, MNCs wishing to play globally in these industries need to strike deals with local partners.

EXAMPLE 12.11

National telecommunication markets are often closely regulated. Thus, if a European telecommunications firm wants to sell its services in regulated markets such as the one in India, the best strategy would be to strike cross-border deals with local firms. This will reduce the regulatory scrutiny faced by the firm. U.K.-based Vodafone acquired a stake in Hutchison Essar for USD 10.9 billion in 2007 to enter the Indian mobile phone services market. Vodafone also has a minority investment of 10 percent in another firm, Bharti.

MNCs also strike deals with local firms in anticipation of adverse regulation. Thus, they preemptively try to deflect either the enactment of adverse regulation or its application. This happens because MNCs create an alignment of interest between themselves and local entities; these entities will stand to lose along with the MNCs and will therefore exert influence to protect the MNCs. Thus, MNCs will want to align themselves with powerful constituencies such as labor unions and bankers.

Achieving Economies of Scale or Avoiding Redundancies

Firms want to be larger in order to fund large "entry" costs such as R&D expenses and to achieve economies of scale in production and distribution. Estimates indicate, for instance, that major pharmaceutical firms spend more than USD 1 billion annually on R&D. This feature alone drives many pharmaceutical firms toward mergers and JVs: The purpose of these deals is to cut redundancies and to achieve scale in R&D. Another industry in which scale is important is the automobile industry. Estimates place the cost of developing a new model at USD 1 to 2 billion. High development costs lead firms to seek scale: Models can be developed only if unit volume is sufficiently high.

EXAMPLE 12.12

Pharmaceutical firms face high (fixed) R&D expenses. If two firms have overlapping R&D, a merger can provide synergies. The merger of Astra AB (Sweden) and Zeneca Group PLC (United Kingdom) in 1999 exemplifies this concept. Through merger, these European pharmaceutical firms expected to reduce redundancies in R&D and save hundreds of millions of dollars annually.

Offering More Comprehensive Solutions to Customers

Another motive for international deals is to help firms offer a portfolio of products to their customers. When customers face transaction costs in assembling solutions—a bundle of products that satisfies a certain customer need—firms have incentives to broker deals with other firms to put together a product portfolio. Solutions help in two ways. They reduce transaction costs for customers, and they help firms achieve product differentiation and increase gross margins. Firms therefore go "shopping" to find partners or targets for acquisition that can provide complementary products.

EXAMPLE 12.13

In 2006, the Japanese financial firm Nomura acquired Instinet—a leading electronic communications network (ECN)—from the private equity firm Silver Lake Partners. Nomura sells financial products to individual as well as institutional clients. The Instinet platform, which allows electronic trading between large investors, rounds out Nomura's product portfolio, and positions it to compete with other large financial firms.

Achieving Global Distribution or Sourcing Capabilities

Setting up global distribution or sourcing systems is often quite challenging: firms face many difficulties including local regulations and cultural differences. For example, if a New Zealand winery wants to distribute its wines in the United States, it must negotiate a maze of (antiquated) federal and state laws that date back to Prohibition times. Suppose an Australian winery has already gained expertise in distributing wines in the United States. A deal (alliance or acquisition) between the New Zealand and Australian firms may make business sense. This is especially true if the two firms offer complementary products: Perhaps the Australian firm sells red wines and the New Zealand firm sells white wines.

EXAMPLE 12.14

The global wine industry is fragmented with tens of thousands of producers. One firm—U.S.-based Constellation, located in Rochester, NY—seeks a dominant position by acquiring businesses around the world. By these acquisitions, Constellation diversifies its portfolio and enhances its ability to source as well as distribute wine. Among its successes are New Zealand wineries Kim Crawford and Nobilo, makers of the popular white-varietal sauvignon blanc. By acquiring these wineries and maintaining production assets and people, both parties benefit. Original owners stay on and focus on wine production. Constellation focuses on distribution.

12.3 The Joint Venture: Description and Examples

MNC use of joint ventures
MNCs form joint ventures for various reasons: to share technology, to produce, to sell, to procure supplies, and even to conduct R&D.

Joint ventures (JVs) are free-standing entities created by two firms to achieve specific business purposes. JVs range from simple to complex. A simple JV may be one that aggregates negotiating power to procure reliable supplies for two firms. Complex ones may involve the design, production and marketing of an array of products.

JVs are very common in cross-border situations for many reasons.

- When an MNC wants to operate in certain developing nations such as Vietnam, the JV is often the only solution because the outright purchase or even the majority purchase of a local business is prohibited. Also, the business landscape in developing countries is so different that foreign firms, even if permitted to, cannot effectively develop their own business infrastructure.

- A JV allows financing at the local level. This may have some advantages. First, because of incentives, local financing may be less costly. Second, local financing may allow the use of equity in compensation contracts. Third, local financing serves to mitigate currency risk as well as country risks such as those of blocked currency and government takeover.

Joint Ventures: Types and Examples

1. **Complementary technology JV.** In today's world, products are often quite complex and require optimal combinations of various technologies. When a firm finds itself searching for pieces of a puzzle while completing the design of a product, it is compelled to enter into licensing or JV agreements with firms that offer the missing pieces. These JVs often design products and eventually distribute them. The U.S.-based private firm Synaptics and U.K.-based Zytronic created a JV in 2001 to jointly develop computer interface products. Synaptics provided expertise in touch sensing and software; Zytronic provided expertise in optical filters and glass sensors.

2. **Production JV.** Firms may have complementary skills in producing a product and thus create a production JV. Fiat (Italy) and Tata Motors (India) established a JV in 2007 to manufacture cars in India. This JV benefited from Tata's local knowledge and Fiat's engine and small-car technology.

3. **Sales JV.** This type of JV is often motivated by the desire to obtain economies of scale in distribution or to round out a product portfolio. Two or more firms that want to jointly sell certain products may form a JV. This type of JV does not contain R&D or design elements and focus on the marketing function. For example, the JV Verizon Wireless was formed by the U.K. firm Vodafone Airtouch (a combination of the U.K.'s Vodafone and U.S.'s Airtouch) and the U.S. firm Verizon (a combination of Bell Atlantic and GTE) to provide wireless services in U.S. markets. This unit now serves tens of millions of customers.

4. **Concentration JV.** In industries such as automobiles and telecommunications, the level of fixed costs is very high. Thus, firms search for ways to obtain economies of scale. They can achieve scale by combining their manufacturing activities with another firm in the same industry. A JV of this type is similar to a production JV; the difference occurs in the motive

of scale; production JVs occur because of complementary skills, while concentration JVs occur simply to raise output and cut costs. General Motors, for instance, created a JV with Fiat (Italy) to produce small engines. One may also consider the example of Verizon to be one motivated by the desire for concentration; the JV was able to address a market of more than 50 million customers, thereby achieving considerable economies of scale.

5. **R&D JV.** Many industries require large investments in R&D to develop products. In this context, firms may want to combine their R&D efforts for two reasons. First, they may want to avoid redundancies in R&D efforts and make them more efficient. Second, firms may want to diversify away the inherent risk of R&D in which the "hit" rate is typically quite low. In a JV of this sort, R&D efforts between firms are coordinated and combined to produce benefits for the two firms. In some cases, the coordinated efforts are maintained at the respective firms; in others, the efforts are conducted in a joint location. An example is the agreement between the U.S. biotech firm Medarex and the European pharmaceutical firm Novo Nordisk. Under the terms of this agreement, Novo Nordisk will develop and commercialize any human antibody products that may result from this alliance. Medarex will receive certain payments up front and expects to receive milestone payments as well as royalties on commercial sales of products resulting from the alliance.

6. **Supply JV.** Firms may join forces to procure supplies. This can be achieved either by using the JV to purchase required supplies or to manufacture them. The former often is accomplished through business-to-business (B2B) networks such as ones pioneered by Ariba; a prominent but unsuccessful example is Covisint that brought together automakers to jointly source parts. An example of the latter—with the JV actually producing a component—is one between Volkswagen and Sanyo (announced in 2008) to produce lithium-ion batteries. Volkswagen has other such agreements to produce these batteries, most recently with China's BYD (announced in 2009).

Challenges in Implementing and Sustaining a Cross-Border JV

As mentioned earlier, JVs are more complex than licensing, distribution, or other agreements. This is so because many JVs conduct the full spectrum of corporate activities including financing, product design, production, and distribution. A cross-border JV adds the complexities arising from cultural differences and misalignment of incentives. Very few JVs last more than five years. Some of the reasons for failure are as follows:

- The MNC and the local partner may have diverging preferences concerning business models. This may create disagreements over operational issues such as inventory management, credit policy, and distribution methods.

- The MNC and the local partner may have disagreements over corporate governance issues. This is especially a problem when the local partner is a governmental agency; in such cases, government officials may exercise control over the firm in undesirable ways.

- The MNC and the local partner may have disagreements over changes in financing and investment strategies.

- In joint ventures in which the MNC provides intangible assets (intellectual property), disputes may occur over the local partner's use of such assets.

Valuing a JV or an Alliance

JVs may be valued using standard capital budgeting techniques. See the following example.

EXAMPLE 12.15

Bloom, a U.S. pharmaceutical firm, enters into an R&D JV with a biotech firm based in the United Kingdom. The terms of the agreement are as follows:

- The U.K. firm is to receive an up-front payment of GBP 100,000.

- A major milestone is expected in two years with a 60 percent probability of success. In this event, Bloom is expected to pay GBP 200,000. The research and development (R&D) work would then be completed in a year and the product would be launched three years hence after obtaining the necessary regulatory approval. The probability of regulatory approval is 50 percent. If all goes well, the drug would be launched in six years from today.

- Bloom expects gross revenues (net of direct expenses and selling expenses) to be USD 1,000,000 a year for a period of six years.
- Indirect expenses are expected to amount to USD 200,000 annually.
- Bloom is expected to pay royalties of 3 percent of gross revenues.
- Spot GBPUSD = 1.50; minimal change is expected in the foreseeable future.
- Bloom has a cost of capital of 12 percent and pays no taxes.

Solution: See below.

Joint Venture Valuation (Bloom)

Inputs

t = 0 payment	
Upfront payment (GBP)	100,000
t = 2 payment	
Milestone payment (GBP)	200,000
Probability	60%
t = 6 onward	
Gross revenues (USD)	1,000,000
Indirect expenses (USD)	200,000
Royalty on gross revenues	3%
Cost of capital (USD)	12%
Taxes	0%
GBPUSD	1.50
GBPUSD future changes	0%

	Cash Flows (USD)		
	t = 0	*t = 2*	*t = 6–11*
Upfront (convert to USD)	−150,000		
Milestone (convert to USD)		−300,000	
Gross revenues			1,000,000
Royalty (3%)			−30,000
Indirect expenses			−200,000
(Total) cash flow (CF)	−150,000	−300,000	770,000
× Probability	100%	60%	30%
= E(CF)	−150,000	−180,000	231,000
PV factor at 12%	1.00000	0.79719	2.33292
PV	−150,000	−143,495	538,905
NPV	**245,410**		

Note: The PV factor for cash flows 6–11 is the product of a six-payment annuity factor and a five-period single-sum factor.

Discussion: This calculation is from Bloom's perspective. Note that the up-front and milestone payments are in GBP, while the benefits of the project are in USD cash flows. The milestone payment and the recurring operational cash flows are contingent on success; therefore, they are adjusted by the probability of success. The probability of meeting the milestone is 60 percent, and the probability of generating subsequent cash flows is 30 percent (= 60% × 50%). The cash flow stream is converted into USD values to apply the U.S. cost of capital of 12 percent. The value of this JV to Bloom is USD 245,410.

JV dissolution
The *dissolution of a JV* is preplanned and executed through the exercise of a call or put option given to one of the JV partners.

JVs can also contain real options. One option frequently encountered is the option to take full control of the business at the end of a certain period. There are two ways to structure this option:

- **Call option.** The local partner is given the option to take over the JV's assets at a future date at a prespecified price. Because the MNC has a short position in this option, the option value must be subtracted to calculate overall project NPV.

EXHIBIT 12.2
Comparison of Mergers and Joint Ventures

Characteristic	Joint Venture	Merger
Horizon	Medium term (3–7 years); exit is preplanned and relatively easy	Long term; exit is costly and difficult
Nature of assets or business	Easily separable from MNC, usually includes tangible assets (e.g., plant and equipment) or easily identifiable intellectual property (e.g., patent)	Not easily separable from MNC, usually includes intangible assets (e.g., brands, business processes)
Regulatory environment	Local government may allow only JV and disallow mergers (or greenfield projects) in certain industries	Open economies are conducive to mergers
Intellectual property (IP) protection	JVs occur when the MNC has reasonable assurances its IP is secure	When an MNC's IP is not secure in a JV, the MNC would prefer to engage in a merger
Overall cost	Low to moderate transaction costs; may entail exit costs	High transaction and transition costs; target firms are usually bought at a premium

- **Put option.** This structure is somewhat rare and occurs when the MNC has bargaining power. The MNC preserves the right to sell its share of the JV to the local partner at a pre-specified price. In contrast to the call option, the put option increases project NPV.

12.4 International Mergers

Cross-border mergers typically involve firms from two different countries combining their organizations to create a new corporate entity. For our discussion purposes, we use the term *mergers* to encompass various forms of mergers and acquisitions (M&A) including the acquisition of (1) entire firms through a stock acquisition and (2) divisions or substantial portions of a firm through an asset acquisition. The latter can be achieved through a cash deal while the former can also be achieved through a stock deal.

Mergers differ from JVs (and strategic alliances) because they are more permanent, irrevocable, and costly. Mergers—especially large mergers—are irrevocable in the sense that a firm's resources (financial and strategic) are fully committed to the transaction. There is considerable pressure to make the merger work well. Hence, firms do not have the "option to abandon." This is best illustrated in the ill-fated Daimler-Chrysler merger. It took a considerably long time—with associated cumulative losses—before sufficient willpower was found to de-merge. Exhibit 12.2 summarizes these and other salient differences between mergers and JV.

- **Transaction and transition costs.** Mergers are costly. The two kinds of merger costs are **merger transaction costs** and **merger transition costs**. Transaction costs—the more visible component—involve investment banker fees, accounting fees, legal expenses, and other direct expenses required to conduct a transaction. These costs are typically incurred premerger. Post-merger, the firm incurs transition costs (for restructuring and integration) that are often much higher than transaction costs. These costs involve expenses related to the integration of various systems such as payroll, accounting, and information systems. Transition costs also include various forms of payouts to employees such as adjustments for existing stock options.

EXAMPLE 12.16

A merger is a complicated business and requires specialized intermediaries. A large financial and legal advisory infrastructure (located primarily in New York City) supports merger activity. Thomson Financial reports that aggregate financial and legal advisory fees alone in a single year (2007) are estimated at almost USD 50 billion. Compared to total deal volume of roughly USD 5 trillion, financial and legal advisory fees are about 1 percent. Important firms providing financial advice include Goldman Sachs, Morgan Stanley, Citi, JP Morgan Chase, and UBS (household names all). Important firms providing legal advice include Skadden, Arps, Slate, Meagher and Flom; Allen and Overy; and Sullivan and Cromwell.

Top Global M&A Advisers (2007)

Adviser	Rank	Fee Income USD (millions)	Number of Deals	Market Share (fee income)
Goldman Sachs	1	3,147	421	7.1%
Morgan Stanley	2	2,574	392	5.8%
Citi	3	1,961	460	4.5%
JP Morgan Chase	4	1,952	363	4.4%
UBS	5	1,920	391	4.4%
Credit Suisse	6	1,587	345	3.6%
Merrill Lynch	7	1,539	286	3.5%
Lehman Brothers	8	1,298	243	2.9%
Deutsche Bank	9	1,072	232	2.4%
Rothschild	10	925	330	2.1%

Source: Thomson, *Mergers and Acquisitions Review,* 2007. http://www.thomsonreuters.com/business_units/financial/league_tables/merger_acquisition/.

merger synergy
To accommodate the high transaction and transition costs of a merger as well as the premium usually demanded by target shareholders, *merger synergy* should exceed 40 percent of firm value.

- **Acquirer's perspective.** From the acquirer's perspective, in addition to transaction and transition costs, the merger premium—the additional amount paid to target shareholders beyond prevailing share prices to effect the merger—must also be considered. Research indicates that premiums of 30–40 percent are required in cross-border mergers.[5] Thus, for a merger to make sense from the acquirer's perspective, potential benefits (synergies) must exceed the sum of transaction costs, transition costs, and merger premium. A rule of thumb for a cross-border merger states that merger synergy (the present value of additional cash flow arising from cost savings and revenue enhancements) must comfortably exceed 40 percent of the premerger target value. The fact that cross-border mergers are increasingly prevalent (see Exhibit 12.3) indicates the presence of such high levels of benefit.

Conducting Large Cross-Border Mergers

In the past, mergers and acquisitions were constrained by the size of the transaction. A firm wishing to take over another firm valued at say USD 10 billion was required to arrange cash or debt/equity financing for the same amount. This proved to be a challenging task. Today, almost all large mergers are conducted using stocks. For instance, in the merger between Chrysler and Daimler, Chrysler shareholders received the shares of the new firm Daimler-Chrysler.

EXHIBIT 12.3
Cross-Border M&A: Number and Value of Deals over USD 1 Billion
The secular increase in cross-border M&A has been affected by the technology crash of 2000 and, more recently, by the credit crisis of 2006–2007.

Source: Table I.3 from United Nations Conference on Trade and Development (UNCTAD), *World Investment Report,* http://www.unctad.org/en/docs/wir2006_en.pdf (accessed August 15, 2009).

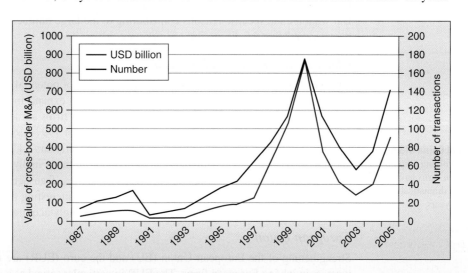

[5] For example, see Robert Harris and David Ravenscraft, "The Role of Acquisitions in Foreign Direct Investment: Evidence from the U.S. Stock Market," *Journal of Finance* 46, no. 3 (1991), pp. 825–844. This study—based on the early cross-border merger wave—finds that U.S. targets in cross-border mergers receive a 13 percent higher premium compared to U.S. targets in domestic mergers. The study also notes that a relatively higher proportion of cross-border mergers are in R&D-intensive industries.

EXHIBIT 12.4
National Pride Over a Juice Maker?

Faced with a stagnant soft drinks market in the United States, The Coca-Cola Company has been aggressively seeking growth opportunities abroad. The Chinese market in particular offered great promise. The growth rate for soft drink consumption was expected to be more than 10 percent in 2009. To further penetrate the Chinese market in 2008, Coca-Cola struck a merger agreement with the Chinese juice maker Huiyuan Juice Group Ltd. This proposed USD 2.4 billion transaction would have been Coca-Cola's largest overseas acquisition. Coca-Cola was attracted to this deal because the fruit and vegetable juice market in China offered an even greater growth rate than carbonated drinks and Huiyuan was a respected national brand in this segment. Both firms were strongly in favor of this merger and were looking forward to reaping synergies. But the Chinese Ministry of Commerce blocked the merger, ostensibly on antitrust grounds. Market observers attribute this reaction to nationalistic feelings. Huiyuan was a home-grown brand and it appeared as though Chinese officials would prefer to keep these brands away from foreign ownership.

Examples of large international mergers include the following:

- **Petroleum industry.** BP Amoco PLC (United Kingdom) and Arco Atlantic Ritchfield Co (United States).
- **Automobile industry.** Renault (France) and Nissan (Japan).
- **Pharmaceuticals.** Astra AB (Sweden) and Zeneca Group PLC (United Kingdom).
- **Communications.** Vodafone Group PLC (United Kingdom) and Airtouch Communications Inc. (United States).
- **Financial services.** Deutsche Bank AG (Germany) and Bankers Trust (United States).
- **Publishing.** Thomson (Canada) and Reed Elsevier (United Kingdom -Dutch) and Harcourt (United States).
- **Energy.** ScottishPower PLC and Pacificorp (United States).

Although many large cross-border mergers have occurred lately, significant impediments remain. First, almost all nations prohibit or closely regulate takeovers of firms in industries such as utilities (e.g., airlines, power) and defense. Second, nations have their own antitrust laws; even if laws are similar, enforcement may differ. Third, nationalistic feelings (see Exhibit 12.4 for an example) may force decision makers to prohibit mergers even if merger proposals concern nonsensitive industries and have no antitrust problems.

Important Drivers for Recent Cross-Border Mergers

Earlier in the chapter, we discussed general reasons for mergers and other related transactions. But what are the specific reasons contributing to the large number of cross-border mergers in recent years? See the discussion of important drivers.

Globalization and the Rise of Asia

Globalization has the dual effect of increasing the size of potential markets and making access to these markets easier. Thus, firms are encouraged to expand internationally. Asia provides an interesting example. Three factors have made Asian firms attractive targets in cross-border mergers since 1999. First, the emerging markets crisis of 1997–1998 depressed market values. Second, Asian economies have been on a tear in recent years—China and India had GDP of about 8 to 10 percent—offering many market opportunities. Finally, Asian countries have liberalized and allowed foreign takeovers in certain industries. Transactions involving Asian targets have increased manyfold in the recent decade. A very interesting recent development is Asian outbound M&A: Firms in India and China are increasingly acquirers of foreign firms.

India and China M&A
M&A involving *Chinese* and *Indian* firms have increased dramatically in recent years.

European Union

Strengthening of the European Union (EU) and the euro (EUR) are reasons behind numerous mergers involving European firms. The EUR in particular served as a catalyst for many reasons. First, the EUR makes it possible for firms to conduct operations across European nations with much lower transaction costs. Second, the emergence of the EUR and the corresponding strengthening of capital markets have allowed firms to obtain funding for mergers much more easily. Third, the EUR promises to quicken the convergence between various economies in Europe,

EXHIBIT 12.5
Cross-Border M&A
by Private Equity and
Hedge Funds

Source: Table I.6, "United Nations
Conference on Trade and Develop-
ment (UNCTAD), *World Investment
Report 2006,* http://www.unctad.org/
en/docs/wir2006_en.pdf (accessed
August 15, 2009).

Year	Number of Deals		Value	
	Number	Percent of Total	USD (billions)	Percent of Total
1987	43	5.0	4.6	6.1
1988	59	4.0	5.2	4.5
1989	105	4.8	8.2	5.9
1990	149	6.0	22.1	14.7
1991	225	7.9	10.7	13.2
1992	240	8.8	16.8	21.3
1993	253	8.9	11.7	14.1
1994	330	9.4	12.2	9.6
1995	362	8.5	13.9	7.5
1996	390	8.5	32.4	14.3
1997	415	8.3	37.0	12.1
1998	393	7.0	46.9	8.8
1999	567	8.1	52.7	6.9
2000	636	8.1	58.1	5.1
2001	545	9.0	71.4	12.0
2002	478	10.6	43.8	11.8
2003	649	14.2	52.5	17.7
2004	771	15.1	77.4	20.3
2005	889	14.5	134.6	18.8

thereby offering firms a more homogenous market. Fourth, firms transact in a fairly stable currency, an improvement over pre-EUR currencies such as the Italian lira and the Spanish peso. The
issues of transaction costs and capital markets are perhaps the most important of these reasons.

Private Equity and Hedge Funds

These funds are emerging as an important force in cross-border M&A. Private equity funds
(PEF) are backed by capital from financial institutions such as pension funds, banks, insurance companies, and other large institutions (e.g., universities) and wealthy investors. Hedge
funds (HF) are unregulated mutual funds serving the needs of wealthy investors and financial
institutions. One key difference is that hedge funds typically trade in and out of positions. This
means that HF—unlike PEF that typically have 5- to 10-year horizons—have less interest in
corporate control. Statistics show that these PEF and HF account for nearly 20 percent of all
cross-border M&A (see Exhibit 12.5). Unlike MNCs that use cross-border M&A to acquire
mostly own-industry or related-industry assets (horizontal or vertical mergers), PEF and HF
are opportunistic and seek any undervalued assets.

USD Weakness

Recent patterns of U.S. inbound and outbound cross-border mergers indicate that the dollar
weakness has had an effect on mergers. During 2006–2007, the EUR rose significantly against
the USD. Compared to 2004–2005 when inbound and outbound mergers were roughly equal,
during 2006–2007, inbound mergers far exceeded outbound mergers. This phenomenon linking
currency values and M&A activity was earlier noted in academic studies.[6]

EXAMPLE 12.17

Assume that an Italian construction materials firm wants to penetrate U.S. markets by purchasing a U.S.
target with a market capitalization of USD 400 million. Suppose the Italian firm became aware of this
target in 2005 when the EURUSD rate was at 1.30. At this rate, the target is worth EUR 308 million. The
Italian firm waits for an opportune moment and notes in late 2007 that the EURUSD is about 1.5. Assuming the USD price of the target has not changed, the Italian firm finds that the EUR value of the target
is now EUR 267 million. This translates to a saving of EUR 41 million. Perhaps at this price, the target is
affordable for the Italian firm. This behavior on the part of the acquirer is no different from European
consumers' evaluation of the cost of a U.S. vacation: An unusually high number of Europeans visited the
United States in 2007 because of the weak USD.

[6] Harris and Ravenscraft (1991) show that currency values play an important role in cross-border mergers.

Overcapacity

The last decade has been characterized by overcapacity in certain mature industries such as automobiles and steel. Overcapacity leads to deterioration in prices, increases in average unit costs, and consequently losses. Share prices and debt ratings also fall, and firms are unable to obtain financing for capital expenditures. This situation calls for what is euphemistically referred to as *rationalization*. Firms need to identify unproductive assets such as plants using older technologies or plants in areas with high labor costs and obtain salvage value. Firms also must reengineer their operations to make their workforce and management more productive. A downsizing of the workforce is an inevitable consequence of overcapacity. Sometimes such restructuring actions require a catalyst; mergers often play this role.[7] The Arcelor-Mittal Steel Merger in 2006 is an example of a merger resulting from industry overcapacity.

Sarbanes-Oxley Act of 2002

The Sarbanes-Oxley Act of 2002 is landmark legislation that makes it more costly for foreign firms to obtain financing and list their shares in U.S. exchanges, thereby reducing the use of cross-listing.[8] Because of this adverse consequence, many foreign firms, especially those from emerging markets, may view a merger with a U.S. firm as a relatively attractive method of tapping U.S. markets for capital.[9] The U.S. merger partner (usually the acquiring firm) becomes a conduit for financial resources.

Challenges for Cross-Border Mergers

While the opportunities for cross-border mergers are many, MNCs should not underestimate the challenges encountered in implementing mergers. The difficulties that Daimler experienced in assimilating Chrysler should be a warning to firms interested in cross-border mergers. In this section, we list some of the important challenges.

Regulatory Barriers

M&A barriers
Cross-border mergers face *regulatory barriers* as well as *cultural barriers*.

Cross-border mergers often go through a complex regulatory approval process. Many nations, especially smaller nations and developing nations, have enacted legislation to ban foreign ownership of their firms. In certain cases, foreign ownership is permitted as long as it does not obtain majority control of the firm. These barriers are consequences of intense nationalistic feelings. But the problem does not lie just with such small and developing nations. Many pro-business Western nations such as France, Germany and the United Kingdom as well as Asian nations such as Japan also erect regulatory barriers. Because firms face regulations in multiple jurisdictions, the costs of responding to regulatory action can be substantial. Both firms and regulatory authorities are cognizant of this problem. In fact, there is a movement to unify the global regulation of mergers. It remains to be seen whether this movement will lead to fruition.

EXAMPLE 12.18

The EU has a strong regulatory apparatus for mergers involving European firms or non-EU firms with substantial operations in Europe. The apparatus triggers scrutiny when worldwide sales of the combined entity exceed EUR 5 billion (a relatively low threshold). As with regulators in the United States, EU regulators look for concentration (market power) and adverse impact on consumers. But other issues such as environmental impact and employment impact are also considered. The EU has set a one-month time limit for approval of most mergers, but in the case of big mergers, the probe is extended by another four months. The EU has not been shy about demanding concessions from merger partners. This was the case with many large mergers such as Astra/Zeneca, AOL/Time Warner, MCI/WorldCom,

---

[7] Michael Jensen, "The Modern Industrial Revolution, Exit, and the Failure of Internal Control Systems," *Journal of Finance* 48, no. 2 (1993), pp. 831–880.

[8] J.D. Piotroski and S. Srinivasan "The Sarbanes-Oxley Act and the Flow of International Listings," Working Paper, University of Chicago, 2007.

[9] Bill Francis, Iftekhar Hasan and Xian Sun, "Financial Market Integration and the Value of Global Diversification: Evidence for United States Acquirers in Cross-Border Mergers and Acquisitions," *Journal of Banking and Finance* 32 (2008), pp. 1522–1540. This article discusses the attractiveness of a merger with a U.S. firm for a firm from segmented markets.

and Seagram/Vivendi. For example, in the AOL/Time Warner merger, AOL was forced to relinquish its links with Germany's Bertelsmann. In a famous case involving two U.S. firms—General Electric and Honeywell—despite approval from U.S. authorities, EU regulators killed the deal.

Cultural Barriers

There are obvious difficulties in combining two different cultures and styles of management. This difficulty became apparent in the Daimler-Chrysler merger. Market observers note that Chrysler's aggressive management style did not mesh with Daimler's more conservative approach.

Corporate Governance Differences

Corporate governance structures may differ. For example, the structure of the board of directors differs from country to country. In Germany and other continental countries following the dual-tier board structure, the supervisory board is required to have labor union representatives. Norms regarding executive and employee compensation may also differ. (These issues were discussed in Chapter 1.)

Valuation of Cross-Border Mergers

From an acquirer's perspective, the evaluation of a merger target is nothing short of a giant capital budgeting exercise. The target's business opportunities—across multiple products and divisions—must be analyzed and the future cash flows estimated. Typically, the estimation period for cash flows is about five years. Cash flows are estimated over this period, and, as in project analysis, a salvage or terminal value is assumed at the end of this period. The present value of all cash flows including the terminal value provides an estimate of the target's value to the acquiring firm. Finally, the merger's value (that is, the transaction value) is calculated as the difference between the target's value and the price paid for it.

A challenging issue in merger valuation is the estimation of the synergy between the acquiring firm and the target. Mergers are often initiated because of potential synergies between two firms. Synergies occur from the combination of assets of two firms. Thus, the acquiring firm's influence on the target must be assessed. For instance, the target firm could be a poorly managed firm; after the merger, the acquiring firm could install some of its managers in the target to improve its management. The effects of these restructuring activities must be assessed to determine the target's cash flows.

EXAMPLE 12.19

Timberline, a U.S. lumber firm, is considering the purchase of a Canadian firm for Canadian dollar (CAD) 6,000 (all values in millions). A financial analysis over a four-year horizon indicates that stand-alone after-tax cash flows of CAD 1,000 are subject to synergies of 20 percent and the after-tax terminal value of CAD 4,000 is subject to a synergy of 25 percent. Timberline's weighted average cost of capital (WACC) is 10 percent. CADUSD = 0.90. Assume that interest rates in CAD and USD are 4 percent and 2 percent, respectively (annual compounding). Calculate the NPV of the transaction to Timberline with and without consideration of synergy. Assume that the Canadian firm has no debt to be repaid.

Solution: See below.

Timberline's Merger Valuation

Purchase price	6,000	CAD millions
Timberline's WACC	10%	USD
Target's annual CF	1,000	CAD millions
Annual CF synergy	20%	
Target's terminal value	4,000	CAD millions
Terminal value synergy	25%	
Interest rate (CAD)	4%	
Interest rate (USD)	2%	

	Cash Flows in Millions (CAD, USD where noted)				
	t = 0	*t* = 1	*t* = 2	*t* = 3	*t* = 4
A. Without Synergy					
Purchase price	−6,000				
Annual CF		1,000	1,000	1,000	1,000
Terminal value					4,000
CF w/o synergy	−6,000	1,000	1,000	1,000	5,000
CADUSD	0.9000	0.8827	0.8657	0.8491	0.8327
CF (USD)	−5,400	883	866	849	4,164
NPV at 10 percent (USD)	**−400**				
B. With Synergy					
Purchase price	−6,000				
Annual CF		1,200	1,200	1,200	1,200
Terminal value					5,000
CF with synergy	−6,000	1,200	1,200	1,200	6,200
CADUSD	0.9000	0.8827	0.8657	0.8491	0.8327
CF (USD)	−5,400	1,059	1,039	1,019	5,163
NPV at 10 percent (USD)	**713**				
Synergy (USD)	**1,113**				

Note: CADUSD is forecasted using IRP. (See Chapter 5 for details.)

Discussion: NPV to Timberline with and without synergy equals −USD 400 and USD 713, respectively. Synergy equals the difference between these two values and equals USD 1,113. The Canadian firm's stand-alone value (that is, without synergy) is USD 5,000 (add purchase price of USD 5,400 to NPV of USD negative 400). The U.S. firm cannot bid lower than this value. The maximum bid is USD 6,113 (add NPV of transaction of USD 713 to purchase price of USD 5,400).

Other Issues in Evaluating a Foreign Target

The following are additional issues to consider in valuing a cross-border merger target.

Target's Debt

Because mergers usually involve the purchase of outstanding shares of the target firm, a primary objective of merger valuation is to determine the target's share price. Recall the Timberline example in which we applied capital budgeting principles to determine the Canadian target's overall value. Suppose the target has outstanding debt. The value of this debt must be subtracted from estimated firm value to arrive at equity value. Equity value divided by the number of shares provides an estimate of share price. Throughout, calculations must consistently produce output in the same currency.

Discount Rates

The overall cost of capital (WACC) is used to discount free cash flows and the salvage value. As with capital budgeting problems, there may be asymmetries in the cost of capital. Thus, the target's value may be different for various interested parties. Valuation asymmetries indicate violations in the international Fisher effect caused by segmented markets and temporary disturbances in markets. The target may have a higher value to the acquirer because of a lower cost of capital from the acquirer's perspective. Alternatively, if the acquirer's cost of capital is higher, the merger would typically be unattractive.

Taxes

Taxes may also cause an asymmetry in value. If an MNC is considering a target in a low tax country, it is possible for the value of the target to the MNC to be lower than the target's local value. Unless synergies are large, the acquirer may not find the target attractive.

Terminal Value

It is not unusual for terminal values to exceed 50 percent of the target's total value. Thus, mistakes in assessing terminal values can be potentially disastrous. If the business involves the use of fixed assets that have an active secondary market, then reasonably precise estimates can be obtained. However, if the salvage value primarily comprises the value of intangibles such as goodwill, then estimates may be subject to considerable errors.

Real Options

Earlier, you learned that real options are frequently encountered in cross-border transactions. To value these options, the acquiring firm must assess the nature of the real option (e.g., does it involve new investments or does it involve exiting an investment?), the current value of the assets in question, the transaction that would trigger the exercise of the real option, and the conditions under which this exercise would occur. (See discussions in Chapter 9 for further information on this topic.) A key input is the standard deviation of the (implied) volatility factor that triggers exercise of the real option. Commonly used proxies are the standard deviation of macroeconomic factors such as the gross national product (GNP), inflation, and currency rate. If the real option concerns producing and selling a product, one may also use the standard deviation of product demand (same or similar product) as a proxy. See Appendix 12 for an example of the real options approach to valuing a merger.

Alternative Valuation Methodologies

discounted cash flow (DCF) and price-earnings (PE) method
The *discounted cash flow method* is used to value merger targets. An alternative is the *price earnings method.*

It would be wise for firms to use alternate methods to assess a target's value. The **discounted cash flow (DCF)** method used in the Timberline example is a favorite method, but firms also use other methods. These alternate methods typically relate price or value to financial metrics such as earnings or sales and are known as "multiples" methods. A common multiples method is the **price-earnings (PE) method**. PE multiples can be calculated for the target and compared against benchmarks. A low PE for the target relative to benchmarks indicates undervaluation; this provides an opportunity for the acquirer to buy the target at an attractive price. Other methods involve price to sale ratios (PS) or market-to-book value ratios (MB).

EXAMPLE 12.20

A potential target is trading at a PE multiple of 15, and its competitors are trading at a multiple of 20. Estimate the maximum merger premium without incorporating synergy. Next, assume a synergy equivalent to 10 percent of the target's earnings. What is the maximum premium assuming synergy?

Solution: For ease of calculations, assume that the firm's current earnings per share (EPS) are USD 1.

Current price = USD 15 (because PE = 15)
Benchmark price = USD 20 (because competitors' PE = 20)
Maximum merger premium = 20/15 − 1 = 33.3 percent

But synergies imply potential EPS = 1 × (1 + 10%) = 1.1
Revised benchmark price = 1.1 × 20 = USD 22
Maximum merger premium = 22/15 − 1 = 46.7 percent

Discussion: Most managers use multiple methods. The NPV method is the most commonly used but is often supplemented with the PE method.

Importance of Due Diligence

Due diligence is the process by which data are accessed to confirm and validate inputs used by the acquiring firm. In a friendly acquisition, following the expression of interest by a potential acquirer (usually via a nonbinding bid), the target sets up a "data room" with help from its investment advisers. Typically, the acquirer already has estimates of baseline value (stand-alone value of firm), synergies, and various costs. The data room is used to confirm these estimates. In a hostile acquisition, because the target does not provide financial data to the potential acquirer, the due diligence process is much more challenging, and it becomes more important to use the services of financial advisers. In a cross-border situation in which data are more difficult to obtain, most deals are friendly. But even when data are available in a friendly transaction, differences in information and accounting systems can subject the interpretation to precision errors.

Summary

- International alliances and acquisitions occur when firms located in two or more countries combine to conduct joint business activity. These transactions range in complexity from simple procurement deals to complex ones such as mergers or joint ventures. MNCs conduct these transactions to penetrate new markets, to source technology and capabilities, and to reap the benefits of scale and scope.

- Licensing deals mainly occur in the context of technology transfers from one firm to another; hence, these transactions are prevalent in high-technology industries.

- Procurement contracts are common in most manufacturing-related industries. More comprehensive outsourcing contracts allow firms to focus on their core competencies by outsourcing products, services, and processes.

- Strategic alliances are complex medium- to long-term arrangements in which firms cooperate on a range of activities including product development and marketing activities.

- Joint ventures create stand-alone organizations; these are convenient vehicles for firms to penetrate foreign markets.

- Mergers are complex transactions in which two firms combine to create a new entity. Because mergers involve large transaction and transition costs, significant synergy is necessary for mergers to occur.

- Cross-border mergers face many challenges including differences in culture and management styles, the need for regulatory approval, and differences in corporate control mechanisms.

- Mergers and joint ventures are valued by discounting free cash flows over a finite horizon and by incorporating an estimate of terminal value. Difficulties include cost of capital asymmetries, precision errors in assessing salvage values, difficulties of assessing real options, and evaluation of synergies.

Questions

1. **Licensing Agreement.** What are licensing agreements? In what industries are they commonly found? Why? Give examples to support your answer.

2. **Form of Alliance.** The Rochester Corporation is a U.S.-based firm specializing in digital imaging. Its technologies have applications in diverse industries including document production/duplication, health diagnostics, security systems, and pharmaceutical research. The firm seeks to increase its worldwide revenues. Explain what forms of alliances it can pursue in Europe to achieve its objectives.

3. **Form of Alliance.** Per capita spending on pharmaceuticals in India is among the lowest in the world. Arya is one of a handful of generic drug makers active in this market. The Indian national income is growing at a rate of 8 percent annually, and Arya expects a higher than proportional increase in the Indian drug industry. What are possible alliances that Arya can strike with an Italian pharmaceutical MNC?

4. **Cross-Licensing Agreement.** How does a cross-licensing agreement differ from a regular licensing agreement? In what industries are these agreements commonly found? Why? Give examples to support your answer.

5. **Outsourcing.** The contract manufacturing industry is relatively obscure (not a fashionable one to talk about) but an important one (at least in the recent decade). Global firms such as Singapore's Flextronics and Taiwan's Quanta are members of this industry. What do these firms do, and who are their customers? What are business/economic concepts that explain the development of this industry?

6. **Outsourcing.** What is business process outsourcing (BPO)? Why do firms seek it? Who are its providers?

7. **Outsourcing.** Customer support is an integral element of both the product and service industries. Often customer support is delivered via telephone. One firm that has developed a market niche in this industry is Sutherland (located in Rochester, New York). Sutherland uses employees in foreign locations such as the Philippines to provide services to major U.S. corporations. These offshore employees work on behalf of Sutherland's clients to provide customer support. Can you speculate on reasons Sutherland selected the Philippines as one of its key countries?

8. **Outsourcing.** Explain why outsourcing has become a political issue in the United States lately. Use your general business knowledge to answer this question.

9. **Strategic Alliances.** What are strategic alliances? How do they differ from other forms of alliances such as licensing and JV?

10. **Strategic Alliances.** The airline industry offers many examples of strategic alliances. The leading private airline of India, Jet Airways, signed an agreement with a leading U.S. airline, American Airlines, to code share flights and hook up their networks to offer connectivity to customers. Both airlines have extensive domestic networks but few flights between the United States and India. Can you explain why this alliance makes sense for both partners?

11. **Joint Venture.** What is a JV? What are its various forms? Provide cross-border examples of various forms of JV.

12. **Joint Venture.** All foreign automobile firms operating in China (for example, Toyota, Honda, General Motors, Volkswagen) use a JV with a local partner as the organizational form. Speculate why this is the case.

13. **Joint Venture.** When firms take on local partners in JVs, what are its typical risks? How can these risks be mitigated?

14. **Minority Ownership.** It is common for large technology firms to take 5 to 20 percent equity stakes in small emerging firms in adjacent businesses. What is the formal term used to describe these investments? What are the motives for doing so?

15. **Mergers.** Why do mergers occur in waves? What merger waves have occurred in the past (list name and approximate date)? Discuss the most recent wave in more detail.

16. **Motives for Cross-Border Mergers.** Characterize the frequency and importance of cross-border mergers. Discuss important drivers of these mergers. What are your predictions for the next decade?

17. **Entities Involved in Cross-Border Takeovers.** Private equity funds have emerged as important players in cross-border takeover activity. The as yet uncompleted merger of Expro provides a recent example. Expro is a U.K.-based oil services firm. In 2008, Halliburton, a well-known Houston-based oil services firm, made a bid to acquire Expro. However, a bidding war ensued when the private equity firm Candover also expressed interest. What are private equity firms (PEF)? How do takeovers by PEF differ from takeovers by firms such as Halliburton? Why are PEF increasingly interested in cross-border investments?

18. **Target Valuation.** The most common method for valuing a merger target is the DCF method, which involves discounting cash flows to determine target value. A newer method using option pricing theory is gaining in importance, especially concerning small targets in uncertain foreign markets. Explain why using option theory in these circumstances might be appropriate.

19. **Merger Costs and Implementation Issues.** The CFO of an MNC makes the following statement: "We rarely take over foreign firms. We rely instead on JVs to launch foreign operations." What is the plausible logic behind these assertions? Would you agree with this statement if it were made by the CFO of a European auto firm? What if the firm is a U.S. software firm?

Problems

1. **Distribution Agreement.** A Philippine firm wishes to distribute coconut-based food products in the United States. The U.S. distributor demands an up-front payment of USD 50,000 and 10 percent of sales revenue. Assume that over a period of five years, the Philippine firm achieves annual revenues of $250,000. Assume that all expenses (excluding distribution costs, which are 10 percent of revenues) amount to 75 percent of revenues. The discount rate for USD cash flows is 10 percent. What is the NPV (USD) to the Philippine firm?

2. **Distribution Agreement.** A Taiwanese electronics manufacturer considers an agreement with Arrow Electronics to distribute its products in Europe, where it has no presence and where it sees no possibility of creating a sales organization by itself. Arrow demands an up-front payment of EUR 1 million and 10 percent commission on all sales. The Taiwanese firm estimates sales of EUR 12 million annually over the three years of the agreement. Another firm, Zebra Electronics, offers to distribute the products but requires no up-front payment and only a percent of sales as commissions. What is the break-even commission percent that makes the two offers equivalent? Assume that both Arrow and Zebra will achieve the same level of sales. Also assume zero taxes and a discount rate of 12 percent.

3. **Distribution Agreement.** Sanfro, a Swiss pharmaceutical firm, wishes to market its new cholesterol medication in the Eastern European market. It is considering a distribution agreement with a Czech firm for a period of five years. Marcel Kleiber, Sanfro's CFO, is unsure of the advantages and disadvantages of entering into the distribution agreement and wishes an NPV analysis. He has obtained the following estimates of cash flows for two scenarios: going solo (A) and using a distribution agreement (B).

   Revenues. Under scenario A, Sanfro expects revenues of Swiss franc (CHF) 5 million each year for the first two years followed by CHF 10 million each year for the remaining three years. Under scenario B, Sanfro expects revenues of CHF 10 million each year for all five years.

   Distribution expenses. In scenario A, Sanfro needs to set up a sales organization in Eastern Europe. By spending a minimum amount of CHF 2 million up front, Sanfro expects to establish such an organization. This sales organization will incur expenses of CHF 1 million each year. In scenario B, Sanfro pays 20 percent of its revenues to its Czech partner.

   Miscellaneous data. You may assume that direct expenses are 10 percent of sales and include manufacturing costs as well as shipping expenses. Assume no taxes. Assume that the discount rate is 7 percent.

   a. Estimate NPV of scenarios A and B. What is your recommendation to Mr. Kleiber?

   b. Calculate the break-even payment percent to the Czech partner.

4. **Outsourcing Contract.** A U.S.-based heavy equipment producer is considering the outsourcing of a component in China. The firm estimates a requirement of 1,500 units of the component each year. Based on an internal analysis, the cost of producing the component in-house is USD 125 per unit. A Chinese firm offers to make this component for USD 100. The shipping cost is expected to be USD 10 per component. The U.S. firm will bear the shipping cost. The Chinese firm offers a three-year contract at a fixed price. Assume a discount rate of 10 percent. What is the NPV of savings from outsourcing?

5. **Outsourcing Contract.** DMW, a German auto manufacturer, is considering the sourcing of certain components from India. The firm estimates a requirement of 120,000 units a year. The component is currently manufactured in-house at a cost of EUR 40. The Indian firm offers a five-year agreement to manufacture this component for rupee (INR) 2,100 per unit. The German firm also bears shipping costs of EUR 2 per component. Assume a discount rate of 10 percent. Spot EURINR equals 60.

   a. What is the NPV of savings from outsourcing?

   b. Assume that the INR steadily increases in value against the EUR each year. What is the break-even annual percent change in the value of INREUR? (That is, by what percent can the INR change in value each year for the outsourcing contract to stop making sense?) [*Hint:* Because of a constant change in INREUR, annual cash flow (CF) would take the form of a growing (declining) annuity; the objective is to calculate the rate of decline for this annuity.]

6. **R&D Joint Venture.** Merck—a major U.S. pharmaceutical firm—considers an R&D JV with Biocon, a biotech firm in India. Using the following terms of the agreement, estimate the NPV from Merck's perspective.

   Payments to Indian firm for development work. Biocon is to receive an up-front payment of INR 50 million. A major milestone is expected in three years with a 40 percent probability of success. In this event, Merck is expected to pay Biocon INR 100 million. The R&D work would then be completed in a year and the product would be launched three years hence (that is, seven years from now) after obtaining the necessary regulatory approval. The probability of regulatory approval is 60 percent.

   Revenues and expenses. Merck expects revenues (net of direct expenses and selling expenses) of USD 20 million a year for a period of six years (that is, years 6–11). Indirect expenses are expected to amount to USD 1 million annually. Merck will also pay Biocon royalty of 3 percent of gross revenues.

   Other data. Spot USDINR equals 40 and is expected to vary little in the next few years. Merck has a cost of capital of 9 percent and pays no taxes.

7. **Production and Sales JV.** Fiat—an Italian auto firm—signs a production agreement with Tata—an Indian firm—to manufacture a local version of its Uno car. Under the terms of the agreement, Fiat would share its small car technology. Tata contributes its production capacity as well as distribution systems. Fiat is affected by the following terms of the agreement:

   Initial investment. Fiat does not make any cash investment. It provides only its IP. The JV does not have any capital equipment on its books and, hence, there is no depreciation or salvage value.

   Revenues. Over each of the project's five years, the JV expects to sell 100,000 cars at a price of Indian rupees (INR) 1.4 million each.

   Expenses. The JV incurs direct costs of production and distribution of INR 0.9 million per car. Tata, not the JV, bears indirect costs.

   Payments to Tata. Tata bears the fixed cost of production and distribution, but the JV pays Tata 10 percent of revenues as compensation.

   Share of profits. The JV repatriates 50 percent of profits to Fiat each year.

   Other data. Spot EURINR equals 60. Assume that the INR is expected to depreciate by 1 percent a year. Fiat's cost of capital is 11 percent. Assume Indian corporate income taxes of 20 percent with withholding taxes of 5 percent. Also assume that there are no additional Italian taxes.

   a. What are the JV's profits each year?

   b. Estimate cash flows to Fiat and NPV.

   c. Fiat is interested in an alternate structure for the JV by which it obtains only a licensing fee per auto sold and has no share of profits. Assume that the fee triggers a 10 percent withholding tax in India. Again, there are no additional taxes in Italy. Calculate the fee per car that makes the two structures equivalent.

8. **Merger Evaluation.** A Canadian mining firm wishes to acquire a Brazilian copper producer. The current market value in terms of the Brazilian currency denomination (BRL) of the Brazilian firm is BRL 7 billion. Most mergers of this nature require a takeover premium of 25 percent. Also, the Canadian firm must pay transaction costs of CAD 250 million and incur a cost of CAD 150 million to integrate the Brazilian firm's operations into its own operations. Estimate the total cost of the acquisition. Assume spot CADBRL equals 2.

9. **Merger Evaluation.** A potential target is trading at a PE multiple of 12, and its competitors are trading at a multiple of 16.

   a. Estimate the maximum merger premium without incorporating synergy.

   b. Assume a synergy equivalent to 20 percent of the target's cash flows. What is the maximum premium in the presence of synergy?

10. **Merger Evaluation.** Elf Aquitaine, a French integrated oil company, wishes to expand its scope by acquiring the U.S. oil services firm Bushwhacker (NASDAQ: BUSH). The target is an all-equity firm with 200 million shares outstanding; the most recent closing price was USD 23.68. Elf estimates a stand-alone intrinsic value of USD 28.50 a share and potential synergies of USD 5.25 a share. Most mergers are consummated when an acquirer pays a 25 percent premium that helps induce target shareholders to tender their shares. Also, a merger such as this one usually incurs transaction costs of USD 100 million. These costs include investment banker fees as well as costs incurred by Elf to internally pursue the merger transaction. Elf also estimates an integration cost of USD 150 million. Evaluate whether it is worthwhile for Elf to pursue this acquisition by answering the following questions or doing the following:

    a. What is Bushwhacker's current market value?

    b. Evaluate whether a 25 percent takeover premium would satisfy Bushwhacker's shareholders given the circumstances (compare takeover price assuming this premium with intrinsic value).

    c. How much is Bushwhacker worth to Elf? How much does it cost? What is the NPV of the transaction?

    d. An analysis of merger rules and previous rulings indicates a 20 percent chance that regulators will not approve the merger. The decision will be known only after Elf has already incurred merger transaction costs. Should Elf initiate the merger?

11. **Merger Evaluation.** Hewlett Packard (HP), a U.S. firm, is considering the purchase of a German IT services firm to boost its service revenues in the Continent. The purchase price is expected to be EUR 2.2 billion. A five-year horizon analysis indicates that stand-alone annual after-tax cash flows of EUR 0.3 billion are subject to synergies of 15 percent, and the after-tax terminal value of EUR 1.5 billion is subject to a synergy of 20 percent. The WACC of the U.S. firm is 10 percent. EURUSD equals 1.50. Assume that interest rates in EUR and USD are 4 percent and 2 percent, respectively (annual compounding).

    a. What is the stand-alone value of the German firm?

    b. What is the value of the German firm to HP?

    c. What is the synergy generated by HP

    d. What is the premium offered by HP compared to stand-alone value?

    e. What is the NPV of the transaction to HP?

    f. Assume that investment banking fees and other transaction costs are USD 100 million. Is the transaction still valuable to HP?

Extension

1. **Target Valuation Using Option Pricing Theory.** Consider a potential target in a foreign country. It is young firm with the potential flexibility to expand its product line. Assuming no expansion, the firm is valued at EUR 40 million. Depending on macroeconomic and industry demand conditions (volatility estimated at 25 percent) in the next two years, the firm may have the possibility to invest an additional EUR 100 million. The second-stage investment of EUR 100, were it to occur today, would be premature and generate an NPV of only EUR 8 million. The firm wishes to wait and see market developments before exercising its option to make the second-stage investment. Estimate total firm value. Assume that the risk-free rate of interest (continuous compounded) is 4.1 percent. (See Appendix 12 for an explanation of using the option pricing model to value merger targets.)

Case

Clover Machines: *Chinese Joint Venture*

As its emerging markets strategy unfolds, Clover Machines seeks to penetrate China. The Chinese market is in many ways similar to the Indian market. Farms are small and demand exists only for low-cost and low-margin equipment. But the Chinese construction market offers great potential for Clover. Growth rates during past years are around 10 percent, and the market is expected to reach a size of USD 20 billion in the next few years. Anecdotally, people have claimed that the Shanghai skyline boasts the highest number of cranes of any city in the world. Further, Beijing is undergoing a boom that is also related to the recent Olympics. Published reports also indicate a host of highway and railway projects. Clover is particularly attracted to outlays of USD 160 billion toward railway projects during the next five years. These projects require specialized equipment and provide opportunities for selling rotary drilling rigs, excavators, concrete pump trucks, and loaders. Clover believes it has design advantages in some of this equipment.

But there is also fierce competition in China. A host of Japanese, Korean, European, and local competitors have been raising output and slashing prices. Also, Caterpillar, a leading U.S. firm, is very active in this market and has substantial local production capability. Because of price competition, local production (at lower cost than in most other countries) is on the rise. With the exception of high-end equipment, Clover finds itself unable to compete effectively in these markets. To facilitate entry, Clover is contemplating a joint venture (JV) with Hunan Construction Machines (HCM), a Chinese firm.

Brian Bent, Clover's CFO, is studying a proposal submitted by Yujie Han, who was assigned to report on business opportunities in China. Mr. Han's report identifies the following benefits of conducting business with HCM:

- HCM produces low-end machinery but has built capabilities in servicing both railway and roadway projects (as opposed to commercial construction). HCM is also aware of bidding and procurement procedures in this industry.

- HCM has 10 years of manufacturing experience in China and has a factory near Shanghai employing 500 workers.

Mr. Bent reviews the proposal, which calls for added capacity in HCM's existing factory to meet the JV's needs and has a few concerns. The location is not in one of the special economic zones (SEZ) established by China to attract foreign investment. A factory located in an SEZ gets a multitude of tax breaks for the first four years it earns profits. Mr. Bent wonders whether HCM's intellectual property (IP) and business contributions are sufficient to warrant giving up half of the JV's potential profits. Furthermore, in China, as in many other emerging markets, there appear to be concerns about JV partners expropriating a firm's IP.

Mr. Han's report also presents the following contractual and cash flow details:

- The JV would produce specialized equipment geared toward the transportation industry. Project life is five years.

- HCM would contribute land as well as a factory. Clover would contribute equipment costing CNY 200 million as well as working capital of CNY 50 million. Although HCM and Clover would be equal partners, Clover would receive full salvage value from its investment as well as recovery of working capital at the project's end. Likewise, HCM is returned its own capital investment.

- Revenue projections in the first five years are CNY 200, 200, 300, 350, and 400 million, respectively.

- Direct expenses would be 40 percent of sales.

- Proprietary technology owned by Clover would be used. In return, the JV would pay licensing fees to Clover equaling 5 percent of sales.

- Overheads would be CNY 50 million each year.

- Chinese income is taxed at 20 percent. Assume that the Chinese government imposes a 10 percent withholding tax on all remittances including license fees. Assume that U.S. taxes of 35 percent are applied on license fees as well as Clover's share of the Chinese taxable income, but all Chinese taxes (withholding plus 50 percent of income taxes) are counted in the foreign tax credit. Assume no income taxes, Chinese or U.S., on salvage value.

- The dividend policy calls for annual disbursement of all cash flows.

- The capital equipment provided by HCM would be fully depreciated. Clover's contributions would be depreciated straight line over a period of four years.

- Expected salvage value related to Clover's capital expenditure has an after-tax value of CNY 100 million.

- USDCNY equals 6.4506. The CNY is expected to appreciate annually by 4 percent.

- Clover's discount rate for similar domestic projects is 10 percent.

Mr. Bent is anxious to see the analytical work supporting the JV proposal as well as a thorough discussion of various advantages and disadvantages. Please use a spreadsheet to show your calculations.

Appendix 12

Valuation of Real Options in Cross-Border Mergers

Recall the discussion of real options in Chapter 9 and their valuation in Appendix 9B. This appendix extends those concepts to cross-border M&A valuation. Recall from these previous discussions that real options provide "triggers" for firms to behave opportunistically and extract value in a changing world.

Cross-border mergers provide many potential option-related triggers. A firm may acquire a seemingly loss-making firm in a foreign country. But this acquisition may provide a variety of options as follows:

- If consumer demand rises in the foreign market, the firm can quickly introduce a variety of products.

- If the country's currency value decreases, the firm may shift production to that country.

- By learning how to conduct business in the country, the firm may decide whether or not to make further investments or shift to another country.

- If the foreign firm develops new technology, the firm may consider transferring that technology to its domestic markets.

The following example shows how to apply a standard option pricing model (Black-Scholes) to value real options in an acquisition.

EXAMPLE 12.21

A U.S.-based MNC considers a potential target in a foreign country. It is a young firm with a single product and potential flexibility to expand its product offerings. Assuming no expansion, the firm is valued at USD 25 million. Depending on macroeconomic and industry demand conditions (volatility estimated at 30 percent) in the next three years, the firm may have the possibility to invest an additional USD 10 million to obtain capabilities to market a second and related product. The current value of these new assets is USD 12 million and provides an NPV of USD 2 million, but the firm wishes to wait to see market developments before exercising its options. Estimate total firm value. Next, assuming a market value of debt of USD 4 million and 5 million shares outstanding, calculate per share value. Assume that the USD risk-free rate of interest (continuous compounding) is 3.5 percent.

Solution: The option to expand is evaluated using the Black-Scholes option pricing framework. The five inputs are as follows:

Option Pricing Input	Explanation
S = 12 million	The present value of new assets if the foreign firm chooses to invest in a related product. But this value is based on current market conditions. Value in the future may change depending on prevailing market conditions.
X = 10 million	The additional investment required to market the related product.
t = 3	The length of time available for making the decision of whether or not to proceed with the related product.
σ = 30%	A measure of volatility in external conditions that determine whether the firm should invest in the related product.
r = 3.5%	Because all cash flows and values are in USD, one must use the USD risk-free rate of interest.

Using the Black-Scholes model with the preceding inputs, we find an option value of USD 3.962 million (for details, see Appendix 9B). This implies that:

Total firm value = USD (25 + 3.962) million = USD 28.962 million

Equity value = USD (28.962 − 4) million = USD 24.962 million

Value per share = USD $\dfrac{24,962,000}{5,000,000}$ = USD 4.99

Discussion: The traditional discounted cash flow method produces a value of USD 27 million. Two components add up to this value: NPV of 25 million assuming no expansion and NPV of 2 million for expansion (invest 10 million and obtain assets worth 12 million). The option method produces a higher value of USD 28.962 million. The difference of USD 1.962 million represents the option's time value. The target benefits from delaying its investment in new assets because of high volatility (30 percent) in environmental variables.

CHAPTER THIRTEEN

International Trade

The credit crisis of 2007–2008 claimed an unlikely victim: small U.S. exporters. Their clients, especially in the Far East, encountered difficulty in obtaining letters of credit needed to import the goods. Merchandise trade—the import and export of goods—was impacted. For example, Cross Creek Sales, a small sawmill in Georgia that sells kiln-dried lumber, had orders postponed or canceled by certain Chinese customers because of their inability to get letters of credit. What are letters of credit? More generally, what are problems that importers and exporters encounter, and what are procedures for solving these problems and conducting trade effectively?

International trade occurs in every imaginable product and in an increasingly large volume. Merchandise trade alone in 2008 exceeded USD 14 trillion (despite the crisis) composed of millions of individual transactions. One sees a variety of procedures (payment methods, financing techniques) because of time (to fulfill contracts) and distance (between purchaser and seller) considerations. Payment methods range from the simple (prepayment or open account) to the complex (letter of credit or documentary collections). What are these methods, and what criteria do firms use to select among them? International trade also depends on the availability of financing for various parties. Exporters need financing so that they can put monies up front to produce products. Importers need financing so that they can purchase these products for subsequent sale. What methods do importers and exporters use? These issues are addressed in this chapter.

We start with firm-level (micro- or corporate finance) issues and then move to national and global (macro- or policy) issues concerning trade. In the latter half of the chapter, we discuss how governments measure, regulate, and encourage trade; we also discuss the role of global institutions such as the World Trade Organization (WTO) in fostering trade. International trade brings nations together but also divides them. Managers need to understand the complex relationships between nations because the macroenvironment ultimately affects firm-level business.

In particular, we discuss the following in this chapter:

- Problems such as time lags and informational asymmetry experienced by importers and exporters.
- Methods of trade such as the letter of credit that are attempts to solve some problems encountered in trade. Explain how firms choose between these alternatives.
- The creation and use of the banker's acceptance.
- Various methods of financing exports and imports.
- Differences in trade methods between advanced and developing nations.
- The balance of payments system and how to measure international trade and capital flows.
- Current trends in world trade, especially pertaining to the U.S. situation.
- The institutional framework supporting international trade.

13.1 Import and Export: Shipment and Payment

Importers and exporters face unique risk factors, primarily because they do not know each other well and because of problems of long-distance contracting. A variety of contracting mechanisms that regulate shipment and payments have evolved to address these risk factors.

In this section, we start by identifying risk factors and proceed to describe various payment mechanisms.

Risk Factors

Exports and imports are more complicated than domestic transactions. These transactions are subject to many problems.

Shipment Time

Many international transactions require goods to be transported using cargo ships. In addition to the journey's length, the following cause delays: time for transit to the port, to clear customs at the port of exit, to wait for the ship, to load the ship, to unload it, to obtain customs clearance at the port of entry, and to move the shipment to the importer's premises.

EXAMPLE 13.1

Garment production is a labor-intensive business. So, it is no surprise that low-wage countries such as India, China, Bangladesh, and Sri Lanka are major exporters. But these nations are quite far from customers in the West. When an Indian exporter sends a shipment of garments from Tirupur, India, to a department store in Chicago, the United States, it is not unusual for actual delivery to take one or two months.

Counterparty Risk

The counterparty risk pertains to the nonperformance of a transaction's contractual terms. In particular, the exporter is concerned about the risk of the importer's nonpayment on receipt of the goods. The physical distance separating the two entities contributes to a lack not only of information about counterparties but also of ability to properly enforce contracts.

Product Quality Risk

The importer faces product quality risk because the goods received may not meet specifications. The payment may have been made prior to receipt of goods, leaving the importer little recourse. Even if the payment is withheld until receipt of goods, an importer may have made important commitments with its customers that would be in jeopardy if the goods prove to be of insufficient quality.

EXAMPLE 13.2

Electronics components are principally manufactured in Asian countries such as Taiwan, Malaysia, and China. Many producers are small and recently started their business. Western importers are wary of prepaying for goods sourced from unknown exporters; anecdotal stories of how firms "disappear" abound. Even if goods are produced and shipped, product quality remains a serious issue.

Currency Risk

No matter which currency the invoice stipulates, one or the other or both parties are subject to currency risk. If an Indian garment exporter invoices a shipment to a U.S. importer in rupees (INR), the U.S. importer faces risks that the INR would appreciate against the USD. If instead the invoice currency were the USD, the Indian exporter would bear the currency risk. Most international transactions are currently conducted in benchmark invoice currencies such as the USD, euro (EUR), pound (GBP), and yen (JPY); nevertheless, some parties bear currency risk. In Chapters 6 and 7, you learned that this type of currency risk is known as *transaction exposure* and is straightforward to measure and control.

Regulatory Burdens

Most countries subject exporters and importers to significant regulation. Even trade between so-called free-trade nations can have complex procedures. Governments impose rules and regulations on trade for various reasons including economic protectionism, health and safety, national security, and taxation.

EXAMPLE 13.3	Agricultural products in particular face high levels of regulation. For example, the importation of cured meats (e.g., salami from Italy) into the United States is primarily prohibited but, when allowed, is highly regulated by the U.S. Department of Agriculture. Likewise, Europeans and Asians are concerned about consuming U.S. beef containing antibiotics and hormonal additives.

Financing

A critical concern for trade is financing, primarily because of considerable shipment time. Because payments are often made after the actual delivery of goods, a long shipment time lengthens the exporters' cash cycle. A *cash cycle* is defined as the lag between the time a business pays for its raw materials and supplies and the time it receives cash for its sales. Even an extra month in the cash cycle can financially stress firms with low amounts of working capital and inadequate financing opportunities. This is especially true of small firms in emerging economies with limited financial resources.

Summary of Risk Factors

time lags and **informational asymmetry**
Because of *time lags* and *informational asymmetry,* international transactions have more risks than domestic transactions.

These problems in international trade can be consolidated into two main ones: time lags and informational asymmetry.

- *Time lags* occur in international transactions because of geographical distance and other factors. Shipments take time. Preshipment contracting can also cause delays; normal steps required in contracting a sale, such as the initial enquiry, discussion of specifications, invoicing, and negotiation of prices, might take much more time in an international sale. The time lag either creates or exacerbates other problems such as the financing problem. Even currency risk would be reduced if transactions were completed sooner.

- *Informational asymmetry* occurs because importers and exporters do not know each other well. A U.S. exporter of capital equipment may be concerned about the lack of information about a particular Turkish importer. A garment manufacturer in Bangladesh may be concerned about a French department store and its business methods. This lack of information directly leads to problems such as product quality and default risks. Solutions to these problems—discussed next—are imperfect and increase transaction costs.

Payment Methods Not Involving an Intermediary

A number of international transactions are between affiliates who know each other, eliminating problems of informational asymmetry. Even in transactions involving nonaffiliates, the counterparties may have a long history of contracting with each other and know the other party well. Counterparty knowledge and trust eliminate many risk factors. Consequently, the counterparties turn their attention to minimizing transaction costs rather than risks. This results in the use of contracting mechanisms without involving intermediaries such as banks.

use of simple payment methods
If the *counterparties* know each other, they can arrange for a simple payment method without the involvement of intermediaries.

Open Account

With an open account transaction, the importer and exporter have an understanding that payment will be made according to an agreed-upon schedule following the shipment and receipt of the goods. Open accounts usually occur when parties have contracted before and have built a foundation of trust. Furthermore, open accounts are used when the parties expect a series of transactions. Thus, if the importer defaults on a particular payment, she risks losing the exporter's business; her reputation in the marketplace is also at stake. This may be a sufficient deterrent to nonperformance. In economic terms, open accounts occur when the benefit of defaulting on a payment is less than the present value of future benefits in a relationship. This implicit safeguard is known as *relational protection*. Open accounts are cost effective because contracting parties do not need the services of a third party to mediate risks. This reduces transaction costs.

Consignment

The consignment method is used when the importer wishes to purchase goods for immediate resale and desires low inventory risk. In this method, the exporter retains title to the goods even after the importer receives them; the importer is required to pay the exporter only when he sells the goods to a third party. This method is similar to the open account method because the exporter relies on the importer's integrity. A key consideration in this method is inventory risk. If the goods become obsolete and lose value, the exporter bears the consequences. Such inventory risks are magnified in an international context. Thus, the consignment method is riskier than the open account method from the exporter's perspective and for this reason is rarely used except between affiliates.

EXAMPLE 13.4

One special context in which the consignment method is used is when the exporter is anxious to market a new product and sends the first few units on consignment so that the importer can use them as demonstration models and make initial sales. Italian and German textile machinery manufacturers use this method to target customers in Asia. They send a few units on consignment to a local sales agent and may subsidize this agent's participation in local exhibitions. Potential costs of default are traded off against the potential gains of market entry.

Prepayment

In the prepayment method—also known as the *telex transfer (T/T)* or *cash advance* method— the importer pays for the merchandise by wire transfer prior to shipment. This method offers the simplicity of the open account method. In terms of risks, however, the prepayment method differs from the open account method. An exporter using the open account method bears the (default) risk of not being paid for the shipment. An importer using the prepayment method bears the risk (product quality) of not receiving the goods or receiving the wrong ones. Thus, the choice between the open account and prepayment methods hinges on the trade-off between default and product quality risks. If the default risk is lower, the open account method is appropriate; if the product quality risk is lower, the prepayment method is appropriate. Find a comparison of these unmediated payment methods in Exhibit 13.1.

Payment Methods Involving an Intermediary

counterparties do not know each other
When *counterparties do not know each other,* intermediaries assist by contributing knowledge, enforcement ability, and risk management skills.

When counterparties do not know each other, informational asymmetry creates various problems. Complex contracting solutions are required to solve these problems. A primary consideration is default risk that exporters face: The creditworthiness of the importers is in question. A logical solution calls for a third party or intermediary to provide guarantees.

Intermediary Value Proposition

The following conditions are conducive to the use of an intermediary:

- **Knowledge.** The intermediary has better information about the importer's creditworthiness. Usually, the intermediary assuming default risk is a bank that has a long-standing relationship with the importer. Better information translates to a more precise estimate of risk and, hence, an increased ability to bear that risk. In contrast, an exporter who has inadequate knowledge of an importer may assume the worst and thus be reluctant to transact.

- **Enforcement ability.** The intermediary has a better ability to enforce the importer's liability. Banks, which serve as the intermediary in a majority of cases, have legal and collection departments that can effectively deal with collection issues.

EXHIBIT 13.1
Comparison of Unmediated Payment Methods

Method	Risks to Importer	Risks to Exporter	Transaction Costs	Setting or Context
Open account	Product quality	Default, currency, interest rate	Low	Repeat customer (reputational protection)
Consignment	None	Default (importer), currency, interest rate, inventory	Medium (potentially high if goods are returned)	Interaffiliate or with new product facing uncertain markets
Prepayment	Default (exporter), product quality	None	Low	Small orders

- **Risk management.** The intermediary has ways to diversify and mitigate default risk. By conducting hundreds of transactions, the intermediary is able to diversify default risk across different importers.

Letter of Credit

A time-tested payment method for import/export using an intermediary involves the use of a document called the **letter of credit (L/C)**. This payment method, also known as the *documentary credit* method, requires the following process. An importer, after negotiating the price and terms, approaches a banker and asks for the banker to issue an L/C. This document describes the sales transaction and guarantees payment to the exporter on the fulfillment of certain conditions. The exporter is named as the *beneficiary* in the L/C. The usual conditions are that the exporter ships the goods by a certain date, obtains the **bill of lading** specifying that the goods have been loaded onto a ship/aircraft and presents the bill of lading and other ancillary documents (e.g., insurance coverage) to the bank issuing the L/C. The L/C also specifies the payment mechanism: Usual choices are sight drafts or time drafts drawn by the exporter and payable by the importer's bank. (We explain the concept of drafts later in this chapter.) The key feature of an L/C is the guarantee that the bank issuing it provides; this guarantee is made on behalf of the importer. The various documents involved in an L/C transaction are discussed next (also see Exhibit 13.2 depicting the flow of documents and the resulting payment).

Letter of Credit Documents

L/Cs are known as *documentary credits* because payment is conditional on receipt of the following documents:

- **Bill of lading.** The bill of lading (BL) is the most important document specified in the L/C. It is essentially a receipt issued by the transportation company (also known as *shipper* or *carrier*) indicating the goods shipped and whether the transportation charges have been prepaid. If the goods are shipped by sea, the document is called an *ocean bill of lading;* if shipped by air, it is called an *airway bill.* The carrier issues this document to the exporter which in turn presents it to the importer's bank for payment. A BL can be more than a mere receipt. It can also be used to convey the title to goods shipped. The bank issuing the L/C holds the BL until the importer makes the reimbursement. A BL conveying title is known as an *order BL;* one without this feature is known as a *straight BL.* BLs typically include the following information: brief unverified description of the merchandise, names of the exporter and importer, ports of shipment and arrival, date of shipment, and whether the freight charges have been paid.

- **Commercial invoice.** The exporter issues this document that describes the terms of the sale to the importer. It contains a detailed description of the goods, shipment method, shipment information including weights and dimensions, price, terms of payment, and names/addresses of the contracting parties.

EXHIBIT 13.2
L/C: Payment and Document Flows

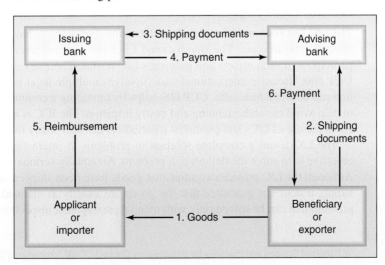

- **Insurance documents.** In most transactions, insurance is obtained against risk of damage to goods while in transit. The exporter obtains insurance documents from the insurance company. These documents specify the goods insured, nature of risks insured, and insurance company's liability.

- **Miscellaneous documents.** There may be additional documents such as the certification of the goods prior to shipment, packing lists to assist customs authorities, and certifications to export control and other regulatory authorities.

When assuming the default risk of an importer, the bank issuing the L/C requires a deposit to cover the amount of the liability. More commonly, however, the bank has an ongoing relationship that is of value to the importer. Thus, the importer's incentives are to satisfy its obligation under the L/C. With customers of good standing, banks often use the L/C as the context to extend credit; we discuss this later in this chapter.

Role of Banks

L/C transactions

Banks play a vital role in
L/C transactions.

Because L/C transactions span two countries, usually more than one bank is involved. The bank originating the L/C, often the importer's bank, is known as the **issuing bank**. Another bank, known as the **advising bank**, serves as a conduit between the issuing bank and the exporter. This bank conveys the L/C to the exporter and assists in presenting the required documents for payment. In a few cases, especially when dealing with unknown issuing banks in high-risk countries, exporters demand that a local bank (i.e., in the exporter's country) jointly assume the default risk; the local bank that co-guarantees the payment is known as a **confirming bank**. The advising bank generally serves as the confirming bank. Naturally, all banks in this contractual chain charge fees known as *issuing, advising,* and *confirming fees,* respectively. Each fee component is approximately 0.1 percent of transaction value. In certain high-risk situations, fees can be much higher. For example, if the importer is in a high-risk location, confirming fees can be as high as 5 percent.

Types of Letters of Credit

An **irrevocable L/C** does not allow the terms of the contract to be changed without the beneficiary's consent. The presumption is that L/Cs are irrevocable. Revocable L/Cs are rare and quite risky for the exporter: in fact, the central benefit of an L/C is lost in these cases. Some L/Cs allow the beneficiary, at her discretion, to transfer benefits to a third party; these L/Cs are known as **transferable L/Cs**. These are particularly useful for intermediaries who resell goods to a foreign buyer; in this case, the transferable L/C allows the eventual buyer to issue a credit to intermediaries, who in turn use a portion of the credit to source the goods and keep the remainder as a profit.

Letter of Credit Regulations

The L/C has been used for decades. Over time, conventions have been developed for their effective construction. The International Chamber of Commerce (ICC) has been an active participant in such efforts and publishes L/C norms. The most recent iteration is known as **UCP 600**.[1] Because international trade involves multiple legal jurisdictions, dispute resolution can be a real headache. UCP 600 helps by providing a common framework for contracts to help avoid misunderstanding and costly litigation. The ICC is also a source of information about the use of L/Cs and publishes a periodical devoted solely to documentary credits.

The L/C is not a complete solution to problems in international trade. The L/C's main objective is to solve the default risk problem. An equally serious problem is product quality. Although the L/C provides comfort that goods have been shipped as indicated by the bill of lading, it does not guarantee that the goods are exactly as claimed. This is unfortunately a problem that can be solved only with manual preshipment inspection.

---

[1] *ICC Uniform Customs and Practices for Documentary Credits UCP 600,* International Chamber of Commerce, 2006.

Letters of Credit versus Documentary Collections

L/Cs are expensive. Rough estimates of various fees (issuing, advising, confirming, etc.) put the cost of one at 0.25 percent of transaction value with minimum charges of at least USD 1,000. Because of these costs, MNCs use the open account method in transactions that have relational protection. But what if such protection is not available? Is there an alternative mechanism that is less costly than the L/C yet provides some of its benefits?

Documentary Collection

A potential alternative to the L/C, the **documentary collection** method is similar to the L/C method in that it intertwines the performance of the parties with each party taking sequential steps in turn toward settlement (see Exhibit 13.3). The exporter ships goods without requiring any documents from the importer. However, the importer cannot get the title to the goods until it arranges for payment. *Documents against acceptance* occur when the importer receives the title to the goods on acceptance of a draft; the actual payment will be made many days after the importer receives title. The more common *documents against payment* occur when the title is received only on actual payment; this method is less risky from the exporter's perspective. A banker intermediates by holding the documents providing the title until the importer makes the payment. The banker's role in this transaction is simpler than in the case of the L/C, in which the banker assumed issuing, advising, and confirming roles. Critically, with documentary collections, the bank is not assuming any liability. For this reason, banker's fees for documentary collections are much smaller, often less than USD 200.

Documentary collections require fewer documents than L/Cs. This is a significant advantage in many respects. We have already mentioned lower transaction costs as a benefit. A second benefit is lower execution risk. Estimates show more than 50 percent of all L/Cs are flawed and, in a few cases, payment is actually refused. Costly renegotiations take place to rectify problems. This does not appear to be a problem with documentary collections.

Given the higher costs and complexity of L/Cs, why do some firms continue to use L/Cs?[2] The obvious reason is that L/Cs offer more protection to the exporter than documentary

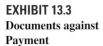

documentary collections
Documentary collections are simpler and less costly than L/C transactions.

EXHIBIT 13.3
Documents against Payment

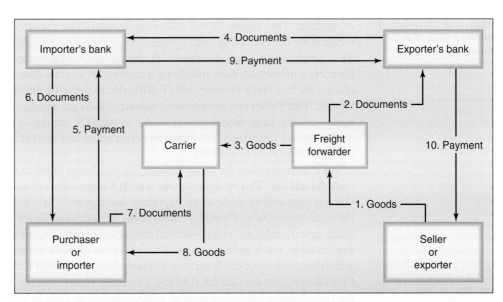

Note: Goods go from exporter to freight forwarder to carrier to importer. Documents go from freight forwarder to the exporter's bank to the importer's bank to the purchaser to the carrier. The importer's bank releases documents only upon receipt of payment, and the carrier releases goods only upon receipt of the documents. Payment flows from importer to importer's bank to exporter's bank to exporter.

[2] Ronald Mann, "The Role of Letters of Credit in Payment Transactions," *Michigan Law Review* 98, no. 8 (August 2000).

collections. Recall that under L/Cs, payment is contingent on a specified list of documents. With documentary collections, payment is contingent on the will of the importer; should the importer decide to not take delivery for whatever reason, the exporter remains with an inventory of unsold goods in a foreign country.

However, there are other, more subtle reasons to use the L/C:

- It might provide a signal about the importer's quality. This signal may regard more than the payment for the current transaction. Indeed, many firms use an L/C for the first few transactions with a new customer in a foreign country, after which they use less costly methods such as open accounts. To initiate this relationship, however, the seal of approval from a reputable banker may be important. Evidence suggests that bankers impose strict screens prior to issuing L/Cs.

- The L/C may provide legitimacy to a transaction. This may be important in countries where money laundering is a problem. So, importers from these countries may signal their legitimacy through L/C usage.

- The L/C also provides collateral benefits in obtaining permits and loans. This is especially relevant in developing nations such as Sri Lanka and Pakistan where L/Cs provide financial status to a business and allow easier access to business permits (e.g., importing equipment) and loans.

These advantages help explain why L/Cs are more prevalent than documentary collections, especially in developing nations where information on parties may be sketchy and concerns such as those involving government controls and financing are relevant.

The Banker's Acceptance

Recall that the L/C specifies the payment amount and method. Two payment alternatives are the time draft and the sight draft. A *draft* is an order (or demand) issued by one party to another party to pay a certain sum of money. In the context of the L/C, the exporter draws the draft demanding that the issuing bank (or, equivalently, the importer) pay a certain sum of money to the exporter. A *sight draft* stipulates that the payment be made when the draft is presented under the conditions specified in the L/C. A *time draft* stipulates that the payment be made at a future point in time, typically 30 or 60 days following the presentation of documents.

banker's acceptance

The *banker's acceptance* is often the result of an L/C transaction.

If the payment mechanism specified in the L/C is a time draft, it often leads to a banker's acceptance. This occurs in the following manner. The exporter sends various documents required by the L/C along with a time draft to the issuing bank through the advising bank. The issuing bank accepts the time draft, thereby creating a *banker's acceptance (BA)*. This is basically a promissory note specifying a payment at a future date. Elsewhere in this book, we discuss the fact that a Treasury bill (T-bill) reflects the government's promise to pay a certain amount (face value) at a certain date (maturity). BAs are similar to T-bills. When a reputable bank—usually large money center banks in the U.S. setting—creates a BA, it becomes a money market instrument. BAs have an active secondary market; this enables the exporter to liquidate them prior to maturity.

An important reason for using banks as intermediaries in international transactions is to mitigate default risk. This is certainly true with BA transactions in which banks offer a guarantee that payment will be made to the exporters. An important development in the 1990s changed the value proposition offered by banks in BA transactions. Governments and private insurers made export-credit insurance—default risk protection for exporters—more widely available. For example, when Indian automobile component manufacturers ship components to global auto firms, they often use insurance available from the Export Credit Guarantee Corporation. Consequently, the demand for BAs fell. One study reports that the level of outstanding BAs in the United States fell from a level of USD 50 billion in 1990 to USD 10 billion in 2000.[3]

---

[3] Ken Cyree, James Lindley, and Drew Winters, "The Effect of Substitute Assets on Yields in Financial Markets," *Financial Management* 36 (2007), pp. 27–47.

13.2 Import and Export Financing

Because of geographical distances and contractual complexities, imports and exports create a long cash cycle (number of days between cash outflow and cash inflow) for exporters and/or importers. For example, if the open account payment method is used, the exporter pays for raw materials, produces and ships the output, and then must wait for the importer to receive the goods and pay. This imposes a heavy working capital burden on the exporter. With other methods, the exporter's cash cycle burden is partially transferred to the importer. At the other end, importers also face their own working capital requirements: They also pay for goods and only later receive revenues by selling these imported goods. In this section, we discuss financing techniques to provide working capital for imports and exports.

Import Financing with Letters of Credit

L/Cs were originally devised to solve the default risk problem. However, their usage today suggests other benefits such as financing. Often issuing banks provide financing to importers in conjunction with the issuance of the L/C. This is especially the case in developing nations where sources of financing are limited. The mechanics of this loan are as follows:

- The exporter presents the L/C and supporting documents, and the issuing bank settles the liability on behalf of the importer.
- The importer does not reimburse the bank right away. An arrangement is made to repay the amount (with interest) at a later date.
- The importer repays the loan at maturity. This date may coincide with receipt of cash flows from its customers.

This method of financing is especially useful if the importer is obtaining components used in manufacturing a product. The importation of components occurs early in the cash cycle and triggers financing needs. When components are obtained and used in products that are later sold, receipts from customers are used to settle the loan. The use of L/Cs as a financing mechanism is one of the factors explaining their widespread use despite the high transaction fees charged by banks. Importers who are using L/Cs primarily as a financing vehicle must consider L/C-related fees as part of financing costs.

EXAMPLE 13.5

An importer obtains components from a foreign supplier for USD 50,000. The L/C fees of USD 1,250 are payable immediately. The components are expected to arrive in a month. The L/C stipulates payment by a sight draft. The importer's bank is willing to meet the payment specified in the L/C and advance the amount to the firm for a period of two months at a stated rate of 9 percent (annual compounding). Calculate the cost of financing.

Solution: As a first step, solve the loan payment:

Loan repayment $= 50,000 \times (1 + 9\%)^{2/12} = 50,723$

Recall that cost of financing equals the internal rate of return (IRR) of financing cash flows. The following table shows cash flows and resulting IRR.

Cost of Financing with Letter of Credit

Month	CF without Fees	CF with Fees
0	0	−1,250
1	50,000	50,000
2	0	0
3	−50,723	−50,723
Monthly cost = Internal rate of return (IRR)	0.72%	2.03%
Annual cost = (1 + Monthly cost)^{12} − 1	9.00%	27.28%

Discussion: Assuming the L/C has no utility other than financing, the true cost of financing is 27.28 percent. If the L/C has considerable value as a payment mechanism, then the cost of financing is between 9 percent and 27.28 percent and perhaps closer to 9 percent. If, for instance, government regulations require the use of L/Cs as payment mechanism, the marginal cost of the loan is only 9 percent.

Export Financing with Letter of Credit and Banker's Acceptance

L/C and export financing
Garment exporters in Tirupur (India) often use the *L/C* for obtaining a *loan* and only then begin production.

Exporters may also need financing. L/Cs can be used in obtaining export financing. Because L/Cs are viewed as sale authentication devices, an exporter can submit the L/C to a banker and obtain a loan. As with import financing using L/Cs, export financing with L/Cs is important to small firms and to firms in developing nations where financing is costly and/or difficult to obtain. For example, many garment exporters in Tirupur (India) begin garment production only after obtaining an L/C. To provide working capital for production (to meet payroll, to buy yarn, to pay for knitting services, to pay for dyeing and other processing, etc.), they obtain bank loans using the L/C.

Exporters can also use the BA as a source of financing. The exporter can discount or sell the BA in the secondary market. In this transaction, the exporter effectively obtains a loan from BA investors. The following example shows how to calculate financing costs for a BA.

EXAMPLE 13.6

Assume that an exporter obtains a two-month draft with a face value of USD 50,000. The acceptance fee (also known as *stamping fee*) is USD 300 payable immediately. Suppose the banker is willing to discount the BA at a rate of 6 percent (simple interest terms). Calculate the cost of financing inclusive of the stamping fee.

Solution:

Amount realized by exporter $= USD\ 50,000 \times \left(1 - 6\% \times \dfrac{2}{12}\right) - 300 = USD\ 49,200$

Because maturity value = FV in 2 months = 50,000

Implied cost of financing (annual) $= \left(\dfrac{50,000}{49,200}\right)^{12/2} - 1 = 10.16\%$

Discussion: Even if there are no acceptance fees, the true cost will be higher than 6 percent. This is so because the 6 percent rate of interest is applied on the future value (FV), not the present value (PV), thereby overcharging interest.

Loans and Guarantees from Export-Import Banks

ex-im banks
Most nations have established *ex-im* banks to assist importers and exporters.

Nations have a vested interest in international trade: It generally increases the welfare of their citizens. Accordingly, many nations have established institutions that assist imports and especially exports by providing information, financing (loans and guarantees), and insurance. These institutions are often organized as banks-cum-insurance firms and are known as **export-import banks** (or simply **ex-im banks**).

EXAMPLE 13.7

In its annual report for 2007, the U.S. Export Import Bank reports that it made 2,793 authorizations for a total of USD 12.6 billion in loans, guarantees, and export credit insurance. Some of these authorizations are large such as the billions provided to support the sale of Boeing aircraft in India and China. Others involve modest amounts and support small U.S. exporters such as Air Tractor, a Texas-based firm exporting agricultural and fire-bombing aircraft mostly to Latin American markets. Most nations today have similar institutions (e.g., the Export Credit Guarantee Corporation of India). See http://www.exim.gov/about/reports/ar/ar2007/Index_IR.html (accessed December18, 2008); and www.ecgc.in.

Other Trade-Financing Techniques

Other financing methods in the context of international trade are discussed next.

Preshipment and Preorder Financing

Earlier we discussed the way L/Cs might be used to obtain postorder preshipment financing. But even prior to obtaining orders and resulting L/Cs, exporters may need working capital financing. This is especially important for small firms, newly started firms, and growing firms. Banks are the main source of this financing; but bank financing, unless collateralized by fixed assets, is usually difficult to obtain. Many governments wishing to encourage exports offer financing schemes that can alleviate the situation.

Accounts Receivable Financing

A type of postshipment financing, accounts receivable financing is particularly relevant when firms use the open account method and/or extend liberal credit terms to their customers. For example, firms using terms such as net 60 (payment due in 60 days after shipment or receipt of goods) often have large receivables positions. Banks may be willing to use the accounts receivables as collateral and provide financing. Because of risks in converting receivables to cash, banks typically advance only a portion of the value of the receivables and charge high rates of interest.

Factoring

The exporter can arrange to transfer the accounts receivable to a third party, usually a bank or a finance company, known as the *factor*. In return, the factor pays the exporter the discounted value of the receivables. Thus, this is equivalent to obtaining financing and helps firms reduce their other sources of financing such as bank debt. Factoring is different from accounts receivables financing in that assets are actually transferred to the factor. Factoring is usually done without recourse, meaning that the factor assumes all risks such as currency, default, and country risks; exceptions are made only for billing disputes. In some cases, factoring is conducted with recourse, meaning that the exporter assumes all risks; this method may be appropriate when the exporter is interested only in obtaining financing, not in the transfer of default and other risks.

13.3 Measuring International Trade

This section discusses the measurement and reporting of trade statistics. We discuss why governments measure trade and the accounting method they use to calculate trade-related flows. We also discuss recent international trade data.

Governments measure international trade for many reasons.

- First, governments can provide information to their citizens about trends in international business. For instance, if the government of a country specializing in textiles learns that the international trend is toward increased purchase of garments by European countries, the textile industry of that country could use this information to increase capital expenditure to prepare for future demand.

- Second, based on collected trade information, governments set public policy such as taxation, import/export procedures, quotas, and restrictions and create tax-free zones and regulations concerning banking. For example, if a government finds that in a particular export industry, a competing country has increased market share, then provisions such as export tax credits can be considered. The government also can help by providing more infrastructure (e.g., port facilities) for this industry.

- Statistics on trade patterns can also provide evidence of direct and indirect trade restrictions imposed by governments. This information is useful in trade negotiations.

EXHIBIT 13.4
U.S. Current Account, 2007 (USD billion)

Source: U.S. Department of Commerce at *http://www.bea.gov/ international/index.htm#bop* (accessed July 10, 2008).

	Exports	Imports	Difference
Goods	1,148	1,968	−820
Services	497	378	119
Income receipts	818	736	82
TOTAL	2,463	3,082	−619
Unilateral transfer			−113
CURRENT ACCOUNT			−732

For these reasons, in the United States, the Department of Commerce collects trade data and disseminates them freely through its Web site and publications. Global organizations such as the International Monetary Fund (IMF) and especially the WTO also have incentives to measure international trade.

The Balance of Payments Accounting System

The United States has an elaborate accounting system to measure trade as well as other transactions between U.S. entities and foreign entities. This overall system is known as the **balance of payments**. Information on these accounts is publicly available from the Bureau of Economic Analysis (www.bea.gov).

The most visible component of the balance of payments account is the current account. As Exhibit 13.4 illustrates using U.S. data for 2007, the components of the current account are:

- **Goods.** These are merchandise exports and imports. Examples of U.S. exports are agricultural exports such as corn and soybeans to China. Automobiles are examples of U.S. imports.
- **Services.** Services include items such as travel, passenger fares, royalty and license fees, and other private services. An example of a U.S. export is travel expense incurred by foreigners while traveling in the United States. Examples of U.S. imports are royalty and license fees paid by U.S. firms to foreign firms.
- **Income receipts.** These are income flows arising from cross-border investment in assets. An example of U.S. exports is the payment of dividends from foreign corporations to U.S. citizens. An example of U.S. imports is the payment of interest by U.S. firms to foreign entities.
- **Unilateral transfer.** This relatively minor item primarily comprises U.S. government grants and private remittances.

The current account is often discussed in three levels (values from exhibit 13.4):

balance of trade
The *balance of trade* equals the difference between the export and import value of goods.

- **Balance of trade (BOT) (Level I).** The difference between goods exports and imports is known as the **balance of trade (BOT)**. A negative (deficit) BOT indicates that a country imports more than it exports. This is the most visible and discussed statistic from the current account. This number is often reported in newspapers to the population at large. In 2007, the U.S. BOT was negative USD 820 billion.
- **Balance of goods and services (BOGS) (Level II).** BOGS expands the definition of trade to include services in addition to goods. The **balance of goods and services (BOGS)** for the United States can be calculated as BOT (negative USD 820 billion) plus the value for services (positive USD 119 billion) and equals negative USD 701 billion.
- **Balance of current account (Level III).** This is the overall balance in the current account and includes the balances in goods, services, income, and unilateral transfers. The current account balance for 2007 is negative USD 732 billion.

The balance of payments uses the double-entry accounting method. Hence, overall accounts are always in balance. The current account balance (or discrepancy) is perfectly offset by the financial account balance, which reflects cross-border purchases and sales of assets. The simplest way to understand this is as follows. Assume that U.S. exports and imports are USD 300 and USD 200, respectively. This would imply a current account balance of USD 100. This balance would be reflected in an increase in the U.S. holdings of foreign assets or currency by USD 100. See Appendix 13 for detailed data on the U.S. financial position in 2007 and further explanation of the current and financial accounts.

Trends in International Trade

The World Trade Organization (WTO) publishes annual statistics on world trade. The most recent data (see Exhibit 13.5) indicate that in the decade of the 2000s, world trade grew at an annual rate of 5.5 percent, while global gross domestic product (GDP) grew at only 3 percent. Thus, a larger part of global business activity is now conducted across borders. The key category of traded goods is manufactured products. But it is noteworthy that even agricultural products—once produced solely for local consumption—are traded in good amounts.

exporters and importers
Asians are the leading exporters, *North Americans* are the leading importers, and *Europeans* conduct the largest amount of intraregion trade.

Which regions engage actively in international trade? See Exhibit 13.6 for the level of trade in 2007 and exporting and importing regions. In intraregion trade, Europe tops the list with trade of USD 4,244 billion. Asia is next, followed by North America. In interregion trade, Asia to North America is the largest category with USD 756 billion. Considering total exports, the largest exporters are Europeans. Considering only exports to other regions, Asians are the largest exporters. The largest importers are Europeans, but if one excludes intraregion imports, North Americans are the largest importers.

EXHIBIT 13.5
Annual Percentage Change in Global Trade versus Production & GDP (2007)

Source: 2008 International Trade Statistics (WTO). http://www.wto.org/english/res_e/statis_e/its2008_e/its2008_e.pdf (accessed December 17, 2008).

	2000–2007	2005	2006	2007
World merchandise exports	**5.5**	**6.5**	**8.5**	**6.0**
Agricultural products	4.0	6.0	6.0	4.5
Fuels and mining products	3.5	3.5	3.5	3.0
Manufactures	6.5	7.5	10.0	7.5
World merchandise production	**3.0**	**3.0**	**3.0**	**4.0**
Agriculture	2.5	2.0	1.5	2.5
Mining	1.5	1.5	1.0	0.0
Manufacturing	3.0	4.0	4.0	5.0
World GDP	**3.0**	**3.0**	**3.5**	**3.5**

EXHIBIT 13.6   Global Trade: Origin and Destination, 2007 (USD billion)

Origin	Destination							
	North America	South and Central America	Europe	Commonwealth of Independent States	Africa	Middle East	Asia	World
North America	951	131	329	12	27	50	352	1,854
South and Central America	151	122	106	6	14	9	80	499
Europe	459	80	4,244	189	148	153	434	5,772
Commonwealth of Independent States	24	6	288	103	7	16	60	510
Africa	92	15	168	1	41	11	81	424
Middle East	84	4	108	5	28	93	397	760
Asia	756	92	715	80	91	150	1,890	3,800
Total	**2,517**	**451**	**5,956**	**397**	**355**	**483**	**3,294**	**13,619**

2008 International Trade Statistics (WTO). http://www.wto.org/english/res_e/statis_e/its2008_e/its2008_e.pdf (accessed December 17, 2008.)

EXHIBIT 13.7

**U.S. Merchandise
Exports and Imports**

Source: www.bea.gov. (accessed
June 20, 2008).

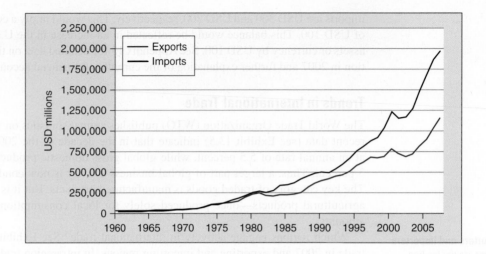

Imports and exports are increasing not only for developing countries that are undergoing rapid transformation but also for mature economies such as that of the United States. The data in Exhibit 13.7 show merchandise exports and imports for the United States over the last 30 years. One can note a dramatic increase in both exports and imports. The annual rate of growth of both is approximately 15 percent. In addition, a yawning gap between imports and exports exists, indicating a widening BOT deficit.

Is a BOT deficit a bad thing? Economists view international trade as the engine for global growth. Despite this consensus on trade, there is much anguish and controversy in the United States over the persistent BOT deficit in recent decades. There are many points of view here. The political perspective is that a BOT deficit increases unemployment and, hence, is undesirable. Obviously, when a country imports goods and services, it is shifting employment to overseas locations. This point has not escaped the attention of labor union leaders and opportunistic politicians. Economists, however, are not so quick to condemn BOT deficits. When deficits are caused by growth in a country, they may indicate a sound economy.[4] In addition, economists point to many years of surpluses prior to 1971 and indicate that trade deficits and surpluses are cyclical. Nevertheless, a persistent deficit may be deemed troublesome.

13.4 Trading Blocks and Agreements

An interesting post-World War II development is the emergence of multilateral trade agreements. They have played a large role in the growth of world trade. In this section, we discuss the role played by agreements such as the WTO agreements and the North American Free Trade Agreement (NAFTA). Because of their important status, we focus on the WTO agreements, which were known as the **General Agreement on Tariffs and Trade (GATT)** until 1995.

General Agreement on Tariffs and Trade and World Trade Organization Agreements

GATT (later WTO) was one of the most important postwar developments. More than 100 countries, accounting for more than 90 percent of world trade, joined to sign the initial world trade agreement in 1947. The purpose of this and subsequent agreements (initially known as GATT and later as the WTO) was to promote world trade by reducing trade barriers and preventing unilateral actions by member countries. By all objective measures, such as the amount of trade

[4] K. Chrystal and G. Wood, "Are Trade Deficits a Problem?" *Federal Reserve Bank of St. Louis Review*, January/February 1988, 3–11.

EXHIBIT 13.8
Ten Benefits of the WTO Multilateral Trading System

Source: http://www.wto.org/english/thewto_e/whatis_e/10ben_e/10b00_e.htm (accessed August 17, 2009).

1. The system helps promote peace.
2. Disputes are handled constructively.
3. Rules make life easier for all.
4. Freer trade cuts the cost of living.
5. The system provides more choice of products and qualities.
6. Trade causes incomes to rise.
7. Trade stimulates economic growth.
8. The basic principles make life more efficient.
9. Governments are shielded from lobbying.
10. The system encourages good government.

and the level of tariffs, these agreements have been a tremendous success. Refer to Exhibit 13.8 for benefits of trade proclaimed by the WTO; some, such as the improved standard of living, are obvious, but others, such as benefits to governments, are less obvious.

Membership

WTO

The *WTO* has more than 150 members.

Currently, there are more than 150 member countries in the WTO. A country wishing to join makes a formal application and is subject to review. The review may take about five years. An initial review evaluates the consistency between the applicant's trade laws and policies and those of the WTO. The terms of entry are then worked out. Negotiations are conducted, often at the bilateral level between the applicant and prominent WTO members, to resolve issues. Agreements typically call for transitional steps and concessions by the applicant over market access. The most famous recent entry is China in 2000 after nearly 15 years of arduous negotiations.

WTO Rounds

The GATT/WTO agreements have evolved over time. Successive rounds of negotiations have increasingly eliminated various forms of unfair trade practices and have covered more goods and services. The first six rounds, starting with the 1947 Geneva round and ending with the 1964–1967 Kennedy round, focused on tariff reduction, admittedly the first order of business. The seventh round, Tokyo 1973–1979, expanded coverage to nontariff measures such as quotas. The 1986–1994 Uruguay round, which is the most recently completed round and the basis for existing WTO rules, is the most ambitious and expanded the scope of coverage to items such as intellectual property and services. The current round, known as the Doha round, was launched in 2001 but has not yet led to any agreements. Following the Uruguay round, there have been negotiations for tariff-free trade in agriculture, information technology products, and financial services. We discuss some of the key WTO agreements and initiatives next.

Antidumping Agreement

Dumping is said to occur when a company exports a product at a price lower than the one that its home market normally charges. Article 6 of the WTO agreements allows member countries to take certain actions when it can demonstrate that dumping has unfairly harmed domestic industries. The most common antidumping action is to charge extra import duties to bring the price of the products in line with market prices. The WTO specifies methods for assessing the impact of dumping, the amount of extra duties to be charged, and the duration of the action.

Subsidies and Countervailing Measures

The problem of subsidies is quite different from the problem of dumping, although the effects and remedies are similar. Dumping is the result of corporate action while subsidies result from governmental action. The WTO classifies subsidies as prohibited, actionable, and nonactionable. *Prohibited subsidies* clearly distort international trade. Examples include subsidies that require certain export targets. *Actionable* subsidies occur in the gray area between prohibited and nonactionable subsidies: If member states can prove "serious prejudice" (usually when an ad valorem subsidy exceeds 5 percent), they can challenge the subsidy with the WTO. When subsidies are proven to be actionable or prohibited, countries can assess countervailing duties. Nations are permitted to have *nonactionable* subsidies. These are either (1) nonspecific subsidies or (2) specific subsidies for industrial research and precompetitive developmental activity. In special cases, subsidies are allowed for developing nations or disadvantaged regions.[5]

U.S. Concerns

The United States has been instrumental in pushing for agreements in key areas such as services, intellectual property rights, and e-commerce.

- **Services.** The General Agreement on Trade in Services (GATS) is specifically geared to cross-border sales of services. WTO members have made specific commitments to open their service markets to free trade. This agreement applies to items such as services sold by banks, insurance firms, telecommunication firms, hotels, and transportation companies.

- **Intellectual property rights.** The United States is probably the nation with the biggest stake in the area of intellectual property rights. Patents and copyrights on products such as pharmaceuticals, semiconductors, and computer and networking equipment are vital for U.S. businesses. Recent trade discussions have focused on these issues.

- **E-commerce.** Business conducted over the Internet or an electronic medium is referred to as *e-commerce*. This is a relatively new field with major players such as Amazon.com and eBay pushing the frontier. The field is rapidly evolving with projections of high revenue growth rates and a large market size in the near term. Given the novelty of the field, trade issues are ill defined at the moment, but countries try to keep ahead of the curve.

The North American Free Trade Agreement and Other Regional Agreements

NAFTA came into existence in 1994 with the objective of phasing out all tariffs on industrial products and most of those on agricultural products traded among Canada, Mexico, and the United States. This phaseout was expected be achieved over a period of 10 to 15 years. In particular, NAFTA imposes more restrictions on Mexico's ability to erect trade barriers than allowed by existing trade regimes; some of the products influenced by NAFTA include machine tools, medical devices, semiconductors, computers, and telecommunications and electronic equipment. NAFTA also attempts to remove nontariff trade barriers such as the import licenses that Mexico used to create a de facto quota system.

NAFTA was also expected to make exports from Mexico easier by removing duties and restrictions on the U.S. and Canadian side. In fact, one of the great fears of U.S. labor was that U.S. firms would set up factories in Mexico and close operations in the United States; this caused a significant amount of protest when NAFTA was implemented. Especially in the United States, there were concerns that Mexico would be able to export more but would not increase imports to the same extent; these fears were largely proven untrue, as both Mexican imports and exports surged following NAFTA (see Exhibit 13.9).

In addition to NAFTA, other regional agreements or associations exist. One successful regional association is the Association of Southeast Asian Nations (ASEAN). It was started in 1967 with the participation of five Asian countries: Indonesia, Malaysia, the Philippines, Singapore, and Thailand. Currently, this organization encompasses all 10 countries of Southeast Asia, and its sphere of activity encompasses economic and political aspects. The importance of ASEAN is indicated by the facts that more than 500 million of the world's citizens live in this area and that some of these countries are moving rapidly up the ladder to first-world status.

[5] See http://www.wto.org/english/docs_e/legal_e/ursum_e.htm for a summary of agreements from the Uruguay round (accessed September 12, 2008).

EXHIBIT 13.9
NAFTA's Effect on
Mexican Exports and
Imports

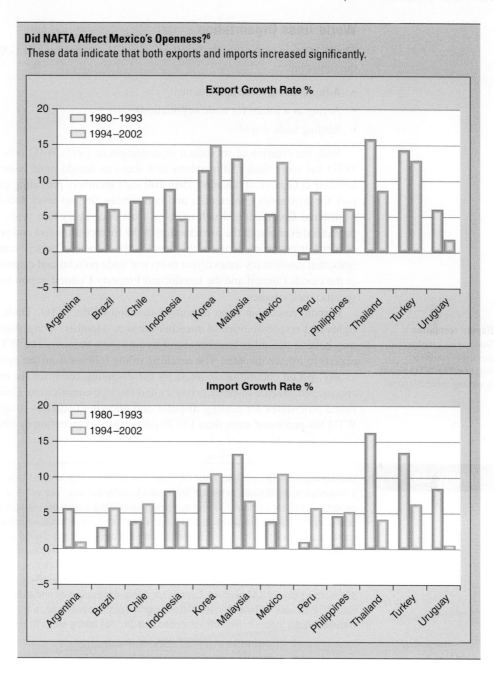

Did NAFTA Affect Mexico's Openness?[6]
These data indicate that both exports and imports increased significantly.

13.5 Global Organizations Influencing International Trade

Earlier we discussed the importance of global agreements such as GATT/WTO. In this section, we focus on the organization created to administer these agreements: the WTO. We also discuss the roles of other organizations such as the International Monetary Fund and the World Bank.

[6] M. Kose, Guy Meredith, and Christopher Towe, "How Has NAFTA Affected the Mexican Economy? Review and Evidence," Working Paper, IMF, 2004.

World Trade Organization

The WTO was created in 1995, following the Uruguay round of GATT. Its mission includes the following[7]:

- Administering trade agreements.
- Acting as a forum for trade negotiations.
- Settling trade disputes.

With the creation of its formal organization in 1995, WTO now supersedes GATT. The WTO has more than 150 members and seeks to decide most issues on a consensus basis. Located in Geneva, it has more than 500 staff members providing the organization and support for its various conferences and committees. Its top-level decision-making body is the Ministerial Conference, which meets at least once every two years. These meetings are the publicized events with the participation of the finance ministers and possibly the heads of state of member countries. Beneath this level is the General Council, consisting of trade bureaucrats, that meets many times a year to review trade policies and disputes. Subcommittees, such as the Goods Council and the Intellectual Property Council, report to the General Council on specific policy issues.

dispute resolution
Trade among nations inevitably results in *disputes*. The WTO assists in settling these disputes.

Dispute resolution is an important function of the WTO. Trade agreements outline the rights and responsibilities of member nations. Members bring disputes to the WTO when they believe that other members have treated them unfairly. The WTO appoints independent experts to rule on disputes. The resulting ruling follows from the agreements in place as well as any special commitments made by the disputing countries. In most cases, countries are encouraged to settle disputes privately and through consultation. Failing this, there are established procedures for settling disputes and allowing countries to appeal WTO rulings. The WTO has processed more than 150 disputes since its inception in 1995.

EXAMPLE 13.8

War between the United States and Canada? The lumber war that came to a head in 2001 resulted from a long-simmering dispute between these two friendly nations. The value of Canadian annual lumber exports—used for commercial and construction-related purposes—is approximately USD 7 billion a year. The Canadians are presumed to have a cost advantage because most Canadian lumber is harvested from government-owned (Crown) lands in contrast to the United States, where private lands are used. Stumpage fees in Canada are assumed to be lower because of this arrangement, which was accused of being a subsidy. The U.S. Department of Commerce concluded that the amount of the subsidy was 19.13 percent. The United States imposed a countervailing duty of 18.79 percent and an antidumping duty of 8.43 percent. Canada challenged these duties and asserted they were inconsistent with WTO as well as NAFTA rules. After lengthy legal proceedings, a truce was finally called in 2006 with the United States calling off the duties and Canada taking steps to limit its lumber exports.

Source: Chi Carmody, "Softwood Lumber Dispute (2001–2006)," *The American Journal of International Law* 100, no. 3 (2006), pp. 664–674.

International Monetary Fund

The International Monetary Fund (IMF) came into existence in 1945 following the postwar Bretton Woods conference. The IMF explicitly states that its mission is to facilitate the expansion and balanced growth of world trade and to oversee the international payment system. Thus, issues such as international trade, currency stability, and balance of payment issues fall within its purview. One of its key activities is to provide financial assistance to any of its 185 member countries (as of 2007) that may be experiencing balance of payment problems. Most of these commitments are currently to nations in the troubled regions of Africa, Asia, and eastern Europe.

---

[7] See the WTO Web site at www.wto.org for more information.

The IMF is not to be confused with the World Bank, which has very different objectives and is usually oriented to fostering development in the poorest nations. The IMF is much more involved in trade and currency issues and is not so concerned about assistance related to education and infrastructure.

Sometimes the IMF's actions in economic crises such as the emerging markets crisis of 1997–1998 are controversial. The IMF is known to couple financial assistance with prescriptions concerning countries' fiscal and monetary policies. It insists that it has no authority over the economic policies of member countries, but critics point out that its financial aid often comes with strings attached. Countries such as Malaysia were bitter critics of the IMF during the Asian crisis, although it is not clear how much of this criticism has to do with political pandering to domestic constituencies.

The IMF is financed by its members. Members are allotted financing quotas or subscription money depending on their national product. The United States is by far the largest contributor, providing nearly 20 percent of the IMF's capital. Voting power is closely tied to the financing quota, and consequently, the United States has the most influence on IMF decisions.

United States

The *United States* is the largest and most influential member of the IMF.

World Bank

The **International Bank for Reconstruction and Development (IBRD)**, also known as the *World Bank,* was established in 1944. Unlike the IMF, the World Bank's objective is to help developing nations by advancing loans and grants. Most loans are offered at market rates without any subsidy. By issuing bonds in global debt markets, the World Bank is able to obtain financing that may not be available directly to small developing nations. Some loans to the poorest of nations are offered, however, from a special pool of money at low or zero interest rates.

In 2006, the World Bank's outstanding loans totaled USD 46 billion. While this amount may be small in the context of developed nations such as the United States, it is sufficient to provide meaningful assistance to Latin American countries such as Bolivia, African countries such as Madagascar, and Asian countries such as Sri Lanka.

EXAMPLE 13.9

In a typical month, the World Bank processes more than 25 loans and grants. The following is an example of a grant and a loan from June 2008.

- Grant of USD 94 million to Cote d'Ivoire for providing emergency urban infrastructure. The grant is to be used for projects in the following areas: water supply, sanitation, solid waste management, and roads.
- Loan of USD 20 million repayable in 40 years to Nicaragua for developing micro- and small-scale businesses. The loan is to be used to enhance the competitiveness of these business enterprises by providing grants and financial services and fostering the dissemination of information.

In addition to lending for development or to alleviate poverty, the World Bank attempts to enhance the business environment of developing nations by using the following tools:

- **The International Finance Corporation (IFC).** IFC promotes private sector investment in developing countries through investment and advisory activities. IFC serves as an investor and an honest broker and helps to reassure foreign investors, local partners, and creditors. IFC advises businesses entering new markets. It also advises governments to provide a more hospitable business environment, to create effective and stable financial markets, and to privatize inefficient state enterprises.
- **The Multilateral Investment Guarantee Agency (MIGA).** Foreign direct investment is an important driver of growth in emerging economies. MIGA's mandate is to promote foreign direct investment by offering political risk insurance (guarantees) to investors and

lenders and by providing skills and resources to help emerging economies attract and retain this investment.

- **The International Center for Settlement of Investment Disputes (ICSID).** ICSID provides facilities for the settlement—by conciliation or arbitration—of investment disputes between foreign investors and their host countries.

G8

G8, or the **group of eight nations**, includes seven major OECD nations—the United States, Japan, Germany, France, Italy, the United Kingdom, and Canada—and Russia. The economic ministers of these eight nations meet annually to discuss issues such as currency values and international trade. These meetings have been held since 1975, when six of these countries held the first meeting in Rambouillet, France. This is an informal group that serves more to initiate than to consummate discussions of important issues.

The meetings in Heiligendamm (Germany) in 2007 and Hokkaido (Japan) in 2008 focused on energy. A key outcome is the International Partnership for Energy Efficiency Cooperation, which brings together the G8 countries, China, India, South Korea, and the European Union. The Hokkaido agenda included four items: oil prices, the value of the Chinese yuan, the environment, and the global credit crisis.

The G8 is an evolving institution. Unlike the IMF or the WTO, it has no constitution, mission statement, or formal organization. However, a structure is gradually beginning to take shape. In addition to the annual meetings that stress economic issues, the G8 is organizing ministerial forums to target specific areas such as unemployment, crime, energy, and terrorism. Ad hoc meetings focus on specific issues or countries. Task forces are also created on an ad hoc basis to provide information on topics such as money laundering. The membership itself, although largely unchanged, accommodates the participation of other countries such as China, India, Brazil, Mexico, and South Africa. The G20 meeting held at Pittsburgh (United States) during September 2009 is a harbinger of things to come.

Summary

- Import and export transactions contain fundamental problems of time lags and informational asymmetry. Many risks such as those related to currency, counterparty, and product quality occur because of these underlying problems.

- The letter of credit (L/C) is a system by which the exporter obtains payment upon completing certain tasks such as the shipment of goods. This method of trade has high transaction costs because it involves banks as mediators and guarantors.

- Other trade methods include the open account method in which payment is made after receipt of goods at the discretion of the importer and the documentary credit method in which title to goods passes to importers only after they make the payment.

- Banker's acceptances (BAs) occur when time drafts used to pay exporters are accepted by a banker on behalf of the importer. Banker's acceptances are money market instruments with liquid secondary markets.

- Both importers and exporters require financing. Importers require it to pay for goods purchased. Exporters require it because of the lag between incurring production costs and receiving payment from importers. Importers and exporters use various mechanisms, often involving banks, to finance trade.

- Nations collect and disseminate trade information. The United States displays trade information using the balance of payments accounts. There are two key accounts: the current account, which measures current flows such as merchandise flows, and the financial account, which measures changes in ownership of assets such as stocks and bonds.

- The World Trade Organization is an important organization that promotes world trade. In part due to its efforts, trade increased dramatically in the second half of the 20th century.

Questions

1. **International Trade.** What does the term *international trade* mean? What is the formal list of activities encompassing it? Does this coincide with what the average citizen understands about it?

2. **Problems in Merchandise Trade.** Consider the import and export of goods. What are some problems in a transaction between counterparties that are not affiliated with one another? Which of these problems remain even if the two parties are affiliated?

3. **Problems in Merchandise Trade.** A privately held Chinese toy manufacturer wishes to purchase a sophisticated machine tool from a small private firm in Illinois. The equipment is custom made and must be ordered two months ahead of shipment. Assume that it takes three weeks for the equipment to be transported from the factory in Illinois to the manufacturer's facility in China. Describe some of the problems in structuring a contract between these two parties.

4. **Currency Risk in International Trade.** Explain why currency risk occurs for one or both counterparties in international trade. In answering this question, consider the following scenarios.

   a. Scenario A. An Indian garment manufacturer orders a computerized embroidering machine from a German manufacturer for EUR 600,000. The time from order to delivery is three months.

   b. Scenario B. A U.K. retail chain orders cooking implements (pans, utensils) from a Chinese manufacturer for USD 400,000. Delivery is scheduled in two months.

5. **Product Quality Risk.** Explain why product quality risk is heightened in international trade between unaffiliated entities. What are some remedies to this problem?

6. **Payment Methods.** Gattoni Rubinetteria, an established Italian bathroom fixtures manufacturer, seeks to expand its sales to the Indian and Chinese markets. The building boom in these two nations has given Gattoni the opportunity to aggressively expand its markets. You have the following additional information. The average shipment is expected to be worth EUR 400,000. Half of the shipments are expected to be to repeat customers. What method of payment should Gattoni demand from its customers?

7. **Payment Methods.** Compare the open account, telex transfer, and consignment methods of payment. Evaluate risks to the two parties as well as transaction costs involved. Consider transactions between an olive oil producer in Lazio, Italy, and a large chain of gourmet food stores in the northeast United States. Which method would you suggest and why? Assume that the two parties have no prior transactions.

8. **Letter of Credit.** What is a letter of credit (L/C)? Who issues and it and why? Who is the applicant? Who is the beneficiary? What problems of international trade does the L/C solve?

9. **Letter of Credit.** Explain how payment is made for a purchase using an L/C. What are the exact steps and the documents used? What can go wrong in these steps? What are the possible remedies if things go wrong?

10. **Role of Banks in Letter of Credit.** Explain the role of banks in L/C transactions. How are these banks compensated?

11. **UCP600.** What is UCP600, and what is its role in international trade?

12 **Documentary Collections.** Explain two forms of documentary collections and how they work. What are the advantages and disadvantages relative to L/Cs?

13. **Banker's Acceptance.** What are banker's acceptances (BAs)? How do they occur and in what context?

14. **Financing with Letters of Credit:** Paul Trading Corporation, an Irish importer and distributor of garments, transacts with Century Garments of Tirupur, India. Explain how both parties can use L/Cs as financing tools.

15. **Balance of Payments.** What system of accounts does the U.S. government use to measure transactions (trade and capital) between its citizens/businesses and foreign entities? What are the key subaccounts, and what do they measure?

16. **U.S. Trade Status.** Obtain trade statistics from the Department of Commerce Web site to answer these questions:

    a. What is the most recent trade deficit? Give monthly and annual figures.

    b. What are the two countries with which the United States has the highest deficits? Why?

    c. How does the United States fare with trade in services? Which country purchases the most services from the United States?

17. **Levels of the Current Account.** What are the three levels of the current account, and what do they measure? Which level is most often reported in the press and why?

18. **WTO.** What is the WTO? What issues were discussed in the most recent round of talks? What are some recent actions the WTO has taken?

19. **Regional Agreements.** What is the role of regional trade agreements in international trade? Name several of them and assess their relative importance. Are regional agreements becoming less or more important?

Problems

1. **L/C Financing.** An importer obtains components from a foreign supplier for USD 400,000. The L/C fees of USD 1,500 are payable immediately. The components are expected to arrive in a month. The L/C stipulates payment by a sight draft. The importer's bank is willing to meet the payment specified in the L/C and advance the amount to the firm for a period of two months at a stated rate of 11 percent assuming annual compounding.

   a. Ignoring L/C fees, what are the cash flows? What is the annual financing cost?

   b. Incorporating L/C fees, what are the cash flows? What is the annual financing cost?

2. **L/C Financing and Currency Effect.** Argentina has a high per capita consumption of leather jackets. Styles demanded are similar to European styles. An Indian leather exporter is considering shipping tanned leather to an Argentinean leather garment manufacturer. The shipment is invoiced for USD 600,000. The goods can be shipped immediately and will take a month to arrive in Argentina. The Argentine firm takes out an L/C to facilitate this transaction. It pays fees of Argentine peso (ARS) 3,000 for the L/C. The L/C stipulates payment by a sight draft. The importer's bank is willing to meet the payment specified in the L/C and advance the USD amount to the firm for a period of four months at a stated rate of 5 percent assuming annual compounding. Assume also that spot ARSUSD = 0.3294 and that the ARS is expected to weaken against the USD at the rate of 6 percent a year.

   a. Identify all L/C-related cash flows for the Argentinean firm.

   b. Using information on the expected annual change in the value of ARS, calculate its expected value at the time of the loan (month 1) and at the time of the repayment (month 5). [*Hint:* Use compounding principles to infer the rate at which ARS weakens for the one- and five-month intervals, respectively.]

   c. Convert all cash flows identified in (a) into ARS. What is the annual financing cost (IRR)?

3. **BA Financing.** Assume that an exporter obtains a two-month draft with a face value of USD 100,000. The acceptance fee (also known as *stamping fee*) is USD 500 payable immediately. Suppose the banker is willing to discount the BA at a rate of 5 percent (simple interest terms). Calculate the cost of financing inclusive of the stamping fee.

4. **Balance of Payments.** You obtain the following data on the U.S. balance of payments. Using your knowledge of this accounting system, please fill in the missing values and identify/calculate the three levels of the current account.

U.S. Current Account, 200X (*USD billion*)

	Exports	Imports	Difference
Goods	1,200	2,000	?
Services	?	300	100
Income receipts	700	?	50
TOTAL	?	?	?
Unilateral transfer			−75
CURRENT ACCOUNT			?

5. **Current Account Levels.** You obtain the following data on the U.S. balance of payments.

U.S. Current Account, 200X (*USD billion*)

	Exports	Imports	Difference
Goods	1,500	?	?
Services	?	300	−100
Income receipts	?	600	50
TOTAL	?	?	?
Unilateral transfer			−125
CURRENT ACCOUNT			−300

    a. Using your knowledge of this accounting system, please fill in the missing values.

    b. Identify/calculate the three levels of the current account.

Case

Clover Machines: *Eyes on the Doha Round*

According to the World Trade Organization (WTO), world merchandise exports of agricultural products in 2006 were nearly USD 1 trillion and constituted 8 percent of world trade. Since the year 2000, trade in agriculture has increased at a rate of 10 percent annually, equaling or bettering growth rates for industrial sectors such as autos and textiles. Laura Brooks, Clover's CEO, was thinking about the future for global agriculture and the role Clover could play in that future. In fact, Laura was looking at WTO statistics (see Case Exhibit 13.1) on major exporters.

The future does appear bright. But there were some storm clouds on the horizon. The Doha round of WTO talks—started in 2001—was at a critical stage. Brazil, Russia, India, and China, using their newly found economic muscle, exerted pressure on the United States and European Union (EU) to reduce or eliminate farm subsidies. In principle, the United States and EU have subsidies of about USD 40 billion and USD 100 billion, respectively, but recent spikes in agricultural prices have dramatically reduced the need for actual subsidy. Regardless, developing countries continue to press the case, fearing future situations in which subsidies may actually be employed. In retaliation, the United States and EU called for developing countries to reduce or eliminate tariffs on industrial goods. During the summer of 2008, some tense exchanges between participants occurred. Mr. Pascal Lamy, the WTO's leader of the Trade Negotiations Committee, warned that "time is running out."

CASE EXHIBIT 13.1

	USD (billions)	Share in World Exports				Annual Percentage Change			
	2006	1980	1990	2000	2006	2000–2006	2004	2005	2006
European Union	95.31	—	—	10.1	10.1	10	14	7	9
United States	92.66	17.0	14.3	12.9	9.8	4	4	4	12
Canada	44.23	5.0	5.4	6.3	4.7	4	19	3	7
Brazil	39.53	3.4	2.4	2.8	4.2	17	27	14	13
China	32.54	1.5	2.4	3.0	3.4	12	9	19	13
Australia	22.18	3.3	2.9	3.0	2.3	5	35	−4	5
Thailand	21.58	1.2	1.9	2.2	2.3	10	13	4	21
Argentina	21.33	1.9	1.8	2.2	2.3	10	13	12	11
Indonesia	18.32	1.6	1.0	1.4	1.9	15	27	16	30
Russian Federation	17.06	—	—	1.4	1.8	14	13	20	16
Malaysia	15.57	2.0	1.8	1.5	1.6	12	14	2	16
Mexico	14.69	0.8	0.8	1.6	1.6	8	13	13	17
India	14.41	1.0	0.8	1.2	1.5	14	8	26	34
New Zealand	13.24	1.3	1.4	1.4	1.4	10	24	7	2
Chile	11.49	0.4	0.7	1.2	1.2	10	22	11	14

Source: International Trade Statistics 2007, www.wto.org.

Ms. Brooks wondered about the following issues related to her firm's future:

1. The firm has already embarked on a strategy for global operations with a new emphasis in emerging markets. Do trade statistics support this strategy?
2. In addition to countries already targeted by Clover, what other countries should it consider? Why?
3. What implications do current trade tensions have for Clover? Would their successful resolution help or hurt Clover's initiatives in selling agricultural machines worldwide? More generally, what is the connection between trade in agricultural products and demand for Clover's machines? What is the connection between farm subsidies and demand for machines?
4. Does the information presented in this case have anything to say about Clover's construction business?

Appendix 13

A Primer on U.S. International Transactions

The purpose of this appendix is to explain the following fundamental relationship concerning international trade:

Exports − Imports = United States purchases of foreign assets − Foreign purchases of U.S. assets

Current Account   Financial Account (previously called *capital account*)

A country that exports more gets to invest more in foreign assets. A country that imports more has more foreign ownership of its assets. This relationship between trade (left-hand side of the equation, also called the *current account*) and financial transactions (right-hand side of the equation, also called the *financial account*) is best explained using the 2007 balance of payment accounts of the United States (see Exhibit 13.10 for account details).

In 2007, the current account balance (the difference between lines 18 and 1) was *approximately* equal to the financial account balance (the difference between lines 55 and 40). Note that the official accounts reproduced here use negative values for U.S. imports and U.S. purchases of foreign assets. Ignoring these signs:

$$\text{Exports} - \text{Imports} = 2,463,505 - 3,082,014 = -618,509$$

$$\text{U.S. purchases of foreign assets} - \text{Foreign purchases of U.S. assets}$$
$$= 1,289,854 - 2,057,703 = -767,849$$

EXHIBIT 13.10   **U.S. International Transactions in 2007 (millions of dollars)**

Line	(Credits +; debits −)	2007
	Current Account	
1	**Exports of goods and services and income receipts**	**2,463,505**
2	Exports of goods and services	1,645,726
3	Goods, balance of payments basis	1,148,481
4	Services	497,245
5	Transfers under U.S. military agency sales contracts	16,052
6	Travel	96,712
7	Passenger fares	25,586
8	Other transportation	51,586
9	Royalties and license fees	82,614
10	Other private services	223,483
11	U.S. government miscellaneous services	1,212
12	Income receipts	817,779
13	Income receipts on U.S.-owned assets abroad	814,807
14	Direct investment receipts	368,275
15	Other private receipts	444,299
16	U.S. government receipts	2,233
17	Compensation of employees	2,972
18	**Imports of goods and services and income payments**	**−3,082,014**
19	Imports of goods and services	−2,345,984
20	Goods, balance of payments basis	−1,967,853
21	Services	−378,130
22	Direct defense expenditures	−32,820
23	Travel	−76,167
24	Passenger fares	−28,486
25	Other transportation	−67,050
26	Royalties and license fees	−25,048
27	Other private services	−144,375
28	U.S. government miscellaneous services	−4,184
29	Income payments	−736,030
30	Income payments on foreign-owned assets in the United States	−726,031
31	Direct investment payments	−134,414
32	Other private payments	−426,515
33	U.S. government payments	−165,102
34	Compensation of employees	−9,999
35	**Unilateral current transfers, net**	**−112,705**
36	U.S. government grants	−33,237
37	U.S. government pensions and other transfers	−7,323
38	Private remittances and other transfers	−72,145
	Capital Account	
39	**Capital account transactions, net**	**−1,843**

(*continued*)

Line	(Credits +; debits −)	2007
	Financial Account	
40	**U.S.-owned assets abroad excluding derivatives (outflow)**	**−1,289,854**
41	U.S. official reserve assets	−122
42	Gold	0
43	Special drawing rights	−154
44	Reserve position in the International Monetary Fund	1,021
45	Foreign currencies	−989
46	U.S. government assets other than official reserve assets	−22,273
47	U.S. credits and other long-term assets	−2,475
48	Repayments on U.S. credits and other long-term assets	4,104
49	U.S. foreign currency holdings and U.S. short-term assets	−23,902
50	U.S. private assets	−1,267,459
51	Direct investment	−333,271
52	Foreign securities	−288,731
53	U.S. claims on unaffiliated foreigners reported by U.S. nonbanking concerns	−706
54	U.S. claims reported by U.S. banks, not included elsewhere	−644,751
55	**Foreign-owned assets in the United States, excl. derivatives (inflow)**	**2,057,703**
56	Foreign official assets in the United States	411,058
57	U.S. government securities	230,330
58	U.S. Treasury securities	58,865
59	Other	171,465
60	Other U.S. government liabilities	5,342
61	U.S. liabilities reported by U.S. banks, not included elsewhere	108,695
62	Other foreign official assets	66,691
63	Other foreign assets in the United States	1,646,645
64	Direct investment	237,542
65	U.S. Treasury securities	156,825
66	U.S. securities other than U.S. Treasury securities	573,850
67	U.S. currency	−10,675
68	U.S. liabilities to unaffiliated foreigners reported by U.S. nonbanking concerns	156,290
69	U.S. liabilities reported by U.S. banks, not included elsewhere	532,813
70	**Financial derivatives, net**	**6,496**
71	**Statistical discrepancy (sum of above items with sign reversed)**	**−41,287**
	Memoranda	
72	Balance on goods (lines 3 and 20)	−819,373
73	Balance on services (lines 4 and 21)	119,115
74	Balance on goods and services (lines 2 and 19)	−700,258
75	Balance on income (lines 12 and 29)	81,749
76	Unilateral current transfers, net (line 35)	−112,705
77	Balance on current account (lines 1, 18, and 35 or lines 74, 75, and 76)	−731,214

http://bea.gov/international/index.htm#bop (accessed December 16, 2008).

Discrepancy

The current and financial account balances as just calculated are not equal because of the following discrepancies (bolded items in Exhibit 13.11):

- Unilateral current transfers (line 35).
- Capital account transactions (line 39).
- Financial derivatives (line 70).
- Statistical discrepancy (line 71).

Of these items, unilateral current transfers (primarily private U.S. grants to overseas entities) and statistical discrepancy (measurement error, or the plug figure in the accounts) are relatively large values.

Components of the Current Account

The current account has three components: goods, services, and income from assets. In addition to goods or merchandise (exported or imported), the current account includes various services such as transportation, royalties, license fees, and other private services (e.g., consulting services). Also included are income flows such as dividends from cross-border holdings of assets. Overall, the United States has a deficit because it imports more goods than it exports. In the other two categories, services and income, the United States actually has a surplus, but it is much smaller than the deficit in goods.

Components of the Financial Account

The financial account reflects flows related to acquisition of cross-border real and financial assets. These two components are labeled as "direct investment" and "foreign securities," respectively. In 2007, because of the U.S. deficit in the current account, foreign investments in U.S. assets were more than U.S. investments in foreign assets.

Note that the financial account reflects only "financial flows" or current purchases or sales of assets. Information about the total value of cross-border assets (that is, outstanding amounts) and how this value changes from year to year is not available in the financial account as reported above but is made available in other reports. For example, the total value of cross-border assets in 2007 included as its components the value for 2006, the financial flows for 2007, and the change in value (because of asset price and currency changes) during the year. This additional information concerning the country's international investment position and that of the current and financial accounts are available at *http://bea.gov/international/index.htm#bop*.

CHAPTER FOURTEEN

International Taxation and Accounting

Taxes are at least one-third of gross domestic product (GDP) in most countries. Do MNCs—favorite targets of tax authorities because of their considerable cash flow—pay taxes passively, or do they strategize, structure their organization, and design contracts to minimize taxes? Because taxes are important for most business organizations, they play an even more important role in cross-border decisions as a result of the interaction of tax systems of multiple countries; this offers the corporate manager a complex environment with great benefits to making the right decision. Decisions concerning taxes make significant differences to corporate value and, hence, are of great concern to the financial manager. Basic taxation concepts were introduced earlier in discussions concerning capital budgeting. This chapter offers a more in-depth analysis of international taxation; it is the key focus of the chapter.

A second topic discussed in this chapter is accounting, which, along with taxes, is often combined in a single corporate function known as the *controller function*. International accounting issues are of interest to managers as well as investors. Accounting is the language that brings together firms and their investors. But this language varies globally. In this chapter, we explain why differences occur in national accounting systems. This knowledge is useful not only to investors attempting to evaluate corporate performance but also to corporations engaged in investment activity. We also discuss accounting issues surrounding activities that are distinctively characteristics of MNCs such as cross-border operations, currency conversion and hedging; we identify issues that are of importance to MNCs in general and provide specific accounting details of relevance to U.S-based MNCs. As with taxes, firm strategies are related to accounting. Accounting does matter, not simply as a costly and necessary activity, but also because its methods (choices) determine how firms hedge, conduct business with their subsidiaries/affiliates, and write contracts. This chapter introduces some of these concepts.

The specific topics addressed in this chapter are:

- Various types of taxes paid by MNCs.
- Ways in which international tax treaties attempt to harmonize tax collection efforts and promote global economic activity.
- Ways in which various kinds of taxes and credits affect MNC cash flows.
- Strategies that MNCs can use to mitigate taxes and maximize corporate value.
- The importance of accounting information in corporate governance.
- Ways in which accounting systems differ around the world and how recent efforts to harmonize or bring these systems into agreement are proceeding.
- The importance and features of the international financial reporting standards.
- Ways in which U.S. MNCs account for issues such as hedging and currency translation.

14.1 Taxation of MNCs: An Overview

MNCs are subject to more types of taxes than are domestic firms. In this chapter, we provide an overview of various taxes such as corporate income taxes and value added taxes and provide information on the distribution of tax collection across countries.

Jurisdiction and Taxable Entities

Tax systems are characterized by their definition of jurisdiction and taxable entities.

Jurisdiction

In determining taxable income, nations must consider the issues of (1) country of incorporation and (2) location of the business activity. These are two basic approaches:

- With the *territorial* approach, a country taxes all income derived from activity in its territory whether it is generated by its own citizens/businesses or foreign citizens/businesses.

worldwide income approach
The United States uses a *worldwide income approach* to taxes. U.S. firms therefore are potentially subject to double taxation.

- With the worldwide income approach, in addition to taxing all entities (domestic or foreign) on income generated within its borders, a country taxes its citizens and businesses on worldwide income.

We can immediately see the potential for double taxation in the latter approach. A U.S-based MNC operating in Germany would potentially face double taxation because the United States uses the worldwide income approach: Income earned in Germany is subject to taxation in both countries. Tax treaties between nations, such as the one between the United States and Germany, mitigate the problem of double taxation. We discuss tax treaties in a later section.

Source Income

Tax systems also differ in how they respond to the source of the income and whether such income has already been taxed. For example, would a corporation as well as its shareholders be liable for income taxes if the corporation earns income and distributes it as dividends?

- The *separate entity* approach independently considers each entity for tax determination. In countries following this system such as the United States, shareholders pay taxes on dividends received from corporations even though corporations have already paid taxes on income.
- The *integrated system* approach corrects for such multiple taxation on a single source of income.

MNCs are concerned with this issue for two reasons. First, MNCs themselves are investors in other firms and may receive dividends and other income flows. Second, MNCs are affected because taxes paid by investors ultimately affect the cost of capital. The latter is perhaps a more important consideration. The implication is that MNCs must consider taxation faced by their investors in making payout as well as financing decisions.

Various Types of Taxes MNCs Face

MNCs face a variety of taxes, including income taxes, withholding taxes, goods and service taxes, and excise duties/taxes.

Domestic and Foreign Corporate Income Taxes

Corporate **income taxes** by far represent corporations' largest tax liability. An MNC pays domestic corporate income taxes in the country of incorporation and foreign corporate income taxes in countries where it has business activity through affiliates and subsidiaries. Large U.S.-based MNCs pay income taxes in scores of countries and have dedicated tax personnel on their payroll to monitor tax matters. National corporate tax rates range from 20 percent to 40 percent (see Exhibit 14.1).

Foreign Withholding Tax

Many countries impose **withholding taxes** on capital-related payments such as dividends and interest paid by domestic entities to foreign entities. Unlike normal income taxes, this taxation is triggered by transactions, and the tax amount is automatically withheld. Thus, when a foreign subsidiary makes a dividend payment to an MNC parent, it triggers withholding taxes and results in a lower after-tax amount received by the parent.

EXHIBIT 14.1
Selected Foreign Income
and Withholding Taxes

Source: PricewaterhouseCoopers,
"Corporate Taxes, Worldwide Sum-
maries," available at *www.pwc.com*
(accessed December 2, 2008).

Country of Parent MNC	Foreign Country/ Location of Subsidiary	Foreign Corporate Tax	Withholding Tax on Dividends	Withholding Tax on Royalties
United States	India	40%	15%	10%
United States	China	25%	10%	10%
United States	Germany	34%	0%	0%
United States	United Kingdom	30%	5%	0%
United States	Russia	24%	5%	0%
United States	Brazil	34%	0%	15%
Korea	India	40%	15%	15%
Japan	India	40%	10%	10%
Australia	China	25%	10%	10%
Germany	China	25%	10%	10%
China	Ireland	12.5%	0%	10%
Germany	Ireland	12.5%	0%	0%
Italy	Brazil	34%	15%	15%
Spain	Brazil	34%	10%	10%

This table contains typical marginal tax rates faced by large nonfinancial MNCs. Rates may vary depending on factors such as income levels, industry, location, and so on. For specifics, see the original source.

Goods and Services Taxes and Value Added Taxes

MNCs pay sales taxes when they buy and sell materials, products, and services. By definition, a *sales tax*—also called a **goods and services tax (GST)**—is a tax imposed on a sale
transaction. This tax is often applied at a flat rate on sales revenue. When an MNC purchases
raw materials and components, it pays sales tax as part of the purchase price. When an MNC
sells items, it collects sales tax from its customers and passes it on to tax authorities.

Sales taxes are administered in most countries. Even in the United States, which relies less
on sales taxes than other taxes, individual states collect sales taxes ranging from 2 to 10 percent. European nations have far higher levels of sales taxes. To mitigate the disincentives of
multiple levels of sales taxes, many of these countries have resorted to using the **value added
tax (VAT)** that uses the concept of marginal value to determine a taxable amount. Consider an
MNC that purchases raw materials, processes them, and sells the resulting finished product.
The MNC pays sales taxes on the purchase of raw materials. When the MNC sells a finished
product, the tax authorities assess sales taxes only on the value the MNC added. Thus, this
system ensures that a product that undergoes various stages of production is taxed only once
and that total taxes paid equals taxes that would have been paid had taxes been assessed only
once at the point of the last sale.

EXAMPLE 14.1

A European manufacturer purchases raw materials for a pretax price of euro (EUR) 10. It sells the
finished goods for a pretax price of EUR 15. If the VAT is 10 percent, calculate taxes for the two transactions. Demonstrate that total taxes are 10 percent of final product price.

Solution:

Transaction	Beginning Value	Ending Value	Value Added = Ending − Beginning	VAT @ 10 Percent
Raw materials purchased for EUR 10	0	10	10	1.00
Finished product sold for EUR 15	10	15	5	0.50
TOTAL			EUR 15	EUR 1.50

Discussion: Identification of beginning and ending values for each step in the value chain is key to a
VAT calculation. The ending value in a particular step is the beginning value of the next. This ensures
that the overall tax is a constant percent of the final product's value.

Customs and Excise Duties

The government of many countries, including the United States, levies special taxes such as
customs and **excise taxes** on certain imported and/or luxury items. An MNC requiring such

goods as inputs to products or services bears an additional burden. The taxes are imposed for protectionism and/or wealth transfer and were used much more commonly in the past. Over time, countries have eliminated or reduced these taxes to encourage economic activity; nevertheless these taxes remain in most countries.

EXAMPLE 14.2

Consider an MNC with a subsidiary in India that requires certain capital equipment from Japan for a new project costing yen (JPY) 60 million. The subsidiary must consult the Indian government's taxation rules. In many instances involving importation of equipment, countries impose customs duties. Suppose the equipment under consideration is a taxable item and requires a 10 percent customs duty. The Indian subsidiary pays customs duties equaling JPY 6 million. Assuming that JPYINR (yen in terms of rupee) equals 0.5, this equals taxes of INR 3 million. This increases the project's fixed costs and its break-even point.

Other Taxes

Other local and real estate taxes may also apply to MNCs. In countries such as Germany, city taxes are considerable. In addition, MNCs must pay social security taxes in many countries. Although these taxes may not be as high as corporate income taxes, they may collectively add up to significant amounts.

Refer to Exhibit 14.2 for the ways various countries belonging to the Organization for Economic Cooperation and Development (OECD) collect taxes. In the average OECD

EXHIBIT 14.2

Tax Structure, OECD Nations (2006)

Source: www.OECD.org
(accessed 2008-08-15)

Country	Taxes as Percent of GDP	Tax Structure: Percent of Total Taxes					
		Personal Income	Corporate Income	Social Security Employee	Social Security Employer	GST	Other
Australia	31.2	40.2	18.2	0	0	28.5	13.1
Austria	42.6	22.7	5.4	13.8	15.8	28.2	14.2
Belgium	45.0	30.6	8.0	9.9	18.6	25.0	7.8
Canada	33.5	35.1	10.3	6.2	8.5	25.9	14.1
Czech Republic	38.4	12.7	12.4	9.5	27.0	31.2	7.2
Denmark	48.8	50.7	6.5	2.3	0.1	32.7	7.7
Finland	44.2	30.5	8.1	4.8	20.3	31.7	4.6
France	43.4	17.0	6.3	9.3	25.3	25.6	16.5
Germany	34.7	22.8	4.5	17.6	19.8	29.2	6.1
Greece	35.0	13.8	9.4	13.9	16.0	37.1	9.7
Hungary	38.1	17.8	5.8	6.3	23.4	40.8	5.8
Iceland	38.7	36.9	3.3	0.2	8.1	41.1	10.4
Ireland	30.1	27.4	11.9	4.8	9.3	37.8	8.8
Italy	41.1	25.4	6.9	5.5	21.1	26.4	14.7
Japan	26.4	17.8	14.2	16.2	17.1	20.0	14.6
Korea	24.6	13.6	14.3	12.1	8.6	36.3	15.0
Luxembourg	37.8	17.8	15.3	12.4	12.6	30.4	11.4
Mexico	19.0	24.6	—	16.5	—	55.5	3.4
Netherlands	37.5	16.4	8.2	18.3	11.2	32.0	14.0
New Zealand	35.6	41.0	15.5	0	0	33.8	9.7
Norway	44.0	23.5	22.6	7.3	13.0	29.7	3.8
Poland	34.4	12.0	5.8	40.9	—	36.0	5.2
Portugal	34.5	15.9	8.3	9.3	21.4	38.6	6.5
Slovak Republic	30.3	9.3	8.1	9.4	28.0	39.8	5.4
Spain	34.8	17.7	9.8	5.4	24.4	28.0	14.7
Sweden	50.4	31.4	6.3	5.6	22.5	25.8	8.5
Switzerland	29.2	34.8	8.6	11.4	11.0	23.7	10.5
Turkey	31.3	14.9	7.3	8.4	10.7	47.7	11.1
United Kingdom	36.0	28.7	8.1	7.7	10.4	32.0	13.1
United States	25.5	34.7	8.7	11.6	13.3	18.3	13.4
EU average	39.7	24.6	8.2	9.4	16.6	30.7	10.6
OECD average	*35.9*	*24.6*	*9.6*	*8.5*	*14.9*	*32.3*	*10.1*

international differences in taxes
The United States relies on *income taxes*. In contrast, the EU relies on *GST*. Overall, taxation is higher in Europe than in North America or Asia.

country, taxes form 35.9 percent of GDP. In fact, OECD reports that this figure has been rising in recent years. The highest rate of taxation occurs in Scandinavian countries (nearly 50 percent), and the lowest occurs in Asian countries (about 25 percent). The structure of taxes varies a great deal. For example, countries in Europe rely on GST/VAT taxes more than the United States does: EU countries on average obtain 30.7 percent of their taxes from this category, while the comparable value for the United States from sales taxes is 18.3 percent.

14.2 Tax Harmonization

MNCs engage in foreign direct investment (FDI) as well as international trade, subjecting themselves to taxes in multiple jurisdictions. Nations wish to encourage MNC activity, not deter it by duplicating taxes on income. Tax treaties express this desire. This section discusses tax treaties and an essential ingredient for treaty implementation—foreign tax credits.

International Tax Treaties

In general, tax treaties have the following provisions:

- Specification of types of income that will not be taxed to avoid double taxation.
- Reduction of withholding taxes on items such as dividends, interest, and royalties.
- Explicit specification of tax credits and their application to various types of incomes as a mechanism to reduce double taxation.

The purpose of tax treaties is not only to reduce the incidence of double taxation, but also to protect the rights of individual nations in regard to taxation and to provide corporations predictability with respect to taxes. The latter point is important because corporations make investments in anticipation of future benefits; knowledge of future taxes is important in calculating future cash flows.

The OECD has been at the vanguard of promoting tax treaties and has published a model treaty for reference purposes. Some provisions of the model **tax treaty**, applicable to business income, are included in Exhibit 14.3. Nations have used this template, initially published in 1963 and now updated, as the basis for their tax treaties. The United States, after some initial resistance, has now signed treaties with more than 60 nations. Details of these treaties can be obtained from IRS publications.

EXHIBIT 14.3
Model U.S. Tax Treaty Provisions Concerning Business Income

Source: www.OECD.org (accessed December 12, 2008).

1. The business profits of an enterprise of a Contracting State shall be taxable only in that State unless the enterprise carries on business in the other Contracting State through a permanent establishment situated therein. If the enterprise carries on business as aforesaid, the business profits of the enterprise may be taxed in the other State but only so much of them as are attributable to that permanent establishment.

2. Subject to the provisions of paragraph 3, where an enterprise of a Contracting State carries on business in the other Contracting State through a permanent establishment situated therein, there shall in each Contracting State be attributed to that permanent establishment the business profits that it might be expected to make if it were a distinct and independent enterprise engaged in the same or similar activities under the same or similar conditions. For this purpose, the business profits to be attributed to the permanent establishment shall include only the profits derived from the assets or activities of the permanent establishment.

3. In determining the business profits of a permanent establishment, there shall be allowed as deductions expenses that are incurred for the purposes of the permanent establishment, including a reasonable allocation of executive and general administrative expenses, research and development expenses, interest, and other expenses incurred for the purposes of the enterprise as a whole (or the part thereof which includes the permanent establishment), whether incurred in the State in which the permanent establishment is situated or elsewhere.

EXAMPLE 14.3

The U.S. tax treaty with China, for instance, has the following features:

- U.S. or Chinese corporations would pay income taxes only in their home countries except when they have created cross-border permanent establishments.
- In the case of a cross-border permanent establishment, the treaty specifies methods for assessing taxable income, allowable expense deductions, and prohibited deductions.
- A detailed specification of how China and the United States would tax cross-border enterprises such as joint ventures (JVs).
- Specification of the nature of the tax credits allowed by both countries.

Foreign Tax Credits

tax treaties

Most *tax treaties* allow MNCs to use foreign income taxes as credits against domestic income taxes.

Foreign tax credits are the key mechanism used to mitigate double taxation. Tax treaties define and list creditable taxes that typically include corporate income taxes as well as withholding taxes. It is not common, however, for VAT or GST to be included in this category. Generally,

$$\text{Foreign tax credit} = \text{Foreign income tax} + \text{Withholding tax}$$

The foreign tax credit mechanism works as follows. An MNC determines whether it has triggered payment of domestic taxes. This occurs in one of two scenarios. Its wholly owned foreign subsidiary has earned income, or its partially owned foreign affiliate (e.g., JV) has distributed or remitted income. In either scenario, tentative domestic taxes are calculated based on the MNC's foreign taxable income. The tax credit offsets tentative taxes and reduces payment to the MNC's domestic tax authorities.

$$\text{Actual domestic income tax} = \text{Tentative domestic income tax} - \text{Foreign tax credit}$$

EXAMPLE 14.4

A foreign subsidiary produces taxable income of USD 10 million and remits all of its cash flows to its U.S. parent. Assume foreign income and withholding taxes of 25 percent and 5 percent, respectively. Domestic tax is 35 percent. The tax treaty between the two nations specifies that foreign income and withholding taxes are creditable items. What is the domestic tax liability?

Solution:

Foreign taxable income = 10,000,000

Foreign income tax = 10,000,000 × **25%** = 2,500,000

Before withholding tax remittance = 10,000,000 − 2,500,000 = 7,500,000

Withholding tax = 7,500,000 × **5%** = 375,000

Foreign tax credit = 2,500,000 + 375,000 = 2,875,000

Domestic tentative income tax = 10,000,000 × **35%** = 3,500,000

Actual domestic income tax = 3,500,000 − 2,875,000 = 625,000

Sometimes, foreign subsidiaries reinvest earnings and remit only partial earnings to the parent. Partial remittance also results when the MNC only partially owns the subsidiary. Domestic taxes are generally leveled only on the amounts actually repatriated. The remittance percent is applied on subsidiary taxable earnings to determine the tax base for domestic income taxes.

EXAMPLE 14.5

Consider the information provided in the previous example. Assume that the firm follows a 50 percent remittance policy. Calculate cash flows and taxes.

Solution:

Foreign taxable income = 10,000,000

Foreign income tax = 10,000,000 × **25%** = 2,500,000

Before withholding tax remittance = **50%** × (10,000,000 − 2,500,000) = 3,750,000

Withholding tax = 3,750,000 × **5%** = 187,500

Foreign tax credit = (**50%** × 2,500,000) + 187,500 = 1,437,500

Domestic tentative income tax = (**50%** ×10,000,000) × **35%** = 1,750,000

Actual domestic income tax = 1,750,000 − 1,437,500= 312,500

In the previous examples, domestic taxes are higher than foreign taxes. Consider the reverse. Depending on the rules for tax credits, a firm may have an excess amount of foreign tax credit. Two tools are available for dealing with this situation. First, for a particular year, the firm can average its taxes across countries; thus, it may use excess tax credits from one country against the tax liability from another. Second, by using tax carryforwards and carry-backs, excess tax credits in a particular year may be offset against tax liabilities in the closest past and future years.

Alternative Tax Scenarios and Effective Tax Rates

In this section, we discuss four possible tax scenarios and provide a comprehensive example explaining differences. To facilitate exposition, use the following notation:

$$T^* = \text{Foreign tax rate}$$
$$T^W = \text{Withholding tax (foreign)}$$
$$T = \text{Domestic tax rate}$$
$$T^{Eff} = \text{Effective (total) tax rate}$$

Double Taxation

In this scenario, an MNC first pays taxes to a foreign government, repatriates income to its home country, and faces a second round of taxation. No foreign tax credit is allowed. The effective tax is the sum of the foreign and domestic taxes. This is the *pre-tax-treaty scenario,* and it has been rectified in most country pairs. The equation for the effective tax rate is:

$$T^{Eff} = T^* + T$$

Foreign Tax Deduction

Some countries may offer partial mitigation of double taxes by allowing firms to deduct foreign taxes in calculating their home taxable income. In this scenario, the firm pays home taxes not on subsidiary taxable income but on the subsidiary after-tax income. Thus, some reduction is available compared to the double taxation scenario. A USD 1 of taxable subsidiary earnings becomes equal to an after-tax amount equaling $(1-T^*) \times (1-T)$. This implies an effective tax rate of

$$T^{Eff} = 1 - (1 - T^*) \times (1 - T)$$

Foreign Tax Credit

In this scenario, subsidiary taxes are full offsets against parent taxes. If the foreign tax rate is less than the domestic tax rate, the MNC pays the differential. Instead, if the foreign tax rate is higher, no additional taxes are due in the home country, but there is no refund either.

So, the effective tax rate is the maximum of the foreign and domestic tax rates as in the following equation:

$$T^{Eff} = \text{Max}(T^*, T)$$

Withholding Taxes and Foreign Tax Credit

This scenario was modeled in the previous section. Because withholding taxes are applied on after-tax remittances, the total foreign tax as a percent of taxable income equals $1 - (1 - T^*) \times (1 - T^W)$. Assuming a foreign tax credit on withholding as well as foreign income taxes, the effective tax rate is:

$$T^{Eff} = \text{Max}(1 - (1 - T^*) \times (1 - T^W), T)$$

EXAMPLE 14.6

A U.S.- based MNC conducts business through an overseas subsidiary and remits all earnings to the parent. The firm faces income tax rates of 30 percent in the foreign country and 40 percent in the United States. Subsidiary revenues and expenses are USD 10,000 and USD 6,000, respectively. Calculate taxes and the effective tax rate for the following four scenarios:

Scenario I. Zero withholding tax and no foreign tax credit or deduction.

Scenario II. Zero withholding tax and a foreign tax deduction.

Scenario III. Zero withholding tax and a foreign tax credit.

Scenario IV. A 10 percent withholding tax and a foreign tax credit.

Solution: See below.

Effective Tax Rate Comparison

	Scenario			
Tax Parameters	**I**	**II**	**III**	**IV**
Foreign tax	30%	30%	30%	30%
Domestic tax	40%	40%	40%	40%
Withholding tax	0%	0%	0%	10%
Tax deduction/credit	None	Deduction	Credit	Credit
Subsidiary Cash Flows				
1 Revenues	10,000	10,000	10,000	10,000
2 Expenses	6,000	6,000	6,000	6,000
3 Taxable Income	4,000	4,000	4,000	4,000
4 Foreign taxes (30%)	1,200	1,200	1,200	1,200
5 Remittance, before tax	2,800	2,800	2,800	2,800
6 Withholding tax (10%)	0	0	0	280
Parent Cash Flows				
7 Remittance, after tax	2,800	2,800	2,800	2,520
8 Domestic taxable income	4,000	2,800	4,000	4,000
9 Tentative domestic tax (40%)	1,600	1,120	1,600	1,600
10 Foreign tax credit = 4 + 6			1,200	1,480
11 Actual domestic tax	1,600	1,120	400	120
Tax Summary				
12 Total taxes = 4 + 6 + 11	2,800	2,320	1,600	1,600
13 Effective tax rate = 12 ÷ 3	70%	58%	40%	40%

The effective tax rate can also be directly calculated by using formulas. These calculations are:

Scenario I. $T^{Eff} = T^* + T = 30\% + 40\% = 70\%$

Scenario II. $T^{Eff} = 1 - (1 - T^*) \times (1 - T) = 1 - (1 - 30\%) \times (1 - 40\%) = 58\%$

Scenario III. $T^{Eff} = \text{Max}(T^*, T) = \text{Max}(30\%, 40\%) = 40\%$

Scenario IV. $\text{Max}(1 - (1 - T^*) \times (1 - T^W), T) = \text{Max}(1 - (1 - 30\%) \times (1 - 10\%), 40\%) = 40\%$

Discussion: Subsidiary pretax income is 4,000. In scenario I, the subsidiary pays taxes of 1,200 and remits 2,800. The parent pays taxes on the subsidiary-level taxable earnings of 4,000 and pays taxes of 1,600. In scenario II, because of a deduction, the parent pays taxes only on 2,800, reducing the tax burden somewhat. In scenario III, because of a credit equaling foreign tax of 1,200, the parent pays only domestic taxes of 400. Thus, credits are more valuable than deductions. In scenario IV, subsidiary level taxes are higher because of withholding taxes, but all foreign taxes (totaling 1,480) are used to offset domestic taxes. Because domestic taxes are higher than the combined foreign taxes, scenario IV results in the same overall tax as scenario III.

credits versus deductions
Tax *credits* are not the same as tax *deductions*. Credits lead to lower taxes than deductions.

14.3 Tax Minimization Strategies

Some of the strategies MNCs use to minimize taxes are to:

- Set prices in intrafirm cross-border transfer of components/services/products in such a manner to maximize deductions in high-tax locales.
- Use hedging to maximize the probability of utilizing tax deductions.
- Locate assets in low-tax jurisdictions (tax havens).

We cover these and other strategies in this section, emphasizing the setting of transfer prices.

Transfer Pricing

MNCs conduct thousands of transactions each year with their affiliates and subsidiaries in foreign countries. The prices at which these intracompany transactions are conducted are known as **transfer prices**. MNCs can strategically use transfer prices to achieve many objectives, important among them being tax minimization.

transfer prices
Transfer prices can be used to shift income from high-tax countries to low-tax countries.

Transfer prices can be used to shift income from high-tax countries to low-tax countries. Transfer prices serve to reallocate taxable income between units of the MNC operating in different countries. Consider a U.S. parent with a subsidiary in Turkey; the parent sells components to the subsidiary. By lowering transfer prices, the MNC can shift taxable income from the United States to Turkey. This may be advantageous, for instance, if the Turkish subsidiary has a tax holiday during which it does not pay any taxes in Turkey. Such a shift of income also makes sense if the Turkish tax rate is lower than the U.S. rate. Instead, if the Turkish tax rates were to be higher than the U.S. tax rates, it would make sense to increase transfer prices to shift income from the Turkish subsidiary to the U.S. parent.

EXAMPLE 14.7

A U.S. MNC sells 1,000 units of a product to its Turkish subsidiary for USD 10,000. The parent incurs direct and indirect expenses of USD 4,000 and USD 2,000, respectively. The subsidiary only incurs an indirect expense of USD 5,000; its direct expense equals the transfer price of USD 10,000. The subsidiary sells the product for USD 20,000. If U.S and Turkish taxes are 30 percent and 40 percent, respectively, evaluate the merit of increasing the transfer price to USD 12 per unit.

Solution: See below.

Using Transfer Prices to Reduce Taxes

Inputs

Existing transfer price = USD 10
U.S. MNC sells 1,000 units to Turkish subsidiary for USD 10,000.
Proposed transfer price = USD 12

	Taxes (%)
United States	30%
Turkey	40%

Continued

A. Existing Scenario

	Subsidiary	U.S. MNC	Total Taxes
Revenues	20,000	10,000	
Direct expenses	10,000	4,000	
Indirect expenses	5,000	2,000	
Taxable income	5,000	4,000	
Taxes	2,000	1,200	3,200
Earnings	3,000	2,800	

B. Revised Transfer Price Scenario

	Subsidiary	U.S. MNC	Total Taxes
Revenues	20,000	12,000	
Direct expenses	12,000	4,000	
Indirect expenses	5,000	2,000	
Taxable income	3,000	6,000	
Taxes	1,200	1,800	3,000
Earnings	1,800	4,200	

Discussion: The MNC saves USD 200 in taxes by increasing the transfer price from USD 10 to USD 12. The savings also can be calculated as follows:

$$\text{Tax savings} = \text{Units} \times \text{Change in transfer price} \times \text{Difference in tax rate}$$
$$= 1,000 \times (12 - 10) \times (40\% - 30\%)$$
$$= \text{USD 200}$$

Tax strategies involving transfer prices depend on marginal tax rates. One should not determine transfer prices based on published tax rates or even on average tax rates that apply to an MNC. This is so because items such as the depreciation and debt tax shields influence marginal tax rates. In the example just discussed, even if the U.S. tax rate is higher than the Turkish tax rate, shifting income to the United States may make sense if the firm has unused tax shields in the United States.

Firms do not have *carte blanche* in setting transfer prices. National tax authorities are increasingly clamping down on this practice. In the United States, **section 482** gives the IRS the authority to regulate income, deductions, credits, or allowances of taxpayers to prevent tax evasion. Firms are required to derive arm's-length transfer prices by using stipulated methodologies. However, the IRS realizes the difficulties of benchmarking intracompany transfer prices. Arm's-length prices are not always available, especially when goods and services are firm specific. Nevertheless, MNCs must be aware of transfer pricing regulations in multiple jurisdictions to avoid violations and penalties.

regulations and penalties Governments are waking up to the misuse of transfer prices. They are tightening *regulations* and increasing *penalties* for misuse.

The issue of transfer prices is a complex one because of its link to other corporate issues. For example, when a firm operates in a country with a high level of political and economic risk, the use of transfer prices to shift money away from the country may be beneficial. Transfer prices also have effects on incentive contracts; in this context, the ideal transfer price needs to reflect market values to provide the correct managerial signals and incentives. This factor could therefore be a firm-level constraint on the use of transfer prices to minimize taxes.

Other Methods to Minimize Taxes

Taxes may also be minimized through hedging, tax havens, restructuring remittances and other methods.

Hedging Strategies

The distribution of taxable income over time and across countries determines the present value of taxes an MNC pays. As discussed in Chapter 7, reducing the variance of taxable income will lower the overall tax burden. Taxable income varies over time because of some key

EXHIBIT 14.4
Characteristics of
Successful Tax Havens

- Low or zero corporate income and withholding taxes.
- Low or zero taxes on passive incomes such as dividends and interest.
- Well developed and sophisticated banking infrastructure.
- Stable currency.
- Privacy.
- Low country risk.
- Transparent regulatory framework allowing unhindered business activities.

underlying factors such as variability in the competitive environment and economic cycles, execution risk, interest rate risk, and currency risk. Some of these factors, specifically the interest rate and currency factors, can be controlled by using hedging. This in turn will reduce the present value of taxes.

Tax Havens

Tax havens are countries such as Switzerland with very low corporate and withholding taxes (see Exhibit 14.4). MNCs can use affiliates in tax havens to minimize their total tax burden. One popular way to save taxes is to route dividend payments from foreign subsidiaries through tax havens. Thus, a U.K.-based MNC with a subsidiary in Taiwan can route dividend payments through its affiliate in the Bahamas, another tax haven. The dividend payment can be allowed to remain in the tax haven affiliate for a period of time long enough to save money by deferring taxes in the United Kingdom as well as to exploit the low rates of taxes on interest income in tax havens. The competition among nations engaged in the tax haven business is fierce. Switzerland has long been famous for its tax-free status and its financial privacy, but it is now facing competition from many other nations including Caribbean nations such as Bermuda, the Netherlands Antilles, and the Cayman Islands. Concerns about illegal uses of tax havens remain. Efforts are underway to make tax havens comply with international standards regarding supervision, transparency, and money laundering.

Optimal Use of License Fees and Other Payments from Subsidiaries

Royalty and license fees are often tax deductible for foreign subsidiaries. Especially when the foreign income tax rate is higher than the rate in the country of the parent, an MNC can minimize taxes by increasing royalty and license fees. In particular, the use of these fees is preferable to the use of dividends to repatriate income, because dividends can be paid only from after-tax funds. Another advantage of these fees is that they are politically less visible than dividend payments in developing countries; thus, they can help a firm mitigate political risk.

Miscellaneous Methods

MNCs can use other methods including these:

- Diversify their tax base across countries. This allows them to manage their taxes more effectively by averaging them and by reducing the impact of high taxes in certain countries.
- Use tax credit carryforwards and carrybacks to offset the tax credit against tax liabilities.
- Conduct many transactions involving the generation of capital gains and losses. By timing these transactions, MNCs can manage the volatility of taxable income and thus minimize their tax liability.

14.4 International Accounting Overview

Accounting systems provide tools for performance measurement in a firm. This has internal as well as external "corporate control" uses. Internally, the firm uses performance metrics in applications such as compensation contracting and risk management. Externally, accounting provides the means for communicating with the firms' investors. In this section, we provide an overview of accounting as a corporate control mechanism and discuss differences between various national accounting systems.

Accounting as a Corporate Control Mechanism

The traditional view is that accounting is a system for documenting a firm's current financial position. There are two reasons for this point of view. First, governmental authorities are interested in a reliable accounting of transactions primarily as away to facilitate tax assessment. Second, the separation of ownership and control in most corporations means that owners want financial information to monitor the cash transactions conducted by managers. These demands imposed requirements of transparency and reliability on accounting information. *Transparency* refers to the quick and timely transfer of information, and *reliability* refers to the integrity of the information.

This monitoring function has evolved over time. Shareholders—no longer satisfied with a mere list of cash transactions—want financial information necessary to value the firm. They desire information about current business activities as well as future prospects. Some examples of desired data items are impairment of assets the firm owns, provisions for future taxes and other liabilities, and knowledge of the firm's contractual assets and liabilities. Modern accrual-based accounting is a vehicle for conveying such information. Research supporting this perspective of accounting indicates the following: accrual-based accounting earnings are much more reliable in predicting future cash flows than are cash-based earnings numbers; accrual-based accounting earnings have a higher correlation with share price changes than operating cash flows.

Other stakeholders have also imposed their demands on accounting. A firm's creditors have special needs. Because creditors' benefits are capped by the value of interest and principal payments, they are more interested in evaluating downside risk than upside potential. Thus, creditors demand conservative accounting information that more quickly reveals unfavorable news than favorable news. This means, for instance, that impairment of asset values is reflected more quickly than are enhancements to asset values.

While accounting systems attempt to respond to these various demands, they have some inherent limitations. For example, accounting can be geared to record cash transactions effectively but cannot be easily adapted to reflecting important items such as contractual agreements. Also, firms walk a fine line in providing information to their investors while keeping information away from their competitors; for example, firms may be reluctant to provide sales figures on certain products. Finally, the demands of certain stakeholders may take precedence over the demands of some others; accounting cannot be all things to all people.

Differences in Accounting Standards and Incentives

Accounting systems of various nations differ in form, application, usage and enforcement. These differences are attributable to various factors:

- **History.** The history of a country influences its accounting system. Countries with a colonial past typically adopt systems associated with a colonial power. For example, accounting standards in Singapore are strongly influenced by the U.K. model of accounting.
- **Capital markets.** The development of capital markets is strongly related to demands placed on accounting information. In highly developed capital markets, increased informational demands are placed on accounting systems.
- **Governments.** Governments may have a strong influence on accounting systems. For example, a government that is motivated to reduce fraud and maximize tax collections may be motivated to promote a rigid and reliable accounting system that may not be as sensitive to the informational needs of investors.
- **Globalization.** Globalization has its impact on accounting. Firms need cross-border investors to diversify their capital base. They can do so partly by responding to the informational needs of these investors.

Code versus Common Law

A theoretical perspective consistent with the factors identified accounting differences between countries following code and common law traditions.[1] **Code law** or codified law occurs from governmental processes. Many European countries such as Germany, France and Italy as well as Japan have codified law. **Common law** occurs from individual action in the private sector and is market driven. Anglo countries such as the United Kingdom, United States, and Australia fall in the common law camp. The business environments of code and common law countries differ significantly. A key difference is the greater prevalence of arm's-length contracting in common law countries; this contrasts with the greater prevalence of private contracting in code law countries. This distinction guides accounting practice. In common law countries, accounting originates from the private sector (e.g., demand by investors) with the help of self-regulating bodies such as the Financial Accounting Standards Board (FASB) in the United States. In code law countries, accounting originates from government action and is tied to issues such as tax collection; information to investors is not such a high priority. Research indicates that common law accounting reflects economic income better than code law accounting. Further, common law accounting is much quicker to reveal adverse news; this is especially important for bondholders, who need to understand downside risks. In sum, common law accounting appears to offer more transparency to investors.

code and common law
Code law countries have very different accounting systems compared to *common law* countries.

Accounting in Emerging Markets

Accounting systems in Asian countries such as India, China, Malaysia, Singapore, Thailand, and Hong Kong demonstrate the promise and shortcomings of accounting in developing nations. Many Asian nations have been influenced by their colonial past and have adopted aspects of Anglo-American accounting. Nevertheless, the contracting environment is quite different in these countries for the following reasons:

- **Family control.** In countries such as Hong Kong, wealthy families control many firms by holding the majority of voting shares. Relevant financial information is more efficiently transmitted internally through informal means. Unlike the situation in the United States, the demand for external reporting is relatively low.

- **Weak enforcement.** Countries such as Thailand have weak enforcement systems. There have been hardly any lawsuits against managers or accountants for fraud and misrepresentation involving financial statements. This is in contrast to the United States, where litigation over accounting information is quite common.

- **Underdeveloped financial markets.** National securities markets in countries such as Malaysia are small and underdeveloped. Thus, there is a lack of pressure from shareholder groups for good governance and transparent accounting.

- **Government control.** In countries such as China, the government is a partner in many business enterprises. This is quite unlike the situation in major OECD countries.

International Financial Reporting Standards

This section discusses the origins of international standards, their differences with U.S. GAAP, and prospects for their adoption.

Origins of International Standard Setting

Not surprisingly, there is a movement to harmonize national accounting practices. In 1973, the International Accounting Standards Committee (IASC) was formed following agreement between professional accounting bodies from influential countries such as the United States,

---

[1] R. Ball, S. P. Kothari and A. Robin, "The Effect of International Institutional Factors on Properties of Accounting Earnings," *Journal of Accounting and Economics* 29 (2000), pp. 1–51.

the United Kingdom, Germany, France and Japan. IASC's membership—which includes members of the International Federation of Accountants—currently exceeds 100. The stated goals of the IASC and its successor, the **International Accounting Standards Board (IASB)** are[2]:

- To develop, in the public interest, a single set of high quality, understandable and enforceable global accounting standards that require high quality, transparent and comparable information in financial statements and other financial reporting to help participants in the world's capital markets and other users make economic decisions.
- To promote the use and rigorous application of those standards.
- To bring about convergence of national accounting standards and international accounting standards to high-quality solutions.

IASB and IFRS

After reorganization in 2001, the IASB replaced the IASC as the international standard setter. The IASB is governed by the not-for-profit IASC Foundation (group of trustees) and is assisted by an external advisory committee and by an interpretations committee. Standards—previously known as *international accounting standards (IAS)*—are now known as **international financial reporting standards (IFRS)**. These accounting standards—the older IAS and the more recent IFRS—are analogous to the **Statement of Financial Accounting Standards (SFAS)** found in the U.S. setting.

Current Use of IFRS

IFRS

IFRS are gaining in popularity and are expected to displace U.S. GAAP eventually.

IFRS standards are rapidly gaining worldwide importance. Stock exchanges (and stock market regulators) around the world have allowed or mandated the use of IFRS in the following ways[3]:

- Many exchanges allow foreign firms to use IFRS in lieu of their national standards. Examples include exchanges in Argentina, Australia, Germany, Hong Kong, Malaysia, and Spain.
- Some exchanges mandate the use of IFRS for foreign firms. Examples include exchanges in Austria, Jordan, and Bangladesh.
- Some exchanges allow domestic firms to use IFRS in lieu of national standards. Examples include exchanges in the Netherlands, Poland, Slovenia, and South Africa.
- Some exchanges mandate domestic firms to use IFRS. Examples include exchanges in China (B shares only), Cyprus, Austria, Estonia, and the Czech Republic.

Future of IFRS

The future for IFRS appears bright. Most large European firms have shown the way by adopting IFRS. U.S. firms are increasingly interested in IFRS. In late 2008, the U.S. Securities and Exchange Commission (SEC) released a proposed roadmap for adoption of IFRS by all U.S. public firms. Assuming certain conditions are satisfied—convergence efforts between IFRS and U.S. **generally accepted accounting principles (GAAP)**, IFRS education and dissemination, and so on, certain U.S. firms may be allowed to report using IFRS as early as in 2009. According to this roadmap, all U.S. firms are expected to use IFRS by 2016. Because IFRS adoption has a significant impact on Sarbanes-Oxley compliance and information systems, many U.S. firms are preparing to stay ahead of the curve. Audit firms anticipate that global firms will form the initial wave of IFRS adopters among U.S. firms. One interesting advantage to these firms would be the uniform use of IFRS in all subsidiaries and affiliates and the resulting reduction in accounting and auditing costs.

---

[2] See www.iasb.org.

[3] See http://www.iasplus.com/country/useias.htm for a list of countries and standards for public and private firm accounting. Because of rapid changes in standards adoption, please check this and other Web sites to obtain current information.

IFRS versus U.S. GAAP

First, considering the broad picture, one perspective is that the two accounting systems are similar and that there is greater convergence over time. But there is another perspective that IFRS is fundamentally different because it is in many ways more general (that is, more principles based) and offers less industry-specific guidance. Second, at the technical level, there are many differences in areas such as revenue recognition, inventories, property, plant and equipment, and intangible assets. For example, under IFRS, the cost of inventory is determined using first-in first-out (FIFO) or weighted average cost methods, and the use of the last-in first-out (LIFO) method is prohibited; U.S. GAAP allows all these methods.[4]

Consequences for Investors

Would adoption of high quality standards such as U.S. GAAP or IFRS lead to better and more transparent information? Investors need to beware of accounting labels.[5] Research on accounting systems in Asian countries indicates low levels of transparency despite claims that countries have adopted U.S. or IFRS standards. This evidence reinforces a fundamental truth about the quality of accounting systems: Reporting quality may be influenced by formal standards, but it is ultimately influenced by practice (that is, by demand and supply factors). The institutional framework of a nation is always more influential than its declared accounting system.

14.5 Currency-Related Accounting Issues

This section discusses the complexities of currency related accounting and how GAAP responds to these issues. In particular, you learn how currency effects are aggregated and reflected in an item called the **foreign translation adjustment (FTA)**.

Issues MNCs Face in Accounting for Foreign Operations

We learned that accounting information in general and financial statements in particular have many uses including the structuring of incentive contracts and providing information to markets. Thus, it is important for financial statements to reflect the firm's financial position accurately. This may be challenging when the financial statements are initially constructed in a foreign currency and require translation to the reporting currency. The fundamental decision is whether to use historical foreign exchange rates (historical method) or spot exchange rates (current rate method) to translate foreign values to reporting values. In various countries, accounting codes and standards mandate the method to be followed. But before we consider the standards applicable to U.S. MNCs, it is instructive to understand the various accounts and the problems inherent in the use of the current and historical rate methods.

Monetary Assets and Liabilities

Monetary assets are cash and near-cash assets of the firm. Near-cash assets may include bank deposits and investments in marketable securities. Monetary liabilities are items such as accounts payable and loans due for repayment in the short term. Considering the alternatives of using historical or current foreign exchange rates, the consensus is in favor of the latter.

Other Current Assets and Liabilities

These are items such as inventory and accounts receivable. The main distinction between this category and the preceding category is that these are not liquid items since they are real

---

[4] See the following report by a major accounting firm for a detailed list of differences between IFRS and U.S. GAAP: "IFRS Compared to U.S. GAAP," KPMG, May 2008.

[5] R. Ball, A. Robin and J. Wu, "Incentives versus Standards: Properties of Accounting Income in Four East Asian Countries," *Journal of Accounting and Economics* 36 (2003), pp. 235–270.

instead of financial items. Consider the example of inventory. There are advantages and disadvantages of using the current method. While the current foreign exchange rate will capture any changes in the value of the foreign currency, its use may obscure changes in the foreign currency value of the assets. Lets assume that a U.S. MNC has an inventory of materials in India with a book value of INR 5,000; this asset was generated when the INR was trading at INR 40 per USD. If the INR depreciates to INR 50 per USD, the current rate method would indicate a drop in inventory value. But this may not be realistic, as the foreign currency value of the inventory may have also risen because of inflation. In fact, the presence of purchasing power parity (PPP) would argue against the use of the current method and support the use of the historical rate method.

Long-Term Debt

This item represents long-term borrowings from private markets (e.g., bank debt) or public markets (bonds and debentures). Even though this is a long-term item, it has the characteristics of a monetary item. Thus, the current rate method would be preferable here.

Revenue and Expense Items

These are items such as sales, direct expenses, overheads and depreciation. Sales and expense items could potentially be measured using the current method or a variation of the current method that uses the average currency rate during the period; the concept of a historical rate does not exist for these items. Depreciation tries to measure the economic loss of value in using an asset. The current method may be problematic for translating depreciation in cases when the foreign currency depreciates in response to inflation; in such a scenario depreciation would understate the implied replacement value or the true loss of economic value.

U.S. Regulations: SFAS 52

In the United States, the most recent accounting standard regarding foreign exchange translation is the **Statement of Financial Accounting Standards (SFAS) 52**, which became effective in 1981. SFAS 52 applies in situations where a U.S.-based MNC conducts operations in a foreign country using the currency of that country and accounts for such activity using the same foreign currency. The MNC can choose to define the foreign currency as the *functional currency*, and once an initial choice is made, it cannot easily be reversed unless the economic situation changes.

Current Rate Method

SFAS 52

For U.S. firms, the *current rate method* prescribed by *SFAS 52* is the most prevalent method for translating foreign income and assets.

When a firm chooses a foreign currency as the functional currency, SFAS 52 prescribes the following method to translate the accounts into the USD:

- Assets and liabilities are translated at the current exchange rate, the exchange rate prevailing when financial statements are derived. Equity is translated at historical rates.
- Income statement items are translated at the time when such items are recognized.
- Dividends are translated at the rate prevailing on date of payment.
- Foreign translation adjustment (FTA) amounts for a reporting period—the sum of translation gains and losses—are accumulated in a special subaccount connected to the equity account called the cumulative translation adjustment (CTA).

EXAMPLE 14.8

The following demonstrates the use of the current rate method of translating net assets. The accounts of a U.S. MNC's Canadian subsidiary are presented. The USD values flow into the consolidated statement of the parent. Below is a simplified example with the objective of explaining the source of the foreign translation adjustment in consolidated accounting statements.

Translation of Net Assets Using the Current Rate Method of SFAS 52

	CAD Denominated Amounts ($t = -1$)	USD Value		Translation Gains/Losses
		CADUSD = 0.80 ($t = -1$)	CADUSD = 0.90 ($t = 0$)	
Assets				
Cash	10,000	8,000	9,000	1,000
Accounts receivable	5,000	4,000	4,500	500
Inventory	3,000	2,400	2,700	300
Plant and equipment	22,000	17,600	19,800	2,200
Total assets	40,000	32,000	36,000	
Translation effects of assets				4,000
Liabilities				
Accounts payable	4,000	3,200	3,600	400
Short-term debt	6,000	4,800	5,400	600
Long-term debt	10,000	8,000	9,000	1,000
Translation effects of liabilities				2,000
Equity, including cumulative translation adjustment	20,000	16,000	18,000	
Total liabilities and net worth	40,000	32,000	36,000	
FTA = Translation effects of assets − Translation effects of liabilities				2,000

Discussion: At the current rate, the assets produce a total translation gain of USD 4,000, while the liabilities produce a translation loss of USD 2,000. On a net basis, the MNC has an FTA of USD 2,000 (=4,000 − 2,000). This value flows into the equity account, increasing its value from USD 16,000 to USD 18,000. The equity account component reflecting currency effects is known as the cumulative translation adjustment (CTA). Other components of the equity account, however, are reflected at historical currency values.

The preceding example focused on translating net assets. In general, under the current rate method of SFAS 52, the FTA for a year has two components: net assets (*NA*) and net income (*NI*). The following equation is a good approximation of FTA in practice[6]:

$$FTA = \underbrace{NA_{t-1} \times (S_t - S_{t-1})}_{\text{Translation of Net Assets}} + \underbrace{NI_t \times \left(S_t - \frac{S_t + S_{t-1}}{2}\right)}_{\text{Translation of Net Income}}$$

EXAMPLE 14.9

On January 1, 2008, the Chinese subsidiary of a U.S. firm has assets of CNY 56 million and liabilities (excluding equity) of CNY 42 million. During the year 2008, the subsidiary earned a net income of CNY 8 million. The January 1 and December 31 values of CNYUSD are 0.16 and 0.17, respectively. Calculate the *FTA*.

Solution:

$$FTA = NA_{t-1} \times (S_t - S_{t-1}) + NI_t \times \left(S_t - \frac{S_t + S_{t-1}}{2}\right)$$

$$= (56 - 42) \times (0.17 - 0.16) + 8 \times \left(0.17 - \frac{0.17 + 0.16}{2}\right)$$

$$= \text{USD } 0.18 \text{ million}$$

[6] For example, see Henock Louis, "The Value Relevance of the Foreign Translation Adjustment," *The Accounting Review* 78, no. 4 (2003), pp. 1027–1047.

> *Discussion:* The CTA will increase by USD 0.18 million. In this example, since the CNY increased in value, there is a positive translation effect. Does this mean that the economic position of the firm is stronger? Research shows that this is not the case. Economic effects (measured by stock returns) often are opposite to that of the *FTA*. For example, if a foreign currency weakens, FTA < 0, but a firm that manufactures abroad and sells domestically may have positive economic effects.

The current rate translation method is the predominant method. There are two situations where an alternate method—the temporal rate method prescribed by SFAS 8—is used:

- **When the MNC operates in a country with a high rate of inflation (>100 percent over a three-year period).** The temporal rate method distinguishes between monetary and nonmonetary items. The former are remeasured at current exchange rates and the latter are remeasured at historical rates. Also, income statement items are remeasured at average rates. Resulting adjustments are posted to net income.

- **When the USD is deemed the functional currency of the foreign subsidiary.** Here also the temporal rate method is applied.

14.6 Derivatives Accounting

Until the late 1990s, corporations reflected their derivatives transactions and positions as off-balance-sheet items. This created difficulties for investors trying to understand risks of investing in corporations. While the predominant corporate use of derivatives was in hedging, numerous instances of firms losing tens of millions of dollars in derivatives positions heightened investor anxiety. FASB undertook the challenge of accounting for derivatives in 1996. Two years later, after considerable deliberation, SFAS 133 was released. In this section, we discuss challenges in derivatives accounting and features of SFAS 133 that address some of these issues.

Accounting Issues

Accounting for derivatives is challenging for the following reasons:

- **Valuation complexity.** Derivatives are complex instruments. Many currency and interest rate derivatives used by corporations require complex valuation models. Most accountants are not prepared for this challenge and it may take considerable corporate resources to implement accounting procedures.

- **Lack of market prices.** Many derivatives used by corporations are private contracts. Even if they are traded, they have low levels of liquidity. Market prices when available may be unreliable.

- **Notional versus market value.** The notional (i.e., face) value of derivatives has very little to do with their market value. For example, if a firm engages in a large currency forward transaction, at inception, the notional value (amount of currency to be bought or sold) is very large, while the market value is zero. How is this reflected in accounting?

- **Earnings volatility.** Corporations engage in simple hedges in which they try to protect values of short-term assets such as accounts receivable, currency positions or marketable securities. However, they also engage in hedging to reduce economic exposure; these are often long-term hedges that attempt to protect the cash flows of the corporation. In these cases, there may be an apparent mismatch in timing between value changes in the derivatives position and the actual cash flows being hedged. There is a fear that this mismatch will increase the volatility of accounting earnings and actually discourage firms from hedging.

SFAS 133
MNCs routinely use derivatives for hedging currency and other risks. If U.S.-based, they follow *SFAS 133* for hedge accounting.

Types of Derivatives Hedges

After considerable research and discussion, in 1998, FASB released **SFAS 133**, titled *Accounting for Derivatives Instruments and Hedging Activities*. SFAS 133 defines various types of derivatives covered by the statement and identifies four uses/situations:

- **Fair value hedges.** These hedges attempt to protect the market value of a recognized asset or liability or a firm commitment. Usually, these are monetary assets/liabilities and receivables/payables/inventory. Losses and gains in the derivatives as well as the underlying hedged item are recognized in earnings. By definition, these changes are of opposite signs. In effective hedges, earnings are affected only by a small amount. For hedges to qualify for this accounting treatment, certain preconditions must be met. Firms must specify ex ante the asset or liability to be hedged, the objective of hedging and the expected effectiveness of the hedging instrument.

- **Cash flow hedges.** These hedges attempt to protect the future cash flows of the firm. FASB refers to these cash flows as "cash flows of a forecasted transaction." Because of the long-term nature of this hedge, the accounting treatment is more complex. Derivatives gains and losses are initially reported outside of earnings as a component of Other Comprehensive Income (OCI). When the forecasted events finally affect earnings, derivatives gains and losses—initially parked in OCI—are reclassified into earnings. As with fair value hedges, firms must meet preconditions for implementing this accounting treatment.

- **Foreign currency hedges.** These are to be treated either as fair value hedges or cash flow hedges depending on the situation. Usually, transaction exposures are hedged using fair value hedges, and operating exposures are hedged using cash flow hedges.

- **Speculation.** This is the simplest accounting scenario. The derivatives are marked to market and the gains and losses recorded periodically. Firms dislike this method of accounting for derivatives used in hedges because of timing differences between recognition of derivatives losses and gains compared to underlying asset losses and gains. Thus, earnings potentially become more volatile. However, some firms may prefer not to go through the "hoops" for qualifying their hedges as fair value or cash flow hedges.

Effects of SFAS 133

This accounting standard tracks two issues: (1) reflection of derivative gains and losses in income and (2) synchronization of value changes in derivatives and the hedged item. As with most regulations, there are associated costs. We do not yet have robust estimates of what compliance with SFAS 133 costs firms. But there are indications that small firms are finding it burdensome and some are choosing not to hedge as a consequence. Large firms also are modifying their hedging behavior and are trading off hedging benefits versus accounting ease and impact on earnings volatility. MNCs are sometimes caught between the proverbial "rock and a hard place." Exposures left unhedged may have adverse consequences, but hedging requires costly accounting procedures.

EXAMPLE 14.10

Provisions of SFAS 133 have been adopted internationally. IAS 32 and 39, both revised in 2003 and effective from 2005 offer disclosure similar to SFAS 133. In addition to the types of hedges recognized in SFAS 133, the IAS standards also define portfolio hedges of interest rate risk and hedges of a net investment in a subsidiary. Two key differences are: IAS allows macrohedging (hedging of multiple exposures generally from a firm-level perspective) and mandates more stringent classification and disclosure of all financial instruments. Experts deem that IAS and U.S. standards offer more similarity than differences and expect even greater convergence in the future.

Summary

- MNCs pay various taxes including domestic and foreign income taxes, VAT, GST, excise taxes, and customs duties.
- MNCs, by paying taxes in multiple countries, are potentially exposed to double taxation. Some countries offer relief from double taxation with tax deductions and credits for foreign taxes.
- Many countries have signed tax treaties that reduce the tax burden of MNCs by eliminating the double taxation of income. The foreign tax credit is an important mechanism used to mitigate double taxation.

- MNCs use various strategies to minimize their global tax burden. Strategies include the use of transfer pricing and tax havens. Transfer pricing is useful in shifting income from high-tax areas to low-tax areas; however, this is subject to the tax rules of various countries. Tax havens are countries such as Switzerland and the Bahamas that impose low or zero taxes; by flowing income through these countries, MNCs defer or eliminate certain taxes.

- Accounting information is important for effective corporate governance. MNC accounting can differ depending on the country of incorporation. Global differences in accounting systems are explained by factors such as history, the structure of capital markets, and the influence of governments.

- Accounting standards are converging. International Financial Reporting Standards (IFRS) appear to be gaining momentum. Many nations allow firms to use IFRS instead of their national standards for financial reporting.

- MNCs face special accounting issues in the areas of currency translation and derivatives. Currency translation for U.S. firms is guided by SFAS 52 and requires the use of the current exchange rates to translate most income statement and balance sheet items. Derivatives accounting in U.S. firms is guided by SFAS 133, which allows, under certain conditions, the synchronization of gains and losses in the two sides of a hedge (derivative and hedged item) in order to minimize earnings variability.

Questions

1. **Taxation Jurisdiction.** What are territorial and worldwide income approaches to taxation? What approach does the United States use? Which of the two approaches leads to double taxation?

2. **Taxable Entities.** What are the separate entity and integrated system approaches to taxation? Which of these approaches leads to double taxation?

3. **MNC Taxation Taxonomy.** What are various taxes paid by MNCs in their global operations? List and explain.

4. **Emerging Markets versus Developed Country Taxation.** "Watch out for local (town) taxes in Germany. . . ." The subsidiary manager was thus warned by the CFO of the U.S. parent. Are there country- and region-specific taxes that an MNC must pay attention to? What taxes are used by emerging countries more than developed markets? On the contrary, what are taxation strategies of developed nations?

5. **Overall Tax Burden.** What do OECD statistics tell us about the share of GDP attributed to taxes? How does the United States fare on this metric compared to European countries and emerging economies?

6. **Distribution of Tax Revenues.** How does the United States differ from other countries in its distribution of tax revenues? What types of taxation are important in the United States relative to other countries and what types are less important?

7. **Rationale for Tax Treaties.** Why do nations sign tax treaties? What are typical features of tax treaties? Are MNCs facilitated or hindered by tax treaties? Explain.

8. **Foreign Tax Credits.** Explain how a typical foreign tax credit (FTC) system works. What is its purpose? Who are beneficiaries of FTC? What are some practical difficulties in implementing FTC provisions?

9. **Credits versus Deductions.** The treasurer of an MNC states, "A foreign tax deduction is worth less than half of a foreign tax credit." Using equations or logical statements, demonstrate the validity of this statement for typical tax situations faced by MNCs.

10. **Transfer Pricing Regulations.** Who regulates transfer pricing methods? What U.S. regulations are applicable to transfer pricing? If there is one universally accepted transfer pricing method, what is it?

11. **Transfer Pricing.** Assume that an MNC runs afoul of country A's regulations while satisfying those of country B. Officials in country A force the company to change its transfer prices. What are potential ramifications?

12. **Tax Minimization.** Explain two tax minimization strategies (other than transfer pricing) that can be adopted by an MNC.

13. **Accounting Standards.** Honeywell is a diversified industrial firm. One of its key divisions makes machines for factory automation. To boost its capability in the area, Honeywell wishes to take over a mid-sized Singaporean firm that specializes in robotics. The CFO establishes a team to scrutinize data on the Singaporean firm and develop a plan for the takeover. A key concern is interpretation of the financials. Singapore supposedly follows IAS, which are similar to U.S. GAAP. What are some pitfalls of assuming that accounting methods of the target are similar to U.S. accounting methods? Explain.

14. **Currency Translation.** What are FTA and CTA (SFAS 52)? Using your knowledge of different types of currency exposure from previous chapters, explain the scope of these measures. In other words, what types of exposure do they measure, and what is their limitation?

15. **Derivatives Accounting.** A CFO giving a talk to MBA finance and accounting students in a famous school in Boston says, "Well, if you'd like to work for MNCs, you'd better obtain more than passing familiarity with SFAS 133." Elaborate and explain this statement.

16. **SFAS 133.** According to SFAS 133, derivatives (and hedges) are placed in four categories. Based on the category, different accounting regulations apply. In particular, consider the category of "fair value hedges." Explain what this category means and its importance to MNCs. Also explain why firms need to expend resources (that is, manpower or consulting dollars) to satisfy accounting and other provisions contained in this category.

Problems

1. **VAT.** Spain imposes a 20 percent VAT on goods and services. Mingus, a U.S.-based MNC, purchases raw materials to produce and sell shampoo and other cosmetics. Assume that in a given month, purchases of raw materials equals EUR 200,000 and sales equals EUR 600,000.

   a. Complete the following table to indicate VAT on the purchase and sale transactions.

   b. What are the pretax and after-tax (gross) profit?

Transaction	Begin Value	End Value	Value Added = End − Begin	VAT @ 20 percent
Raw materials purchased for EUR 200,000				
Finished product sold for EUR 600,000				
Total				

2. **No Tax Credit Scenario.** A foreign subsidiary produces taxable income of USD 500,000 million and remits all after-tax cash flows to a U.S. parent. Assume foreign income and withholding taxes of 20 percent and 10 percent, respectively. The domestic tax rate is 35 percent. There is no tax treaty between the two nations.

   a. Calculate foreign income tax and after-tax income.

   b. Calculate the withholding tax and after-tax amount remitted to parent.

   c. Calculate domestic income taxes.

   d. What is the overall tax burden in percent terms?

3. **Tax Credit Scenario.** A German firm has a profitable subsidiary in China that makes a remittance of after-tax income. Assume that this subsidiary produces taxable income of

CNY 40 million and remits all after-tax cash flows to its German parent. Assume Chinese income and withholding taxes of 25 percent and 10 percent, respectively. Assume a German tax of 40 percent. A tax treaty between the two nations allows the German firm to use Chinese tax payments as a credit against German taxes. Assume that the exchange rate for remittance as well as tax calculations is EURCNY equals 9.86.

   a. Calculate foreign income tax and after-tax income.

   b. Calculate the withholding tax and after-tax amount remitted to parent.

   c. What is the foreign tax credit?

   d. Calculate tentative and actual domestic income taxes.

   e. What is the overall tax burden in percent terms?

4. **Partial Remittance.** A fully owned Russian subsidiary of a U.S. oil company (Dallas Rigs) has ruble (RUB) 500 million of taxable income during a particular year. Dallas plans to pay Russian corporate income taxes of 24 percent and remit 40 percent of the remainder to the parent. The rest is being pumped back into the firm for new projects. Assume that the Russian tax authorities also charge 5 percent withholding taxes. The U.S. tax rate is 35 percent. Assume that a tax treaty exists between Russia and the United States and that all Russian taxes are eligible for a foreign tax credit.

   a. Using a spreadsheet format, show all taxes paid by Dallas in Russia and in the United States.

   b. Calculate the overall tax burden.

5. **High Foreign Taxes.** An Italian firm has a fully owned Brazilian subsidiary. Brazil has corporate income and withholding taxes of 34 percent and 15 percent, respectively. Trace the path of EUR 1 of taxable income as it exits Brazil and enters the accounts of the Italian firm. What are the various taxes? Assume Italian taxes of 32 percent. Assume a tax treaty provides recognition of all Brazilian taxes as a tax credit in Italy.

6. **Tax Credit versus Tax Deduction.** Assume foreign and domestic income tax rates of 20 percent and 30 percent and zero withholding taxes.

   a. If the country follows a system of giving a tax *deduction* for foreign taxes, what is the overall tax burden of an MNC with foreign income?

   b. If the country follows a system of giving a tax *credit* for foreign taxes, what is the overall tax burden of an MNC with foreign income?

7. **Transfer Pricing.** An Irish MNC sells 200 units of a product to its Brazilian subsidiary for EUR 200,000. The parent incurs direct and indirect expenses of EUR 40,000 and EUR 60,000, respectively. The subsidiary incurs only an indirect expense of EUR 25,000; its direct expense is equal to the transfer price. The subsidiary sells the product for EUR 1,500 each. If Irish and Brazilian taxes are 10 percent and 35 percent, respectively, evaluate the merit of increasing the transfer price to EUR 1200 per unit.

8. **Transfer Pricing Risk.** A U.S-based MNC is concerned about its transfer pricing policy. It ships a ready-to-assemble product to its subsidiary in India. The Indian subsidiary is currently charged USD 250 per product; this price has already been scrutinized and approved by transfer pricing officials. The firm is debating the merits of increasing the transfer price by USD 50. However, its auditors indicate a 50 percent probability of an audit by Indian tax authorities. Experience by other companies show that Indian transfer pricing officers are successful in 20 percent of their audits. Penalties are usually set at 25 percent of assessed value of the end product, which in this case is USD 400. Analyze these data and advise the firm. Assume that U.S. and Indian tax rates are 30 percent and 40 percent, respectively.

9. **Foreign Translation Adjustment.** A U.S. firm has a French subsidiary. The table below provides details of assets and liabilities of the subsidiary in the local currency (EUR thousands). Assume that the EURUSD rates are 1.30 and 1.40 at the beginning and end of the year, respectively. Calculate the amount of the foreign translation

adjustment that occurs in the parent's books because of its French subsidiary's assets and liabilities.

Subsidiary Assets and Liabilities in Local Currency

	EUR Denominated Amounts ($t = -1$)	USD Value		Translation Gains/Losses
		EURUSD = 1.30	EURUSD = 1.40	
Assets				
Cash	2,000			
Accounts receivable	500			
Inventory	3,000			
Plant & equipment	7,000			
Total assets	12,500			
Translation effects of assets				
Liabilities				
Accounts payable	2,000			
Short-term debt	4,000			
Long-term debt	2,500			
Translation effects of liabilities				
Equity, including cumulative translation adjustment	4,000			
Total liabilities and net worth	12,500			
Translation adjustment = Translation effects of assets – Translation effects of liabilities				???

10. **Foreign Translation Adjustment.** Assume that U.S. MNCs translate assets and liabilities at current rates and net incomes at average rates. The Indian subsidiary of a U.S. firm has current assets, fixed assets, current liabilities, and long-term debt of 20, 100, 40, and 30, respectively (INR millions all). Also during the year, the subsidiary earned an income of INR 20 million. Assume that beginning and ending values of USDINR are 43 and 41, respectively. Calculate the foreign translation adjustment.

11. **Foreign Translation Adjustment.** Assume that U.S. MNCs translate assets and liabilities at current rates and net incomes at average rates. A U.S-based MNC has subsidiaries in India, Russia, and Italy. The following table lists relevant figures from the subsidiaries' accounting reports for the year 200X. The beginning of the year values of USDINR, USDRUB, and EURUSD were 40, 20 and 1.50, respectively. Assume that the three currencies—INR, RUB, and EUR—changed during the year against the USD by 10 percent, −8 percent and 12 percent, respectively.

Account	India (INR million)	Russia (RUB million)	Italy (EUR million)
Current assets	15	50	4
Fixed asset	45	100	6
Current liabilities	20	40	2
Long-term liabilities	0	20	3
Net income	8	12	1

a. What is the FTA arising from each subsidiary?

b. What is the overall FTA? Suppose the parent's consolidated books have a CTA value at the beginning of the year of USD 44 million. What is the ending value of CTA?

Extension

1. **Tax Minimization and JV activity.** Tidepool, a U.S.-based MNC, is setting up a 50-50 JV in India to manufacture home appliances. Tidepool intends to supply its technical know-how. The Indian firm brings its knowledge of running factories in India as well as distribution capabilities. Tidepool's CFO is concerned about the structure of the JV. In particular he is interested in the issue of royalty payments. He has read a research report indicating that the use of royalty payments to compensate a JV partner for its technological input may save on taxes.

   a. What is the alternative to using royalties to extract cash from the JV? Which alternative involves lower taxes? Explain.

   b. Are there any potential difficulties in transfer of royalty back to the United States?

   c. Are there any potential difficulties concerning incentive contracts at the Indian JV?

   d. How would the JV partner respond to demand for royalty payments from the U.S. firm?

   e. Evaluate the statement attributed to a tax official in an emerging economy: "Royalty payment to an MNC parent is just another form of stealing from the national treasury. Unscrupulous MNCs use royalty payments to practically bring down taxes to zero and we have to regulate this behavior. If you think about it carefully, you will note that it is just like transfer pricing in its effects...."

Case

Clover Machines: *Minimizing Global Taxes*

As Clover's global operations increased in size and scope, it started paying more attention to issues concerning taxation. Last year, the firm paid a total of USD 200 million in taxes. Foreign taxes were 10 percent of the total, reflecting almost proportionately Clover's foreign business. But Clover's globalization means that it is exposed to a broad variety of foreign taxes ranging from corporate income taxes to excise duties to local taxes. Brian Bent, Clover's CFO, wonders whether it would make sense to create a team of managers to address taxation issues and to develop a tax strategy for Clover. An alternative would be to hire a professional firm such as PricewaterhouseCoopers or KPMG to perform this function.

Mr. Bent is worried about resources expended on tax planning—whether allocated internally or outsourced. He is also worried about being distracted from core operational issues. He wonders whether savings in taxes could offset the resources needed for achieving these savings. In other words, should Clover minimize taxes, or should it minimize the sum of taxes and related transaction costs?

A particular area of concern for Mr. Bent is transfer pricing, identified by most experts as the key area of concern in international accounting and taxation. As Clover moves to fine-tune its global operations and sourcing components from various countries, transfer pricing is suddenly on the radar screen. The Indian operation is an example of the range of issues that Clover faces. Clover operates a JV in India producing and selling agricultural machinery. Over time, Clover realized that certain cost advantages were available if the Indian JV could be used to also make some critical components for use in its U.S. production line. Although the Indian corporate tax rate at first blush appeared low, Clover quickly realized that aggregate Indian taxes (including local taxes and excise duties) were higher than U.S. taxes. There was an economic advantage to using a low transfer price out of India.

Prior to 2001, India had few transfer price regulations. But new regulations, first enforced in 2003, raised the bar quickly. India largely adopted OECD guidelines but added its own twist to the regulations. As in the United States and largely in alignment with OECD regulations, India insisted on arm's-length prices. But Indian authorities requested substantial documents—exceeding requests in the United States—proving that this was indeed the case. In a few cases, cost-plus prices were allowed, but Indian subsidiaries of U.S. firms were asked to show healthy markups even if the parent did not make high profits on the final product. Any transaction exceeding USD 3.75 million was automatically audited and Indian transfer pricing officers (TPOs) were given wide powers to impose additional taxes and penalties.[7] TPOs were even given powers to revisit earlier audits that were successful and impose new taxes. A significant percent of audits results in adjustments unfavorable to the corporation. To make matters worse, when unfavorable tax adjustments are made in India, it is not always the case that correlative relief is offered by U.S. authorities.

The situation in India is hardly unique, as many governments around the world are gaining awareness of transfer pricing issues and using regulations to protect their tax revenues. As Mr. Bent ponders the various issues, he seeks answers to the following:

1. Construct plausible scenarios in which Clover faces higher Indian taxes than U.S. taxes. Why are the data on taxes presented in the text not uniformly relevant to all corporations?

2. Discuss the trade-off between tax savings and transaction costs. What is your recommendation for Clover?

3. Should Clover's ex ante objective be minimization of taxes or minimization of tax-related hassles? In answering this question, refer to facts pertinent to the Indian situation presented in the case.

4. Based on your general understanding of taxes, comment on the following: "Clover needs to minimize taxes by selecting appropriate countries for its operations, selecting the right organizational structure (subsidiary or JV) in addition to selecting the right transfer prices."

5. Using information from the IRS's Web site or other sources (e.g., http://www.irs.gov/irm/part4/ch46s03.html#d0e562342), briefly summarize how the IRS would evaluate the sourcing of components from Clover's affiliate in India. Comment on the comparison between controlled and uncontrolled transactions.

---

[7] Hardev Singh and Saurabh Dhanuka, "How to Survive a Transfer Price Audit in India, *TP Week International Tax Review,* tpweek.com (accessed July 2008).

CHAPTER FIFTEEN

International Portfolio Investments

We conclude this book with a discussion of cross-border investments in financial assets. Unlike previous chapters focusing on investments by corporations, this chapter focuses on investments by individual investors and financial institutions. Although this book is geared toward corporate financial decision making, this investment-oriented topic is relevant. This is so because corporate financial managers must understand issues faced by their providers of capital, their investors. Capital market equilibrium brings together demand and supply forces. Corporations demand capital and investors supply capital. Both issues are relevant to students of corporate finance.

This topic is also important because it addresses another important dimension of globalization: the integration of financial markets. Interestingly, governments have allowed the integration of goods markets even before they allowed the integration of financial markets. Thus, international investing is an evolving phenomenon that is of great importance to private citizens and by extension to corporations.

The (Markowitz) theory of diversification is important to modern corporate finance. In Chapter 6, we discussed the way this theory helps corporate managers assess and control currency risk. In this chapter, we explain how investors use the same important theory to make optimal asset allocation decisions. The key financial concept studied in this chapter is international diversification; it can improve the risk-return trade-off of investor portfolios. We follow this theoretical discussion with a practical discussion of how investors actually achieve international diversification in their portfolios. We discuss practical issues concerning international investment vehicles such as American depositary receipts (ADRs), mutual funds, hedge funds, exchange-traded funds (ETFs), and derivatives. We discuss international equity investments as well as international debt investments. Finally, we consider investments in developed as well as developing economies.

In particular, this chapter focuses on:

- Two reasons for investing abroad: profit motive and risk-reduction motive.
- Empirical data on the correlation between foreign assets and domestic assets and implications for global investing.
- Various constraints that increase transaction costs, lower returns, and increase risk in international investing.
- Ways in which investors can invest in overseas equities, including investments in individual stocks and funds.
- Differences between investments in developing countries and in developed countries.
- How investors can invest in the debt instruments of foreign issuers.
- Environmental changes affecting the world of investing.

15.1 Why Invest Internationally?

Investors like return and dislike risk and thus make investing decisions by balancing risk and return. Financial theory uses mathematical models to describe this behavior. Investors add assets appropriately to their portfolios and optimize based on resulting portfolio return

(r_p) and portfolio risk (σ_p). Various methods are used to evaluate investments. One popular method, known as the **Sharpe index (SI)**, is expressed as:

$$SI = \frac{r_p - r_f}{\sigma_p}$$

Sharpe index
The *Sharpe index* is used to evaluate the risk-return trade-off of an investment or portfolio.

In the Sharpe index, the numerator reflects the return or profit net of the risk-free return (r_f). The denominator reflects risk. The ratio thus reflects return per unit of risk. Investors seek the highest possible index value.

International investments can potentially increase SI in the following ways:

- **Profit.** By increasing portfolio returns, international investments can increase the numerator.
- **Risk reduction.** By decreasing the standard deviation of portfolios, international investments can decrease the denominator.

We explain these two benefits next.

Profit Motive

international investments
International investments can potentially provide *higher profits* (reward) than domestic investments.

As with MNCs, investors seek profitable overseas investments. For a variety of reasons—growing economies, insufficient capital, inefficient markets—international investments may offer higher returns than comparable-risk domestic investments.

Growing Economies

There is a great disparity in national growth. As with corporations, certain economies are mature with low gross domestic product (GDP); others are emerging or growing with high GDP. Investments in high-growth countries are potentially of interest to investors, assuming prices are not overly inflated. In the 1970s and 1980s, Asian economies such as Japan, Hong Kong, Singapore, and Malaysia offered many investment opportunities. In recent years, Brazil, Russia, India, and China—the so-called BRIC nations—have taken center stage. It is inevitable that other countries—perhaps in Africa or South America or eastern Europe—will offer opportunities in the future. One interesting feature of emerging stock markets is that returns are skewed to the right. This means that the incidence of high returns is larger than normal. It is not unusual to see years with returns of 50 percent or more.

Insufficient Capital

Many countries grapple with the problem of insufficient capital. Various reasons such as government controls, insufficient investor protection, and corruption lead to this condition. A natural consequence of insufficient capital is high return potential (that is, a high cost of capital). Businesses hunt scarce capital by offering a premium in returns. Investors from mature countries may be attracted to invest in such nations.

Inefficient Markets

In efficient markets, asset prices are fair and offer only a normal rate of return consistent with risk. In inefficient markets, asset prices may be abnormally low or high at least temporarily. With the possibility of investing in various foreign markets, investors seek markets that are inefficient. They take long positions in markets with abnormally low prices and short positions in markets with abnormally high prices. Which markets are likely to be inefficient? Small, developing markets with unique risk factors (e.g., political risk) are likely to offer opportunities because of market inefficiencies.

Currency Play

Investors also seek profit from a different source: the currency. Currency markets go through secular trends in the short and medium term. In the years preceding the credit crisis of 2007–2008, the USD declined significantly against emerging market currencies such as the BRL and CNY. Investors betting on such trends may allocate part of their portfolio to assets denominated in these currencies.

| **EXAMPLE 15.1** | The world's most famous and richest investor, Warren Buffett, also known as the Oracle of Omaha, runs a unique investment firm, Berkshire Hathaway, listed on the New York Stock Exchange (NYSE). In the early 21st century, well before the USD fell to all-time lows against the euro (EUR) and other currencies, Mr. Buffett declared that the USD 150 billion fund was making significant investments in foreign currencies either directly or indirectly through foreign assets. Mr. Buffett reasoned that the USD was in secular decline and wanted to take advantage of that trend. |

Risk-Reduction Motive

effect of low correlations
International investments usually *reduce portfolio risk* because of low correlation between various markets.

Earlier we noted that a key determinant of portfolio risk is the correlation between assets. When uncorrelated assets are combined, risk reduction results. International investments often offer uncorrelated assets to an investor. Hence, allocating part of a portfolio to international investments, even if these investments do not offer abnormally high returns, can improve a portfolio's risk-return trade-off (SI).

Correlations

Investors interested in equity investments note that the correlations between national equity markets are low to moderate. See Exhibit 15.1 for correlations reported in a recent study. The correlations reported are U.S.-centric and use foreign returns that have been converted to USD basis. The highest correlation reported is 0.69 (United Kingdom and Germany). Most correlations (16 of 28) are between 0.3 and 0.5. The highest correlations are those between the U.S. and European markets. The lowest correlations occur between Japan and Western markets.

A word of caution in interpreting correlations: Methods and results vary. Moreover, correlations appear sensitive to time periods. One interesting result reported in many studies is that correlations in stock returns are increasing. Perhaps this is an inevitable consequence of financial globalization. As correlations rise, the benefit of global diversification decreases. But the benefits of international diversification remain compelling.

EXHIBIT 15.1
Stock Market Correlations

Source: Li Yang, Francis Tapon, and Yiguo Sun, "International Correlations across Stock markets and Industries: Trends and Patterns 1988–2002," *Applied Financial Economics* 16 (2006), pp. 1171–1183.

	United States	Austria	Canada	Germany	France	Hong Kong	Japan	United Kingdom
United States	1.00							
Austria	0.45	1.00						
Canada	0.68	0.47	1.00					
Germany	0.55	0.37	0.44	1.00				
France	0.48	0.40	0.28	0.58	1.00			
Hong Kong	0.54	0.44	0.62	0.47	0.26	1.00		
Japan	0.35	0.41	0.36	0.32	0.26	0.34	1.00	
United Kingdom	0.66	0.52	0.52	0.69	0.51	0.52	0.46	1.00

| **EXAMPLE 15.2** | Assume three possible scenarios I–III with associated probabilities of 40 percent, 40 percent, and 20 percent, respectively. The stock market returns of country X in these three scenarios are 30 percent, −10 percent, and 20 percent, respectively. The stock market returns of foreign country Y (converted into the currency of X) are 36 percent, 0 percent and −10 percent, respectively. Calculate the correlation between the stock returns of X and Y. |

Solution: See below.

Correlation Computation

◇	A	B	C	D	E	F
1						
2			**Home X Country**		**Foreign Y Country**	
3	**Scenario**	**Probability**	**Return**	**Deviation**	**Return**	**Deviation**
4	I	40%	30%	18.0%	36%	23.6%
5	II	40%	−10%	−22.0%	0%	−12.4%
6	III	20%	20%	8.0%	−10%	−22.4%
7						
8	Mean		12.0%		12.4%	
9	Variance			0.03360		0.03846
10	Standard deviation			18.33%		19.61%
11	Covariance			0.02432		
12	Correlation			0.6765		

Note: Calculation of mean, variance, and sigma is explained in Chapter 6. Additional steps are as follows. Covariance equals the sum of the product of {probability, deviation (X) and deviation (Y)}. Correlation equals covariance divided by the product of the two standard deviations. See the following equations:

Covariance = 40%(18%)(23.6%) + 40%(−22%)(−12.4%) + 20%(8%)(−22.4%) = 0.02432

Correlation = 0.02432/(18.33% × 19.61%) = 0.6765

Discussion: This is an example of the use of probabilistic (ex ante) data to calculate correlations. Other methods use time-series data; slightly modified formulas are required. The result indicates a correlation of 0.6765 between X and Y—a relatively high correlation. It is high because the deviations are of similar sign in two of the three scenarios.

Portfolio Standard Deviation

As in Chapter 6, we use correlations and other inputs to calculate the standard deviation. As a first step, calculate the portfolio variance using the following equation:

$$\sigma_p^2 = w_1^2\,\sigma_1^2 + w_2^2\,\sigma_2^2 + 2w_1w_2\,CORR\,\sigma_1\,\sigma_2$$

The standard deviation (sigma) is the square root of the variance.

EXAMPLE 15.3

Consider the previous example concerning countries X and Y. An investor located in country X wishes to invest equally in the stocks of X and Y. Demonstrate the benefits of diversification for this investor. Assume that the risk-free rate of interest in country X is 5 percent.

Solution: Recall that X and Y have standard deviations of 18.33 percent and 19.61 percent, respectively; the correlation is 0.6765. Hence,

$$\sigma_p^2 = w_1^2\,\sigma_1^2 + w_2^2\,\sigma_2^2 + 2w_1\,w_2\,CORR\,\sigma_1\,\sigma_2$$

$$= (50\%)^2\,(18.33\%)^2 + (50\%)^2\,(19.61\%)^2 + 2(50\%)\,(50\%)\,(0.6765)\,(18.33\%)\,(19.61\%)$$

$$= 0.03017$$

$$\sigma_p = \sqrt{0.03017} = 17.37\%$$

Also, calculate the Sharpe index (SI) for (1) domestic investment only and (2) international diversification with equal proportions in X and Y. Recall that X and Y have mean returns of 12.0 percent and 12.4 percent, respectively.

$$SI = \frac{r_p - r_f}{\sigma_p}$$

Domestic only:

$$SI = \frac{12.0\% - 5\%}{18.33\%} = 0.3819$$

With international diversification:

$$r_p = 50\% \times 12\% + 50\% \times 12.4\% = 12.2\%$$

$$SI = \frac{12.2\% - 5\%}{17.37\%} = 0.4145$$

Discussion: Comparing the international portfolio sigma of 17.37 percent with the domestic portfolio sigma of 18.33 percent, we note a risk reduction of 0.96 percent. The international portfolio sigma of 17.37 percent can also be benchmarked against a hypothetical international portfolio that has no diversification benefit (that is, the correlation = +1). This hypothetical no-diversification portfolio would contain the following amount of risk:

$$\sigma_p = 50\% \times 18.33\% + 50\% \times 19.61\% = 18.97\%$$

Thus, imperfect correlation reduces sigma by 1.60 percent.

Diversification improves the risk-return trade-off. The SI increases from 0.3819 to 0.4145. In this example, the increase in SI is caused by both a reduction in risk and an increase in return.

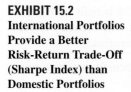

EXHIBIT 15.2
International Portfolios Provide a Better Risk-Return Trade-Off (Sharpe Index) than Domestic Portfolios

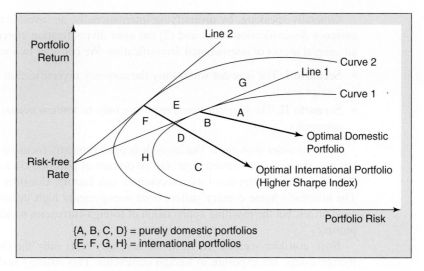

{A, B, C, D} = purely domestic portfolios
{E, F, G, H} = international portfolios

Investments in emerging markets are especially compelling from the risk-reduction standpoint. These markets have the lowest correlations with U.S. or European equity markets. In recent years, U.S. investors have recognized this and other benefits of emerging markets (for instance, the incidence of high returns). In the opinion of some experts, these benefits outweigh the higher than normal propensity for emerging markets to crash (e.g., Mexico in 1994 and various Asian markets in 1997–1998).

Graphical Depiction of International Diversification

Exhibit 15.2 summarizes our previous discussion concerning international diversification. An investor restricted to domestic assets or portfolios will be limited in both obtaining return and decreasing risk. The set of possibilities available to this investor is contained within Curve 1 in the diagram. For instance, possibilities include points {A,B,C,D}. Of course, the investor will strive to select the best portfolio possible by evaluating the SI of various combinations. This means that he would ultimately select the portfolio identified by the point of tangency between Line 1 and Curve 1. Note that the slope of Line 1 equals the SI of this optimal portfolio.

In contrast, an investor considering international assets and portfolios will be unconstrained in obtaining return and decreasing risk. This investor will consider possibilities contained within Curve 2. For instance, possibilities include points {E,F,G,H}. Of course, this investor too will strive to optimize based on SI and will therefore select the portfolio identified by the tangency between Line 2 and Curve 2. The slope of Line 2 equals the SI of the optimal international portfolio. Because the slope of Line 2 is higher than the slope of Line 1, the optimal international portfolio is superior to the optimal domestic portfolio.[1]

Currency Diversification Considerations

Recall our portfolio calculation in the Risk-Reduction Motive section. The expected return is calculated from the perspective of the home country investor after converting the cash flows to the home currency (USD in the case of U.S. investors). Similarly, the sigma is calculated by considering the distribution of rates of return after conversion to the home currency. This means that there is an implicit currency effect and the more explicit foreign market effect. Our previous calculation did not separate these two effects.

[1] See advanced finance texts for a more detailed discussion of portfolio theory (e.g., Stephen Ross, Randolph Westerfield, and Jeffrey Jaffe, *Corporate Finance* [New York: McGraw Hill, 2008]). In these texts, more specific terminology is developed. For example, the upper-left portion of the curves depicted in Exhibit 15.2 is known as the *efficient set*. Also, the line connecting the risk-free rate with the optimal portfolio is known as the *capital market line (CML)*. Portfolio theory links investor behavior to asset pricing models such as the capital asset pricing model (CAPM).

Generally speaking, by diversifying internationally, an investor can benefit from (1) the currency diversification effect and (2) the asset diversification effect. The currency effect is an integral aspect of international diversification. We consider two scenarios:

- **Scenario I.** The investor wants only the currency diversification benefit, not exposure to foreign assets.
- **Scenario II.** The investor wants exposure only to foreign assets, not exposure to foreign currencies.

First, consider scenario I. The investor is predominantly focusing on the domestic market but may desire a small investment (say 10 percent of portfolio) in foreign currencies as protection against country-level macroeconomic risk factors. Consider the following situation: The investor's home country suffers from unexpectedly high inflation. This would depress asset prices, but the resulting appreciation of foreign currencies would provide compensatory profits.[2]

Next, consider scenario II. In it, the investor wants only the diversification offered by foreign assets, not exposure to foreign currencies. This strategy is difficult to implement in practice because the purchase of foreign assets automatically provides exposure to foreign currencies. However, certain sophisticated financial techniques can be used to implement this strategy. In conjunction with a foreign investment, one could use derivatives such as currency futures and currency options to hedge the currency effect. In practice, because of difficulties in hedging currency risk, most U.S. investors retain currency risk when investing in foreign equity.

15.2 Barriers to International Diversification

Standard portfolio theory suggests that investors hold a global market portfolio that is weighted by the relative value of various national markets. Thus, if U.S. assets compose 35 percent of the global portfolio and Japanese assets compose 15 percent, this theory would indicate that an investor holds 35 percent U.S. assets, 15 percent Japanese assets, and so on. This theory would also apply uniformly to all the citizens of the world. The investor's nationality should in principle not affect portfolio composition.

But we know that investors do not behave in this fashion. Even in the most globally oriented country, the United States, investors focus primarily on domestic assets. In 2005, U.S. equity market capitalization was roughly 40 percent of world market capitalization. Yet U.S. investors had more than 80 percent of their equity portfolio in domestic equity (see Exhibit 15.3). The situation in other countries with the possible exception of some European countries is even further removed from optimality. This phenomenon of underrepresenting foreign investments is known as the **home bias**. Since 2000, however, home bias has declined significantly. The increase of foreign assets in investor portfolios appears to be a secular trend.

Why is home bias significant? We next examine barriers to international investing that may potentially explain the home bias.

home bias
Globally, investors structure portfolios mostly with domestic assets. This *home bias* may be due to barriers in international investing.

Currency Risk

One concern of investors in international investments is currency risk. In an earlier chapter, we noted that domestic currency returns of a foreign investment (r) can be expressed as:

$$r = (1 + r^*) \times (1 + s) - 1$$

Here, r^* equals the return of the asset in the foreign currency, and s equals the change in the foreign exchange rate.

---

[2] B. Solnik, "Global Asset Management," *Journal of Portfolio Management* 24 (1998), pp. 43–51.

EXHIBIT 15.3
Home Bias, 2005
Estimates (USD
millions)

Source: Piet Sercu and Rosanne
Vanpee, "Home Bias in International
Equity Portfolios: A Review," Working Paper, Katholieke Universiteit,
2007. Available at SSRN: http://ssrn.
com/abstract=1025806.

Country	Domestic Market Cap	Foreign Assets	Foreign Liabilities	Domestic Equity Holdings	Market Cap in World Market (percent)	Domestic in Total Equity (percent)	Home Bias
Argentina	47,590	9,558	1,971	45,619	0.1	82.7	82.6
Australia	804,015	126,418	158,336	645,679	1.9	83.6	81.7
Austria	126,309	63,566	36,647	89,662	0.3	58.5	58.2
Belgium	286,326	202,205	86,028	200,297	0.7	49.8	49.1
Brazil	474,647	2,809	99,706	374,941	1.1	99.3	98.1
Canada	1,482,185	363,067	296,496	1,185,688	3.5	76.6	73.0
Chile	136,493	23,016	5,942	130,551	0.3	85.0	84.7
Colombia	50,501	1,009	1,186	49,315	0.1	98.0	97.9
Czech Republic	53,798	4,386	6,549	47,249	0.1	91.5	91.4
Denmark	187,161	88,038	39,293	147,868	0.4	62.7	62.2
Egypt	79,509	898	4,513	74,996	0.2	98.8	98.6
Finland	228,266	64,471	117,041	111,225	0.5	63.3	62.8
France	1,769,569	529,289	600,072	1,169,497	4.2	68.8	64.6
Germany	1,221,106	528,153	507,419	713,687	2.9	57.5	54.6
Greece	145,121	8,326	28,003	117,117	0.3	93.4	93.0
Hong Kong	1,054,999	227,834	119,234	935,765	2.5	80.4	77.9
Hungary	32,576	1,749	13,297	19,279	0.1	91.7	91.6
India	1,069,046	36	100,805	968,242	2.5	100.0	97.4
Indonesia	81,428	93	17,275	64,153	0.2	99.9	99.7
Israel	122,578	8,169	35,864	86,714	0.3	91.4	91.1
Italy	798,073	416,446	242,896	555,177	1.9	57.1	55.2
Japan	5,542,716	408,575	929,135	4,613,580	13.2	91.9	78.7
Korea	718,011	13,913	187,502	530,508	1.7	97.4	95.7
Malaysia	180,518	1,550	23,240	157,278	0.4	99.0	98.6
Mexico	239,128	3,041	75,378	163,750	0.6	98.2	97.6
Netherlands	575,843	478,427	349,158	226,685	1.4	32.1	30.8
New Zealand	40,593	21,785	8,194	32,398	0.1	59.8	59.7
Norway	190,952	125,677	54,982	135,971	0.5	52.0	51.5
Philippines	39,818	184	5,696	34,122	0.1	99.5	99.4
Poland	93,602	1,671	14,754	78,848	0.2	97.9	97.7
Portugal	75,066	15,762	19,714	55,352	0.2	77.8	77.7
Russia	527,022	336	48,128	478,894	1.3	99.9	98.7
Singapore	257,341	67,592	54,970	202,370	0.6	75.0	74.3
South Africa	549,310	60,756	58,874	490,436	1.3	89.0	87.7
Spain	959,910	122,870	185,435	774,475	2.3	86.3	84.0
Sweden	420,953	202,216	124,792	296,161	1.0	59.4	58.4
Switzerland	935,448	357,270	400,885	534,563	2.2	59.9	57.7
Thailand	123,885	1,217	25,746	98,139	0.3	98.8	98.5
Turkey	161,538	90	26,503	135,034	0.4	99.9	99.5
United Kingdom	3,058,182	992,737	1,217,227	1,840,956	7.3	65.0	57.7
United States	17,000,805	3,317,705	1,664,493	15,336,311	40.5	82.2	41.7
Venezuela	7,316	405	586	6,729	0.0	94.3	94.3
Total	41,949,250	8,863,315	7,993,970	33,955,281	100		

Note: Home bias (last column) equals the difference between the previous two columns.

EXAMPLE 15.4

Consider a U.S. investor purchasing a German asset for EUR 100. At a current spot rate of EURUSD equals 1.60, this investment costs USD 160. It is liquidated a year later at EUR 110, implying an asset return of 10 percent. However, assume that at this time, the EURUSD equals 1.52, reflecting a depreciation of 5 percent. What return did the investor earn?

Solution:

$$r = (1 + r^*) \times (1 + s) - 1$$
$$= (1 + 10\%) \times (1 - 5\%) - 1$$
$$= 4.5\%$$

Alternatively,

$$r = \frac{110 \times 1.52}{100 \times 1.60} - 1 = 4.5\%$$

Discussion: The currency depreciation of 5 percent reduces home currency returns. The resulting return of 4.5 percent can be approximated using the equation $r = r^* + s$. Using this simpler equation, $r = 10\% - 5\% = 5\%$.

Based on the simpler form of the return equation ($r = r^* + s$), we can derive the variance (total risk) of a foreign investment as follows:

$$\sigma^2\,(r) = \underbrace{\sigma^2(r^*)}_{\substack{\text{Asset}\\\text{Risk}}} + \underbrace{\sigma^2(s)}_{\substack{\text{Currency}\\\text{Risk}}} + \underbrace{2 \times \sigma(r^*, s)}_{\substack{\text{Covariance}\\\text{Risk}}}$$

The three terms on the right-hand side are asset risk, currency risk, and covariance risk, respectively. We explain these risk factors and provide an example.

Asset Risk

Asset risk is the fundamental risk factor and reflects the risk that the local investors bear of the foreign asset. If the asset is a foreign stock, the risk would be assessed based on the variation in the asset's local (i.e., foreign) currency-denominated prices. Depending on the type of the asset or the country, this risk factor could be high or low. Asset risk includes micro (firm-specific and industry-specific) as well as macro (country-specific) effects.

Currency Risk

The second risk factor is currency risk. Earlier (Chapter 6) we discussed this issue in the context of corporate investments. Investors whose home currency is a stable one such as the USD or EUR are especially concerned about this risk factor when investing in foreign countries with risky currencies.

Covariance Risk

covariance risk
The *covariance risk* factor will increase overall risk in a foreign asset if a high positive correlation between the asset and the currency exists.

Investors are also sensitive to the risks conveyed by the covariance term in the preceding equation. For example, U.S. investors in Thai assets noted that during the emerging markets crisis of 1997–1998, asset values as well as the Thai baht lost value. This implies a positive correlation between the value of the Thai currency and the value of Thai assets. Thus, the risk of investing in Thai assets was greater than that implied by the mere consideration of asset and currency risks. This situation is unfortunately true for many foreign assets, specifically for investments in small economies (or markets) where factors affecting currency values (e.g., country risk factors) also affect asset values. In some instances, however, a negative covariance risk offsets currency risk (net currency effect is zero or negative) and makes a foreign investment fairly safe: The following example illustrates this interesting possibility.

EXAMPLE 15.5

A U.S. investor is considering an investment in Mexico. The asset has a local currency standard deviation (asset risk) of 25 percent. The standard deviation of MXNUSD (Mexican pesos) is 8 percent. Assume that the correlation between the asset and MXNUSD is –0.3. Estimate total risk. Determine whether the investment is riskier for a U.S. investor compared to a local (Mexican) investor.

Solution:

$$\sigma^2\,(r) = \sigma^2(r^*) + \sigma^2(s) + 2 \times \sigma(r^*, s)$$
$$= (25\%)^2 + (8\%)^2 + 2 \times (-0.3) \times 25\% \times 8\%$$
$$= 0.0625 + 0.0064 - 0.0120$$
$$= 0.0569$$

$$\sigma(r) = \sqrt{0.0569}$$
$$= 23.85\%$$

Discussion: Because of negative correlation between asset and currency, covariance risk mitigates asset and currency risks, far more than currency risk in particular. The resulting total risk to a U.S. investor is less than the risk to a local investor. In such situations, hedging away currency risk from the investment would be pointless.

Government Controls and Taxes

government controls
Myriad *government controls* deter investments in certain foreign markets.

Many governments control investments by foreigners in local assets. The following are examples of government controls:

- **Outright ban.** Some governments, usually in small countries with closed economies, ban foreigners from owning assets. National pride often motivates this. Governments may also fear that foreigners will amass economic power or that foreign businesses will exploit local citizens.

- **Ownership limits.** Many governments allow foreign ownership of assets but only in a limited manner. For example, many governments restrict foreign ownership of local firms to no more than 50 percent of equity. Such restrictions could be motivated by factors such as the desire to have local control of businesses and to prevent an excessive outflow of corporate earnings.

- **Taxes and fees.** Governments may impose various taxes, including withholding taxes and transaction fees, to discourage the foreign ownership of local assets.

- **Regulations.** Governments may impose restrictions even on entities with permission to invest in local assets. For instance, many governments allow foreign institutional investors (FII) to make investments but in a controlled and regulated manner.

- **Market access.** The channels through which foreign investors can purchase local assets can also be regulated. For instance, only certain state-owned banks can be named as agents for such transactions. Or certain mutual funds may be designated as investment vehicles for foreigners.

- **Repatriation controls.** Governments may impose controls and/or taxes on the flow of dividends and other payments to foreign investors. This is often the case in countries with current account deficits and balance of payments problems.

- **Exchange rate controls.** Governments may mandate unfavorable foreign exchange rates for repatriation of money.

The net effect of government controls is an increase in transaction costs for investors. Additionally, investors bear risks that the controls themselves will change over time. Investors evaluate overseas investment opportunities by estimating after-tax and after-transaction-cost returns.

Informational Asymmetry

Information is a key ingredient in the investment process. Lack of information about foreign corporations leads to two negative effects:

- Investors will perceive a higher level of risk because the lack of information creates uncertainties about projected outcomes.

- Monitoring foreign managerial activity becomes difficult and, hence, increases agency costs.

The problem of informational asymmetry is in part due to differential accounting systems. In Chapter 14, we noted that in addition to differences in accounting standards, differences in the application of these standards create difficulties for international investors. For example, investors accustomed to conservative accounting practices in the United States cannot rely on similar rapid reflection of negative information in accounting reports in many foreign countries.

Accounting reports are not the only way to disseminate corporate information, however. In the U.S. setting, the following additional methods are used:

- **Earnings calls.** Firms communicate with the investment community through earnings calls during which corporate officials answer questions from financial analysts. Today, these calls are available to all investors through the Internet.

- **Other SEC filings.** U.S. firms are required to file reports with the Securities and Exchange Commission (SEC) when "material" information becomes available. (See http://www.sec.gov/answers/form8k.htm for an explanation of SEC 8-K filings.)

- **Interactions with investor community.** Firms also interact with financial analysts, although recent regulation prohibits private contacts. This has forced firms increasingly to use their corporate Web sites to communicate with their investors. Some chief executive officers (CEOs) and chief financial officers (CFOs) also appear on TV financial shows to discuss corporate issues, and some even write blogs to disseminate information.

- **Press releases.** Finally, when confronted with significant news about future earnings (especially negative news), firms provide information through press releases.

Overall, non-U.S. firms use these diverse methods of information dissemination less frequently compared to U.S. firms. However, there appears to be a convergence in global information dissemination practices.

Corporate information is also available from noncorporate sources. Investors use information and reports created by financial analysts working in investment banks. They are known as *sell-side analysts* because a key motive for publishing reports is to generate stock transaction commissions for these banks. Although the value of much of this information is questionable, the recommendations of a few influential analysts tend to influence market prices. Recently, much of this analysis became available to investors over the Internet. Web sites such as Yahoo, Bloomberg, and Wall Street Research Network disseminate this information to investors. The level of information about non-U.S. firms on the Web is also increasing.

Corporate Governance

Recall from discussions in Chapter 1 that *corporate governance* refers to the set of arrangements, internal and external, that enable the operation and monitoring of corporations. Key to the governance of corporations are the rights of stockholders and their power in directing its course by selecting the board of directors and voting on key issues such as financing and mergers. Internal arrangements include the institution of the board of directors and the use of mechanisms such as incentive contracts. External mechanisms include transmitting accounting reports, monitoring by governmental agencies, monitoring by stockholders, and the market for corporate control.

The U.S. (or Anglo-Saxon) model of corporate governance relies on the following elements and is friendlier to equity investing than are other models:

- Stockholders have the right to elect directors and to participate in significant decision making such as mergers and new financing. These stockholder inputs are solicited in the proxy statement mailed annually.

- The board of directors, often composed of a significant number of independent outside directors, looks after stockholders' interests and curbs managerial opportunism.

- Laws protect stockholders' rights by entitling them to access corporate information and enabling them to take legal action against inefficient or fraudulent managers.

- A transparent accounting system and frequent communication from firms help reduce the informational asymmetry between managers and owners.

- A vibrant market of corporate control makes possible the takeover of firms by hostile means if necessary.

- An active capital market constantly evaluates firm performance.

Investors in corporate securities are sensitive to governance arrangements. Corporate asset values suffer when governance fails. Failures have occurred in many countries and dampen the enthusiasm for international investing. In many developing countries such as the Czech Republic, we see egregious acts such as the transfer of wealth from minority stockholders through mechanisms such as asset sales at below market prices.

corporate governance

Poor *corporate governance* can be a deterrence in certain markets.

The United States has not been immune to corporate governance failure. In the last decade, three important scandals occurred: the failure of Enron and other large corporations around 2000, the options backdating scandal of 2006, and the credit crisis of 2007–2008. Although the credit crisis is generally not perceived as a governance crisis, one needs to remember that much of the problem can be traced to the failure of internal controls in large firms such as AIG and Citicorp.

Global Crises and Contagion

global crises

Global crises induce high correlation between markets and negate the diversification benefits of global investing.

Global crises such as the emerging markets crisis of 1997–1998 have discouraged investments in emerging markets. The prolonged slump in the Japanese markets—once 40 percent of world market capitalization—also has encouraged European and U.S. investors to look to home markets or at most to Western markets. These crises along with the more recent credit crisis of 2007–2008 had a widespread effect on financial markets. The principal effect is a strong positive correlation between national stock markets. Recall from earlier discussions in this chapter that the *raison d'être* for international investing is imperfect correlation between markets. This advantage is lost during a global crisis.

EXAMPLE 15.6

The emerging markets crisis of 1997–1998 originated in Thailand, arguably a small and unimportant economy, but quickly spread around the world. A "perfect storm" of factors contributed to the worldwide spread of this crisis: excessive government debt, government control of currency values at excessively high levels, lack of adequate regulation of banks, and currency speculation by hedge funds. At one point, market watchers had hoped that the crisis would be contained in a few Asian countries. However, after Russia succumbed to the crisis, most Western countries also experienced the crisis. Although U.S. stocks were not drastically affected—barring a meltdown during the third quarter of 1998—globally diversified stock portfolios did little to protect investors.

The phenomenon of equity markets crashing together seems to have repeated during the credit crisis of 2007–2008. See Exhibit 15.4 for the pattern followed by five key equity markets. The overall picture shows all five markets crashing together, especially in the second half of 2008. When the crisis first came to light in 2007, certain emerging markets, such as those in Brazil and India, were considered unaffected. Later, however, when the crisis deepened, all markets took a hit.

EXHIBIT 15.4
Credit Crisis of 2007–2008

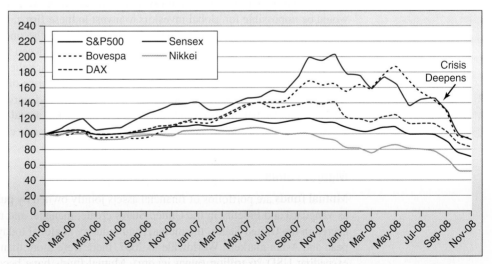

The indexes are S&P 500 (United States), Bovespa (Brazil), DAX (Germany), Sensex (India), and Nikkei (Japan). To facilitate comparison, all indexes were set equal to 100 at the beginning of the period.

15.3 International Equity Investments

We have seen the importance of adding foreign assets to one's portfolio. Among foreign assets, the most interesting category is equity investments. A host of factors, including interest rates, inflation, currency values, county risk, and technology, affect equity markets in unique ways. Equity investments carry considerable risks but also the promise of correspondingly high returns. Although risks appear high because national markets respond differently to different factors, equity also offers considerable potential for portfolio risk reduction. Thus, foreign equity offers potential for increasing an investor's risk-reward trade-off (SI). In this section, we discuss various ways in which investors in general and U.S. investors in particular can invest in global equity instruments.

Investors can potentially purchase shares of foreign companies directly. However, such trades must be routed through a foreign brokerage firm and may be required to comply with foreign regulations. Because of these difficulties, transaction costs—consisting of custodial fees as well as regular components such as commissions and bid-ask spreads—can be very high. Most investors, therefore, do not follow this route. In this section, we discuss other means of investing in foreign equity such as depository receipts, mutual funds, and ETFs.

Depository Receipts

In an earlier chapter, we discussed how firms use **depository receipts (DRs)** to list their shares and raise capital in the United States through American depositary receipts (ADRs) and in global markets through global depository receipts (GDRs). We consider here the demand for DRs from U.S. and other investors and discuss their advantages and disadvantages as investment vehicles. Recall from discussions in Chapter 10 that DRs are pseudoshares issued by depository institutions and backed up by a certain number of actual shares of foreign firms. This allows the value of the original shares to flow directly into the value of the receipts. This arrangement is similar to that in mutual funds when the net asset value of the asset holdings flows through to fund holders. Unlike a mutual fund, however, depository receipts allow holders to exercise their shareholder voting rights; also, holders can trade receipts in secondary markets.

variety in ADR listings
ADRs offer a wide variety of foreign equity investments to U.S. investors.

As of June 2008, the NYSE listed 418 ADRs from 45 different countries. BRIC nations, Canada, Japan, and many European nations are featured prominently in this list. Many ADRs, such as Philips, Sony, Nokia, and Daimler, are household names. As an avenue for profit or diversification, however, countries as well as companies off the beaten track offer more potential. The ADR list contains companies such as an Irish aircraft leasing company, an Israeli department store, an Indian copper producer, a Greek tanker operator, and a Chinese educational services firm. The list of Brazilian ADRs listed on the NYSE (see Exhibit 15.5) provides the reader an idea of the diversity and depth of ADR markets. Without ADRs, it would be impossible for global investors to invest in these firms.

How do markets value depository receipts relative to the underlying shares? Generally speaking, because arbitragers can exploit discrepancies between DR prices and the prices of actual shares to make arbitrage profits, DR prices closely track the value of underlying shares. For instance, if a DR is trading for a higher price than the price of the underlying stock, arbitragers (especially, large institutions) short-sell the DR and purchase the underlying stock. Research shows that the difference between DR prices and actual share prices rarely exceeds 1 percent. A related finding is that the correlation between price changes in DRs and original shares is close to 1: They are perfect substitutes.

Mutual Funds

Mutual funds are portfolios of financial assets jointly owned by public investors. Firms such as Vanguard and Fidelity in the United States create, manage, and market mutual funds. Pioneered in the United States, the mutual fund industry is global today and is penetrating European and Asian markets. Worldwide in 2007, there were more than 65,000 funds with assets exceeding USD 26 trillion (www.ici.org). Mutual funds have become the main vehicle for investments in financial markets. Although mutual funds have increased in popularity, some

EXHIBIT 15.5
Brazilian ADRs Listed
on NYSE (June 2008)

Source: www.nyse.com (accessed
June 20, 2008).

Issuer	Symbol	Industry
Aracruz Celulose S.A.	ARA	Bleached eucalyptus pulp products
Banco Bradesco S.A.	BBD	Private banking
Banco Itaú Holding Financeira S.A.	ITU	Banking
Brasil Telecom Participações S.A.	BRP	Telecommunications
Brasil Telecom S.A.	BTM	Telecommunications
Braskem S.A.	BAK	Petrochemicals
Companhia Brasileira de Distribuição	CBD	Food retail
Companhia de Bebidas das Americas (AmBev)	ABV	Beverages
Companhia de Saneamento Básico do Estado de São Paulo	SBS	Water utility
Companhia Energetica de Minas Gerais-Cemig	CIG	Electric utility
Companhia Paranaense de Energia-COPEL	ELP	Electricity generation
Companhia Siderurgica Nacional (CSN)	SID	Steel manufacture/distribution
Companhia Vale do Rio Doce (CVRD)	RIO	Iron ore production/distribution
CPFL Energia S.A. (CPFL)	CPL	Electricity generation
Embraer-Empresa Brasileira de Aeronáutica S.A. (Embraer)	ERJ	Aircraft design/manufacture
Gafisa S.A.	GFA	Construction
Gerdau S.A.	GGB	Steel production
GOL Linhas Aéreas Inteligentes S.A. (GOL)	GOL	Airline
Perdigão S.A.	PDA	Food production
Petróleo Brasileiro S.A.-PETROBRAS	PBR	Oil and gas
Sadia S.A.	SDA	Food production
TAM S.A.	TAM	Airline
Tele Norte Celular Participações S.A.	TCN	Telecommunications
Tele Norte Leste Participações S.A.	TNE	Telecommunications
Telebras HOLDRs	TBH	Telecommunications
Telecomunicações de Sao Paulo S/A-Telesp	TSP	Telecommunications
Telemig Celular Participações S.A.	TMB	Telecommunications
TIM Participações S.A.	TSU	Telecommunications
Ultrapar Participações S.A.	UGP	Industrial group/Gas district
Vivo Participações S.A.	VIV	Cellular telecommunications
Votorantim Celulose e Papel S.A. (VCP)	VCP	Pulp and paper production

experts have been concerned about underperformance. Academic studies show that the average mutual fund underperforms relative to benchmarks such as the S&P 500 index.

Domestic Fund Categories

Mutual funds are typically invested in the following domestic asset categories[3]:

- **Short-term government security investments or investment-grade corporate paper.** This category offers the highest level of safety for principal amounts and carries very low interest rate risk because of the assets' short maturity.
- **Medium- to long-term government security investments.** This category has a low to zero default risk but may have moderate to high levels of interest rate risk.
- **Medium to long-term corporate bonds.** In addition to interest rate risk, this category has exposure to default risk depending on the investment grade selected. Some of these funds labeled as "high yield" are invested in junk bonds.
- **Growth stocks.** This category of equity funds is typically invested in stocks having above average growth prospects for revenues and earnings (usually more than 10 percent). Usually this category is invested in medium- and large-cap growth stocks and may contain exposure to many MNCs.

[3] The Web sites of leading fund families such as Fidelity and Vanguard provide good information on types of funds.

- **Income stocks.** These funds contain low-growth stocks that often pay dividends. Many of these stocks may also be labeled as value stocks.
- **Small-cap stocks.** These funds typically invest in small high-growth stocks. It is well known that average growth rates are high for small-cap stocks. These are often much riskier investments than medium- and large-cap growth stocks.
- **Sector funds.** Mutual funds in this category (pioneered by Fidelity) invest solely in a particular industry. Typical sector funds cover high-tech industries such as communications, software, wireless, semiconductors, networking, and biotechnology. Some of these industry groups have a great deal of international exposure. This is perhaps the riskiest category of mutual funds.
- **Index funds.** These funds try to replicate the results of an index such as the Standard and Poor's 500. Some large index funds passively invest in all shares in an index; others use optimization techniques and invest in a subset of index shares.

International Fund Categories

In the last two decades, hundreds of funds invested solely in international assets have been introduced. These funds offer a convenient way for investors to get exposure to international equity. One problem is that international funds do not offer the same array of investment types as domestic funds. Nevertheless, the following types of international funds are available:

- **International bond funds.** Although the variety of international bonds is large in terms of issuers, currency, and option features, these funds by and large focus on large low-risk issuers and USD-denominated bonds.
- **Emerging market debts.** These are typically invested in bonds issued by the governments of developing countries and carry a high yield because of country risk. Most of these bonds are denominated in USD.
- **Regional equity funds.** These well-diversified funds are invested in regions such as Europe, Latin America, and Asia Pacific.
- **Country equity funds.** These are investments in specific countries and are thus quite risky because of exposure to country risk.

Open- versus Closed-End Funds

The selection of international mutual funds includes a critical choice between open-end funds and closed-end funds. **Open-end mutual funds** allow new (net) investments to change the size of the fund; thus, a large inflow of money into the fund requires its managers to purchase additional assets or to increase the fund's cash portion. Therefore, the number of shares in an open-end fund varies. **Closed-end mutual funds** fix an initial level of assets and do not allow any new inflow or outflow. However, shares of closed-end funds are listed in exchanges, enabling fund investors to buy and sell shares and change their investment levels. These two fund types have their advantages and disadvantages. Closed-end funds are suited for country funds because investments in countries such as India and China are regulated and are therefore not very liquid. An open-end fund with a large net inflow will have difficulty in purchasing assets in these illiquid markets; large outflows are probably even more problematic because prices may fall precipitously in illiquid markets. The problem with closed-end funds is that their values deviate from net asset value (NAV) depending on current investor sentiment. Thus, funds trade at a discount or at a premium to NAV. This situation exposes the investor to an additional risk factor, namely the risk of changes in the discount or premium. In 2008, many closed-end country funds traded at a discount.

country funds
Most *country funds* are closed-end funds. Investors can buy and sell shares in these funds easily through their brokerage accounts.

EXAMPLE 15.7

On July 11, 2008, the Morgan Stanley India Investment Fund (NYSE: IIF) closed with a market price of USD 21.98 and an NAV of USD 24.15. What is this closed-end fund's premium or discount?

Solution:

$$\text{Discount} = \frac{21.98 - 24.15}{24.15} = -8.99\%$$

Index Funds

In response to empirical evidence of chronic mutual fund underperformance, the industry has turned to passive investing methods. Open-ended index funds—consistent with academic theory calling for investments in market indexes—debuted with the enormously successful Vanguard Index 500 fund. A vast array of competing funds tracking a variety of indices such as the NASDAQ 100, the Russell 2000, and the Wilshire have been issued. After success in replicating domestic U.S. indices, fund companies turned their attention to overseas indices, primarily Morgan Stanley capital international (MCSI) indices, but these index mutual funds were primarily regional funds. For example, Vanguard has index funds tracking indexes for Europe and Asia/Pacific. Investor demand for country-level index mutual funds was left unsatisfied. However, a newer investment vehicle (exchange-traded funds) emerged to satisfy this need.

Exchange-Traded Funds

ETFs

ETFs—a relatively new method of investing—offer an efficient way to invest in foreign equity.

Investor demand for country-level funds led to an innovation in 1996 when Barclays (in partnership with Morgan Stanley) created a series of country-tracking **exchange-traded funds (ETFs)** known as *world equity benchmark shares (WEBS)*. ETFs are interesting and innovative investment vehicles combining the best traits of open- and closed-end mutual funds (see Exhibit 15.6). Like open-end mutual funds, their investments are allowed to vary. For example, when indexes change, ETFs can change their investment levels. More important, like open-end funds, there is a process for new investment and redemption—through a complex process involving creation units[4]—that disciplines prices to faithfully reflect NAV. As with closed-end funds, investors can buy or sell shares in stock exchanges. Barclays later rebranded WEBS as iShares.

Country ETFs are passive investment vehicles that seek to track well-publicized benchmarks such as the MSCI indexes. MSCI indices are value-weighted country indexes constructed along the lines of the S&P 500; this is an advantage because tracking value-weighted indexes requires fewer transactions than tracking price-weighted indexes such as the Dow Jones Industrial Average (DJIA). Other competing international ETFs, notably ones known as *basket of listed depository receipts (BLDRS)* that track Bank of New York Mellon ADR indexes, have been issued in the 21st century.

ETFs have the following advantages over international mutual funds:

- **Liquidity.** ETFs are exchange traded and hence offer more liquidity to investors. Mutual funds often constrain the number of transactions; this is not the case with ETFs.

- **Low transaction costs.** Transaction costs are lower not only because they are passively managed but also because they use sampling and optimization techniques to form country portfolios. However, portfolios with a small number of securities require complicated mathematical algorithms and may have tracking errors.

- **Tax efficiency.** ETFs offer more tax efficiency than most mutual funds. When actively managed mutual funds buy and sell stocks, they generate capital gains and losses. During good years, capital gains lead to payouts and trigger personal taxes for investors. Turnover ratios for many actively managed mutual funds exceed 100 percent: This is an indication of tax inefficiency.

- **No load.** Unlike most open-end mutual funds, ETFs have no front-end loads or deferred sales charges; unlike some closed-end mutual funds, ETFs do not trade at a discount.

- **Low management expenses.** Country ETFs are managed cost effectively and provide very good tracking relative to benchmark indexes. Studies indicate that the correlation between iShares and benchmark indexes is higher than that between closed-end country funds and benchmarks.

---

[4] Institutional investors, at a wholesale level, can create and redeem units. This means that large investors can transact directly with the fund at NAV rather than at market prices. For instance, if market price for a particular fund is higher than NAV, large investors can purchase directly from the fund at NAV and sell at higher market prices. This type of arbitrage forces market prices to equal NAV.

EXHIBIT 15.6

These Wild and Crazy ETFs Could Help Tame Your Portfolio

Source: Jonathan Clements, *The Wall Street Journal* (Eastern edition), December 19, 2007, p. D1.

The hype is finally justified.

Wall Street has rolled out some 600 exchange-traded index funds, those stock-market-listed products that have exploded in popularity. Many, however, merely mimic existing mutual funds—or are so narrowly focused that they're of little use to prudent investors.

But lately, all that's changed. ETF sponsors have launched intriguing funds in four key sectors, offering ordinary investors some great new ways to diversify.

—Foreign real estate. You likely have the bulk of your money in blue-chip U.S. stocks and high-quality U.S. bonds. Your goal: Lower your portfolio's risk level by adding investments that might post gains when these two core holdings are suffering.

On that score, foreign real-estate stocks look like a winner. "As the saying goes, all real estate is local," quips investment adviser Larry Swedroe, author of *Wise Investing Made Simple.* "International real estate has a very low correlation not only with U.S. risks, but also with their local stock markets."

While there are some conventional mutual funds focused on foreign real-estate stocks, the ETFs on offer are especially appealing if you're looking for a low-cost index fund. The past year has seen the launch of funds such as iShares S&P World ex-U.S. Property (symbol: WPS), SPDR DJ Wilshire International Real Estate (RWX) and WisdomTree International Real Estate (DRW). These funds charge just 0.48% to 0.6% in annual expenses.

—International small caps. Among international small-stock mutual funds, there are some good options—but many are closed to new investors.

Now, investors have a handful of ETFs to choose from, including iShares MSCI EAFE Small Cap (SCZ), SPDR S&P International Small Cap (GWX) and WisdomTree International Small Cap Dividend (DLS), which levy 0.4% to 0.6% in annual expenses.

If you own blue-chip U.S. stocks, foreign small companies are a much better diversifier than foreign large-cap companies, Mr. Swedroe argues. "If you think about General Motors and Daimler, they're both global companies," he says. "But a local German restaurant chain or a local grocery chain will be much more affected by what's happening in the German economy."

—Commodities. ETF sponsors have unveiled a slew of commodity funds, such as iShares S&P GSCI Commodity (GSG) and PowerShares DB Commodity (DBC). Also, check out iPath Dow Jones-AIG Commodity (DJP) and iPath S&P GSCI Total Return (GSP), two "exchange-traded notes" from Barclays Bank that trade like ETFs.

"A lot of people will buy energy stocks and commodity stocks and think they're getting diversification," says Nelson Lam, an investment adviser in Lake Oswego, Ore. "But you want to go for the commodities, not the commodity stocks."

Mr. Lam owns PowerShares DB Commodity, which charges 0.83% a year, including brokerage expenses. To avoid tax hassles, he advises holding the fund in a retirement account.

—Foreign bonds. If you have a large bond portfolio and relatively little in foreign stocks, foreign bonds are a great way to diversify.

Problem is, the mutual-fund choices are a little disappointing. These funds often have fairly steep annual expenses, and some hedge their currency exposure. This hedging means the funds aren't as good a diversifier, because they may not rally when U.S. turmoil causes the dollar to tumble.

Enter SPDR Lehman International Treasury Bond (BWX), an 11-week-old ETF that charges 0.5% in annual expenses and doesn't hedge its currency exposure. The fund will be buffeted by both currency and foreign interest-rate swings. But that makes it the sort of erratic performer that could fare well when U.S. investments are struggling.

Intrigued? Remember, we're talking here about volatile investments. My advice: Don't stash more than 10% of your total portfolio in any of the funds mentioned above. In fact, a 5% allocation is probably plenty.

- **Low tracking error.** Country ETFs also tend to have a lower correlation with the S&P 500 than closed-end funds have because they track the NAV faithfully and are not influenced by investor sentiment in the United States. This enhances the diversification effect.

Derivatives

Large investors and institutions have another avenue for international investments: derivatives. As we discussed in Chapter 3, prices of options and futures track the prices of the underlying assets. This feature of derivatives implies that investors can use options and futures on foreign assets/indexes to gain international exposure.

Many options and futures contracts are based on foreign equity indexes. Examples include:

- FTSE-100 (UK stock index) futures traded on the London International Financial Futures and Options Exchange (LIFFE).
- CAC-40 (French stock index) futures traded on LIFFE.
- DAX-30 (German stock index) futures traded on the European Exchange (EUREX).
- Options on the Hong Kong Index and Japan Index traded on National Association of Security Dealers Automated Quotations (NASDAQ).
- Options on the China Index traded on Chicago Board Options Exchange (CBOE).
- Options on MSCI ETF (world stock index) traded on CBOE.

This list includes exchange-traded derivatives. As noted in Chapter 3, investors often find a wider variety of derivatives in the over-the-counter (OTC) markets. Both exchange-traded and OTC derivatives are perhaps more useful to large investors; small investors usually prefer mutual funds and ETFs for their foreign exposure.

U.S. MNCs

A frequently overlooked but effective way to invest in overseas assets is to invest in U.S. MNCs such as Boeing, Coca-Cola, General Electric, and so on. Many of these MNCs have considerable assets in foreign countries. Even when they do not directly own assets, they have investments through subsidiaries, affiliates, and joint ventures (JVs). These overseas activities are so important that more than half of the profits of many of these firms result from overseas sales.

An investor may consider U.S. MNCs equivalent to a portfolio of domestic and foreign assets. Achieving international diversification through MNCs has many advantages:

- The MNCs serve as allocators of capital and search out the best global opportunities, saving investors the effort of searching for appropriate global equities in which to invest.
- It is easy to obtain information on MNCs. Thus, there are fewer informational asymmetry problems.
- Transaction costs are very low because of the large size of MNCs and of their average trading volume.
- The quality of corporate governance is well known and is of high quality. This results in lower agency costs.

Hedge Funds and Private Equity Funds

hedge funds
Wealthy investors have the option of investing abroad through *hedge funds* and *private equity funds.*

Hedge funds are largely unregulated versions of mutual funds, and many of them invest in foreign assets. A tremendous growth in hedge fund assets occurred in the last decade. Today there are more than 1,000 hedge funds with more than USD 100 billion of assets under management. The key difference between mutual funds and hedge funds is that hedge funds cater to wealthy investors with net worth exceeding USD 1 million and are run as a private partnership having no more than 100 investors.

Hedge funds avoid the regulatory scrutiny focused on mutual funds because of their private nature. The presumption is that individuals investing in hedge funds monitor the fund's activities more than mutual fund investors do; thus, regulators allow the unhindered functioning of hedge funds. Typical constraints faced by mutual funds in the areas of leverage, concentration of assets, and short-selling do not apply to hedge funds. For example, mutual funds are allowed to use leverage (i.e., borrowing) only for up to 50 percent of their asset worth; this constraint does not apply to hedge funds.

The management of hedge funds also differs considerably from that of mutual funds, which has implications for fund performance.[5] Two differences are worth noting here.

- First, hedge fund managers invest a considerable portion of their wealth in the funds they manage. In this respect, hedge funds are similar to venture capital funds. This personal investment aligns the incentives of managers and fund investors; however, this may make the manager poorly diversified and risk averse or cautious in investment strategy.

- Second, most hedge funds offer incentive contracts to their managers. On average, managers receive a 1 percent management fee and 14 percent of profits after certain minimum level of profits has been realized. While this structure of compensation may induce excessive risk taking, it also provides strong incentives for performance.

Taken together, these two differences explain why hedge funds on average outperform mutual funds. However, research also notes that hedge funds do not appear to outperform passive benchmarks such as indexes.

Hedge funds have caught the imagination of the investing public. Because of high leverage and risky investments, some hedge funds produced triple-digit investment returns in certain years. But there have also been spectacular failures. In fact, the emerging markets crisis of 1997–1998 wiped out one particularly famous fund, Long-Term Capital Management. This fund was considered the superstar of hedge funds prior to its demise. It was run by some of the most famous traders on Wall Street and used the mathematical and economic expertise of Myron Scholes (of Black-Scholes fame) and Robert Merton (another derivatives guru). This particular event is noteworthy because regulators (including the U.S. Federal Reserve) feared that the failure of this fund would cause global panic because of the numerous derivatives positions that would be defaulted, affecting counterparties around the world.[6] Market watchers with long-term memory should surely view recent events concerning AIG (in 2008) with a sense of déjà vu! **Private equity funds (PEFs)** differ from hedge funds because they invest in nonpublicly traded assets such as start-ups, mature but private firms, and real estate. PEF, once primarily domestic operations, now venture across borders in search of high returns. For example, U.S.-based venture capital funds (a form of PEF) now actively venture into countries such as China in search of investments. As with hedge funds, only large investors and institutions are able to invest in PEF. A key advantage of PEF to investors is that they provide access to nontraditional assets such as real estate and infrastructure projects as well as early-stage firms.

15.4 International Bond and Money Market Investments

While equity investments form the glamorous component of international investing, one should not overlook investments in international bonds. There are essentially three instrument categories to consider:

- **Government bonds issued by major Organization for Economic Cooperation and Development (OECD) nations such as Germany, France, Japan, and the United Kingdom.** These bonds are generally denominated in the currency of the nation issuing the bonds. The credit ratings tend to be quite high, although some nations' bonds are rated lower than those in the United States.

- **Corporate bonds issued by MNCs in their respective national markets or in the Euro markets.** These are usually large issues, primarily by firms such as General Electric that have high-quality ratings. Corporate bonds are generally riskier than bonds issued by major OECD governments.

[5] C. Ackerman, R. McEnally, and D. Ravenscraft, "The Performance of Hedge Funds: Risk, Return and Incentives," *Journal of Finance* 54, no. 3 (1999), pp. 833–874.

[6] PBS TV aired the documentary-drama based on the LTCM story titled "The Trillion Dollar Bet." Also see Roger Lowenstein, *When Genius Fails: The Rise and Fall of Long-Term Capital Management* (New York: Random House).

- **Bonds issued by developing nations such as Mexico, India, and Brazil.** These bonds contain an element of country risk because many of these nations have unstable economic and/or political systems.

One benefit offered by foreign debt instruments is high returns. Additionally, foreign debt may be desirable because of exposure to foreign currencies; this may offer diversification benefits in a portfolio. Emerging market debt can be a very interesting play on the fundamentals of the respective countries. Often, large country risk premiums are built into the yields of emerging market debt. When fundamentals improve, the yields have the potential to decrease dramatically, often by hundreds of basis points. This, in turn, can translate into large capital gains for investors. In fact, research shows that emerging market debt is a close substitute for emerging market equity.[7] The correlation between debt and equity returns in emerging countries can be as high as 0.90.

Investors can also consider money market instruments (e.g., Eurocurrency) that are usually safer than international bonds. Default risk is often minimal: Issuers usually are of high quality, and the maturity is short enough to prevent the development of an adverse situation. These investments are important ways to invest in foreign currencies. Earlier we discussed the benefits of adding some currency assets to a domestic portfolio. International money market instruments offer this benefit.

15.5 What the Future Holds

The future is bright for international investing. In this section, we discuss three phenomena: the rise of equity culture around the world, the rapid fall of barriers to investing, and globalization in the financial services industry. As we ponder these issues, we should also keep in mind that the credit crisis of 2007–2008 was more severe than initially thought and may upset established trends in international investing.

The Rise of Equity Culture

Equity culture is a term used to define the propensity of people to invest in equity instruments. Nowhere is this culture more evident than in the United States. Especially in the last two decades, Americans have wholeheartedly embraced the risks and rewards of investing in individual stocks or in stock mutual funds. Almost every American has some exposure to the stock market through either personal assets or pension funds (401k and 403k accounts).

The rest of the world does not display an equity culture to the same extent. This is despite the fact that the savings rate is high in European nations and in Japan. In Europe, citizens traditionally invest their savings in bank accounts and in real estate; many wealthy Europeans have two or three homes, and some hold offshore bank accounts. In Japan, a country with perhaps the highest savings rate in the world, citizens use post office savings accounts as the main vehicle for savings. The situation concerning equities is perhaps even worse in developing countries. In India, for instance, a significant part of a family's savings is invested in gold and other jewelry. More generally, in developing countries, citizens seek safety in real estate. The absence of well-functioning financial markets in many countries is a hindrance to the development of an equity culture.

This situation is changing rapidly, however. In Europe, for instance, as governments work toward the convergence criteria for the European Union, they are forced to reform or even dismantle legacy pension systems. Europe, like the United States, is also aging rapidly, with citizens anticipating the prospect of financing long retirements. These changes are influencing Europeans to consider equity investments. In developing countries such as the BRIC nations, interest in equity investments is rapidly rising.

There is one cloud on the horizon. The credit crisis of 2007–2008 wiped out trillions of dollars of value for equity investors. The long-term effects of this crisis are unknown at this time.

[7] J. Kelly, L. Martins, and J. Carlson, "The Relationship between Bonds and Stocks in Emerging Countries," *Journal of Portfolio Management,* Spring 1998, pp. 110–122.

The Rapid Fall of Barriers to Financial Globalization

In the last two decades, the number of investments by U.S. investors in foreign stocks and bonds has increased tremendously. While U.S. investors initially focused on investments in Canada and a few European countries such as the United Kingdom, U.S. investors today have investments in many parts of the world including developing countries. While this interest in global investments is the result of many factors, a key reason is the fall of explicit barriers such as capital controls and taxation.

The U.S. markets are perhaps the world's most unfettered financial markets. Even there, however, historic regulations such as the ones separating commercial and investment banking have hindered the growth of the financial services industry. Recently, such barriers have continued to fall as the lines between various entities offering financial services continue to blur. Such developments not only offer more convenient bundling of financial services but also permit the creation of new and innovative services.

In Europe, especially since 1992, banks and other financial institutions have been allowed greater freedom to conduct cross-border transactions. Subtle barriers remain, but large-scale consolidation of financial institutions in Europe is an encouraging sign. Financial markets in emerging economies are much more constrained, but, as with Europe, there are signs that changes are on the way. Again, the credit crisis of 2007–2008 has led to discussions about restructuring the global financial system, and there is uncertainty about actions governments will take in this regard.

The Globalization of the Financial Services Industry

The financial services industry comprises banks, brokerages, insurers, and other financial companies that provide various services to individual and institutional clients. Major changes have occurred in this industry in recent times. Some changes were caused by regulations and others by market forces and technology. In the United States, for instance, commercial banks have lost ground as investors sought money market funds for short-term investments and stock and bond mutual funds for long-term investments. Brokerage houses have also seen their share of turmoil. While the number of brokerage accounts and the volume of assets managed have risen, traditional brokerages have lost business to the upstarts such as Schwab and the newer Internet-only brokerages such as E*Trade and TD Ameritrade. The financial services landscape in the United States has also been shaped by numerous mergers, the most spectacular being the merger that brought together the brokerage concern Salomon Smith Barney, the global bank Citicorp, and the insurance firm Travelers. This and other mergers have allowed firms to bundle financial services and market them as never before.

Europe is going through a major revolution also. Private citizens are increasingly managing their own financial assets (e.g., pension assets). The landscape is shifting rapidly and is creating a boom in the financial services industry.[8] Changes are perhaps even more dramatic in developing countries that until recently had practically no financial services industry to speak of. But with the opening of markets under the World Trade Organization and other agreements, alliances are being struck between local firms and European or U.S. firms. In India for instance, U.S. firms such as Morgan Stanley and Merrill Lynch have established joint ventures with Indian firms to offer financial products such as mutual funds.

The credit crisis of 2007–2008 has dramatically changed the landscape of the financial services industry. Venerable firms such as Lehman Brothers either declared bankruptcy or merged with other entities. Giant firms such as Citicorp and AIG have been crippled. A wave of mergers and restructurings is now in motion. According to the track record of the financial services industry and its response to various crises, one would expect financial innovation to result and a more globalized financial services industry to emerge. It is an interesting moment to be a student of international finance.

---

[8] For a complete discussion of financial services in the Eurozone, see I. Walter and R. Smith, *High Finance in the Euro-Zone* (Upper Saddle River, NJ: Prentice Hall, 2000).

Summary

- International investments offer both profit and risk-reduction potential. Optimal cross-border allocations can improve investors' risk-return trade-off.

- Investors have faced some hurdles such as currency risk, government controls, taxes, and informational asymmetry.

- U.S. investors have many ways to invest in global equity. Hundreds of mutual funds invest in international stocks. Hedge funds provide high net worth investors even more attractive possibilities. Investors wishing to manage their own stock portfolios may also consider depository receipts, which are pseudoshares that mimic foreign stocks. Newer alternatives include ETFs and various derivative instruments.

- U.S. investors also have access to international bonds and money market instruments though mutual funds. This may offer beneficial exposure to foreign currencies.

- The future for international investments is bright with the development of the equity culture, the fall of barriers, and the rise of the financial services industry.

Questions

1. **Profit Motive.** Much has been said about the risk-reduction motive for foreign investments. But what about the profit motive? What are compelling factors that indicate the profitability of foreign investments?

2. **Inefficient Foreign Markets.** *Inefficiency* may be bad word for economists but is a beacon to investors. Evaluate the proposition that certain foreign markets are inefficient. What are some indicators for inefficient markets?

3. **Currency Play Motive.** Some investors regard foreign equities as a currency play. Explain this perspective on international investing.

4. **Risk-Reduction Motive.** Explain the risk-reduction motive for investing in foreign assets. Which type of foreign assets is more likely to reduce risk, and which is less likely?

5. **Correlations between Stock Markets.** A colleague makes the following remark: "Global stock markets are quite homogeneous. A Taiwanese semiconductor firm is no different from a U.S. firm in the same industry. Ditto for Swiss pharmaceuticals, Japanese auto firms, and so on. What is the point of global diversification?" Respond to this position using data as appropriate to make your points.

6. **Sharpe Index.** Explain the use of the Sharpe index to evaluate a foreign investment. What are the inputs? Be precise in identifying inputs. For example, identify the currency (local or domestic) in which amounts are measured.

7. **Sharpe Index.** Apparently, Czech investors also use the Sharpe index (SI). Published values of the SI for various Czech stocks in Czech databases and journals appear significantly higher than the SI for U.S. stocks. Does this mean that U.S. investors should buy Czech stocks? Explain your position.

8. **Asset and Currency Correlation.** A U.S. investor is considering an investment in Thailand. The investor has studied portfolio theory in graduate school and explains her rationale as follows: "For U.S. investors, Thai stocks—exporters primarily—offer a unique profile. The negative correlation between the bhat and the stock market—because companies tend to do well when the bhat is down—offers built-in diversification." Evaluate the merits of this position.

9. **Diversification and Currency Effects.** Grace Slick, a pension fund manager, seeks investment opportunities around the world. In keeping with the organization's goals, she seeks investments with low correlations with the existing primarily U.S. stock portfolio. After considerable research, Ms. Slick notes an interesting phenomenon in certain countries. The local currency stock returns have very low correlation with

U.S. stocks, but after converting to USD, the returns appear to have stronger correlations. She is wondering whether there is a way to avoid the unsavory currency effect. Please advise Ms. Slick.

   a. Is it plausible that some countries exhibit the effects identified here (that is, low correlation when measured in local currency but higher correlation in converted values)? Speculate on country characteristics that produce this effect.

   b. What are practical ways to structure portfolios to benefit from the local correlation between USD and local currency-denominated returns of foreign assets without being affected by currency effects?

10. **Home Bias.** What is the home bias in international investing? Give examples. In regard to it, how does the United States compare with European countries?

11. **Government Controls.** What are the ways in which governments regulate inbound and outbound investments? What are the effects of these regulations?

12. **Depository Receipts.** An investment manager makes the following observation: "I would like to invest in ADRs, but there are slim pickings. There are not many companies, and the few that are listed seem to be rather blah, the usual MNCs like Sony and Honda, you know. . . ." Respond to the manager.

13. **Mutual Funds versus ETFs.** Evaluate the advantages and disadvantages of international investing using mutual funds and ETFs.

Problems

1. **Correlations.** Norman Phelps is a portfolio manager for a foundation that had traditionally made domestic (U.S.) investments. He wishes to investigate the benefits of adding foreign stocks to his equity portfolio to improve its risk-return profile. In particular, Mr. Phelps is interested in assessing whether Japanese stocks are beneficial because of their imperfect correlation with U.S. stocks. Collecting the USD values of a Japanese portfolio as well as data on a U.S. portfolio, Mr. Phelps first calculates returns. Next he calculates standard deviations and the covariance between the portfolios. He notes that the standard deviations of U.S. and Japanese portfolios are 20 percent and 15 percent, respectively. The covariance is 0.0066.

   a. What is the correlation between U.S. and Japanese stock returns?

   b. What can you conclude regarding the merit of investing in Japanese stocks to diversify the portfolio?

2. **Correlations.** The following table provides forecasted data pertaining to investments in A (domestic stock portfolio) and B (foreign stock portfolio, returns calculated in domestic currency).

Scenario	Probability	Return A (Domestic)	Return B (Foreign)
I	30%	10%	15%
II	30%	30%	10%
III	40%	−5%	0%

   a. Calculate standard deviations of A and B as well as the correlation between A and B.

   b. Comment on the diversification potential between A and B.

3. **Portfolio Standard Deviation.** Research reported in the chapter shows that the correlation between the U.S. and Japanese stock markets is 0.35. Assume that the standard deviations of the two markets are 15 percent and 18 percent, respectively. All statistics pertaining to the Japanese market use return data converted into USD. An investor redeploys USD 10 million out of a USD 40 million U.S. stock portfolio into Japanese stocks.

   a. What is the variance of the revised portfolio?

   b. What is the standard deviation of the revised portfolio?

   c. Based solely on portfolio standard deviation, do you think this is a good move?

4. **Sharpe Index.** The following table provides forecasted data pertaining to investments in P (domestic stock portfolio) and Q (foreign stock portfolio, returns calculated in domestic currency). Assume the domestic rate of interest is 5 percent.

Scenario	Probability	Return P (Domestic)	Return Q (Foreign)
I	30%	10%	20%
II	30%	30%	10%
III	40%	−5%	2%

a. Calculate standard deviations of P and Q as well as the correlation between them.

b. Form a portfolio containing equal proportions of P and Q. What is the portfolio standard deviation? Calculate the Sharpe index (SI) of the portfolio. Is this an improvement over the SI of P?

c. Interpret your results and form conclusions for foreign investments.

5. **Sharpe Index.** A U.S. investor is considering two stocks and wishes to select one of them for his portfolio. Data on these stocks follow. Assume that the U.S. risk-free rate is 6 percent.

Stock	Country	Average Return Past 5 Years	Standard Deviation
A	United States	12%	30%
B	Poland, listed as ADR	14%	50%

a. Calculate the Sharpe index for each stock.

b. Which stock would you prefer for your portfolio? Explain.

c. Would you give special consideration to B because it is a foreign stock? Explain.

6. **Currency and Asset Returns.** A U.S. investor notes that a closed-end mutual fund invested in the Indian stock market provided a return of 22 percent during 2006. The investor wonders about the currency contribution to this investment return and wishes to decompose it into currency and asset components. She obtains the following information about USDINR: values are 44.92 and 44.11 at the beginning and end of year, respectively. Which equation can she use to decompose domestic returns of a foreign asset? Calculate its components.

7. **Currency and Asset Returns.** A wealthy U.S. investor—Arturo Diaz—with a USD 20 million portfolio engages an asset manager whose favorite strategy is to invest in no more than 10 stocks. Last year, the manager selected an interesting stock for the portfolio: a Brazilian telecommunications firm listed on the NYSE as an ADR. Mr. Diaz notes that the stock did very well and made a 42 percent return. He wonders if this was just due to the strength of the Brazilian real (BRL) and wishes to decompose asset and currency returns. He notes that the beginning and ending values of USDBRL for the year are 2.139 and 1.779, respectively. Perform appropriate calculations to decompose the returns.

8. **Currency and Asset Returns.** A U.S.-based hedge fund purchases a French asset for EUR 10,000. Its current spot rate is EURUSD 1.58. Assume that a year later, the investment is liquidated for EUR 10,500. Assume that the spot rate at that time is EURUSD 1.48. What return did the hedge fund earn? Demonstrate two methods of answering this question.

9. **Foreign Investment Risk Decomposition.** Assume that BRIC countries have been doing well lately. Of these four nations, China has been attracting the most attention. Russia appears to get the least attention. A U.S. investor who believes in being a contrarian is considering an investment in Russia. The asset under review has a local currency standard deviation (asset risk) of 30 percent. The standard deviation of (ruble) RUBUSD is 8 percent. Assume that the correlation between the asset and RUBUSD is −0.2. Estimate total risk. Determine whether the investment is riskier for a U.S. investor compared to a local (Russian) investor. Explain your results.

10. **Foreign Investment Risk Decomposition.** A U.S. investor considers adding shares of a Dutch firm to her portfolio. Shares of this firm trade in the Euronext exchange and have a local currency (EUR) standard deviation of 24 percent. The standard deviation of EURUSD is 12 percent. Assume that the correlation between the asset and EURUSD is 0.4. Estimate total risk. Determine whether the investment is riskier for a U.S. investor compared to a local (Dutch) investor. Explain your results.

11. **Foreign Investment Risk Decomposition.** A private equity fund (PEF) considers an infrastructure project in Sri Lanka. It is a two-year project that involves the construction of a resort and provides a liquidating cash flow only when assets are handed over to a local partner. A complex formula using Sri Lanka rupee (LKR) and U.S. dollar (USD) determines the final payoff to the PEF. A financial analyst constructs four equally likely scenarios for this payoff and associated values of USDLKR (see the following table). Assume that the initial investment is USD 20 million and spot USDLKR is 100.

Scenario	Payoff (LKR million)	Spot USDLKR
I	2,000	100
II	2,500	110
III	3,000	110
IV	4,000	120

   a. Calculate asset return from Sri Lankan and U.S. perspectives.

   b. What are the values of asset risk, currency risk, and covariance risk for each?

12. **Foreign Investment Risk Decomposition.** A Swiss investor is considering a foreign investment that offers equally likely local currency returns of −5 percent and 45 percent. These returns are independent of currency returns, which are equally likely to be −10 percent and 10 percent.

   a. Construct a table showing all possible scenarios and asset returns from the perspectives of locals as well as the Swiss investor.

   b. What are the values for asset risk, currency risk, and covariance risk?

   c. What is the correlation between (local currency) asset and currency returns?

Case

Clover Machines: *Deliberations at Brickleys*

While sipping his after dinner glass of port, Ian Bell, a junior analyst with the leading British wealth management firm Brickleys, wonders whether a high-risk strategy would pay off with career advancement. A week ago, his boss, Kevin Petersen, who manages a large Saudi account, instructed Mr. Bell to search for a way to diversify the portfolio into emerging market assets. A host of straightforward solutions awaited Mr. Bell. Numerous BRIC stocks (in GDR form) traded on the London Stock Exchange. Furthermore, Brickleys would have absolutely no difficulty in accessing ADRs traded on the NYSE. Direct investments in foreign exchanges were a bit trickier, but given the size of the client's account, even this alternative was possible. But Mr. Bell was mulling the idea of suggesting that the Saudi client invest in shares of Clover Machines. Was this too outlandish a suggestion? Would this help or hurt his career?

Before he could submit a formal report to Mr. Petersen, Mr. Bell wished to find answers to the following questions quickly:

1. What is Clover's emerging markets strategy? Is exposure to emerging markets expected to increase or decrease? What are the subcomponents (that is, specific countries) of Clover's

emerging markets exposure? What are specific factors that can either benefit or hurt Clover because of its emerging markets exposure? Does this analysis indicate a high correlation between Clover's stock price and prices of other more traditional emerging markets assets? [*Note:* One has to refer to previous Clover cases to determine part of this answer.]

2. If the client finds the idea of investing in Clover interesting, are there ways to convert the investment into a purer play on emerging markets?

3. At the present time, Clover does not have many "fixed assets" (that is, plant and equipment) in emerging markets. Does this mean that Clover is not a good emerging markets play?

4. Would the fact that Clover is a U.S. firm present exposure to the USD? In particular, the Saudi client may be concerned about excessive USD exposure. (Can you articulate why?) Suggest ways to address this concern.

5. Assuming that the analysis of Clover's business indeed demonstrates a significant play in emerging markets, what are some additional points that Mr. Bell can use to justify the Clover investment?

LIBRARY, UNIVERSITY OF CHESTER

A

arbitrage   Arbitrage is based on the intuitive "buy-low sell-high" rule. When an asset or its synthetic equivalent (a combination of other assets producing equivalent cash flows) is traded at differential prices, the arbitrager buys at the low price and sells at the high price.

arbitrage, covered interest arbitrage (CIA)   A way to exploit the interest rate spread between currencies. Typically, one borrows the low-interest currency, converts to the high-interest currency, makes a deposit to earn the high-interest, and repays the low-interest loan at maturity. A forward contract is used to perform the future conversion of the high-interest currency into the low-interest currency. The low-interest currency is also known as the funding currency, and the high-interest currency is also known as the target currency.

arbitrage, locational   A currency arbitrage transaction based on a particular currency selling at differential prices in two different locations.

arbitrage, triangular   A currency arbitrage transaction based on inconsistent currency quotes involving three currencies.

B

balance of goods & services (BOGS)   BOGS is the difference between export and import values for goods and services.

balance of payments   The (U.S.) accounting system that measures trade and financial transactions between U.S. entities and foreign entities. Key components are the current account and the financial (or capital) account.

balance of trade (BOT)   BOT is the difference between goods exports and imports. A negative (deficit) BOT indicates that a country imports more than it exports. This is the most visible and discussed statistic from the current account.

banker's acceptance (BA)   An IOU issued by a large bank; occurs in the context of international trade transactions.

bank loan, line of credit   A line of credit is a flexible financing arrangement. In this financing method, firms negotiate parameters such as the maximum amount, interest rates, and fees. As funding needs arise, firms draw on this line of credit.

bank loan, syndication   Syndicated bank loans are large bank loans made by a consortium of banks.

bank loan, term loan   Term loans are unsecured loans made for a specified period of time at a fixed interest rate.

Bank of International Settlements (BIS)   An umbrella organization for national central banks; assists central banks and disseminates banking and other financial information.

base currency   In a currency quote, the base currency is the currency that is being bought or sold.

bid-ask spread   The difference between the prices at which a market maker will buy (bid) and sell (ask) a particular currency.

bill of lading (BL)   A receipt issued by the transportation company (also known as *shipper* or *carrier*), indicating the goods shipped and whether the transportation charges have been prepaid. The bill of lading is usually a requirement for payment under the terms of a letter of credit.

bond equivalent yield (BEY)   In a context of U.S. bonds paying semiannual coupons, BEY equals the semiannual yield times 2.

break-even analysis   In the context of project NPV, break-even analysis is the identification of threshold values of inputs such as units sold for generating positive project NPV.

Bretton Woods agreement   This 1944 agreement sought to stabilize the world monetary system by fixing the value of the USD against gold at USD 35 per ounce and anchoring other currencies to the USD. The International Monetary Fund was created with oversight responsibilities for the international monetary system.

BRIC   Brazil, Russia, India and China; these nations are at the vanguard of developing nations.

C

capital asset pricing model (CAPM)   A model linking return to risk. Among other applications, used to calculate the cost of equity.

capital asset pricing model, international (ICAPM)   The international version of the CAPM. A global equity portfolio or index is used as the market index.

capital controls   Taxes and other impediments to the flow of capital across borders.

carry trade   Also known as uncovered interest arbitrage, carry trade is similar to covered interest arbitrage with one exception. A forward contract is not used for the future currency conversion, so there is no "cover."

Chicago Mercantile Exchange (CME)   A leading derivatives exchange in the United States.

Clearing House Automated Payment System (CHAPS)   A U.K.-based communications network that facilitates settlement of currency trades.

Clearing House Interbank Payments System (CHIPS)   A U.S.-based communications network that facilitates settlement of currency trades.

code law   This is a legal system whose laws arise from governmental processes.

commercial paper (CP)   Short-term debt instruments issued by large, high-quality corporations and financial institutions. CP issued in the U.S. and Euro markets is referred to as *USCP* and *ECP*, respectively. CP that is backed by pools of assets is known as *asset-backed CP* or *ABCP*.

common law   This is a legal system whose laws arise from the private sector and that is market driven.

comparative advantage theory　A theory, first advanced by 19th-century economist David Ricardo, which explains why countries engage in international trade. Countries produce and export goods in which they have a relative advantage in one of the factors of input (technology, raw materials, labor or capital).

cost of capital　The (percent) return demanded by investors when financing a firm.

cost of debt　The (percent) return demanded by creditors when financing a firm.

cost of debt, all-in　The cost of debt, calculated from the firm's viewpoint, after issue costs have been considered.

cost of equity　The (percent) return demanded by shareholders when financing a firm.

counterparty risk　In financial contracts such as derivatives, the risk that one of the two parties will default.

country risk　Political, regulatory, and economic risks affecting operations in a foreign country.

cross rate　The value of a foreign currency in terms of another foreign currency.

currency intervention　Actions taken by central banks to increase or decrease a currency's value.

currency system, fixed　A system in which a nation fixes its currency value. As a practical matter, values are fixed to a commodity such as gold or to another currency. Variations include the pegged currency system.

currency system, floating　A system in which a nation allows the value of its currency to be freely set by market forces.

current account convertibility　The conversion of currencies for conduct of trade. This is a precondition for free international trade.

D

depository receipts (DRs)　These are pseudoshares (receipts) issued by a financial institution based on a depository of original shares. The value of these pseudoshares mimics the value of the original shares. When issued in the United States, they are known as *American depository receipts (ADRs)*. When issued simultaneously in more than one market, they are known as *global depository receipts (GDRs)*.

derivatives　Financial contracts whose cash flows and value derive from some underlying financial asset or commodity or index.

discount rate　Rate used to discount cash flows in order to find PV.

distribution agreement　A contract allowing a firm to use distribution channels owned by another firm.

documentary collection　An alternative to the L/C; under this method, a banker mediates and hands over title to goods to the importer upon payment (cash or acceptance of draft).

dual listing　The listing of equity in a domestic as well as a foreign stock exchange.

E

electronic funds transfer (EFT)　MNCs use electronic systems such as the U.S.-based automated clearing house (ACH) to transfer funds to affiliates, subsidiaries, and customers/suppliers.

Eurobond　A long-term debt instrument issued in the Euro markets.

Euro Commercial Paper (ECP)　A short-term debt instrument issued by corporations in the Euro markets.

Eurocurrency market　A subset of the international money market where lending and borrowing of currencies occur outside of their respective countries.

Eurodollar　The main component of the Eurocurrency market; involves short-term debt transactions denominated in USD.

Euro markets　A generic term used to indicate an international market. Eurocurrency and Eurobond markets are important components.

European Central Bank (ECB)　The European counterpart of the U.S. Federal Reserve. The ECB oversees EU monetary policy and manages the value of the EUR.

European Monetary Union (EMU)　With its origins in the 1957 Treaty of Rome and the creation of the European Commission (EC) in 1967, major European nations integrated their monetary system. This ultimately led to the creation of the euro (EUR) in 1999.

European Union (EU)　The formal union of European nations created by the Maastricht Treaty of 1992. A key component was monetary union. The European Central Bank was created to oversee this aspect of the union.

exchange rate, real　An exchange rate that has been corrected for changes in price levels (inflation).

exchange-traded fund (ETF)　Like a mutual fund, ETFs are portfolios owned by the public. An ETF is similar to a closed-end mutual fund in that its shares are traded on an exchange. But unlike a closed-end mutual fund, redemptions or new investments are possible as long as they are conducted in wholesale lots.

export-import bank (ex-im bank)　These are usually government-run or government-backed institutions that assist imports and especially exports by providing information, financing (loans and guarantees), and insurance.

exposure　In the context of international finance, this refers to how the MNC is affected by currency changes.

exposure, economic　The effect of currency changes on all cash flows of the firm. This is total currency exposure.

exposure, operating　The effect of currency changes on the firm's operating cash flows.

exposure, transaction　The effect of currency changes on the firm's currency holdings as well as any near-term contractual cash flows in foreign currencies.

exposure, translation　The effect of currency changes on the firm's (translated) financial statements. This type of exposure is also known as *accounting exposure*.

F

factoring   Factoring involves the sale of receivables to third parties known as *factors*. Banks and financing companies serve as factors.

Federal Reserve Bank   The central bank of the United States; oversees the monetary system and currency markets.

Fedwire   A U.S.-based communications network operated by the Federal Reserve system that facilitates settlement of currency trades.

financial slack   Financial slack represents the capacity to source financing—especially short-term financing—as needed.

Fisher effect (FE)   A theory indicating that the nominal interest rate is made up of two components: the real interest rate and the rate of inflation. Also see *international Fisher effect*.

floating rate note (FRN)   A medium-term debt instrument issued by corporations and financial institutions in the Euro markets; the coupon is determined by LIBOR or other reference rates.

foreign direct investment (FDI)   FDI represents the cross-border investments in real assets. MNCs perform a majority of FDI.

foreign tax credit (FTC)   A credit for foreign taxes paid by an entity (MNC) on foreign-source income; this credit offsets the domestic income tax liability. FTC regulations are governed by tax treaties between countries as well as by national tax regulations.

foreign translation adjustment (FTA)   The application of accounting procedures such as U.S. GAAP (e.g., SFAS 52) results in the FTA, which is a measure of the currency impact on net income and net assets.

forward   An agreement to buy or sell an underlying asset at a future date for a predetermined price.

forward discount premium   The percentage by which the forward price of an asset differs from its spot price.

forward parity   Also known as unbiased forward rates, this theory indicates that forward rates are unbiased estimates of future spot rates.

forward rate agreement (FRA)   An agreement to obtain a loan at a future date. Eurocurrency futures are the exchange-traded equivalent of FRAs.

futures   Forward contracts traded on exchanges. (See the definition of a *forward*.)

G

General Agreement on Tariffs and Trade (GATT)   GATT is the predecessor to the WTO. Prior to 1995, the multilateral agreements between nations (facilitated by WTO's predecessor) were known as GATT agreements.

generally accepted accounting principles (GAAP)   These are accounting practices in the United States based on standards issued by the U.S.-based Financial Accounting Standards Board (FASB).

globalization   The cross-border movement of goods, money or people; the integration of nations.

gold standard   A monetary system that either uses gold itself as money or uses gold reserves to support currency value.

gravity theory   A theory which states that bilateral trade is high when countries have physical proximity and when their economies are of similar size.

Group of Eight nations (G8)   G8, or the Group of Eight nations, includes seven major OECD nations—U.S., Japan, Germany, France, Italy, U.K., and Canada—and Russia. The economic ministers of these eight nations meet annually to discuss issues such as currency values and international trade.

H

hedge   The use of derivatives to control (currency) risk.

hedge, forward   The use of forwards to control (currency) risk.

hedge, money market   The preemptive purchase or sale of a foreign currency in anticipation of a future transaction. This affords protection against future changes in the value of the foreign currency.

hedge, option   The use of options to control (currency) risk.

hedge funds   Hedge funds are largely unregulated versions of mutual funds, and many of them invest in foreign assets. Hedge funds are unregulated because only a small number of wealthy investors hold shares.

I

imperfect markets theory   A theory that explains why international trade occurs. Because imperfect markets block the cross-border movement of inputs to a product, countries specialize only in certain products and trade with one another to obtain others.

industry agglomeration theory   A theory of industry location explaining why certain industries take root in certain locations. Key variables are input availability and positive externalities such as shared knowledge.

Interbank market   The main market in which foreign currencies are traded; banks are the main participants in this electronic market.

interest rate parity (IRP)   An equilibrium condition where the interest rate differential is equal to the forward-spot differential. When this condition holds, covered interest arbitrage is not profitable.

International Accounting Standards Board (IASB)   The main international accounting organization; IASB promulgates accounting standards known as *international accounting standards (IAS)* or *international financial reporting standards* (IFRS).

International Bank for Reconstruction and Development (IBRD)   The IBRD is more commonly known as the World Bank. This bank provides assistance to developing nations in the form of loans and technical assistance.

international financial reporting standards (IFRS)   These are accounting standards promulgated by the IASB. These standards formerly were known as *international accounting standards (IAS)*.

international Fisher effect (IFE)   Also known as the Fisher open hypothesis (FOH), the IFE states that national differences in interest rates are determined by differences in inflation rates.

International Monetary Fund (IMF)   An international organization with oversight of the global monetary system; provides loans and technical assistance to members at times of crisis.

J

joint venture (JV)   A business entity created by two corporate partners. The JV is a freestanding firm with its own management and assets.

L

lagging   Deferring the timing of a cash flow to synchronize it with other flows.

law of one price (LOP)   An equilibrium condition in which products are sold for the same prices in different countries, after controlling for currency values.

leading   Advancing the timing of a cash flow to synchronize it with other flows.

letter of credit (L/C)   A document drawn by the importer's banker that describes the sales transaction and guarantees payment to the exporter on the submission of shipping and other documents.

letter of credit, advising bank   This bank serves as the conduit between the exporter and the issuing bank. This bank conveys the L/C to the exporter and assists in presenting the required documents for payment.

letter of credit, confirming bank   If the L/C issuing bank is unknown or small, the exporter may ask for another bank to provide a co-guarantee. This co-guarantor is the confirming bank.

letter of credit, irrevocable   This type of L/C cannot be modified without the consent of the beneficiary (exporter).

letter of credit, issuing bank   This is the bank issuing the L/C and is usually the importer's bank.

letter of credit, transferable   This type of L/C allows the beneficiary (exporter) to transfer benefits to a third party.

licensing agreement   A contract allowing a firm to obtain technology or intellectual property from another firm for a fee.

lockbox   Lockboxes are collection points established near clusters of customers so that payments can be received and processed quickly.

London Inter Bank Offer Rate (LIBOR)   The reference rate for the Eurodollar market; calculated and disseminated by the British Banker's Association.

M

margin account   Also known as *performance bonds*, these accounts represent collateral set up by traders in financial assets (especially futures).

mergers, transaction costs   These costs are typically incurred premerger and include investment banker fees, accounting fees, legal expenses, and other direct expenses required to conduct a transaction.

mergers, transition costs   Postmerger, the firm incurs transition costs (for restructuring and integration) that include expenses related to the integration of various systems such as payroll, accounting and information. Transition costs also include various forms of payouts to employees such as adjustments for existing stock options.

mergers and acquisitions (M&A)   A merger occurs when two firms combine to form a new entity. An acquisition occurs when one firm acquires another; the target firms loses its identity and becomes part of the acquiring firm. In practice, the terms *mergers* and *acquisitions* are used synonymously or put together using the acronym *M&A*.

minority ownership   A minority ownership occurs when one firm purchases less than 50% of the (vote-bearing) shares of another firm. In practice, most minority investments involve a 10% investment.

multinational corporation   A large firm with subsidiaries and affiliates in many foreign countries.

mutual funds   Mutual funds are portfolios of financial assets jointly owned by public investors.

mutual funds, closed-end   This is the alternative to the open-end structure for a mutual fund. Shares of a closed-end fund are traded on stock exchanges. The number of shares in a fund does not change over time. In other words, redemptions or new investments are not possible.

mutual funds, open-end   This is the most common structure for a mutual fund. Funds can flow in and out of it, and the asset size can change correspondingly.

N

netting   Canceling out positive and negative cash flows (in a currency) to reduce currency risk (and the number of transactions). Netting can be performed on an intracompany or intercompany level. Also, netting can be bilateral (between two parties) or multilateral (between many parties).

new trade theory   A trade theory which explains why nations import as well as export the same product. The simultaneous import and export occurs because consumers want variety and producers want scale, so nations only produce specific variations of the product but in large enough quantities for export.

New York Stock Exchange (NYSE)   The leading stock exchange in the United States and now part of the global firm NYSE Euronext, which operates stock and futures exchanges worldwide.

nondeliverable forward (NDF)   A forward contract whose settlement is made using the cash equivalent of the underlying asset.

North American Free Trade Agreement (NAFTA) A trade agreement involving Canada, Mexico, and the United States signed in 1994.

O

OLI model Proposed by Dunning, the OLI model explains that firms become MNCs because of ownership, location and internalization advantages.

option, call A contract providing the right but not the obligation to *buy* an underlying asset at a future date for a predetermined price known as the *strike price.*

option, financial A financial contract providing the option to buy (call option) or sell (put option) an underlying asset.

option, put A contract providing the right but not the obligation to *sell* an underlying asset at a future date for a predetermined price known as the *strike price.*

option, real A business situation that allows an entity (e.g., an MNC) to act flexibly (that is, the entity has two or more alternatives) and to extract positive cash flow.

option, real, abandon This real option occurs in the context of a firm's project and allows the firm the ability to abandon the project if conditions so dictate. As with other real options, the key is to structure operations flexibly, so the abandonment is made possible.

option, real, alter operating scale This real option occurs in the context of a firm's project and allows the firm to change the project's scale. To create this option, a firm creates excess capacity as well as flexibility in its sourcing and production.

option, real, growth This real option occurs in the context of a firm's project and allows the firm to expand on an initial foray by launching related projects. MNCs obtain this option when they set up operations in foreign countries to gain local knowledge and capabilities; this makes it possible for them to activate future growth.

option pricing model This usually refers to the original model for pricing stock options proposed by Black and Scholes. Variations of this model are used to price currency options.

outsourcing In the global context, outsourcing (also known as *offshoring*) refers to the use of foreign providers for components, products, or services.

P

political risk An important component of country risk; the political situation in a foreign country can impact an MNC's operations. Insurance against this risk is widely available.

Porter's Diamond A theory of industry location explaining why certain industries take root in certain locations. Key variables are factor conditions, demand conditions, related industries and industry structure and rivalry.

private equity funds Private equity funds are similar to hedge funds in that only a small number of wealthy investors hold shares. They differ from hedge funds because they invest in nonpublicly traded assets such as start-ups, mature but private firms, and real estate.

product life cycle theory A firm-level or country-level theory of trade which states that firms or nations seek international markets for their products after having exhausted potential in domestic markets.

purchasing power parity (PPP) An equilibrium condition concerning price levels and currency values. PPP is the same as the law of one price (LOP), except that PPP refers to aggregate price levels, while LOP refers to prices of individual products. PPP comes in two forms, absolute and relative. Relative PPP (also referred to as PPP) does not require equivalent price levels, but requires that the inflation differential is reflected in currency changes.

R

remittances In an international finance setting, this refers to cash flows remitted by subsidiaries to MNC parents.

S

Section 482 This is the Internal Revenue Service (IRS) section governing transfer prices for U.S.-based firms.

securitization Securitization involves the issue of financial instruments using nontraded assets as collateral. Specifically, pools of homogeneous assets are created and financial instruments are issued backed by these assets. Cash flows from securitized assets are used to make interest and principal payments on these financial instruments.

sensitivity analysis An analysis of how changes in an input variable affect results. In the context of project NPV, sensitivity analyses would focus on inputs such as units sold, prices, cost per unit, and currency values.

SFAS 52 This U.S. accounting standard pertains to currency translation.

SFAS 133 This U.S. accounting standard pertains to derivatives and hedges.

Sharpe index The reward-to-risk ratio (or risk-return trade-off) of an investment or portfolio.

Smithsonian agreement Signed in 1971 in response to a currency crisis faced by the United States and other nations. The Smithsonian agreement attempted to resurrect the gold standard, but the rapid breakdown of the agreement ultimately paved the way for major Western nations to float their currencies.

Society for Worldwide Interbank Financial Telecommunications (SWIFT) An international communications network that facilitates settlement of currency trades.

statement of financial accounting standards (SFAS) These are accounting standards issued by the U.S.-based Financial Accounting Standards Board (FASB). These standards form the basis for U.S. Generally Accepted Accounting Principles (GAAP).

strategic alliances Strategic alliances are broad agreements between companies to share resources, develop products, or market products. They differ from licensing and distribution agreements in that they are less specific, involve more than one product or issue, and are often for a longer term.

structured notes   Structured notes are straight notes (medium-term debt instruments) augmented with derivative-like features.

swaps   Financial contracts involving the exchange of interest payments. The most common type is the interest rate swap—called the *plain vanilla swap*—that involves the exchange of interest payments based on a fixed rate of interest (prespecified) for interest payments based on a floating rate (e.g., LIBOR). Another common swap is the currency swap in which an entity exchanges interest payments in one currency for interest payments in another.

T

tax, excise   Special taxes or duties imposed on certain goods.

tax, goods & services (GST)   Also known as *sales tax,* GST is imposed on the sale of goods and services.

tax, income   Firms and individuals pay this tax on income.

tax, value added (VAT)   VAT is a special form of GST. At each step of the value chain, the tax is applied only on the marginal value generated.

tax, withholding   When an MNC's foreign subsidiary repatriates income back to the parent, the income becomes subject to the withholding tax.

tax treaty   This is a bilateral agreement that simplifies tax rules and mitigates double taxation. A key provision in most tax treaties relates to the foreign tax credit.

terms currency   In a currency quote, the terms currency is the currency that is being used to buy or sell the base currency.

transfer price   In the context of MNC operations, a transfer price is the price at which inputs or products are transferred between the parent and subsidiaries. Because tax rates differ internationally, the choice of the transfer price affects overall taxes.

tunneling   Expropriation of assets from firms by majority shareholders to the detriment of minority shareholders and other stakeholders.

U

UCP 600   A document issued by the International Chamber of Commerce outlining procedures for documentary credits such as the L/C.

V

value-at-risk (VaR)   The maximum likely losses in a given asset or situation or business. In other words, VaR indicates potential future losses so that decision makers can be prepared ahead of time.

vehicle currency   An intermediate foreign currency through which another foreign currency is bought or sold; the USD often serves this role.

venture capital   Financing for the start-up phase of firms, usually provided by a specialized financial intermediary known as a *VC firm.*

W

weighted average cost of capital (WACC)   An average of costs of financing components, such as debt and equity, weighted by their relative proportions in the capital structure; used as discount rates to determine project NPV.

World Trade Organization (WTO)   An organization of more than 100 nations; strives to monitor and increase international trade.

INDEX